JEREMIAH

Smyth & Helwys Bible Commentary: Jeremiah

Publication Staff

Publisher and President
Cecil P. Staton, Jr.

Executive Vice-President
David Cassady

Vice-President, Editorial
Lex Horton

Senior Editor
Mark K. McElroy

Book Editor
P. Keith Gammons

Art Director and Book Designer
Jim Burt

Assistant Editors
Griff Hogan, Kelley Land, Erin Smith

Smyth & Helwys Publishing, Inc.
6316 Peake Road
Macon, Georgia 31210-3960
1-800-747-3016

Library of Congress Cataloging-in-Publication Data

Fretheim, Terence E.
Jeremiah / by Terence E. Fretheim
p. cm. — (Smyth & Helwys Bible Commentary, 15)
Includes bibliographical references and index.
ISBN 1-57312-072-3
1. Bible. O.T. Jeremiah—Commentaries. I. Title. II. Series.

BS1525.3 .F74 2002
224'.2077—dc21

Library of Congress Control Number: 2001054919

SMYTH & HELWYS BIBLE COMMENTARY

JEREMIAH

TERENCE E. FRETHEIM

SMYTH&HELWYS
PUBLISHING, INCORPORATED • MACON, GEORGIA

PROJECT EDITOR
R. SCOTT NASH
Mercer University
Macon, Georgia

OLD TESTAMENT
GENERAL EDITOR
SAMUEL E. BALENTINE
Baptist Theological Seminary
at Richmond, Virginia

NEW TESTAMENT
GENERAL EDITOR
R. ALAN CULPEPPER
McAfee School of Theology
Mercer University
Atlanta, Georgia

AREA
OLD TESTAMENT EDITORS
MARK E. BIDDLE
Baptist Theological Seminary
at Richmond, Virginia

AREA
NEW TESTAMENT EDITORS
R. SCOTT NASH
Mercer University
Macon, Georgia

KANDY QUEEN-SUTHERLAND
Stetson University
Deland, Florida

RICHARD B. VINSON
Baptist Theological Seminary
at Richmond, Virginia

KENNETH G. HOGLUND
Wake Forest University
Winston-Salem, North Carolina

ART EDITOR
FRED WHITEHURST
Georgia State University
Atlanta, Georgia

ADVANCE PRAISE

After a long absence of Jeremiah commentaries, we are currently happily experiencing a revival in Jeremiah studies and a variety of new commentaries. Among the more important of these is this offer by Terence Fretheim, perhaps the premier biblical expositor of his generation. Fretheim is thoroughly grounded in critical study, but his commentary is no weary repetition of that learning. Here speaks a lively believer attentive to the current world and convinced of the pertinence of the texts to that world. The welcome outcome is an effective connection between text and world made by Fretheim as well as can be made by any contemporary interpreter. Fretheim's contribution is a major presence in the new Smyth & Helwys commentary series that holds immense promise for critical, faithful exposition.

—*Walter Brueggemann*
Columbia Theological Seminary

This perceptive commentary benefits from Terence Fretheim's attention to theological substance and to stylistic detail. Readers will be well served by his mediating position between maximalist and minimalist interpretations of the book of Jeremiah, as well as by the rich analysis of the prophet's understanding of God.

—*James L. Crenshaw*
Duke University Divinity School

Terence Fretheim's commentary makes the book of Jeremiah accessible and appealing for readers at this crucial time in our history. Like no other commentary, this one illuminates the suffering of God and the suffering of creation in the book of Jeremiah. Fretheim draws out from the text the interconnections of human actions, political realities, and ecological well-being. He calls Jeremiah an assaulter of the mind, a champion of the poor, and a prophet of divine anguish.

Balanced scholarly judgment characterizes this commentary. Fretheim finds in the figure of the prophet neither a fiction nor a precise historical character but a persona who embodies God's voice, God's pathos, and God's love.

The commentary is beautifully written, clearly designed, and sprinkled liberally with interpretive voices and perspectives other than Fretheim's own. The book will make a wonderful companion for any reader of Jeremiah, and this biblical text will be a central resource for the work of recovery and critical analysis after the September 11th tragedy.

—Kathleen M. O'Connor
Columbia Theological Seminary

Few interpreters of Scripture go so quickly and well to the heart of the matter as does Terence Fretheim. Nowhere is that more clearly demonstrated than in his clear and articulate comment on the book of Jeremiah. Fretheim's long wrestling with the God of the Old Testament has been brought to bear effectively on his interpretation of that ancient God-wrestler, Jeremiah. If one wants to hear the word of the Lord afresh in the study of this most important prophet, Fretheim's commentary gives the reader a whole new set of ears for careful listening.

—Patrick D. Miller
Princeton Theological Seminary

CONTENTS

ABBREVIATIONS USED IN THIS COMMENTARY

Books of the Old Testament, Apocrypha, and New Testament are generally abbreviated in the Sidebars, parenthetical references, and notes according to the following system.

The Old Testament

Genesis	Gen
Exodus	Exod
Leviticus	Lev
Numbers	Num
Deuteronomy	Deut
Joshua	Josh
Judges	Judg
Ruth	Ruth
1–2 Samuel	1–2 Sam
1–2 Kings	1–2 Kgs
1–2 Chronicles	1–2 Chr
Ezra	Ezra
Nehemiah	Neh
Esther	Esth
Job	Job
Psalm (Psalms)	Ps (Pss)
Proverbs	Prov
Ecclesiastes	Eccl
or Qoheleth	Qoh
Song of Solomon	Song
or Song of Songs	Song
or Canticles	Cant
Isaiah	Isa
Jeremiah	Jer
Lamentations	Lam
Ezekiel	Ezek
Daniel	Dan
Hosea	Hos
Joel	Joel
Amos	Amos
Obadiah	Obad
Jonah	Jonah
Micah	Mic

Nahum	Nah
Habakkuk	Hab
Zephaniah	Zeph
Haggai	Hag
Zechariah	Zech
Malachi	Mal

The Apocrypha

1–2 Esdras	1–2 Esdr
Tobit	Tob
Judith	Jdt
Additions to Esther	Add Esth
Wisdom of Solomon	Wis
Ecclesiasticus or the Wisdom of Jesus Son of Sirach	Sir
Baruch	Bar
Epistle (or Letter) of Jeremiah	Ep Jer
Prayer of Azariah and the Song of the Three	Pr Azar
Daniel and Susanna	Sus
Daniel, Bel, and the Dragon	Bel
Prayer of Manasseh	Pr Man
1–2 Maccabees	1–2 Macc

The New Testament

Matthew	Matt
Mark	Mark
Luke	Luke
John	John
Acts	Acts
Romans	Rom
1–2 Corinthians	1–2 Cor
Galatians	Gal
Ephesians	Eph
Philippians	Phil
Colossians	Col
1–2 Thessalonians	1–2 Thess
1–2 Timothy	1–2 Tim
Titus	Titus
Philemon	Phlm
Hebrews	Heb
James	Jas
1–2 Peter	1–2 Pet
1–2–3 John	1–2–3 John
Jude	Jude
Revelation	Rev

Other commonly used abbreviations include:

ad loc.	at the location discussed
AD	*Anno Domini* ("in the year of the Lord")
(also commonly referred to as CE = the Common Era)	
BC	Before Christ
(also commonly referred to as BCE = Before the Common Era)	
C.	century
c.	*circa* (around "that time")
cf.	*confer* (compare)
ch.	chapter
chs.	chapters
d.	died
E.	English
ed.	edition or edited by or editor
eds.	editors
e.g.	*exempli gratia* (for example)
et al.	*et alii* (and others)
f./ff.	and the following one(s)
gen. ed.	general editor
H.	Hebrew
ibid.	*ibidem* (in the same place)
i.e.	*id est* (that is)
LCL	Loeb Classical Library
lit.	literally
n.d.	no date
rev. and exp. ed.	revised and expanded edition
sg.	singular
trans.	translated by or translator(s)
vol(s).	volume(s)
v.	verse
vv.	verses

Additional written works cited by abbreviations include:

AB	Anchor Bible
ABD	*Anchor Bible Dictionary*
ANET	*Ancient Near Eastern Texts*
BA	*Biblical Archaeologist*
BAR	*Biblical Archaeology Review*
BHS	*Biblia Hebraica Stuttgartensia*
BRev	*Bible Review*
BZAW	Beiträge zur Zeitschrift für die alttestamentliche Wissenschaft
CBQ	*Catholic Biblical Quarterly*
DH	Deuteronomistic History
DSS	Dead Sea Scrolls
Dtr	Deuteronomist

HAR	*Hebrew Annual Review*
HUCA	*Hebrew Union College Annual*
IBC	Interpretation: A Bible Commentary for Teaching and Preaching
ICC	International Critical Commentary
IDB	*Interpreters Dictionary of the Bible*
JB	Jerusalem Bible
JBL	*Journal of Biblical Literature*
JEDP	Yahwist-Elohist-Deuteronomist-Priestly
JPS	Jewish Publication Society
JSOT	*Journal for the Study of the Old Testament*
KJV	King James Version
LXX	Septuagint = Greek Translation of Hebrew Bible
MDB	*Mercer Dictionary of the Bible*
MT	Masoretic Text
NAB	New American Bible
NEB	New English Bible
NICOT	New International Commentary on the Old Testament
NIV	New International Version
NRSV	New Revised Standard Version
OAN	*Oracles Against the Nations*
OTL	Old Testament Library
REB	Revised English Bible
RSV	Revised Standard Version
TEV	Today's English Version
TNK	Tanak = Hebrew Bible
VT	*Vetus Testamentum*
VTSup	Supplements to Vetus Testamentum
WBC	Word Biblical Commentary
ZAW	*Zeitschrift für die alttestamentliche Wissenschaft*

AUTHOR'S PREFACE

Jeremiah is an enigmatic and extraordinarily difficult book. It taxes one's interpretive capacities at every turn, whether the issues are literary, historical, or theological. The book also has had a way of getting inside my person — even my dreams! — and interrupting long-cherished directions of thought. Having arrived at the end of this project, I am convinced that I have only begun to understand its complexities.

Yet, for all of Jeremiah's complexity, a certain coherence is observable. I have been especially attentive to the theological perspectives of the book, and that will be evident at every turn. The portrayal of the God of Jeremiah is particularly challenging and I have been concerned to work with this material in such a way that it can continue to inform faith and life. It is hoped that teachers and preachers of these texts will be aided in a special way.

Work on this commentary would not have been possible without the help of many persons. I wish to express my appreciation to students at Luther Seminary and McCormick Theological Seminary, who have responded to this material in earlier forms. I am also grateful to the Administration and Board of Directors of Luther Seminary for granting a sabbatical leave. Special thanks are due to my editors, Scott Nash, Mark Biddle, and Samuel Balentine, whose encouragement and assistance have been invaluable.

Finally, and especially, my gratitude goes to my wife, Faith, to whom this book is dedicated. Her unfailing support through many fits and starts with this material is immeasurable.

Terence E. Fretheim

SERIES PREFACE

The *Smyth & Helwys Bible Commentary* is a visually stimulating and user-friendly series that is as close to multimedia in print as possible. Written by accomplished scholars with all students of Scripture in mind, the primary goal of the *Smyth & Helwys Bible Commentary* is to make available serious, credible biblical scholarship in an accessible and less intimidating format.

Far too many Bible commentaries fall short of bridging the gap between the insights of biblical scholars and the needs of students of God's written word. In an unprecedented way, the *Smyth & Helwys Bible Commentary* brings insightful commentary to bear on the lives of contemporary Christians. Using a multimedia format, the volumes employ a stunning array of art, photographs, maps, and drawings to illustrate the truths of the Bible for a visual generation of believers.

The *Smyth & Helwys Bible Commentary* is built upon the idea that meaningful Bible study can occur when the insights of contemporary biblical scholars blend with sensitivity to the needs of lifelong students of Scripture. Some persons within local faith communities, however, struggle with potentially informative biblical scholarship for several reasons. Oftentimes, such scholarship is cast in technical language easily grasped by other scholars, but not by the general reader. For example, lengthy, technical discussions on every detail of a particular scriptural text can hinder the quest for a clear grasp of the whole. Also, the format for presenting scholarly insights has often been confusing to the general reader, rendering the work less than helpful. Unfortunately, responses to the hurdles of reading extensive commentaries have led some publishers to produce works for a general readership that merely skim the surface of the rich resources of biblical scholarship. This commentary series incorporates works of fine art in an accurate and scholarly manner, yet the format remains "user-friendly." An important facet is the presentation and explanation of images of art, which interpret the biblical material or illustrate how the biblical material has been understood and interpreted in the past. A visual generation of believers deserves a commentary series that contains not only the all-important textual commentary on Scripture, but images, photographs, maps, works of fine art, and drawings that bring the text to life.

The *Smyth & Helwys Bible Commentary* makes serious, credible biblical scholarship more accessible to a wider audience. Writers and editors alike present information in ways that encourage readers to gain a better understanding of the Bible. The editorial board has worked to develop a format that is useful and usable, informative and pleasing to the eye. Our writers are reputable scholars who participate in the community of faith and sense a calling to communicate the results of their scholarship to their faith community.

The *Smyth & Helwys Bible Commentary* addresses Christians and the larger church. While both respect for and sensitivity to the needs and contributions of other faith communities are reflected in the work of the series authors, the authors speak primarily to Christians. Thus the reader can note a confessional tone throughout the volumes. No particular "confession of faith" guides the authors, and diverse perspectives are observed in the various volumes. Each writer, though, brings to the biblical text the best scholarly tools available and expresses the results of their studies in commentary and visuals that assist readers seeking a word from the Lord for the church.

To accomplish this goal, writers in this series have drawn from numerous streams in the rich tradition of biblical interpretation. The basic focus is the biblical text itself, and considerable attention is given to the wording and structure of texts. Each particular text, however, is also considered in the light of the entire canon of Christian Scriptures. Beyond this, attention is given to the cultural context of the biblical writings. Information from archaeology, ancient history, geography, comparative literature, history of religions, politics, sociology, and even economics is used to illuminate the culture of the people who produced the Bible. In addition, the writers have drawn from the history of interpretation, not only as it is found in traditional commentary on the Bible but also in literature, theater, church history, and the visual arts. Finally, the *Commentary* on Scripture is joined with *Connections* to the world of the contemporary church. Here again, the writers draw on scholarship in many fields as well as relevant issues in the popular culture.

This wealth of information might easily overwhelm a reader if not presented in a "user-friendly" format. Thus the heavier discussions of detail and the treatments of other helpful topics are presented in special-interest boxes, or Sidebars, clearly connected to the passages under discussion so as not to interrupt the flow of the basic interpretation. The result is a commentary on Scripture that focuses on the theological significance of a text while also offering the reader a rich array of additional information related to the text and its interpretation.

An accompanying CD-ROM offers powerful searching and research tools. The commentary text, Sidebars, and visuals are all reproduced on a CD that is fully indexed and searchable. Pairing a text version with a digital resource is a distinctive feature of the *Smyth & Helwys Bible Commentary.*

Combining credible biblical scholarship, user-friendly study features, and sensitivity to the needs of a visually oriented generation of believers creates a unique and unprecedented type of commentary series. With insight from many of today's finest biblical scholars and a stunning visual format, it is our hope that the *Smyth & Helwys Bible Commentary* will be a welcome addition to the personal libraries of all students of Scripture.

The Editors

HOW TO USE
THIS COMMENTARY

The *Smyth & Helwys Bible Commentary* is written by accomplished biblical scholars with a wide array of readers in mind. Whether engaged in the study of Scripture in a church setting or in a college or seminary classroom, all students of the Bible will find a number of useful features throughout the commentary that are helpful for interpreting the Bible.

Basic Design of the Volumes

Each volume features an Introduction to a particular book of the Bible, providing a brief guide to information that is necessary for reading and interpreting the text: the historical setting, literary design, and theological significance. Each Introduction also includes a comprehensive outline of the particular book under study.

Each chapter of the commentary investigates the text according to logical divisions in a particular book of the Bible. Sometimes these divisions follow the traditional chapter segmentation, while at other times the textual units consist of sections of chapters or portions of more than one chapter. The divisions reflect the literary structure of a book and offer a guide for selecting passages that are useful in preaching and teaching.

An accompanying CD-ROM offers powerful searching and research tools. The commentary text, Sidebars, and visuals are all reproduced on a CD that is fully indexed and searchable. Pairing a text version with a digital resource also allows unprecedented flexibility and freedom for the reader. Carry the text version to locations you most enjoy doing research while knowing that the CD offers a portable alternative for travel from the office, church, classroom, and your home.

Commentary and Connections

As each chapter explores a textual unit, the discussion centers around two basic sections: *Commentary* and *Connections*. The analysis of a passage, including the details of its language, the history reflected in the text, and the literary forms found in the text, are the main focus

of the *Commentary* section. The primary concern of the
Commentary section is to explore the theological issues presented
by the Scripture passage. *Connections* presents potential applica-
tions of the insights provided in the *Commentary* section. The
Connections portion of each chapter considers what issues are relevant for teaching and suggests useful methods and resources.
Connections also identifies themes suitable for sermon planning and
suggests helpful approaches for preaching on the Scripture text.

Sidebars

The *Smyth & Helwys Bible Commentary* provides a unique hyper-
link format that quickly guides the reader to additional insights.
Since other more technical or supplementary information is vital
for understanding a text and its implications, the volumes feature
distinctive Sidebars, or special-interest boxes, that provide a wealth
of information on such matters as:

- Historical information (such as chronological charts, lists of kings
  or rulers, maps, descriptions of monetary systems, descriptions of
  special groups, descriptions of archaeological sites or geographical
  settings).

- Graphic outlines of literary structure (including such items as
  poetry, chiasm, repetition, epistolary form).

- Definition or brief discussions of technical or theological terms
  and issues.

- Insightful quotations that are not integrated into the running text
  but are relevant to the passage under discussion.

- Notes on the history of interpretation (Augustine on the Good
  Samaritan, Luther on James, Stendahl on Romans, etc.).

- Line drawings, photographs, and other illustrations relevant for
  understanding the historical context or interpretive significance
  of the text.

- Presentation and discussion of works of fine art that have
  interpreted a Scripture passage.

Each Sidebar is printed in color and is referenced at the appropriate place in the *Commentary* or *Connections* section with a color-coded title that directs the reader to the relevant Sidebar. In addition, helpful icons appear in the Sidebars, which provide the reader with visual cues to the type of material that is explained in each Sidebar. Throughout the commentary, these four distinct hyperlinks provide useful links in an easily recognizable design.

Alpha & Omega Language

This icon identifies the information as a language-based tool that offers further exploration of the Scripture selection. This could include syntactical information, word studies, popular or additional uses of the word(s) in question, additional contexts in which the term appears, and the history of the term's translation. All non-English terms are transliterated into the appropriate English characters.

Culture/Context

This icon introduces further comment on contextual or cultural details that shed light on the Scripture selection. Describing the place and time to which a Scripture passage refers is often vital to the task of biblical interpretation. Sidebar items introduced with this icon could include geographical, historical, political, social, topographical, or economic information. Here, the reader may find an excerpt of an ancient text or inscription that sheds light on the text. Or one may find a description of some element of ancient religion such as Baalism in Canaan or the Hero cult in the Mystery Religions of the Greco-Roman world.

Interpretation

Sidebars that appear under this icon serve a general interpretive function in terms of both historical and contemporary renderings. Under this heading, the reader might find a selection from classic or contemporary literature that illuminates the Scripture text or a significant quotation from a famous sermon that addresses the passage. Insights are drawn from various sources, including literature, worship, theater, church history, and sociology.

Additional Resources Study

Here, the reader finds a convenient list of useful resources for further investigation of the selected Scripture text, including books, journals, websites, special collections, organizations, and societies. Specialized discussions of works not often associated with biblical studies may also appear here.

Additional Features

Each volume also includes a basic Bibliography on the biblical book under study. Other bibliographies on selected issues are often included that point the reader to other helpful resources.

Notes at the end of each chapter provide full documentation of sources used and contain additional discussions of related matters.

Abbreviations used in each volume are explained in a list of abbreviations found after the Table of Contents.

Readers of the *Smyth & Helwys Bible Commentary* can regularly visit the Internet support site for news, information, updates, and enhancements to the series at <**www.helwys.com/commentary**>.

Several thorough indexes enable the reader to locate information quickly. These indexes include:

• An *Index of Sidebars* groups content from the special-interest boxes by category.

• An *Index of Scriptures* lists citations to particular biblical texts.

• An *Index of Topics* lists alphabetically the major subjects, names, topics, and locations referenced or discussed in the volume.

• An *Index of Modern Authors* organizes contemporary authors whose works are cited in the volume.

INTRODUCTION

The book of Jeremiah is the longest book in the Bible (in terms of words and verses) and is certainly one of the most complex. The complexity of the book is evident in several ways, including its structure and flow of thought, the person and role of the prophet, the historical setting of its individual texts, its understanding of God, and its relationship to a much shorter Greek version. [Carroll on Jeremiah] Yet, for all of the book's difficulty, its depth of reflection on divine action and human response, as well as the range and rigor of its rhetoric, has kept the book very much alive in the religious communities that recognize its canonical stature. Indeed, its language of "new covenant" has left its mark on the very name of the larger biblical collection to which it belongs.

Carroll on Jeremiah

The book of Jeremiah is long, complex, and difficult. To the modern reader it appears to be a repetitive mess, a mixture of prose and poetry, in no particular order, but containing traces of attempts to collate and give some order to parts of the material.... The reader who is not confused by reading the book of Jeremiah has not understood it!

Robert P. Carroll, Jeremiah (OTG; Sheffield: JSOT Press, 1989), 9.

JEREMIAH IN HISTORICAL CONTEXT

The book of Jeremiah is introduced by a brief description of the historical context in which Jeremiah's words were spoken (1:1-3), namely, the period leading up to the fall of Jerusalem to Babylon in 587 BC and its immediate aftermath. This event was a watershed moment in Israel's history and the book of Jeremiah centers on that event with all of its complex social, political, economic, military, and religious dimensions. [Focus on the Fall of Jerusalem] [Israel in the Ancient Near East]

A chronology of this period can be sketched on the basis of various biblical and nonbiblical sources, though the book of Jeremiah itself is

Focus on the Fall of Jerusalem

That Babylon so filled the scene during Jeremiah's ministry can be seen in the fact that Babylon and Nebuchadrezzar are explicitly mentioned more than two hundred times in chs. 20–52 (and implicitly elsewhere; Assyria is named only four times). The role that Judah's kings play in Jeremiah also reveals this focus; the closer in time the kings are to the fall of Jerusalem, the more attention they are given in the book. Hence, only one text speaks of oracles delivered in the time of Josiah (3:6), and Jehoiakim plays an active role only in 26:20-23 and 36:1-31 (and Jeremiah never encounters him directly); Zedekiah, however, is given a prominent role and is the only king with whom Jeremiah personally engages.

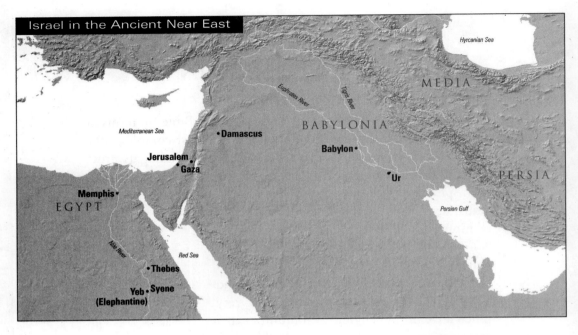

Israel in the Ancient Near East

only of partial help in this task. Some Jeremiah texts present a relatively straightforward recounting of the fall of Jerusalem (see 39:1-10; 52:1-30) or specify a certain chronology (e.g., 24:1; 25:1-3; 26:1; 27:1). Other passages, however, are almost completely devoid of specific historical reference (see chs. 2–20, 30–31), and the attempt to date many of these oracles more specifically has been sharply contested. William Holladay, for example, seeks to date Jeremiah's oracles with some precision, but most interpreters understand that such exactitude is not possible, indeed may be unfaithful to the text itself (a perspective followed in this commentary).[1] The book, especially the poetic oracles with their numerous metaphors, often presents the historical situation, not as "factual history," but in more impressionistic terms (see below). Moreover, the various perspectives of the editors of the book have certainly colored the telling of these events (see below). The following general sketch of the historical setting of the book is commonly accepted and will serve our purposes at this point.

Assyria was the dominant power in the region during the century and more prior to Babylon's ascendancy; its armies decimated the North in 722 BC (see 2 Kgs 17) and subjugated the South (Judah). As Assyrian power weakened over the course of the seventh century, the political and religious landscape of Judah changed in significant ways. Under King Josiah (640–609 BC) significant reforms were undertaken and some opportunity for independence presented itself, but these developments proved to be fleeting, especially when Josiah was killed in battle with the Egyptians (2 Chr 35:25 speaks of Jeremiah's lamenting reaction to his death). Babylon began to overshadow Assyria in Israel's larger world and then decisively defeated its armies at the battle of Nineveh (612 BC). Babylon under Nebuchadrezzar (who ascended the throne in 605 BC) set its sights on further conquests; it defeated Egypt and its allies at Carchemish (in northern Syria) in 605 BC and secured control of the region.

In the years following the death of King Josiah in 609 BC incompetent kings led Judah to ruin. [The Last Kings of Judah] Among them King Jehoiakim stood out; his contemptuous response to Jeremiah's warnings by personally destroying Baruch's scroll (36:1-32) may be a representative behavior (see 26:20-23; 22:13-19). When Jehoiakim rebeled against Babylonian rule (601 BC), Babylon moved against Jerusalem. Jehoiakim died in the siege and his son Jehoiachin, who reigned only three months before Jerusalem fell (598–597 BC), was exiled to Babylon along with many leading citizens (see 22:24-30). Jehoiachin in exile remained the titular head of Israel; he was alive in Babylon at the end of the book of Jeremiah (52:31-34; 561 BC).

The Babylonians put Zedekiah, Jehoiachin's uncle and another son of Josiah, on the throne. In the following decade King Zedekiah dithered away any good will Israel may have had with Babylon. Zedekiah was the only king with whom Jeremiah interacted in person, at least according to the book. The prophet persistently counseled Zedekiah to submit to the yoke of Babylon (21:1-14; 27:12; 32:1-5; 34:1-7; 37–38), but the king ignored him and rebelled. Babylon came against Jerusalem, razed the city and temple, humiliated the Davidic king, and sent him and other Judahites to join their compatriots in exile in Babylon (39:1-10; 52:1-30; 587 BC).

Nebuchadrezzar appointed a leading Judean citizen, Gedaliah, to govern Judah (from Mizpah, north of Jerusalem). Jeremiah, who was not exiled to Babylon because of his counsel of nonrebellion, became involved in advising those who were left in the land. Within a few years, however, anti-Babylonian zealots assassinated

The Last Kings of Judah

The length of Jeremiah's ministry is remarkable in that it takes place over the course of the reigns of the last five kings of Judah and one governor. While two of the kings reigned for less than a year, this length of time is witness to his staying power through periods of great tension and hardship, both for himself personally and for his community. The rulers and key events during their reigns are:

Josiah (640–609 BC)
Jehoahaz (609 BC)
Jehoiakim (609–598 BC)
Babylon under Nebuchadrezzar establishes hegemony in the region with its defeat of Egypt (and Assyria) at the battle of Carchemish (605 BC). Jehoiakim rebels against Babylon, an act which leads to the subjugation of Jerusalem.
Jehoiachin/Coniah (598–597 BC)
Judah/Jerusalem falls to Babylon in 597 BC and the first deportation of citizens to Babylon occurs.
Zedekiah (597–587 BC)
Zedekiah's rebellion against Babylon leads to the destruction of Jerusalem and the temple, followed by a second deportation.
Gedaliah (587-582? BC)
This Babylon-appointed governor is assassinated by anti-Babylon conspirators, leading to a third deportation to Babylon while still others flee to Egypt, taking Jeremiah with them.

Gedaliah and more Judeans were exiled to Babylon (582 BC?). Other Judeans, ignoring Jeremiah's counsel, migrated to Egypt and forced the prophet to accompany them (40:7–44:30).

The presentation of the history of Israel in the book of Jeremiah ends in the middle of things; ambiguity reigns and no resolution of these disturbing and devastating events is in view. The future of the people of God hangs in the balance. God has made promises, but fulfillment lies beyond any horizon visible to the community to whom Jeremiah is written.

The Primary Issues of the Book of Jeremiah and the Rhetorical Strategies Used to Address Them

The importance of knowing at least the broad outlines of this historical situation for the interpretation of Jeremiah cannot be exaggerated. At the same time, the introduction of the book (1:1-3) specifies that the intended readers have already experienced these events; the history in and of itself will not be news to them. These verses, which indicate that the fall of Jerusalem has already occurred, provide a lens through which the book is to be read. The historical setting for the *book* in its present form (however late its final editors are dated) is a time when Israel had been scattered across the ancient Near Eastern landscape, from Egypt to Babylon and beyond. Even more, however much later editors appropriated this material in order to speak to new situations in the life of the people of God, from the book's own standpoint those newer situations do not include a time after Israel's restoration to the land (538 BC). For all the promises about Israel's future fortunes (e.g., chs. 30–31, 50–51), they remain unfulfilled from the perspective of the book.

These opening verses (1:1-3) mean that the original audience for the *book* of Jeremiah is fundamentally different from the audience for the *preaching* of Jeremiah (even if many people are a part of both audiences). The word for that audience is not about religious matters that float above the maelstrom of life. The book is addressed to a particularly horrific situation in the life of the people of God and is to be interpreted in terms of that specificity. The fall of Jerusalem is such a disastrous event for Israel because every aspect of its life is so deeply affected (see the poignant cries in the book of Lamentations). This includes the devastation of the city and country, the death and traumatization of many citizens (including women and children), the exile of key leaders to

Babylon, and the loss of two institutions that had centered Israel's life for centuries—the temple and the Davidic kingship.

The book of Jeremiah is most basically concerned to address itself in as forthright a way as possible to pressing questions voiced by the survivors of this debacle, most of whom are probably in exile in Babylon. Given these implied readers, the book is not primarily concerned to transmit the words and deeds of Jeremiah as such, but to use the heritage of Jeremiah to address the ongoing spiritual and religious needs of a devastated and questioning community. Their most compelling question is one that regularly punctuates the text either explicitly or implicitly (e.g., 5:19; 9:12; 13:22; 14:19; 16:10; 22:8): "Why is the land ruined and laid waste like a wilderness, so that no one passes through?"

The responses to this and related questions (e.g., What might have been? What will the future be?) are the decisive contribution of the book of Jeremiah for its implied readers. The reason these disastrous events took place is most basically rooted in the nature of the God–Israel relationship. The book stakes a theological claim that these events occurred, not because Israel's God was incompetent or uncaring, but because the people of God were unfaithful and their own God would not, indeed could not, remain indifferent, for the future of the *creation* was at stake. At the same time, the effect desired in readers of the book was not simply informational. Walter Brueggemann's statement regarding the intended effects of the preaching of Jeremiah would apply in a general way to the book, namely, "to have an impact on persons, to impinge upon perception and awareness, to intrude upon public policy, and to evoke faithful and transformed behavior."[2] I would add: the intended effect is to bring to shamed and hurting exiles a clear word about the kind of God who is present and active on their behalf. This divine engagement means that, despite the people's unfaithful past and desperate present (which must be squarely confronted), God will act to make all things new.

What rhetorical strategies are used in Jeremiah that could have such an effect on the intended audience? What would this rhetoric do to those who read it? For one thing, words are used with considerable passion and energy, not only through striking images and metaphors, but in the forms and patterns of the language itself: "in exclamations and interjections, in emphatic particles, in passionate shouts and urgent expostulations and warnings, and, above all, in extraordinarily striking assonances."[3] This use of language conveys a sense of urgency and deep concern. [Brueggemann on Jeremiah's Language]

Brueggemann on Jeremiah's Language

The situation of the people is such that language "must not be conventional, reasonable, predictable, or expected. It must shock people's sensitivity, call attention to what is not usually noticed, break the routine, make statements with ambiguity so that people redescribe things that have long since seemed settled, bear surpluses of power before routine assessment."

Walter Brueggemann, "The Book of Jeremiah: Portrait of the Prophet," in *Interpreting the Prophets*, ed. J. L. Mays and P. J. Achtemeir (Philadelphia: Fortress, 1987), 118.

In addition, the frequent change of speakers and exchange among speakers gives to the entire book a dialogical character. This dialogue conveys a sense of urgency as various voices get into the conversation about the nature of the crisis at hand and what to do about it. The people are often quoted, in interaction with both Jeremiah and God (e.g., 3:22b-25; 8:19; 14:19-22). Individuals (usually community leaders) are often in conversation with Jeremiah, and with God, though usually through the intermediation of the prophet (e.g., 21:1-7). The prophet and God are often in lively and urgent communication, with regard to both personal and community matters (e.g., 12:1-6; 15:15-21); though God's word begins the relationship (1:4-5), both take the initiative in the ongoing interaction. The God of Jeremiah not only speaks, but listens, and is open to taking new directions in view of what is heard (e.g., 18:7-10).

The dialogue is especially revealing of the highly conflicted character of perspectives and relationships. Who speaks the truth regarding the nature of the situation and God's will with respect to it? The prophet-to-prophet interaction is particularly important to note, for claims regarding who has the true word of God for these implied readers are highly contested, not least among the exiles themselves (see especially chs. 27–29). But opposition to Jeremiah and the word of God stems from virtually every quarter—from his family and friends (11:18-23; 12:1-6), kings and other governmental officials (20:1-6; 26:1-24; 36:1-31; 37-43), the "remnant of Judah" (42–44), and the people more generally (e.g., 15:10). The conflict that began early in Jeremiah's career persisted throughout his ministry and continued into the very situation of the implied readers. It would be crucial for them to learn how to discern the truth amid the cacophany of voices claiming to know the will of God, and this story of conflict was designed to make them aware of the options and to help them sort things out. Their future was at stake.

From a different perspective, language is used in Jeremiah in a starkly realistic way. These texts tell the truth about the situation and do so in an unsparing way through the use of vivid portrayals, piercing images, and harsh, outrageous metaphors. This unrelenting realism and these shocking metaphors are used for all levels of the divine-human relationship, but especially the people's infidelity and their experience of judgment.

Regarding the people's infidelity, they had been unfaithful to their relationship with God, both with respect to their life of faith and worship and of their relationships with one another. The primary metaphor used for the God–Israel relationship is marital. The marriage began very well (2:2-3) but was soon violated as people and leaders alike became idolatrous (2:5-13). Shocking sexual imagery is used to depict this infidelity (see 2:20, 23-24, 33; 3:1-9, 13, 20; 4:30; 13:27) as well as the divine judgment (13:22-26). Because Israel is "wife" in this metaphor, the infidelity is described one-sidedly in terms of female behavior and has been rightfully evaluated as degrading to women, whether then or now (see commentary on the several texts). Suffice it to say here that this imagery was likely used for its shock value, particularly in view of the predominantly male audience. It was a way to bring sharply home to readers the depth of their unfaithfulness.

With respect to Israel's failure in interhuman relationships, the metaphors used are also barbed and biting, designed to get to the heart of things in a hurry. Adulterous Israelite men are likened to lusty stallions, neighing for their neighbors' wives and trooping to brothels (5:7-8). Wealthy Israelites are likened to fowlers; they are scoundrels who set traps and catch human beings by stealing the goods of the less fortunate to fill their own pantries and growing fat and sleek in the process (5:26-27). They are legal sharks who misuse the court system, draining the lifeblood of the innocent poor (2:34) and failing to come to the defense of the widow and orphan (5:28). They use their tongues like a bow and arrow, speaking lies and slandering even their own family and friends (9:3-6). There is no commandment that remains unbroken (7:9), and yet they claim innocence (8:6). Again, the sharp metaphors are designed to get under the skin and expose the inner rottenness that infects all their relationships. Given this rhetoric the readers would not be able to claim innocence or argue that God or even life itself has somehow been unfair to them.

Regarding the experience of judgment, the rhetoric is designed for different purposes. The devastating experience in and through which readers have gone is not downplayed. Considerable energy and passion is used to portray a community that has experienced a disaster approximating a nuclear nightmare (see 4:23-26). While the text commonly speaks of these events in future terms, readers would recognize that they have already experienced them and continue to bear their effects.

The text repeatedly speaks of those realities that caused this suffering, especially evident in the recurring phrase, "sword, famine, pestilence" (e.g., 14:12, 16; 15:2). These words are repeated *ad nauseam*; "famine" occurs more than thirty times; "sword" more than seventy times (along with numerous other words for instruments of war); "pestilence/disease" more than twenty times. Words such as "death," "destroy/destruction," "devour," "break," "scatter"—of adults and children, military and civilian—are common. Even more graphic language is used for those who die: their bodies are not buried (or are disinterred) and are used for dung or become food for birds and beasts (7:33; 8:1-3; 9:22; 16:4; 19:7; 34:20) and even for members of their own families and neighbors (19:9)! Repeated words such as "waste," "ruin," and "desolation" speak of the devastating effect upon their entire environment—homes, cities and towns, birds, animals, vegetation, and land. All of this incessantly repeated language gives full rhetorical recognition of the hell through which the readers have gone; they will be able to recognize their own experience in all of its gory and tragic details in the text itself.

Even more, the language Jeremiah used to portray this disaster includes reference not only to external realities but also to their internal effects. Common words, often occurring in clusters for maximal effect (e.g., 25:9; 42:18)—"horror," "shame," "disgrace," "curse," "hissing," "taunt," and "derision"—say something not only about how others perceive them but also, especially when thinking about shame in that culture, about their own depleted sense of self. James Muilenburg has catalogued the "terminology of adversity" in Jeremiah, and the range of frequency of the language of pain and suffering is truly remarkable.[4] His categories include the following: sickness and wounds (e.g., 30:12-15); travail and anguish (e.g., 4:31); horror, terror, desolation (e.g., 12:10-11); abandonment, rejection, alienation (e.g., 14:19-21); grief and mourning (e.g., 6:26; 31:15). The pain of readers is thereby put on full public display for all to see and hear and in a way that is both wrenching and realistic.

That this painful experience of the people is so fully acknowledged in both its external and internal aspects is of great importance; only when this is done—and done publicly—can any positive words about the future begin to take hold among the readers. The several dimensions of the lament psalms, which so straightforwardly voice the cries and acknowledge the pain and the hurt, both self-inflicted and enemy-inflicted, with all of the internal and external effects, certainly lies in the background of the use of this language.

No wonder it is often said that the book of Jeremiah is filled with tears. It is notable that not only the tears of the people are put on public display (often in their own words, e.g., 14:19-22), so also are the tears of the prophet and the tears of God (e.g., 4:19; 8:18–9:1; 9:10, 17-19; 10:19; 12:7; 13:17; 14:17; 20:14-18; 23:9). What becomes so apparent in the book is that readers could see that neither God nor God's messenger remained aloof and unaffected by what they have had to go through. The same or similar language is used for the tears of all those involved in this disaster.

Abraham Heschel has been most articulate in lifting up the tears of prophet and God.[5] Others have followed his train. Regarding the prophet, Muilenburg speaks strikingly of "his capacity for empathy, both social and cosmic, his profound sympathy with his own people, despite their waywardness and infidelity, his ability to identify himself interiorly with their afflictions."[6] The prophet's suffering is not simply empathetic and personal, however; the prophet embodies the suffering of God. I have spoken at length of the tearful speeches of God in Jeremiah, tears because the people have been unfaithful to the relationship and tears because of the suffering the people are having to undergo.[7] The suffering of God, however, despite all the heartache at the people's infidelity, is not a passive, enervating suffering; God's suffering is of such a nature that it enters powerfully into the lives of people where they are and works to transform their mourning into joy (31:13-17). The tears of the people are fully recognized; their desperate situation is named for what it is. But because of the suffering of the prophet and God, their tears will not have the last word.

Another unusual rhetorical detail in the book is the naming of over fifty different individuals from the time of Jeremiah's ministry, often with specific family connections. Almost all of these names occur in chapters 20–45. Whereas chapters 2–20 are dominated by oracles directed to the people as a whole, chapters 20–45 focus on various officials and religious leaders. Of what import is this interest in familial detail and in narratives that portray them in action? For one thing this narrative detail shows how widespread was the rejection of the prophet and his word; every level of Israelite society was resistant. And through the telling of stories, and not just giving oracular prophetic pronouncements, memories can be jogged and this wholesale rejection can be given a "real life" status. A *story* of resistance can have greater potential impact on those who lived through this time. From a post-fall perspective such a portrayal of individuals and their stories would also make clear that there are no innocents among the exiles. A few persons are lifted up and given a positive stature (e.g., 26:24; 38:7-13), perhaps to show that the people were not somehow fated to speak and act as they did and to suggest that there is a faithful remnant upon which a new community can be built. There may also be some interest here in putting into place the families and individuals who would or would not be leaders of a post-restoration community. These specifics, as well as the numerous chronological references, may also serve the rhetorical function of anchoring the narrative in specific persons, times and places so that appeals cannot be made to faulty memories.

In this connection we note the considerable amount of narrative material that speaks of the prophet and his work. After a period of time in scholarship during which the person of the prophet was given front-page attention, with special focus on the confessions,[8] there has been a recent tendency to decenter Jeremiah and emphasize the word that he speaks.[9] But the pendulum has now swung too far in the other direction. The existence of so many narratives calls us back to the prophet as agent of the word of God (the degree to which the life of the prophet is idealized is beside the point; see below). The narratives want to say, at the least, that the word of God does not arrive on the human scene in a disembodied way; that word is spoken by human beings and their abilities and character count with respect to how that word is handled and proclaimed. Human beings with their gifts make a difference to God and to the word that is spoken. Even more, the word of God is conveyed not simply in the words that are spoken but also in and through the prophets' actions (of which the symbolic acts are but one sort) and through the persons that they are, through their very humanity. [Von Rad on the Person of the Prophet]

Finally, how might we evaluate the rhetorical strategies in the book? How effective were (are) they? Might they serve as models for other times and places? Are they (always, often) meant to be taken literally? How much of a role does hyperbole or irony or even humor play? Were (are) all of the metaphors of God appropriate?

Von Rad on the Person of the Prophet

Jeremiah serves God not only with the harsh proclamation of his mouth, but also with his person; his life becomes unexpectedly involved in the cause of God on earth. Thus, now—and in Jeremiah this is something new—the prophet not only becomes a witness of God through the strength of his charisma, but also in his humanity; but not as one who triumphs over the sins of mankind, not as one overcoming, but as a messenger of God to mankind breaking under the strain. Hence, Jeremiah's life here becomes a forceful witness, his suffering soul and his life ebbing away in God's service becomes a testimony of God.

Gerhard von Rad, "The Confessions of Jeremiah," in *A Prophet to the Nations: Essays in Jeremiah Studies* (Winona Lake IN: Eisenbrauns, 1984), 346.

Are some of them exhausted, no longer possible to be used? The metaphors of violence, patriarchy, and perhaps even misogyny come to mind. But the evaluative questions become even more pressing: What kind of God is this who uses such coarse and violent language and who speaks and works in ways that issue in such suffering and displacement? And what kind of person must the prophet be who agrees to be the agent for such language and action?

The Portrayal of Jeremiah and the Tradition in which He Stands

Generally speaking, the book portrays Jeremiah as a prophet who has personally received a word from God regarding the divine purposes with respect to Israel and its larger world, has been called to speak that word in a public way, and who obediently, though reluctantly takes up that task.

Considerable scholarly disagreement exists, however, regarding the extent to which the book's portrayal of Jeremiah corresponds to reality. Basic to this debate are two observations: the book is unique in the considerable amount of material that speaks of the person of Jeremiah; at the same time, the book itself expresses no interest in biography or autobiography per se (witness the absence of reference to his birth or death). To construct a portrayal of Jeremiah, the interpreter has the difficult task of seeking to weave a fabric from bits and pieces of various sorts laid out in an uncertain order over the course of the book. It may be legitimate for readers to attempt to do this, but they should be aware that they are then using the book in a way in which it was not written to be used.

Rembrandt's Portrait of Jeremiah

Perhaps no other artist captures the depth of the human psyche better than Rembrandt van Rijn. In this painting, Jeremiah is portrayed amid the destruction of a smoldering Jerusalem; yet, he is strangely illuminated by a glowing light. Underlying his deep sense of lament, perplexed in the midst of his prophetic obedience to God, Jeremiah leans on the "Word," with his left arm leaning on a book of Holy Scripture. The vessels of gold and glitter from a previous prosperous temple site, perhaps symbols of self-offering, have been reduced to a few gathered remains. His use of subtle tonal modulations reflect Rembrandt's use of light and dark (chiaroscuro) to create a sense of God's Presence as if emanating from the depths of the ruins.

Rembrandt van Rijn. *Jeremiah Lamenting the Destruction of Jerusalem.* 1630. Oil on Panel. Rijksmuseum, Amsterdam. (Credit: Super Stock, Inc)

A traditional approach to this issue, still well represented among modern scholars, is that the book narrates the story of the ministry of a prophet named Jeremiah who lived during a tumultuous period of Israel's life. The assumption is that the reader can determine the setting of the individual texts and construct a consistent portrayal of the prophet in his historical context.[10] A more recent approach, represented by Carroll especially, claims that such a reconstructive task goes beyond the evidence available.[11] For him, the book presents an idealized character; Jeremiah is essentially a literary figure, with only shadowy links to historical reality.

Brueggemann and others seek to move between these two extremes, correctly in my estimation.[12] As is true to a greater or lesser degree with the presentation of any historical figure, the portrayal of Jeremiah reflects both the speech and action of an actual individual and a literary construction by editors or authors informed by varying perspectives. The book presents us with both a powerful personality *and* an interpretation of his role and significance. Because the editors are inevitably selective and have been shaped by their perspective on the past and the pressing issues they seek to address, Jeremiah emerges as both more than and less than the actual historical prophet. [Truth and Historicity]

Truth and Historicity

It is important to say that, though considerable uncertainty exists regarding the extent to which the book reflects the "facts" regarding the prophet and his life situation, truth is not necessarily related to historicity. Truth can be conveyed through a variety of types of literature, including idealized portraits of prophetic figures.

According to the chronology the book provides (see 1:1-3; 25:1-3; 36:1-2), Jeremiah's prophetic ministry lasts for over forty years. It begins with his call in 627 BC in the thirteenth year of Josiah (see 1:2; 25:3), though that has been disputed,[13] and ends several years after the fall of Jerusalem in 587 BC (see chs. 42–44). There seems to be no good reason not to accept this chronology in a general way. Jeremiah's ministry thus begins at a time of great promise under King Josiah and his reforms, though it is not clear how Jeremiah is related (if at all) to these efforts (see 2 Chr 35:25), and it ends with the country and its treasured institutions in ruins and its people scattered across the region.

Jeremiah has a priestly lineage, and this probably informs the character of his message to some degree. He is a native of Anathoth (1:1), a village three miles northeast of Jerusalem in the territory of the tribe of Benjamin. He is a descendant of the tribe of Levi through the priest Abiathar, one of the two priests appointed by David to oversee Israel's religious life (1:1; 2 Sam 20:25). Abiathar was banished to Anathoth by Solomon (1 Kgs 2:26-27) because of his support of Solomon's brother Adonijah as David's successor.

The descendants of the other chief priest, Zadok, were thus in charge of the temple during the centuries after Solomon, and at the time of Jeremiah; they would have been supporters of the Davidic monarchy.

So Jeremiah belongs to a family of priests that had long been out of the loop of religious authority in the land. He was thus an "outsider" with a pedigree and was raised in a village where his family had long been settled; it is reasonable to think that they had maintained a critical stance with respect to the religious and royal establishment. Jeremiah's various critical references to the temple and to matters such as sacrifice may stand in this critical tradition (e.g., 6:20; 7:1-22). But it seems unwise to claim that his sharp criticism entails rejection of such religious institutions (see 33:17-26 and God's promise regarding the levitical priesthood). At various points his ministry is carried out in proximity to the temple (chs. 7, 26), and some think he could have been a priest, or a cultic prophet, that is, a prophet with responsibilities in association with the temple worship.[14] But this seems unlikely in view of his heritage; he may rather have intruded publicly into these areas to make his point as vividly as possible.[15]

Regarding his royal connections, Jeremiah often comes into conflict with Josiah's successors, though he is reported to have had direct personal contact only with King Zedekiah. His efforts were rewarded by much condemnation and derision from these kings as well as from other authorities and the populace as a whole (see chs. 26, 36). Interpreters often make much of Jeremiah's opposition to a "royal–temple ideology" (this is a key element in Brueggemann's interpretation of the book),[16] but some caution is in order.

Jeremiah does subject the kings to sharp attacks in the concentrated passage in 23:10-30, but in the major section that focuses on indictment and judgment (chs. 2–20) kings are rarely singled out (Manasseh in 15:4, but he is from a previous generation). Kings do come in for criticism more directly in chapters 21–45 and their responses are directly related to the fate of the nation. This judgment is unrelenting, however, only with respect to King Jehoiakim (22:18-19; 26:20-23; 36:20-31). Jeremiah expresses hostility toward Jehoiachin in 22:24-30, yet the final form of the book ameliorates this judgment with a positive note (52:31-34). Jeremiah's most personal relationship with a king (Zedekiah) is marked by frustration and disappointment, yet less than full condemnation; indeed the prophet holds out positive possibilities (e.g., 27:12; 34:4-5; 38:17-18).

Moreover, several statements about the kingship suggest a positive value (22:1-4), including the approval of Josiah's way of ruling (22:15-16). Jeremiah's hopes are shaped in terms of a new David (23:5-6; 30:9; 33:14-26; cf. 30:21). In fact, 33:17-26 refers to the unconditional character of the Davidic covenant and the divine commitment thereto is stated in the strongest of terms—as firm as the creation itself. Jeremiah's sharpest words about individual kings seem not to be grounded in a blanket condemnation of the Davidic kingship as such. It is often claimed that many or all of these positive statements did not originate with Jeremiah himself. This may be so, but that is a speculative claim; clearly the book's final editors want to characterize the message of Jeremiah for readers in these terms.

Jeremiah is consciously linked to Israel's prophetic heritage. The only full quotation of a text from the prophetic literature (26:18) explicitly links him to the prophet Micah (Mic 3:12). Connections with Hosea, a northern prophet, are often noted, especially the use of the marital metaphor for the God–Israel relationship and sexual imagery for Israel's infidelity (cf. Hos 1–3), as well as the stress upon the pathos of God in response (see Hos 6:4; 11:1-9). Though Jeremiah's focus on issues of social justice does not match that of Amos or Isaiah, his concern is lively enough to continue that tradition (see Jer 5:25-28; 7:5-6). Jeremiah's witness to God's use of Babylon as both agent and recipient of judgment (see below) parallels Isaiah's understanding of Assyria (see Isa 10). The conflict with false prophets, which often centers Jeremiah's attention (e.g., 6:13-15; 14:13-16; 23:9-32; 27-29), stands in the tradition of Micah 3:5-6 (cf. Hos 9:8-9; Isa 28:7-10; Zeph 3:4). Examples could be multiplied, but these are sufficient to show that there is a self-conscious linkage of Jeremiah to an existing prophetic heritage. Jeremiah is not unique nor, for all the opposition he faces, does he stand alone (see 26:20-23).

Particularly because of the connections made to Deuteronomy (see below), commentators make much of Jeremiah's links to Moses.[17] Yet, the various correspondences that are drawn seem often to be strained. Parallels between Jeremiah's call (1:4-10) and that of Moses (Exod 3:1-6) have often been noted, yet the differences are profound regarding the nature of the commission (except in general terms); the similarities may be more due to conventional ways of narrating call experiences than conscious linkage. The reference in Deuteronomy 18:18 to God raising up a prophet and putting words into his mouth probably lies in the background of Jeremiah 1:9 (see 15:16; Ezek 2:8-3:3).[18] At the same time, there is only one mention of Moses in the book (15:1) and surprisingly few explicit references to the Sinai covenant (11:2-10; 22:9; 31:32) or even the Law (e.g., 5:5; 6:19; 7:5-9; 9:13; 16:11; 26:4; 32:23). Certainly the Law plays an important role in Jeremiah, particularly as the grounds for the indictment of the people (e.g., 7:8-10). At the same time, certain emphases in Jeremiah go well beyond Moses, not least the "new" covenant that sets aside the Mosaic form (31:31-34), a "new" constitutive act of God that depreciates the exodus (16:14-15; 23:7-8), the continuing claims regarding the promissory covenants of Abraham and David (see commentary on chs. 32–33), and an understanding of God that is much more relational and filled with pathos than that of the Deuteronomist.

Regarding matters of a more personal nature in the portrayal of Jeremiah, several are noted in the book; yet, they are mentioned not out of biographical interest, but in the service of the word of God that Jeremiah brings. We are told that he was not married, had no children (16:2) and did not participate in mourning rites or community feasts (16:5-9), but this was done at the command of God to serve as a symbolic act (see commentary at ch. 13). In obeying God's command in these respects, the prophet not only prefigured the end of these experiences for the people of Israel but also portrayed, indeed embodied what God's own experience of abandonment and the loss of community was like (12:7; 14:8).[19] We are also given glimpses into Jeremiah's concern for personal safety (37:20; 38:15). These references suggest that his courageous stand on behalf of the word of God is not undertaken with total disregard for personal well-being and his complaints indicate that he would rather not have had to bear the painful pressures brought upon him by his antagonists.

This reference brings us to Jeremiah's several laments or confessions (see commentary at chs. 11–12). A consistent theme in the laments is Jeremiah's complaint to God regarding the opposition he faced (e.g., 11:19-20; 20:10-12). Specific testimony is given to efforts made by his opponents to silence him, including trial, arrest, and imprisonment (e.g., 26:10-19; 36:26; 37:11–38:6), though he was not without supporters (26:24; 38:7-13). Resistance to him and the message he brings continues until the end of the narrative (ch. 44). Again, this information is not provided for biographical purposes, as real as the experiences may well have been; rather, the prophet's experience of rejection and his lamenting his situation were understood to mirror *God's* experience at the hands of the people. Even more, because the prophet not only spoke God's word, but embodied it, God's experience becomes Jeremiah's experience. As God was rejected by the people, so also the prophet who spoke and embodied God's word was resisted and renounced by them. Jeremiah's laments, whatever their roots in his personal life, thereby have become a proclamation of the word of *God* to the audience for whom these chapters were written.[20] [Heschel on the Prophet]

Heschel on the Prophet

An analysis of prophetic utterances shows that the fundamental experience of the prophet is a fellowship with the feelings of God, *a sympathy with the divine pathos*, a communion with the divine consciousness which comes about through the prophet's reflection of, or participation in, the divine pathos . . . . He lives not only his personal life, but also the life of God. The prophet hears God's voice and feels his heart. He tries to impart the *pathos* of the message together with its logos.

The prophet's inner life was not wholly his own. His emotional situation reflected the divine relation to Israel: compassion as well as anger. What he felt was not always original with him.

The prophet does not see the world from the point of view of a political theory; he is a person who sees the world from the point of view of God; he sees the world through the eyes of God.

Abraham Heschel, *The Prophets* (New York: Harper, 1962), 26, 125, 138.

The last picture readers are given of Jeremiah finds him condemning the idolatry of his compatriots in Egypt (43:8–44:30). The time of his death is left unreported; the place of his death is probably Egypt.

The portrayal of Jeremiah is developed even further beyond the borders of the book. The tradition of Jeremiah as a "weeping prophet" is reinforced by 2 Chronicles 35:25 and is extended by the Septuagint's (LXX) preface to Lamentations (1:1), which ascribes the book to Jeremiah. In Jewish literature, later legends imagine varying accounts of his ministry in Egypt and Babylon as well as Palestine, both before and after the exile. Baruch, the Letter of Jeremiah, and 2 Maccabees (2:2-8; 15:14-16) continue the tradition within the deuterocanonical books (see also Sir 49:4-7), as do the pseudepigraphical 1 Esdras (1:28), *Lives of the Prophets, Paralipomena of Jeremiah*, and *2–4 Baruch*. It may also be noted that Jeremiah is given more attention than any other prophet in both Josephus and Philo; in contrast, Jeremiah is mentioned in the Qumran texts relatively infrequently.

In the New Testament, the prophet is mentioned three times, all in Matthew (2:17; 16:14; 27:9), but only the first reference is clearly understood, citing Jeremiah 31:15 in connection with Herod's slaughter of the innocents. Citations of Jeremiah texts in the New Testament are relatively infrequent. The most famous use of Jeremiah are the references to the new covenant in 1 Corinthians 11:25; 2 Corinthians 3:5-6; and Hebrews 8:8-12, 10:16-17 (see the commentary at 31:31-34). Revelation 18 has several direct references to Jeremiah 50–51, especially in using language regarding Babylon to speak of Rome (see also Rev 7:17; 13:9-10). Other allusions may be noted, such as the "den of robbers" (Jer 7:11 and Mark 11:17); "find rest for your souls" (Jer 6:16 and Matt 11:29); "boasting" in the Lord (Jer 9:23-24 and 1 Cor 1:31; 2 Cor 10:17); and Paul's being set apart before he was born (Jer 1:5 and Gal 1:15).

The Structure of Jeremiah

The structure of the book of Jeremiah, while clear in some respects, is finally something of a puzzle.[21] Several factors contribute to this difficulty, including the less than obvious development of thought, the lack of a consistent chronological ordering, the references to various scrolls and other writings, and the differences between the Hebrew Bible and the LXX (see below). That the book is clearly a collection of materials emergent in various times and places could mean that the book as a whole has been somewhat haphazardly arranged; scholarly difficulties in discerning a precise structure may well be revealing of this reality.

Within the book itself there are some signs of specific collections of material. Chapter 36 speaks of two scrolls, but we cannot be certain which portions of the present book are being referenced (see below). In 30:2 we are informed of a "book," commonly called the Book of Comfort/Consolation, a smaller collection of oracles of hope and promise; it is probably to be identified with chapters 30–33, but some think only chapters 30–31 are to be included. Chapters 46–51 consist largely of oracles against the nations (OAN); they likely constituted a separate collection at some point (see below on their placement in the LXX), and some think that the "book" of 25:13 refers to this collection (others identify it with the scroll in ch. 36 and to all or most of chs. 2–24). These signs of collections within the book suggest that it has been composed at least in significant part by bringing together originally separate blocks of material (see below).

The concern for dating at many different points in the book (28 instances) opens up the question of a possible chronological arrangement. Yet, the various parts of the book are not in chronological order; for example, 21:1-2 is dated close to 588 BC; 24:1 dates that chapter soon after 597 BC; the next chapter is dated in 605 BC (25:1). Moreover, hardly any concern for chronology is present in chapters 2–20 (3:6 speaks generally of the time of Josiah). While a greater chronological concern exists in chapters 21–45 (e.g., 25:1; 26:1; 27:1; 28:1; 36:1), no pattern seems evident. Such mixed chronological references suggest that other factors have been more decisive in arranging the material.

Stylistic devices have also been thought to provide clues to the arrangement of the book. For example, recurring words/phrases at key points have been noted. Jeremiah's reference to the womb of his mother in 1:5 and 20:18 has been considered an *inclusio* for chapters 1–20;[22] on other hand, the repetition of the commissioning verbs of 1:10 in 24:6 could be said to bracket chapters

1–24. Or, the references to the ancestral promises and restoring Israel's fortunes in 30:3 and 33:26 have been said to bracket the Book of Comfort. Yet, perhaps the phrase "the days are surely coming" in 30:3 and 31:38 serves this function for a shorter book. Perhaps all of these bracketing devices played an organizing role at one or another stage in the formation of the book, but we cannot be certain.

Various collections according to theme suggest editorial arranging: 2:1–4:4 (sin and repentance); 7:1–8:3 (cultic matters); 14:1–15:4 (drought and war); 18:1–19:15 (image of potter and clay); 21:11–23:6 (royal house and city); 23:9-40 (prophets); 27–29 (prophets and Babylon); 37–38 (Jeremiah and Zedekiah); and 40:7–41:18 (community without Jeremiah). Yet, such topical arrangements do not seem to be carried consistently throughout the book or with any overall framework in mind.

The pivotal role played by chapter 25 in the book has suggested a plausible arrangement for the entire book. Most scholars are agreed that 25:1-14 (or the bulk of it) constitutes a summary and conclusion to the first half of the book (or perhaps chs. 2–20). Especially helpful is the further idea that the entire chapter constitutes a "hinge" for the book as a whole.[23] On the one hand, the chapter summarizes the first half of the book with its focus on the judgment against Israel (vv. 1-11; vv. 8-11 constitute the oracle). On the other hand, the chapter anticipates the OAN at the end of the book with its general oracles against the nations (vv. 15-38), especially the demise of Babylon, anticipated in vv. 12-14, 26 (cf. chs. 50–51). The judgment of Israel is not the end of God's work; indeed, God's agent for that judgment (Babylon) shall itself be judged and Israel will be delivered and return home (chs. 50–51 could thus be considered climactic). This consideration then doubles back to the first chapter and picks up the theme of Jeremiah as a "prophet to the nations" (1:10). This role of Jeremiah among the nations is picked up especially in the more personal references in 25:15-17 and 51:59-64. This point of continuity across the entire book of the word of God spoken against the nations provides, finally, a word of hope for Israel.

It seems best then to divide Jeremiah into two major blocks of materials (chs. 2–24, 26–51, with ch. 25 as a hinge), to which is attached an introductory chapter (1) and a concluding epilogue (52). The latter bracket the book in its final form; they provide the call of Jeremiah and a summary of the most basic historical situation that both book and prophet address, dating from 597 BC

(52:1) to 561 BC (52:31-34). The latter verses anticipate a positive future, especially when viewed through the lens of chapters 50–51.

The division of Jeremiah into two major blocks of material has often been elucidated in terms of their respective emphases on judgment and deliverance.[24] Though this is an appropriate observation in terms of the number of texts that are devoted to these two themes, it can be misleading. The first half of the book contains several strong oracles of unconditional future salvation (3:15-18; 12:14-16; 16:14-15; 23:5-8), even climactically so (24:4-7, 25:12-14). These announcements are indeed amplified in the second half of the book, but the latter does not introduce a new theme.

Emphasis on the discontinuity of two halves of the book can neglect the fact that the second half of the book contains many narratives that *illustrate in specific terms* the resistance of specific groups and individuals to the word of God of that Jeremiah speaks more generally in the first half of the book (chs. 26–29; 34; 36–44; these in turn have been anticipated in 20:1-6 and 21:1-7). This move from the general to the specific must also be emphasized in thinking through the factors behind this division of the book.

One additional factor may be noted regarding this division. The people of Israel as a whole tend to be indicted in the first half of the book, but the climactic vision of chapter 24 first introduces a division *within the community*, between the exiles in Babylon and other Israelites.[25] This issue of the identity of the true people of God within Israel receives focused attention in the second half of the book, with its interest in prophetic conflict and the future of the exiles in Babylon (27–29), the perfidy of those remaining in the land (34, 37–38), the exception of the Rechabites (35), and the denunciation of the "remnant of Judah" that goes to Egypt (41–44). The future of Israel in the plan of God lies with those in Babylon (from where they will return to the land of promise, 50–51).

The organization of the materials *within* the two major blocks of chapters 2–24 and 25–51 is contested.[26] We only give a basic outline at this point, suggesting relationships as the commentary proceeds. Chapters 2–24 may be divided into chapters 2–6, 7–10, 11–20, and 21–24. Chapters 26–51 may be divided into chapters 26–35, 37–45 (with ch. 36 constituting a hinge), and chapters 46–51. [Outline of the Book of Jeremiah]

Having made these observations, there may be a point in the absence of a clear overall structure. If the book is understood as a *collage*, a work of art in which materials of various kinds are thrown

Outline of the Book of Jeremiah

onto a screen, then the intended effect is achieved by an imaginative profusion of different genres, images and metaphors, life settings, and personal encounters. This would match the use of language more generally (see above). That is, the book does not present an argument in any usual sense or a clear historical development but seeks to achieve its objective by a kaleidoscopic look at a highly complex situation from a myriad of angles. The resultant portrayal is highly impressionistic, perhaps even surreal, and leaves the reader with a sense of the situation that is much more effective than a photograph or linear argument could achieve. As such, the book conveys the remarkable complexity of the situation for readers who had to come to terms in a personal way with this period in their history.

The Formation of the Book of Jeremiah

The formation of the book of Jeremiah has been the subject of considerable debate. Scholars generally agree that Jeremiah achieved its present form over an extended period, continuing well beyond the time of Jeremiah himself. But the details regarding the growth of the book, including the amount of material to be ascribed to the prophet, are contested.[27] [Luther on Jeremiah]

Luther on Jeremiah

So, it seems as though Jeremiah did not compose these books himself, but that parts were taken piecemeal from his utterances and written into a book. For this reason we must not worry about the order or be hindered by the lack of it.

Martin Luther, "Preface to the Prophet Jeremiah," in *Luther's Works* (vol. 35; Philadelphia: Fortress, 1960), 280-81.

The dispute regarding how much material goes back to Jeremiah himself corresponds to that of the portrayal of the prophet (see above). Traditionally, scholars have accepted the claims of the book itself, and hence assign more material to Jeremiah than to later editors and, moreover, seek to determine the historical setting for most (if not all) texts.[28] Others scholars emphasize to a greater or lesser degree the use of Jeremiah's words by later editors who seek to speak to new situations and who often idealize the prophet in so doing.[29] The result of this later usage is that the actual words of Jeremiah are not considered recoverable and the amount of reliable material about the person of Jeremiah is minimized. From this angle, the original Jeremiah and his historical setting are not certainly available except in very general terms. A mediating position on this point is comparable to that noted above regarding the portrayal of Jeremiah; material originating with Jeremiah or dependent upon his work, though not able to be determined in any precise way, has been combined with later editorial reflections. But, in any case, given the highly speculative character of the enterprise, interpreters of Jeremiah should expend little effort in seeking to sort out what may or may not go back to the prophet himself.

The complexity of the development of the book of Jeremiah is evident in several ways. The following features can help us better understand the matter, though issues of formation will finally remain elusive.

1. *Claims the Book Itself Makes.* The book itself reports some details regarding its formation, especially chapter 36. The chapter is probably not a straightforward historical account but has been built up over time from an unknown nucleus. Yet, its basic framework, unique among the prophets, can be relied upon in a general way. The chapter ascribes the committal to writing of Jeremiah's preaching to divine initiative and dates the undertaking to 605 BC, the fourth year of King Jehoiakim (36:1-3). This timing may be due to key political events associated with the rise of Babylonian hegemony in the region (see above); Judah's future hangs in the balance. This writing takes place about midpoint in Jeremiah's ministry, so at least half of the present book is apparently not included in this scroll. Yet, at this point the die is understood to have been cast regarding the shape of Israel's future (see commentary, especially on 36:27-31).

Jeremiah commissions Baruch the scribe to write at his dictation all the words that God had spoken to him (36:4). In other words, what had existed only in oral form is here committed to writing; writing is seen as a secondary, but significant development. Later, after the destruction of this scroll, he will dictate a second scroll and "many similar words were added to them" (36:32). [Jeremiah and Baruch]

Jeremiah and Baruch

Baruch, a somewhat shadowy figure, is commonly thought to be a companion of Jeremiah (they went to Egypt together, 43:3-6) and his amanuensis. This is the only clear case of a prophet having such a companion (see Isa 8:17). Given the role of Baruch in the transmission of Jeremiah's oracles, being explicitly linked both to the first scroll and the second scroll with its additions (36:4, 32), he is often given a considerable role in the composition of the book. It has been claimed that he not only wrote down the oracles dictated to him by the prophet but is also responsible for the third person narratives regarding the activities of the prophet. Though the latter writing activity may reflect actual authorship, it is sheer speculation and should not be pursued in any precise way.

The relationship between Jeremiah and Baruch is further developed in later Jewish literature (e.g., the Deuterocanonical book Baruch), and there is some tendency to read that legendary material back into the life of Jeremiah. What Jeremiah says about the relationship between the two figures is no doubt the beginning of that legend (see commentary at chs. 32; 36; 43; 45).

Seal of Baruch

The first scroll contained the oracles of Jeremiah delivered from the beginning of his ministry to this moment (627–605 BC; see 25:3; 45:1). The words are described as oracles of judgment that provided an occasion for the people of Israel to repent and return to the Lord, a return that God desired because God prefers forgiveness to judgment (36:2-3). Yet, it remains unclear exactly which parts of the present book of Jeremiah were written on the first scroll (or were added to the second scroll). Perhaps they included the poetic oracles of chapters 2–24, or significant parts thereof. Jeremiah 25:1-14, the summary of part I of the book, is usually thought to speak of these oracles (see above). In addition, as noted above, there are references to other writings within the book (25:13, a possible reference to the first or second scroll), including some ascribed to Jeremiah himself (29:1, 30-32; 30:2; 51:60-63).

These various references to written documents give Jeremiah (and Baruch) credit for originating important parts of the book. At the same time, no claim is made that they are responsible for the entirety of Jeremiah. In fact, the writings that are referenced have been dispersed at several places in the book. This suggests that later editors have gathered such collections, pieced them together, and introduced their own levels of interpretation, understanding themselves to be true to the heritage of Jeremiah.

2. *The Identification of Speaker.* Sometimes the book presents the words of Jeremiah in the first person, whether in his call or other receptions of the word of God (e.g., 1:4, 11; 13:1, 8; 14:11; 15:1; 28:1), in interaction with God (e.g., 4:10; 6:11a, 26; 10:19, 23-24; 11:18-20; 12:1-4), or in response to the effects of God's action (e.g., 4:23-26; 15:10). At other times, the narrative is *about* Jeremiah, presented in the third person; this is especially the case in prose sections and in the last half of the book (e.g., 7:1; 11:1; 14:1; 25:1; 27:1). In these cases, another writer/editor seems to be telling readers about the prophet. To make matters more complicated, sometimes the texts where the first person is used are interwoven with materials in the third person (e.g., 11:1, 6, 9; 14:1, 11; 25:1, 15; 28:1, 5; 36–45). At other times, readers cannot clearly sort out whether it is God or Jeremiah who is speaking (4:19-22; 8:19–9:3).

A straightforward reading of these differences suggests that we have to do with a combination of words from Jeremiah himself (or so it is claimed) and reports about Jeremiah by others. While Baruch has been understood to have a significant role in transmitting these materials, it seems more likely that, whatever his role, several editors have been at work on this material over an extended period of time. The force of those texts that intermingle first and third person reference to Jeremiah may witness to a strong sense of continuity between Jeremiah himself and subsequent interpretations of his life and work.

3. *The LXX Version of Jeremiah.* One type of evidence for understanding the book of Jeremiah as having developed over time is the difference between the LXX and the Hebrew text (MT).[30] These differences suggest that there was no fixed book of Jeremiah for many (unknown) years. Fragments of Hebrew texts linked to both Greek and Hebrew versions have been found among the DSS—evidence that demonstrates the continuing existence of both versions over a long period of time and their relative antiquity.

Many of the differences between MT and LXX are not especially important, but they are significant enough to have prompted no little reflection on the formation of Jeremiah. The major differences include the following. The LXX version of Jeremiah is one-seventh (14.7% of 52 chapters) shorter than the MT. The MT and LXX have the same number of chapters, but the LXX has fewer verses and words. The MT has 3,097 words the LXX does not have; the latter has 307 words the former does not have. The LXX has less repeated material than the MT (see below). The LXX also has a different arrangement of some chapters. Most important is the placement of the OAN; they occur in chapters 46–51 in the MT but in the LXX they are placed in the middle of the book—as with Isaiah 13–23 and Ezekiel 25–32—after 25:13a (and in a different order from the MT). One effect of this difference in the LXX arrangement is that chapter 45—reporting Jeremiah's word to a disconsolate Baruch—becomes his last word in the book, though dated in 605 BC (as is 25:1; 36:1); it is then followed by a somewhat shorter version of chapter 52 (51:64b is missing in the LXX).[31]

In its translation of biblical books, the LXX normally expands on the MT. The unusual shortened form of the text in the LXX of Jeremiah suggests that it was translated from an earlier version of the Hebrew rather than being a later shortening of the Hebrew (probably in Egypt, where a shorter Hebrew text had been preserved from expansive editing). Among the examples that suggest this conclusion are these: Jeremiah is called the prophet only four times in the LXX, but thirty times in the MT. This suggests some development in thinking about the stature of Jeremiah as a prophet. Also, the phrase "oracle of the Lord" occurs much more frequently in the MT, which also has more epithets for God (e.g., 35:13). These expansions in the MT suggest that theological and/or liturgical factors were at work in the later transmission of the material. If the LXX is a translation of an earlier version of the Hebrew text (no longer extant) than the one we now have, this would indicate that the Hebrew Jeremiah continued to grow for some (unknown) period of time until it reached its present form.

4. *Doublets and Recurring Phrases.* A prominent literary feature of Jeremiah is the presence of numerous doublets (repeated texts) and recurring phrases.[32] This phenomenon may be revealing of the complexity of the editorial process through which Jeremiah has passed. Over fifty doublets have been noted (e.g., 6:13-15= 8:10-12; 10:12-16=51:15-19; 11:20=20:12; 15:13-14=17:3-4; 16:14-16=23:7-8; 23:5-6=33:14-16; 23:19-20=30:23-24; 30:10-11=46:27-28; 49:19-21=50:44-46). The repeated verses are often given a fresh interpretive cast by the new context in which they have been placed (e.g., 23:19-20 is a word of judgment against Israel; in 30:23-24 other nations are the probable addressee). In other cases, readers are presented with earlier material that is developed in differing ways (e.g., 7:1-15 with 26:1-6; 26:1-3 with 36:1-3; 39:4-10 with 52:7-16).

Scholars continue to puzzle over this literary phenomenon more generally and over the interpretation of the individual repeated texts in their respective contexts. The repetitions in whole or in part may conceal some sort of editorial framework, tying various parts of the book together, but that is not clear. We note the doublets in this context because the sheer number of repeated verses, often with fresh interpretations by virtue of their new contexts, suggests that later editors have been at work and have honored the material they have inherited by seeking to use it in new ways.

5. *Poetry and Prose.* Another factor that affects reflection about the formation of Jeremiah is the combination of poetry and prose; they are often intermingled in Jeremiah, but poetry dominates in the first half of the book, prose in the second half. Prophetic oracles are often presented in poetic form, but they are also accompanied by prose passages providing interpretive comment (e.g., 5:18-19). Prophetic oracles also occur in prose in accounts of what the prophet did (e.g., 35; 44). It is commonly suggested that the prose material in chapters 2–20 was written in light of later reflection on these events and in support of the poetic oracles (see below).

6. *Deuteronomic Language and Perspective.* Scholars have observed that a number of Jeremiah passages have a style, vocabulary, and perspective similar to that of the book of Deuteronomy and the Deuteronomistic History (=Joshua, Judges, Samuel, Kings; often referred to as Dtr). For example, see the focus on covenant in 11:1-17 or the ending of the book (ch. 52), which does not mention the

prophet, but bears a strong family resemblance to the ending of Dtr (2 Kgs 24:18–25:30). As for their form, these texts are in prose and commonly supplement or interpret poetic sections. As for their content, the concern with infidelity to Yahweh is especially strong; the issue is centered in the first commandment and a breakdown in the relationship between God and people. At the same time, some prose texts also convey hopeful signs that witness to a God who is prepared to move into a positive future in spite of the mistakes of the past (e.g., 3:15-18).

Arguments against such a deuteronomic editorial hand have been presented (e.g., the presence of a common style and perspective in Seventh-century Judah that Jeremiah himself might have appropriated). It seems likely, however, that editors that had been at work on other literature (such as Dtr) have had their hand in Jeremiah. These prose expansions witness to subsequent use of the Jeremiah material in the community, probably in the wake of the fall of Jerusalem (see below).[33] At the same time, separating out this material in any precise way is speculative and, in any case, these materials have become so much an integral part of the present book that Jeremiah would not be Jeremiah without them.

7. Scholarly Reconstructions. In view of this textual data several scholarly theories have been offered as to how Jeremiah might have grown into its present form. These formulations are not unlike the source-critical hypothesis regarding the Pentateuch (JEDP). The stages in the growth of Jeremiah could be understood both in terms of separate sources that have been brought together (see above on written texts) as well as ongoing revisions of existing forms of Jeremiah. Three primary sources have been commonly isolated:

A. *The poetic oracles*, especially in chapters 2–25 (commonly designated Source A). In view of 36:1-4 and 25:1-11 these may correspond to the material recorded by Jeremiah's secretary, Baruch. At the same time, the ascription of the poetry to Jeremiah is dependent on the mention of him in the editorial framework and the prose sections. Also to be noted is that these oracles do not mention Jeremiah's actual confrontations with the various kings of Judah (see 22:6-30), a concern that is prominent in chapters 26–45.

B. *The prose accounts of the ministry of Jeremiah*, at least parts of which may have been written by Baruch, commonly referred to as source B (e.g., 19:1–20:6; 26–29; 32; 34–45). While too selective to be a biography, these texts do chronicle key aspects of Jeremiah's ministry. The presence of so much biographical material in the book gives rise to questions about how it functions as prophecy. As noted above, it probably shows that the word of God is understood to be conveyed not only in and through what the prophet said, but also in the person the prophet was. His very life conveyed a word of God.

C. *Expansions by Deuteronomic Theologians.* These later editors, working after the fall of Jerusalem, expanded the oracles of Jeremiah, especially in chapters 1–25, so as to make them more applicable to a subsequent generation (commonly known as source C). Key texts often assigned to these editors include: 7:1–8:3; 11:1-17; 13:1-11; 14:1–15:24; 16:1-13; 17:19-27; 18:7-12; 19:1–20:6; 21:1-12; 22:1-5; 24; 25:1-13a; 26–27; 29:10-20; 32:1–33:13; 34:8-22; 35:12-19; 36:28-31; 37:1-2; 39:1–40:6; 42:7-22; 44–45. In addition, numerous shorter pieces are included (e.g., 1:15-16, 18-19; 3:6-14; 5:18-19; 8:19b; 17:2b-3a).

While there are increasing tendencies to regard this schematic as too mechanistic an understanding of the growth of the book, most scholars recognize a basic distinction between the oracles of Jeremiah and the work of later editors of various sorts over an extended period of time. In thinking about the complexities of the formation of the book, William McKane offers a helpful hypothesis. He speaks of a "rolling corpus" in the growth of the book; a nucleus of texts is built up over time by other texts, and this process in turn generates further reflections.[34] All of this is presented in a somewhat haphazard way, suggesting that the book in its present form is not the product of a single editor who shapes the book finally according to some particular schematic. "We are dealing with a long, complicated, untidy accumulation of material extending over a very long period, to which many people have contributed."[35] The coherence of the book that results from this work must not be exaggerated nor the book's obscurities underestimated.

Another helpful perspective is that of Brevard Childs; he is concerned less with historical issues than with the book in its final, canonical shape.[36] He does make a distinction between material original to Jeremiah and that of later editors but claims that it is the combination of the two that reveals the heart of the canonical form of the book. For example, in a general way the original Jeremiah is more concerned about words of judgment, the later editors are more centered on words of promise. Together they constitute a tension-filled judgment-promise theme for the book as a whole.

This double theme is made evident immediately in the call of Jeremiah (see the six verbs in 1:10) and shapes the book in a general way. The first twenty-five chapters in the book emphasize uprooting and destroying judgment, while chapters 26–52 move more toward planting and building up the community (but see above on the structure of Jeremiah).

The later editors made these editorial moves, not basically in order to demonstrate Jeremiah's predictive accuracy (no such claims are made, not even in ch. 52; though see 2 Chr 36:21-22), but in the interest of interpreting the significance of Jeremiah's words to their own audiences (see above). These later developments are important theologically, for they reveal an understanding that Jeremiah's words continue to speak to audiences that live on the far side of the original historical context. They enabled an understanding of what had led to this disaster, how they might face the tragedies that had so deeply affected their community and which in turn might guide them in thinking through means to ensure that it would not happen again. Even more, the words of hope provided some glimmer of assurance that God's judgment, as severe as it proved to be, was not God's last word to Israel, but that God had a remarkable future in store for them.

Themes in Jeremiah

The question of the theological coherence of the book of Jeremiah has often been the subject of scholarly debate. Certain characters appear regularly across its pages (God; Jeremiah; the people of Israel), but the question has been raised as to whether they or the perspectives they represent are coherently presented (let it be noted that problems of coherence are often rooted in the *interpreter's* theological perspective).[37] Various efforts have been made to distinguish among differing perspectives in the book, for example, between the theology of the prophet himself and that of one or more editors of the book. Yet, because we cannot certainly separate out the prophet's theology from that of later editors, and because the editors probably understood their own perspectives to stand in the tradition of Jeremiah, it seems best to seek to speak of the theology of the book as we now have it. In this task, while coherence should not be forced, more continuity may be available than is commonly thought. [Keeping Track of Jeremiah's God]

That God is made such a prominent actor in Jeremiah is not an inference drawn from the historical data, but is reflective of long held theological convictions about the presence and activity of God

Keeping Track of Jeremiah's God

Whatever we might think about issues of coherence, the sheer complexity of Jeremiah's God will no doubt create tensions within the reader. One of the more complex aspects of the book of Jeremiah is the violence associated with its theology; we hear some of the sharpest condemnations to be found anywhere in the prophets. You wonder how readers could pick themselves up off the ground after having heard them. On the other hand, we hear clear and ringing promises that God's commitment to Israel will not fail. How could readers keep the judgment oracles and the salvation oracles together? That fact that the intended readers lived between the experience of judgment and the fulfillment of the promise is important in seeking to sort this issue through.

These complex theological realities suggest that readers keep track of what is said about God as they read. What kind of God is this? It is not enough just to ask about God; the question is more specific: what *kind of God* is portrayed here? And then, remembering that your own views of God will impinge upon these reflections, is Jeremiah's kind of God your kind of God? If not, in what ways does Jeremiah's God differ from yours and what do you do with those points of difference? Do you, for example, leave them aside and appropriate the God of Jeremiah selectively, picking and choosing (perhaps unconsciously)? What criteria do you use to make such decisions?

In thinking about such questions, keep track of the images and metaphors that are used to speak of God and God's activity. For example, can the sexual metaphors used for divine judgment be appropriated as a word of God for our own time? Is Jeremiah's God too angry and/or insufficiently compassionate? Does Jeremiah's God get carried away? Are Christians now exempt from such harsh divine judgment talk, however much we may claim that the indictment of sin continues to be appropriate? If not, as is surely the case, why not?

in Israel's life story. The prophet and those who gathered and edited these texts believed themselves to have the God-given capacity to see the "something more" in these events. In other words, God's will had been specifically revealed to the prophet (and others) and that enabled the capacity to discern God's purposes in and through what was happening in these tumultuous times. At the same time, no simple theological interpretation would do, for God and God's prophet(s) were at work in and through all the social and political realities that were a lively force in this situation. And so God's word in Jeremiah catches up to all dimensions of life, both those of Israel and those of other peoples with whom Israel has to do. [Israel's Actual History and Confessed History]

The following are leading theological claims that inform the writing and editing of the book of Jeremiah.[38]

1. *God and Creation.* God "made the earth" (Jer 33:2; cf. 10:12-13=51:15-16; 27:5; 32:17) and continues to uphold the "fixed orders" of creation (31:35-36; 33:20, 25). Such "fixed orders" refer to the great rhythms of creation (the sea, sun, moon, stars, day, night; see Gen 8:22). But, notably, this language does not bespeak a mechanistic world or a divinely determined one, for the land can become desolate and mourn, the animals and birds can be swept away (12:4), and human behaviors can wreak havoc in God's good creation, and with impunity (12:1). God does not "control" or micromanage the world, however much God's actions are deemed to be effective.

Israel's Actual History and Confessed History

The much-discussed question of the relationship between Israel's actual history and its confessed history is often raised in this connection. The texts need not be literally descriptive of the events surrounding the fall of Jerusalem in order to speak the truth about God's purposes and actions and be theologically and religiously significant. Yet, if no links exist between the confession and Israel's actual life, at least in its broad strokes, then the confession itself does become problematic. Even though the reported events may not be able to be finally verified, their general happenedness is important. Moreover, God's activity should be linked not only to the events themselves but also to the confessional activity of Jeremiah and the later editors who interpret these events. Only God's act in the gift of faith enables the confession that God has acted in Israel's external world.

This perspective regarding the creation entails an openness for genuine creaturely decision-making and (lack of) responsiveness. Again and again in Jeremiah, the people are given choices that will shape their future, which in turn will shape the future of all other creatures, indeed the future of God (God will do different things depending upon what creatures do). The various "if, if not" constructions (12:14-17; 17:24-27; 21:8-10; 22:1-5; 38:17-18; 42:9-17) demonstrate such an openness to the future. God "plants" the people, but it is they who take root, grow, and bring forth fruit (12:2). What creatures "grow up into" and the fruit they bear make a difference both for themselves and for their world, for good or for ill. People can make God's "pleasant portion a desolate wilderness" (12:10); the God who is "near" and "far" (23:23) can be "far from their hearts" (12:2); and Babylonian armies can exceed their divine mandate, with devastating effects upon land and people (12:14, "evil" neighbors; see 25:11-14; 51:24). From another perspective, there is room for an incalculable and frustrating randomness in God's created order (e.g., Jer 12:1, the "way of the guilty" can prosper; Eccl 9:11 speaks of "chance" for such realities), so that no theory of retribution (or any other theory) can explain the way the world works (even for the Deuteronomists).

Jeremiah's relational God has created a relational world. An interrelatedness exists among all creatures for Jeremiah (and for Israel). The world could be imaged as a giant spider web. Every creature is in relationship with every other, such that any act reverberates out and affects the whole, shaking the entire web in varying degrees of intensity. This understanding may be illustrated by the virtual drumbeat of Jeremiah that moral order affects creational order, though not mechanistically or inevitably. Again and again, we read how human sin has an adverse effect upon the earth, indeed upon the entire cosmos. Because of human wickedness it does not rain (3:3; 2:12; 5:24-25; 14:4), the land is made desolate (12:10-11; see 23:10), the animals and birds are swept away (12:4; see 4:25; 9:10;

14:5-7; Hos 4:3; Zeph 1:3), and the land is polluted (3:2, 9; 16:18; see 2:7; Isa 24:5) and mourns (12:4; see 4:28; 23:10; Isa 24:4-7; 33:9; Hos 4:3: Joel 1:10-20)—to God! (12:11). Indeed, the entire "earth...heavens" seems to be reduced to a precreation state of being (4:23-26), though that very context (v. 27) insists that no "full end" of the earth is in view. Modern understandings of the interrelatedness of the ecosystem connect well with these insights.

An important claim of Jeremiah is that God "fills heaven and earth" (Jer 23:23-24). At the least, this means that God is present and relational to everything in creation that is not God, whether "near by" or "far off" (in creaturely terms). Inasmuch as God "fills heaven and earth," the latter exist as realities to be filled; hence, all creatures are a genuine "other" to God. Given the comprehensive character of "heaven and earth," the divine relationship with the other is not limited to the human sphere. God as the "God of all flesh" is one formulation in Jeremiah that moves this relationship beyond the human (32:27; see Gen 9:15-17). Moreover, that the desolate land mourns *to* God (12:11; see 4:28; 23:10; Joel 1:10, 20) demonstrates that it has a relationship with God that is independent of God's relationship to the human (see Job 38-41; Pss 104:21, 27; 145:15-16; 147–148). That God in turn addresses the land (16:19; see 22:29) also evidences such an independent relationship.

Such language regarding the nonhuman cannot be reduced to figurative speech, poetic license, or worshipful exuberance. Rather, this language of interresponsiveness shows that God's presence to and relationship with the earth and its creatures is more than external; there is an inwardness or interiority characteristic of the earth and its creatures such that a genuine relationship with God exists. To speak in this way does not necessarily lead to a panpsychism or vitalism, only that some kind of *internal* relationship with God is claimed.[39]

This considerable detail regarding the importance of creation in Jeremiah provides the theological grounding for the understanding of Jeremiah as "a prophet to the nations" (1:5, 10) as well as the variety of ways in which the nations become the subject of various oracles (especially chs. 25, 46–51). Because God is the God of all creation, God is the God of all peoples and nations. God is present and active among them, even though they may not recognize this to be the case (it is just such activity that enables insights such as 22:8-9). Moreover, God's purposes for all creation include these various peoples (cf. 12:14-17; 18:7-10), whether as agents for judgment or deliverance (see below), as objects of judgment (chs. 10; 25; 50–51), or as objects of divine deliverance (see 3:17; 4:2; 16:19-21; 46:26; 48:47; 49:8, 39).

2. *A God of Pathos.* The relational God of Jeremiah is no aloof God, somehow present but detached. God is a God of great passions (pathos); deep and genuine divine feelings and emotions are manifest again and again. Sorrow, lament, weeping, wailing, grief, pain, anguish, heartache, regret, and anger all are ascribed to God in Jeremiah.[40] While these divine passions are focused on an unfaithful people, the earth and its creatures also get caught up into God's vulnerable heart. To God, Israel and its land are "my house…my heritage…the beloved of my heart…my vineyard…my portion…my pleasant portion" (12:7-10; see Ps 50:10-11). This recurrent "my" shows that the relationship God has with people and land is not perfunctory in character; God is deeply involved in their life and is profoundly affected by that engagement.

At the same time, this display of divine pathos is no sentimental or romantic matter. God manifests not only sorrow (3:19-20; 9:10, 17-18; 12:7; 13:17) but also sword-wielding anger (12:12-13; see 4:26; 7:20 and often; see above on rhetorical strategies). Indeed, into the midst of this language of closeness and possession comes the strong expression of hate (12:8; see 44:4; Amos 5:21; Hos 9:15). As we know from close interhuman relationships, the sharp juxtaposition of love-and-hate language indicates something of the trauma of this broken relationship for God. These are divine emotions of great intensity, evidencing the depth to which God's own "heart and soul" are affected (see 32:41).

An angry God is a difficult concept for moderns, not least because God in anger is made responsible at least in part for the human devastation and environmental degradation. Take 4:23-26, "I looked on the earth, and lo, it was waste and void…all the birds of the air had fled…the fruitful land was a desert…before the Lord, before his fierce anger" (see also Jer 7:20; 10:10; 21:5-6; 44:22; 51:29, 43; more generally, see 2:15; 4:7, 20; 7:34; 45:4; 50:46; cf. Isa 13:13; 24:18-20). In Jeremiah 12:11-13 the land is made desolate and produces thorns even though wheat has been sown—because of "the sword of the Lord" and "the fierce anger of the Lord."

The anger of God is always *provoked* by creaturely words and deeds (e.g., 7:18; 8:19; 32:29-32).[41] Anger is a divine response not a divine attribute; if there were no sin, there would be no anger. The sin most in focus in Jeremiah is infidelity, unfaithfulness within Israel's relationship with God. The dominant metaphor is marital, assuming a deep intimacy between God and people; the images used are often graphic (e.g., 3:1-5; 13:20-27). In "unpacking" this metaphor, the anger (mixed with other emotions) felt by a spouse at a partner's unfaithfulness may be used to signal something of the depth of the feelings of God. The juxtaposition of anger over the breakdown of a close relationship and sorrow over its personal and public effects, not least on the land, is evident in 12:7-13 (another striking text is 9:10-11; the verb in v. 10 has God as subject, see NRSV footnote). The Godward side of wrath is always grief; and a striking thing about the God of Jeremiah is that both the grief and the anger are revealed to the prophet, who puts both on public display. Readers must distinguish anger and grief but never separate the two in any interpretation of these texts.

These texts insist that this grieving/angry God bears some responsibility for the wasted land and cities, but how to refine such a claim is no easy task. Consideration of two additional matters, each of which is implicit or explicit in Jeremiah, will help us sort this matter out: the relationship between sin and consequence and the issue of agency.

3. *Sin and Judgment.* How one thinks about sin and judgment in Jeremiah shapes one's thinking about the aforementioned matters. The relationship between them is conceived in intrinsic rather than forensic terms. Jeremiah's call account sets the issue: disaster (*rā'āh*) breaks out because of the people's wickedness (*rā'āh*; 1:14, 16). This understanding may be observed in various formulations (note the image of "fruit," as in 12:2). God brings disaster (*rā'āh*), which is "the fruit of *their* schemes" (6:19; see 14:16). God gives to all "according to their ways, according to the fruit of their doings" (17:10; see 32:19). In other words, *rā'āh* issues in *rā'āh*. Like fruit, the consequence grows out of (or is intrinsic to) the deed itself. God introduces nothing new into the situation, and so the consequence can be designated by the same word as "sin/evil."

This reality can also be observed in the use of the verb *pāqad*, "visit." Its translation as "punish" in NRSV is often problematic, as in 21:14: "I will punish you according to the fruit of your doings." A more literal translation catches the thought more precisely: "I will visit upon you the fruit of your doings" (see 5:9; 14:10). These formulations show that God mediates the consequences of that which is already present in the wicked situation. The people's sin already has had a significant level of "negative fallout" on the land, given the interrelatedness of all creatures; God's mediation of the effects brings those consequences to completion, though the agency issues cannot be factored out in any precise way. In other terms, God's anger and withdrawal is a "seeing to" the moral order for the sake of justice and a future for the land. It is no favor to land or people to let evil and its ill effects go unchecked. But God's way of resolving the problem does not entail a flick of the divine wrist—a "quick fix." To provide for a positive future for the land God uses another strategy; God enters deeply into the realities of sin and evil—including experiencing the very suffering that people and land experience (see above)—and breaks them open from within.

This understanding of judgment is supported by the fact that, while there is a personal dimension to divine anger, wrath is also impersonally conceived in Jeremiah (and elsewhere, e.g., Num 1:53; 16:46). Wrath "goes forth" because of their *rāʿāh* (4:4=21:12; 23:19), "is not turned away" (4:8; 23:20), "bursts upon" (23:19), or "is poured out upon" (7:20; 10:25; 42:18), the effect of which may include environmental degradation. In this way of thinking, wrath is an effect that grows out of a violation of the moral order of God's creation. God's personal anger may be said to be a "seeing to" this movement from deed to consequence that is the moral order.

4. *God Works Through Means and the Accompanying Violence.* God works in Israel's world through means, including human beings—as individuals and communities, both within and without the community of faith—and, potentially, all other creatures. This is the case for both judgment (Nebuchadrezzar) and deliverance (Cyrus). Moreover, the language used for God's actions in Jeremiah is often conformed to the means that God uses (see below), one effect of which is the ascription to God of an inordinate amount of violence.

Some scholarly statements regarding agency tend to discount the genuine role that the Babylonian armies play; it is as though God is the only real agent. But readers must not diminish the distinction between God and God's agents or discount the stature and the very real power of that human army. Just how God is involved in this activity cannot be factored out with precision; however, 51:11 may contain a clue with its reference to God as having "stirred up (*hēʿir*) the spirit of the kings of the Medes" (cf. Zech 1:14; Jer 6:22; 25:32; 50:9, 41; 51:1; Isa 13:17; 41:25; 45:13; Ezek 23:22; Joel 4:7).

In determining to work through means, God chooses to be dependent on that which is not God to carry out the divine purposes in the world. This is a risky move for God because it links God with the character and activities of the chosen instruments. God does not perfect people before working through them, which means that one must not necessarily confer a positive value on the results (following the pattern of the evaluating work of God, who places a negative value on some Babylonian activity).

Conformation of Divine and Human Actions

📖 Generally, note the virtual absence of God talk in descriptions of the fall of Jerusalem (39:1-14; 52:3b-30); they are also uncommon in the oracles against Babylon (chs. 50-51). Some violent actions are also ascribed to both Jeremiah and God (cf. 1:10 and 24:6; 25:15-29).

God's Action	*Nebuchadrezzar/Babylon/Others*
Jer 13:14—I will dash (*nps*) them	Jer 48:12— they will break in pieces (*nps*)
—I will not pity (*hml*), or spare (*hus*) or have compassion (*rhm*)	21:7—he will not pity (*hml*), or spare (*hus*) or have compassion (*rhm*)
—when I destroy (*šht*) them (also 13:9; 9:15; 13:24; 18:17; 30:11)	36:29—he will destroy (*šht*); see 51:25; 52:8; 23:1-2
—I will scatter (*pûs*) 24:9; 27:10	—have scattered (*pûs*) the flock 50:17; cf. 23:2
—I will drive them away (*ndh*)	Israel driven away (*ndh*) by Assyrians and Babylonians
21:5—I will fight against you (*lhm*)	21:2—he is making war against us (*lhm*)
21:6—I will strike down (*nkh*)	21:7—he shall strike them down (*nkh*)
21:14—I will kindle a fire (*yst*)	32:29—they will kindle (*yst*) a fire
49:20—God has plan (*y's*) and purpose (*hšb*)	49:30—Nebuchadrezzar has plan (*y's*) and purpose (*hšb*)
49:38—God will set (*śîm*) his throne	43:10—Nebuchadrezzar will set (*sîm*) his throne
19:11 (+)—God will break (*šbr*) the people	43:13 – Nebuchadrezzar will break Egyptian holy objects
25:9—those slain (*hll*) by the Lord	51:49—Babylon must fall for slain of Israel by his (king of Babylon) hand
27:8—Until I have completed its destruction	
12:12; 47:6—sword of the Lord (see 14:12; 15:9)	20:4—they shall fall by the sword of enemies
25:8; 49:19—God imaged as a lion	4:7; 5:6—foe from the north like a lion
29:4, 7, 14—God sends into exile (*glh*)	29:1 (and often) —Nebuchadrezzar sends into exile
29:17—God will pursue (*rdp*) them	39:5; 52:8—Chaldeans will pursue them
30:3; 31:20—I will bring them back to land	42:12—he will bring them back to land
—I will have mercy	—he will have mercy

Remarkable correspondences exist between God's actions and those of Nebuchadrezzar.[42] [Conformation of Divine and Human Actions] I lift up several of these texts. The "sword of the Lord" (12:12; see 47:6), which God "summons" and "sends" (25:16, 29), refers to human beings wielding the sword (6:25; 20:4). The judgment of God is mediated through the Babylonian armies or, later, the enemies of Babylon (the "weapons of his wrath," 50:25). A striking juxtaposition of God and the means God uses is evident in 13:14 and 21:7; both God and Nebuchadrezzar "will not pity, or spare, or have compassion" in the destruction of Jerusalem.

What conclusions might one draw from this common fund of language? Such harsh words appear to be used for God because they are used for the actions of those in and through whom God mediates judgment. God's language in 27:8 puts the matter in a nutshell, "I have completed its destruction by his hand." In view of this mediation, God refers to Nebuchadrezzar as "my servant" (25:9; 27:6; 43:10). Others whom God designates "my servant" in Jeremiah are David, the prophets, and Israel! In some sense God has chosen to be *dependent* on Nebuchadrezzar in carrying out that judgment.[43] Exodus 3:8-10, where both God and Moses (often called "my servant") bring Israel out of Egypt, could function as a paradigm for such considerations.

Servant language is also used for the birds and animals of the land in Jeremiah; they will "serve" the king of Babylon in his judgmental work (27:6; see 28:14; they are parallel with the sword in 15:3). Such an understanding is present also in Jeremiah 12:9 (see 7:33; 16:4; 19:7). The animals may be used as metaphors for the Babylonians (e.g., 4:7; see Isa 56:9), but these texts speak of the agency of the animals themselves. One may also note God's command to cut down the trees to make siegeworks (6:6) or the use of the hot wind (4:11; 22:22) and fire (5:14). Indeed, desolation of the land as an effect of human iniquity is used by God as an instrument of judgment (3:2-3; 5:24-25; 14:2-12). "Victim" language is sometimes used for these effects on the land and its animals, but this insufficiently recognizes the "vocation" to which God calls them in service of the divine purposes, a vocation that may entail suffering. One might compare God's use of wind, waves, clouds, and darkness in judgment of the Egyptians in Exodus 14–15; these nonhuman creatures become the *savior* of the human!

As Nebuchadrezzar is identified as God's servant,[44] so, at the time of the return from exile, another "unchosen" one, King Cyrus of Persia, will be identified as God's "anointed one" or "messiah" (Isa 45:1-7). As with Cyrus (Isa 45:4),[45] Nebuchadrezzar does not know Yahweh. The coalescence of God's actions and those of Nebuchadrezzar are abundantly clear in these texts. God will bring Babylon's armies against Israel and destroy them (and their neighbors). God may be said to be the ultimate agent in these events, but not in such a way that the power of other agents is less than real.

That God does not "control" Nebuchadrezzar is shown by the fact he overreaches and exceeds the divine mandate (25:11-14; 51:24; see Isa 47:5-7); he is no puppet in the hands of God. That God is not the only effective agency in these events is made clear by the divine judgment on Babylon (25:12-14; 50-51; see Isa 47:6-7; Zech 1:15, "while I [God] was only a little angry, they made the disaster worse"; note also the statement of divine regret in Jer 42:10, "I [God] am sorry for the disaster"). In effect, Babylon goes beyond its proper judgmental activities, and commits iniquity itself in making the land an "everlasting waste." It is assumed (as with

Barton on Amos's Oracles Against the Nations

John Barton's helpful comments on Amos could also apply to Jeremiah's oracles against Babylon: "...He was appealing to a kind of conventional or customary law about international conduct which he at least believed to be self-evidently right, and which he thought he could count on his audience's familiarity with and acquiescence in . . . at a crucial place in his message he sees moral conduct as a matter of conformity to a human convention held to be obviously universal, rather than to the overt or explicit demands of God."

John Barton, *Amos's Oracles against the Nations: A Study of Amos 1:3–2:5* (Cambridge: Cambridge University Press, 1980), 2.

---

the OAN generally) that there are moral standards that should be known by the nations and to which they are held accountable.[46] [Barton on Amos's Oracles Against the Nations] This divine judgment on Babylonian excessiveness shows that God did not micromanage their activities; they retained the power to make decisions and execute policies that flew in the face of the will of God. Hence, the will and purpose of God, indeed the sovereignty of God, active in these events is not "irresistible."[47] In some sense God risks what the Babylonians will do with the mandate they have been given. One element of that risk is that God's name will become associated with the violence, indeed the excessive violence of the Babylonians.[48]

Another factor to be considered here are those texts wherein God calls Jeremiah to bring a word of nonviolence through Israel's submission to Babylon (see chs. 27–29; 38:17-18). This divine command, which intends to reduce the violence, was announced after the Babylonian subjugation of Jerusalem in 597 BC and before the fall and destruction of 586 BC. With a political realism, God announces that, if Israel would not rebel against Babylon, its future would take a less violent course. In other words, Babylon would function as an agent of divine judgment in different ways, depending upon how Israel responded to the call for nonviolence. Israel's own resorting to violence would lead to its experience of even greater violence as well as to the fuller association of God with such violence.

To recapitulate, God is not the sole agent with respect to the downfall and devastation of Israel; God acts in and through the agency of Babylon. At the same time, the latter will certainly act as kings and armies in that world are wont to act. That is predictable and God (and other observers) knows this from experience with conquerors such as these. This portrayal of God is a kind of extreme realism regarding what is about to happen to the people. And when the people do experience the pillaging, burning, and raping of the Babylonian armies, readers can be sure that they were real agents. Jeremiah also makes this witness when it describes the actual destruction of Jerusalem (chs. 39; 52) in terms that hardly mention God.

These striking parallels suggest that *the portrayal of God's violent action in Jeremiah is conformed to the means that God uses.* God is portrayed in terms of the means available. God thereby accepts any fallout that may accrue to the divine reputation ("guilt by association").

This perspective is testimony to a fundamentally *relational* understanding of the way in which God acts in the world. There is an ordered freedom in the creation, a degree of openness and unpredictability, wherein God leaves room for genuine human decisions as they exercise their God-given power. Even more, God gives them powers and responsibilities in such a way that *commits* God to a certain kind of relationship with them. This entails a divine constraint and restraint in the exercise of power in relation to these agents (Babylon overdid it!). These texts in Jeremiah are testimony to a divine sovereignty that gives power over to the created for the sake of a relationship of integrity.

5. *God and Prophet.* We have already spoken in several of the above contexts regarding the relationship between God and Jeremiah. Here we lift up Jeremiah's role as agent of God. We have seen above how there is a remarkable conformation of the language used for divine action and the action of the means that God uses. In addition, there is a striking conformation of the language used by God and God's prophet. For example, Jeremiah's laments often petition God to visit his enemies with various judgments (11:20; 12:3; 15:15, 17; 17:18; 18:21-23; 20:12; also 6:11; 10:25), language that God also uses. The correspondences between the speech of Jeremiah and God indicate something of the range of conformation. [Conformation of God's Speech and Jeremiah's Speech]

One question that arises from the statistics in the accompanying sidebar is how the situation with God and Jeremiah relates to that of God and the Babylonians. Does God use such violent language because that is the language God's prophet uses? This would be similar to what happens in any proclamation of the word of God in any age; God becomes associated with the language the preacher uses. This is certainly true at some basic level for God's words in the book of Jeremiah; they are presented in human language. God does not micromanage the written or spoken words, but is linked to them by virtue of the claim that God's word is being spoken or written. That God criticizes Jeremiah's language (15:18-19) could suggest this approach, though God never criticizes him for the violence of his language. The task would certainly be much easier if we

Conformation of God's Speech and Jeremiah's Speech

GOD'S SPEECH	JEREMIAH'S SPEECH
Wrath (*ḥēmāh*, 4:4; *zaʿam*, 10:10)	Filled with *God's* wrath (6:11), indignation (15:17).
—pour out wrath (*špk*, 6:11; 14:16)	—Pour out wrath (10:25)
Slaughter (*harēgāh*, 7:32; 19:6)	Set them apart for slaughter (12:3).
Vengeance (*nāqām*, 5:9, 29; 9:8)	Let me see *your* vengeance upon them (11:20; 15:15; 20:12)
Shame (*bôš*, 2:26), dismay (*ḥtt*, 8:9)	Let my persecutors be shamed, dismayed (17:18; 20:11)
Bring evil/disaster (*rāʿāh*, 4:6; 6:19; 11:23)	Bring upon them evil/disaster (17:18)
Break this people (*šbr*, 19:11) doubly (16:18)	Break them with *double* destruction (17:18)
Give sword, famine (11:22; 14:12; 15:2, 9)	Give them sword, famine (18:21)
"Therefore" (18:13+)	Therefore+announcement of judgment (18:21)
Childless, widowed (6:11b-12; 15:7-9)	Let wives become childless and widowed (18:21)
Young men die by sword (12:22)	Let young men die by the sword (18:21)
Suddenly (*pitʾōm*, 15:8)	Bring marauder suddenly (18:22)
Crying Out (*zāʿaq*, 11:11-12; 25:34)	May a cry be heard (18:22)
God will not listen after repentance (14:7-11)	Do not forgive their iniquity (18:22)
Trip up, stumble (*kšl*, 6:15, 21; 8:12)	Let them be tripped up (18:23; 20:11)
"Time" of visitation (6:15; 10:15; 11:12-14)	"Time of anger" (18:23; cf. v. 17)
Violence, destruction (6:7)	Must shout, "violence and destruction" (20:8)
Weariness (15:6)	I am weary (6:11; 20:9)
They will not prosper (*śkl*, 10:21)	They will not succeed (20:11)

could say that the violent language of God has been conformed to the violent language of Jeremiah. Perhaps it would be more accurate to appeal more generally to the interactive character of the God–Jeremiah relationship, so that who learns from whom is not so clear.[49]

Many interpreters have had difficulty with Jeremiah's outbursts for their harsh and unforgiving nature and sought to explain them (away) in one fashion or another, usually appealing to Jeremiah's humanity. This is a human being in deep anguish. But these texts say more than that; their language is not simply to be evaluated: "he's only human." However much Jeremiah's language corresponds to that of psalms of imprecation, it cannot simply be ascribed to outbursts over his suffering at the hands of his enemies. Jeremiah's language has been explicitly shaped by God's language;

God's judgment has become his judgment. Jeremiah has become conformed to the wrath of God.

6. *Jeremiah as Prophet of Hope.* For all the language of divine judgment, eminently deserved by an unfaithful people, God loves Israel with "an everlasting love" and continues to be faithful to those who have experienced judgment (31:2). In Heschel's words, "God's attachment to Israel is eternal"; "Beyond all indignation and imprecations lay the certainty that Israel as God's creation would abide, Israel would exist"; "The rule of Babylon shall pass, but God's covenant with Israel shall last forever." It was "only in the certainty that His mercy is greater than His justice that the prophet could pray: 'Though our iniquities testify against us, act, O Lord, for Thy name's sake'" (14:7).[50] Such convictions are at least in part grounded in Jeremiah's claim that the Davidic promises are still in place through all that has happened (33:14-26), which in turn are grounded in God's commitment to Israel's ancestors (7:7; 11:5; 16:15; 30:3; 33:26). God's promises will not fail; they will never be made null and void as far as God is concerned. Though a rebellious generation may reject the God of the promise and remove themselves from the sphere of fulfillment, God's promise can be relied on absolutely.

It is this understanding of divine faithfulness to promises made that finally shapes the rhythm of the book of Jeremiah. Hence the book includes words of salvation integrated throughout, amid words of judgment (3:15-18; 12:14-16; 16:14-15; 23:5-8; 24:4-7), and not just in the last half of the book. Indeed, God's saving actions are in view from the beginning in the call of Jeremiah (1:10); God will build and plant this people, come what may. The conditional features associated with deliverance (e.g., 7:5-7; 18:7-8; 22:1-5; 24:8-10; 38:17-18; 42:10) pertain to a look back at Israel's possibilities before the final act of judgment fell. What might have been! Once Judah and Jerusalem are devastated and the exiles scattered, then the promises are stated in an unconditional way (e.g., 31:1-6, 31-34; 32:37-41; see commentary on these texts).

God will establish this future for Israel in a unilateral way; this future is finally not dependent on anything that Israel does. God will make a new covenant with Israel and so write the Law in their hearts that there will be no further need for teaching (31:31-34). God "will make an everlasting covenant with them, never to draw back from doing good to them" (32:40) and God "will give them one heart and one way, that they may fear me for all time" (32:39; cf. Ezek 11:19-20; 36:26-27). This God will do, come what may, but it will happen only on the far side of a refining fire.

NOTES

[1] William Holladay, *Jeremiah 2* (Philadelphia: Fortress, 1989), 15-25.

[2] Walter Brueggemann, "The Book of Jeremiah: Portrait of the Prophet," in *Interpreting the Prophets*, ed. J. L. Mays and P. J. Achtemeier (Philadelphia: Fortress, 1987), 117-18.

[3] James Muilenburg, "The Terminology of Adversity in Jeremiah," in *Translating and Understanding the Old Testament*, ed. H. T. Frank and W. L. Reed (Nashville: Abingdon, 1970), 60.

[4] See Muilenburg, "Terminology."

[5] Abraham Heschel, *The Prophets* (New York: Harper, 1962), both generally and in his chapter on Jeremiah (103-39).

[6] So Muilenburg, "Terminology," 60.

[7] Terence Fretheim, *The Suffering of God: An Old Testament Perspective* (Philadelphia: Fortress, 1984), 107-37.

[8] Classically, see J. Skinner, *Prophecy and Religion* (Cambridge: Cambridge University Press, 1922). Regarding the confessions in particular, see Gerhard von Rad, "The Confessions of Jeremiah," in *A Prophet to the Nations: Essays in Jeremiah Studies* (Winona Lake IN: Eisenbrauns, 1984), 339-47.

[9] For an example, see Robert Carroll, *Jeremiah* (Philadelphia: Westminster, 1986).

[10] For example, Holladay, *Jeremiah 2*, 25-35. The standard presentation of this perspective is that of J. Skinner, *Prophecy and Religion*.

[11] See Carroll, *Jeremiah*, 55-64.

[12] See Walter Brueggemann, *A Commentary on Jeremiah: Exile and Homecoming* (Grand Rapids: Eerdmans, 1998), 11-12; Idem., "The Book of Jeremiah: Portrait of the Prophet," in *Interpreting the Prophets*, ed. J. L. Mays and P.J. Achtemeier (Philadelphia: Fortress, 1987), 113-29. In the same volume, see also James Crenshaw, "A Living Tradition: The Book of Jeremiah in Current Research," 111-12.

[13] For example, Holladay, *Jeremiah 2*, 25-26.

[14] See Carroll, *Jeremiah*.

[15] For an extensive discussion of the relationship between Jeremiah and the other books of the Old Testament, see Holladay, *Jeremiah 2*, 36-70.

[16] See Brueggemann, *Jeremiah*, 6.

[17] For the issues and the literature, see L. Stulman, *Order Amid Chaos: Jeremiah as Symbolic Tapestry* (Sheffield: Sheffield Academic Press, 1998), 158-65.

[18] For the various links between Moses and Jeremiah and for Deuteronomy and Jeremiah, see Holladay, *Jeremiah 2*, 38-39, 53-63. See also E. W. Nicholson, *Preaching to the Exiles: A Study of the Prose Tradition in the Book of Jeremiah* (Oxford: Blackwell, 1970).

[19] For the development of this understanding, see Fretheim, *The Suffering of God*, 156-57.

[20] Ibid., 157-59.

[21] For several helpful efforts to consider the structure, see *Troubling Jeremiah*, ed. A. R. P. Diamond, K. M. O'Connor, and L. Stulman (Sheffield: Sheffield Academic Press, 1999), especially the essays by Stulman, Kessler, and Carroll. See also L. Stulman, *Order Amid Chaos*.

[22] See J. R. Lundbom, *Jeremiah: A Study in Ancient Hebrew Rhetoric* (Missoula MT: Scholars Press, 1975); W. L. Holladay, *The Architecture of Jeremiah 1–20* (Lewisburg, PA: Bucknell University Press, 1976).

[23] See M. Kessler, "The Function of Chapters 25 and 50–51 in the Book of Jeremiah," in *Troubling Jeremiah*, 64-72.

[24] For example, see Stulman, *Order Amid Chaos*, 23-98.

[25] On this issue, see C. Seitz, *Theology in Conflict: Reactions to the Exile in the Book of Jeremiah* (Berlin: de Gruyter, 1989).

[26] For a detailed argument regarding the structure within these two major divisions, see Stulman, *Order Amid Chaos,* 23-98.

[27] For a helpful survey of Jeremiah scholarship up to 1984, see Leo Perdue, "Jeremiah in Modern Research: Approaches and Issues," in *A Prophet to the Nations: Essays in Jeremiah Studies*, ed. L. G. Perdue and B. W. Kovacs (Winona Lake, IN: Eisenbrauns, 1984), 1-32. See also J. Crenshaw, fn. 12; A. R. P. Diamond, "Introduction," in *Troubling Jeremiah*, 15-32.

[28] For example, Holladay, *Jeremiah 2*, 25-35.

[29] For example, Carroll, *Jeremiah*, 65-82.

[30] For a thoroughgoing study of their relationship, see J. G. Janzen, *Studies in the Text of Jeremiah* (HSM 6; Cambridge: Harvard University Press, 1973).

[31] The idea of S. Delamarter, "But Who Gets the Last Word?" in *Bible Review*, 1999, 34-45, 54-55, that this placement promotes the role of Baruch (and the MT demotes him) is unlikely for several reasons, not least the image of Baruch as one engaged in self-pity.

[32] For a study of these doublets and recurring phrases, see G. Parke-Taylor, *The Formation of the Book of Jeremiah: Doublets and Recurring Phrases* (Atlanta: SBL, 2000).

[33] See E. Nicholson, *Preaching to the Exiles*.

[34] William McKane, *A Critical and Exegetical Commentary on Jeremiah* (2 vols.; ICC; Edinburgh: T. & T. Clark, 1986), lxxxiii.

[35] William McKane, quoted in Carroll, *Jeremiah*, 43.

[36] Brevard Childs, *Introduction to the Old Testament as Scripture* (Philadelphia: Fortress, 1979), 342-54.

[37] On the impact of the theology of readers on questions of coherence, see Fretheim, "The Character of God in Jeremiah," forthcoming.

[38] These materials are drawn from two of my articles: Terence Fretheim, "The Earth Story in Jeremiah 12," *Readings from the Perspective of Earth*, ed. N. Habel (Sheffield: Sheffield Academic Press, 2000), 96-110, and "The Character of God in Jeremiah," forthcoming.

[39] For detail, see Terence Fretheim, "Nature's Praise of God in the Psalms," *Ex Auditu* 3 (1987): 17-31.

[40] See Heschel, *The Prophets* (New York: Harper and Row, 1962); Fretheim, *The Suffering of God*.

[41] See Heschel, *The Prophets*, 279-98, for a fine discussion of divine wrath. See also Terence Fretheim, "Theological Reflections on the Wrath of God in the Old Testament," in *Horizons in Biblical Theology*, forthcoming.

[42] For further reflections on these matters, see Terence Fretheim, "The Character of God in Jeremiah," forthcoming.

[43] On issues of divine dependence on the human, see Terence Fretheim, "Divine Dependence on the Human: An Old Testament Perspective," *Ex Auditu* 13 (1997): 1-13. Brueggemann's perspective on this issue is stated in his *Jeremiah*, 106 (see 463): God is "not dependent on what is in the world." See also Fretheim, "Creator, Creature, and Co-creation in Genesis 1-2," in *All Things New: Essays in Honor of Roy A. Harrisville*, ed. A. Hultgren et al., Word and World Supplement I (1992), 11-20.

[44] For the issues, see T. Overholt, "King Nebuchadrezzar in the Jeremiah Tradition," *CBQ* 30 (1968): 39-48.

[45] It is helpful to note that the granting of mercy could take place through the king of Babylon (42:11-12). Both the removal of peace and mercy (see 16:5; 21:7) and its restoration are thus related to his agency.

[46] On this issue of "natural law," see John Barton, *Amos's Oracles against the Nations: A Study of Amos 1:3–2:5* (Cambridge: Cambridge University Press, 1980).

[47] Contrary to Brueggemann, *Jeremiah*, 222.

[48] See John Sanders, *The God Who Risks: A Theology of Providence* (Downer's Grove IL: InterVarsity, 1998).

[49] It might be suggested that Jeremiah's sharp statement to God in 20:7 constitutes, at least in part, a critique of the word he was called to bring. This seems doubtful. Yes, God duped him with respect to the call, but he recognizes that action for what it was and he has done what he was called to do in the full knowledge of the deception. *Deception recognized* changes the equation, and he never intimates that the word he was called to proclaim was a false word (see commentary).

[50] So Heschel, *The Prophets*, 110, 127, 129, 298.

THE CALL OF JEREMIAH

1:1-19

This chapter consists of two major segments, a superscription (vv. 1-3) and the call of Jeremiah (vv. 4-10), with associated visions (vv. 11-16) and charges and promises to him (vv. 17-19).

COMMENTARY

Superscription, 1:1-3

These introductory verses inform readers of several basic matters needed to interpret the book properly: (a) the historical situation in which Jeremiah worked; (b) his family origins; (c) that God's word has been spoken to and through Jeremiah; (d) that the book is directed to readers who have experienced the fall of Jerusalem and the exile. [Superscriptions]

1. Jeremiah's ministry is dated from 627 BC (the thirteenth year of Josiah's reign, see 25:3) until shortly after 587 BC (the fall of Jerusalem). Several chapters speak to a situation subsequent to the fall of Jerusalem (e.g., 42–44) and extend his ministry beyond the conventional forty years. Jeremiah's ministry is dated in terms of royal figures. [Kings of Judah] Yet, while kings set the time and place, they do not set the agenda. In fact, God's word will often speak against them, their policies, and their practices.

Setting the book within this historical framework informs readers that "the words of Jeremiah" are to be interpreted in terms of these key events in Israel's life. His words provide an interpretation of these events for those who survived them (the implied readers). Hence, however much the preaching of Jeremiah is rooted in these times and

> **Superscriptions**
>
> The introductions (or superscriptions) to prophetic books commonly contain these elements (cf. Isa 1:1; Amos 1:1; Mic 1:1):
>
> 1. Title ("The words of Jeremiah")
> 2. Personal background ("son of Hilkiah, of the priests who were in Anathoth in the land of Benjamin")
> 3. Reception of God's word ("the word of the LORD came")
> 4. Historical setting of the prophecy ("in the days of Josiah . . . Jehoiakim . . . Zedekiah . . . until the captivity of Jerusalem")
> 5. Whom the prophecy concerned (see 1:5, 10)

Kings of Judah

 The reigns of the kings mentioned in this introduction are:

1. Josiah (640–609 BC); the "thirteenth year" is 627 BC
2. Jehoiakim (609–598 BC)
3. Zedekiah (597–587 BC); the fall of Jerusalem and the beginning of the exile are dated in the eleventh year and the fifth month of his reign.

Two other kings, who reigned for less than one year during Jeremiah's ministry, are mentioned in the book: Shallum/Jehoahaz (609 BC) and Jehoiachin/Jeconiah (598–597 BC). To this list could be added Gedaliah, the governor installed by the Babylonians after the fall in 587 BC. Hence, Jeremiah related to five kings of Judah and one governor over the course of his ministry. Much of his preaching had to do with the "powers that be," and his words were uttered at considerable risk to his own life.

---

places, his "words" are now directed to a new, postdestruction audience (see below).

2. Remarkably little is said about the person of Jeremiah in this introduction. The focus is on his family of origin and on his being a receptor of the word of God (spelled out initially in vv. 4-19). Jeremiah comes from a priestly family of the city of Anathoth (near Jerusalem), though his precise links to the priesthood are uncertain (perhaps the family of Abiathar, 1 Kgs 2:26-27). This certainly means that he was well educated and deeply rooted in the long story of Israel with its God. This background will show itself in his sophisticated use of the Hebrew language, his knowledgeable use of the theological tradition, and his own personal relationship with God. The times of his birth and death are not reported. This lack of concern is one factor alerting readers not to become caught up in trying to reconstruct a biography of Jeremiah (see **Introduction**). As will become evident, matters that speak of his personal story are offered for theological rather than for (auto)biographical reasons. Jeremiah is important to the exiles because it is claimed that his "words" still speak to them in that situation.

3. The historical situation and the personal background of the prophet are important because *God's word* has been spoken to a particular person and into this particular moment in history. This word of God is an embodied word; it has taken up residence in a chosen individual at a particular time and place. At the same time, because what follows has to do fundamentally with "the word of the LORD," its contents break the boundaries of time, place, and even the prophet himself (hence the importance of the "book" in Jeremiah, see ch. 36).

4. As noted, the readers to whom this book is directed have experienced the fall of Jerusalem and exile. We do not know who wrote this introduction to the book of Jeremiah or when it was written. We are only told that it was written sometime after the fall of Jerusalem and the beginning of the Babylonian exile ("the end of the eleventh year of Zedekiah," v. 3). These events are also the note on which the book of Jeremiah ends (ch. 52); hence they provide brackets for the book as a whole.

This seemingly insignificant point is important for how one reads the *present* book of Jeremiah. Though Jeremiah preached at various times over the course of some forty years before 587 BC, the entire book is to be read with the understanding that Jerusalem had *already* fallen to the Babylonians. This disaster and the subsequent exile were an incontrovertible fact for the first (and subsequent) readers (see **Connections: The Opening Verses of Jeremiah and the Reader**). Though there were, no doubt, forms of the book earlier than what we have now (see **Introduction**), the present form of Jeremiah is the only form about which we can be certain and which we are invited to interpret.

The Call of Jeremiah, 1:4-19

The call proper (vv. 4-10) is followed by two visions (1:11-12, 13-16; the NRSV break between v. 13 and

Donatello's Jeremiah

Later moved to the Museo dell'Opera del Duomo (museum of Florence Cathedral), this work originally filled one of the niches on the campanile (bell tower) of Florence Cathedral alongside four other prophets done by Donatello. Though this interpretation of Jeremiah is consistent with the medieval tradition of showing the prophets reading and contemplating the Word of God from their scrolls, the sculptor introduces elements of the Greco-Roman classical tradition alongside it. With the inclusion of toga-like drapery and short hair, the artist has associated the prophetic voice with the look of a Roman orator.

Donatello's sense of the naturalism of the body is noteworthy in this piece. The exposed, full-bodied arm and the organic shifting of the body's weight are elements of this naturalism. Yet, it is Donatello's uniqueness of vision that stands out with this piece (and the other prophets). The deep-set, inward look, the extreme exposure of the right shoulder and the prominence of the straining neck—all are details that seem to point to the bodily experience of the prophet's vision. The scroll being held by Jeremiah's left hand is conceived as if supported by and emanating from the left side of his body. The fusion of the prophetic voice and the Word of God are one.

Donatello (1386–1466). *The Prophet Jeremiah*. 1423–1427. Museo dell'Opera del Duomo. Florence, Italy. (Credit: Alinari/Art Resource, NY)

v. 14 is unfortunate), concluding with a divine charge and promise to Jeremiah (vv. 17-19). Jeremiah is the speaker throughout (vv. 4, 6-7, 8, 11-14); he recalls an earlier call event (how much time has passed?) in which God's words to him play such a key role (vv. 5, 7-8, 9b-10, 11a, 12, 13a, 14-19). This call is most fundamentally a vocation to speak the word of God to Israel (vv. 7, 9, 12, 17). This occasion was doubtless a very personal moment for Jeremiah, but its significance was such that his faithful response would in time affect the entire ancient world.

Verses 4-19 are a single unit in their present form, though they were experienced at different times (see "the second time," v. 13). Its component parts are held together by key themes. The "word" God puts in Jeremiah's mouth will be watched over by God (vv. 9, 12). Jeremiah is to speak what God commands (vv. 7, 17) regarding "kingdoms" (vv. 10, 15); he is not to be afraid (vv. 8, 17), for God will be with him to deliver him (vv. 8, 19). The phrase "the word of the LORD came to me," common in the prophets (e.g., Joel 1:1), is a stock phrase for revelatory activity in both call and visions (vv. 4, 11, 13; see also "today" in vv. 10, 18). This repetitiveness suggests that the common distinction made between call and visions can be overplayed. Vision is an appropriate word for the call proper as well. While a "seeing" component is not present in vv. 4-10, God's hand touching Jeremiah's mouth (v. 9) is a comparable "visionary" phenomenon. In each of the component parts of the text, God speaks and Jeremiah responds.

The report of the call of Jeremiah is outlined according to an available literary convention for speaking of such matters. [The Call Narratives] The report is similar to the call of Moses in Exodus 3–4. This similarity has invited readers to compare the ministries of Moses and Jeremiah, particularly regarding matters of law and covenant. Yet, basic differences are evident. Moses' commission is specific—to bring Israel out of Egypt; Jeremiah's commission is more wide-ranging, and focuses on judgment for Israel rather than salvation. Moreover, while other nations play a prominent role in each of their calls (see Jer 1:5, 10, 15), their roles are quite distinct. For Moses, Pharaoh and the Egyptians are the *targets* of God's judgment; for Jeremiah, Nebuchadrezzar and the Babylonians are usually God's *instruments* of judgment.

The Call Narratives

The calls of the prophets (and other leaders) commonly contain these elements (cf. Exod 3:1-12; Judg 6:11-24; Isa 6):

Encounter (1:4)
Introductory Word (1:5a)
Commission (1:5b, 10)
Objection (1:6)
Reassurance (1:7-8)
The Sign (1:9-10, 11-16)

Norman Habel, "The Form and Significance of the Call Narratives," ZAW 77 (1965): 297-323

Verses 4-10 narrate Jeremiah's call, yet not in a narrowly informational sense. The call assures readers that Jeremiah's ministry is grounded in *God's* initiative, not his own. Moreover, when seen through the lens of their own recent history, the truth of his message is impressed upon them. Readers would be able to see themselves and their recent history as the key reason for Jeremiah's call. Jeremiah was called because of them! The readers are the "them" of v. 8, the ones who threatened Jeremiah and from whom he must be delivered (vv. 18-19). The readers are those who worshiped other gods and became the object of God's judgment in and through other nations (vv. 15-16). With this visionary introduction, readers would be able to see more clearly that it was their apostasy that had occasioned the judgment. At the same time, the call narrative holds up a word of hope for them; its subject is God.

Literarily and theologically, key metaphors used in this chapter will recur throughout the book. The six verbs/images that set Jeremiah's commission (v. 10) are picked up in 12:14-17; 15:7; 18:7-9; 24:6; 31:4-5, 28, 38, 40; 32:41; 42:10; 45:4; 49:38. God is the subject of these verbs in every case except 1:10, and this exception shows how *Jeremiah's* word is effective in accomplishing *God's* work. Of special import for exiled readers would be the two positive metaphors related to community building and a return to the land (build; plant). From its very first page, the book of Jeremiah signals that the prophet's word will not simply be about judgment, however powerful that word will prove to be. No word of judgment will be God's final word to Israel (see **Connections: Events, the Reader, and God**).

Hence, while the call narrative serves as a literary and theological introduction to the words that follow and helps readers to interpret them properly, these connections are not basically an intellectual exercise. The visions serve to bring home to readers that these prophetic words pertain to them—an apostate, yet not finally rejected people of God.

The Call Proper, 1:4-10

God informs Jeremiah in a vision that while he was still in the womb of his mother, God had chosen (="knew," as in Gen 18:19; Amos 3:2) him to be a prophet and set him apart (=consecrated) for this task. Isaiah 49:5 and Galatians 1:15 speak in comparable terms of the servant and Paul. [An Egyptian Parallel] The parallel phrases ("before I formed you" and "before you were born") indicate that this divine decision was made before Jeremiah was fully formed in

An Egyptian Parallel

A striking Egyptian parallel to v. 5 is found in a saying by the god Amun regarding Pharaoh Pianchi (25th dynasty, 751–730 BC): "It was in the belly of your mother that I said concerning you that you were to be ruler of Egypt; it was as seed and while you were in the egg, that I knew you, that [I knew] you were to be Lord." Such a saying, over a century before Jeremiah, shows that such pre-birth understandings of a divine call were not peculiar to Israel.

M. Gilula, "An Egyptian Parallel to Jeremiah I 4-5," VT 17 (1967): 114.

the womb, but not prior to his conception. God is understood to be active *with the mother* in forming the child in the womb (also in Job 10:8-12; Ps 139:13-16; cf. different translations of the difficult v. 16); both God and mother are effective agents (see Gen 17:16). This divine decision does not predetermine that Jeremiah's life will follow a certain course, come what may. Jeremiah, in objecting (v. 6), understands that that decision is resistible, as does his later lament regarding having been born in the first place (see commentary on 20:7-18) (see **Connections: Events, the Reader, and God**).

To be commissioned as a prophet "to the nations" is unique among prophetic calls and is to be understood in light of v. 10 (see 25:13; 36:2; 46:1). This is not a call to "mission work" among the nations, but a commission to proclaim a word to Israel that will catch up the future of other nations (especially Babylon), potentially in both a positive and negative sense (see 12:14-17; 16:19-21;18:7-10; 25:9-32; 46–51). This word about the nations carries a theological claim. [God and the Nations]

Jeremiah's objection (v. 6) may be a literal reference to his youth ("boy" can mean child or young man; cf. 1 Sam 3:1) or a conventional reference to humility (cf. Solomon in 1 Kgs 3:7).[1] His lack of speaking ability is the focus of the objection in any case (see Moses, Exod 4:10). God sets aside the objection, specifying that God will make the decisions as to the audience and will give him

God and the Nations

Linking God's purposes with the chosen people to "nonchosen" kings and nations such as Babylon is a remarkable theological claim. God has to do with all the peoples of the world, not just Israel. God is present and active among all nations, whether they realize it or not. Yet God does not act in a micromanaging way, as is shown by Babylon later being condemned by God for being too destructive (25:12). And this word of God is effective in the lives of these nations, whether realized or not.

For God to be against Israel and for Babylon is not a very comfortable theological reality, especially if we were to apply the same point across the centuries to individual Christians or to the church. But we are assured that even in judgment, when God is against those of us who have been divinely chosen (often in and through those who are not "chosen"), in the final analysis God is for us (Rom 8:31-39).

the words he is commanded to speak (see Deut 18:18). As is typical of calls (see Exod 3:12; Judg 6:16, 23) and divine appearances, generally (see Gen 26:24)—whether fear has been voiced or not—God tells him not to be afraid. God will be present with him and provide for him in times of trouble (vv. 8, 17-19; see 15:20 and the consoling words in 30:10-11). God's response in v. 8 intimates that the word will meet opposition ("them"), and this is explicitly filled out in vv. 17-19.

Within the call vision, God, appearing in human form, touches Jeremiah's mouth with his hand (see Isa 6:7) and explains the meaning of that gesture: "I have put my words in your mouth." (The same language used for Moses in Deut 18:18 is used for the prophet.) Jeremiah later speaks of having eaten God's words (15:16; cf. 5:14). God later speaks of Jeremiah as one who "shall serve as my mouth" (15:19; cf. this language for the relationship among God, Moses, and Aaron in Exod 4:15-16; 7:1-2). The language of eating is important in thinking about the relationship between prophet and God (see **Connections: Eating the Word of God**). The effect of the word "implanted" in the body of the prophet is that he is given a certain stature regarding the nations of the world (including Israel). The word of God he embodies will enable him to shape their future, not with a sword that a king or warrior might wield, but with the word that is "sharper than any two-edged sword" (Heb 4:12) and "like a hammer that breaks the rock in pieces" (Jer 23:29).

The word of God that Jeremiah embodies is a powerful reality. The six metaphors that shape Jeremiah's word to the nations (v. 10) are used at varying points in what follows (see above for texts). Four of the metaphors have reference to the effect of words of judgment on the nations (pluck up; pull down; destroy; overthrow) and two to the effect of words of salvation (build; plant). The word of God is understood to have the capacity to judge and to save, to kill and to make alive (Deut 32:39). These metaphors are drawn from three spheres of life, presented in chiastic fashion [Chiasmus in 1:10] — agriculture (pluck up; plant), construction (pull down; build), and royal–military (destroy; overthrow). The latter are strong verbs of destruction (e.g., Judg 9:45) (see **Connections: Events, the Reader, and God**).

Chiasmus in 1:10

AΩ The *ABCĆBÁ* inversion (or chiasmus) provides one explanation for the order of these verbs. The agricultural terms (A) enclose construction terms (B), which in turn enclose the military terms (C).

To pluck up (A)
To pull down (B)
To destroy (C)
To overthrow (Ć)
To build (B́)
To plant (Á)

Watching and Word

Watching will be God's responsibility, not Jeremiah's. He does not have to worry and wonder about the success of the word (though he apparently does, 17:14-18; 18:19-23); he is only to be faithful in speaking and embodying that word. Noteworthy in this image of watching is the idea that God's word is not understood to proceed on its own to effect what has been said once it has been spoken. God must go with that word and attend to ("watch") that word as it makes its way through minds and hearts in order to bring about what God purposes (see Isa 48:3; for a

discussion of word, see Terence Fretheim, "Word of God," *ABD* [6 vols.; Garden City: Doubleday, 1992], 6: 961-68). Words, once spoken, can have all kinds of effects on people; God must attend to that word so that its effects correspond to the will of God.

And so, for example, in interaction with human beings, God may have to make adjustments in how a word is brought to completion so that it fulfills the divine intention (see 18:7-10). And, of course, God's word can be resisted and often is (see **Connections,** ch. 23).

Two Visions, 1:11-16

The two visions have certain elements in common (cf. the visions in 24:1-10; Amos 7:7-9; 8:1-3). In each case, God asks Jeremiah what he sees (vv. 11, 13), the prophet replies (vv. 11, 13), and God interprets their significance (vv. 12, 14-19). The objects seen are recognizable from daily life, but are visionary images and could not have been photographed. The basic purpose of the visions is to provide reassurances for Jeremiah in the face of the opposition he will encounter in announcing the coming disaster. God will be with him and with his word. Jeremiah is assured that he does not proceed only on his own resources.

Cooking Pots

Pottery vessels, such as the jug shown here and the one mentioned in Jeremiah, were used for storage, transportation, cooking, eating, drinking, and presenting offerings. In essence, a jug such as this was a prevalent commodity in every aspect of life. Thus, Jeremiah's prophecy suggests an upheaval of all that is familiar and comfortable, to be replaced by that which is foreign and excruciating. (Credit: Scott Nash)

A word-play centers the first vision (vv. 11-12). The object seen is a branch (or twig) of an almond tree (Heb., *šāqēd*), one of the first trees to blossom in the spring. This issues in an interpretation that God is watching (*šōqēd*) over his word so that as the twig will blossom (early), so God will effect what Jeremiah speaks, and soon (see the use of this "watchword" in 5:6; 31:28; 44:27). [Watching and Word]

The second vision (vv. 14-16) goes into more detail about the content of the word of God. The object seen is apparently (scholars disagree on details) a pot used for boiling water/food, tilted or overturned away from the north and spilling its scalding contents toward the south. This is interpreted to mean that disaster will flow out of the north—at God's call!—in the form of foreign armies and engulf (NRSV "break out") all the inhabitants of Israel (see **Connections: Sin and Judgment**).This "foe from the north" that will conquer, judge, and rule over all Israel (="set their thrones . . . at the gates," v. 15) is often mentioned in chapters 4–10 (e.g., 4:6). This foe is not specifically identified as Babylon until 25:9 (see 20:4-6; 21:4-7). Jeremiah may have been purposely or necessarily indefinite (threats to Israel commonly came from this direction, most recently Assyria); in either case the enemy is given an ominous character. But the readers, given their experience, would make the identification with Babylon without hesitation.

Idolatry is the specific sin cited in v. 16. Idolatry means to "forsake" Yahweh for other gods, which are no more than "the work of their [the readers'!] own hands" (see 2 Kgs 22:17). The reference to idolatry signals to the reader that the first (and second, in some traditions) commandment is the key issue for God. All other sins to be cited along the way in Jeremiah's oracles are symptomatic of this rupture in the readers' relationship with God (for one connection, see 16:11). Infidelity is the most basic metaphor that Jeremiah will use for this breakdown in Israel's relationship with God.

Divine Charge and Promise, 1:17-19

In concluding the encounter, God specifies Jeremiah's responsibilities in the face of opposition and assures him of divine presence and deliverance. War metaphors are dominant; Jeremiah will be like a city under siege. This imagery sets up the book in terms of a great conflict, and from two different angles. On the one hand, the people fight against the prophet, while Jeremiah is a passive resister (e.g., 11:19). Yet, on the other hand, the words Jeremiah uses, which often contain violent images (e.g., 13:20-27), indicate a rhetorical strategy that assumes that God is fighting against Israel (see 23:29).

The forces who will "fight against" Jeremiah (and God) comprise every type of religious and political leader, including "the people of the land" (=all other citizens), in effect "the whole land" (v. 18). Though their resistance will be powerful, God impresses upon Jeremiah the seriousness of his responsibility and gives him the "weapons" necessary for the task. God has armed him with the word of God for this confrontation, which will make him more impregnable than traditional methods (fortifications of bronze and iron) used by cities (Jerusalem may be in mind, v. 15) to protect themselves in times of siege. Such a comment about Jeremiah also recognizes the presence of a faithful remnant among the unfaithful majority.

Yet Jeremiah could fail. Jeremiah for his part will have to be ready for battle (="gird up loins"), stand tall, and not hold back any of the words God commands him to speak. If he does not do this, he could be "broken" by the opposition (terrified or panicked, see 49:37), and then God would make that very failure (the same verb is used, *ḥtt*) evident for all to see (see 15:19-20). This is not a threat, but a matter-of-fact reminder of the way God's world works—private failure will often lead to public failure.

At the same time, God assures Jeremiah that he is not alone in this task. Whatever may happen along the way, he (and the word he brings) will not *finally* be defeated—an already existent reality to exiled readers who had opposed Jeremiah. As for his own life, he will be rescued from the onslaughts of his antagonists (v. 19; anticipated in v. 8). This promise may refer to texts such as 26:10-19 and 38:1-13 (cf. 45:5) and suggests that Jeremiah does live through the destruction of Jerusalem. But this is not a word that promises Jeremiah some kind of trouble-free life; indeed, God's rescue implies trouble.

CONNECTIONS

The Opening Verses of Jeremiah and the Reader

The nature of the opening recollection of the book (vv. 1-3) means that the original audience for the *book* of Jeremiah was fundamentally different from the audience for the *preaching* of Jeremiah (even if many people were a part of both audiences). The raping and ravaging Babylonian armies and the destruction of Jerusalem and its temple were a lively memory, and the shaming realities of exile were a present experience. Because the readers' situation in exile was so different from what it had been at the time of the original preaching, the words of the prophet carried a different force for them. The readers (including every subsequent generation) were to hear Jeremiah's preaching not so much as past event, but as present word of God to them.

Take this example: The judgment on Jerusalem announced by the prophet was not something to anticipate; it was to be remembered and pondered regarding its continuing importance. Such announcements remained the word of the LORD, but that word was now addressed to a different situation in the life of God's people. We would belittle the texts to suggest that their import was basically to show readers that, say, recent historical events demonstrated the accuracy of Jeremiah's talk about the future. Hanging over the entire book is the recurring theological question of 5:19:

"Why has the LORD our God done all these things to us?" (9:12; 16:10; 22:8; Deut 9:24; 1 Kgs 9:8; see **Introduction**). Reading Jeremiah should enable readers to answer this question and to shape their lives into the future in terms of it.

Events, the Reader, and God

As metaphors, the six verbs of 1:10 do not speak with precision about what will occur in the future. They are somewhat open-ended regarding the effect of the word of God. They leave room for new developments in the historical process and in the relationship between God and Israel. That twice as many metaphors are used for judgment suits well the preponderance of judgment oracles that follow, and would certainly resonate with the experience of exiled readers. Hence, these four metaphors portray that which has already been experienced by the readers. On the other hand, the positive words are not yet descriptive of any experience of the exiles, but would be especially welcome to them, containing a hopeful word from God. [Brueggemann on the Call Narrative]

Looking back, exiles (and other readers) can discern that God's purposes were indeed effected in and through what happened to Israel in destruction and exile. But such hindsight does not warrant conclusions that this ending was predetermined, either in a general way or in terms of Jeremiah's ministry in particular. There does come a point when, to use a boating metaphor, Israel's disastrous trip over the falls does become inevitable. The prophet does discern when the pull of the waterfall makes it impossible to prevent the boat from going over, when those on the boat may not yet realize it (e.g., 4:28). But the calls for repentance in Jeremiah (e.g., 3:11–4:4) suggest that that disastrous future was not necessarily in place from the beginning.

Brueggemann on the Call Narrative

Walter Brueggemann's language is helpful here. God's word works "harsh endings," but also "amazing beginnings." "God can work newness, create historical possibilities *ex nihilo*, precisely in situations that seem hopeless and closed." God's final word to the people of God is not the word of judgment. At the same time, several of Brueggemann's claims in his discussion of the call narrative need qualification. He speaks of the "overruling" freedom of Yahweh, or a God who "[micro?]manages," or that the purposes and word of God are "irresistible." These statements are made in view of the basic assumption of the book that the events of judgment have already happened. It is certainly the case that, from the perspective of the readers, "no escape is available . . . the ending will not go away . . . [they and] we only wait and watch for the ending to materialize." But the reader, in seeking to understand God's role in these events, is not thereby given permission to make a theological jump from "these events *have* occurred in the purposes of God" to "these events *had* to occur."

Walter Brueggemann, *A Commentary on Jeremiah: Exile and Homecoming* (Grand Rapids: Eerdmans, 1998), 23, 25-26.

Indeed, I would claim that the book of Jeremiah has continuing importance for readers (then and now) precisely because their futures are (normally) not set in stone and because a past word of God (e.g., regarding repentance) may once again prove to be a lively word of possibility. How people respond to the word of God does in fact shape their future, as well as the future of others. At the same time, there may come a point in the course of the lives of individuals or communities or nations when a certain kind of future does become inevitable, when it may be too late for repentance to shape the future in a positive way. But even if this disaster should occur, the remarkable word of Jeremiah is that no trip over the falls is final. Israel's God is the kind of God who picks the people up from the rocks below the falls and continues to be about the business of building and planting for the future, even when there does not seem to be much left to work with. And, then, in this continuing journey down the river, the call to repentance remains important.

Eating the Word of God

That Jeremiah is commissioned to be a prophet before he is born says something important about the relationship between the person and the calling. While this claim may have been to counter any challenge to Jeremiah's status as prophet,[2] a finer point is that the distinction between prophetic office and prophetic person is virtually collapsed. Jeremiah does not cease to be a person in his own right, but being a prophet defines his person from the very beginning; it is the very essence of his being. He is decisively shaped by God, not simply to be a certain kind of speaker, but a certain kind of person. Hence, he no longer has a private life that can truly be called his own; he goes without wife and children and the normal run of social activities (16:1-9; 15:17).

This understanding is extended in the commission given to Jeremiah (vv. 9-10; cf. 15:19). The word of God is placed directly into Jeremiah's mouth. It is not necessary for Jeremiah to hear what he is to say; the word is transferred into his very being. This process is graphically portrayed in Ezekiel 2:8–3:3. The prophet thus ingests the word of God; the word of God is thereby enfleshed in the very person of the prophet. He embodies the word of God; indeed, the prophet becomes the word of God ("you are what you eat"). In this connection, the bodily language for God ("hand") is striking. Even for God's self the word is embodied! The prophet/God ambiguity of subject in many of Jeremiah's speeches (e.g., 8:18–9:3) is a further indication of this reality. This may also be seen in that Jeremiah is the subject of the verbs in v. 10, while God is the subject of these verbs elsewhere in Jeremiah (see texts above). Or, a text such as 25:15 (cf. Amos 9:1), where Jeremiah is commanded to "make all the nations to whom I send you" drink the cup of wrath, demonstrates the merging of prophetic acts and divine acts. As will become apparent, all of Jeremiah's actions are to be understood not as (auto)biography, but as embodied word of God. [Von Rad on Eating the Word of God]

Von Rad on Eating the Word of God

Gerhard von Rad properly warns against taking these texts "in too spiritual a way. . . . The entry of the message into their physical life brought about an important change in the self-understanding of these later prophets. (We may ask whether the entry of the word into a prophet's bodily life is not meant to approximate what the writer of the Fourth Gospel says about the word becoming flesh.)"

Gerhard von Rad, *Old Testament Theology* 2 vols. (New York: Harper & Row, 1965), 2:91-92. For these reflections more generally, see Terence Fretheim, *The Suffering of God: An Old Testament Perspective* (Philadelphia: Fortress, 1984), 152-53

Sin and Judgment

It is important to note that the Hebrew word *rāʿāh* occurs twice in this segment (vv. 14, 16), and often in the book, and is commonly translated in two different ways (NRSV, "disaster" and "wickedness, evil"). This verbal linkage makes it clear that the judgment the Israelites will experience flows out of their own deeds. While this linkage can be properly understood in terms of the proverbial phrase, "What goes around, comes around," it is important that God is not removed from the connection between sin and consequence. Yet judgment is not something new that God introduces into the situation (as is commonly thought to be the case in retributionary understandings); rather, God mediates the consequences that are already intrinsic to the evil deed itself.

This dynamic understanding of sin and its effects is common in the book (and the Old Testament more generally) and will often be marked in the commentary (see also **Introduction**). Three clear examples are the following: 6:19, disaster is "the fruit of their schemes"; 14:16, "I will pour out *their* [author's emphasis] wickedness upon them"; 21:14, "I will punish you according to the fruit of your doings." The translation "punish" in 21:14 is problematic, however. In every such case in Jeremiah (in RSV or NRSV), the verb "punish" translates the Hebrew word *pāqād*, the everyday word for "visit." A more helpful translation of 21:14 (and similar texts), which recognizes that retribution is not involved in the divine action, would be, "I will visit upon you the fruit of your own doings."

Such a translation more clearly recognizes that God mediates the consequences that are already present in the wicked situation. In other terms, God thereby sees to the moral order—a reality God has built into the very structures of creation in terms of which human deeds, whether good or wicked, rebound upon the perpetrator's heads, though not in any mechanistic or inevitable way. Similarly, the noun "punishment" (in RSV or NRSV) is usually a translation of the Hebrew word *p^equdāh*, "visit(ation)" (e.g., 11:23).

NOTES

[1] See Robert Carroll, *Jeremiah: A Commentary* (Philadelphia: Westminster, 1986), 98-99.

[2] Ibid., 98.

ISRAEL'S INFIDELITY

2:1–3:5

Indictment for Infidelity and Call to Repentance, 2:1–4:4

Jeremiah 2:1–3:5 is commonly thought to be a part of the larger unit
2:1–4:4. The structure of this unit consists of an indictment of Israel
for its unfaithfulness to Yahweh (2:1–3:5) followed by a call to repentance (3:11–4:4; 3:6-10 is a personal word to the prophet). In the
chapters that immediately follow (4:5–10:25), the theme of divine
judgment through the instrumentality of a "foe from the north" pre-
dominates (e.g., 4:6). The movement in this larger unit is thus:
indictment, call to repentance, and (that having failed) announcement of judgment.

Within the unit 2:1–4:4, a break is sometimes made after 2:37
(rather than 3:5) because of the prominent use of the word "[re]turn"
throughout 3:1–4:4. Yet the people are not actually called to return
in 3:1-5, and the personal address to Jeremiah in 3:6-10 suggests a
break at this point. It seems best to regard 3:1-5 as a "swing" section
that continues 2:1-37 and anticipates 3:6–4:4. These difficulties in
discerning the flow of thought are certainly due to the disparate origins of the various segments.

The addressee of these verses is laid out in a way that has defied
scholarly clarification. Scholars commonly consider 2:1–4:4 to reflect
Jeremiah's early career because of the concern for the northern
kingdom. Josiah's efforts to reunify Judah and Israel may be especially
in view (see 3:6, 14, 18; 2 Kgs 22–23). ("Israel" may refer to the
northern kingdom, as in 3:6-12, or, usually, the people of God as a
whole, as in 2:3.) The present text may consist of an older body of
material originally addressed to the northern kingdom, but it is now
overlaid with components with a southern provenance.

The entire text (2:1–4:4) is to be proclaimed "in the hearing of"
Jerusalem (v. 2). This salutation could refer both to the Jerusalem of
pre-destruction times and the exilic audience (on the latter, see Isa
40:2; 51:17). After an initial premise (vv. 2-3), the word is addressed
to both Judah and Israel (2:4–3:5). Israel may refer to those who had
fled to the south at the time of the fall of the north in 722–721 BC
and were included among the exiles (hence "families," v. 4). Then,
after a personal word to Jeremiah (3:6-10), the North and South are

A Multigenerational Audience

AΩ In view of an exilic audience composed of people from both North and South, the preaching of Jeremiah is understood to speak to both communities, *both* in the past and the present. This double reference to past and present can be seen in the interchanging reference to "ancestors" (2:5-6) and the multigenerational "you" who is the object of God's direct address (2:9; see 3:25, "we and our ancestors"; 14:20). This "generation" is also directly addressed in 2:31. This duality of reference may explain the interchange of feminine singular "you" (2:2, 17-25; 2:33–3:5; see "daughter" in 6:2; 8:19) and masculine singular/plural "you" (2:4-16, 26-32). The "you" includes both those who heard Jeremiah and those who now read these materials (there would be some overlap). The exiles would understand the "you" in terms of their situation, both past and present.

individually addressed (3:12; 4:3), calling for repentance in both cases. The unit is punctuated throughout with the phrase, "(Thus) says the LORD (God of Hosts)" (e.g., 2:2-3, 5, 9). But neither this phrase nor the addressee citations seems to separate literary units in a precise fashion. [A Multigenerational Audience]

Another historical factor to be considered is that Egypt is still a threat. Babylon is not mentioned, and while Assyria may still have some power (2:18; see Lam 5:6), its menacing presence has passed (see the recollections in vv. 14-15, 36). Some scholars connect the material to a time close to the Egyptian campaign of 609 BC. Others seek to assign various snippets of texts to various contexts. No firm conclusions can be drawn, except to place the general setting in the last years before the fall of Jerusalem. In any case, closer specificity on this historical point is unimportant for the present form of the text. These verses have been shaped to speak to an exilic audience that has already experienced the fall of Jerusalem and the Babylonian exile.

COMMENTARY

The basic character of the section 2:1–3:5 is that of a divine lament, common in Jeremiah (see also 3:7, 19-20). Many scholars refer to this text as an "accusation speech" (cf. v. 9) or a "covenant lawsuit" (cf. Mic 6:1-8). But this claim has been rightly disputed.[1] While some formal "lawsuit" elements are present, the accusation is part of a larger rhetorical pastiche in which divine lament is especially prominent (cf. the use of accusation in human laments, e.g., 12:1-4; Pss 44; 73–74; Isa 63–64). One might think of this rhetoric as preaching that rehearses a painful dispute between God and Israel over the issue of fidelity. Several links to the divorce law in Deuteronomy 24:1-4 exist (see 2:5, 7; 3:1), but the interpreter should not reduce this material to legal or formal categories or settings (as is often done with "covenant," a word not used here) (see **Connections: A Dialogical Relationship**).

The flow of thought within this unit is not altogether clear, but consists basically of an opening divine memory of the "honeymoon" with Israel (vv. 1-3), followed by an explosion of metaphors—especially the marital metaphor—that speaks with great intensity about the breakdown of the marriage (2:4–3:5). This material interweaves reflections, questions, accusations, complaints about enemies, and other matters, as is characteristic of human laments (see Ps 13). [A Word to Exilic Readers]

A Word to Exilic Readers

The divine concern for exilic readers in this passage is not simply to review the past (though that is important), but to chart some possible ways of moving into the future together on the far side of judgment. The judgment has already befallen Israel, but that this (reshaped) word once again is used to address exilic readers means that they are to understand that the God with whom they are in relationship is concerned about these sorts of matters. That they still can hear God addressing them in this text means that, whatever the depths of judgment they have experienced, God has not rejected them. At the same time, God is profoundly concerned about their being faithful in the relationship.

Virtually every indictment that God brings forward in this section has to do with the first/second commandment; only in 2:34 do issues of social justice come into play. Only when the issue of the relationship with God has been clearly laid out as the fundamental problem do such *symptoms* of that brokenness appear (here and later). The marital metaphor assumes elements of promise and commitment on the part of both parties. The indictment focuses on the breaking of this commitment by Israel by having intimate relations with other gods. Given this focus, little is said about future judgment (2:36-37; past judgment is evident in 2:14-16), and even then Babylon is not specifically in view. That will come later (20:4-6 for the first time), but now the call to repentance is front and center (3:11–4:4), and a promised future is stated with great clarity (3:15-18).

This section presents "an anatomy of evil, documented with evidence of past and present sins."[2] This is a vivid depiction of the human predicament. As presently situated prior to the calls for repentance in 3:6–4:4, this material is preaching designed to elicit repentance, not to write Israel's epitaph. Yet, while it was probably originally spoken at a time (well) before the fall of Jerusalem when repentance was still possible, in its present form it now can function in such a way only for (exilic) readers.

A Divine Memory, 2:1-3

The word of God to Jeremiah begins with a marital metaphor (v. 2) and moves briefly to an agricultural/religious metaphor (v. 3). The former dominates in this section of Jeremiah, but both metaphors assume that Israel has fully committed itself to Yahweh and is to be devoted only to him. The text focuses on God's remembrance of the marriage with Israel in its early years. How good the relationship used to be! This memory of God occasions suffering in God because the present relationship is so different. How things have changed! Israel's devotion and love as a young bride during the wilderness wanderings were remarkable (not perfect, but comparatively speaking; see Deut 32:10-18). But infidelity is now the rule. The people of God have strayed and "stubbornly followed their own hearts" rather than God, going after other lovers (2:5; 9:14; 13:10). Yet, because God's relationship with Israel is marked by God's love and devotion and not simply by Israel's, there is hope for the future.

Israel had been set apart (="holy") by God as the first of God's chosen ones among the nations, like the first fruits from the harvest that people set apart as an offering to God (see Num 18:12-13; Deut 26:1-2; cf. Israel as firstborn in 31:9). Remarkably, God harvested first fruits "in a land not sown"! It is striking that Israel is considered to be a gift not only set apart *by* God, but also *for* God. This relationship with Israel was not one-sided, with benefits only for Israel. For God, too, this relationship that included Israel's devotion (*ḥesed*) was a gift. Hence, the disloyalty that Israel has shown cuts all the more deeply into the heart of God. If Israel had not meant so much to God, these developments could have been received and handled in a more objective way. [The Divine Lament]

The "harvest" metaphor envisages peoples other than Israel who also belong to God. God begins with Israel within a purpose that is global in its ultimate scope. Israel's election is an initially exclusive move for the sake of a maximally inclusive end. The image of harvest continues with reference to enemies who tried to "eat" the first fruits (first fruits were not to be eaten; see 5:17); that is, they attacked Israel and plundered its possessions (e.g., the Amalekites; Exod 17:8-16). But God's protective hand sheltered the beloved. Such a profanation of the first fruits reserved for God (see Lev 22:1-2) made these nations guilty, and they experienced disaster (*rā'āh*). But now, given the breakdown in the relationship with God, Israel's enemies simply have their own way (vv. 14-19). Recall that, for readers, the fall of Jerusalem has already passed

The Divine Lament

In this text God raises a deeply personal matter in a highly intense and emotion-filled encounter. An intimate relationship has broken down, and this has engendered strong feelings of anger and hurt on God's part (see **Introduction**). No legal analysis can begin to do justice to this situation for either God or Israel, not least because God is open to going beyond the law in resolving the issue (see at 3:1-5, 15-18). To lift up the divine lament in these opening verses is important for interpreting the book as a whole. Jeremiah begins with a portrayal of God in deep pain and anguish. Later images of wrath and judgment are to be interpreted within this lament context that the beginning of the book provides (and often returns to). The book of Isaiah also begins with a divine lament, using a parental metaphor (1:2-3) to speak of the disjunction between past and present. (Terence Fretheim, *The Suffering of God: An Old Testament Perspective* [Philadelphia: Fortress, 1989], 115-16.)

Harvest

The gnarled roots, the energy of growth, and the enduring stamina of the olive trees may have attracted Vincent van Gogh. He executed fifteen paintings of olive trees within a year of his death. Today, the olive tree remains a powerful symbol of harvest in the Middle East. In spite of the ravages of war, Palestinian and Israeli farmers, alike, continue the tradition of the olive harvest that has endured for generations.

Vincent van Gogh. *The Olive Trees.* 1889. Oil on canvas. 36.5"x29". The Minneapolis Institute of Arts. Minneapolis, Minnesota. (Credit: The William Hood Dunwoody Fund/The Minneapolis Institute of Arts)

(1:3). The original idyllic relationship between God and Israel has ended in disaster for *Israel,* both in the past and now again in the recent present.

The lack of reference to Sinai or the covenant in the rehearsal of the story that follows in vv. 6-7 is notable. The wilderness wanderings begin in pre-Sinai times (Exod 15–18). The marriage between God and Israel is understood to be a pre-Sinai reality; God refers to Israel as "my people" throughout Exodus 1–18 (e.g., 3:7; cf. 4:22). The covenant at Sinai formalizes an already existing relationship and is mentioned infrequently in Jeremiah (see 11:2-10; 22:9; 31:32; 34:15-18; Moses occurs only at 15:1). The covenants with Noah and David are mentioned almost as often (e.g., 31:35-37; 33:14-26). To be true to Jeremiah, covenant language should not be overused in thinking through this imagery. In any case, the covenant texts in the Old Testament more generally recognize that adherence to the Sinaitic covenant did not absolutely determine Israel's relationship to Yahweh; see, for example, Moses' arguments (e.g., Exod 32:13).

On Changing Gods, 2:4-13

With this divine memory of the "honeymoon" in view, God responds to the present, broken state of the relationship. This rupture is signaled by the new address to both Judah and the families of Israel (v. 4; cf. Judah in v. 28)—both covered in the phrase "in the hearing of Jerusalem" (2:2). In the verses that follow, God's recollections, and interactions with the people, including questions (rhetorical and otherwise) and accusations, tumble over one another as integral parts of the divine lament.

Initially, readers hear God complaining in the form of a question: "What did your ancestors find wrong with me?" (v. 5; this language is used in divorce proceedings, Deut 24:1). For exilic readers, the

Ancient Israelite Creeds

Much attention is given these days to the biblical narrative (story) as that which makes the characters (such as God) come most alive and reveals their identity most clearly. God's identity is narrated, not reduced to attributes or abstractions. At the same time, the biblical texts refuse to be content with narratives in their portrayal of God. Non-narrative genres, which gather claims about God, are more important for this discussion than commonly recognized. Two major types of such "credal" genres are used in the Old Testament. One focuses on divine acts (e.g., Deut 26:5-9; Josh 24:5-13), and Jer 2:6-7 follows in this tradition. (This genre is emphasized particularly in the work of Gerhard von Rad.) A second credal genre articulates those claims about God in more abstract ways (e.g., Exod 34:6-7). The reader of Jeremiah should be alert to Jeremiah's dependence upon both of these types of confessions, and consider the question: What kind of God is presented in Jeremiah?

"ancestors" would recall all prior generations, not merely those of ancient times. God's question seems to be rhetorical, with the answer self-evident: God committed no wrong in the relationship to occasion Israel's forsaking the marriage to "marry" other gods (and hence Israel could not apply the divorce law of 24:1-4).

Yet this approach may understate the import of God's question. Israel does in fact accuse Yahweh (e.g., 2:35; 3:5) and so the question of 2:5 could be construed as God's invitation to engage in a dialogue—to get the problem out on the table. God's question could be a real question. As such, God's question catches up exilic readers (see the exiles' questions in Lam 5:20-22). From another angle, this is a genuine "why?" question for God (as in vv. 29-32). Given God's exemplary participation as spouse, it is a mystery even to God why Israel would run after other gods. The latter are "worthless things" with no substance to them (*hebel*, perhaps a play on the word Baal; cf. vv. 8, 11, where the economic metaphor is also used; 2 Kgs 17:15). Because the people will inevitably become like that which they follow and worship (as in Hos 9:10; Ps 135:18), why would they choose to shape their lives in terms of that which is insubstantial?

In being unfaithful to the relationship, the ancestors no longer inquired about their most basic story and traditions—God's gracious actions on their behalf in the exodus from Egypt and the treacherous—*note the emphasis*—wilderness wanderings (v. 6). [Ancient Israelite Creeds] This strong wilderness language would connect with the exiles (see Isa 35 for the transformation of the wilderness). In the absence of Israel's testimony, God bears witness to having brought Israel into "my land," the productive garden that was the land of Canaan (2:7; Exod 34:6-7 also places the people's

Baal and Canaanite Religion

Canaanite religious practice played a significant role in the development of Israelite infidelity. According to the books of Kings, this religion gained entry into Israel's life, especially under the program and policies of King Jeroboam, the first king of the northern kingdom (Israel; 1 Kgs 12:25-33). But it was under Ahab and Jezebel that a virulent form of Canaanite religion threatened the very future of the North and, in time, the South (see 1 Kgs 16:31-34).

Canaanite religion was polytheistic. Chief among the deities was El, the high god of the Canaanite pantheon, who presided over that world of gods. Most well-known among these deities to readers, then and now, was Baal, whose consorts included Anat (and Astarte and Asherah). Their mating was believed responsible for overcoming the powers of death and enabling a renewal of life, especially as evidenced in the rains and the fertility of the soil. Every year this drama was reenacted, and the people participated in the associated rituals, which were often of a sexual nature. A blending of religious practices was common (syncretism) and deeply compromised Israel's commitment to Yahweh alone. The sexual imagery used in Jeremiah to speak of the relationship between Israel and God (and other deities) is ultimately derived from religious practices associated with the worship of Baal and Israel's infidelity relating thereto. Idolatry is imaged as spiritual adultery; at the same time, the sexual practices associated with participation in Baal worship mean that the sexual imagery also has a literal reference.

Baal with Thunderbolt. 1700–1300 BC. Bas-relief on limestone stele. From Ugarit Syria. Louvre, Paris. (Credit: Erich Lessing/Art Resource, NY)

Baal-Hammon (Credit: Mitchell G. Reddish)

confession—in the third person—in the mouth of God in the wake of apostasy). In v. 7, notably, God makes a switch from the ancestors to the present audience ("you"; cf. v. 5), thereby collapsing the distinction between the ancestors and the present readers (see also 3:25; 14:20). Their own infidelity matched that of their ancestors; readers could not escape from this indicting word of God by laying the blame on them (see 31:29-30).

The religious leaders were no better than the people; the most important types are singled out (v. 8). Priests did not inquire of the LORD (see v. 6a); scribes or Levites taught the Law without trust/fear ("know") in God; political leaders (shepherds) did not rule effectively; and prophets were prophesying the word of Baal. [Baal and Canaanite Religion] No one escaped from Jeremiah's word! All alike had forsaken the LORD and forgotten the confessional tradition—all became as bankrupt as the idols they worshiped (reinforcing the point made in v. 5; cf. v. 11). This divine

Identification of Place Names

• Cyprus—an island nation in the Mediterranean Sea, about sixty miles off the coast of Canaan; it was a center for maritime trade.

• Kedar—a league of tribes in the north Arabian Desert, east of the Jordan River, which controlled trade routes in that region (see 49:28-33; Ezek 37:21).

• Memphis—a former capital of Egypt on the Nile, fifteen miles south of Cairo, famous for its handicrafts and culture.

• Tahpanhes—an Egyptian city in the Delta region, with a garrison to protect the frontier against invaders; it was a likely place for Israelite consultations with Egyptian officials regarding alliances against Babylon. After the fall of Jerusalem, Israelites fled here as well as to Memphis (43:7–44:1).

assessment of the breakdown in relationship issues in an accusation (v. 9), typical of human laments to God (as with Jeremiah, 12:1). Only in this case, the grounds for the accusation are clear: Israel has forsaken Yahweh by turning to other gods. The people's infidelity is so deep-seated that this judgmental divine response is set for generations to come (v. 9). Notably, the "you" that God accuses here are not the ancestors, but the readers, who have just experienced such judgment!

That Israel would "change gods" is something unparalleled in that world. Readers (the "you" of vv. 7, 9) are invited to see for themselves that this is so (v. 10): take a survey at key trading centers to the east (Cyprus) and to the west (Kedar). [Identification of Place Names] Both would be in a position to hear of such changes and assess exchanges. For other nations, changing gods is unheard of, even though no real gods are involved! Reinforcing the economic metaphor (vv. 5, 8), Israel has exchanged its wealth or glory (=God; see Ps 3:3) for bankruptcy (v. 11).

The heavens are invited to be witnesses to this appalling and shocking evil (cf. Isa 1:2), as they had witnessed the initial love. The common translation "be desolate" (v. 12) could also be rendered "be dry"—give no rain. This reference should be linked with the following water metaphors (v. 13) and the adverse effect on the land (see **Connections: Israel's Sin and Its Ecological Effects**). Indeed, the heavens are to witness *two* evils: Israel has forsaken Yahweh (also 2:17, 19), the fountain/spring of living water (see 17:13; Isa 55:1; John 4:10-14). Also, Israel has taken up with other gods, cisterns that have cracked plaster and can hold no water (for possible marital links, see Prov 5:15-23). Ironically, they have dug cisterns to conserve water (without success) whereas the spring flows naturally. The water metaphors focus on Yahweh as an ongoing source of life (an ever-flowing natural spring) in contrast to other gods, which, in

The Cistern in Shiloh. Shiloh, Israel. (Credit: Erich Lessing/Art Resource, NY)

spite of appearances, are no life-giving resource at all (vv. 12-13). Note that in spite of their infidelities, God calls Israel "my people" (vv. 11, 13, 31-32) and "children" (3:14, 22) and is still identified as "your God" (vv. 17, 19) and "your master"(=*ba'al,* 3:14; see at v. 8). Once again, exilic readers are in view.

Israel Exposed, 2:14-19

When the marriage relationship was in good order, Israel was protected from marauders (v. 3), But no longer, as God's six rhetorical questions in vv. 14-19 demonstrate. Israel (both North and South) is identified as neither a slave nor a homeborn servant (born within a household, hence a slave in perpetuity). Yet Israel has "become plunder" (war loot) to the nations roundabout and now serves them (as also for the exiles). The answer to God's "why" question in v. 14 is in vv. 17 and 19—the people have forsaken Yahweh. This note is ironically related to the people's words in v. 20; their declaration that they will not serve Yahweh has resulted in their serving other nations—a new kind of bondage.

As the exiles would read vv. 15-16, both Assyria and Babylonia may be in view (=lions, see 4:7; Amos 3:12). These nations have "eaten" their prey, Israel (see 2:3; 5:17), by devastating the land and decimating the population (in 721 BC for the North, 587 BC for the South). In addition, the exiles will remember (v. 16 switches back to the second person, "your" head) how Egypt, represented by two key cities (Memphis and Tahpanhes), wreaked havoc with the Davidic "crown," a metonym for Israel itself (a reference to Josiah's death in 609 BC?; see [Identification of Place Names]).

The people became dependent on the "waters" of the ordinary rivers of Egypt and "Assyria" (v. 18; a general reference to a Mesopotamian power, which the exiles would interpret as Babylon; see Lam 5:6), rather than the "living water" (v. 13) that God can supply. This dependence may refer to political alliances (see Isa 30:1-5). Yet, given the references to apostasy and the water metaphors, this development is symptomatic of a more basic infidelity (the infiltration of idolatrous practices from these countries may also be in view). The fundamental issue for Israel is religious, not political, but that problem skews relationships in every walk of life.

The devastation wrought by these nations on Israel is evidence that Yahweh has been forsaken (vv. 17, 19; cf. v. 13). Exilic readers are in view: "you" have brought this upon "yourself" (the second person continues throughout the chapter). Israel has brought these effects upon itself, even though God's leading had been constant (v. 17). Verse 19 continues this note of *self*-infliction. Israel's *own* wickedness/evil (*rā'āh]* is used twice) has resulted in this chastisement—it has not been imposed by God from without (see 1:16 and **Connections** there; 5:25; 6:19; 21:14). The reference is to past, present, and potential consequences (vv. 17, 19). Israel's own apostasies have turned back on them and made them the victim of plundering neighbors. The irony is that by forsaking Yahweh and seeking the gods of other peoples, they are thrown into exile among these very nations. This changed reality for Israel is stated by means of rhetorical questions (vv. 14, 17-18), but a response is nevertheless invited by the questioning mode. Readers would find these questions highly pertinent from their devastating situation in exile (v. 17 is one answer to questions such as those stated in 5:19 and elsewhere).

Israel's Apostasy Detailed, 2:20-37

This segment details the divine claims regarding Israel's infidelity in vv. 5-19 (see vv. 13, 17, 19). The address to "you" would catch up exiled readers once again. God catalogs in graphic terms how Israelites have forsaken their LORD and interacts with their communications. God's rhetorical strategy in the use of such an array of images—often gross, offensive, even sarcastic images—may have been to get Israel's attention. Imagine a modern preacher using these images in a Sunday morning sermon! At the same time, these images function at a deeper level (see **Connections: Use of Female/Sexual Imagery**).

Listen to the explosion of emotional language. God uses these telling images to portray an Israel that has "sprawled and played the whore" on every high hill, the usual place for Baal altars (v. 20; see Hos 4:13; Deut 12:2; see [Baal and Canaanite Religion]). Israel is "a wild ass . . . in her heat sniffing the wind" for smell of the urine of the male ass, easily available for sexual activity to anyone who comes along (v. 24). Israel has made love to strangers (v. 25; see Deut 32:16) and, given past infidelities at Baal shrines on the part of their ancestors, considers trees and stones to be their parents rather than God (v. 27). Israel is so skilled at infidelity that they have even taught prostitutes how to ply their trade (v. 33)! This unremitting imagery continues in 3:2-3. Israel has "played the whore with many lovers . . . where have you not been lain with? . . . by the waysides you have sat waiting for lovers, like a nomad" or, we might say, a street-walker. Jeremiah's sexual imagery is to be understood both literally (it was an integral part of Baal religious practice) and spiritually—being unfaithful to Yahweh and turning to other lovers (gods). What kind of impact might this imagery have had on exilic readers? The strategy might have been to elicit repentance.

Other metaphors of unfaithfulness are interwoven with these sexual images (vv. 21-27): (a) Israel has broken the yoke (constraints) provided by the Law and declared its independence (v. 20; see the irony at v. 14; Exod 24:7); (b) though God planted Israel as a choice vine, it has become a wild vine, bearing obnoxious fruit and sour wine (v. 21; see Isa 5:1-7; Deut 32:32-33; Ps 80). This has been Israel's choice, not God's; (c) though Israel has attempted to wash itself clean with strong cleansers, the stain is so deep-seated that Israel cannot wash it away (v. 22; see Isa 1:16; Ps 51:2, 7, where God does the washing). Israel's rituals of repentance have not been matched by a true admission of guilt, as their claims of v. 23 show; (d) Israel is a young camel, running off in all directions without purpose (v. 23); (e) the people (and all their leaders) are like thieves; they will be shown to have acted shamefully when, it is assumed, they are caught (vv. 26-27; see 2:36; 6:15; 8:12). Their activities with other lovers will be shown to be a shameful thing; they have turned their backs to God rather than their faces (v. 27). In acting shamefully, they will be shamed (vv. 36-37).

Interwoven with these divine complaints and accusations is a series of nine (!) direct quotations from the people themselves (see **Connections: A Dialogical Relationship**). The quotations begin in v. 20 with their declaration that they will not serve God, which God agrees has occurred (cf. the slavery language of v. 14 for the irony). Yet, in response to God's charges in vv. 20-22, they also say they have not gone after the Baals and have not made themselves impure (v. 23a). Or, better (given the admission in v. 25), they claim that their syncretistic practices have not in fact defiled them.

God's response is straightforward: Look at the evidence and see (="know") what "you" have done. They have prostituted themselves in the valleys (the valley of Hinnom near Jerusalem may be in mind, 7:31-32) as well as on the hills (vv. 23b-24; cf. v. 20). This has become a "way" of life for them, like a young camel flitting off in all directions. The people are to recall (v. 25) that God has commanded them to quit such wandering (wearing out their shoes) in waterless places (cf. "living water" in v. 13), but the people contemptuously respond by saying, "No use! no! [NAB]." Having been presented with these images, the people here admit what they seemed to deny in v. 23. Making love to strange gods has become

A Compulsive Will

If the people's claim in v. 25 is "we can't," as seems likely, this amounts to an admission of bondage to sin, or at least a resignation to being "a compulsive devotee of the Baalism who has no rational control over her behavior . . . addicted to idolatry." Given this statement, the claim to innocence in v. 35 need not be contradictory; it could be ironic. Or it could be an illustration of unstable self-perception. Or, most likely, it is revealing of an addictive personality, claiming innocence for actions that are beyond personal control: I cannot be blamed for what I cannot help but do! This verse is linked to a common theme of stubbornness and an "evil will," e.g., 3:17; 18:12; see 5:21; 6:10; **Connections**, ch. 5.

William McKane, *A Critical and Exegetical Commentary on Jeremiah* (2 vols.; ICC; Edinburgh: T. & T. Clark, 1986), 56.

so habitual that they cannot (will not?) stop it (v. 25). [A Compulsive Will]

Still another quotation from the people relates to their changed religious commitments (v. 27a); they claim that a tree and a stone, rather than Yahweh, are father and mother to them (see Deut 32:18, where *God* is the rock who gave them birth). As objects of Canaanite worship (see [Baal and Canaanite Religion]), the tree normally represented the female deity Asherah, and the upright stone (a phallic symbol) the male deity Baal. By having the people reverse their significance, God may mock their ignorance of their new gods. In any case, this is shameful, even silly activity, but so deadly serious.

In so turning to other gods, the people have turned their backs to God rather than their faces (v. 27). In their syncretism they may think they can have both worlds. And so, when they get into trouble and want God's help, they turn their faces back to Yahweh and plead for salvation (see Ps 3:8). "The pagan deities are nothing but fair-weather gods."[3] God ironically responds (v. 28) by asking why they do not turn to these ("your"!; cf. the "your" in vv. 17, 19) gods in such a time (cf. the similar irony in Deut 32:37-38; the use of this language in lament, Pss 42:3, 10; 79:10; Joel 2:17). Even the people apparently realize that these gods—as numerous as their towns (as in 11:13)—have no power to save (see 10:1-16). The powerlessness of these gods would have been sharply evident to exilic readers (see 2 Kgs 18:34), especially those who had continued in their syncretistic ways.

Sexual Imagery

Sexual imagery was often visible in religious sanctuaries in antiquity as a sign of the fertility associated with certain deities. These choregic monuments from the Sanctuary of Dionysos on the island of Delos reflected the connection often made between Dionysos and fertility.

In vv. 29-32, filled with lament language, God responds in a general way to the people's complaints that their God has neglected them. Complaints per se are not declared illegitimate (laments are filled with them). But they are out of order when the complaining is done by those who have been rebellious and unfaithful (v. 29), who say they are free from any commitments and will worship Yahweh no more (v. 31). They have not responded positively to discipline (see 5:3; 7:28; 17:23; 32:33) and instead have killed the prophets sent to turn them back to God (v. 30; the historical reference is uncertain, cf. 26:20-23; Neh 9:26; Amos 2:12, Matt 23:29-31; Acts 7:51-53). As they have acted like lions toward the prophets, so lions will consume them (2:15; 4:7); their actions rebound on their own heads.

Charging the people (the present "generation" of readers!) to listen, God addresses further questions to them (vv. 31-32). Two of the questions are rhetorical. God has not been a wilderness or a dark land to Israel (though questions have been raised, 2:35, and some could interpret v. 30a in these terms!). Rather, God has graciously delivered Israel from these realities again and again (v. 6). Girls do not forget their jewelry or brides their wedding dresses, but the people have long forgotten God. But God's "why" questions (vv. 29, 31c) are neither rhetorical nor informational. They are existential questions. God is genuinely baffled that the rebels would complain against him and mystified that they would declare their freedom from God and pursue other lovers (see Isa 5:4). The parallel drawn in this extension of the marital metaphor is sharp— God and bridal jewelry/attire! The people would never forget these symbolic signs of the marriage, but they forget their spouse (see Deut 32:18). The lament of God is so poignantly stated here (see [The Divine Lament])

God returns to sharp, accusing words of infidelity. Israelites are so skilled at pursuing lovers that even prostitutes can learn from their ways (v. 33). These images of unfaithfulness are carried over into the theme of justice in v. 34. Israel's killing of the poor (who did not break the law of thievery in Exod 22:2-3) is described as having left their "lifeblood" (see 19:4; 22:17) on Israel's clothing. Israel's unfaithfulness to God includes both sexual promiscuity and murder, and both God and the poor are violated. Israelites violate the innocent and then claim innocence for themselves (v. 35). [Heschel on Justice as Personal]

Heschel on Justice as Personal

Justice is not important for its own sake; the validity of justice and the motivation for its exercise lie in the blessings it brings to man [*sic*!]. For justice is not an abstraction, a value. An act of injustice is condemned, not because the law is broken, but because a person has been hurt. What is the image of a person? A person is a being whose anguish may reach the heart of God.

Abraham Heschel, *The Prophets* (New York: Haper, 1962), 216.

The final verses of chapter 2 lift up two more quotations of the people. In spite of this litany of the people's infidelity, they persist in declaring themselves without sin, claiming that God has turned his anger away from them (v. 35). These quotations issue in the sharpest word of judgment in the chapter (vv. 35-37; anticipated in v. 26). God judges them precisely because they claim to be innocent, that they have no sins to confess. The particular consequence cited fits the nature of the sin of infidelity (especially in that culture). The effect will be a public shaming, a violation, by the Egyptians as had been done to the North by the Assyrians (vv. 15, 18, 36; see 13:20-27) (see **Connections: Use of Female/Sexual Imagery**). They have been caught in the act and they will be publicly shamed (like a thief), and this will happen to their political and religious leaders as well as to the people generally (v. 26; cf. 1:18). Israel will be put to shame by the very peoples with whom it had been "gadding about," casually seeking alliances and exchanging gods (v. 36a). This shaming will be publicly visible when the Israelites come away from battle with the Egyptians with their hands on their heads (a sign of defeat and surrender). This will be a sign that those peoples (Egypt) are not trustworthy and that no success will come through alliance with them (v. 37).

The Divorce, 3:1-5

In 3:1-5, the issue of divorce is explicitly brought to the discussion. These verses are a swing section, connecting 2:1-37 with 3:6–4:4. Continuing from chapter 2 is God's use of questions, the startling sexual imagery, and the divine response to what the people have been saying (see above at 2:20-37) (see **Connections: Use of Female/Sexual Imagery**). In addition, this section introduces the language of "return" (v. 1), though not yet repentance, which will be a leading theme of the next section (3:6–4:4). This section also continues the parental metaphor for the God-Israel relationship (v. 4; cf. 2:30); this metaphor is combined with the marital metaphor in 3:6–4:4 (e.g., 3:19). The metaphor "friend of my youth" (v. 4) is used for a husband in Proverbs 2:17, and invites reflection on the mutuality in this relationship; here it has reference back to the early years of marriage (as in 2:2).

The divorce law of Deuteronomy 24:1-4 is assumed in v. 1, and continues the marriage metaphor (see also Hos 2:7, which speaks of Israel returning to her husband). The law stated that a husband who had divorced his wife for cause could not remarry her if she had been remarried and then divorced or widowed. To do so would defile the land itself. Basic to 3:1-5 is this reality: Israel has left her husband, Yahweh, and "married" another (Baal). This move entails divorce from the first husband, namely, Yahweh. This divorce action has formally occurred with respect to the northern kingdom (3:8), and seems to be as good as done with respect to Judah (Isa 50:1 denies that a divorce has occurred).

God's questions raise the issues at stake in this situation (v. 1). The law is clear that the man cannot remarry ("return to") his former wife. The law is clear that such an action would pollute the land even further than it has been—"greatly" (3:2-3; 2:7). The law is clear that the (unfaithful) wife cannot decide to return to her first husband. And the situation is clear: Israel has habitually prostituted itself wantonly with many lovers, graphically evident at the Baal shrines on the hills (see [Baal and Canaanite Religion]). Its actions have been public, aggressive, and opportunistic, like those of a nomad hawking his wares by the side of the road. And, stubbornly (the forehead, v. 3; see Ezek 3:7; Isa 48:4), Israel has pursued this course, showing no shame whatsoever (see 2:26, 36; 6:15; 8:12). On the basis of the law, no renewal of the relationship between God and Israel is possible.

Another effect of infidelity is the pollution of the land for lack of rain (3:3; see Amos 4:5-9). Moral order has adversely affected cosmic order (see Deut 11:13-17). This point is ironic, for it was thought that consorting with Baal would assure rain and fertility; in fact, the opposite has occurred.[4] But even this experience did not drive Israel back to Yahweh, the one who gives the grain, the wine, and the oil (Hos 2:8) (see **Connections: Sin and Its Ecological Effects**).

Even the complaining prayers of the people recalling "the good old times" (cf. 2:2) are insufficient to overcome the (divorce) law and turn back the anger of God (vv. 4-5; see **Introduction**), given the obvious fact that they "have done all the evil they could" (v. 5). Prayers without repentance from such a people will not be heard. Are the people dependent for this hope on a conviction such as Psalm 103:9, where God is confessed as one who will not keep his anger forever? This language may have the exiles particularly in mind (see Lam 5:20-22). An exilic concern would be that persistent evil could mean an ongoing experience of divine anger, or perhaps the sense that they have had their chance with God and that has now passed.

Everything points to the impossibility of there being a remarriage (a restoration of relationship) in this case, *if* one is to obey the law. But, then, in a stunning move, God decides to ignore the "if" in the section that follows, with its repeated invitation to Israel to return (see 3:15-18) (see **Connections: Can God Break the Law?**).[5] God has determined that for the sake of the relationship with Israel, the divorce law must be broken. Relational issues supersede legal issues for God. If a renewed relationship with his people is possible, God will break the law! This divine move is anticipated already in 3:1, where God asks whether "he" (God!) will "return" to Israel! With the emphasis on *Israel's* "return" in what follows (14 times!), this initial question implies that *God's turning toward Israel* is necessary for Israel's turning (cf. the turning of Jeremiah and God in 15:19 and of Israel and God in 31:18-19). [Returning, Human and Divine] The remarkable reality for the exiles is that God is still prepared to break the law, and the call to repentance can still be heard for them in these verses. God is not done with these people, no matter how harsh the judgment.

Returning, Human and Divine

A key point is made here: God will return so that Israel is able to return. Without this divine move, Israel's repentance would not be possible. God has given Israel the space and the power to repent, but the people reject that possibility. Repentance is never simply a matter of human initiative.

CONNECTIONS

A Dialogical Relationship

One characteristic of Jeremiah, more generally, is its fundamentally dialogical character, especially between God and the prophet (for the people, see 3:22b-25; 14:7-9, 19-22). The word from God in this segment, however, seems to be simply laid on the people, with no possibility for a defense. Perhaps so; if there were once such a time, it is no longer available. Yet a dialogical relationship seems to be evident, albeit one step removed. Various responses from the people to *earlier* forms of the God-Israel dialogue are incorporated by God into the discourse (2:20, 23, 25, 27, 31, 35; 3:4-5; indirectly in 2:29); the peoples' own language is often interpreted by God to be self-incriminating, but it is their language. Israel's responses prove to be confusing (cf. vv. 23a, 35 with v. 25b), illusory, self-serving, and self-condemning, but God's language is interactive. In addition, an extensive reply from the people is recorded in 3:21-25. Moreover, what the people did *not* say, but should have, is noted in 2:6, 8.

This character of the material is important to observe in view of exilic readers and their perception of the nature of the relationship with God. To this end, an invitational language appears at numerous points (2:5, 10-11a, 14, 17-19, 21, 23-25, 28-32; 3:1-2, 4-5); whatever its function for original hearers, this language now calls for responses from *readers*. This type of language is continuous with the calls to repentance in 3:12–4:4. Generally speaking, this dialogical interaction is revealing of the kind of relationship God and Israel have. What people have to say counts with God; God takes their response—both positive and negative—into account in shaping the next stages of word and deed. The genuineness of this dialogue demonstrates that Israel has to do with a God who is not capricious and unresponsive, but at the same time will hold the people accountable for the character of their participation in the relationship. It will become evident that the people (especially Jeremiah) can hold God accountable as well.

Can God Break the Law?

In terms of the law in Deuteronomy 24:1-4, Israel has no right to return to the marriage with Yahweh. In other words, the law provides no way into a future for Israel with Yahweh. The law, strictly interpreted, means permanent divorce from Yahweh. The only way for the relationship between Yahweh and Israel to be continued would be on the basis of promise and grace.

On the other hand, according to the law, God—though not remarried—cannot return to the remarried, but divorced, wife. According to the law, there is no need for God even to think about such a possibility; God would be just and fair with Israel by simply obeying the law. But God, because of who God is and the kind of relationship God has established with Israel, cannot simply leave it at that point. God cannot simply say, "I must obey the law," and walk away from the people of Israel. Israel can bring nothing to the table to force the hand of God. But, wonder of wonders, God allows Israel a place at the table! God, because of love for Israel, is filled with pathos over what has happened and cannot let Israel go. God is not simply open to restoration; God makes moves that make restoration possible, even through and beyond judgment. This is shown both in the calls to repentance (3:12-14, 22) and in the promises of 3:15-18. [A Legal Perspective?]

A Legal Perspective?

This analysis shows that this section of Jeremiah must not be understood in narrowly legal terms, for God explicitly sets aside the law in this case. God is not bound to Torah in any static sense; for God, the personal and relational factors at stake override the strict application of the law. To use lawsuit or other legal language for the basic understanding of this text is to treat the matter in much too formal and legalistic a way. At the same time, enough of those categories are used to show that God's response to Israel is just and fair. God's "mercy is greater than His justice."

Abraham Heschel, *The Prophets* (New York: Harper, 1962), 298.

Israel's Sin and Its Ecological Effects

Israel's infidelity has had adverse effects on the very land itself (see **Introduction**). The reader is invited to think in environmental terms—moral order affects cosmic order (v.7b; see 2:12; 3:1-3; 4:23-28; 9:10; 12:4; 14:1-6; Deut 24:4). God has been faithful and Israel has not, with negative consequences for the entire creation. Israel has given up a garden for a wilderness of its own making. When the story of God's graciousness no longer shapes Israel's story, its life becomes a wilderness one more time. And the defiled land vomits them out into an exilic wilderness (a common theme, e.g., Lev 18:24-30).

It is confessed that God is the one who brings rain, but it should be recalled that it was drought and the absence of material blessing that drove at least some people to the worship of Baal (see 44:15-19). So the issue is not as clear-cut as the texts might suggest; the worship of Yahweh would not inevitably mean the absence of drought and consequent prosperity. It is important to note that the damage to the environment in v. 3 occurs without any reference to divine action; the consequences are intrinsic to the deed (as also at 1:16; 2:17, 19; and especially ch. 12; Hos 4:1-3).

The Use of Female/Sexual Imagery

In the context of the divine lament, these sexual images are more than an effort to gain attention. The marital metaphor with which the chapter began continues throughout this section; the images all focus on infidelity. Jeremiah is dependent on an already existing tradition, perhaps especially Hosea (e.g., 1–3; 4:10-15; cf. Isa 62:3-5; Ezek 16; 23; Eph 5:25-33; Rev 2:4-5; 21:2), who picks up on the sexual imagery of Canaanite religion and "baptizes" it for use to speak of the God-Israel relationship. Because of the linkage to actual sexual practices in Baal religion, the metaphor functions in both spiritual and physical terms.

Yet Jeremiah explores the images in an even more intensive way. In terms of the human analogue, these images are true to life, reflecting the actual experience of spousal betrayal (see also at 13:20-27).[6] The image used for Yahweh and Israel is that of a husband who has been betrayed by his wife and all the anger and frustration that would follow from that. In that culture, the subjection of the wife to the husband would also have intensified the response of the husband, who would be shamed in the larger culture because of what his wife had done. Readers are invited to think of feelings they might have—anger, distress, frustration, hurt—if their spouse proved unfaithful. Such language is believed able to reflect the deep feelings of God at Israel's infidelity. The divine anger, disappointment, and pain are made publicly available by the prophet's insights into the interior life of God. Such insights into how God feels about the infidelity are concerned not to generate a "feeling sorry" for God, but to elicit repentance. [Shame]

Shame

AΩ Jeremiah's use of shame language (usually *bôš*) is also linked to these images. Shame language is more common in Jeremiah than in any other biblical book (e.g., 2:26, 36; 3:3, 24-25; 6:15; 7:19; 8:12; 9:19; 10:14). Shame is a deeper reality than embarrassment; it has to do with being more than doing—what persons *are* more than what they do. The common approach to these texts tends to focus on issues of guilt (because of what people have done), but the shame language points to adverse effects at greater depths in the human person (e.g., 2:25). In resolving this issue for Israel, God must go beyond forgiveness, as important as that is (e.g., 31:34). What is needed is a more comprehensive "healing," which touches the whole person and restores human dignity and integrity (see 3:22; 6:14=8:11; 30:17; 33:6).

NOTES

[1] See the analysis of William Holladay, *Jeremiah 1* (Hermeneia; Philadelphia: Fortress, 1986), 73-77; for a contrary view, see Robert Carroll, *Jeremiah: A Commentary* (Philadelphia: Westminster, 1986), 117, 123.

[2] Peter C. Craigie, Page Kelley, and Joel F. Drinkard Jr., *Jeremiah 1–25* (WBC 26; Dallas: Word, 1991), 45.

[3] Holladay, *Jeremiah 1,* 105.

[4] Robert Carroll, *Jeremiah* (Philadelphia: Westminster, 1986), 143.

[5] Walter Brueggemann, *A Commentary on Jeremiah: Exile and Homecoming* (Grand Rapids: Eerdmans, 1998), 43.

[6] See especially Renita Weems, *Battered Love: Marriage, Sex, and Violence in the Hebrew Prophets* (Minneapolis: Fortress, 1994).

REPENTANCE AND RETURN

3:6–4:4

This section (with the swing segment, 3:1-5) is a unit centered on the theme of repentance. The verb "return, repent" (*šûb*) is repeatedly used. God calls for both Israel and Judah to repent (3:11-14, 22; 4:1-4), and their apostasy is recalled by both God (vv. 6-11, 13, 20-21) and people (vv. 23-25). Interwoven with these materials are a word of promise (vv. 15-18), a divine soliloquy (vv. 19-21), and a repentance ritual (vv. 21b-25). [Theme and Variations]

An original northern setting is often suggested (see at 2:1–4:4), but the present text has been shaped to speak to exiles. The theme of returning to Zion (v. 14) assumes the fall of Jerusalem. The prose sections (3:6-11, 15-18, 24-25) are often thought to be a later reshaping of the text for new readers. The call for repentance is a call to exilic readers; the repentance ritual in 3:21-25, whatever its original role, now functions as a model for their repentance, and the promises of vv. 14-18 are provided as motivations to that end.

This section develops several themes from 2:1–3:5. The graphic sexual images continue, now with reference to Israel, the northern kingdom (3:6, 8-9, 13), as do the marital (3:20) and parental imagery (3:14, 19, 22). The use of quotations is ongoing (3:22b-25; cf. 3:16; 4:2), but the confession of sin is new (cf. 3:22b-25 with 2:23, 35). This confession is often considered insincere; I consider it a genuine development if linked to potential usage by exiles.

Theme and Variations

Daniel Berrigan employs a metaphor that may capture some of the "disjointedness" of chapters such as these:

Accustomed as we are to a linear "before and after," we are somewhat set off kilter with the disinterest of the prophet in precise narration, event following event. . . . He will refer, almost in passing, to massively important events: invasions, defeats, exile, and return. But the record kept, if such a term is useful, is a matter of heart rather than mind, of resonance and inference rather than logic. His method might be called musical in the classical sense. A theme is announced, and left largely unexplored. A second and perhaps a third theme follow. Then the variations take over; each theme in turn is played upon again and again, with nuances: detailed, playful, serious, meandering, inviting, awakening. So in the prophets too, much is left to ourselves, unsaid, inferred through metaphor and simile, prose and poetry. A headlong imprecation, followed by a pause, tender, childlike. There are great outpourings of emotion, variations of anger, sin and consequence, mercy and repentance.

Daniel Berrigan, *Jeremiah: The World, the Wound of God* (Minneapolis: Fortress, 1999), 18-19.

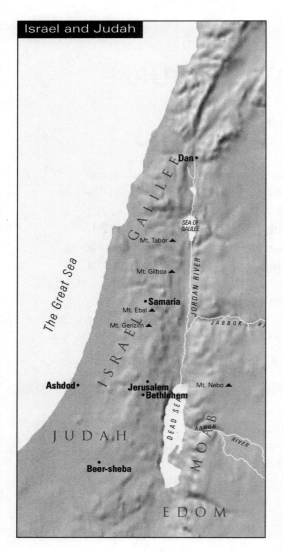

Israel and Judah

The divine soliloquies (3:7, 19-20), comparatively rare in the Old Testament, are also new. The imagery of sisterhood for the relation between Israel and Judah is unusual (3:8-10).

COMMENTARY

Israel and Judah Compared, 3:6-11

This prose section is commonly considered a later commentary on chapters 2–3, though its ascription to the time of Josiah (3:6, unique in Jeremiah) may be related to his attempts to unite North and South (see 2 Kgs 23), clearly a long-range agenda item for Jeremiah (e.g., 3:18). The reference to Israel, the northern kingdom, continues through at least v. 11 and possibly v. 13. This section is a private divine communication to Jeremiah and includes a report of a divine soliloquy (v. 7; as also 3:19-20). In the present form of the book, this section is a word of God to its readers; it enables them to see something of the content of the communication between God and the prophet, in this case a glimpse into the internal divine agony regarding the unfaithfulness of the people.

This segment compares Israel and Judah regarding issues of fidelity (cf. Ezek 16; 23), rehearsed in language similar to 2:1–3:5. Israel's failure to repent resulted in God giving her a bill of divorce, that is, destruction and exile (721 BC). But the pathos of God (v. 7) in relation to Israel continues, for the call to repentance (vv. 12-13) implies that the divorce, while real, is not final. The assumption is that northerners had not been annihilated; they continued to live in the North, in exile, and as refugees in the South. Interestingly, that God thought Israel would return suggests the lack of absolute foreknowledge on God's part (3:7; see 3:19-20).

This summary of northern experience is then compared to that of the South (Judah). Though Judah saw what had happened to Israel, Judah did not learn from this experience and continued in its unfaithful ways (cf. vv. 8-10 with 2:1–3:5). Judah did engage in rituals of repentance, but they were not wholehearted (3:10). Judah cannot even repent properly! Judah is adjudged to be more guilty than Israel (v. 11; also in 23:13-14; 7:12-15 is more even-handed). This must have been startling, even subversive language for the typical Judean (at any time). After all, the North had fallen long ago and rightfully so, given the weight of its idolatries (see 2 Kgs 17). That the passage implies acquittal for the North is doubtful in view of the call for repentance that follows.[1] [Degrees of Infidelity?]

Degrees of Infidelity?

This contrast between Judah and Israel is not a matter of a heavenly moral measuring rod, calculating degrees of infidelity. The comparison is a rhetorically stark way of saying that Judah is not more righteous than Israel. Judeans may have made this claim in a dispute among the exiles regarding who was most to be blamed for what had happened.

The Call to Repentance, 3:12-14

Is the call to repentance real after the seeming absoluteness of the divorce announced in the prior text? The texts on repentance follow a report from the time of Josiah (3:6), but in their present context they are not simply reports on past failures. The language of promise inserted in the middle of the calls to repentance (3:14-18) assumes the fall of both Israel and Judah. And so the call to repentance, whatever its force as an earlier message of Jeremiah (that did not issue in repentance), is now represented as a word to exiles, for whom repentance is possible.

Verse 12 reports a divine command to Jeremiah to proclaim a call to repentance toward the North. This could have reference to northerners scattered in the wake of the fall of Samaria a century earlier (wherever they are). More likely, at least in the present text, the word "North" refers to Babylon (see 3:18; 4:6) and to exiles from both Judah and Israel. If so, the address to "Israel" in v. 12 refers to all the people of God (as is usual in Jeremiah). God, having learned from the experience with Israel in view of Judah's greater guilt, reaches out anew to all exiles. God invites them to repent, return home, and be incorporated into God's new Jerusalem (see Hos 3:5; 14:1-7; the verb *šûb* carries a double meaning of repent and return home).

The promise regarding a population increase and settlement "in the land" in 3:16 assumes a postfall, pre-return situation (see 30:18-22). The "in those days" (twice) and "at that time" phrases (3:16-18) assume that the return to Zion has not yet occurred. Some scholars think that Judah is called to repent only in 4:3-4. But others correctly think that Judah (at least) is called to repentance in v. 14 (and v. 22), for vv. 15-18 include Jerusalem and

Judah in their promissory word. The shift to "return" in masculine plural in v. 14 (it is feminine singular in v. 12) and the use of "children" (cf. 3:19, 21-22; 2:30) are often noted, but their import is uncertain. It seems best to think of vv. 12-14 as catching up *all* the people of God.

Amid a repeated call to repentance, vv. 12-14 are punctuated by the phrase "says the LORD." This repetition suggests that the readers can be assured that: (a) God is merciful (v. 12), or better, faithful (*ḥāsîd*, and that this applies to them in their dire straits; (b) God's anger will not last forever (v. 12); this is a specific response to the people's question in 3:5 (cf. 2:35) and would be a lively concern of the exiles (see Lam 5:20-22); (c) repentance is still possible, even given God's knowledge of the depths of their sinfulness (v. 13); (d) the promise of return (v. 14) does indeed come from the LORD.

Repentance is possible for Israel only because God is merciful and is open to a new future with this spouse, moving against the grain of what the Law stipulates (see at 3:1). God could have adhered strictly to the Law and walked away, never to return. God calls Israel to acknowledge that they have been unfaithful to God (the imagery of infidelity from 2:1–3:5 is summarized in v. 13) and have not *listened* to God's voice (through the prophets; see 7:21-26; 2 Kgs 17:13-14). [Listen or Obey?]

Listen or Obey?

AΩ The translation "obey" rather than "listen" for *šᵉmaʿtem* in v. 13 (NRSV, which translates this verb both ways in 22:21) does not connect as well with preaching that consists of more than law. Active listening entails potential dimensions of the people's response that obeying does not.

The second call to repentance and return (v. 14; both senses of the verb *šûb* are present) uses striking language, lost in the common translation "I am your master." The verb is *baʿal*, which can mean "rule over" or "be a husband to someone" (see Deut 21:13; the noun means "husband," "ruler," or the god Baal). In view of the context, this word does not represent a shift to master/slave imagery, but heightens the pervasive marital imagery (so also 31:32; similarly Hos 2:16-20; cf. the mixing of parental/marital metaphors in 3:19-20). Yahweh, not Baal, will be Israel's husband again (despite the Law)! This reconciling divine move is the "return" of God that is questioned in 3:1; God breaks the Law in order to have Israel as spouse again (see at 3:1-5 and **Connections** there).

God holds out the promise of a return to Zion (v. 14; see 16:14-15=23:7-8; 31:6, 12; 50:4-5). As noted, the return to Zion assumes that the fall of Jerusalem has already occurred; this would catch up exiles from both North and South. The reference to "one from a city and two from a family (tribe)" is not entirely clear, but probably does not refer to an individualized repentance.[2] Rather,

Israel's Shepherds

Shepherds were a common image for the rulers of Israel (see 10:21) and other nations (see 12:10; King Cyrus of Persia is called a shepherd in Isa 44:28). They had become known for their lack of wisdom and fidelity in the care of their flock (see 10:21; 50:6-7). Jeremiah returns to this contrast between unfaithful and faithful shepherds in 23:1-4. Again, he distinguishes between those who have not attended the sheep and scattered them and those who will gather the people of God from among the nations and rule as God would rule. God calls himself the shepherd, in effect the "shepherd of shepherds," in 23:3-4 and 31:10 (see Ezek 34). This promise is to be linked to the Davidic ruler, as the juxtaposition of 23:4 and 23:5 shows (see 2 Sam 5:2; Ezek 34:23), and the eternalness of the Davidic covenant (33:14-26).

Credit: Mitchell G. Reddish

this language refers to the devastating effects of judgment and exile; typically, only a few from various social entities will survive to return (which proves to be the case).

A Promised Future Back Home, 3:15-18

Verse 15 flows directly from v. 14b; the "you" refers back to "children," and exilic readers would understand themselves to be addressed. Verses 15-18 spell out what the return to Zion (Jerusalem) in v. 14 will entail "in those days" for both Israel and Judah (v. 18) (see **Connections: Promise and Repentance**). God will give Israel shepherds that are pleasing to him (=after my own heart; note the divine heart, see 32:41), unlike the shepherds of 2:8. Links to the Davidic tradition are clear (see Ezek 34). These leaders will instruct (=feed) the people in ways that lead them to a new understanding of their relationship with God and others (see 23:1-4; Isa 11:1-3). [Israel's Shepherds] They shall multiply and increase in the land, as they once did in the land of Egypt (Exod 1:7) in fulfillment of the divine command in creation and promises to the ancestors (Gen 1:28; 17:1-8).

In addition, the ark of the covenant, probably destroyed by the Babylonians, is not to be rebuilt or even remembered (see 17:12). [The Ark of the Covenant] As for the reasons, two directions of thought may be present. For one, the ark as container of the Law (see Deut 10:1-5) will not be needed, because the Law will no longer be an external reality, but will be written on the heart (anticipating

The Ark of the Covenant

The ark was a portable sanctuary from Israel's wilderness days (see Exod 25:10-15). The ark was the place of God's special presence among the people, guiding them through the wilderness. It also served to house the two tablets of the Law (Deut 10:8) and hence had a specific link to the Sinai covenant. David recaptured the ark from the Philistines, brought it to Jerusalem, and built a house for it (2 Sam 4–6). This was a means that David used to unify the northern and southern tribes. King Solomon brought it into the Holy of Holies of the temple, where it symbolized not only the place of God, but the throne of God in the midst of his people (1 Kgs 8:1-13). The ark was probably destroyed by the Babylonians when they razed the temple, but no specific mention is made of its destruction.

31:31-34). Two, the ark as the throne of divine presence (Exod 25:10-22) will not be needed, because God's throne would now be a personal presence in Jerusalem (3:17; see Ezek 48:35), accessible to the entire community of the faithful, not just in the Holy of Holies with its limited access. The ark will not even be missed, so real will the presence of God be in the city! Jeremiah never clarifies whether this means no new temple as well (see 30:21; Ezek 40–48). It seems unlikely that this is a reference to God's general presence in a community of people apart from a specific place (note that Jerusalem is not spiritualized, 31:38-40). This command may also be linked to the unification of North and South in 3:18; the ark would no longer be an issue of contention.

Several other features of this image of the new Zion are evident. All the nations shall gather to Jerusalem (see 16:19-21; Isa 2:1-5; Mic 4:1-5; Ps 22:27), and they (the nations!) will no longer have stubborn and evil wills (used elsewhere to describe Israel, e.g., 7:24); this is a remarkably global perspective (12:14-17 assumes a less profound change; the nations could resist). And the nations will no longer trouble Israel! This perspective will be reinforced by the interest in what Israel means for the nations in 4:2. Finally, a division between North and South (Israel and Judah) will no longer exist; they shall return from the land of exile and live together peacefully in the land of promise.

Verse 18 makes clear that this promise is made with the exile in mind, as "together" Judah and Israel return from the north (see 3:12; cf. Ezek 37:15-23 for a comparable hope). So exiled readers would understand this promise as related to their future. Is this promise conditioned upon their repentance (v. 14)? Or is this a sure promise that serves to motivate their repentance (see **Connections: Promise and Repentance**)?

A Divine Lament, 3:19-22a

Verses 19-22 are a divine soliloquy in the form of a lament. They are parallel in part to v. 7, addressed to the North; the texts both speak of God as having thought that Israel would do something that it did not do. What role do these verses have in this context? Though they may originally have followed 3:5 (links with God as Father and the use of feminine singular "you") or 3:14, they now follow up on the promise. This placement could suggest that the call to repentance in v. 14 has been refused, and this is God's response. The time for the fulfillment of the promise has not yet arrived.

More likely, the divine lament is parallel to the promise; it is another dimension of the call to move the people to repentance, and it is revealing of the kind of God who makes the promise. This divine pathos is rooted in love and faithfulness. Because God yearns for the future just promised (vv. 14b-18), God laments that it could not have come to be before, but now it is possible only "in those days" beyond disaster and exile. The God who once gave Israel "a pleasant land" thought the relationship would work, but it has not; at the same time, the prior verses indicate that this gift of "land" is promised for the future (v. 18). These verses present to the people a look into the divine heart so that they might see the extent to which their rejection has had an effect upon God. In these verses, the tension "tears at the heart of God, who yearns, but who will not be mocked, trivialized, or used."[3]

The lament focuses on the memory of God and the suffering occasioned by the divine encounter with a recalcitrant people. God had thought that Israel, given the status of "children" and placed as heirs in a beautiful land (now polluted, see vv. 1-3; 12:10), would call God its Father *and* would not rebel (*šûb*) against that parenting (v. 19) (see **Connections: Divine Foreknowledge and the Will of God**). Note that Israel is placed "among" God's children (are the nations in view here again?). They had called God their Father (3:4), but in the context of rebellion. But, switching back to the marital metaphor (v. 20), Israel has betrayed its relationship to God like an unfaithful wife to her husband. [God's Broken Heart]

Might such a glimpse into the heart of God move Israel to repentance? Verses 22b-25 suggest that this indeed was (at least

> **God's Broken Heart**
>
> 📖 What intimacy God desired in his relationship with the people, and what disappointment is expressed here! The dreams of God have become broken dreams. The depths of this disappointment are expressed in the use of both parental and marital metaphors. While literary purists might deplore the mixing of these metaphors, the effect is to intensify the pathos. God has been rejected both as parent and as husband! God is like a person who has been rejected not only by a spouse, but by his children as well. God suffers the effects of a broken relationship at multiple levels of intimacy. (See Terence Fretheim, *The Suffering of God: An Old Testament Perspective* [Philadelphia: Fortress, 1984], 116.

potentially) Israel's response to God's call for repentance in v. 22a. But whose "voice" and "weeping" are heard in v. 21? It could be Israel's (so NIV), sorrowful that they have forgotten God and perverted their life's journey. Or, more likely, the "voice" is God's, whose weeping (following from vv. 19-20) is reported by Jeremiah, who in turn quotes God's call to repentance in the first person in v. 22a (see NRSV colon at v. 21). If the latter, God would be weeping *for* Israel's children (rather than NRSV "of," it may be an objective genitive, as with Rachel's weeping, 31:15) because they have forgotten him.[4]

By its very nature, this call from God would give the exiles hope for the future, for it reveals a God who desires to heal them of their infidelities (literally, their turnings). Note that God speaks of healing rather than forgiveness; healing is a more comprehensive and holistic divine action—including forgiveness—that affects the entire person and more fully speaks to issues of shame (see [Shame]; Hos 6:1-3; 14:4).

A Ritual of Repentance, 3:22b-25

A ritual of repentance follows (vv. 22b-25), the prose elements of which are commonly considered to be a late addition (v. 24 again assumes the fall of Jerusalem). Whatever their origin, these verses must finally be interpreted in terms of exilic readers. But several questions arise. Do the people speak these words (as in 14:7-9, 19-22), or is this a "wish list" for God? A parallel with Hosea 14:1-3 is commonly drawn, where God speaks the words that God hopes to hear from the people. Yet, unlike Hosea 14:1-3, no language in this text specifies that these are God's words. It is best to take them as Israel's words. But, then, is this genuine repentance or pretense (as in 3:10)? These words and actions may have been insincere if prayed by pre-destruction Israel, but the text now seems to reflect a genuine repentance on the part of the exilic community or at least gives the repentant ones words to speak.

In this ritualized scenario, the people "come" to God at a sanctuary, professing and confessing that: (1) "you are the LORD our God" (as in 31:18-19), who alone can bring "salvation" to Israel; (2) their orgiastic religious practices on the hills/mountains (where many Baal shrines were located; see [Baal and Canaanite Religion]) were a delusion; (3) the effects of the shameful thing (a reference to Baal) that—ironically, given Baal's supposed skills—devoured everything, including children and animals, for which their ancestors worked (on "devour," see 5:17; 50:17). Note the repeated "from our youth"; that is, from the beginning of Israel's life the infidelity has been constant. All the wasted years! The people confess their sin of not listening to the voice of God (through the prophets)—denied in 2:35—and undergo a public shaming (see 2:26, 36). The striking image of lying in a bed of shame, covered with the blankets of dishonor, is drawn from the images of infidelity (on shame, see [Shame]).

Another View on Repentance, 4:1-4

What then of God's response in 4:1-2? Is God informing them that they have not yet gotten the repentance right? Are these "conditions for return"?[5] Is this a list of additional things they have to do if they are going to be saved from judgment?

Though 4:1-2 is sometimes considered a call to repentance, the list of conditions (vv. 1-2a, as NRSV)[6] functions in quite different terms. It spells out not only what repentance itself entails and some of the actions that repentant people do, but also their practical effects on *others*. The "then" of v. 2b refers to the positive effects that will take place "if" Israel: (a) returns "to me"; (b) sets aside its abominations (=idolatrous practices) from the presence of God (at the sanctuary); (c) does not waver in its recommitment to Yahweh (or its resolve to put away syncretistic practices); (d) and swears its oaths in the name of Yahweh (rather than other gods?), truthfully and justly (in contrast to false swearing, 5:2). In other words, vv. 1-2a drive toward the point made in v. 2b: if Israel does these things, then the *nations* (!) will benefit by their association with Israel (see at 3:17, where all nations come to Zion). [Blessing for the Nations]

The last segment (4:3-4) is another "swing" section (see 3:1-5). It summarizes the point of the previous section regarding repentance (the addressee is essentially the same as at 2:1-2). It also introduces the theme of judgment to follow.

Blessing for the Nations

Especially striking in 4:1-2 is that no benefits are said to accrue to Israel! Lifted up for attention is the thought that Israel is God's instrument in and through which blessing will come to the nations—a reference to well-being in every sphere of life. Even more, all these peoples who are blessed will glorify God (see Ps 47:9). Carroll puts it well: "Israel's turning means the transformation of the nations." The inclusive perspective of God's purposes for all peoples is in place here (see 3:17; 12:14-17; 16:19-21) and reinforces the strong place that the nations and the creation more generally have in Jeremiah (see **Introduction**). Once again, the meaning of Jeremiah's calling to be a prophet to the nations is evident (1:5, 10). The language used in v. 2b is drawn fundamentally from the *Abrahamic* covenant (see Gen 12:3; 22:18; 26:4; Ps 72:17). This text is one of several links in Jeremiah to Genesis materials having to do with creation, blessing, and the promises to the ancestors (see chs. 32–33).

Robert Carroll, *Jeremiah* (Philadelphia: Westminster, 1986), 156.

Two images are used to speak of the call to repentance. The first stresses more outward realities; the second uses an image that cuts into a person and removes those impediments to being a member of the people of God. The people are first to break up their unplowed soil (see Hos 10:12) to rid it of thorns and briars (Isa 5:6). By so doing, they will not sow their seed among thorns on unprepared and hard ground (see Matt 13:7; Mark 4:1-9) and will be better able to get a good crop.

Second, the people are to circumcise (=remove the foreskin of) their hearts—the person as a thinking, deciding individual—to the LORD, a metaphor for repentance (see 9:26). The image of circumcision is important for what it says about the nature of repentance; it is not an easy word spoken, a New Year's resolve, giving up something for Lent. It is a cutting that makes for blood and pain, and the effect of such suffering is the reintegration into the community of faith, a new beginning. [Circumcision as God's Work]

The summons to repentance concludes with a warning (repeated in 21:12). If the people do not repent, they will suffer the evil effects of their actions. Note that God's unquenchable wrath is spoken of in impersonal terms; it will "go forth like fire" (see 7:20; 17:27; 23:19; 30:23; Amos 5:6; Num 1:53; 16:46). From the perspective of the exilic readers of Jeremiah, judgment was an already experienced reality. So, for them, this warning has to do not simply

Circumcision as God's Work

Interestingly, v. 4a could also be translated "be circumcised by the LORD." The verse would then retain the ambiguity of subject we have seen with the verb "return" (see 3:1) and maintain the tension evident in the changing human and divine subjects of circumcision in Deut 10:16; 30:6. Repentance on the part of the people is not possible without God's "return" to be at work on their hearts. At the same time, God's work is resistible; one could refuse to repent, or repent "lightly" (see 6:14). To depict Israel as an uncircumcised male in spiritual terms claims that Israel no longer belongs to the covenant community simply on the basis of an external cutting. Only repentance of sin can complete the act of circumcision that enables one to continue to be a member of the community of faith. Unrepentant people remove themselves from the sphere of promise, a move that God will honor, but only after major efforts are made to heal the breach.

Heschel on the Wrath of God

One of the most helpful treatments of God's wrath is located in Abraham Heschel's *The Prophets*. This quote is from a section titled "The Evil of Indifference":

The prophet's angry words cry. The wrath of God is a lamentation. All prophecy is one great exclamation; God is not indifferent to evil! He is always concerned, He is personally affected by what man does to man [*sic*]. He is a God of pathos. This is one of the meanings of the anger of God: the end of indifference! The message of wrath is frightful, indeed. But for those who have been driven to the brink of despair by the sight of what malice and ruthlessness can do, comfort will be found in the thought that evil is not the end, that evil is never the climax of history. . . . Man's [*sic*] sense of injustice is a poor analogy to God's sense of injustice. The exploitation of the poor is to us a misdemeanor; to God, it is a disaster. Our reaction is disapproval; God's reaction is something no language can convey. Is it a sign of cruelty that God's anger is aroused when the rights of the poor are violated, when widows and orphans are oppressed?

Abraham Heschel, *The Prophets* (San Francisco: Harper & Row, 1962), 284-85.

with a past experience, but also with a future that would continue that judgment. [Heschel on the Wrath of God]

CONNECTIONS

Promise and Repentance

The placement of this promise in the final redaction of Jeremiah is important for thinking through how it functions for exiles. The promise links back to the building and planting in the call of Jeremiah (1:10) and anticipates later promises (e.g., 23:1-8; 30–32). This is a real promise, an incredibly creative possibility, an unbreakable commitment, sure as the faithfulness of God (see Jer 31:35-37). This is what it will be like "in those days"—no ifs, ands, or buts. The people can absolutely rely on this promise. And this can serve as motivation for repentance/return. The promise itself is not conditioned on anything that the people do, though they can reject the promise-keeper and not participate in the fulfillment that will certainly come to pass.

The placement of the promise at this point in Jeremiah may soften the message of gloom and doom that follows, but that is not the point. Nothing must take the edge off the deathly seriousness of Israel's failure (chs. 2–3) and experience of judgment (see chs. 4–10). Keeping the promise of salvation and the announcement of judgment firmly together is crucial for Jeremiah. This is not an "illogically" placed text. God's word of judgment is in the service of God's *saving* will and purpose. Life is possible for this people only by passing through death. God's keeping of this promise lies on the far side of a devastating but refining judgment, a judgment already experienced by the readers.

In the larger context of Jeremiah, repentance is not a condition for participation in the return to Zion (and not an historical one either, at least in thinking about individuals). In Jeremiah, God himself will see to the "condition"! God will put a new heart and a new spirit within them (24:6-7; 32:36-41), and they shall "all know me" (31:34). This new covenant will be of such a character that infidelity will no longer be possible (see 3:17). The promises will be fulfilled, come what may (see [Circumcision as God's Work]).

God's promises will not fail; they will never be made null and void as far as God is concerned. Though a rebellious generation might not live to see the fulfillment of the promises because they have rejected God, the promise can be relied upon. The promise is an everlasting one, unconditioned from God's perspective. The promise is always there for the believing to cling to, and they can be assured that God will always be at work to see that it will be fulfilled.

Divine Omniscience?

Texts such as these do not call divine omniscience into question, only an understanding of divine foreknowledge as absolute. God knows all there is to know (omniscience), but there are future human contingencies that are not yet available for knowing absolutely, even for God. The philosophical issue of whether absolute foreknowledge does or does not entail predestination (an issue that is undecidable, at least at present) does not come into play. The issue is not an abstract notion, but specific texts wherein specific divine words are spoken about the future. That God shares such words with the prophet, who proclaims them publicly, may be intended to counteract any notion on the part of exiles that God knew all along that, say, judgment would happen and didn't inform them about it, and hence the calls to repentance were unreal.

Divine Foreknowledge and the Will of God

God's soliloquies in 3:7 and 3:19 are unusual in that they suggest that God was actually uncertain as to how the people would respond in a given situation. God is depicted as thinking that the people would respond positively to their initial election or that they would return after a time of straying. But events proved that God's outlook on these futures was too optimistic. The people did not respond as God "thought" they would. What God "thought" would happen did not occur. This suggests that God's knowledge of future *human* action is limited to some degree. God's future is depicted as somewhat open-ended in relationship with human beings. God speaks of a past divine thought regarding Israel's future; one might say that, regarding such matters, God thinks in terms of possibilities or probabilities, not absolute certainty.

There are several other texts in Jeremiah that assume such a divine understanding of the future. These are the "either-or" texts (see at 22:1-5). Generally, it may be said that God knows what *God* will do in the future, but in these texts there are alternative futures presented, and God's future action is specifically said to be dependent on decisions that the people make. [Divine Omniscience?]

From another angle, one might think of these statements in 3:7 and 3:19-20 as revealing of God's will for Israel. But God's will does not get done. God wills a faithful relationship with the people, but they have resisted that will of God and become faithless. The will of God is resistible, and Israel has succeeded in doing just that. The only other interpretive option with this material would be to say that Israel's infidelity (or sin more generally) is the will of God. But, if so, then God's uncompromising *condemnation* of Israel's actions is out of order. It is best to understand that Israel's sin has been *against* the will of God; as a consequence, God's hopes for Israel have been dashed, and God's will for their positive future has been frustrated.

NOTES

[1] Contrary to William McKane, *A Critical and Exegetical Commentary on Jeremiah* (2 vols.; ICC; Edinburgh: T. & T. Clark, 1986), 66.

[2] Contrary to Ronald Clements, *Jeremiah* (IBC; Atlanta: John Knox, 1988), 36.

[3] Walter Brueggemann, *A Commentary on Jeremiah: Exile and Homecoming* (Grand Rapids: Eerdmans, 1998), 45.

[4] Cf. William Holladay, *Jeremiah 1* (Philadelphia: Fortress, 1986), 123.

[5] Brueggemann, *Jeremiah,* 48.

[6] For different possibilities, see Holladay, *Jeremiah 1,* 126-27. Modern translations vary, e.g., NAB.

DISASTER THREATENS ISRAEL

4:5-31

God Will Not Turn Back, 4:5–6:30

What questions did the exiles find most pressing in light of the fall of Jerusalem, the destruction of temple and kingship, and exile? The question in 5:19 sums it up: "Why has the LORD our God done all these things to us?" In other terms, what is the proper *interpretation* of what happened? It is assumed that God has been involved in what has happened (so also 14:19; 22:8; this assumption is not made in the questions of 9:12; 13:22). The issue is *why* God has done these things. The short answer is stated clearly: idolatry or spiritual infidelity.

To portray this reality, this section (as well as 2:5–4:4) is almost exclusively focused on the *religious* failures of the people. [The Nature of the Problem] To get at this, a series of vignettes is sketched that looks at this tragedy from various angles, using various metaphors, rather than presenting the material in a strictly linear fashion. It is hoped that readers would thereby gain some understanding with respect to the past and some guidance for shaping the future.

This section consists of a rhythm of indictments followed by announcements of judgment (regularly but not always introduced by "therefore"). Several prose sections have been inserted into the predominantly poetic material in almost hit-or-miss fashion (4:9-12, 27; 5:18-19); these commonly assume the fall of Jerusalem and are often considered to be commentary on Jeremiah's oracles, reinterpreted for

---

The Nature of the Problem

Given the reality of the "foe from the north," remarkably little is said in this segment (or in the first half of Jeremiah) regarding military policies or decisions. Moreover, the readers are not invited to engage in a political or social analysis of the situation. In fact, issues of social justice seldom come explicitly into view (see 2:34; 5:26-28). Explicit personal failures are no more common than instances of social injustice (e.g., adultery and lying, 5:7-8; 9:3-9). Given the common perception of the brunt of the prophetic message and the reality of an Amos or even an Isaiah, this is surprising. It would appear that Jeremiah (not unlike Hosea) understands the problem to be more systemic in nature, namely, religious infidelity, manifested especially in idolatry. Specific individual and social sins are understood to be symptomatic of this more fundamental issue. And so attention is centered on the heart of the problem. As Walter Brueggemann writes, "Caring ethics without a core covenantal commitment is not possible." Perhaps "not possible" is too strong, given the moral expectations God has for the "non-chosen" nations, but from within Israel's covenantal relationship the point is essentially correct.

Walter Brueggemann, *A Commentary on Jeremiah: Exile and Homecoming* (Grand Rapids: Eerdmans, 1998), 69.

a new time and place. This reinterpretation, however, is the only form of Jeremiah's message of which we can be certain. The interactive character of the relationship between God and Jeremiah is prominent in this section (see Jeremiah's personal response to God in 4:10, 19-21; 5:3-5; 6:10-11).

The marital imagery used in chapters 2–3 is almost entirely missing in this section (see 4:30). The pain and anguish of God is not as often in evidence behind a furrowed brow. The primary pathos evident here is anger. Yet, as we know from Jeremiah as a whole, the godward side of anger is grief (see **Introduction**), which is evident in several texts. For example, the remarkable statements of suffering in 4:19-21 (cf. 8:18–9:2; 9:10, 17-19) express the pain of God as much as the prophet. Moreover, still present in this section are those divine questions, rhetorical and otherwise, that give us a glimpse into the anguish of God's heart. How long (4:14, 21; cf. 4:30)? How can I pardon you (5:7)? Shall I not punish them for these things (5:9, 29; 9:9)? It is as if God were saying: I've looked for a rationale to stay the judgment, but I can find no good reason to do so.

In the midst of the unrelenting indictments and announcements of judgment, a word of hope is barely heard through the gloom. There is nothing like 3:15-18, yet noted here and there is a word that the judgment will not bring a "full end" to God's relationship

---

Metaphors in 4:5–6:30

AΩ Focusing on 4:5–6:30, metaphors drawn from the sphere of warfare are especially prominent (4:5-6, 13, 16, 19-21, 29; 5:15-17; 6:1, 4-7, 22-23, 25). But the range of metaphors is remarkable: wild animals—lion, leopard, wolf, swift eagle (4:7, 13; 5:6); hot wind (4:11-12); clouds and wind (4:13); watchers of a field (4:17); cosmic catastrophe (4:23-26); vineyard strippers (5:10; 6:9); fire (5:14); eaters (5:17); shepherds with flocks (6:3). The metaphors for the wicked people are also rich: lusty stallions (5:7-8); prostitute's clothing and cosmetics (4:30); birdcatchers (5:26-28). Metaphors of the anguish of the people suffering judgment are also present, e.g., a woman giving birth (4:31). The use of such lively metaphors has the rhetorical function of impressing the issue upon the minds of readers in a way that no more abstract or literal language can.

with Israel (4:27; 5:10, 18). These qualifications of total judgment may be later additions, but for the editors (and exilic readers!) this note is understood to be implicit in the *original* word of judgment. Israel does have a future that shines through all the doom and gloom, but only on the far side of a refining fire that will wreak horrific devastation.

The imaginative use of metaphors—especially for the coming judgment—invites reflection on these events from various angles. Over the course of these chapters, these metaphors describe a *relentlessness* in the advance of the enemy. The section begins with that advance (4:5-7), continues to be voiced throughout (4:16-17, 20, 29; 5:15-17; 6:1-8, 22-23; cf. 8:16-17; 9:21), and will come to a climax in the announcement of 10:22. [Metaphors in 4:5–6:30]

It is not accidental that images of warfare predominate in this section. God's agent of judgment is an enemy "from the north" (4:6), first introduced in Jeremiah's call (1:13-15). Though not explicitly identified as Babylon until 25:9 (see 20:4-6), exiled readers would make this identification from the beginning. For these readers, these materials have an embodied enemy in mind, with real weapons and incredible military power. This is not disembodied literature, always applicable to every situation.[1] These prophecies, addressed to both Israel and Judah, are commonly dated early in Jeremiah's career. But because this historical setting is nowhere set forth in an explicit way means that such *specifics* should not play a central role in interpretation. It is sufficient to know that the situation is generally associated with the fall of Jerusalem. The reality of Israel's situation is grim and grave. Exilic readers know the horrendous character of the actual experience and wonder about its continuing effects on their life and their relationship with God.

It has been suggested that these texts reflect a "chaos tradition."[2] While this text gives ample (and often neglected) testimony to the importance of creation in Jeremiah, how one speaks of chaos is important (see **Connections: The End of the World?**).

COMMENTARY

This section, addressed to Judah and Jerusalem (as in 2:2; 4:3), describes the situation that threatens Israel "from the north" (4:6) and spells out the disastrous effects that that invasion will have on every form of life. In fact, this invasion will be so devastating that an "end-of-the-world" scenario is sketched in 4:23-26.

This section begins by alerting "Zion" to the threat (4:6) and ends with "Zion" gasping for breath (4:31). Scholars disagree on which verses are in prose and which are in poetry (e.g., 4:9-12, 27 are prose in NRSV, poetry in NAB). It is common to understand 4:5-31 as a series of announcements of judgment with two interludes (4:9-12, 19-26). But the language of "announcement of judgment" is not fully adequate to describe this material. The judgment is in process, and its devastating impact on land and people is described in horrendous detail. The exiles are being told that God did warn the people of a coming disaster (an important matter for their ongoing assessment of the kind of God with whom they have to deal) and their actual experience is being described.

The interpretation of this section is made more difficult by the use of quotations from people and prophet(s) and the uncertain identity of the speakers. In v. 10, the Hebrew text ascribes the words to Jeremiah ("I said"; so NRSV); the Greek text ascribes it to the (false) prophets of v. 9 ("they will say"; so NAB). The Hebrew text is the more difficult reading and should be followed. The last phrase in v. 13 is spoken by either people or by the prophet on their behalf. The identification of the "I" ("my"; "me") in vv. 19-31 is uncertain (see below). God is clearly the "I" in 4:11-12, 17, 27-28; 5:1, 7, 9, 14-15, 18-19, 22, 26, 29, 31; 6:2, 8, 12, 15, 17, 19-21, 27. Jeremiah is the "I" in 4:10; 5:4; 6:10-11, 26.

A Foe from the North, 4:5-8

These verses are a warning from God *to* the people because of God's anger *at* the people (as in 6:1, 8; in 6:17 they ignore the alarm)! God seeks to provide some protection for them from God's own agents of judgment. It is as if, having pulled the trigger of anger, not even God can hold it back (see 4:28) and, given the kind of God this is, God reaches out in some concern for the people now that the judgment is actually in process. God is "bringing disaster (*rā'āh*) from the north" (v. 6), and *God* gives the people the words to interpret what is happening (v. 8). This enemy is called a "lion" (v. 7), language used in 2:15 and 5:6 (see 5:17; 50:17), and it is clear that God's anger is at work in and through these marauding armies and that people and land will be devastated.

[Is God the "Real Agent" Here?]

God tells Jeremiah to warn the people (the verbs are plural in vv. 5-6) about this threat by sounding the ancient equivalent of an air raid siren. They are to raise a standard to Zion (a signal to flee to Jerusalem), blow the trumpet, shout, and urge everyone to leave

Is God the "Real Agent" Here?

Walter Brueggemann makes several theological claims regarding issues of agency in this text that should be challenged. For example: "The army may be Babylonian, but the real agent is Yahweh." Such a statement discounts the genuine role that the Babylonian armies play; they are no less "real" than Yahweh. That they will later be judged by God for overreaching (25:12-14) shows that they are not puppets of God. Brueggemann's subsequent phrase, "the wounded warrior [God] has become invading army," is helpful so long as one does not diminish the distinction between God and God's agents or discount the stature and the very real power of that human army.

Brueggemann seems to guard against this understanding when he says: "The rule of Yahweh is not done 'supernaturally,' but through historical agents," though he goes on to speak as if only Yahweh were the "real" power in this situation. I cannot see any theological space between "supernatural" and God as the only "real agent." Consider also this idea voiced by Carroll: "It is not simply the invading army which carries out this destructive enterprise; it is Yahweh who destroys the community." This, too, could be misinterpreted. The texts do not suggest that God somehow acts on a parallel track or supplements the devastating work of the Babylonian armies with some other form of unmediated action. God is active in these events, but God acts in and through the Babylonians, and not in a micromanaging way.

Walter Brueggemann, *A Commentary on Jeremiah: Exile and Homecoming* (Grand Rapids, Eerdmans, 1998), 54, 56, 70.

Robert Carroll, *Jeremiah* (Philadelphia: Westminster, 1986), 163.

---

the countryside and small towns quickly. They are to flee to the relative safety of the fortified cities, especially Zion. The enemy is on its way! In addition, they are to engage in rituals of penitential lament. God invites the people not to plead to have God's anger turned back (as in Joel 1), for it is too late, but to recognize that very reality—and possibly to save some (in line with the less than a "full end").

Is God Deceptive?, 4:9-12

These verses assume that judgment is in process; it is just a matter of time before the enemy has overwhelmed them—"on that day" and "at that time" (vv. 9, 11) have already occurred from the perspective of readers. When the siege begins (v. 9), political and religious leaders will be immobilized by the onslaught and utterly fail the people, lacking any resources to be of help. The prophets would be astounded (v. 9), probably because they believed they had been uttering the word of God.

Verse 10 calls into question the legitimacy of the prior divine warnings and call for public lamentation (vv. 5-8), especially in view of the certainty of the judgment voiced in v. 9 (see vv. 11-12, 28). Why did God urge Israel to do these things (which could be interpreted as supporting the claims of the false prophets) if the judgment was inevitable? Jeremiah (the speaker, see above) is voicing a question raised by exiles (and perhaps those mentioned in v. 9). It is also a genuine question for Jeremiah. How would God respond to the question (see **Connections: Has God Been Deceptive?**)?

Verses 11-12 introduce a new metaphor with respect to God's judgment through the enemy from the north: a hot wind (cf. fire in 4:4; lion in 4:7). God's judgment may be *like* the oppressively hot, life-sapping desert wind called the sirocco, but it is much worse. The purpose of God's wind ("from me") will not be to cleanse or to winnow (clear the chaff away). The very strong wind will effect a thoroughgoing judgment; the grain will be swept away with the chaff. Verses 11-12 are words from God that will be spoken (by Jeremiah?) as Jerusalem is experiencing devastation; God is active in and through the armies for purposes of judgment (see [Is God the "Real Agent" Here?]). At the same time, and this is important, God still refers to Israel as "my people"; God does not understand that the relationship has ceased altogether (see also 4:22; 5:26, 31; 6:14, 26-27).

The Enemy Is Near, 4:13-18

God, through Jeremiah, invites the people to look (v. 13) and to listen (vv. 15-16) for the signs of approaching disaster (cf. chs. 2–3). Look at the storm clouds on the horizon; the enemy of the north with its swift horses and chariots is at Jerusalem's gates. They will experience the whirlwind (a storm) because they have sown the wind (see Hos 8:7). The people respond by lamenting "we are ruined"; they have no hope (NAB has the people speak all of v. 13). Such a response would fit the exiled readers' situation as a statement of their present plight.

But God (see v. 17, "says the LORD"; returning to a theme in 3:6–4:4) urges the people of Jerusalem (and the exiles) to cleanse themselves, that is, repent of the evil (*rā'āh*) "within you," that is, in their heart, so that they might be delivered (see Isa 1:16). Expressing God's lament, Jeremiah responds to the people's lament: how long will they continue to devise wickedness in their hearts (v. 14; see vv. 19-21)? The call for repentance does not assume that deliverance from the enemy is still possible, for v. 12 has claimed that the time of cleansing is past. Some other form of salvation that would see them through the disaster may be in mind, some amelioration of the devastation. For exilic readers such a deliverance would fit their situation precisely.

The prophet proceeds to cite reasons for the urgency. Israel is called to listen to the voices of the people in the northern part of the region (v. 15; v. 16 quotes what they are saying, see NAB). Dan is one of the northernmost cities in Israel and Mt. Ephraim is a reference to the mountains there; they would have gotten the word about the approaching enemy first. These northerners are giving Jerusalem advance notice that the destroyers "from a distant land" are on their way. They will lay siege to the cities of Judah and shout their war cries against Jerusalem. Indeed, the enemy has now encircled Jerusalem; there is no escape (v. 17). The enemies who have been watched for by Israel have now become the "watchers" of Israel (see 1:12).

The reason for this onslaught is clear: Israel has rebelled against the LORD. Israel cannot blame bad politics, poor economics, or lack of luck. Israel has brought this disaster upon itself by what is in its own heart (vv. 14, 18; in 2:19 the words "evil/disaster/doom [*rāʿāh*]" and "bitter" refer to Israel's apostasy). Note that God has only facilitated the effects of Israel's own evil deeds. This is *your* disaster! The disaster has penetrated to your very hearts—now filled with fear and foreboding—because your heart is where the evil (*rāʿāh*, v. 14) is lodged. The judgment penetrates as deeply as their wickedness. The people's evil (*rāʿāh*) issues directly in their disaster (*rāʿāh*). The consequence is intrinsic to the deed; it has not been imposed on the people by God (see **Introduction**).

Personal Anguish at Creational Devastation, 4:19-31

These verses are sometimes said to be a representation in the mind of prophet/God regarding what is about to happen. Yet the bulk of the description is in the present and past tenses. Exilic readers would understand these verses as descriptive of past experience. The anticipation of the judgment and the judgment itself have been elided in view of what, for the readers, has already occurred.

The audience for vv. 19-22 is uncertain, but there is no indication that it has changed from Judah/Jerusalem (v. 5; see vv. 11, 14). Verses 19-21 are usually said to be Jeremiah's privately expressed emotions (to God) in response to the devastating effects of God's judgment. Yet the speaker of vv. 19-21 is difficult to discern. God's speech surrounds this text (vv. 17-18, 22), while "my" tents and "I cannot keep silent" suggest the words are Jeremiah's (or, possibly, Jeremiah representing the people; see 10:19-20; 30:12-15). This elision of speakers suggests that the anguish felt by God is experienced and expressed by the prophet at the disaster for Israel (see **Connections: The Anguish of Prophet and God**).

Into the midst of this lament, God recounts the key factors that have led to the disaster (v. 22; cf. 8:4-7); the emotion-filled voices of God and prophet are contrasted with the people's foolish nonchalance about these devastating developments. Once again, the word *rāʿāh* is used; evil leads to evil. The people not only do evil, but they are also skilled at it (v. 22)! That so much language associated with wisdom and understanding is used at this point is remarkable. What the people have done is a matter not simply of doing evil and not doing good, but of conduct that is not wise, is not informed by generally available understandings of what it means to do good. Note that these references to stupidity are not specifically related to law and covenant, but to the wisdom tradition, wherein the knowledge of God is a central element (cf. Prov 1:7, "the knowledge of God is the beginning of wisdom"). On the basis of everyday common sense, this people should have known better what it means to do good and shun evil (this kind of argument underlies the oracles of judgment against the nations in chs. 25, 46–51).

Verses 23-26 are remarkable in their depiction of the effects of the divine judgment (see **Connections: The End of the World?**). This description may continue the more private dialogue of vv. 19-22, but it could also be a public statement. The four-fold "I looked" provides a haunting rhythm to the depiction of the catastrophe. Verse 26 pointedly states that the devastation has to do with the fierce anger of God (see at 4:4; **Introduction**); but the context makes clear that the prior reality is what the people have done. The consequences of human sin are cosmic in their scope. [Moral Order and Cosmic Order]

Moral Order and Cosmic Order

The effect of the moral order on the cosmic order is once again made clear (see 2:1–3:5; 12:4; **Introduction**). That the world is so interconnected holds up the high level of importance of human words and deeds for the continuing health of the environment. That human sin and evil can have such wide-ranging effects in the world of nature is sobering. That the world does not come to a full end (v. 27) is important for other claims of Jeremiah (31:35-37; 33:14-26) and also signals that the cosmic imagery, while devastating, is not to be taken in a fully literal sense (cf. Amos 8:9-10; Joel 2:1-11; Nah 1:2-8). Yet there is a certain literalness that must not be discounted, and our own more recent experience with environmental devastation verifies the truth of this.

Images from the creation account in Genesis 1–2 are prominent in vv. 23-26. The earth has returned to a situation of "waste and void" (Gen 1:2). Or, in terms of Gen 2:5, the earth has become a wilderness once again (note the absence of water). The heavens no longer have any lights. The mountains and hills are no longer established in their places; earthquakes may be in mind (see Ps 46:2-3). The earth has no human (and animal?) inhabitants at all, and the birds have disappeared (cf. 9:10; **Connections** at 12:4). The earth is a wasteland, and cities are in ruins (note the historical linkage). This is a portrayal of reality before God ordered the heavens and earth and brought into being the various creatures. The word of God is active once again (4:28), but this time in wrath.

Those who separate vv. 23-26 from vv. 27-28 tend to do so because it is thought that v. 27 takes away from the stark end of creation in vv. 23-26. Hence, it must be a late "pious" addition to qualify the harshness of vv. 23-26. Those who retain v. 27 engage in some exegetical gymnastics in order to keep the starkness of vv. 23-26. Brueggemann, for example, considers v. 27 "an expression of uncertainty on Yahweh's part, wrought out of Yahweh's yearning not to destroy . . . as though God cannot fully accept God's own poetic rendition of judgment."[3] But there is no language of uncertainty in v. 27. God is clear on this point. While no specific idea of the remnant is present in this text, it does reflect the situation in which exilic readers found themselves. Though the judgment was catastrophic, they still lived! Their life meant that God had kept the promises regarding the orders of the world (see chs. 31:35-37; 33:14-26). This word about God not making a full end is a virtual refrain, picked up again in the next chapter (5:10, 18).

Verse 28 portrays the dirge-like response of the (still existent!) heavens and earth to what has occurred—a mourning and a "wearing" of funeral black. The entire cosmos is in mourning over what has occurred! The cosmic mourning is in order because the devastation is certain. As if to make sure that this judgmental decision of God is final, v. 28 lists a series of strong verbs: God has spoken and will not turn back from the decision. God will not "repent" or "change his mind"—this will be Israel's future. God does repent at other times and places—even in the Jeremiah tradition (18:7-10; 26:3, 13, 19; see Jonah 3:9-10), but not in this situation.[4]

Just as vv. 23-28 envision the effects of the judgment on the larger environment, vv. 29-31 focus specifically on the awful effects on daily life that the *people* have (had) to endure. As if in response to this decision of God not to turn the judgment back, vv. 29-30 describe Israel's varying responses to the enemy, using three different metaphors. The identity of the "I" in v. 31a is uncertain; it is probably best to think of both God and Jeremiah (note that Jerusalem is directly addressed as "the desolate one" in v. 30).

One response is to flee. Every person seeks to escape from the cities, to find places among rocks and bushes to hide from the marauding horsemen and archers (see Isa 2:19-21; contrast God's advice to flee to the fortified cities, 4:5-8). Another response is to dress up, bejewel themselves, and put on make-up like a prostitute (v. 30; see chs. 2–3; Ezek 16:26-29; 23), hoping to seduce the marauders (perhaps through political compromise or sexual politics) in order to avoid death. But they do not realize how unattractive they are and that they have no real charm to share. Their potential lovers (political lovers) reject their enticements and kill them instead. A third response is anguished moaning over pains and hurts so sharp that it is like the experience of the birth of a first child (before anesthesia!). Israel is left with its hands outstretched, screaming for help, but no help comes as it sinks exhausted in the killing fields. Remarkably, God still uses the word "daughter" for the people of Israel (v. 31); Israel is still God's people (see vv. 11, 22). Through the use of this language, God/prophet voice a lament over the suffering they have to endure. The language of giving birth among murderers could be a hopeful sign (cf. Isa 42:14). But new life will be possible only through death.

The language used to describe the event is such that exiled readers will recognize their own experience and their anguished and tortured fall at the hands of the Babylonian armies. To read these materials is to relive that horrendous experience, an important step on the way to healing.

CONNECTIONS

Has God Been Deceptive?, 4:10

Several (overlapping) interpretations of 4:10 seem possible. One, Jeremiah accuses God of being deceitful (as in 15:18; see 14:13; 20:7). The immediate context (vv. 5-8) seems to assume that, for *God,* genuine safety could be found in Zion, and God would respond to the laments (and hence the false prophets' words would have proved correct). Yet God's word in v. 9 indicates that, in fact, this activity would prove fruitless (see also v. 28). And so Jeremiah's word about deception may relate to the incongruity between vv. 5-8 and v. 9. This interpretation may be correct, but it remains to be asked whether Jeremiah is accurate in his assessment.

Two, Jeremiah's charge refers to the false prophets, mentioned in v. 9, but with the understanding that God has inspired them to be deceptive through their words. The false prophets have spoken the words cited in v. 10, "It shall be well with you." This could be related to 14:13-15, where Jeremiah may again charge God with deception through false prophets, a charge that God denies. It is possible that God uses (prophetic) deception as a means to blind people to the dangers in order to hasten the judgment (see 1 Kgs 13; 22; Ezek 14:9). But, if this is the case, what is one to make of the *indictment* of the false prophets for speaking peace when there is no peace (5:12-13, 31; 6:13-15=8:10-12; 14:13-16; 23:16-17; 27:9–28:17; 29:8; 37:9, 19; see Lam 2:14)? If God is being deceptive through them, this pervasive indictment would introduce another layer of deception, for God actually wants them to say what they're saying. But these texts make abundantly clear that the prophets are deceiving themselves. Multiple layers of deception would raise the question of the deceitfulness of all God's words, and Jeremiah's status as a prophet who did not deceive becomes problematic. One might qualify this point and say that God is charged with deceit just for permitting them so to speak.[5] But then, of course, God could be blamed for *anything* that God permits.

Three, the interpretation adopted here is that Jeremiah is genuinely voicing the complaints of the people (and those mentioned in v. 9). Certainly many believed that God had inspired those prophets and that they were speaking the truth; and so for them, in view of events, the problem lies with God. Given their question, it becomes a genuine question of Jeremiah. How would God respond to this complaint?

The Anguish of Prophet and God

The suffering of prophet and God are so linked that it is difficult to sort out the speaker; no sharp distinction between God and prophet should be made. As if with one voice, prophet and God express their anguish over the suffering of the people.[6] [Divine Anguish as Rhetorical Strategy]

This anguish is felt both physically and emotionally; "anguish" is more literally a reference to a churning stomach. The anguish is both anticipatory of the judgment to come and of a judgment that has already occurred, given the language of vv. 23-26. Note the repeated emphasis upon looking (vv. 21, 23-26) and hearing (vv. 19, 31). The devastation that fills the prophet's senses is so thoroughgoing that modern readers might think of a nuclear holocaust (vv. 20, 23-26). The vision speaks not only of personal tents and their curtains (=tent-flaps), but the whole land of Israel (v. 20); indeed the very cosmos itself is swept away by the whirlwind of God's judgment. The sounds and sights of war fill the scene—trumpets, alarms, shouts, standards, the noise of horsemen and archers, the cries and anguish of suffering people.

Divine Anguish as Rhetorical Strategy

While the emotions so evident in vv. 19-22 may not have been publicly voiced, they are now integrated into a public document. These words are the word of God, or at least have become so, to exiled readers. What was the rhetorical strategy that issued in the sharing of these emotions with *that* audience? Why would it be important for the exiles to see this side of the prophet and their God? These words reveal that the harsh words of judgment are not matched by an inner harshness. Words of judgment are not proclaimed joyously, but reluctantly and with great anguish. The godward side of the word and deed of wrath is grief. More generally, this sharing of the emotions of prophet and God reflects a deeply relational understanding of God.

Jeremiah's Lament

Here, the "embodied anguish" of Jeremiah has been reduced to feigned anguish as this German Romantic print takes on the air of an operatic set. The "stage backdrop" is typical of the conception of many of the German artists working in Rome in the early 19th century. The pristine, geometric architectural forms and shapes are reflective of the Nazarene interests in a return to art of the early Renaissance. The group was referred to as Nazarenes because of their stated commitment to return to a simplified Christian art. Their art was influenced by German medieval art and early Italian Renaissance painting. Carolsfeld has depicted Jeremiah's lament over the destruction of Jerusalem within the environs of a simplified, antique cityscape. Something of the German medievalizing aspect of this work may be seen with the swooning damsels in distress.

Julius Schnoor von Carolsfeld. *The Lamentations of Jeremiah.* 19th century. Woodcut. *Das Buch der Bucher in Bilden.* (Credit: Dover Pictorial Archive Series)

This vision of the effects of war is so filled with terror that God and Jeremiah are wracked with pain over what has happened to people and land. The prophet is an enfleshment of the emotions of God over what has occurred and what may yet occur. It is common to interpret these verses in terms of the prophet's representative suffering on behalf of Israel.[7] But another approach seems preferable. Texts such as these (see also 8:19–9:3) should be interpreted in terms of the prophet's embodiment of God's anguish. The prophet suffers in his role as a servant of God. It is true that Jeremiah's anguish parallels that of the people (see 4:31), but so does God's.

Both God and prophet enter into the anguish of the people. In taking this approach to such texts, the prophet's anguish becomes a word of *God* to the people (exilic readers) and not a word of the *people* to God. In hearing Jeremiah, the people should be able to see how God has entered into the anguish of the people's situation and made it God's very own.[8]

The End of the World?, 4:23-27

The devastating effects on the earth depicted in vv. 23-26 are not due to an explicit divine decision, for God introduces nothing new into the situation. As 6:19 puts it, these effects are the "fruit of their own schemes." This is *rāʿāh* (4:18) as the effect of human *rāʿāh* (4:14; see **Introduction**). At the same time, God is in some sense complicit in the environmental degradation (see at ch. 12). The Babylonian armies are complicit as well, and their actions wreak chaos, but they are not the incarnation of a chaos monster or in the service of some supernatural evil force. They themselves will be held accountable and suffer judgment because of their arrogance and violence (see 25:12-14; 50–51).[A Chaos Tradition?]

Is this language hyperbolic, as is commonly claimed (an exaggeration for rhetorical effect)? Or is this simile/metaphor, indicating what Israel's judgment would be *like*? Either assessment may discount the *creational* effects of human wickedness. Verse 27 summarizes the point being made; the *whole earth* is "a desolation." That is, Israel's sin has these kinds of cosmic effects (see **Connections** at ch. 12). This segment could be called a vision that Jeremiah has into a possible future for the creation, given the extent of the devastation. But this text is not a prophetic prediction; from the perspective of exilic readers, it has already happened. In its most basic sense this prophecy depicts the fall of Israel. It is a vivid portrayal of what that event "looked" (note the emphasis) like and felt like for everyone concerned. At the same time, it remains a pertinent vision for any time and place. Human sin can have such effects! In the last generation in particular, moderns have come to accept this interconnection of human behaviors and adverse effects on the environment as a truism. This is a vision of what human sin *could*

A Chaos Tradition?

The portrayal in vv. 23-26 does not depict a return to an original chaos that had been kept under control through the centuries. This is an effect of God's wrath (see 4:4), not some triumph of existent chaotic forces. (See Terence Fretheim, "The Book of Genesis" [*NIB*; 12 vols.; Nashville: Abingdon, 1994], 1:356.) These verses are no testimony to such forces; they witness to the adverse effects of *human wickedness* on the creation. To ascribe these effects to some resurgent power of chaos is to diminish the depth and breadth of human sin and its cosmic effects (not unlike "the devil made me do it"). There may well be imagery used in these texts drawn from a "chaos tradition" that serves the creation-wide scope of what is at stake here, but there is no explicit or implicit dualistic perspective at work.

do to the ecosystem, some signs of which are clearly in evidence. It is conceivable that the damage has already been done and that vv. 23-26 in fact express a vision of our future; perhaps it is "too late." But we speak and act as if this were not the case.

These adverse effects on the creation are to be related to the rejuvenation of creation in texts such as 31:1-14 (cf. Isa 35). But even with a new creation (see Isa 65:17-25), continuities with the old remain. Those texts that speak of a new creation are very much this-worldly; they, too, constitute a vision for the future. [Heschel on Verses 23-26]

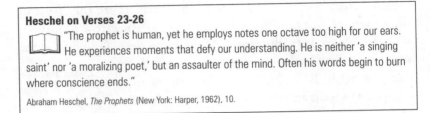

Heschel on Verses 23-26

"The prophet is human, yet he employs notes one octave too high for our ears. He experiences moments that defy our understanding. He is neither 'a singing saint' nor 'a moralizing poet,' but an assaulter of the mind. Often his words begin to burn where conscience ends."

Abraham Heschel, *The Prophets* (New York: Harper, 1962), 10.

NOTES

[1] Walter Brueggemann at times speaks in ways that make the historical situation irrelevant, e.g., *A Commentary on Jeremiah: Exile and Homecoming* (Grand Rapids: Eerdmans, 1998), 53, even if his overall analysis recognizes the historical rootage of the material.

[2] See the discussion in Leo Perdue, *The Collapse of History: Reconstructing Old Testament Theology* (Minneapolis: Fortress, 1994), 141-46.

[3] Brueggemann, *Jeremiah*, 60.

[4] On distinctions in the theme of divine repentance, see Terence Fretheim, "The Repentance of God: A Key to Evaluating Old Testament God-Talk," *HBT* 10 (1988): 47-70.

[5] So Peter C. Craigie, Page Kelley, and Joel F. Drinkard Jr., *Jeremiah 1–25* (WBC 26; Dallas: Word, 1991), 74.

[6] So Terence Fretheim, *The Suffering of God: An Old Testament Perspective* (Philadelphia: Fortress, 1984), 160.

[7] See, e.g., Abraham Heschel, *The Prophets* (New York: Haper, 1962), 119-22.

[8] This point of view is laid out in Fretheim, *The Suffering of God*, 159-62.

WHY HAS GOD DONE ALL THESE THINGS TO US?

5:1-31

This chapter consists of a series of indictments (5:1-5, 10-13, 20-28) followed in each case by a "therefore" (stated, vv. 6, 14; implied, v. 29), which introduces judgment oracles (5:6-9, 14-17, 29-31). A prose interlude (5:18-19), usually thought to have been added later, reinforces the indictments (and those of earlier chapters). This interlude provides the question with which the chapter, indeed the book, is fundamentally concerned: Why?! By means of its question and answer form (see 9:12; **Introduction**), these verses make clear that the divine judgment is not a capricious divine move, but has its basis in the people's infidelity. At the same time, this interlude restates an assurance stated in the poetry (5:10; see 4:27) that God would not make "a full end" of Israel. [Less Than a "Full End"]

The divine lament also finds its place in this chapter behind questions addressed to readers (5:7, 9, 22, 29, 31). These divine questions, which interact with human comments (vv. 2, 4-5, 12, 19; see v. 24), are not simply rhetorical questions. The questions in vv. 7, 9, and 29 reveal a God who has earnestly sought another way into the future, but finally and reluctantly comes to a point where a future without disastrous judgment is not possible. These questions are also genuine questions for the exilic readers. From the perspective of their experience of the destruction, do they think that God has been unfair for taking this course of action? Can they think of any other course of action that God might have taken? The questions in v. 22 reveal a

---

Less Than a "Full End"

The theme of less than a "full end" (4:27; 5:10, 18) may well be a later editorial perspective, but its presence establishes something basic about the meaning of judgment for the book of Jeremiah. Whether such a note was a part of Jeremiah's preaching or not, the editors, by inserting these (and other) qualifications to the judgment, *interpreted* Jeremiah's preaching in these terms, making explicit what they thought to be implicit (at least). The judgment of God was not understood to be a final word about the people of Israel, but a dark journey through which the people must pass because of their unfaithfulness. But God would be there throughout the devastation, making sure that there would be a remnant with which to begin again. This qualifying theme sounds through all the doom and gloom of chs. 4–5 and provides a reassuring word for those exiles who thought their experience might mark the end of Israel as God's people.

divine wonderment at their nonchalance in the face of a God who has created the world and provided boundaries for the negative forces of creation. Behind the question in v. 31 stands a God who asks what resources they will have available when the destruction falls. The mere asking of the questions reveals a God who is deeply concerned about their future.

The problem of the identification of the speaker persists from the previous chapter. The interchange of speakers (God; Jeremiah; people) continues to give evidence for the dialogical character of this material, revealing again something basic about the character of the God with whom readers have to do. The many quotations from the people may serve to trigger the memories of the exiles of those tumultuous years (see **Connections** in ch. 2).

COMMENTARY

How Can I Pardon You?, 5:1-9

God ("I") speaks in vv. 1-2 and commissions heralds (see v. 20; 4:5-8, including Jeremiah; the "you" is plural, which may also catch up the memories of exilic readers). They are to traverse the streets and squares of Jerusalem in search of a righteous person (v. 1; see 2:10; Zeph 1:12). This is not an instruction to take a literal census of the righteous in the city, but to search their minds and name names. Moreover, this instruction to find "one person" is not to be understood strictly in terms of quantity, for Jeremiah, Baruch, and others (see 26:24; 26:20) could be named. The "one" hyperbolically (see also the "all" and "everyone" in 5:5-6) stresses how pervasive the infidelity has become. The issue at stake is much the same as that addressed by Abraham in Genesis 18:22-33. Are there sufficient numbers of righteous to constitute a critical mass that might (in time) turn the city back to faithfulness? For the sake of the presence (and potential impact) of these righteous ones, God would pardon the *city* (so also 5:7a). This "pardon" is a *corporate* matter and focuses on sparing the *city* from destruction, not forgiving each individual within the city (see **Connections: Can One Person Save the City?**). The result of this "research" is one answer to the question "Why?" in v. 19.

In this "census," God seeks persons who "act justly" (with respect to their neighbor) and "seek to be faithful [NRSV, "truth"]" (to God). Relationships with both God and neighbor are in view (the "way" in vv. 4-5 includes both; specifics on both are given in

vv. 7-8). The people mouth proper confessional statements (v. 2), such as when they swear by the name of their God when they give oaths (for whatever reason). But this God-language is full of pretense, for in their daily lives they are neither just nor faithful. As 5:7 makes clear, they are actually swearing by the "no gods" to whom they have given their real allegiance. [On Using the LORD's Name]

Jeremiah responds to God in vv. 3-5a. He acknowledges that God looks for fidelity in the people. To that end, God has disciplined them in various unspecified ways (see 2:30), but they have learned nothing. In fact, such experiences have only hardened them in their ways, and they remain adamant in their refusal to return to God (see **Connections: Israel's Stubborn Heart**). Jeremiah suggests that those who respond in this way are only the ordinary people (="poor"), and they remain set in their ways because they do not know the Law of God ("way" in vv. 4-5 is a more general term for a pattern of life that the Law specifies concretely). He then determines to go ("I will go" rather than "let me go") to more educated and prominent citizens; certainly they will know the way and follow the Law.

On Using the Lord's Name

Swearing falsely in the Lord's name is a theme that occurs in this segment of Jeremiah (4:2; 5:2; 7:9; cf. 12:16). Berrigan's comments are especially apt:

> "They swear falsely" (v. 2) is a common tactic (then and now). That is, they invoke God, but only in furtherance of a shady deal. Thus a spate of sacred smog is released on the air, wonderfully obscuring the truth of the issues at hand. In the short run, the tactic works well, not merely in the wide world of wheeling and dealing, but in "religious" circles as well. In such a way, those who embody such virtues as justice and truth can be put to the door. And seldom has bad faith worn a more innocent face! . . . Alas for truth. We see instead a culture and climate in which duplicity, betrayal, doublespeak, surreptitious dealing, guile, treachery, and low cunning are the "normal" tools of political discourse. The chefs of chicanery proceed to marinate the above admirable qualities in a bland of religious fakery. Thus, for example, "family values" become the sanctified code for a nouveau brand of fascism.

Daniel Berrigan, *Jeremiah: The World, the Wound of God* (Minneapolis: Fortress, 1999), 25-26.

One wonders why Jeremiah thought he could discover faithfulness more readily among the prominent citizens than the ordinary folk; he is probably being ironic, given his indictment of leaders elsewhere (see 2:26). Verse 5b may be Jeremiah's (or, possibly, God's) comment on the results of the prophet's search: Everyone was unfaithful and, in rebellion, had thrown off all the constraint that the Law provides ("yoke" and "bonds" are agricultural images; they restrain, guide, and protect the animals, see 2:20). For exiled readers, there could be no escape in this sweeping judgment; they were included in the "all," even if they were righteous.

The opening "therefore" in vv. 6-9, with God speaking, follows from the prior indictment of unfaithfulness and introduces the word of judgment. The metaphors used for judgment by foreign armies are drawn from the world of wild and dangerous animals (lions [2:15; 4:7], wolves, and leopards; see Hos 13:7-8; Hab 1:8); their "watching" is linked to God's watching in 1:12 (see 4:17).

There may be a literal element as well in this reference to the wild animals (see 27:6; **Connections**, ch.12). The effect of their ferocity is brutal and uncompromising; instead of the order provided by restraints, wild animals will have their way with the people. They ("everyone!") will be mauled and torn to pieces; indeed, as 5:17 states, their children, crops, livestock, vines, and fruit trees will all be eaten up. The verbs in v. 6 indicate that these effects are already in process (see NAB).

Still, enfolded in this announcement are further words of indictment, both in general terms ("transgressions" and "apostasies"; "forsaken me") and with specificity (giving oaths in the name of other "no gods"; committing adultery by frequenting houses of prostitution and coveting the wives of their neighbors). In playing out the metaphor of lusty stallions, God uses language that is sharp, even sarcastic. Though God had satisfied their hunger, their sexual appetites were ravenous for that which violated the marital relationship. The infidelity that Israel had shown in its relationship with God expressed itself in unfaithful human relationships. Infidelity had become a way of life. (Note that while infidelity in Jeremiah is often imaged in terms of female sexuality [e.g., 3:1-3], here the actual inter-human infidelity is imaged in male terms.)

Divine questions play a key role in vv. 7, 9 (the questions in v. 9 become a refrain in this section of Jeremiah, 5:29; 9:9; see above on the questions). [Questions for Exiles] The questions are addressed to Israel as a mother with children ("you" plural, v. 7; the third plural address in v. 9 refers back to "your children" in v. 7). God's questions are rhetorical in the sense that, given the situation described, God does not have the option of pardoning Jerusalem (see v. 1) or of not "judging" them. At the same time, the word "how" in v. 7 has the ring of a lament about it (see 9:19; Hos 11:8); God would prefer to pardon them and would prefer not to follow through on the judgment. God agonizes that this is not an option (it does become an option on the far side of judgment, 31:34). The heart of the reason for not pardoning is stated in vv. 3, 7; they are obdurate, "have refused to repent," and "have forsaken me" (see 2:13, 17, 19).

Many translations of v. 9 are problematic. The verb commonly (here and elsewhere in Jeremiah) translated "punish" is *pāqād*, which is the everyday word for "visit." [Punish, Punishment in 5:9, 29] The

Questions for Exiles

Whatever function these questions may have had before the fall of Jerusalem, they are now questions to exilic readers. The exiles are invited to think back and consider the options with which God was presented in that time and to realize anew the questioning and agony through which God was going with respect to the shape of their future. It would be important for exiles to see this divine reluctance, that their God had tried to find another way into the future for them besides judgment. This view of a reluctant-to-judge God could be grounds for hope that a more positive future for them would remain a divine concern.

Punish, Punishment in 5:9, 29

AΩ Most occurrences of "punishment" (in NRSV and elsewhere) translate words for "sin," especially ʿāwôn; most occurrences of "punish" (in NRSV and elsewhere) translate pqd, "visit." The translations "punish, punishment" are deeply problematic. They suggest that God introduces something new (e.g., a penalty) into the situation, when in fact the consequences grow out of the deed (see **Introduction**).

Whether "these" in 5:9a and 5:29a refers to the previously noted sins (so NRSV; NAB) or people (see William Holladay, *Jeremiah 1* [Philadelphia: Fortress, 1989],

182, though Holladay's sense is different) should be decided in favor of the latter in view of the usual use of the preposition ʿal with reference to the people following the verb pāqad (e.g.,11:22; 21:14). This would make the line parallel to "nation such as this" in v. 9b. One could translate "Upon these people I will visit [their sins]." The sense, as commonly elsewhere in Jeremiah, is that God will visit the people's sins upon them. If it be insisted that "these" refers to the sins, then the translation should be, "for these things I will visit [them]," which could be argued on the basis of 9:9 (where the additional word bām has reference to the people).

---

sense is that God will visit their iniquities upon them; God will mediate the effects that grow out of their own deeds (6:19 and often). The verb *nāqam*, translated "bring retribution" in v. 9b (NRSV), is also translated "avenge myself" (so RSV; NIV) or "take vengeance" (NAB). The verbs *pāqad* and *nāqam* are also parallel in 11:20-22 and 15:15. To introduce the idea of "retribution" into these texts is problematic in view of the act-consequence perspective so pervasive in Jeremiah (see **Introduction**). God's use of the reflexive ("myself") suggests that this divine mediation of the consequences of sin has to do with God's being true to himself, that is, true to the moral order that God has established in the creation. The sense is that God will not remain unresponsive in the face of these infidelities for the sake of God's commitment to the created order (note the creation themes in 4:23-26; 5:22-24; 9:10-11).

Infidelity Leads to Exile, 5:10-19

The rhythm of vv. 1-9 is repeated in vv. 10-17, though more episodically, given the shift in speakers. [The Speaker in Verses 10-19] Included are a commission (v. 10; this time to the invading armies, as often in the OAN, e.g., 50:14-16, 21), an indictment (vv. 11-13), and an announcement of judgment (vv. 14-17). The sharp statement of judgment, which sounds total in v. 17, is reassuringly qualified in vv. 18-19 (returning to a theme of v. 10), but still severe—exile to a foreign land.

In the divine commission to the armies, the image used for Israel is a vineyard, a common metaphor for the people of God (2:21; 6:9; 12:10; Isa 5:1-7). The strong language, "they

The Speaker in Verses 10-19

AΩ The speaker throughout vv. 10-19 may be God. More likely, however, vv. 12-13 are spoken by Jeremiah, singling out the false prophets, to which God responds in v. 14 (the phrase, "because you [NRSV footnote] have spoken this word," could be a reference to what Jeremiah has said *about* the prophets in vv. 12-13). There is clearly a shift in audience in God's speech, from foreign armies (v. 10), to Jeremiah (v. 14), to the people (vv. 15-17; for unknown reasons, "you" is plural in v. 15a and singular in vv. 15b, 17).

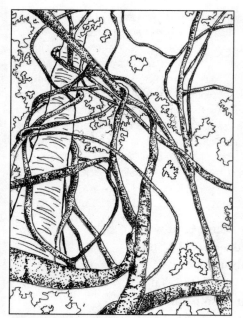

Vines and Branches

[both northern and southern kingdoms] are not the LORD's," must be interpreted in view of the less than "full end" phrase.[1] While the relationship is broken because of Israel's faithlessness, it is not irreparable or without a future (see Isa 54: 7-8). Rather, the branches—the growths on the vines that have accumulated over the years (infidelities, v. 11; cf. 3:20)—are to be stripped away. Even if one were to deny a distinction between vines and branches[2] and claim that the destruction is total, that does not necessarily carry the sense of finality. From the perspective of exilic readers, the issue obviously was not annihilation, but what the past meant and what the future would be.

As noted, Jeremiah is the likely speaker of vv. 12-13. Both verses have been thought to be a quotation of the people; v. 13 would thus be a judgment on all prophets, even Jeremiah (see REB). Yet the content of the quotation in v. 12 is remarkably similar to other speeches of the false prophets (e.g., 6:13-15; 14:13-16; 23:17), so that v. 13 follows naturally as a judgment on them. The false speaking is a misplaced confidence that God would not act against them, would not mediate the negative effects of their sins ("evil," *rāʿāh*), whether of famine or invasion. For Jeremiah, their words are not God's word, but only "wind" (the Hebrew word is *rûaḥ*, which plays on the word used for spirit, a source of prophetic inspiration, e.g., Isa 61:1). The idiom is similar to the modern "windbag" (see Isa 28:7-10; Mic 2:11). The phrase, "thus shall it be done to them," carries the sense that they will inherit the "wind," a metaphor for foreign armies (see 4:11-13; 13:24; 22:22), just as they have blown their wind on the people (cf. Hos 8:7). In other words, what goes around, comes around.

The announcement of judgment follows in vv. 14-17 ("therefore"). Because the people have spoken lies and the prophets have spoken windy words, God is making Jeremiah's words a fire (see 1:9, where God puts the word in Jeremiah's mouth; 15:16). Fire is a metaphor for God's word (23:29; see 20:9) *and* a metaphor for the invading armies and the devastation they leave in their wake (see 4:4; 6:29; 11:16; 15:14); that is, Jeremiah's fiery word of judgment will be effected through them. Using the metaphor of wood for the people, the fire of God's word/the armies will consume them. The ancient, long-enduring, foreign language-speaking "nation" from far away (v. 15; its identity is left open-ended for readers to fill in) will "eat up" everything of value (like fire, v. 14)—food, children, livestock, and fruit trees (v. 17). The repetition pounds the point home: the social order as they have known it will disappear. Hyperbolically, every member of this nation is a mighty warrior, and they have emptied all of their quivers, whose emptiness mirrors the effect of their arrows—open graves (v. 16). They will destroy all the cities, even those which are fortified (including Jerusalem). The people have put their trust in these cities—not least because God has told them to flee there (4:5; see 8:14, where they realize that these cities will not protect them)!

Verses 18-19 speak again of less than a "full end" (v. 10; 4:27) and voice a question raised by exilic readers (9:12 and often): Why has God done all these things to us? The response to be given to the people has two aspects. One, their infidelity explains the destruction (forsaking "me," see v. 7). Two, their being in a foreign land (Babylon) is understood in "what goes around, comes around" terms. As they served alien gods in their own land, so they shall serve "strangers" in an alien land. The "strangers" are probably Babylonians (see 30:8), but could also be foreign gods (see 2:25; 16:13).

An Appalling and Horrible Thing, 5:20-31

The rhythm of indictment and announcement of judgment continue, and various questions from God punctuate this segment. The readers are directly addressed with questions (vv. 22a, 31), inviting responses; the question of v. 29 (see v. 9) is in the third person. [The Audience as "You" and "Them"]

These verses are once again addressed to both Israel (=the house of Jacob) and Judah. The identity of the one called to address Israel in v. 20 is unclear (the imperatives are plural as in v. 1 and 4:5-8; they are probably heralds, but include exilic readers in some sense), but the content of the message is clear. God's people have a stubborn and rebellious heart and have turned away from the LORD (v. 23); they have

The Audience as "You" and "Them"

AΩ The mixture of second person ("you") and third person ("they") throughout vv. 20-31 is typical (e.g., ch. 7). The effect of this rhetorical strategy is to elide the generations (with some overlap, no doubt)—participants in the destruction of Jerusalem and the exiles who look back on that experience. The present readers ("you"; vv. 21-22, 25, 31) are invited to look back and evaluate God's evaluation of "them" (vv. 23-24, 26-31). This strategy catches up the readers in the word of God that continues to be spoken, and does not allow the readers to put these matters behind them. This word of God has been shaped to be a word for the postdestruction generation.

eyes and ears but do not see and hear (v. 21; see Isa 6:9; Matt 13:14-15; in this respect, they are like the idols they worship, see Ps 115:4-7). In language drawn from the wisdom tradition (see Prov

1:7), the people's stubbornness is ascribed to their foolishness and senselessness (v. 21; see 4:22; 10:8). The problem is not one of ignorance, however, as if to say that with a little more knowledge, the issue could be resolved. The language is relational; the issue is that they do not know the LORD, which leads to a foolish life of evil rather than good (see 4:22). Even direct questions regarding an expected posture—fear and trembling—before the holiness of God go unheeded (v. 22a). This stubbornness and rebelliousness is sharply stated in v. 23; they have gone their own way, with no regard for their Creator. With the repetition of the language of v. 21 in 6:10 (having ears but not hearing), it is clear that the people are not *able* to respond positively to the call to repentance (see 2:25 and **Connections: Israel's Stubborn Heart**).

Earlier in Jeremiah, Israel is said to have neglected the confession of God as their redeemer (2:6-7); here their failures are associated with a neglect of the confession of God as creator (5:22, 24; see **Introduction**). On the one hand (v. 22), they do not acknowledge that God has created the world order in such a way that the forces of chaos (=sea) are contained within boundaries of sand and rock (see 31:35; Job 38:8-11). Israel's very life is dependent upon this ordering, restraining work of God. Israel should "tremble" before a God who has created such a world, but they do not. This is evidence that they are blind and deaf to the work of God among them. Indeed, they have trespassed the bounds set for them in the Law (v. 24; see v. 5), and hence they have proved more rebellious than the raging sea.

On the other hand (v. 24), the people do not acknowledge that their God is the one who gives the rains (see Hos 2:8-11; 6:3) and who has promised the seven weeks of harvest between Passover and Pentecost (Lev 23:10-17; see Gen 8:22), during which rain was not common. The implication is that Israel has been looking (fruitlessly) to other gods for these blessings. Their infidelities ("iniquities" and "sins"), however, mean that these blessings will not be forthcoming, depriving them of the very good for which they long (v. 25; 3:2-3; 12:4). Moral order has had an adverse effect upon cosmic order (see [Moral Order and Cosmic Order]).

The indictment takes a new turn in vv. 26-28 (anticipated in 2:34), as God denounces the people (but note the "my," and in v. 31) for their treacherous treatment of the poor and disadvantaged (see Isa 1:23)—an infrequent theme in Jeremiah (see [The Nature of the Problem]). At the same time, distinctions are made among Israelites. Only some are named "scoundrels" or "criminals." Yet, while only such people are condemned here, their actions affect the

Heschel on Prophetic Interference

In a sense, the calling of the prophet may be described as that of an advocate or champion, speaking for those who are too weak to plead their own cause. Indeed, the major activity of the prophets was *interference*, remonstrating about wrongs inflicted on other people, meddling in affairs which were seemingly neither their concern nor their responsibility. A prudent man is he who minds his own business, staying away from questions which do not involve his own interests, particularly when not authorized to step in—and prophets were given no mandate by the widows and orphans to plead their cause. The prophet is a person who is not tolerant of wrongs done to others, who resents other people's injuries. He even calls upon others to be the champions of the poor.

Abraham Heschel, *The Prophets* (New York: Harper, 1962), 204-205.

---

entire "nation" (v. 29). The presence of the righteous (see 5:1) is minimal in comparison, and so the entire people—even the poor and the needy—suffer the consequences of the worst among them (see **Connections: Can One Person Save the City?**).

God's rhetoric is scathing! [Heschel on Prophetic Interference] These criminals are likened to fowlers—bird catchers that set traps for birds; the keys to bird catching are careful planning, lying in wait for opportunities, and hidden nets, which are quickly sprung to capture unwitting birds. These scoundrels are like those traps; they seek to catch human beings—devising schemes that can trap people unawares, so as to enrich themselves (see Prov 1:11-14). So much wealth is built upon the backs of the poor and the needy! Continuing with an image related to birds, the poor are to these scoundrels like caged birds, whose meager resources are captive to their scheming; through treacherous activities they have filled their houses with loot, with riches procured at the expense of the poor (see Isa 3:14-15). Without regard for limits or boundaries (unlike the sea and the harvests), they neglect issues of justice, refuse to care for the needy, and ignore their rights (contrast Josiah in 22:16). Moreover, this exploitation is not simply a personal matter; it has become institutionalized, particularly in the courts ("judge with justice"; see Deut 16:18-20). In the wake of such individual and communal wickedness, the questions of 5:9 are repeated (see [Punish, Punishment in 5:9, 29]).

Verses 30-31 draw the leaders of Israel into the equation. Appallingly, the leadership of both prophets and priests has failed (see 2:8; 26:7-9); they are imaged as conspiring together to produce a false assurance among the people (see vv. 12-13). Rather than speak out against these wicked schemes and speak the truth about the nature of the evil in the midst, they simply reinforce the people's wishes and contribute further to this injustice. And the people do not care; they love to see their unjust activities approved by the powers that be. They are all in this together. They love to have it so! But their total lack of regard for the negative effects of their actions is short-sighted. What will "you"(!) do when you are visited by overwhelmingly destructive forces? What will you do when the end comes? If you have given any thought to the end! The point is that you will be able to do nothing to stop the onslaught, and you will be swept away.

CONNECTIONS

Israel's Stubborn Heart

The essence of sin for Jeremiah is not individual deeds or words; it is rather to be found in the human will (see 13:23; 17:9). Human beings are not essentially evil, so that they become sin; but their sinfulness is deep and pervasive.

Stubbornness is an important theme in Jeremiah (3:17; 5:23; 6:28; 7:24; 9:14; 11:8; 13:10; 16:12; 18:12; 23:17). It is commonly linked with the language of willfulness (an "evil will [heart]"), and related texts such as 5:3 that refer to Israel's hard faces seem to presuppose that reality. In the interpretation of this theme, the tendency has been to push the issue toward one ditch or another: Either God has determined Israel's behaviors and is in total control of events, or the people's freedom of will is intact until the end. Neither perspective is appropriate for Jeremiah, but it is difficult to find one's way between these ditches. (This issue is similar to the hardening of Pharaoh's heart.)[3]

The illustration used in chapter 1 can help set a proper direction. The history of God's people may be likened to a boat on a fast-moving river, headed for a gorge or a waterfall. As often in history, human decisions and other factors can bring life to a point where there is no turning back, no possibility of getting the boat to the shore before it goes over the waterfall. In such cases, history's possibilities are inexorably narrowed to a single one. Deterministic language can be used to interpret such moments, but it is not a determinism that was in place from the beginning. The trip over the falls was not always the shape of the future, but there may come a point when that plunge becomes inevitable.

In thinking about the fall of Jerusalem, there comes an unidentifiable moment sometime before the fall when that future becomes inevitable. At that point, nothing can be done to turn the boat back from the falls (see 4:28). Even sincere repentance may not be able to stop that future from coming, because it comes too late in the journey to turn the situation around for the *community* (probably the case in 14:7-9, 19-21).

God's involvement in this process may be sketched out in these terms. God was at work in and through the prophets to turn the people to repentance (see 3:12-14), but in its absence that very work of God makes the stubbornness even more obdurate (see 2 Kgs 17:14). In such cases, the continued divine involvement through the prophet has the effect of intensifying the sinful behavior of the people, making it more and more difficult for them to respond positively (it becomes easier and easier to say "no" to God). This kind of divine activity thus drives the boat toward the waterfall until it finally goes crashing over the edge. [God as Judge]

Life then becomes possible only on the far side of the trip over the falls. For Jeremiah, finally, the only future possible for Israel is that God will pick them up off the rocks below the falls and continue the journey. At what point in the ministry of Jeremiah that restoration occurs is impossible to say, but it is clear from 1:3 that the book in its final form assumes that the trip over the falls is inevitable. That future seems to be signaled by several texts, including 5:3 and, especially, 5:23.

God as Judge

AΩ The metaphor of God as judge is often a decisive factor in thinking through divine judgment, and for good reason. At the same time, the metaphor pushes one to think of judgment solely or primarily in forensic terms, as if each judgment were the result of a specific divine decision. Though the language of judgment is associated with the court of law, juridical categories do not fully or sufficiently comprehend the workings of divine judgment. This is true from several perspectives. For one, God's judgment is never simply justice. God is patient, forbearing, and 'slow to anger' (e.g., Jonah 4:2). In terms of straightforward legal thinking, God is much too lenient. For another, judgment is understood fundamentally in relational terms: a relationship is at stake, not an agreement or a contract or a set of rules. God does not bring judgment in terms of a legal statute with sanctions. God does not impose anything new on the judgmental situation, but mediates the consequences of sin.

Terence Fretheim, "Divine Judgment and the Warning of the World: An Old Testament Perspective," *God, Evil, and Suffering: Essays in Honor of Paul Sponheim*, ed. Terence Fretheim and C. Thompson, Word and World Supplement Series 4 (St. Paul MN, 2000) 24-25.

Can One Person Save the City?

The distinction between individual and community is important for this discussion. Jeremiah's prophecy has a fundamental corporate dimension; the issue he is concerned to address finally has to do with the future of Israel as a people. The point of 5:1-5 is that there were an insufficient number of people in Israel to effect a positive future for the community as a whole. A comparable point about "critical mass" is evident in Abraham's intercession on behalf of Sodom and Gomorrah in Genesis 18:22-33 (see Jer 23:14, where Jerusalem is likened to Sodom and Gomorrah; Isa 1:9; Ps 14:2-3; Rom 3:10-12). In the absence of a sufficient number of righteous in the city/nation, even individual righteous persons (for example, Jeremiah) will experience the devastation of the community. This may seem unfair to moderns steeped in individualistic perspectives, but this is the "price" one pays for living in a community from which one often receives *benefits* undeservedly as well. When it comes to corporate justice, there may come a point where radical surgery is needed, even if some righteous individuals get caught up in the judgment. To avoid judgment in such cases would be more intolerable for everyone, for it would allow evil to go unchecked in the life of the world.

Texts such as Jeremiah 5:1-5 witness to the significance of the presence of the righteous in any situation (this is not an apotropaic view).[4] The righteous can subvert the effects of sin and evil from within the city/nation so that the consequences are less severe. Such a point argues against a fatalism among the righteous, the belief that nothing can be done about society's problems, that plays down the potential impact of human activity, or is resigned to sin's consequences. The righteous can indeed make a difference to the future of the neighborhood or nation; they can make a difference to God.

NOTES

[1] Contrary to Walter Brueggemann, *A Commentary on Jeremiah: Exile and Homecoming* (Grand Rapids: Eerdmans, 1998), 60, 65-66, there is no sign that God "struggles" with this qualification.

[2] So Robert Carroll, *Jeremiah* (Philadelphia: Westminster, 1986), 181.

[3] On this issue, see Terence Fretheim, *Exodus* (IBC; Atlanta: John Knox, 1991), 96-103.

[4] Contrary to Carroll, *Jeremiah*, 176.

TAKE WARNING, JERUSALEM

6:1-30

This collection of oracles continues the theme of judgment, though the threat to Judah and Jerusalem is portrayed as more immediate. The invading armies are on their doorstep, and they will not be turned back. [The Structure of Jeremiah 6]

COMMENTARY

The Invader Approaches, 6:1-8

This segment is enclosed by warnings to the people about the coming invasion of the "evil . . . out of the north" (vv. 1, 8). Spoken by God in its entirety (though vv. 1-3 have been ascribed to Jeremiah), the ominous character of the situation is captured in part by quotations from the enemy (vv. 4a, 5) and the beleaguered people (v. 5b). At the same time, lament-like materials are woven into the fabric of the coming disaster (vv. 2, 6b-7).

The chapter begins with God's call of alarm to Israel to flee; the relationship to the comparable call in 4:5-6 is uncertain, but may reflect the mixed messages one hears at such a time (later they will be called to flee from Babylon, 50:8; 51:6). Located just to the north of the city of Jerusalem, the Benjaminites would be the first of those in Jerusalem's environs to face the advance of the destructive enemy (="evil," *rāʿāh*) "out of the north" (see 4:6). Then trumpet warnings

---

The Structure of Jeremiah 6

The structure of the chapter is difficult to perceive. The advance of the "evil out of the north" (v. 1) is portrayed vividly in vv. 1-8 and vv. 22-26, though in the latter Israel's response is more vividly depicted. Interchanges between God and Jeremiah follow in each case (vv. 9-15, 27-30). The middle verses (vv. 16-21) are essentially public statements regarding factors at stake in God's indictment of Israel and the consequent announcement of judgment. Verses 16-17 report two interchanges between God and people, the effect of which is to lay the ground for the indictment to follow. In vv. 18-19, the nations and the natural order are called upon to witness to what has happened. In view of vv. 16-19, vv. 20-21 address the people, with an indictment (v. 20; in the second person) and an announcement of judgment (v. 21; in the third person).

The dialogical character of this chapter is notable, with interchanges reported between God and people (vv. 16-17), prophet and people (vv. 24-26), and between Jeremiah and God (vv. 9-15; 27-30).

are to be sounded in Tekoa and Beth-haccherem, villages just south of Jerusalem (next in line for the armies advancing from the north).

Verse 2 is difficult to translate, but NAB (cf. NRSV footnote) captures one possible sense: O lovely and delicate daughter Zion, you are ruined! God's address to the people of Jerusalem as a daughter is filled with pathos. This most precious child to God is ruined! Oh, that it were not so! But, given the advance of Babylon, this future is now certain. The NRSV, likening Zion to the "loveliest pasture," would link up with v. 3; as a lush pasture, the "shepherds" would set their eyes on it and devour it (see 5:17).

Verse 3 describes the advancing armies with a shepherd metaphor and in terms that are certainly ironic. The peaceful pastoral scene is disquieted as it becomes a camp for an army on the rampage. These generals (=shepherds) with their armies (=flocks) will encircle the city (=pitch their tents around her; see 4:17) and encamp in their places (=pasture); the city will be besieged. The failure of Israel's shepherds (see 5:31) means that other (destructive) shepherds will move in and do their own kind of tending. Shepherds who will truly lead God's people have been promised for the future (3:15), and so that promise hangs in the background of this portrayal. Exiled readers may well wonder about their future under these remarkably different shepherd figures.

In vv. 4-5 God captures the mood of the moment through almost journalistic reports from the battlefront and, probably, from opposing sides. The enemy is quoted in vv. 4a, 5, the people of Israel in v. 4b (some consider it the enemy). The enemy's words show progression in its determination to destroy the city and its important buildings: first they attack at noon and then at night (both unusual moves, for surprise?). In between their words of attack comes the Israelites' lament (cf. the Philistines, 1 Sam 4:7-8); whatever their success in the daytime, the night is coming when they stand little chance.

God's next words (vv. 6-7) are a call to action by the Babylonian armies (as in 5:10; as God will later call Babylon's enemies, 50:14-16, 29). Babylon is God's agent in this situation, but they constitute a real threat and their reflections count. God even makes clear to them that "this is the city" that must be destroyed, urging that trees be cut to make a ramp up the side of the city walls and thereby enter the embattled city. In lament-like tones, God also identifies for Babylon the reasons why this is happening. The city is filled with oppressive, violent, and destructive people! And the effects of this violence ("sickness and wounds"; healed in 30:12, 17) continually come before God in the cries of the poor and needy (see 5:26-28). Israel digs deep into their imaginations to devise ever new and fresh ways to pursue their wickedness, just like ever fresh water bubbles up from deep within a well. Israel's well for generating such behaviors is bottomless. In this catalog of Israel's sins, it is as if God wants to clarify for the Babylonians why the city is being given over to them; they are the instruments of *God's* judgment in this endeavor.

Once again, the warning call goes out to Jerusalem (v. 8), essentially a repeat of the warning of v. 1 to flee the city, to which only a few would respond. This seems not to be some last ditch call to avoid disaster; it may have the object to save a few for the sake of less than a "full end" (see 5:10, 18). At best, some response on their part might soften a blow that is certainly coming (the call in v. 8, usually translated "take warning," could be translated "take corrective action" or the like, see NEB). The phrase in v. 8, translated in the NRSV as "in disgust," may rather have a more anguished sense of God's "soul" (commonly translated "I") being wrenched away or painfully estranged (see NEB; as does God's/Jeremiah's "heart, soul" in 4:19). God's warning may have exilic readers in view, recalling such sorrowful words from God.

Prophetic Weariness, 6:9-15

An interchange between God and Jeremiah centers this segment (cf. 5:1-9). The identity of the one addressed in v. 9 is not altogether clear, however; the plural verb ("they shall glean," NRSV footnote) is combined with a singular verb ("pass your hand"). Verse 9 is probably addressed to Jeremiah in view of his response in vv. 10-11a, but the verse could also be another call to Babylon (see v. 6; 5:10). Both agents may be in view. Using the metaphor of the harvest of the vineyard (see Isa 5:1-7), they are to harvest the "remnant of Israel," that is, those who remain after the first onslaught in 597 BC, as a farmer would go over his vineyard and gather every last grape. This may be a more complete harvest than that envisaged in 5:10. To that end, Jeremiah is to use words—the Babylonians, the sword. An alternative interpretation of v. 9 would be that Jeremiah is to preach so as to save at least a remnant from the vineyard that will be destroyed.[1]

Jeremiah is the speaker of vv. 10-11a (NEB extends his words to v. 12a). As has been made clear in 5:21-23 (see **Connections** there), and as Jeremiah here realizes, the people can no longer respond positively to the word of the LORD (a point reiterated in 7:26-27). So, Jeremiah wonders, probably in some anguish: who is

Full of Wrath

AΩ This language is to be related to the image of Jeremiah's eating the word that God gives him (1:9; 15:16-17; cf. Ezek 2:8–3:3). The most basic dimension of that God-given word is wrath. To be full of wrath means that there is no room in him for any other kind of word from God (as in 15:17; see the image of fire in 20:9; 5:14). He has held back from proclaiming this hard word; he has not wanted to speak it. But he has become weary in holding it back and can no longer do so (as in 20:9). He must get that word out. In this regard he has become conformed to God's own situation (15:6); just as God has become weary of holding back, so also has God's prophet. Weariness is characteristic of both prophet and God, and so is wrath. This should not be interpreted in terms of a clinical compulsion, but of a sense of call that must be fulfilled (see **Connections**, ch. 20).

---

left to listen to what he has to say? They have ears, but cannot hear (5:21; see Isa 6:9; **Connections**, ch. 5). Their ears are closed (lit., uncircumcised; the call in 4:4 proved fruitless). God's word is no longer for them a word of life, a word in which they take pleasure; it is simply an object of scorn. They loathe the word of God! In view of this situation, Jeremiah is full of God's wrath and can hold it back no longer. [Full of Wrath]

God responds to Jeremiah in vv. 11b-12. The "I" of Jeremiah (v. 11a) is elided with the "I" of God (v. 12). God commands Jeremiah to speak this word of wrath even though no one listens. Jeremiah's words are dynamic in that their articulation participates in the actual pouring out of the divine wrath (see 25:15; 10:25, where Jeremiah makes the same request of God; see **Connections** in chs. 4; 25 on wrath). His words are effective in furthering the judgment. Yet Jeremiah does not act alone; his word is not efficacious apart from the continuing activity of God. God's "I" remains a subject as God stretches out a hand against Israel (note the link between God's hand and that of Jeremiah in v. 9). Moreover, a third agency is involved as the "others" (v. 12a; the Babylonian armies) take over the land (see **Connections** in chs. 4; 13 on the issues of agency). In the tradition, God's stretching out a hand has been associated with Israel's salvation (e.g., Deut 26:8); here it is associated with judgment (this theme reappears in 15:6).

The inclusiveness of the object of God's word through Jeremiah is remarkable (6:11b-12; see Ezek 9:6). God's answer to Jeremiah's question of v. 10a includes children, married couples, young and old, indeed the very old (a comparable list occurs at v. 21). It includes the houses, fields, and wives of the male population (v. 12a; see Deut 5:21); this devastation is not simply focused on the male armies. Every person will be adversely affected, and everything they have will be taken away. The inclusion of children in this list is troubling; indeed, they are the first ones mentioned as the object of divine wrath (see **Connections: Children and Wives as Objects of God's Wrath**).

Verses 13-15 (essentially repeated in 8:10b-12) again speak the indictment (vv. 13-15a; cf. vv. 6b-7) and the announcement of judgment (v. 15b). The indictment begins with reference to economic injustice, a specific effect of the neglect and scorn of God's word (v. 10). *Everyone* (see v. 11) is scheming for more money, even if it is (knowingly or unknowingly) built upon the backs of the less fortunate. Israel's leaders ("from prophet to priest" is inclusive of the elite) are engaged in the same enterprise, even though it may involve fraud. Moreover, these leaders are false and have no real sense for the depths of Israel's problem. "It's really not so bad!" The challenge to the claim of "peace" (or, possibly, health) pertains both to a word about relationships with Babylon and an assurance of "peace in our time" (see ch. 28) and a personal and communal sickness of heart (see 3:22; 8:22)—the two of which are related. Israel's wounds are deep, indeed fatal, and these religious leaders treat them in an offhanded way (see 5:30-31). The situation calls for open-heart surgery, and they are applying band-aids! [The Prophets of Peace]

This sharp indictment is directed against the prophets in particular and becomes a virtual refrain in the book (e.g., 4:10; 8:11; 14:13; 23:17). They ought to be ashamed for acting so shamefully; and God names their activities with the strong term "abominations" (see 4:1). In a remarkable image, they do not even know how to blush. That is, their abominable activities had become so much a part of their personal identity that the normal human response in the wake of such shameful behaviors was not forthcoming. So ingrained was their sin that (appropriate) shame had disappeared from their lives. They had lost any reference point outside themselves (e.g., the Law) by which their shame might be recognized. The announcement of judgment follows (v. 15b; "therefore"). These leaders will not be exempted when judgment overthrows Israel; they will fall with everyone else. Once again, the inadequate translation "punish" (NRSV) or "punishment" (NAB) renders the verb *pāqad*, "visit" (see [Questions for Exiles] and **Introduction**). The

The Prophets of Peace

"It is unlikely that the false prophets were shameless charlatans. They were presumably sincere patriots, ardent lovers of the people and zealous in their devotion to state and sanctuary. They as well as the leaders of the state, who had the interest of the country at heart, resented the invectives and exaggerated accusations of Jeremiah and entertained a profound trust in God's attachment to Israel."

The leaders of Israel and certainly the general populace no doubt appreciated the optimism of these prophets and felt assured that they had their best interests at heart. These prophets were considered upstanding members of their community and certainly their sincerity was seldom challenged. Might it be the case in any society, including North America, that only the optimistic leaders are given a hearing and treated with respect? Those who are sharply critical of our most honored sacred and secular traditions and speak out sharply against them are consigned by most citizens to the realm of cranks, there to join Jeremiah.

Abraham Heschel, *The Prophets* (New York: Haper, 1962), 482.

idea is that God will return *their* shameful wickedness back upon their own heads.

Forsaking the Ancient Paths, 6:16-21

Once again, the rhythm of indictment and announcement of judgment (vv. 18, 21, "therefore") shapes this poetic segment (see [The Structure of Jeremiah 6] for the structure of these verses). Verses 16-17 seem to be addressed to exilic readers, recalling the history between Israel and God; God's call to tend to the tradition continues to be pertinent for readers. Will they respond as their forebears have? The verses state the indictment in general, rather than specific, terms by recalling the word that God has provided in the past and how the people have rejected it (vv. 16b, 17b).

God has provided both the Law (v. 16a) and the prophets (v. 17a). For the first, the metaphor of travel on roads is used. The exilic readers are asked to recall how God had invited those who had wandered off onto byroads (18:15; see 7:23-24) to return to the main road on which they had long ago begun their journey (2:2). If they would be alert and inquire regarding long-established, God-given directions for travel, they would see where the good and proper paths are, and this would lead them to rest and refreshment (see Matt 11:29). The phrase "ancient paths" gathers up the themes of God's gracious activity manifest in salvation at the sea, sustenance through the wilderness, and the giving of the Law. The Law was not given apart from God's salvific actions that initiated the journey and sustained the people along the way. But the people refused to walk on the paths provided for the journey (as in 2:20, 25, 31).

Sentinel's Tower
The fortifications of ancient cities typically included a sentinel's tower that granted defenders a commanding view of the roads or plains lying before the walls.

The metaphor of sentinels (v. 17), those who are alert to threats to a city and provide warning through the blowing of the trumpet (see 4:5, 19, 21; 6:1), has reference to the prophets in particular (see Ezek 3:16-21; Hos 9:8). Once again, God's graciousness is evident, warning the people of possible threats to their life. But again, even after having heard the trumpet sound associated with war, they ignore it (see 7:25-26).

These rejections of God's gracious provisions along the journey of Israel's life issue in an announcement of judgment (v. 18;

Offerings in 6:20

Frankincense is an aromatic gum resin obtained from trees of the genus *Boswellia*, used for incense and perfume (Exod 30:34-38; Song 4:6, 14). It is indigenous to southern Arabia, where Sheba was located (see 1 Kgs 10). Sweet cane is the hollow stem of certain grasses or reeds that yield sweet scents and oils. "Burnt offerings and sacrifices" are general terms for a variety of temple offerings. Through the priest, God accepted what the worshiper brought to the sanctuary. By declaring that these expensive offerings are not acceptable, God thereby overrules whatever decisions the priests may have made; no doubt, priests would have declared these pricey offerings acceptable without much reflection.

Frankincense tree. (Credit: Brewton-Parker College)

"therefore"). God calls upon the other nations (!) to hear "the testimony" (rather than NRSV, "congregation," possibly a reference to exilic readers) just reported in vv. 16-17 in the people's own obstinate words; they will shape coming events (NRSV, "what will happen to them"). God also calls upon the earth (v. 19) to hear the word that God is going to bring disaster (*rāʿāh)*. In other words, all other human (nations) and nonhuman (earth; see 2:12; Isa 1:2; Mic 6:1-2) creatures are called upon to listen to the judgment that God will bring against the people and the reasons (testimony) for the disaster. The disaster God will bring is specifically cited as "the fruit of their schemes" (see Prov 1:31). That is, disaster (*rāʿāh)* grows like fruit out of their iniquities (often *rāʿāh*), named here as the people's inattention to God's word and their rejection of God's instruction. God does not introduce the disaster into the situation; rather, God sees to the moral order and mediates the consequences ("fruit") of the people's wickedness (see **Introduction**).

The rhythm of indictment and announcement of judgment continues in vv. 20-21. In the direct question of v. 20a, to which God responds (v. 20b), God rejects the sacrifices that Israel has brought (see 7:21-23; Isa 1:11; 43:24). [Offerings in 6:20] Even more, given the "therefore" that follows in v. 21, these offerings are considered a reason for judgment! The people had gone to great lengths to make sure that they had the best of offerings; they had imported products from distant lands—no doubt at great expense. Perhaps the reason they had made such efforts was to appease the wrath of God (see 2:35; 3:5). [Sacrifice and Appeasement]

God's "therefore" (in the third person, "this people") issues in a striking judgment (v. 21; see Hos 4:5; Isa 8:14-15, where God himself is the stumbling block!). God is going to set up unnamed

Sacrifice and Appeasement

One basic reason that God gave Israel its sacrificial system was to provide a regular means whereby the people could receive life, blessing, and forgiveness. Sacrifices and offerings were not most fundamentally an act of the people, but a rite in and through which God could act on behalf of faithful worshipers. The people's faithfulness was important, for the efficacy of the offerings and sacrifices was a tangible sign of faith, a highly concrete way in which believers could offer themselves to God. But it was God's actions in and through these concrete actions that made them effective for new life. Sacrifices were not a means by which Israel sought to wring blessing out of a reluctant God or to appease or placate the divine anger; they were not given for God, but for the people. Yet, while appeasement was a foreign idea in Israel's sacrificial system, people no doubt often fell into such an understanding (as is true of worship practices in every age). The text at 6:20 (see at 7:1-11; 21-22) may reflect a worship situation where the faithfulness of the worshiper was considered irrelevant to sacrificial efficacy.

---

roadblocks or obstacles so as to make sure *everyone* (cf. v. 11) stumbles and falls and, finally, perishes. This is anything but a call to repentance; at *this juncture* in their history together, God is going to make sure that they do *not* find a way to return to a faithful relationship. The build-up of the effects of evil is too extensive for that; the only way into the future for this people is through fall and devastation. They will have to plummet over the falls (see **Connections** at ch. 5). Exilic readers, having gone over the falls, can only rest back in the promise that God will not make a full end of them and will, in time, come and pick them up from the rocks.

The Invaders Advance and Israel Reels, 6:22-26

The agent of God's judgment is more closely and terrifyingly described in vv. 22-23 (see vv. 1-8; 50:41-43 adapts vv. 22-24 for a foe of Babylon, so that it becomes a salvation oracle for Israel). The foe from the north (Babylon, for readers) is a great nation, a faraway people, but they are now close at hand. They are well equipped, with the best in weapons and horses; they are cruel and will have no pity on the Israelites (see 13:14; 21:7). There are so many of them that their movements sound like the roaring of the sea. Then comes the climactic word: "Against you, O daughter Zion." This phrase, with its sense of "beautiful child," reveals the divine pathos that lies behind this sharp word of judgment.

In vv. 24-26 two voices are heard from the midst of the onslaught from the north. The people speak in vv. 24-25; Jeremiah speaks in v. 26, including himself ("my") among the people ("us"). The people's words bespeak helplessness, anguish, and sheer terror in the face of the advancing armies (for the phrase "terror is on every side," see 20:3-4, 10). There is no escape! Their pain is likened to that of a woman in labor (see 4:31; 30:6; a metaphor for *divine* pain in Isa 42:14). Many exilic readers would no doubt recognize their personal experience in these words. Jeremiah responds by commending rites of lamentation and mourning (v. 26; as in 4:8; cf. 25:34; Amos 8:10). These prayers are not penitential laments (e.g., Ps 51), nor are they rituals of deliverance (e.g., Joel 1:13-14). The time for such rites has passed; the irresistible destroyer is already in the midst of the people. The response to be made is a dirge (as in 9:17-22); it assumes a death, a death filled with suffering and pain; it is as if an only child has been killed. The lovely city of Jerusalem, filled with God's chosen people, is as good as dead. These rituals may in fact have been an experience of postdestruction readers (see Lamentations).

Tested and Rejected, 6:27-30

God's response in v. 27 is directed to Jeremiah personally. God has called him to be a tester of the people of Israel as they move through the refining fires of judgment (see 1:18; Zech 13:9; Mal 3:3). God is the tester elsewhere (e.g., 9:6; 17:10), so that Jeremiah is here recognized as having been given a role that God plays. This dimension of the prophetic call may be linked to 1:5, where Jeremiah is appointed as a prophet to the nations. Like an assayer of the quality of ore, Jeremiah is to determine what will become of the people's character and fidelity under fire (alternatively, to separate the righteous from the wicked). Will the fire serve to refine the people so that they emerge as a renewed people? No, they are too set in their ways so that the silver, that is there (!), cannot be separated out from the dross and can only be rejected.[2]

Verses 28-30 assume that the task of v. 27 has been completed and announce the results; as such, these verses could be said to summarize the previous chapters. The call of Jeremiah has now come full turn, and v. 28 announces the results. These verses are spoken either by Jeremiah or by God. The people cannot be saved, because "all" of them (see 5:1) are stubborn and rebellious; everything they say ("slanders") and do is corrupt. They are so hardened in their ways that they are likened to "bronze and iron" (see **Connections**, ch. 5). The fire of judgment through which they pass is fierce; even a metal such as lead (usually found in silver ore) is consumed by the heat. But the refining process has no salutary effect on this wicked people; finally, the pure metal cannot be separated out in the refining process (see Isa 1:22). They are so wicked that no good use can be made of them, and the tester decides that they can only be discarded as "rejected silver"; in fact, they are rejected by God (see 7:29). The previous verses also make clear, however, that rejection does not mean a "full end" (4:27; 5:10, 18). God finds it necessary to drive the people over the falls to their death; their only hope for the future lies not in what they do or say, but in what *God* does for them. Only the catastrophic fires of judgment and God's creation of a new heart (see 24:7; 32:39) will make a future possible.

CONNECTIONS

Children and Wives as the Objects of God's Wrath

The inclusion of children (playing in the streets!) in a list of those who are the *object* of God's judgment is troubling (v. 12; see v. 21; 9:21; 18:21; 19:9). The text states not simply that children will suffer the effects of the judgment on the community, but that they themselves are singled out for judgment. In God's own words: "Pour it out on the children!" Jeremiah seems to have learned both his rhetoric and its content from God, for a comparable word is heard in his laments (18:21); in that text he calls upon God to give the children of his adversaries over to famine and the sword. This proves to be no rhetorical flourish, as we know from the reality of the destruction itself and its absolutely devastating effect on children (see Lam 1:5, 16; 2:19-21; 4:4, 10; cf. 2 Kgs 6:28-29; Isa 49:26; Ezek 5:10).

Why should children be the object of the wrath of God, let alone suffer for what adults have done? They certainly are undeserving of such suffering. Perhaps one can translate Jeremiah 6:11 so that Jeremiah becomes the subject of the verb: "I must pour it out" (so REB), but that translation option seems an effort to take an easy way out. One can certainly recognize that this material is written in the light of actual experience, whether of the fall of Jerusalem itself or other such military campaigns. One can place this text in an ancient context and bemoan how war was waged in that time. At the same time, we know very well that this way of waging war is a not uncommon modern phenomenon!

The understanding of the wrath of God in more impersonal terms is certainly to be taken into account here (see at 4:4; **Introduction**). Certainly one is to recognize that cannibalism is mentioned in traditional treaty curses (see Lev 26:29; Deut 28:53-57). Certainly this kind of rhetoric is present in the psalms

---

On Being Critical of the Bible

However helpful such comments may be in trying to rationalize what happens to the children, standing squarely before us is the command of God to pour out wrath on the children. Why should children be the *specific* object of the wrath of God, made to suffer for what adults have done? Do not readers have to be critical of the tradition at this point (or even God, if one thinks it to be a direct quote from God)? Should not readers, with great care, stand over against the Bible on matters such as these? Certainly most people would be critical of, say, a modern general who gave his soldiers orders to kill children. Many have recognized that one has to be critical of the patriarchy of the biblical material. Should not greater recognition of the problem of violence in the Bible, evident in this text, be current among its readers? This issue is recognized, at least implicitly, by those who have made choices regarding lectionary texts; texts such as these are not usually read on occasions of public worship. That is a passive response, however. Should not the issue be confronted more directly, not only with respect to the Bible but also in interaction with God? In so doing, readers could stand in the tradition of Abraham (Gen 18:23-25) and Moses (Exod 32:9-13), who brought sharp questions before God regarding the use of violence. And God received these questions without condemning those who spoke them.

---

of imprecation (Pss 109:9-10; 137:9), and even in Jeremiah's laments (e.g., Jer 18:21-23). Certainly we do not want to insist that speakers of laments be held to careful theological formulations and niceties; hurting persons must be allowed to pour out their anger at such times, regardless of the theological fallout. And perhaps we should allow for this in the laments of God as well; God is deeply pained by what has happened to this relationship, with all the sorrow and anger that goes with the breakdown of a relationship of intimacy. But if we do so, then we must tell it like it really is for God, and not dismiss such words by easy appeals to divine mystery. One approach to such language is to say that such divine words are designed to make readers uncomfortable, to get inside them and show what their sin has wrought; to try to escape from the force of the text, that is a typical sinner's response. Yet, it is one thing to be told that our sin has had incredibly negative effects upon the children of the world; it is something else to be told that God commands the abuse.[On Being Critical of the Bible]

A plausible, if not finally satisfactory, response relates to the interconnectedness of life. This is a *communal* judgment; once unleashed, the Babylonian armies will cut down everyone and everything in their path. When it comes to war, everyone, including children, will suffer. Moreover, such agents are not under the control of God, as is evident from God's judgment on Babylon for its overreaching and pride (see 25:11-14; 50:29; 51:24). When it comes to the reality of communal judgment in any time or place, all human beings, regardless of station in life, will be caught up in

Dresden, WW II
During World War II, the
German city of Dresden
was bombed with
incendiary bombs that
resulted in the destruction
of much of the city and the
loss of many civilian lives,
though the city itself was
considered to be of no
strategic importance.

(Credit: The Churchill Society)

the devastation (e.g., the indiscriminate way in which bombs fell on cities like Dresden, Germany in World War II).[3]

Also present in these verses is the pillaging of property; according to v. 12, this includes not only fields, but wives (repeated even more directly in 8:10, with God as explicit subject). Wives were raped in the fall of Jerusalem (Lam 5:11); this text suggests that God, in announcing judgment in these terms, consigns them to such a fate (cf. the divine word of judgment about David's wives in 2 Sam 12:11; they are given over to his neighbors, and their rape is one of the consequences). A response to this form of God's violence needs to be comparable to that raised above regarding children.

NOTES

1 See William McKane, *A Critical and Exegetical Commentary on Jeremiah* (2 vols.; ICC; Edinburgh: T. & T. Clark, 1986), 144-45.

2 See William Holladay, *Jeremiah 1* (Philadelphia: Fortress, 1986), 230-32, on the details of the refining process.

3 For further reflection on this issue, see Terence Fretheim, "The Portrayal of God in Jeremiah," forthcoming.

THE TEMPLE SERMON

7:1–8:3

This segment is commonly said to consist of various prose speeches (e.g., 7:1-15, 16-20, 21-26, 7:27–8:3), but they have now been integrated into a single tapestry. With a few breaks (see vv. 16, 27), the whole should be considered a communication from God to prophet, who is never said to have actually delivered it (contrast ch. 26).

[Jeremiah 7: A Gathering Chapter]

Three divine commands to Jeremiah punctuate the segment (vv. 2, 16, 27-28a), the last two of which inform the sense of the first (Jeremiah does not speak in this chapter). Jeremiah is to speak, but the people will not listen; Jeremiah is not to pray for them, for God will not listen (šmʿ ["listen"] occurs eight times in the chapter). God will not listen anymore because the people have persistently not listened to God (see Isa 59:2). The people of Israel are both directly addressed in the second person (vv. 2-15, 17, 21-25, 29) and referred to in the third person (vv. 18-20, 26, 28-34; 8:1-3; see [The Audience as "You" and "Them"] on this mixture for the sake of exilic readers). In this context, the third person could give evidence of a divine distancing from people and place, reinforced by the use of the phrase "this people" (vv. 16, 33; still "my people" in v. 12) and the accompanying horrors of judgment.

> **Jeremiah 7: A Gathering Chapter**
>
> This chapter is startling in its spiraling movement toward a deathly end. It proceeds from the people gathered at the temple in seeming security, to stark images of death with corpses strewn about the Jerusalem area, to the exile of a fearful few. In some sense the chapter presents the story of the people of Israel, from lively possibilities for a good life on a promised land (vv. 3-7), to resistance, death, and captivity. This chapter might be called a gathering chapter, pulling together some of the key elements from chs. 2–6 and propelling the reader forward into still further indictments and announcements of judgment in chs. 8–10, at which point another gathering prose segment will revisit some of these themes (11:1-17).

The purpose of this chapter is to bring together in a focused way the most basic reasons for the fall and exile of the people of Israel that have been rehearsed in poetic form in chapters 2–6 (per the question of 5:19 and elsewhere). In order to make this point as clear as possible, the chapter progresses at several levels. At one level, the chapter centers on matters relating to worship. Various forms of worship, whether formally appropriate or blatantly idolatrous, are shown to be bankrupt. Where the worship forms may be appropriate (the temple), the understanding of them has deteriorated into a meaningless mantra (see v. 4). Where the worship forms are idolatrous, there seem to be no boundaries to religious imagination and practice, from the worship of various gods and goddesses to child sacrifice (vv. 18, 30-31; 8:2).

At another level, the chapter presents a historical perspective on these matters. The present crisis is not something unusual, but is part and parcel of a long history of failure (vv. 23-26). The people's refusal to listen can be traced back to their earliest days (see 2:5-7), and their history has been punctuated by earlier crises of the same order (v. 12). Indeed, stubbornness, an evil will, resistance, and turning a deaf ear to God have characterized their entire life. But this survey not only rehearses what the people have done, but it also focuses on God's story with this people. God has been remarkably patient, persistently sending prophets to turn them around, desiring to be their God so that it could go well with them. The problem has not been with God's speaking and acting, but with their (not) listening and doing. That God is deeply pained by these developments has been evident in what has preceded (e.g., 2:29-31; 3:19-20) and will be even more evident in the texts that follow (e.g., 8:4-7, 18-22; 9:10, 17-19). At still another level, the chapter presents an almost insurmountable disjunction for readers, with its combination of exhortation and disaster (see **Connections: The Disjunction between Exhortation and Finality of Judgment**).

COMMENTARY

The Temple of the Lord, 7:1-15

Jeremiah 7:1-15 consists of oracles that God commands Jeremiah to give at the entrance to the temple precincts (=gate of the LORD's house, v. 2). These verses are often called "the temple sermon," though only God speaks here. A shorter version (with a somewhat different focus) appears in 26:1-6, where the sermon is dated at the beginning of the reign of Jehoiakim (609 BC), shortly after the death of King Josiah and the deposing of his son Jehoahaz (who ruled for only three months). From 609–605 BC, Israel was under Egyptian control. The specific occasion for the sermon may have been the celebration of a festival, probably Tabernacles, at which time pilgrims came from various parts of the land to worship at the temple. If so, God commissions Jeremiah to deliver this sermon in a very public place to crowds of people.

In vv. 3-7, God (through Jeremiah) calls upon the people to amend their "ways and doings" (an instance of merismus; see also in 18:11; 26:13). The last half of v. 3 is grammatically ambiguous (as is the similar formulation in v. 7). It could have reference to God's presence in the temple: Amend your ways . . . so that I may dwell (or remain) with you in this place (so NAB; cf. NRSV, "and let me dwell with you in this place"). God's staying is dependent on what Israel does, or Israel by its infidelities could drive God away from the temple (see Ezek 8:6). The text could also be construed to mean the following (NRSV footnote): Amend your ways . . . and I will let *you* [the people] dwell in this place, that is, remain in the land rather than go into exile. On this point the speech comes to a close, namely, being cast out of the land (v. 15). A third possibility[1] is to read v. 3 in terms of the first possibility and v. 7 in terms of the second; "this place" is interpreted to mean "temple" in v. 3 and "land" in v. 7.

Most likely, the phrasing in both verses is purposely ambiguous; the one reading focuses on the temple and God's presence; the other focuses on the people's presence in the land. These matters are integrally connected, as vv. 14-15 make clear; both God's presence in the temple and the people's presence in the land are adversely affected by Israel's infidelity. Both God and people leave temple and land. In any case, in the present context of vv. 1-15, what seem like future possibilities (vv. 3-7) have in fact been reduced to one (vv. 14-15): God and people are going to leave "this place," no ifs, ands, or buts (see **Connections: The Disjunction between Exhortation and Finality of Judgment**).

To his announcements of judgment, Jeremiah no doubt often faced this mantra-like response: This is the temple of the Lord (the Hebrew, "they are" [NRSV footnote], probably refers to the various temple buildings). [The Temple of the Lord] Nothing evil can happen to us (as the prophets kept reminding them, 5:12; 6:14)! God will protect us, come what may! But Jeremiah twice pronounces these words "deceptive words"; they conceal a lie (vv. 4, 8; the judgment also placed on the words of the prophets, 14:13-16). That is, the words deceive people into thinking that they are secure, protected from any disaster, regardless of what they say or do (see the comparable formulation in Mic 3:11). Verse 14 reinforces v. 4 in identifying the "deceptive words" in which Israel had come to "trust" (so also v. 8). Israel had come to "trust" in the temple as "a

The Temple of the LORD

The temple enjoyed a central place in the lives of Israelites, and it had become for many a tangible sign of God's continuing favor toward them. In and of itself this was not a problem; think of Josiah's concern for the centralization of the sanctuary in Jerusalem (2 Kgs 23). The people of Israel, however, had also come to believe that the temple (and the city of Jerusalem) was inviolable. That is, because God dwelt in this place, God would protect it (and the people who lived there) from all harm. The heart of the issue is not that the people thought that the temple was God's dwelling place (or called by God's name, v. 10). God had chosen to dwell in this place (1 Kgs 8:12-13); indeed, it was God's *desire* to dwell in this place (Ps 132). The theological problem was that the temple itself became an object of trust and was thought to be a talisman—a charm, a rabbit's foot, a medal of St. Christopher on the dashboard—capable of averting any harm that might threaten their way of life. But the temple (and the city) was not to be confused with the God who dwelt there, as if God's own future were tied to the continued existence of this building. As if to demonstrate this point, that in which they trust will be blown away and no longer be available for their trusting. Misplaced trust issues in disaster for all.

The luxurious appearance of the temple has captured the imagination of artists for centuries. This illustration shows the overall epic grandeur of the temple.

Reconstruction of the Temple of Solomon.
(Credit: Foto Marburg/Art Resource)

safe place" (see v. 10), as a point of "eternal security," rather than in the God who had deigned to dwell in that place.

The admonition of v. 3 is spelled out in more detail in vv. 5-7, and the phrase "deceptive words" of v. 4 is repeated in v. 8, with the additional claim that trust in such lies about the efficacy of the temple will gain them nothing. Verses 5-7 specify what it means for Israel to amend its ways and doings. The audience would not be able to escape the point by picking and choosing the ways they wanted to follow. Nor would they be able simply to mouth some words of repentance. First of all, Jeremiah states the issue positively: Amend your ways, and that means you are to act justly with one another. Then Jeremiah speaks in terms of *specific* prohibitions: Do not oppress the resident alien (often, a refugee), orphan, or widow (see Exod 22:21-24; Deut 10:18-19; 24:17-22); do not shed innocent blood in the land ("this place"); and do not go after other gods, which can only have negative consequences ("hurt").

Notable is the claim about the land, from which the exilic readers had been banished. It is still the land of promise that God gave "forever and ever" (v. 7; see 3:18; 11:5; 14:15; 30:3; 32:22). God has not taken that promise back.[2] But those who are unfaithful thereby remove themselves from the sphere of the promise and will not participate in its fulfillment, except perhaps on the far side of a devastating judgment.[3] (For a comparable formulation regarding God's eternal promise regarding the land and the possibility of eviction, see Deut 4:40; 29–30.) This clause provides a word of hope in the midst of judgment; the exiles can cling to the promise, knowing that God will be faithful. Verse 8 is a turning point. The people had been told not to trust in deceptive words (v. 4), but they paid no heed (vv. 25-27; see 18:11-12): "Here [behold!] you are trusting in such words." The specifics of vv. 5-7 have been persistently violated, and Jeremiah now proceeds to specify both indictment (vv. 9-12) and announcement of judgment (vv. 14-15, "therefore").

Verses 9-11 consist of two rhetorical questions that, in effect, state that the persistent call for amendment of life has not been heeded. These comments drip with irony, even sarcasm. In the first question (vv. 9-10), five of the ten commandments (or a collection on the way to becoming the Decalogue), the most basic requirements for Israel in its relationships with God and neighbor, are cited (see Exod 20:1-17; Deut 5:6-21; note the different ordering). They steal, murder, commit adultery, swear falsely, and worship other gods. And, then, even though they have broken commandments right and left, and continue doing so, they have the audacity to come to the temple, stand before God, and claim they are secure from any negative effects their sins might have. This is an ongoing major disconnect that exists between worship and life (note the appeal in 44:17 that Israel "got away with this" over the course of many years!). [Worship and the Neighbor]

One of the major effects of such an understanding of the temple with its worship and ritual is that responsibilities toward the neighbor may be relaxed and seen to be of secondary import. The net effect of this divorce is stated in the second rhetorical question (v. 11). This house (=the temple), called by God's name (note the repeated reference), has become a den of robbers (see Matt 21:13, and Jesus' use of this phrase in his cleansing of the temple—one more time!).

Worship and the Neighbor

The last-named sin—idolatry—is not simply another on a list, but is the climactic issue, just as in vv. 8-9 (it is the focus in vv. 18, 30-31; note the shortened form of this exhortation in 35:15). The relationship with God is the central issue, but not in isolation from life. This relationship cannot be fostered through, say, religious rituals while the needs of the neighbor go unattended. The link between God and the neighbor is indissoluble. If love of neighbor in these *specific* ways is not practiced, that is a sign that the relationship to God has broken down, and religious rituals in and of themselves are of no value (see also Isa 1:10-17; Amos 5:21-24; Mic 6:6-8).

That is, the temple is made analogous to a hideout for robbers, where they could escape from the authorities and not be threatened with arrest. Then, when the coast was clear, they could again sally forth to do their wicked deeds. But while the obtuse religious leaders may not see what is going on, God does. The ominous reference to God's watching (v. 11b) harks back to Jeremiah's call; it is now time for the one who has been watching over his word "to perform it" (1:12).

Verse 12 concludes the questions by providing an object lesson for the people's consideration of these matters. They are called to remember what happened to Shiloh, the first major religious center for Israel in the land of promise (about twenty miles north of Jerusalem); here the ark of the covenant, God's own dwelling place, had been housed (3:16; Josh 21:1-2; 1 Sam 1:1-9). The story of Shiloh's destruction at the hands of the Philistines some 500 years earlier was no doubt an important memory. The point made is not simply to establish a precedent that God *can* do to Jerusalem as God had done to Shiloh. It is more direct: as it was with Shiloh in the wake of Israel's wickedness, so shall it *now* be with Jerusalem. This assertion has the force of saying that the temple in Jerusalem is like the one in Shiloh; thereby Jeremiah "relativizes the Temple of Jerusalem, rendering it one of at least two such shrines, and thus he tacitly destroys the cosmic dimension which is central to its mythos."[4] The people attack Jeremiah for comparing the fates of Shiloh and Jerusalem in 26:6-9, as if the divine rejection of Shiloh in the North was a sign of God's favor toward Jerusalem and the South. In sanctuaries at both Shiloh and Jerusalem, God had deigned to dwell among the people; but God's own home was not inviolable to God. God would prefer to be homeless than dwell among such a people (see 12:7)! The people had come to "trust" in a house (v. 14). Such misplaced trust in God's place on their part meant exclusion from their own place. For God, this mistrust had gotten to the point where there was no turning back—the judgment must now fall.

Verse 13, with its "and now," pulls together the indictment of the previous verses ("all these things") and introduces the announcement of judgment (vv. 14-15; "therefore"). Because Israel has done these things and has not listened to God's word, even though God had spoken persistently (vv. 23-26 make the same point in more detail), the judgment must now fall. The temple, in which the people trust, and the city/land (given to their ancestors) will be destroyed as was Shiloh. And the people will be cast out of the land, indeed out of God's sight, as had happened to the people of

Israel, the northern kingdom (=Ephraim) in 722 BC (see 1 Kgs 9:7; 2 Kgs 17:23).

The Inevitability of Judgment, 7:16–8:3

In 7:16–8:3 God turns to Jeremiah with special words regarding "this people" (vv. 16, 33). The segment consists of two directives to the prophet (vv. 16, 27-28a), each followed by sharp indictments of the people (vv. 17-19, 30-31) and announcements of judgment (vv. 20, 7:32–8:3; "therefore"). Between these two sections stands a word to the people (vv. 21-26, "you"), rehearsing for them the sorry history of their relationship with God. This segment functions as one part of the rationale for the judgment: God has been patient with them for centuries, but no more.

No More Intercession, 7:16-20

God forbids Jeremiah to pray for this people, restating the point in several ways (v. 16; no pleading; no intercession; no pressing the issue). [No More Intercession] God will not listen to such prayers (as in Isa 1:15; 59:2). This command is a motif in the chapters that follow (11:14; 14:11; 15:1 draw a comparison to Moses [Exod 32:10-14] and Samuel [1 Sam 12:23]). This prohibition is linked to the prior judgment on temple ritual and that regarding sacrifice which follows in vv. 21-22; no religious activity can save Israel at this juncture. The rhythmic word about the people's not listening to God in vv. 24-28 is matched by God's not listening to prayer on their behalf. The prohibition indicates that there is no turning back from the judgment that is about to fall (see 4:28). From the perspective of the exilic readers, this communication of God to Jeremiah reveals some of the behind-the-scenes communication that may help to explain aspects of their recent experience.

No More Intercession

For God to prohibit intercessory prayer is striking (see also 11:14; 14:11; 15:1; see [The Covenant]). For one thing, it shows how the situation shapes the divine word to the prophet; the interpreter cannot generalize this prohibition, as though God in every situation would make such a prohibition. This is a command for this particular time and place. At the same time, for exilic readers, this is an important statement about prayer and their understanding of it in their distressful situation. Prayers are not an automatic entry into the divine mind, as though God were bound to respond positively to prayers whenever they are uttered. Prayers are part of a larger relationship between God and people, and the health of that relationship is important in thinking about the communication that is possible between them. (See Samuel Balentine, *Prayer in the Hebrew Bible: The Drama of the Divine-Human Dialogue* [Minneapolis: Fortress, 1993], 38, and his discussion of this chapter and Jesus' use of it, 279-83.)

The factors that stand behind the prohibition are given to Jeremiah in the form of an indictment and an announcement of judgment (vv. 17-20). In the indictment, God asks Jeremiah to observe what the people are doing in their busy, matter-of-fact way—in both Jerusalem and towns. Note the inclusive reference to male and female adults as well as children (see 6:11); it sounds like "family values" with a religious focus!

The Queue of Heaven

This epithet for goddesses known from several ancient Near Eastern sources, often thought to be identified with the Assyro-Babylonian goddess Ishtar (or her Palestinian manifestation Astarte). She was an astral deity, associated with war and fertility. The Canaanite goddess Anat (a consort of Baal) and other goddesses may also be in mind (the various goddesses were likely local manifestations of the same goddess). The people made cakes in the form of stars for the various rituals (44:19 reports that the cakes bore an image of Ishtar). The

Goddess Astarte in a Window. Ivory. From Arslan Tash (Hadatu), Northern Syria. Phoenician. 8th C. BC. (Credit: Erich Lessing/Art Resource)

worship of such goddesses was introduced into Israel by King Manasseh (2 Kgs 21:1-9) and was revived after the death of Josiah. The Queen of Heaven is also the subject of Jeremiah's later words of judgment to refugees of the Babylonian devastation (44:15-30). That a Babylonian deity provides the focus for the indictment, especially in view of the later text, suggests that whatever pertinence these words may have had for a predestruction audience, they are also directed to the exiles themselves and the temptations they would have faced.

Everyone contributes in some way to the worship of "the queen of heaven" (see 19:5, 13; 32:29); even more, the reference to "other gods" suggests that the people are worshiping a pantheon of deities. [The Queen of Heaven] And it all has become such a normal thing to do! In Berrigan's words, "We have the socializing of sin, its mimetic power, the passage of the quite normal, quotidian activities into perilous areas: the normalization of the abnormal . . . the formerly abhorrent has become the norm."[5]

Israel's infidelity has provoked God to anger. Yet v. 19 seems to contradict this divine claim (and the judgment of v. 20). God states that the people have not really provoked (NAB "hurt") him, but they have provoked themselves "to their own hurt" (NRSV). The latter phrase more literally carries the sense of "to shame their face" (see the theme of shame in 2:26, 36; 3:25; 9:19). The verse does not claim that God has not been provoked to anger at all, but that the people's provocation has had a more severe effect on themselves. [Divine Anger]

Verse 20 moves to the announcement of judgment. God's anger and wrath (note the intensification in the repetition) will burn; it will not be quenched, but will be poured out on "this place" and all living things—people, animals, vegetation. The language of "pour out" is used for divine anger elsewhere (see [Divine Anger]). The Hebrew word for "pour out" in v. 18 is a synonym for that translated "pour out" in v. 20; a "what goes around, comes around" understanding of divine wrath is understood here, facilitated by the point in v. 19. The people have poured out their offerings to other gods, and hence God's anger is poured out against them.

A History of Disobedience, 7:21-26

These additional words of indictment are given by God to Jeremiah to be delivered to the people (so v. 27). These verses set up a contrast between the offering of sacrifices and walking in God's commandments. God's words about sacrifices are sarcastic (see Amos 4:4-5). The invitation to add sacrifices to what they are already offering, probably to God as well as to other gods (v. 18), implies that they can offer as many as they want and it will not do them any good. In fact, such practice will hasten the day of judgment, for it will establish them even more in their infidelity (see **Connections: The Disjunction between Exhortation and Finality of Judgment**). Inasmuch as God did not command the sacrifices in the first place, the practices in and of themselves would not constitute disobedience; it would only be so if other gods were involved (see vv. 9, 18).

Verse 23 seems to take back the point made in v. 22. One might claim that sacrificial acts are included in the Law as part of the "walk only in the way that I command you." But they are not. At

---

Divine Anger

This statement in vv. 18-20 reflects how the divine anger actually works. It is not that God's anger is essentially responsible for the shame and judgment that the people suffer. The people's actions are responsible for these effects; in other words, their shame and suffering are intrinsic to the deed. Note that the anger of God is *provoked*. This kind of language for divine anger is common in Jeremiah (8:19; 11:17; 25:6-7; 32:29-32; 44:3, 8; uniquely, NAB translates 7:18 "in order to hurt me") and reveals several things about God. For one, God is affected, moved, by what the people do. For another, it reveals that anger is not an attribute of God, as if anger were no different than, say, love. Rather, God's anger is contingent. If there were no sin, there would be no divine anger. To say that God is always angry, that anger is integral to the divine identity (just as love is), is finally to fall back into a kind of dualism.

God's wrath being "poured out" (7:20; also 6:11; 10:25; 42:18; 44:6) provides another insight into the divine anger. While there is a personal dimension to God's anger, the divine wrath is also impersonally conceived in Jeremiah (and elsewhere, e.g., Num 1:53; 16:46). Wrath is not only "poured out," but it also "goes forth" because of the people's wickedness (*rāʿāh*, 4:4 = 21:12), like "a whirling tempest" (23:19), "is not turned away" (4:8; 23:20), and "bursts upon" the head of the wicked (23:19). Moreover, wrath is like fire that burns (4:4; 7:20; 15:14; 17:4; 21:12; 44:6). In this way of thinking, wrath is an effect that grows out of a violation of the moral order of God's creation. God's personal anger may be said to be a "seeing to" this movement from deed to consequence that is the moral order (see **Connections** at chs. 4 and 25).

the same time, the absence of such a commandment does not narrow the Law down to moral behavior, as if no ritual commands of any sort are in view. For the people to "obey my voice" is comprehensive, touching all areas of life (see 11:4). The promise "I will be your God, and you shall be my people" is traditional language (e.g., Lev 26:3, 12) and is a refrain in the Book of Consolation (e.g., 30:22), where it functions in a different way in view of the unconditional promise of a new covenant (31:31-34). [How Is Obedience a Condition?]

How Is Obedience a Condition?

The point made here is not that obedience is the condition for Israel to *become* God's people and for God to *become* their God. The tradition recognizes again and again that the people are already God's people before the Law is given (e.g., "let my people go," Exod 1–15). This language carries this sense: Obey my voice, and you will *continue* to be my people. Through infidelity, manifested in disobedience, the people can remove themselves from the sphere of the relationship and its promises. This point is also evident in the phrase, "so that it may be well with you" (language common to Deuteronomy, e.g., 5:33). This is a common motivation given for obeying the Law; for it to "be well with you" is an effect of faithfulness, not necessarily or inevitably, but in general terms.

In vv. 24-26, God specifies that Israel has not listened to God's voice, from the very day that they came out of Egypt (yet, cf. 2:2; see Deut 29–30 for a comparable testimony). This behavior is habitual (and hence God would not listen to prayers on their behalf, v. 16). Again and again—"day after day"!—God has sent "my servants the prophets" to turn them back to the Lord (2 Chr 36:15-16), but they did not listen to that way of mediating the voice of God either. They paid attention to neither the Law nor the prophets (so also at 6:16-17). They turned away from God (=backward) rather than toward God in repentance (as in 2:27). The stubbornness of their "evil (*ra*ʿ) will" and the stiff necks of the people are especially cited (see **Connections**, ch. 5). They follow their own wills rather than the will of the Lord; in fact, it has gotten to the point where no other way of life is possible for them (see at 2:25; 18:12). More recent generations were more stubborn than earlier ones (v. 26); this may be a reference to those who experienced the fall of Jerusalem, but the identity of the "they" that "did worse than" is not made entirely clear. Such a story of Israel's past, especially its most recent past, would clarify for the exilic readers some of the issues that have been at stake for God.

A Horrific Judgment, 7:27–8:3

God tells Jeremiah to speak "all these words" (=vv. 1-26, in the present form of the text) to Israel, but signals to him in advance that they will not listen (v. 27), as has been the case heretofore (6:10, 17; 7:13). (see **Connections: The Disjunction between Exhortation and Finality of Judgment**). Then Jeremiah is called to announce to Israel (v. 28) a kind of final declaration of its situation before God. Israel has not obeyed God and has rejected discipline (see 2:30; 5:3); faithfulness (NAB, see 5:1; NRSV "truth") has disappeared from Israel's life and is no longer evident in what they say. In view of this situation, and drawing on a poetic piece from an unknown source (v. 29), God declares this *generation* of Israelites (importantly, not Israel itself!) to be rejected and subject to wrath. But note that wrath is not the only word for this moment, as God calls for lamentation; grief is the godward side of wrath. As a sign of mourning, God calls on Jerusalem imaged as a woman ("your" is feminine singular) to cut off its hair (see 16:6) and raise a dirge/elegy over the death of Israel (see 6:26; 9:17-21; 31:15). The people, and this directive would also be pertinent to exiled readers, are to lament on the "bare heights," which is where their infidelities were practiced (3:2, 21). The point is similar to the irony of v. 21; as they continue in their idolatrous practices, they should incorporate rites of lamentation.

Once again, reasons for this judgment are specified, which set in motion still another sequence of indictment (7:30-31) and announcement of judgment (7:32–8:3). Israel has done evil (*ra*ᶜ) in God's sight by setting up abominable idols and associated objects (see 4:1; 13:27) in the temple, thereby desecrating the holy place (see 32:34-35). Moreover, they have built the shrine (=high place) of Topheth in the valley of Hinnom and, among other idolatrous practices, have sacrificed their children there. [Topheth] God's claim that such a sacrifice was not divinely commanded (as with others, v. 22) may have been repeatedly and strongly stated in view of interpretations of the law of the firstborn (see Exod 22:29-30) that child sacrifice was commanded by God.

Because of these infidelities, certain judgments are announced (7:32–8:3; cf. 19:6-8 for similar language). These graphic descriptions are written (at least) in view of actual experiences in the fall of Jerusalem. Exilic readers could connect the extreme rhetoric, perhaps earlier dismissed, with the gruesome realities of that experience (see **Introduction**). The book of Lamentations shows just how horrific that time was for Israel.

The days are coming when the shrine will no longer be called Topheth or the valley of Hinnom, but the Valley of Slaughter (or murder), because of all the bodies buried there in the wake of the siege of Jerusalem; they will take up every space! Drawing a

Topheth

AΩ Topheth is an Aramaic word meaning "firepit," and is pronounced with the vowels for the Hebrew word for "shame" (*bōšet*); its name thereby carries an implicit judgment of the activities carried on there. This shrine was in the valley of Hinnom (or Gehenna), immediately west and south of the walls of Jerusalem. Child sacrifice associated with the god Baal (19:5) was among the idolatrous rites carried on at this shrine; practices of this sort are explicitly forbidden in Lev 18:21 and Deut 18:10 (see 19:6-8; 32:35; 2 Chr 28:3; 33:6). Both Ahaz and Manasseh are said to have introduced child sacrifice (2 Kgs 16:3; 21:6), and it was abolished by Josiah (2 Kgs 23:10). How common these rituals were practiced is disputed; they were probably not as widespread as the texts might seem to suggest. (For several viewpoints on this issue, see Robert Carroll, *Jeremiah* [Philadelphia: Westminster, 1986], 221-24.)

gruesome picture (also in 16:4; 19:7; 34:20), all of the corpses of "this people" will be strewn on the valley floor and become food for birds and animals—without human interference. It was an unimaginable horror in that culture for bodies not to be buried and become subject to scavengers (see Ps 79:2-3). God will bring to an end the rhythm of daily life as they know it; there will be no more joyful family occasions, including weddings, anywhere in the land (so also 16:9). Even the land itself shall become a waste (v. 34; see at 3:2-3; 12:1-13). Once again, a rhythm of "what goes around, comes around" is evident; the killing/dead bodies of the children issues in the killing/dead bodies of "this people," and their corpses will lie in the same place as those of the children—Slaughter.

In a gruesome, even ghoulish vein, the judgment speaks of the disinterment of Judah's dead leaders (kings, officials, priests, and prophets are named, and the word "bones" is repeated in each case) and the other inhabitants of Jerusalem (8:1-2). Not even death in the past will have delivered these leaders from the judgment of God (given the history of rebellion, vv. 24-26); even the dead will suffer a most shameful future. In a deeply ironic move, their bones are to be spread before the heavenly bodies and left exposed in order to become dung—a kind of homage or sacrifice. These heavenly bodies refer to astral deities that Israel—and the verbs are piled up at this point—loved, served, followed, inquired of, and worshiped; but they now are powerless to do anything on behalf of Israel. Such practices, introduced under King Manasseh (2 Kgs 21:1-16; cf. 2 Kgs 17:16), were forbidden (Deut 4:19; 17:3), and Josiah had specifically destroyed their priests and shrines during his reform (2 Kgs 23:4-5). In that reform Josiah also disinterred corpses at the sanctuary in Bethel and desecrated altars with their bones (2 Kgs 23:15-20). This practice of disinterment, exposure, and desecration was common in that world, especially in association with the violation of treaties. The final verse (8:3) lifts up the horror of this situation for those who remain alive through such a slaughter. [A Word for Exilic Readers]

A Word for Exilic Readers

In Jer 8:3 the exilic readers come specifically into view ("remnant"); they will wish that they were dead. That the few who had survived the devastation and been driven by God to various places of exile are called "this evil [*rāʿāh*] family" is a sharp word for the readers. They remain under the judgment of God; they remain in exile. But they are alive, and in these texts written for them they read of a God who cares enough to speak a word, however harsh. They will come to know that divine judgment does not exclude divine faithfulness.

CONNECTIONS

The Disjunction between Exhortation and Finality of Judgment

Most readers experience something of a disjunction in moving from vv. 3-7 to vv. 14-15 (and beyond). The chapter starts with admonitions that are seemingly open to the future, with possibilities for amendment of life and continued vitality in the promised land (vv. 3-7). But the sermon quickly evolves into speaking of a future that is no longer open; judgment and exile are certain (vv. 14-15, 20, 32-34; 8:1-3). Efforts to overcome this seeming inconsistency have not been particularly successful. One possible direction is to translate the opening verb in v. 3 as "has said,"[6] or make it a general statement about what God "says" (or "these are the words of"). In either case, one could then consider all of vv. 3-7 to be a quotation of something God has said in the past, with v. 8 beginning the address to the present audience ("here you are"). Another effort[7] considers these elements to be originally discrete, but brought together by editors in order to exhort exilic readers to tend to their life with God so that the past would not be repeated. That may well be a way for readers (both ancient and modern) to appropriate this material, but the text still confronts us with a sermon that provides no real break between the exhortation and the certain judgment. Another angle on the text needs to be pursued.

Verse 27 may be a key to help resolve this issue. God tells Jeremiah that he is to speak "all these words [vv. 1-25] to them, but they will not listen" (Exod 7:2-4 is parallel in some ways). In other words, the call to amend their ways (vv. 3-7) is to be proclaimed with the clear understanding that the people will not listen, as has been the case throughout their history (vv. 25-26; see 35:15, where this exhortation is placed in the mouth of "all my servants the prophets").

But what would be the point of such an exhortation if the end result were known in advance? At this particular juncture in Israel's history, as laid out in chapters 2–6, their future is set in stone; the enemy is at the gates, and God will not turn back (4:28). At such a time, the function of the prophetic word is not only to lay out an interpretation of what is happening in the external world of the audience, but also to reveal (for all to see, not least exilic readers) the deep "stubbornness of their evil will" (vv. 24, 26; note 18:11-12, where the call to "amend your ways" is immediately followed

Levenson on the Temple Sermon

In the temple sermon "we see a denatured form of the old notion of the Temple as a locus of ultimate security. In contrast, Jeremiah asserts the existence of ethical preconditions for Israel's admittance to the central shrine. . . . Not only YHWH, but also Israel is a sojourner in the sanctuary, one whose presence is delicate and fragile and not to be taken for granted. In the building, which 'bears God's name,' (vv. 10, 11, 14) that is, which is his personal property, man comes as a guest and not as a proprietor. The decision to allow man to dwell there (vv. 3, 7) and the decision to place God's name there (v 12) are God's. The Temple exists and functions in the spiritual universe by his grace alone."

Levenson goes on to say, "But Jeremiah's Temple sermon is not a sermon against the Temple. . . . The ethical demands which the prophet issues should not be conceived as an alternative to the Temple. What Jeremiah does oppose is the idea that the divine goodness so evident in the Temple is independent of the moral record of those who worship there, in other words, the effort to disengage God's beneficence from man's ethical deeds and to rely, as a consequence, on grace alone. . . . The grace of God does not mean exemption from the demands of covenant law, from ultimate ethical accountability. Grace and Law belong together."

It is striking to see Levenson's two uses of the phrase "grace alone." In some respects the phrase is appropriate and in other respects it is not. I hear in his second usage some resonance of Bonhoeffer's understanding of "cheap grace."

Jon Levenson, *Sinai and Zion: An Entry into the Jewish Bible* (Minneapolis: Winston, 1985), 166-68.

---

by the uselessness of a positive response in view of "the stubbornness of our evil will"; see 2:25; 5:21; 6:10). The "if" is not an "if" of positive possibilities; it is an "if" that drives home the point that such possibilities no longer exist. Such preaching would have the effect of hardening their stubborn hearts even more (see **Connections**, ch. 5) and bring on the end even more quickly, driving them over the falls. To this end, the prophet is to preach these hard words and not pray. The people are also to continue their idolatrous worship (v. 21), for that too will hasten the end. On the far side of judgment, this kind of preaching will help make sense of what has happened.

On Mercy and Sacrifice

Verse 22 (see Amos 5:25) implies that Israel did not have sacrificial rituals during the wilderness wanderings (though "the day" could be a literal reference rather than the general "when," perhaps even to Exod 15:22-26). This statement is often thought to mean that Jeremiah (and Amos) was not familiar with the divine commands that are now a part of the levitical code (Lev 1–7; these prophetic texts are often used to date the latter to a later time). In 14:12, God indicates that he will not accept their offerings; 17:26, however, speaks of them in a positive light; and they are envisaged for the future (33:18). God has already indicated that the burnt offerings are not acceptable (6:20), but that judgment seems to be related to the faithlessness of those who bring them (see [Offerings in 6:20]). [Levenson on the Temple Sermon]

It seems unlikely that an historical point is being made here. Other scholars make distinctions among commands in the Pentateuch; for example, Exodus ascribes only the Decalogue to the explicit divine command at Sinai; other rituals were given later by Moses. Still others think that specifically individual sacrifices are referenced here rather than the prescribed rituals of tabernacle/temple. That is, the issue focuses on the command given in v. 23 to walk only in the way that God has commanded. But these perspectives draw too fine a point on the matter at stake.

A preferable perspective is brought by those who interpret the text in terms of priority; God prefers mercy to sacrifice, obedience that pervades one's entire life to specific rituals (see Hos 6:6; Mic 6:6-8; Matt 12:7). Verse 22 would not be true in and of itself, but that negation serves the purpose of setting off the more comprehensive concern about obedience in the totality of life in v. 23. (This understanding fits well with the emphases drawn out in vv. 5-6, 9; see [Worship and the Neighbor].) [Heschel on Justice and Ritual]

Heschel on Justice and Ritual

"The world is overwhelmingly rich; the human mind is incapable of paying attention to all its aspects. The painter sees the world in color, the sculptor in form; the musician perceives the world in sounds, and the economist in commodities. The prophet is a man who sees the world with the eyes of God, and in the sight of God even things of beauty or acts of ritual are an abomination when associated with injustice."

Abraham Heschel, *The Prophets* (New York: Haper, 1962), 211-12.

NOTES

[1] See William Holladay, *Jeremiah 1* (Philadelphia: Fortress, 1986), 235-36.

[2] Contrary to Robert Carroll, *Jeremiah* (Philadelphia: Westminster, 1986), 211, "No divine promise is forever."

[3] Walter Brueggemann, *A Commentary on Jeremiah: Exile and Homecoming* (Grand Rapids: Eerdmans, 1998), 77-79, wrongly suggests that judgment stands over against the promises to which God has bound himself.

[4] Jon Levenson, *Sinai and Zion: An Entry into the Jewish Bible* (Minneapolis: Winston, 1985), 167.

[5] Daniel Berrigan, *Jeremiah: The World, the Wound of God* (Minneapolis: Fortress, 1999), 43.

[6] So Holladay, *Jeremiah 1,* 235.

[7] So Carroll, *Jeremiah,* 211.

IS THERE NO BALM
IN GILEAD?

8:4–9:1

Judgment and Tears, 8:4–10:25

These chapters are commonly considered together. The predominant themes of indictment and judgment mediated by the "foe from the north" return to front and center stage as they had been in 4:5–6:30 (see introduction to that section). The relentlessness of that enemy advance comes to a kind of climax with their noise and commotion of 10:22. Two prose sections (9:12-16, 23-26) have been sewn into this predominantly poetic section, and 10:11 is written in Aramaic.

While the continuities with prior sections are considerable, the tone of this section is somewhat different. Lament materials, of both God and Jeremiah, increase in number and punctuate the entire section (8:4-7, 18-22; 9:1-2a, 10, 17-21; 10:19-21). They are revealing of the mind and heart of the prophet and the God whose word cuts so deeply and sharply; they may also be a factor in the somewhat disjointed presentation of this material. The laments soften somewhat the harsh message of judgment, but it is not because the latter is any less clear. It is because readers are given a clearer glimpse into the heart of the one who exercises judgment.

COMMENTARY

Verses 4-13 consist basically of words of indictment, with announcements of judgment interwoven at vv. 9a, 10a, and 12b-13 ("therefore"). At the same time, God's words in vv. 4-9 are imbued with an element of pathos. In a way similar to 2:5, 29-32, the combination of rhetorical question (vv. 4, 8-9) and bewildered question (v. 5) occurs in the indictment. In making a case against a people who refuse to repent ("re/turn" is a key word here; forms of *šûb* are used six times, *niḥam* once), God acts with a wonderment that does not mask an inner anguish over what has happened to the relationship. The focus on the law and instruction in vv. 7-9 balances that on

The Speakers of 8:18–9:1

The identification of the speaker(s) in these verses is difficult. The questioning laments of the people in v. 19b (quoted by the speaker of v. 19a) seem clear enough, as does v. 20 (NRSV places both in quotation marks; NAB only the second; REB only the first). It is possible that v. 22a is also spoken by the people, but that is less certain. A more difficult task for the interpreter is to sort out the speaker in the remaining verses. Is it God or Jeremiah or both? Divine speech markers appear at 8:17 and 9:3, but it is difficult to know to which verses they refer. God is clearly the speaker of v. 19c (NRSV places it in parentheses). It has been usual for interpreters to name Jeremiah as the speaker of the other verses, probably for theological reasons, namely, hesitance or refusal to ascribe grief and hurt to God. A few scholars now name God as the speaker of most if not all of these verses. (See especially Kathleen O'Connor, "The Tears of God and Divine Character in Jeremiah 2–9," *God in the Fray: A Tribute to Walter Brueggemann*, ed. T. Linafelt and T. Beal [Minneapolis: Fortress, 1998], 172-85; Mark Biddle, *Polyphony and Symphony in Prophetic Literature: Rereading Jeremiah 7–20* [Macon GA: Mercer University Press, 1996], 28-31.) I have suggested that readers are not asked to make a sharp distinction between the voice of prophet and the voice of God in these and other lamenting texts; in them we can hear the language of both. (T. Fretheim, *The Suffering of God,* 160-62.) Yet, the voice of God is primary; if Jeremiah speaks these words, it is because God first speaks them. The lamenting prophet embodies the words of a lamenting God. For other texts wherein the mourning of God and prophet are overlaid, see 4:19-21; 10:19-20; 13:17-19; 14:17-18. It is likely that all the protagonists in this situation—people, prophet, and God—voice their laments. The interweaving of speakers gives the text a certain liturgical character, but it may be more accurate to say that we hear a *cacophony* of mourning at Israel's destruction.

worship in 7:1–8:3; both of these central spheres of Israel's religious life have deteriorated into deception and lies.

The last half of this section (8:14–9:1) consists largely of a series of interwoven laments, including those of the people (vv. 14-15, 19b, 20) and prophet and God (vv. 18, 19ac, 21–22; 9:1). [The Speakers of 8:18–9:1] The reason for the lament is sharply stated in vv. 16–17, namely, the relentless approach of a biting, devouring enemy. The end of this unit is difficult to discern; it is probably best to make the break between 9:1 and 9:2, where a switch is made from the prophet/God suffering *with* the people to their suffering *because* of them.

Why Has This People Turned Away?, 8:4–13

Indictment and announcement of judgment predominate in this segment. The point of the rhetorical questions in v. 4 is this: ordinarily, if a person goes away, that person will return; if a person falls, that person will get up again; if a person sins, some regret or remorse is usually forthcoming. In each case, this would be the *natural* thing to do; hence, Israel's behaviors have a fundamentally *unnatural* character to them. Even the birds have natural instincts that bring them back (see Isa 1:3). They know instinctively what to do; Israel does not, even though they have the law (v. 7). The point is not unlike that of 5:22: the sea's boundaries are contrasted with a people whose behavior knows no boundaries. This appeal to parallels among nonhuman creatures indicates that Israel has not only broken its relationship with God, it has transgressed the basic structures of the created order (v. 7). The issue is not simply a matter of sin and redemption; God's very creation is being disrupted (see **Introduction**). Israel has turned away from God again and again, yet refuses to repent/return (see 5:3; 7:24-27); they have fallen, but they refuse to get up again. Even the birds know better!

The next question (v. 5) is a lament-filled divine response in view of God's first questions: Why?! There seems to be no explanation for the people's behavior— even for God (see also 2:29, 31; 8:19)![1] The backsliding is a permanent way of life; they hold fast to falsehood, resisting repentance. God has attended to their needs and listened to their prayers, but hears no honest speaking (v. 6). Individuals do not regret their wickedness (*rā'āh*) or inquire critically into the effects of their own behaviors. They are like a horse that plunges into battle without thought for the possible deadly consequences; they do not seem to be able to do otherwise. Repenting for this people is no longer possible.

In God's judgment the people do not "know" (that is, truly understand and follow) the ways of the Lord, though they have the law/ordinances (*mišpāṭ*) of God (v. 7), as do the scribes (v. 8). These "wise men," who undoubtedly spend their professional lives studying the law (!), are especially in view here, but not exclusively so. [The Wise] Neither the content nor the scope of this "law" is made clear; it is simply identified as "the law (ordinances) of the Lord" (vv. 7-8). Both people and scribes violate that divine order for life. God wonders out loud: how can the scribes understand themselves to be wise, to be following the instruction (*tôrāh*) of God (v. 8)? The scribes have rejected "the word of the LORD" (v. 9); the (spoken) word is not to be set up over against the law here, for they are parallel in 6:19 (see 2:8; Isa 1:10). Their words are lies and they perpetuate falsehoods in their writing and speaking; their activity is at least one factor as to why the "people do not know" (v. 7). These teachers claim to be wise, but—making the point with a rhetorical question—there is no wisdom in them. [How Is the Law a Lie?]

And so God announces a judgment upon the scribes in particular; yet, the prophet and priest are also drawn into the judgment, and the people in general are also in view (vv. 9a, 10; "the least to

The Wise

Jeremiah speaks of scribes here and in 18:18; he himself had a scribe named Baruch (36:32). These individuals were associated primarily with the palace and the temple, and could serve more generally as secretaries. With respect to the palace, they were responsible for civil legislation, the administration of royal affairs, and giving counsel to the king. With respect to the temple, they interpreted priestly law and were teachers of the Torah (see 2:8; in the sense of both law and narrative). The reference to the "pen" indicates that they were working with a written form of the law; but it is not known what body of law this was, and efforts to link it to Deuteronomy are speculative. In any case, they had a central role in the transmission of the tradition to both leaders and the people. Wisdom is used in 9:9 in this general sense, being parallel to the word of God.

How is the Law a Lie?

To be accused of making the law into a lie is a jolting accusation. It seems clear that the scribes are not being accused of rewriting the law and dispensing with the pre-revised version. Moreover, the identity of the "lie" is not centered on their formal or external use of the law (whatever it is). Rather, the issue is their *interpretation* (or commentary) of the law. Now, of course, everyone who uses the law interprets it; to deny that would be just as deceitful. The issue is the *content* of the interpretation, the particular "spin" they put on the law—that is the lie. Theirs is an interpretation that reinforces the message of "peace" and complacency given by the prophets and hence cannot be the word of the LORD (v. 11). Their "soft" use of the law never convicts anyone, never moves people to ask, "What have I done?" (v. 6). They find ways of using the law to conceal the real problem rather than to reveal it. Like the temple, the law in and of itself cannot function as a talisman; how one interprets it is crucial.

---

the greatest"). According to v. 9a, the wise will be put to shame, dismayed, and taken (or ensnared; see Isa 28:13). This seems to be primarily a reference to a judgment on their particular "wisdom"; ensuing events will show them to be anything but wise and their reputations as interpreters will be shattered (see 1 Cor 3:18-20). They will be shamed and dismayed by the inadequacy and misdirection of their instruction with respect to the gravity of the situation, and they shall be taken into exile. Warnings for the exiled readers are certainly implicit in this, especially the need to be discerning regarding the interpretations of the word of God that they hear (explicit in ch. 27). [Berrigan on Wisdom]

According to v. 10a, and here the judgment seems to reach out to include everyone, their wives and their property will be given to others. Verses 10-12 are a virtual repetition of 6:12-15 (v. 10a is similar to 6:12a, while vv. 10b-12 simply repeat 6:13-15; see comment there). For God to give their wives over to other men is, in effect, to give these women over to be raped by others (see 6:11 and **Connections** there; for a comparable judgment of David, see 2 Sam 12:11). This word of God becomes all too real in the fall of Jerusalem (see Lam 5:11; 3:51). This consequence is related especially to the sins of unjust gain and dealing falsely; they have coveted that which is not theirs and so—what goes around, comes around—they will lose that which belongs to them (Exod 20:17).

Verse 13 (its translation is uncertain; cf. NRSV and NIV) draws indictment and judgment together. God is imaged as a gatherer of fruit at harvest time (see Isa 5:1-7; Luke 13:6-9). Working from the

Berrigan on Wisdom

Daniel Berrigan's poem, "We are Wise," captures the relationship of "wisdom" and judgment here very well:

How then declare, "We are wise"
when foolishness crowns your days?

And "God's word dwells in us"—
lo, worldly traffic buzzing?

Priest, prophet, scribe—
anarchic, deceitful, every one.
False healing, meager faith;
a cry: "Peace, peace!" at lip,
and the warrior heart aflame—
sword unsheathed, at the ready.

Day of discord, day of doom.
My wrath
unsheathed, at the ready!

Daniel Berrigan, *Jeremiah: The World, the Wound of God* (Minneapolis: Fortress, 1999), 47.

NRSV translation, God comes to gather in the harvest, and finds no fruit—no grapes and no figs (see the comparable point at 2:21); indeed, the leaves of the vines and trees are withered. Or, alternatively (NIV; NRSV footnote) and more likely, the harvest is an image of judgment and the vines are in this condition because of that very divine action (see 5:11; 6:9). The fruitfulness of the land—a gift from God in creation and in the land settlement (Deut 8:7-10)—has been adversely affected by the people's wickedness: the land has become an unfruitful waste (see 4:26; 7:34; 9:10; 12:4 and **Connections** there; **Introduction**). This effect of their wickedness on the fruitfulness of the land is named divine judgment. The only fruit they bear is the "fruit of their own schemes" (see at 6:19; 21:14; **Introduction**), namely, disaster for themselves and for their entire environment.

Laments Over the Coming Disaster, 8:14–9:1

This segment begins with a question from the people: why are we sitting around in our homes and villages in the face of the Babylonian onslaught? In response, they call on one another to head for the fortified cities (heeding the warning of 4:5), perhaps out of a conviction that they may as well die fighting. And die they will, for all their hopes have been dashed. The people are resigned to the effects of divine judgment, described in various ways: being doomed; being given poisoned water to drink (also 23:15, either a metaphor for deathly experience, an enemy tactic of poisoning wells, or to the "cup of wrath" in 25:15-16); nothing good is happening; and there is no healing or peace, only terror and despair.

The people use similar language in 14:19, where they raise questions as to whether God has completely rejected them. This language could well be reflective of the exiled readers' sense of their situation; there is no healing or peace, for God has doomed them to perish because of their sins. The people's admission that they have sinned against the LORD (v. 16; similarly, 14:7, 20) stands in some tension with v. 6. This is not necessarily an act of repentance, however; it could be simply the mouthing of a current or even a typical interpretation of their situation. From another perspective, they do answer correctly the recurrent question of 5:19 and 9:12 (see **Introduction**). If it is a repentant act, it comes too late to stop the judgment (as in ch. 14); the trip over the falls is inevitable (see **Connections**, chs. 5 and 7).

God responds to the people in vv. 16-17 with no word of deliverance from the relentless judgment. Indeed, the armies from the north are already on their way (exilic readers would understand this to be Babylon). They have entered the land of promise; those in Dan—either the northernmost tribe or its city by that name—have already experienced the invasion. The enemy is now so close that one can almost hear the snorting of their horses and the trampling of their hooves, to which the quaking of the land may have hyperbolic reference. The quaking is probably also a reference to both fearful people and the very structures of the land itself (see 4:24). The enemy has come to devour everything—land, city, and all creatures, as already specified in 5:17. In v. 17, the image of the enemy moves from stallions to snakes—from snorting, trampling terror to creeping, crawling poison—let loose by God himself (actual snakes may also be in view, see Num 21:6; Deut 32:24). Unlike snakes, however, this enemy will not be able to be charmed out of its deadly intentions; its bites will prove to be fatal. This may be linked to the theme of health and sickness (vv. 15, 22).

In vv. 18-22 and 9:1, the lament once again comes to the fore, and the images shift from external threat to internal hurt and sickness. The identification of the speaker in these verses is not always clear; it seems best to recognize several speakers, with God as the primary one (see [The Speakers of 8:18–9:1]). In v. 18 God through Jeremiah expresses grief and the loss of joy or pleasure at these events; God's heart is sick and so is Jeremiah's! In v. 19, the last two lines are clearly a divine lament (NRSV puts it in parentheses and quotation marks, NAB in brackets); it is placed between laments from the people (vv. 19b, 20). In this lament readers once again meet up with the "why?!" of God (see 2:29, 31; 8:5) at the people's provocation of the divine anger with their unfaithful worship of foreign idols. It is a genuine divine "why?"!

The people in v. 19b bemoan the apparent absence of God in the city of Jerusalem and its temple (driven out by their sins, v. 14; see Ezek 8:6). If God were in Zion, it was thought that these things would not be happening to them (see Mic 4:9–10). In view of 2:6, 8, where the people are criticized for *not* asking where God is, these questions should be understood as appropriate in the situation. These would also be questions that exilic readers would ask (Lam 2:7; 5:20-22). Verse 19c makes clear that God is indeed present, but present in wrath, not as the God of a theology that would protect them come what may (see 7:1-15; [Divine Anger]). This is an expression of divine suffering, but a suffering *because* of what has happened to the relationship. [Suffering "because" and Suffering "with"] The people also lament (v. 20) the length of time that they have suffered under the Babylonian siege (through the summer and an

Suffering "because" and Suffering "with"

These verses make an important distinction with respect to the reasons for the suffering of God and prophet. They suffer not simply *with* the people who are suffering, but *because* the people have violated their relationship with God. (On this distinction, see T. Fretheim, *Suffering of God*, 107-37.) The sense of suffering "because" is sharply evident in v. 19c; the people have provoked God with their images and foreign idols. God is revealed not as one who remains coolly unaffected by the rejection of the people, but as one who is deeply wounded by the broken relationship. Judgment is viewed basically in terms of a breakdown in a personal relationship with all its associated effects—all the anger, pain, and suffering that would commonly accompany such a breakdown. In effect, the exiles are invited to look back and see that they have been visited "not with strict and icy indifference of a judge, but with the pain and anger of one whose suit for a personal surrender has been rejected."

The suffering "with" on the part of both God and prophet can also be seen in this text (8:21; 9:1). God does not view what has happened to the people with a kind of detached objectivity. God is not an executioner who can walk away from the judgment thinking, "I only did my duty." Nor is there any satisfaction, let alone celebration, that justice has now been done. However much the judgment is deserved, God does not leave them alone to wallow in the ill effects of their own sins. God turns from the role of judge to that of fellow-sufferer. These two texts seem not simply to be an anticipation of the coming suffering, but a recognition of the actual suffering being experienced. Once again, this would connect well with exiled readers. God, having judged, does not put them out of the picture and go on to other responsibilities.

Links to the NT may be made with respect to both of these dimensions of suffering, the former particularly in the weeping of Jesus over Jerusalem (see Luke 13:34) and perhaps both in Jesus' statement in 19:41–44.

Walter Eichrodt, *Theology of the Old Testament* (2 vols.; Philadelphia: Westminster, 1967), 2:427.

---

apparently failed fall harvest). The reference to the harvest in v. 20 is no simple chronological marker, however; it refers back to v. 13, which speaks of harvest in terms of judgment rather than the joy that comes with the harvest. The fall (New Year) festival, associated with God's kingship, could have been looked to as a time for divine

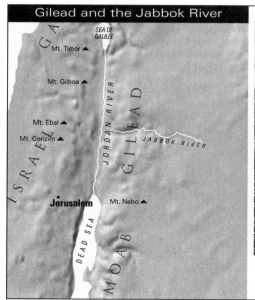

A view of Gilead looking across the Jabbok River Valley.
(Credit: Mitchell G. Reddish)

A Balm in Gilead

Gilead is a region in the Transjordan, north of Moab; it was an area known for its healing resources (balm is a resin from the balsam tree that was applied to wounds; see 46:11; 51:8). This verse is familiar from its use in the spiritual, "There is a Balm in Gilead." This spiritual claims that there *is* a balm in Gilead "to make the wounded whole" and "to heal the sin-sick soul." The song assumes a Christology, namely, that Christ is the "Gilead" where balm can be found; or, alternatively, that Gilead, being across Jordan, is the goal of the life of the Christian. The song rightly connects the "balm" with issues of spiritual sickness, and its effects on the whole person; but one wonders where the lyricist got the idea that there was a balm in Gilead that in fact had such healing powers. While the text claims that there is a balm in Gilead, it also claims that that balm is insufficient to heal what is wrong with Israel. Somewhere along the line, Gilead has gained a symbolic value beyond this text. At the same time, if related to healing texts in the Book of Consolation (30:17; 33:6), the text implies that only God can be a healer of this people. For Christians, Christological connections are close at hand.

Gathering of Balsam Resin. Le Lione des Simples Medicine. ca. 1600. Biliotheque National. Paris, France. (Credit: C.Y./Art Resource, NY)

vindication. But, it comes and goes and judgment remains the order of the day.

After quoting the people in distress (v. 20), God returns (v. 21) to an expression of deep pain at these developments (a suffering *"with"*); the various emotion-laden words reveal various dispositions: hurt, a broken heart, being disconsolate, and dismay. These words are piled up to show the deepest possible grief, such as would be the case at the death of one who is truly loved. If the speaker of v. 22a is God, it reflects a divine wonderment (ironic?) that this people have not availed themselves of the best healing resources available, those in Gilead. [A Balm in Gilead] The first two questions are rhetorical: Yes, there is balm in Gilead; yes, there are physicians there; but, it is implied, they are powerless to restore health to a patient with this kind of illness. The answer to the question "why?" in v. 22b pertains to the nature of the sickness; no conventional healing methods are available for what ails Israel. It will become evident in 30:17 and 33:6 that only God can provide healing for Israel.

> **Cowper on 8:18–9:1**
>
> In his poem "The Time Piece" (*The Task*, Book II) William Cowper begins by using lines from 8:18–9:1 to express the desire to escape to a time when war and other forms of oppression with all their pain and suffering is no more.
>
> O for a lodge in some vast wilderness,
> Some boundless contiguity of shade,
> Where rumor of oppression and deceit,
> Of unsuccessful or successful war,
> Might never reach me more. My ear is pained,
> My soul is sick with every day's report
> Of wrong and outrage with which Earth is filled
> There is no flesh in man's obdurate heart,
> It does not feel for man; the natural bond
> Of brotherhood is severed as the flax,
> That falls asunder at the touch of fire.
>
> *Poems by William Cowper, Esq., of the Inner Temple* (10th ed.; New York: William L. Allison, n.d.), 273.

In 9:1, God is filled with grief; yet, there are no proper means to express the depth of these feelings. [Cowper on 8:18–9:1] If only his head were a spring and his eyes a fountain, such might be sufficient vehicles to let out all the tears, to express the grief that is felt for all the people who have been destroyed (on God's tears, see also 9:17-18; 14:17). This divine grief will not be a short-lived matter; it will continue day and night (see **Connections: The Intensity of the Divine Lament**).

CONNECTIONS

The Intensity of the Divine Lament

As noted in [The Speakers of 8:18–9:1], it seems best to understand 8:18–9:1 as words of grief spoken by God in and through the prophet. Their mournful response at the destruction of Jerusalem is so symbiotic that in everything we hear the anguish of both God and prophet. Jeremiah's grief is an embodiment of God's grief. Exilic readers are here shown the genuine pain of both God and prophet regarding these destructive events. This language reveals that the godward side of anger is grief, not satisfaction; God and prophet are affected in the deepest levels of their being by what has occurred. [Brueggemann on God's Suffering]

God has expressed deep emotions over these developments for the people of Israel in earlier chapters (see 2:29-31; 3:19-20), and that response to the judgment about to fall is now made even more intense in these verses. The refrain-like use of the phrase "my (poor) people" (vv. 19, 21, 22; 9:1, 2) is filled with pathos; the reader can almost envisage God uttering these words with "his head in his hands." To speak of judgment is no joy, for either God or prophet. Readers must not shy away from speaking of the emotional life of God in connection with this text and others; the prophet here makes those divine feelings publicly available for all to see and hear. While not discounting the continuity with human emotions (there is a "yes" in this anthropopathic metaphor), readers should also recognize the "no" and distinguish between divine and human emotions. Such a point of discontinuity would be particularly evident with respect to the passivity and enervation suffering commonly brings in its train for human beings. God, however, is not reduced to passivity or bereft of resources to act in the midst of suffering. Indeed, suffering may be considered a vehicle for divine action. God does not relate to suffering as a mechanic does to a car, seeking to "fix it" from the outside, nor is God like some welfare administrator in a distant office signing vouchers for food stamps. God enters deeply into the suffering human situation and works the necessary healing *from within* (see the paradigmatic Exod 3:7 in this connection).

This is an important word for readers, particularly those who had actually experienced destruction and exile, for it is highly revealing of the kind of God that stands behind the judgment. Readers are not called upon to sympathize with God (see Luke 23:38) or to identify with either God or the prophet in grief (such as in the phrase, "his grief is also our grief"). Nor is it simply a matter of their recognizing that God grieves along with them (as much as this may be the case, see v. 21). At this point, readers are given a glimpse into the heart of the one who brings judgment; the God who brings judgment does so with grief and sorrow. And for God to so enter into the mournful situation means that mourning will not be the last word spoken (see 31:13; see [Suffering "because" and Suffering "with"]).

Brueggemann on God's Suffering

This poetic unit is one of the most powerful in the Jeremiah tradition. It is also one of the most pathos-filled....This is poetry that penetrates God's heart. That heart is marked by God's deep grief. God's anger is audible here, but it is largely subordinated to the hurt God experiences in the unnecessary death of God's people. God would not have it so, but the waywardness of Israel has taken every alternative response away from Yahweh.

Walter Brueggemann, *A Commentary on Jeremiah: Exile and Homecoming* (Grand Rapids: Eerdmans, 1998), 91-92.

NOTE

[1] On the "why" questions for God, see Terence Fretheim, *The Suffering of God: An Old Testament Perspective* (Philadelphia: Fortress, 1984), 56-57.

THE LAMENTS INTENSIFY

9:2-26

This section begins with a lament (v. 2) and links it to an indictment (vv. 3-6) and announcement of judgment (vv. 7-9, "therefore"). This segment is followed by three lamentations over the deadly consequences of Israel's infidelities (vv. 10-11, 17-19, 20-22). Two prose sections reflect upon these events for the sake of exilic readers; the first looks to the past and provides another response to the question "Why?" (vv. 12-16); the second looks to the future with words of reassurance for the faithful and of judgment for the unfaithful (vv. 23-26).

COMMENTARY

Words as Weapons, 9:2-9

In vv. 2-3 (vv. 1-2H) the speaker is God (vv. 3, 6-7, 9), but as in the prior verses, God and prophet are not finally separable. In v. 2, God/prophet expresses a wish for a dwelling place in the desert (rather than the temple!) to which to escape from this people, to "get out of the house" (imagery used by an abused person in Ps 55:4-8)! Grief, yes; but escape and isolation, too. This is no simple suffering with the people; this is also getting some distance from them. It may even reflect a divine/prophetic need to go on a retreat of sorts, perhaps to gain perspective, or just to get out of the line of fire! This is expressed as a divine desideratum (O, that I had . . .), but there is no indication that such a retreat is available, finally.

God's reasons for seeking such a retreat are given in a summary listing of the people's evil doings (9:3). They cover the waterfront of sins—spiritual, moral, social: adultery (probably spiritual infidelity, yet see 5:7), faithlessness (treason!), and lying rather than truthtelling. [Berrigan's "Tears"] The misuse of the tongue is vividly portrayed; the theme of words as weapon begins the indictment in v. 3 and returns in v. 8. Their words/tongues are like bows with arrows aimed at doing harm (see Jas 1:26; 3:1-12). Generally, their lives can be

Berrigan's "Tears"

Tears, tears be my meed [reward],
tears in a desert waste—
the slain, the innocent
laid low, and no recourse!

They prevail, the great ones,
deceitful, deadly,
a plague of arrows.

Each against each, rumor
thick sown as tares—
crafty, vigilant,
doors iron-barred.

What care you, uncaring
of me—you scorners
of love, of law?

Daniel Berrigan, *Jeremiah: The World, the Wound of God*
(Minneapolis: Fortress, 1999), 48.

characterized as moving from one evil to another (v. 3; *rāʿāh...rāʿāh*); they do not know (*yādʿ*) the Lord, that is, they are unfaithful to the marital relationship. The closer the relationship, the deeper the hurt when it is broken.

Verses 4-6 expand on the theme of deceit and falsehood. In the midst of the chaos created by the Babylonian invasion, the audience is warned to be on guard; they cannot trust even those who are closest to them. Trust and truth have become casualties, which leads to even further ill effects, not least the disintegration of the community itself. Where there is no truth there can be no trust and no real community (an important word for the isolated community of exiles, not least in view of the false prophets among them, see ch. 27). The reasons to be on guard are made clear: they act like Jacob, the supplanter (NAB; see Gen 25:26-33; Hos 12:3); they slander and deceive one another; *everyone* lies and (more expansively) no one speaks the truth (v. 5; to "teach one's tongue" is to make it a habit). The indictment concludes with a rhetorical flourish. They have become so weary devoting their moral energy to sinful verbal activity that they have no strength left to repent! Oppression upon oppression! Deceit upon deceit! The decisive point in the last clause of v. 3 is repeated in v. 6: they do not know the Lord (see 8:7)!

But who are these people who are being warned: "beware of your neighbors"? Perhaps they are a righteous remnant; Jeremiah is certainly included in this group, given his own experience of slander on the part of those close to him (12:6; 20:10). Or, this could be a gracious warning to everyone; even in judgment God cares enough about the people to attempt to bring some order to the verbal chaos. Or, more probably, they are the exilic readers (as is certainly the case in vv. 12-16, 23-26); they continue to experience what became commonplace during the siege of Jerusalem (see chs. 27–29).

The word of judgment follows in v. 7 ("therefore"); as often before, the judgment is stated in questioning terms (vv. 7, 9; on the questions in v. 9 see 5:9, 29). God stands as a reluctant judge, making that hesitation clear to exilic readers, even inviting someone to make a contrary case. But what else can God do (see Hos 6:4)? God has tried every other means. God has been persistent in sending warnings over the years (see 7:24-26), but there has

Translating 9:10

AΩ A translation issue presents itself in v. 10. The Hebrew text reads, "I will take up weeping and wailing," with God as subject (so NIV). This reading is to be preferred, and is parallel to the first person verbs of v. 11. The NRSV (cf. NAB), however, follows the Greek and Syriac versions in translating, "Take up weeping and wailing" (the addressee is plural, hence a reference to the community). One likely reason for this translation is form-critical in nature; a call to take up a lament is considered parallel to the calls in vv. 17 and 20. Yet, such a formal consideration seems insufficient to override the Hebrew text. Perhaps another reason is the difficulty of thinking of God in these terms. The Hebrew text more strongly presents God as one who is suffering over the devastating effects on the environment that have been wrought by the Babylonians. At the same time, with the other translation, it could be said that God's call to take up weeping implies a divine pathos to be voiced by the community.

---

been no response. And so, God will refine them and assay (test) them. This metaphor drawn from the practice of iron smelting continues the image used in 6:27-30. Verse 8 loops back and picks up the basic elements of the indictment in vv. 4-6: even though they speak friendly (*šālôm*) words to their neighbors, that is only a façade that hides their deceitful intentions (see 12:2; Pss 28:3; 62:4). They deliberately set out to use their tongues in a way that harms, if not destroys, others. They are like robbers in hiding, waiting for an opportunity to ambush their unsuspecting neighbors and wound them, if not kill them, with their *tongues*. But God's testing will bring their true intentions to light and they will suffer the consequences.

Divine Grief and Judgment, 9:10-11

Verses 10-11 weave in the element of pathos once again. The devastation here is presented as both past (v. 10) and future (v. 11); perhaps the best way to keep these verses together is to posit that the onslaught is in progress. [Translating 9:10] God is portrayed as one who weeps and wails over what has happened to the environment (see 4:23-26); this depiction is continuous with the divine lament themes in this context (8:18–9:3; 9:17-19) and elsewhere (e.g., 3:19-20). A striking element of the divine pathos is present here: God is weeping for the mountains and for the pastures! The reasons: they have been laid waste and become uninhabited; the sounds of livestock are no longer heard; the birds and the animals have disappeared (cf. the descriptions in 4:24-26 and 12:4; **Connections** at chs. 4, 12).

God's judgment on Jerusalem and the towns of Judah through the Babylonian armies will make them a heap of ruins and the towns (comparatively) uninhabited. When armies waged war in those days, they did not confine their activities to the human population but killed the animals and destroyed the foliage. The God who mediates the judgment through these marauders at the same time takes up a lamentation for the disastrous effects these events will have on people and animals, cities and pasturelands. Certainly God is complicit in this ecological disaster, but the prior reality is the sinfulness of Israel. This necessary divine complicity makes for even greater agony on God's part over what has occurred (see **Connections: The Juxtaposition of Grief and Wrath**).

Why?!, 9:12-16

Verses 12-16 are commonly considered to be an editorial expansion of vv. 10-11, focused on "understanding" what has just been said. This prose section is clearly set in a time after the destruction of Jerusalem; see the comparable question with response in 5:18-19; 16:10-13; 22:8-9, also in prose (cf. Deut 29:24-28; 1 Kgs 9:8-9). The questions in v. 12 reflect queries by the exiles, though they are sharply focused on the wasted land (cf. vv. 10-11) in a way that the other texts are not (cf. 1 Kgs 9:8; see discussion at ch. 12). Verse 12a wonders about the meaning of the events of which the prior verses speak; who is wise enough to explain what has happened (see Hos 14:9)? Has God revealed an explanation to anyone? Verse 12b picks up on words and phrases in v. 10 and integrates them into a question regarding the reasons for this disaster. It is striking that these questions are inserted between two texts that are filled with lament, both human and divine. The human questions and divine judgments must be interpreted from within this context so filled with emotion and loss, pain and mourning.

The divine response to the questions (vv. 13-16) is cast in terms that would be familiar to the reader of Jeremiah: an indictment (vv. 13-14) followed by an announcement of judgment ("therefore," vv. 15-16). The indictment is stated in summary terms, picking up on the basic elements of 7:24-26: the people have abandoned the God-given Law and have not walked in its ways and they have not listened to the voice of God (probably a reference to the prophets rather than the Law). Once again (see 7:24) the theme of stubbornness is given prominence; they have persisted in following the dictates of their own hearts and have worshiped the Baals that their ancestors taught them to worship (see 7:9; see **Connections** at ch. 5). Unfaith does get passed on from generation to generation, becomes increasingly recognized as normal, and has

Wormwood and Poisoned Water

Wormwood is a shrub belonging to the aster family. This plant, with its bitter taste and poisonous effects, is used as a metaphor for the experience of destruction and bitter sorrow (Lam 3:15, 19; in Jer 23:15 these metaphors are applied to the false prophets). God is also going to give the people poisonous water to drink (see 8:14), an ongoing problem in that part of the world. The text does not back off from claiming that God is an agent in judgment that leads to these effects. The combination of wormwood and poisonous waters is a deadly brew.

(Credit: Mitchel G. Reddish)

a cumulative effect on the entire society that in time bursts forth in great devastation.

The announcement of judgment follows (vv. 15-16) and is probably to be cast in the past tense.[1] That is, this is an announcement that God gave to the people in the past, recalled here for the sake of responding to the queries of exilic readers. The image is sharp: God is going to feed them with wormwood and poisonous waters. [Wormwood and Poisoned Water] These divine "gifts" are a reversal of God's gift of manna and water in the wilderness (Exod 15:22-25; 16:1-35). God will also scatter the people among the nations, nations unfamiliar to Israel (note the plural; Egypt and Babylon were the most prominent), and pursue them with the sword until they are consumed (see Lev 26:33; Deut 28:36, 64). From the exilic readers' point of view, they have lived and are living with these realities.

Calls for Lamentation, 9:17-22

Verses 17-22 introduce still further laments into this mix of indictment and judgment, including a lament from the people, quoted in v. 18. The effects of the divine judgment are now broadened to include the recollection of divinely commissioned mourning rites associated with the fall of Jerusalem. The situation is desperate for the people of God; v. 19 speaks of ruin and shame, of exile and the destruction of homes. Given the reference to exile ("we have left the land"), this dirge "from Zion" may be articulated by those few left in the city. Alternatively, Zion may be a reference to the people wherever they are scattered.

In v. 17, God calls on the audience (probably exilic readers) to gather the mourning/skilled women to participate in a wake (see Amos 5:16-17). Their mourning is to join the lament of the people of the entire community (v. 19); the effect is weeping on a grand scale. These women are professionals, mourners who represent the entire community at the death of an individual or the destruction of a city (see 22:18). Anything but restrained, their activities would consist of loud crying and frenetic movement. They are called to raise a dirge over "us," so that "our" eyes may run down with tears and "our" eyelids flow with water (see 14:17). The use of the first person plural in vv. 17-18 in a divine oracle means that God is included among the "us," *both* as one who mourns and is mourned for. The professional mourners are to come and weep not only for Israel, but for God as well! In some sense, God has died the death of these people; God, too, goes into exile. Their dirge would initiate the mourning process and others (including God!) would participate in the ritual laments. Parallels to the mourning of deities at the destruction of sacred cities are found elsewhere in the ancient Near East. [Heschel on the Divine Call to Lament]

Heschel on the Divine Call to Lament

Abraham Heschel interestingly probes the interiority of the God who calls others to lament: "Does not the word of God mean: Cry for Israel and for Me? The voice of God calling upon the people to weep, lament, and mourn, for the calamities are about to descend upon them, is itself a voice of grief, a voice of weeping."

Abraham Heschel, *The Prophets* (New York: Haper, 1962), 113.

In v. 20, God calls to these female professional mourners to hear the word of God and receive that word into their very selves. Then they are to teach a dirge to their daughters and neighbors, all to increase the volume of the mourning. The God-given language of the dirge follows in v. 21 and continues in v. 22 (after a renewed introduction in v. 22a, omitted in NAB; some interpreters consider v. 22 a word from God to Jeremiah). The dirge reflects the horrors of the siege of Jerusalem.

Death, the grim reaper (see v. 22), is virtually personified and is depicted as a prowler who enters through windows of houses and kills their inhabitants (see Isa 28:14-22; Hos 13:14). Death is everywhere! Death cuts down ordinary citizens and officials, children and young men. It enters into homes and palaces and cuts off people in the streets and squares. Death cannot be resisted. Corpses will be strewn everywhere, like dung is strewn on the fields as fertilizer (see 8:2; 16:4), like sheaves left behind the reaper to rot in the field. What a song to teach your children! These verses could be an ironic allusion to the myth regarding the Canaanite god of death (Mot) who kills the god Baal and drags him into the underworld. Here the adherents of Baal participate in that death and are strewn across the countryside—all to disappear in time.

On Boasting, 9:23-26

Verses 23-26 are a segment in prose (or partly thereof; NAB scans vv. 23-24 as poetry). Verses 23-24 seem to be unrelated to vv. 25-26, though they may be linked by a common rejection of trust in any virtue, possession, or practice that blurs the centrality of trust in God. Exilic readers appear to be the audience addressed. First, in a wisdom saying in triadic form, God clarifies the nature of the present situation (vv. 23-24). The exiles have experienced the judgment of God in all its death-dealing horror through the actions of Babylonian armies. The "Why?!" questions, calling for wisdom and discernment, have been fielded and addressed (vv. 12-16). But that is not God's only word or last word to the exiles. This could be a general response to a people who did boast in wisdom and riches (see 8:8, 10), but the focus is on the experience of judgment (as in the concern about wisdom in 9:12).

God makes clear that the divine action takes place "in the *earth*" (wherever and whenever), and not in arbitrariness or vindictiveness, but "in steadfast love, justice and righteousness." These words refer to God, *not* to the characteristics of human beings brought about by God's actions.[2] *Even in judgment*, whatever the appearances (such as the violence of the Babylonian armies), God's actions are to be so characterized. The judgment has occurred because God is just and does not let sin and evil go unchecked in the world. But in the midst of the judgment, God's love remains steadfast and God remains faithful to commitments in the relationship with Israel (the basic meaning of "righteousness").

God takes pleasure (!) in acting in these ways, because in so doing God is being true to God's own self. The people are to understand and know that their God is this kind of God. In their knowledge of this kind of God they are to boast (see 4:2). The boasting is, in effect, a confession of faith (see 12:1). The great judgments through which they have passed, and any future events that they might anticipate (vv. 25-26), are not to be ascribed fundamentally to human wisdom or strength or wealth, however much human beings were the agents of God's action. Notably, however, these human "gifts" are not considered negative in and of themselves (!); so the text does not call for a divestment of them, but rather a proper understanding of their status in life. The confession of faith is to focus on God—a God of steadfast love, justice, and righteousness—and not on self or one's own virtues and possessions (see **Connections: Let the One Who Boasts, Boast in the Lord**).

Verses 25-26 are somewhat unclear, but they do continue the theme of trust and provide an assuring word to exiles, albeit in a negative way. The verb translated "attend to" (NRSV) is *pāqad,* a verb that commonly refers to divine visitation in judgment. This judgment probably refers both to the fall of Jerusalem and to the defeat and destruction of the surrounding nations against whom the Babylonian armies had moved (cf. 12:14-17 for another possible connection).

This word about the future focuses on those "who are circumcised only in the foreskin" (so NRSV). The peoples mentioned are remarkable in that "Judah" is simply included on a list, including Egypt, Edom, Ammon, Moab, and certain Arab tribes for whom shaven temples is a religious rite (see 25:23; this practice was forbidden for Israel, Lev 19:27). From the evidence we have, all of these peoples practiced circumcision. All of these nations, including the house of Israel, though circumcised in the flesh, were uncircumcised in the heart. The point seems to be that physical circumcision will not protect anyone, including Israel, in this time of invasion and destruction; hence, it joins a list of religious practices that include the temple and sacrifices (see 6:20; 7:4-15, 21-23). At the end of the day, circumcision or uncircumcision is not what counts, only the circumcision of the heart (see 4:4; Rom 2:25-29; Gal 5:2-5; 6:15). Regarding physical circumcision, Israel stands together with others and not apart. By merging Israel into this larger circumcised group, Israel as a circumcised people is shown to have no special security in the face of the divine judgment. Indeed, "all" the house of Israel is uncircumcised in heart; judgment is inevitable for all.

At the same time,[3] the statement makes no claims about Israel's "chosen status," as if judgment showed that Israel is "no more chosen than any other." Israel is certainly as open to judgment as any other people, perhaps even more so (see Amos 3:2), but God remains committed to this people in and through the worst of the judgments.

CONNECTIONS

The Juxtaposition of Grief and Wrath

It may seem incongruous for readers that God follows a statement of profound grief with an announcement of judgment (vv. 10-11). But these verses are typical of Jeremiah in keeping themes of lament and judgment closely linked. Jeremiah enables readers to see that the internal side of divine anger is grief. To put it too simply, a kind of "this hurts me more than it hurts you" sense pervades the divine judgment. God mediates judgment so that sin and evil do not go unchecked in the life of the world. But God does so at great cost to the divine life.

God's history with these people through the years means that they have been caught up into the divine life and indeed have shaped the divine identity. Because of God's promises to Israel, God will forever be known as the God of Israel. It is precisely because of those commitments that God grieves. [On Divine Freedom]

This seeming incongruity is sometimes used to suggest that Jeremiah presents images for God that "contradict each other." And so, "divine tears put aside punishment...and characterize God in radically different terms from much of the rest of the book." These tears "provide a glimpse of another kind of deity" from that of "the divine punisher and wrathful judge."[4] But anger and tears go together in Jeremiah (see 8:19c in context; 9:10 with 9:11; 9:17-19 with 9:22). To speak of tears and anger together is not contradictory. Rather, these emotions are held together in God, as they commonly are when speaking of people who have suffered the brokenness of intimate relationships. Anger and tears flow together. The predominance of marital metaphors in Jeremiah suggests that he is thinking of just such relationships in developing the character of God.

Another unusual dimension of the divine pathos in vv. 10-11 is that human beings are hardly in view. [Berrigan on Sin and the Environment] The focus of divine suffering is centered on God's other creatures

---

On Divine Freedom

Talk about divine freedom is common in Jeremiah studies, but the way in which the matter is formulated is often problematic. It is very important to affirm that God is free to judge God's own people. At the same time, God's freedom cannot be maintained in an unqualified way for Jeremiah. For God to enter into judgment is not even fundamentally an exercise in freedom. Most basically, God's judgment (or any divine action) is grounded in God's will and purpose for people and world; indeed, judgment may be *necessary* if God would be faithful to that purpose. Judgment may be the only way in which God can do justice to relationships established and to a purpose to which God is committed (see 9:23-24; 29:1-10; 31:1-6; for detail, see Terence Fretheim, "The Character of God in Jeremiah," forthcoming).

The immense agony of the God of Jeremiah is a demonstration that God is not truly free of God's relationship with Israel. If God were completely free of any commitments to Israel, then the judgment would not affect the divine life to the same extent. This means that it is a mistake to think of the God of Jeremiah as "radically free," or similar sorts of formulations. (For example, Walter Brueggemann, *A Commentary on Jeremiah: Exile and Homecoming* [Grand Rapids: Erdmans, 1998], 138; This perspective is also typical of L. Stulman, *Order Amid Chaos: Jeremiah as Symbolic Tapestry* [Sheffield: Sheffield Academic Press, 1998], 178. Stulman also wants to speak of the God of Jeremiah as being in "absolute control," 76, 114. If so, given how unruly Israel is, one would have to score God a crashing management failure!) If God were truly free, God would just get up and leave, for God would have no significant commitments to this people and God would not agonize so over what has happened to the relationship. Given God's promises, God is truly limited by them; God will be faithful.

and the pain of God's heart over their destruction is sharply evident. God has established a relationship with nonhuman creatures

Berrigan on Sin and the Environment

📖 Beings that flew and raced free and sang and bellowed, barked and screeched and roared; all that lends joy to eye and ear and touch and taste, that awes and inspires and renders the seeing heart grateful—entire species have been made to disappear. The oracle is of today, of ourselves.

Daniel Berrigan, *Jeremiah: The World, the Wound of God* (Minneapolis: Fortress, 1999), 49.

that is independent of the human and that relationship is of such a nature that God truly grieves when they suffer (see, e.g., Ps 50:10-11; Job 38–41). There is a sense in which one must say that God bears some responsibility for such degradation of the environment, but that is only because of the prior human wickedness (as vv. 12-16 immediately make clear; see **Connections** at ch. 12).

Let the One Who Boasts, Boast in the Lord

The New Testament picks up on the theme of vv. 23-24 in 1 Cor 1:31; 2 Cor 10:17. The Apostle Paul speaks of the divine strategy in calling people to "proclaim Christ crucified" (1 Cor 1:23). God did not choose people because they were rich and powerful, nor because they were wise and skilled in debate. God chose what is foolish and weak, what is low and despised in the world, so that the focus of their proclamation (their "boasting") would be on Jesus Christ rather than on themselves. The source of life and wisdom and righteousness is to be found, not in human virtues or resources, but in what God has done in Jesus Christ for the salvation of the world. The point for both Paul and Jeremiah is not that human wisdom or strength or resources are of no importance. They have their own value and one thinks of Jeremiah himself (!), but they must finally be in the service of "boasting" in the Lord.

NOTES

1 See William Holladay, *Jeremiah 1* (Philadelphia: Fortress, 1986), 306.

2 Contrary to Walter Brueggemann, *A Commentary on Jeremiah: Exile and Homecoming* (Grand Rapids: Eerdmans, 1998), 100-101; see Robert Carroll, *Jeremiah* (Philadelphia: Westminster, 1986), 247-49.

3 Contrary to Brueggemann, *Jeremiah,* 101-102.

4 So Kathleen O'Connor, "The Tears of God and Divine Character in Jeremiah 2–9," in *God in the Fray: A Tribute to Walter Brueggemann,* ed. T. Linafelt and T. Beal (Minneapolis: Fortress, 1998), 172, 184-85.

A UNIVERSAL FRAME
OF REFERENCE

10:1-25

This chapter consists of two major sections. Verses 1-16 constitute a hymnic interlude with a satirical cast wherein Israel's great and incomparable God, creator of all things, is mockingly contrasted with the idols of the nations (numerous parallels with the Psalms and Isaiah 40–55 exist). This text could be understood as an expansion on the portrayal of God in 9:24; several of its themes are also echoed in 16:19-21.

Verses 1-16 rhythmically move back and forth between doxologies (vv. 6-7, 10, 12-13, 16) and caricatures of the idols of the nations (vv. 2-5, 8-9, 11, 14-15). This litany-like form may reflect liturgical usage, with different voices, providing a variety of contrasts between their God and the gods of the peoples among whom they live. This segment (vv. 1-16) introduces interwoven words of judgment and lament (vv. 17-25) that close off this major section of Jeremiah (4:4–10:25). The theme of "the nations" in vv. 2, 25 provides an inclusion for the entire chapter.

COMMENTARY

An Incomparable God, 10:1-16

This opening section, addressed as it is to the house of Israel, proclaims a word about God and idols pertinent to any time and place. Yet, its content suggests that this is a word especially appropriate for exilic readers, surrounded as they were by idolatrous worship (see parallel texts in Isa 40:18-20; 41:6-7; 44:9-20). A special concern to separate the people of God out from these nations and their idolatrous practices is evident. Among the nations with their false gods, Israel's God is incomparable (vv. 6-7). Israel's God is the "King of the nations" (v. 7; cf. v. 10).

This interest in the nations contributes to an even more comprehensive theme of the section, namely, creation (see **Introduction**).

A Universal Frame of Reference

The chapter begins with a word about "the nations" and that theme pervades vv. 1-10. The chapter ends with a comparable reference to "the nations," and links them to the exercise of the divine wrath for their idolatry and excessive wasting of the people of Israel and their land. This *universal frame of reference* for the chapter is important for the entire book of Jeremiah for at least two reasons.

One, it grounds the preceding oracles of judgment against Israel (chs. 2–9) and what follows within the creation-wide purposes of God. What God is about in such judgmental action is not some local skirmish unrelated to God's larger purposes for the creation (see 5:22). What God is about with Israel is not only typical of God's actions among the nations, it has universal implications. The integrity of the creation itself is at stake (e.g., 4:23-26).

Two, this frame of reference links God's creation-wide purposes with all the other nations. This is especially evident in the repetition of 10:12-16 in 51:15-19, where the judgment of Babylon comes into view. Israel's God is "the King of the nations" (10:7) and this King, who is living, true, and everlasting, is sovereign over the nations, evident in the exercise of wrath (so 10:10). Jeremiah's prayer to God in v. 25 is a plea to God to begin to act against the nations in this regard.

So, whether the issue is judgment against Israel or the nations, God's creation-wide purposes are at work, which will issue finally in a universal salvation—deliverance for Israel and "all the earth" (51:59; see 3:17; 4:2; 16:19-21). Indeed, God's goal is to "give rest to the earth" (50:34). "Then the heavens and the earth, and all that is in them, shall shout for joy" (51:48).

The distinction between Israel's God and the false gods of the nations is specified especially in terms of the created order. The idols are products made by human artisans from things that Israel's God has created in the first place—wood from forests, silver, and gold (vv. 3-4, 9). The idols are silent and inactive; they cannot move or speak or give instruction or walk or make anyone afraid (vv. 4-5, 8; see 14:22). They cannot even do evil, let alone good—no dualistic perspective here (v. 5). God is the living God and eternal; the idols are neither (v. 10). Moreover, God not only created the world in the first place, God also continues to be actively engaged in creative activity (vv. 12-13, 16) (see **Connections: Israel's God and the Prohibition of Images**).

Notably, considerations regarding divine wrath are linked to these creation themes (vv. 10-11, 13, 15). In other words, wrath is understood to be an integral part of the *created order*, in and through which God works in judgment. [A Universal Frame of Reference] God's judgmental actions with respect to Israel are not capricious or unusual; rather, God is thereby being true to the very created order of things. Israel comes into the picture explicitly only at the end of the doxology (v. 16), and even though Israel is God's elect people, they remain subject to these created orders (see Amos 3:2, and the creation themes associated with judgment in Amos 4:13; 5:8-9; 9:5-6).

The chapter begins (v. 2) with a warning to exilic readers to steer clear of (=not learn) the (idolatrous) "way" of other nations (called "customs" in v. 3). Though the diviners and soothsayers of these nations discern omens in the sky that bring fear into the hearts of their people, Israel should not panic or be fearful of them. God does not mince words: these customs of the nations are false!

Brueggemann on Idolatry

In Jeremiah's time as in our own, the critical faith issue is not atheism, but idolatry. In Jeremiah's time the temptation was the attention of the gods of Babylon. In our day the comparable temptation may be the gods of militarism, of nationalism, of naturalism, of consumerism, of technology. In both cases the temptation is to vest one's life hope in the things we ourselves generate, instead of receiving life as a gift from this One who stands beyond us and for us. Characteristically the Bible does not deny the existence of other gods. The Bible makes an assumption that the world is polytheistic. The other gods exist. They have seductive power, but what they lack is power for life. They cannot do anything, and in that decisive test they are utterly unlike Yahweh, who has the power to give life and therefore the power to judge life....The modern form of idolatry is finally autonomy, the sense that we live on our own terms. But such autonomy is a lie. The truth concerns this other One.

Walter Brueggemann, *A Commentary on Jeremiah: Exile and Homecoming* (Grand Rapids: Eerdmans, 1998), 102, 107.

Related examples of such falsehood are given (note the colon in NRSV at v. 3a). They cut down trees from the forest; the wood is worked with an ax by an artisan; others wrap gold and silver sheathing around the wood and fasten it with nails so that it does not fall over (see Isa 40:19-20). And out comes a god (cf. Exod 32:24)! But these gods, contrary to the claims made about them, are like scarecrows placed in a cucumber field to scare the birds away! They should not put the fear of God in anyone! They cannot speak or walk or do good/evil, that is, act in any way at all (cf. 44:15-18; Zeph 1:12, where some claim this is also true of Israel's God). At the same time, it would not be correct to say that no evil is *generated* in those who worship them; the idols do have a kind of power for evil that should not be gainsaid. [Brueggemann on Idolatry]

This satirical presentation of the idols of the nations and their *creaturely* origins is interrupted by a paean of praise to the Creator Lord (vv. 6-7; cf. Exod 15:11; Deut 33:26; Ps 86:8-9). This hymnic piece begins and ends with the claim that no one is like the Lord; in view are both the idols and the "wise" teachers (an ironic point; they are actually "stupid and foolish," v. 8; see v. 14; 8:8-9; 4:22). The incomparability of God is praised, as is God's greatness and strength. God is imaged here in royal terms: Who would not fear (=revere) such a God (see 5:22, where "fear" also carries the sense of being afraid)? Given the kind of God that God is, it is "fitting" (REB; NRSV, "due") that God be revered; it is meet, right, and salutary that this God should be praised. This is an implicit call to worship the true God; so the concern is not simply to reject idolatrous worship.

Following the paean of praise, the text returns to the claim that the idols have been produced out of what God has made (vv. 8-9), and then concludes with another doxological word (v. 10).

Idols from Silver and Gold

The artisans of idols used silver from Tarshish (a seaport, probably in the western Mediterranean) and gold from Uphaz (an unknown site, perhaps a corruption for Ophir; so NAB). Ophir, an unknown site, perhaps in Arabia or Africa, could be reached most easily by ship (1 Kgs 9:28; 10:11); it was famous for its gold (Job 22:24; 28:16; Isa 13:12). These two distant places may suggest that the people made great efforts to procure the best materials for the manufacture of their idols. But even the best materials and the finest craftsmanship could not make a suitable image for Israel's God.

Gold and silver foil-coverd bronze figure of Baal. 23 cm. Canaanite. c. 1900 BC. Christie's. London, England. (Credit: Werner Forman/Art Resource, NY)

For human teachers to suggest that these idols can give instruction is foolish; they are made out of wood (v. 8)! Moreover, the idols are the work of human artisans, who use materials from God's good creation (imported from far-flung ports). [Idols from Silver and Gold] And they drape the idols in blue and purple clothing, also the product of skilled human work. To suggest that human products can create life for their creators is stupid (though all too common in every generation)! That would be like saying that creatures can give life to their creator God. In contrast, Israel's God is not a created being, but true, living, and eternal (v. 10 is a kind of creed regarding the character of God, cf. Exod 34:6-7). This God is Lord over the earth and the nations are subject to God's moral order; they are not in control of the wrath of God, indeed they may be destabilized by it (see at 4:4; **Introduction**) (see **Connections: "The Work of Your Hands"**).

Verses 11-16 (vv. 12-16 are repeated in 51:15-19), with a new introduction, continue the rhythm of contrast between the idols (vv. 11, 14-15) and the living God of all creation, who is also the God of Israel (vv. 12-13, 16). Verse 11 underlines a basic claim of the entire passage: the idols are creatures, not the Creator (see Ps 96:5) and they will perish like all other created things. Hence, the exiles need have no fear of them. That this verse is written in Aramaic (unique in Jeremiah) may serve to highlight the point of the text. The identity of "you" and "them" in v. 11 is not altogether clear. It is likely that the verse is a directive to the exiles to speak these words to the idolaters among them or, possibly, to the idols themselves. If the latter, this verse is an incantation against foreign worship practices that threatened them.[1]

In contrast to the creaturely, perishable stature of the idols, vv. 12-13 hymn God's status as the Creator (see 5:22; 31:35; Ps 104; Prov 8:22-31; Amos 4:13; 5:8-9; 9:5-6). God has created the earth and the heavens and that reveals God's power. The well-ordered structures of the creation reveal God's wisdom and understanding. The word of God is efficacious and has brought into being the waters of the heavens and on the earth. But this God's creative work also continues through all time, drawing on inexhaustible heavenly "storehouses" (see Job 38:22), as can be observed in various weather systems, including mists, wind, lightning, and rain. At the same time, this creative work should not be considered a divine micromanagement of weather systems (Jer 31:35-37 will speak of fixed orders; see **Connections** there; Gen 8:22; **Introduction**). Each of these dimensions of the work of God the Creator stands in contrast to the ineffectiveness of the idols.

Once again, the poetry returns to the idols and their human artisans (vv. 14-15). In contrast to God, the human producers (and worshipers?) of idols are without wisdom and understanding (see v. 8); indeed they are deluded. The results of their work is of such a character and quality that the idols can only bring shame on their makers. The images that they make are contrasted with the prior characterization of God in several critical ways: they are false not true, dead not living, nothingness not reality, and perishable not eternal. The idols, like the idolaters themselves, will perish. This material prepares the way for God's judgment of the nations in chapters 25, 46–51, though those oracles do not often speak of their idolatry (see 48:35).

Verse 16 returns to and concludes the poem with praise, and for the first time brings Jacob/Israel into the picture. The phrase "portion of Jacob" is a metaphor for God. [God as the Portion of Jacob] This divine self-identification in terms of a particular people is a point where another contrast with the idols is made; God has made a

---

God as the Portion of Jacob

AΩ By using this metaphor God identifies himself as Israel's portion; elsewhere the people make this claim (Lam 3:24; Pss 16:5; 73:26; 119:57; 142:5). In saying this, God claims to *belong* to the people of Israel, just as Israel/Jacob belonged to God (="the tribe of his inheritance"; see the language of "portion" in Deut 32:9; Zech 2:12). This is a remarkable statement of the God-Israel relationship, identified in these texts in terms of a *mutual*

belonging. One could even say that God identifies himself as the possession (!) of Israel, just as the land of Canaan was called Israel's portion (see 12:10; Num 18:20). God's ongoing relationship with Israel has meant that the chosen people have been caught up into the divine life and have thereby *shaped the divine identity*. This epithet is God's own testimony to be *forever* known as the God of Israel; by God's own choosing, Israel has become part of the very identity of God.

commitment in relationship to Israel in a way that no idol could make to other nations (see **Connections** below). Notably, this relationship with Israel is expressed in creational terms, which aligns this verse with the emphases of the chapter up to this point; "he is the one who formed all things." The phrase, "the Lord of Hosts is his name," is a typical paean of praise at the conclusion of a hymn and underlines the hymnic character of this material (see 31:35).

The Final Siege, 10:17-25

Once again, the speaker and the audience are difficult to discern. It seems best to consider the entire segment as spoken by Jeremiah, who quotes others, including God (v. 18) and people (vv. 19-20). The range of emotions expressed here mirrors the varied responses to the devastation experienced. The opening imperative (feminine singular; see ch. 2) is initially addressed to those who are living under siege (v. 17) and whose end is sure (vv. 20-21). Verses 19-20 (and even v. 21) are often assigned to the people; they are personified as Mother Zion, who speaks of the loss of her children (similarly, 31:15-19). Yet, the speaker may still be Jeremiah who voices these concerns as a representative of the people (see the parallels between v. 20 and 4:20 and 30:18), at least in vv. 19-20. In v. 21 Jeremiah reflects the divine indictment of the leaders and their experience of judgment. Given the similarities of vv. 19-20 with 31:15-19, the speaker could also be the exilic community (or Jeremiah as representative of them). Verse 22 brings the reader back to the siege mentality of v. 17; the foe from the north is about to devastate cities and land (and loops back to 4:5-6). Verses 23-25 conclude the section with a prayer of Jeremiah.

Verses 17 and 22 seem to be most closely related to the actual experience of the siege of Jerusalem and other cities. Verses 18-21 consist of an interpretation of these events from several perspectives, as the voices of God, prophet, and people are heard (all through Jeremiah). Jeremiah's prayer in vv. 23-25 seems more distantly related to the events, as he responds, apparently after the fact, to the ferocity of the invaders against God's people. In view of the latter, and taking the section as a single whole, these verses could function as a vivid recollection for exilic readers. Through various rhetorical devices they are transported back into the dire situation of city and people and re-experience it.

The meaning of v. 17, while uncertain, anticipates the exile of the populace in v. 18. Those who are under siege and about to go into exile should lift up their "bundle" or bag of possessions and prepare for the journey. Those whom God will sling (like a stone, Judg 20:16) out of the land and onto this journey into exile (through the mediation of the Babylonians) will suffer deep distress throughout this time of upheaval and deportation (see REB, "I shall press them and squeeze them dry").

The deep distress noted in v. 18 is described in vv. 19-20. The language used recalls that of 4:19-20 and 8:18–9:1. The language of pain and wound and suffering is sharply etched to have an impact on exilic readers. In v. 19b, the people seem to make a confession, with a reference to "punishment" (so NRSV), but the imagery is drawn more from the sphere of health (cf. NIV, "sickness"; NAB, "wound"; see 6:7). This is probably a word of resignation in the face of the onslaught, that there is nothing they can do but endure it. And what has happened is specified (v. 20): their tents/homes have been destroyed; their tent-cords/supports have been severed; their children have disappeared, probably killed; nobody is available to help reestablish a home (30:18 in the Book of Consolation returns to this theme).

All these things have happened because Israel's "shepherds" (=leaders; see 3:15; 6:3; 23:1) have been stupid and have not sought a word from the Lord; they have followed their own devices and reaped the consequences (v. 21). Because of these unwise and unfaithful behaviors, they have not prospered and their flock (=the general populace) have been scattered abroad. While the people are not let off the hook, the fundamental factor leading to these devastating developments is laid at the feet of the religious and political leadership of Israel. Then, suddenly, following close on the heels of the statement about failed leadership, the text returns (v. 22; see v. 17) to the clamorous chaos associated with the advancing Babylonian armies. Their goal is to so devastate Israel's cities that the land on which they have been built will be returned to its wilderness character and be home once again for the jackals (see 9:11).

All of these developments become the occasion for a prayer by Jeremiah that is both petition and intercession (vv. 23-25; the Book of Consolation returns to several of these themes, 30:11, 16). This prayer is set in a time after the destruction of Jerusalem (see v. 25b). It is fundamentally oriented toward the future, a future that includes the exiles (for whom the prophet would serve as representative) and the future of those nations that hold the exiles captive, especially the Babylonians.

This prayer begins with a wisdom-like statement about the relationship of God and human beings generally (v. 23). Human beings are finite creatures, not God, and hence they cannot dictate the shape of their own futures; this would certainly be the case for the exiles. They will often be forced to walk in ways they do not choose, ways that have been dictated by others (e.g., their captors). The point does not center on the understanding of God's ways by human beings[2] but about their ability to control their own destiny. The passage makes no claims about *God* as the one with controlling power (cf. Prov 16:9; 20:24), but v. 24 will appeal to God to provide a certain kind of direction for that future.

Then the prayer moves in two directions, inward and outward. As with vv. 19-20, the prophet again speaks as representative of the people. First (v. 24), Jeremiah petitions God with respect to himself (and those like him)—that God might give a particular shape to the future, particularly the future in exile. He asks God to correct or discipline him (no repentance is implied), but in just measure (see 30:11, where God seems to respond positively to this request) and not in anger, so that he is not reduced to nothing (either to disappear into the mists of history or be killed). The exiles had experienced enough of the divine anger; another such experience would wipe them out.

The divine anger now is to be reserved for others! And so, second (v. 25), Jeremiah intercedes *against* the Babylonians (and allied nations). He prays that God would pour out his wrath upon these people who do not know the God of Israel (see 12:16-17; v. 25 is repeated in Ps 79:6-7, a psalm of communal lament dating from the time of exile). The reason for the prayer is sharply stated: these nations have destroyed Israel and have wasted their entire habitat, both homes and land. In other words, they exceeded God's will for the situation, acting too harshly against the people of God. In this regard Jeremiah's anger conforms to God's anger; God declares a comparable future for these nations in later texts (see 25:12-38; 30:16; cf. Isa 47:5-7; see **Connections** at ch. 7).

CONNECTIONS

Israel's God and the Prohibition of Images

Israel usually speaks of its God in language drawn from human experience. God is *believed* to be one who thinks and acts and feels and decides (note that the argument proceeds from the perspective of faith in this God). God has a mouth that speaks, eyes that see, arms that exhibit strength, and hands that create. These anthropomorphisms stand together with the more concrete relational metaphors (e.g., father, king, spouse) in saying something important about God. Israel's God is a relational being, living and dynamic, one whose ways of relating to the world are best captured in the language of human personality and activity. It is, of course, ironic that Christians from time to time have had difficulty with this language, for in Jesus Christ God has acted anthropomorphically in an unsurpassable way.

The importance of such relational and personal language can be seen in texts that speak of the prohibition of images. The commandment regarding the prohibition of images (Exod 20:4; Deut 5:8) is often thought to guard God's transcendence; but it is just as concerned to protect God's relatedness, if not more so. Jeremiah 10:4-5 contrasts idols with Israel's God with regard to moving, speaking, walking, and acting. Comparable contrasts are found in Psalms 115:5-7 and 135:15-18. The implication is that Israel's God is one who speaks and sees and hears and feels and acts. With the idols there is no deed or word, no real presence or activity. In contrast, Israel's God has entered into a relationship with the world that is lively and real. This "real" God, active in Israel and in all of creation, contrasts with the unreality of the idols.

Interpreters also sometimes suggest that the prohibition of images guards God's freedom. But texts such as these suggest that the prohibition is concerned, rather, to protect God's commitment. Idols are remarkably free of commitments, free from issues of faithfulness to relationships established. Israel's God is not free, at least in this sense (see **Connections**, ch. 9). Such an understanding has ethical and vocational implications for those who are called to walk in all of God's ways. Such persons are called to be in genuine relationship with God and others, and certainly not free of commitments but fully engaged on behalf of the welfare of the other. [In the Image of God]

In the Image of God

This understanding of the prohibition of images is continuous with that point where the Old Testament does talk about a legitimate concrete image, namely, the human being made in the image of God (Gen 1:26-28). It is the human being, with all of its capacities for relationships, that is believed to be the appropriate image of God in the life of the world. All other images fail. The New Testament uses this language to speak of Jesus Christ as the image of the invisible God (2 Cor 3:18; 4:4; Col 1:15; Heb 1:3). This human being is the one who reveals God most clearly and decisively.

"The Work of Your Hands"

Several passages in Jeremiah speak of idolatry as the work of human hands (1:16; 10:9; 25:6-7, 14; 32:30; 44:8). John Barton speaks helpfully about this language, indicating that idolatry is finally "a kind of self-help." "However much worshippers might bow down to the idol and acknowledge it as a great power, it was really themselves they were worshipping all the time. They were failing, as Psalm 115 sees it, to distinguish between divine and human power, between heaven and earth, and in the end between the living and the dead. The idols were 'the work of human hands' and as such provided no power genuinely independent of the power that made them, from which any help could be sought."

Barton goes on to say,

> . . . at a rhetorical level it is easy to insist that the Church must take these warnings to heart and must cease to put its trust in anything that "is not God"....we may find ourselves condemning our contemporaries for idolatry by saying that they worship money, or sex, or power; though if we do this we had better make sure we are aware that we could fall under the same condemnation ourselves. My problem with all this is that these forms of rhetoric come rather easily to the lips, and there is always a great danger that we shall use the condemnation of idolatry as an unanswerable argument against whatever happens to be our pet hate, whether in the Church or in the world. How are we to use the language responsibly in analyzing human conduct, so as not merely to manipulate it as a way of claiming and retaining a kind of high moral ground?
>
> Certainly we can only make a wholesome use of the concept of idolatry if we apply it as a form of self-criticism, not as a stick with which to beat others....Opening our eyes to the possibility that we may be self-deluded is always a very difficult task. How do you challenge your own presuppositions and commitments? Yet, the biblical condemnation of idolatry certainly demands that we should try to do this, however difficult it may be.[3]

NOTES

[1] See Robert Carroll, *Jeremiah* (Philadelphia: Westminster, 1986), 256-57.

[2] Contrary to Walter Brueggemann, *A Commentary on Jeremiah: Exile and Homecoming* (Grand Rapids: Eerdmans, 1998), 108.

[3] John Barton, "'The Work of Human Hands' (Ps 115:4): Idolatry in the Old Testament," *Ex Auditu* 15 (1999): 71-72.

A COVENANT VIOLATED

11:1-17

Laments of Jeremiah and God, 11:1–20:18

The opening unit of this section (11:1-17) constitutes the second major block of prose material (see 7:1–8:3), and functions as a kind of swing section. It gathers up the essence of the previous chapters and introduces the next main section of Jeremiah (11:1–20:18). This unit sets out the certainty of the judgment of Israel, in view of which the various laments are especially appropriate. The note of curse begins and ends this section (11:3; 20:18), as Jeremiah speaks of cursing the day of his birth so Israel is described as cursed. The theme of Israel's "conspiracy" against its God (11:9) serves well as an introduction to their conspiracy against Jeremiah in 11:18–12:6 (see also 18:12, 18 for a conspiracy against both God and prophet). God's life is embodied in the prophet's life.

This section of the book consists primarily of a series of interwoven laments from God, prophet, and people that reflect the certainty and decisiveness of the judgment. In so doing, this section portrays in more particular ways various personal interactions among the principals. The laments of Jeremiah are the central feature amid a variety of types of literature. At the same time, the laments of God and people are also integral to these chapters. The interweaving of laments of God and prophet are especially significant. These laments by God, people, and prophet have been anticipated in the first eleven chapters of Jeremiah (e.g., 2:5, 29-31; 3:1-5, 19-20; 4:19-21; 8:4-7, 14-15; 8:18–9:2, 10-11, 17-22; 10:19-21, 23-25). It would be a mistake to speak of the "first" lament of Jeremiah or any other character in 11:18–20:18 (except perhaps as a means of ordering the material in this section). These chapters intensify the laments of the opening chapters and bring them to a screaming climax in the lament of Jeremiah in 20:14-18. Whatever the reader might think of the harshness of the indictments rendered against Israel and the violence of the judgments, the fundamental backdrop of these tumultuous and devastating events is weeping and mourning (see **Introduction**; on the laments, see next section).

Several other types of literature are interwoven with these laments. Narratives centered in symbolic actions/words of the prophet are

Intensification of Dialogue

We have noted the dialogical character of the first ten chapters of Jeremiah (see **Connections** at ch. 2). While the voice of God has been the most prominent in the opening chapters, the voices of prophet and the people interacting with God have also been heard, especially in chs. 8–10. The dialogical presentation of the material now intensifies in chs. 11–20. God not only addresses the human participants (prophet and people), but God is also addressed by them, and often in direct terms. This openness of God to the words of human beings says something very important about both God and the nature of the relationship that God has established with the people of Israel. This relationship is of such a character that God is not the only one who has something important to say. God will take the contributions of the human parties into account in finding a way into the future.

especially to be noted: The linen loincloth (13:1-11); the wine jars (13:12-14); the prophet's personal life (16:1-9); the potter and the clay (18:1-12); the broken earthenware jug (19:1-15); and, in some ways, the persecution of Jeremiah by Pashhur (20:1-6). Interwoven throughout are some oracles of judgment (13:15-27; 14:10-16; 15:1-4; 16:10-13; 17:1-4; 18:13-17); also included are salvation oracles (12:14-17; 16:14-21), several wisdom sayings (17:5-13), and an exhortation regarding the Sabbath (17:19-27). That the oracles of judgment are interwoven with laments of both prophet and God has a great deal to say regarding how the words of judgment are to be interpreted; words of judgment do not stand isolated but are accompanied by grief. [Intensification of Dialogue]

COMMENTARY

The Indictment, 11:1-10

This unit clearly indicates that the announced judgment on Israel has already taken place (v. 8), so it is addressed to the exiles (see 1:3). Though these verses, usually identified as a Deuteronomistic composition,[1] have been linked to the reform of Josiah and the reaffirmation of covenant in 2 Kings 23:1-3, the text itself provides no reference to that occasion. More generally, this preaching regarding the covenant, a rare theme in the book, places Jeremiah in the tradition of the Deuteronomistic portrait of Moses.

This unit rehearses once again the factors that led to the fall of Jerusalem and the exile. This time around, the infidelity of Israel is considered in terms of the language of covenant. [The Covenant] This is the first time that the covenant is explicitly referenced in Jeremiah (cf. 3:16). Its usage suggests that the issue of

---

The Covenant

The covenant at Mt. Sinai is particularly in view (v. 4) and various aspects of traditional covenant talk are brought into focus. Whereas the covenant ritual *concluded* with curses and blessings (see Deut 27–28), this indictment *begins* in these terms, with the curse up front (vv. 3-5; cf. v. 7), and the judgment that the curse entails is woven into the very fabric of the section (vv. 8, 11-12, 16-17). Other components of the covenant ritual include the recital of God's actions on Israel's behalf (vv. 4-5), the stipulations (here stated in general terms, vv. 4, 6-8), and the people's commitment to be obedient (vv. 4, 6-8; cf. Exod 24:1-8; Josh 24). Jeremiah could be said to function as a witness (v. 5); his response is the same as Israel's response to the various curses in Deut 27:15-26, "Amen"). More generally, the word "listen/obey/heed" occurs eight times in the first eleven verses.

It is wise to remember that covenant is a *metaphor* drawn from the sphere of personal and communal relationships; it is not to be literally understood. Hence, God is not *contractually* bound to exact the terms of the covenant. The relationship between God and people is too personally oriented for contractual language to do it justice. Again and again God has been patient with this unfaithful people; God's "mercy is greater than His justice." The responses of God and people to each other are neither legalistically defined nor schematically determined. This understanding is evident in the recurring reference to God's patient "persistence" (e.g., 7:25) in sending the prophets to turn them from their wicked ways.

The book of Jeremiah is usually interpreted in terms of the Sinaitic covenant and Mosaic theology. The common claim of a heavy Deuteronomic editing of the book has reinforced this understanding. Jeremiah is a prophet like Moses. This perspective is often set over against a theology associated with the temple and the Davidic kingship. This direction in Jeremiah research has sometimes resulted in a narrowly channeled interpretation of the book. Even so, the comparative rarity of covenant language in Jeremiah (references to the covenant at Sinai are especially uncommon, see 22:9; 31:32) should caution interpreters not to attempt to read the entire book through the lens of that particular metaphor (see **Introduction**).

Abraham Heschel, *The Prophets* (New York: Haper, 1962), 298.

---

unfaithfulness must be considered from every conceivable perspective, leaving no possibility of escape from the force of the charges. Or, in somewhat different terms, all of the metaphors for Israel's infidelity considered heretofore are brought to a focused climax: Israel has been unfaithful to the covenant with its God.

The unit is structured in the following terms, though transitions are imprecise; this suggests that the chapter has had a complex history (vv. 15-17 are sometimes treated as a supplement to the sermon).[2] The sermon opens with God twice commissioning Jeremiah to bring a word to Judah/Jerusalem (vv. 2-3, 6); the word of God is given in the second person as direct address (vv. 3-5, 6-8). Each of these two segments is introduced with a word to the readers/hearers: "Cursed be anyone who does not heed the words of this covenant" (v. 3); "Hear the words of this covenant and do them" (v. 6). The balance of each segment speaks of the ancestors (vv. 3-5, 7-8). This rhythm of word to readers followed by ancestral references can also be seen in 7:21-26.

A third word of God to Jeremiah (v. 9) does not include the call to speak to the people, and God speaks about Israel in the third person, including both indictment and announcement of judgment (vv. 9-12). Verse 13, which is addressed to Judah in the second person, breaks into this third person discourse with the essence of the issue of infidelity—the worship of gods other than Yahweh. Verses 15-17 consist of another such direct address, this time following upon a personal word to Jeremiah (v. 14).

The dialogical character of the relationship between Jeremiah and God, so prominent heretofore, is still evident in this segment, though Jeremiah only makes one response ("So be it, Lord," v. 5). God and prophet are together regarding the import of this matter. God addresses Jeremiah personally in v. 14, asking Jeremiah not to pray for this people (a recurring request, see at 7:16; 14:11; 15:1). Verses 15-17 immediately follow with God's reasons for making this request; this time they are addressed directly to the people. God's communications with the prophet are not hidden from the people.

Verses 1-2 are confusing in the Hebrew, with "Hear" being an imperative in the plural ("speak" is also plural, in most MSS). It may be that "Hear the words of this covenant" stands as a general divine pronouncement to all, including Jeremiah, as to the word that now follows regarding what God's covenant with Israel entails. And then a specific word to Jeremiah follows: speak to Judah/Jerusalem (reading a singular "speak" with some texts). Alternatively, if both verbs are plural (see 5:1), then God addresses several speakers (perhaps speakers in exile come into view). The word Jeremiah is to speak begins with a word about curse (see [The Covenant]). Because the people of Israel have not in fact heeded or obeyed "the words of this covenant," for Jeremiah to speak these words is, in effect, a recognition that the curse is in effect (see Deut 27:46 for the same word). The curse seems not to be an actual curse spoken by God against Israel, but a *recognition* by God that Israel is cursed because it is unfaithful (see 17:5).

Jeremiah's response (v. 5), "So be it, Lord," is an assent related particularly to the word about curse. The "*words* of this covenant" (v. 2) is explicitly associated with the covenant given to the "ancestors" after the exodus from Egypt (at Mt. Sinai). Note that Exodus 19:6-7; 20:1; 24:3-8 (see Deut 5:5, 22; 6:6) refer to the commandments and related covenantal matters as God's "words." To refer to Egypt as the "iron-smelter" (v. 4) is to use a metaphor for the fires of adversity and the harshness of slavery (see Deut 4:20; Isa 48:10). The emphasis in this recital lies on the graciousness of God's

Mt. Sinai

Mount Sinai is located in the Old Testament Sinai desert, which is in present-day Egypt. The exact location of the mountain is not known, but it is speculated that it is Gebel Musa in the southern Sinai desert. The location, nevertheless, does not carry as much significance as the symbolic nature of the mountain. At the foot of the mount (the Monastery of Saint Catherine is located there today), the Hebrews developed from a mixed multitude of people into a singular nation. Furthermore, Mount Sinai represents the place where the Israelites were given the Torah as well as the instructions for the Tent of Meeting. (Credit: Erich Lessing/Art Resource, NY)

activity on behalf of Israel when it was in dire straits (see **Connections: The Flow of Thought in Verses 1-5**).

Verses 6-8 continue the rhythm of a word to the readers followed by a word about the ancestors. The call, "hear the words of this covenant," is repeated from v. 2, with the addition, "and do them." Hearing is an insufficient response to the word of God; hearing must be accompanied by doing. While this segment is represented as a word to Judah/Jerusalem prior to the fall, v. 8 indicates that the fall of Jerusalem has become a reality. Hence, the call to "hear" and "do" is a word for post-fall readers, both as a recollection of warnings they had received from God and as a present calling.

The word in vv. 7-8 about the ancestors differs somewhat from the word in vv. 4-5. In the latter, the review focuses on the time of the original covenant-making at Sinai. Verses 7-8 extend that word through the centuries. The covenant-making at Sinai had included a warning regarding the implications of not obeying the words of God (the curses), and this warning had been repeated—persistently!—through the years, even up "to this day" (the readers' time). Then a summary statement is made regarding the people's unfaithful response to the command of obeying God's voice (v. 8). They did not obey, indeed they didn't even incline their ears in God's direction; they followed their own stubborn evil (*ra*ᶜ) will/heart (for a similar assessment, see 2 Kgs 17:13-15; on stubbornness, see **Connections** at ch. 5). This negative assessment is made regarding *all* the ancestors, from Sinai to the present (vv. 9-13 will proceed to speak more specifically of the present generation of readers). The result is a build-up of the effects of their evil behavior that finally reaches a point of no return. These effects are God's judgment and the curses of the "words of the covenant" become a reality for Israel. This was the case with the northern kingdom (2 Kings 17) and, from the readers' perspective, their own recent experience.

Verses 9-10 support the judgment of v. 8 with a more specific word about the nature of Israel's unfaithfulness (in the third person). The *present* people of Israel (=exilic readers) have turned back to the iniquities of their ancestors and followed in their steps, disobeying God's words by serving other gods. This "turning back" could suggest that there were periods of renewal in Israel's life, but the basic picture is that of continuing infidelity. The segment opens with an extension of the covenantal metaphor regarding what has happened to the God-Israel relationship, namely, "conspiracy" (a word used in political contexts, e.g., 1 Kgs 16:20). Thinking of covenant in terms of a treaty, the human party to the agreed upon relationship has broken it by conspiring with other gods, to be in service to them rather than Yahweh (see Deut 31:16). The people of Israel have switched their allegiance; using the treaty analogy, that is a matter of treasonous plots against Yahweh (see 18:12).

The Judgment, 11:11-17

As the reader of Jeremiah has come to expect, the indictment is followed by the announcement of judgment (vv. 11-12, "therefore"). From the perspective of exilic readers this would constitute a recollection. In the wake of their iniquities God is going to bring disaster (*rāᶜāh*, following upon the *ra*ᶜ of v. 9) upon them. They will not be able to escape from it; even though they cry out to God (still worshiped in a syncretistic fashion), God will not listen to them (see below on v. 14). God's not listening to the people is correspondent to the people's not listening to God ("what goes around, comes around" thinking is evident here). And, when (not "if"!) they seek the help of the other gods whom they serve by crying out to them, they will not be delivered; these gods are not able to save (*yāšaʿ*) them (see 2:27-28; 14:8; Deut 32:37-38).

Verse 13 returns to the indictment (see vv. 9-10), this time in direct address. The indictment gives specific, if hyperbolic evidence regarding how pervasive their infidelity has been. Their gods are as numerous as their towns; their altars to Baal are as numerous as the streets of Jerusalem. This shift from the third person to the second person makes best sense in view of the exilic readers. Readers might be tempted to distance themselves from the indictment of vv. 9-10; v. 13 brings it home to the readers. This infidelity has not been someone else's problem; it is yours! They will not be able to escape into the proverb, "the fathers have eaten sour grapes and the children's teeth are set on edge," and charge God with unfairness (31:29-30; Ezek 18:2).

Verse 14, with its particular word to Jeremiah, reinforces the announcement in v. 11 that God would not listen to the cries of the people (see Mic 3:4; Isa 1:15). Jeremiah is not to intercede on behalf of this people, for *God* will not listen to them or to him (as in 7:16; cf. 14:11-12; 15:1); this word reinforces the idea that there will be no turning back of the judgment that is to come (see 4:28). [Do Not Intercede for Them!]

Verse 15 abounds with textual difficulties, but the basic point seems clear. It states the reasons for this harsh judgment: such prayers would be at odds with Israel's usual worship practices and their use of worship spaces (="my house"). A comparable point was made in 7:3-11. They have no right to worship in the sanctuary— or pray!—when they spend their time devising treasonous plots/schemes (NRSV, "vile deeds"). Their vows and offerings will

---

Do Not Intercede for Them!

Why would it be necessary or important for God to prohibit intercession? Could not God just ignore whatever prayers Jeremiah happened to offer? One possible reason is that the command seeks to bring the prophet into the fullest possible conformity with the divine will for the situation. God has determined that judgment is inevitable; Jeremiah should speak and act in view of this divine direction. Prohibiting intercession is one way to do that. It would not be good to have God at odds with the prophet, not least because God takes human prayer seriously into account in charting the future (see [Worship and the Neighbor]).

At the same time, one recalls a comparable instruction that God gave to Moses in the wake of the golden calf debacle (Exod 32:10): Leave me alone! But Moses did not leave God alone, and it made a great deal of difference!

Might the repeated instruction to Jeremiah be comparably understood? Had Jeremiah prayed, who knows? The repetition of the prohibition over the course of these chapters (7:16; 11:14; 14:11; 15:1), however, suggests that this situation is quite different from that of the time of Moses. The build-up of wickedness in Israel's life is too far along for prayers to have any salutary effect; judgment is inevitable.

The absence of prophetic prayer also gives exilic readers another factor to consider regarding the "Why?!" of the fall of Jerusalem. The fault cannot be laid at the feet of the prophet, as if to say, "If only Jeremiah had interceded on our behalf, this would not have happened!" God here makes clear that God commanded him not to pray for them and, to reinforce the point, God even refused to listen to their prayers (see at also ch. 14).

not be effective in turning back the judgment that is to fall (see 6:20; 7:22-23; Isa 1:10-17; Amos 5:21-24) any more than Jeremiah's prayers would. When the fall occurs, they will not be able to sing their hymns of praise!

Note that God still calls these treasonous people "my beloved" (v. 15; as in 12:7). Such language is awkward to some of those who seek to amend the text. But there should be no difficulty with such language; it is precisely "my beloved" that is being judged, not anyone else (see Amos 3:2). The God who enters into judgment with Israel does not thereby cease to love them. In fact, God loves this people through the worst of judgments, and will never finally be done with them; God's love for them is "everlasting" (31:3; Isa 54:7-8). God's very identity is bound up with this people (see [God as the Portion of Jacob]).

Verse 16 (the text is difficult), once again phrased as direct address, speaks of God having (in the past) named Israel "A green olive tree, fair with goodly fruit." This metaphor speaks of a people created by God, full of life, and bearing much fruit (see 2:21; 5:10; 6:9; 17:6-8; Pss 52:8; 92:12-15; Hos 14:7). This metaphor remains appropriate for the exilic readers. It is used because it relates to the metaphor utilized for the judgment to be visited upon Israel. A fire has been kindled and, like lightning, will spread rapidly through the tree and consume all of its branches (see Isa 6:13).

Verse 17 brings several of the themes of this segment together in another direct address. The metaphor of the olive tree is picked up in the reference to Israel as one whom God has planted (see 1:10). This God has been provoked to anger (see 4:4) and has now declared evil (*rāʿāh*, as in v. 11) against Israel ("you") for the evil (*rāʿāh*) they have committed, specifically unfaithfulness in worshiping Baal. Note again the understanding of judgment here: *rāʿāh* issues in, grows out of *rāʿāh* (see 6:19; **Introduction**).

CONNECTIONS

The Flow of Thought in Verses 1-5

The command given Israel's ancestors at Sinai to listen to God's voice and obey the commandments (v. 4) sounds like a condition for what follows. If you do this, then "you shall be my people and I will be your God," and the promise to the ancestors regarding the land (see Gen 17:1-8) will be fulfilled. But a more subtle point is being made here. Several pentateuchal texts (e.g., Deut 9:5; 7:7-8) make it clear that the land is given to Israel quite apart from its (un)righteousness. Moreover, that promise was fulfilled, according to this very text (v. 5, "as at this day"), even though the ancestors "did *not* obey or incline their ear" (v. 8; a point also made in Deut 31:21, 27-29).

Moreover, it is eminently clear in the book of Exodus (e.g., 3:7-10) that, *prior* to the giving of the Law, Israel is *already* God's people. The covenant at Sinai does not establish the relationship between God and people, but charts their vocation as God's chosen ones.[3] The point here is not that Israel, through its obedience, would *become* God's people. Rather, the flow of thought runs like this: listen to my voice and do what I command, *and in so doing* you shall show yourself to be my people and, as for my part, I will be your God and perform the oath sworn to the ancestors. Covenant entails commitment on the part of both God and people, a commitment to be true to the relationship in which they already stand. [Covenant: Abraham and Sinai]

The fundamental way in which the people do justice to this relationship is to obey the commandments; the way in which God is true to the relationship is in fulfilling the sworn promises made to this people. God here testifies to having fulfilled sworn promises (regarding the land) even though the people have been unfaithful. Even more, the phrase "as at this day" (v. 5) indicates that, from the perspective of exilic readers, God's sworn promise regarding the land has not been set aside (see "forever" in 7:7; see 30:3; 32:22).

God's promises (of the land in this case) will not fail; they will never be made null and void as far as God is concerned. Though a rebellious generation may not live to see the fulfillment of the promise (witness the old and new generations in the book of Numbers), and may indeed come under the curse because they have rejected God, the promise can be relied upon (see Deut 4:31; 30:1-5). Thus, the promise is an everlasting one, though participation in its fulfillment is not guaranteed to every person or generation. The promise of God is always there for the believing to cling to, and they can know that God will ever be at work to fulfill it.

Covenant: Abraham and Sinai

One common understanding of the Sinai covenant is that God therein established a relationship with Israel. But such an understanding cannot be correct. A close relationship between God and people was already in place before Sinai, as witnessed by the recurring divine references to "my people" (e.g., Exod 3:7, 10; 5:1). The people in Egypt are the inheritors of the promises given to their ancestors (Exod 3:15-17; 6:4, 8), made not only with Abraham, but also with his descendants (Gen 17:7). The "my covenant" of Exod 19:5 is a reference to the only covenant mentioned earlier in the Exodus narrative (Exod 2:24; 6:4-5).

A less comprehensive creative act has occurred at Sinai, within an already existing relationship. These texts suggest that the covenant at Sinai is a specific covenant within the context of the Abrahamic covenant. Sinai may be said to be a closer specification of what is entailed in that relationship in view of what Israel has become as a people and in the light of their recent redemptive experience. This understanding is made clear by Moses in Exod 32:13, where he appeals to the Abrahamic covenant in the wake of the breaking of the Sinai covenant (see also Lev 26:42-45; Deut 4:31; 9:27). The Sinai covenant is thus a matter, not of the people's status, but of their vocation. (For detail, see Terence Fretheim, *Exodus* [IBC; Louisville: John Knox Press, 1991], 209, 256-58.)

NOTES

[1] For a convenient summary, see Peter C. Craigie, Page Kelley, and Joel F. Drinkard Jr., *Jeremiah 1–25* (WBC 26; Dallas: Word, 1991), 168-69.

[2] See Robert Carroll, *Jeremiah* (Philadelphia: Westminster, 1986), 272-74.

[3] See Terence Fretheim, "The Reclamation of Creation: Redemption and Law in Exodus," *Interpretation* 45 (1991): 354-65.

JEREMIAH'S LAMENTS
AND GOD'S RESPONSES

11:18–12:17

This segment consists of two laments from Jeremiah (11:18-20; 12:1-4), each of which receives a response from God (11:21-23; 12:1-17). These laments are voiced in response to threats to Jeremiah's life from those opposed to his ministry. Before taking a closer look at these texts, a general statement regarding Jeremiah's laments is in order.

Several laments of Jeremiah have commonly been identified in the section 11:1–20:18 (see **Introduction**; introduction to ch. 11). They usually include 11:18-20; 12:1-4; 15:10, 15-18; 17:14-18; 18:18-23; 20:7-13, 14-18. Though conventionally called "Confessions," that word is misleading; they are neither confessions of sin nor confessions of faith. The content and form of the Confessions is similar to many lament psalms and, though they have their own special character, they are best interpreted in terms of that genre. [The Lament Psalms] God responds to the first four laments (11:21-23; 12:5-17; 15:11-14; 15:19-21) and perhaps the last (21:1-10). Moreover, God voices his own laments; they are (or could be) identified as 12:7-13; 14:2-6, 17-18; 15:5-9; 18:13-17 and possibly 13:15-17, 20-27. Laments of the people can also be identified (14:7-9; 14:19-22). Jeremiah's laments must not be treated in isolation from their context, and they are especially to be related to the divine laments.

As noted in the introduction to chapter 11, announcements of judgment are woven within and around these laments. A comparable interweaving of the oracles of judgment and laments is present in chapters 2–10. Such a linkage of laments and judgment oracles strongly suggests how the latter are to be interpreted. Whatever

---

The Lament Psalms

That the laments of Jeremiah (and also those of God to a lesser degree) follow a conventional form common to the Psalter is evident in the following constitutive elements (cf., e.g., Psalm 13). They include: invocation; cry to God; complaint with descriptions of suffering and questions to God; petition for help; condemnation of enemies; motivations for God to intervene; confession of trust in God; certainty of a hearing; vows; elements of praise. Not all of these elements are found in every lament psalm nor always in the laments of Jeremiah, but the family resemblance is clear and will become evident as we move through them.

readers might think of the harshness of the indictments and the violence of the judgments, the fundamental backdrop of these tumultuous and devastating events for God, Jeremiah, and people/land is weeping and mourning. The book of Jeremiah is filled with tears (see **Introduction**) (see **Connections: Jeremiah's Laments for Exilic Readers**).

Jeremiah's confessions/laments have spawned a considerable literature.[1] How they are to be interpreted is much debated and the options can only be sketched here. Do these texts voice the laments of the prophet, the community, God, or some combination thereof? Scholars are in no agreement about this question, and the discussion is much affected by how one construes the "person" of Jeremiah in the book as a whole (see **Introduction**).

One perspective considers these laments to be anonymous literature, shaped by pious transmitters of the tradition in the interests of depicting an ideal prophet. Certainly the ongoing transmission of the tradition has shaped these texts so that they are no simple reflection of the life of the prophet. Moreover, efforts to connect these texts with specific situations in Jeremiah's ministry are doomed to failure for lack of evidence and lack of interest in the text itself to do so. At the same time, certain particularities in these laments, especially as they relate to the call of the prophet, suggest some continuity with the ministry of a person named Jeremiah.

A second perspective considers these laments to be grounded in a communal liturgical setting, wherein the prophet serves as mediator of the prayers of the worshiping community. Though this point of view has few adherents, it has properly seen that there is a communal dimension at work in these texts. At the same time, how one voices that communal dimension is important. One communal level relates to the incorporation of these laments into a book written for a community, initially for exilic readers (see **Connections: Jeremiah's Laments for Exilic Readers**). It is not simply that Jeremiah's laments can become the community's laments, however; their status as the laments of prophet and God is retained and as such they carry a particular word of God to readers (see below). Beyond that, these laments are incorporated into a book for a specific community of believers. As such, they can once again carry the laments of members of that community (in my experience, especially the laments of pastors and other religious leaders) and speak a healing word of God into troubled lives.

A third possibility, adopted here, is that these texts are grounded in the personal prayers of the prophet Jeremiah. Because the particularities of the call play such a key role in several of the laments

(15:15-17; 17:16; 18:20; 20:7-10), I find it likely that the life of an actual prophetic figure stands behind them, though no specific historical situations can be discerned. These laments reflect the character of Jeremiah's calling to be the spokesman of God to a people antagonistic to such a word and to the one who bears that word. He feels squeezed between an insistent God and a resistant people. As such, these prayers are blunt, intense, and uncompromising in their voicing of complaints to God regarding this calling from which the prophet is not able to escape. The laments have clearly been shaped by conventional forms of lament such as are found in the Psalter, yet that dependence may be due to the prophet's personal immersion in the lament tradition. At the same time, redactors have worked through these texts, placed their own stamp upon them, and set them in their present literary contexts for communal consideration and usage.

However much these laments may be grounded in the experience of the prophet, they have become something more than that in the canonical process. They are no longer (auto)biography—if they ever were—but proclamation; in and through which readers hear the voice of God. When one considers the prophet's laments alongside the divine laments, readers can see that the prophet does not simply mirror the laments of God but incarnates that divine word.[2] In chapters 11–20, as elsewhere in Jeremiah (e.g., 8:18–9:3), distinctions between the prophet's words and God's words are not always clear; their voices tend to "bleed" into one another. In their common lamenting, they join together in one grand "liturgy" of mourning (for further discussion, see at chs. 15; 17; 18; 20).

COMMENTARY

A Lamb Led to the Slaughter, 11:18-23

The basic structure of this segment consists of a lament by the prophet (vv. 18-20) and a response by God (vv. 21-23). The content of the lament suggests that Jeremiah is being made aware of threats to his life for the first time.

Verse 18 is difficult to translate, but its basic sense is this: Jeremiah recognizes that God ("you") had revealed to him that there were threats against his life. Jeremiah apparently had been unsuspecting (naïve?) of any such schemes. He considers himself to be like a "gentle lamb led to the slaughter," that is, innocent of these plans to take his life, perhaps too trusting of his antagonists.

This metaphor can be linked to other texts that speak of a sacrificial lamb (see Isa 53:7; John 1:29, 36); yet, Jeremiah claims no vicarious import for his suffering, though these texts have innocent suffering in common.

The plots against Jeremiah—a common theme that recurs in chapters that follow (e.g., 18; 26; 36)—are made especially vivid through an actual quotation from the schemers (part of the revelation received?). In its images, the quotation makes a single point: they are plotting to kill Jeremiah. They will destroy the tree that is Jeremiah, not just diminish his life by removing the fruit which serves as his food (lit., "bread"). In cutting down the tree, they will cut him off from the living community. In so doing, they will erase his (good) name from memory. Given the fact that resurrection was not a belief at this point in Israel's life (see Dan 12:2), the remembrance of the name was the only vehicle for immortality. So, this is an act, not simply of killing Jeremiah, but of attempting to obliterate any memory of him in the community.

In response to this threat, Jeremiah pleads that God exercise proper justice against his pursuers (v. 20; see 12:1-4). If God judges justly and tests people to determine what is in their heart and mind, and Jeremiah confesses that God does do this, then God knows that he is innocent and that this plotting is wrong. Hence, God should follow through on the knowledge that God has. The plea for God to execute justice against enemies is a common theme in the lament psalms (e.g., Pss 3:7; 6:10; 7:6). Notably, Jeremiah himself does not take action against his enemies or contemplate such activity. He commits his cause to God, that is, hands the matter over to God for action—a trusting move on Jeremiah's part. The charge that Jeremiah lays against God in 12:1 is not present here. For God to bring "retribution" is for God to see to the moral order so that the evildoers suffer the consequences of their own actions (see 5:9, 29; 9:9).

God directly responds to Jeremiah's lament (vv. 21-23). This prose response identifies (for readers!) that Jeremiah's antagonists are the people of Anathoth—his own family and neighbors. Though the issue between them is never made clear, it has something to do with the content of his speaking. Their basic concern is to stop him from public preaching in the name of Yahweh. God pronounces very specific judgments on those who have threatened to kill Jeremiah. The young will die by the sword, their sons and daughters by famine, and (unlike Israel generally) not even a remnant will remain. God will "visit" (NRSV, "punish") their own deeds upon their heads (v. 22); the last phrase of v. 23 returns to the theme of "visitation" (NRSV, "punishment"), providing an *inclusio* for this key word of judgment. Adding language familiar to readers of Jeremiah, God is going to bring "disaster" (*rāʿāh*) upon them (see **Introduction**; ch. 1).

The Mourning of/for the Land, 12:1-17

Scholars usually do not treat Jeremiah 12 as either a unit or a unity. The chapter is usually divided into three parts: vv. 1-6, 7-13, 14-17. Verses 1-6 are commonly linked with 11:18-23 and these texts are seen together as confessions/laments of Jeremiah (11:18-20; 12:1-4) with divine responses (11:20-23; 12:5-6). Others separate these confessions into two distinct units. I link them here, but consider chapter 12 as a whole as the unit with which to work, recognizing that the history of these verses prior to their present form is very complex (e.g., the prose material in vv. 14-17 is a later addition).[3]

Jezreel Valley

The Jezreel Valley is situated between the Plain of Esdraelon in the west, the Hill of Moreh in the north, Mount Gilboa in the south, and the Jordan River to the east. It is a forty mile long pass with the Jalud River draining to the east and the Kishon River draining to the west. The valley is the epicenter of Israel; it is not only a major corridor in traveling east or west, it is also one of the most fertile locales in all of Palestine, as seen in the photograph. The blessing of fertile land in this valley prospered both upright and evil men alike. (Credit: Mitchell G. Reddish)

From the perspective of the speaker, Jeremiah 12 consists of two parts, Jeremiah's lament (vv. 1-4) and the divine response (vv. 5-17). I keep vv. 7-17 linked to vv. 1-6 and interpret them as a continuation of God's response to Jeremiah's lament, begun in v. 5. One good reason for this linkage pertains to the land. Jeremiah brings his lament to a climax in v. 4, not with a concern about himself (though that concern remains), but with an appeal on behalf of the land and its creatures ("How long!?"). Verse 4 has been an interpretive crux, omitted in whole or in part or linked to what follows, because many have thought it a departure from the argument of vv. 1-3. But if v. 4 is the climactic point of Jeremiah's lament, focused finally on a concern about the land, the verse fits well with vv. 1-3 (see below; it is, of course, quite possible for the wealthy to thrive in a time of drought!). Comparably, God does not respond simply to Jeremiah's more personal issues (vv. 5-6); God also engages Jeremiah's concern about the present situation of the *land* (vv. 7-13) and its future (vv. 14-17). When vv. 7-17, with their focus on the land, are included in God's response to Jeremiah's lament, God does provide something of an "answer" to him in a way that vv. 5-6 alone do not. From the perspective of vocabulary, note that the concern for a land that mourns (vv. 4, 11) and for the land as heritage (vv. 7-9, 14-15) are interlocking themes across the entire chapter.

The Land Mourns!, 12:1-4

In this lament Jeremiah raises the perennial question regarding God's justice in the face of the presence and persistence of evil. [A Sonnet by Gerard Manley Hopkins] In modern terms, Jeremiah raises questions of theodicy. Jeremiah begins somewhat apologetically, but to use courtroom language and to speak of laying charges against the judge (who has had many words of judgment heretofore!) indicates no timidity on his part. He knows God will be shown to be right in these matters; yet, he wants to lay a case before God. His basic question has to do with the continued prosperity of the wicked, the thriving of the treacherous, in spite of all the strong language of judgment that has been uttered (see Job 21:7; Mal 3:15). Given all this judgment talk, this word of Jeremiah suggests his impatience for God to get on with what needs to be done.

The immediately prior context (and God's reply in v. 6) suggests that Jeremiah is thinking primarily of his own family and friends (see also 9:4; 20:10); yet, it would be a mistake to take such a narrow approach. The charge that Jeremiah puts before God (v. 1) is focused on the injustice of the prosperity of the wicked more generally and he urges God to give them their just due (v. 3). But the rationale for his argument is not fully apparent until v. 4 (see above on structure). The lament moves climactically to an appeal to God on behalf of the land and its nonhuman inhabitants (How long?!).

This perspective may be supported by Jeremiah's use of imagery regarding the land in v. 2. The land on which God planted these people (=Israel) is a bountiful land (see 2:7, 21; 11:17). This land has had a life-giving capacity to enable them—even the wicked!—to take root and thrive (v. 2; "it rains on the just and the unjust"). These people appear to be faithful to their relationship with God; they make their confessions as if they believed in the God of whom they speak. But what is heard from them in public does not correspond to the condition of their hearts (see Isa 29:13). In the

A Sonnet by Gerard Manley Hopkins
Thou art indeed just, Lord, if I contend
With thee; but sir, so what I plead is just.
Why do sinners' ways prosper? and why must
Disappointment all I endeavor end?
Wert thou my enemy, O thou my friend,
How wouldst thou worse, I wonder, than thou dost
Defeat, thwart me? Oh, the sots and thralls of lust
Do in spare hours more thrive than I that spend,
Sir, life upon thy cause. See, banks and breaks
Now, leaved how thick! laced they are again
With fretty chervil, look, and fresh wind shakes
Them; birds build—but not I build; no, but strain,
Time's eunuch, and not breed one work that wakes.
Mine, O thou lord of life, send my roots rain.

See Peter Milward, *A Commentary on the Sonnets of G. M. Hopkins* (Chicago: Loyola University Press, 1969), 182-85.

manner of a typical lament, Jeremiah contrasts himself with his enemies (and God's). In a protestation of innocence (see Ps 17:2-5), God has known him, has observed his daily walk, and has tested him (see 11:20), and he has been found faithful (v. 3a). God reads him like a book and what God sees is what Jeremiah is. His words and actions correspond to his core character. But the acts of the guilty and treacherous are bearing the fruits of wickedness (see 6:19; 17:10; 21:14). One fruit is devastation for the land (v. 4), a virtual refrain in Jeremiah (e.g., 2:8; 3:2-3; 9:11; see Hos 4:1-3). The land is not the problem; the issue is the people who live on it. In the wake of their wickedness, the land, which could take the occasional drought in stride (see 17:7-8), has become a veritable dust bowl (see 14:2-6).

In essence, Jeremiah's charge is this: what kind of divine justice is evident here, that the wicked can have such effects on the land and apparently get away with it? In this reading, Jeremiah's personal situation is seen as part and parcel of the situation faced also by the land. Both mourn because of the fruits of the wicked. This concern for the land also links up with a basic question asked by the exilic readers: "Why is the land ruined and laid waste like a wilderness?" (9:12; see also 1 Kgs 9:8).

And so Jeremiah urges God to pull the wicked out of circulation from among God's sheep—violently (v. 3). May they be led to the slaughter as they have led him (11:19)! Jeremiah's sharp words of judgment against his enemies (v. 3b) are typical of the laments (e.g., Ps 109), and the image used is that of setting apart certain sheep from others for slaughter (see Ps 49:14). But with Jeremiah another factor comes into play; this is not simply a personal comment or outburst. When Jeremiah speaks these words, he comes into conformity with the wrath of God (see 6:11; 15:17; see **Introduction**). God has spoken of the judgment of the people in terms of slaughter (7:32; see 19:6; Ps 44:11, 22). Jeremiah picks up this judgment language from God, and in essence agrees with the divine judgment of the matter. But Jeremiah is impatient for God to stay on task. Moreover, the language of slaughter, connecting as it does with Jeremiah's own assessment of what these people have done to him (11:19), participates in a "what goes around, comes around" understanding of the moral order and God's mediation thereof.

Notably, Jeremiah wants God to remove them from the land not only for his sake, but also for the sake of the land. How long must the land mourn?! Only by removing this people from the land can the land be saved. Because of them the land mourns. The grass of *every* field withers. The animals and the birds are swept away. The people deny any connection between this situation and their sin (v. 4c; see 5:12); and they think that God is blind to what they do and any effects that their behavior may have. God is complicit in what happens to the land (v. 7), but this is only because of the prior reality—"the wickedness of those who live" on it (v. 4b; see Ps 107:33-34) (see **Connections: Does God Not Make Things Worse?**).

The translations of v. 4a vary in view of the fact that the same verbal root may mean both "mourn" and "dry up" (see Isa 24:4). But "mourn" is the usual focus of the verbal root and it clearly has that meaning with land as subject in 4:28, where it is parallel with the verb "grow black" (see Joel 1:9-10). Probably both meanings are in view. The verb may pertain concretely to drought and desertification (see the parallel with "wither," also in 23:10). Yet, that reference does not sufficiently attend to the land as a genuine subject in a larger lament-filled context. The land mourns not only because it is drying up, but also because it has been polluted by Israel's infidelities, devastated by foreign invasions, and forsaken by God. The land joins with Jeremiah and God in lamenting what has happened to it. Even the people, stretched to the limit, can join in (14:2).

God's Response, 12:5-17

God's nonjudgmental response first focuses on Jeremiah's personal situation (vv. 5-6; cf. 15:19) and then centers more comprehensively on the land and God's response to the wicked concerning which Jeremiah has complained (vv. 7-13). The initial reply contains an enigmatic reference to the land as a "safe land" (v. 5b; or "land of peace"); it may be a proverbial reference to the land. In v. 12 the land is not at peace (NRSV, "safe") anymore. The point is that the land is a land of peace compared to what it will become; if Jeremiah has difficulty now, how will he fare when he gets all tangled up in the conflicts created by the people at large (="thickets of the Jordan")? If Jeremiah thinks that family/friends (="foot-runners") have been difficult (see 11:18-23), and God admits they have been (v. 6; cf. v. 2b; 11:21-23), what will he do when all the wicked in Israel (=riders on horses) descend on him? God's point is that things will only get worse and Jeremiah should be prepared for that; yet, it is of no little help that God is fully aware of the situation and informs the prophet.

Verses 7-13 continue the divine response to Jeremiah by providing the prophet (and exilic readers!) with a closer look at God's own response to the situation; it is filled with lament language. [Lament with Me!] Note the repeated divine reference to "my"—house, heritage (3x), heart, vineyard, portion, and pleasant portion (vv. 7-8, 10). Again and again, these are people and places that God identifies as his own, and they are devastated (the judgment is in progress). The land, on which Jeremiah's lament finally centered (v. 4), now becomes the focus of divine consideration; appropriately, the wicked are also in view. God's lament over the land matches Jeremiah's lament in v. 4; indeed, the land itself laments and that lamenting has reached the heart of God (v. 11). People have not "laid to heart" the suffering of the land (v. 11), but God's heart (v. 7) has been deeply touched by it

This focus on the land is especially evident in the use of the word "heritage" (*năḥᵃlāh*), God's own possession, used five times in this chapter. [Habel on God's Heritage] Heritage is best focused on the land here, but extended to incorporate the people of the land; both are God's own possession. God's "house" may refer to temple, land, or people (it refers to temple in 11:15, used with "beloved"; see 23:11; 13:11) and all may be in view. God's forsaking is comprehensive in scope; God has left temple, land, and people. Readers would recall that temple and land are interrelated. From this sanctuary, God's special dwelling place in the land, blessings flow out into all the land (e.g., Psalm 132). But if God forsakes the temple (see Ezek 8:6), then it no longer has the capacity for blessing (see **Connections: Divine Abandonment**).

Verse 8 specifies a key factor in this divine move; Israel has become like a lion to God. Heretofore, the lion metaphor has usually been used for the foe from the north that will devour Israel (e.g., 2:15; 4:7; 5:6; see 5:17). But in this text, as in Israel's persecution of the prophets (2:30), Israel has turned on God like a roaring lion, making God its prey. This self-identification of God as prey is remarkable! But God is not a victim, for God has significant resources for shaping the future.

Lament with Me!

Lament, lament with Me!
They rant and raven
and I their prey!

But yesterday
a small silly
birdling they were—
now hawkish, bestriding
high heaven,
intent they are, devouring.

And earth a shambles!
Shepherds trampling the vineyards!
Sowing wheat, reaping thorns—
harvesters of shame!

Daniel Berrigan, *Jeremiah: The World, the Wound of God* (Minneapolis: Fortress, 1999), 64.

Habel on God's Heritage

The word "heritage" (*năḥᵃlāh*) usually refers to the land of Canaan in Jeremiah—as God's gift to Israel or God's own possession (2:7; 3:19; 16:18; 17:4; 50:11). The word may also refer to the people as God's possession (v. 8; 10:16; see Deut 9:29; 32:9). In Jeremiah 12 "heritage" usually refers to the land (vv. 7, 9, 14-15); in v. 8 it refers to the people—whom God hates because they lift up their voice "against me." (On this word, see Norman Habel, *This Land is Mine: Six Biblical Land Ideologies* [Minneapolis: Fortress, 1995], 33-35, 75-96.) Habel understands the word in terms of a God-people-land "symbiosis." The language of "my (pleasant) portion" (v.10) is a variant formulation of *naḥᵃlāh* that reiterates that the land is God's land.

In response God "hates," that is, God treats Israel as enemy and sends in the lions and other wild animals. [God Hates!] Inasmuch as these are animals of the land, to call the land a "victim" is inadequate; the animals bring resources to fight for the land (on the animals as servants, see 27:6). Heretofore, other preying animals have been used to speak, literally and metaphorically, of God's instruments of judgment (wolf, leopard, snakes, 5:6; 8:17). That list is here expanded with the use of hyenas and birds of prey, indeed God calls "all" the wild animals to be instruments of judgment (v. 9). The hyena image in v. 9a (the translation is uncertain) probably implies that the land has been so polluted by its inhabitants (see 2:7; 3:2) that it has become food only for such scavengers. The hyena greedily moves in on its prey while the vultures circle above, and God commands other animals to join in the devouring of Israel (15:3; see 5:17).

Again, a "what goes around, comes around" understanding informs this text. The people have become lions to God, and hence the lions will attack them. They have made God their prey and hence they will become prey. At the same time, the land gets caught in the middle; it too becomes prey.

In vv. 10-13 God speaks of the devastating effect that the foreign armies have had on Israel and its land. God's references to "my" vineyard (see 2:21; 5:10; 6:9; Isa 5:1-7) and "my" portion (see [Habel on God's Heritage]) continue to convey a mournful tone regarding a genuine loss for God. In God's repetitive, personal, and emotion-laden words (vv. 10-11): the land has become desolate, desolate, desolate, desolate! The land gets hit from several sides. One, it suffers from drought, so that farmers reap only weeds and thorns (vv. 4, 13; 3:3; 5:23-25; 14:2-6; see Gen 3:18). Two, Israel's wickedness and neglect adversely affect the land (vv. 8, 11; see 2:7; 3:2-3). Three, invading armies (v. 10; called "shepherds" in 6:3; Israel's own shepherds/kings may also be in view, 10:21; 23:1) trample on the land and its vineyards, destroying crops, making the land a wilderness (vv. 10-11; see 2:15; 4:7, 26-27; 9:10-11; 10:22). They have entered into the land across every caravan route (or every hill, v. 12) and plundered it. Four, God is active in and through all these

God Hates!

AΩ God's response to Israel's turning against God is "hate," a strong word indicating the deep effect that this breakdown of the relationship has had on God. Divine hate does not mean the end of divine love; it means that God must move against Israel—treat Israel as an enemy—for the sake of a possible future to this relationship. Only by going through the valley of death will it be possible to start over with this people again. The build-up of the forces of evil are too great for there to be any other way into the future.

It would not be wise to suggest that God's hate is directed only to the sin and not the sinner. Sin and sinner cannot be so easily separated. For God to treat Israel as enemy is to hate Israel. This does not mean that God ceases to love Israel, but as we know from personal experience, it is possible for a love-hate relationship to exist (see 31:3). That is a proximate analogy for how God responds to this relationship with Israel.

desolating events for the land (vv. 7, 9, 12-13) (see **Connections: Does God Not Make Things Worse?**).

With the additional devastation wrought by the invaders, "no one takes [the land] to heart," that is, neither Israel nor the marauders care what happens to the land. The land mourns but no one mourns for the land! The enemies of Israel compound the effects of Israel's iniquities and have made the land even more of a desolation. "No one is safe" (v. 12) from one end of the land to the other, because the "sword of the LORD" (v. 12), wielded by the Babylonians, mediates "the fierce anger of the LORD" (v. 13).

Verse 13 speaks of these events in terms of the metaphor of planting and harvesting; the image carries a literal element (Israel shall not harvest its own crops, 5:17), but the metaphor of harvesting speaks in more comprehensive terms. Recall that planting and plucking up is a basic image in Jeremiah's call (1:10). The "they" in v. 13 refers to the Israelites and speaks of the effects of the invading armies. Israel will reap thorns, that is, experience the devastating effects of the invasion, which includes but is not limited to the loss of their crops (9:22; cf. 2:3; 5:24; 51:33). The shame before their harvests is not simply shame that the crops have failed, but that their words and deeds have reaped such devastation on people and land.

Verses 14-17, a concluding prose section, speak to a question that exilic readers may have asked: Will the invaders who plundered people and land get away with it? As noted, these verses could also be understood as a response to Jeremiah's lament: How long will the land mourn?! In an exilic context, Jeremiah's question about the wicked (v. 1) would be expanded to include the overreaching Babylonians and their allies and the mistreatment of people and land (see v. 14; 25:11-14; 50:29; 51:24). These marauders have not spoken the last word. God has a future for people and land beyond all of this desolation, and these verses begin to address that. The Book of Consolation will continue this theme, e.g., 30:16, "All who devour you shall be devoured . . . those who plunder you shall be plundered, and all who prey on you I will make a prey" (more positively, see 31:5, 12, 14; 32:41-44; 33:10-13; 50:19). The land will become a "land of peace" again. [A Future for the Land?]

A Future for the Land?

God's purposes in the world must be conceived in relation to the story of all of God's creatures, including the land. Using Isaiah's language (65:17-25; see 11:6-9), God is creating a new earth and it will be populated by animals, vegetation, and people (see Hos 2:18-23). Comparably, the salvation oracles of Jeremiah are remarkably inclusive in their orientation, including non-Israelites (e.g., 3:17; 12:14-17; cf. 29:7) and the land itself (31:5, 12, 14, 27; 32:42-44; 33:10-13; 50:19). When the trumpet sounds, and God rides the cloud chariots into a new heaven and a new earth, the children will come singing, leading wolves and leopards, and playing among the snakes. And they will not hurt or destroy, for God will, finally, "give rest to the earth" (50:34; see Isa 14:7; 51:3).

Continuing the use of the personal "my" (v. 14, see vv. 7-10), God announces judgment on "my evil neighbors." These nations surrounding Israel, especially Babylon, had "plundered" the heritage (so NAB; NRSV "touch" is weak). Notably, God refers to them as "my" evil neighbors; God includes himself in the Israelite community and a resident of its land! The enemies of Israel and its land are God's enemies. The nations that God used to "pluck up" Israel will now themselves be plucked up (see 1:10; 18:7-10). This verb also refers to the people of Israel (=the house of Judah) whom God will "pluck up" (in a positive sense!) from the nations where they have been dispersed. The third usage of this verb (v. 15) seems to refer to all ("everyone") whom God has uprooted in the past, whether the nations or the house of Judah. God will have compassion upon them, and return them again to their heritage/land. Hence, the focus on land is finally not simply on the land of promise, but on the heritage/land of all peoples. God's concern about land has universal dimensions (see the positive words in the oracles against the nations, 46:26; 48:47; 49:6, 39). Jeremiah is truly a prophet to the nations (1:5, 10).

Then, vv. 16-17 seem to refer solely to the "evil neighbors" upon whom God has had compassion and whom he has returned to their homelands. They are to learn the ways of Yahweh as assiduously as they had earlier taught the people of Israel to worship Baal and swear by that god. If they do this, they shall be built up in the midst of God's people (again, see 1:10). If they will not listen, then God will uproot that people from their land and destroy them. This conditional future offered to the other nations is at least in part for the sake of the future of God's own people and God's own land. The implication to be drawn with respect to Israel and the land seems to be this: Never again!

CONNECTIONS

Jeremiah's Laments for Exilic Readers

A key question to be asked is this: of what value are these laments for an exilic audience? Would they understand themselves in terms of the suffering of Jeremiah, and so his laments become their laments, and (when offered) God's responses to him become God's responses to them? Or, is their value primarily in terms of thinking through what Jeremiah had gone through as a prophet? Or, what God had gone through? Or both?

This exilic community has literally been through hell in the recent past. Their wounds are deep, the questions fierce, and the guilt and the shame are openly displayed before any public that cared to notice. What would be the best way to speak the word of God into such a situation? That is a key question for the editors of Jeremiah (see **Introduction**).

It would not do to gloss over the unfaithfulness of the people; that needed to be stated up front for the sake of honesty and integrity about what had happened. That gets done—in spades!

It would not do to suggest that God had been indifferent to such infidelities. In response, God is depicted as a spurned lover, with all the pain, anger, and anguish that goes with such an estranged relationship. The integration of divine lament, indictment, and announcements of judgment portrays for exiles the kind of God with whom they have to do, both then and now.

It would not do to pretend that the community was healthy and strong. And so the great devastation wrought by the Babylonian armies is depicted in great detail. These events had taken a great toll on everyone (see **Introduction**). A forthright presentation of the laments of the people recognizes these realities. But the fact that prophet and God also lament opens up the disastrous present to possibilities for a more positive future.

It would not do to ignore the penetrating questions, the "Whys?" from the valley of the shadow of death, and offer some insipid bromides or easy "answers" to get them through their intellectual crisis. The word of God for such a community needed to bring together both realism and honesty, but at the same give some public indication of the great pain and sorrow that God and prophet had suffered. Only through such an open expression of grief, combined with a word of hope, might there be a way through the gloom of exile and great loss—of children, friends, community, city, temple. To that end, these laments of prophet and God bring a particular word from God to them.

Divine Abandonment

It is striking that, with all these "my" references affirming divine ownership of the land, that God cannot take care of the land any better than this! But God's way of possessing does not entail "control." God delegates responsibility for the land to others, with all the attendant risks, and will not micromanage their handling of their duties, intervening to make sure every little thing is done correctly. This way of relating to people and world reveals a divine

Brueggemann on God's Actions

In thinking about the divine abandonment, it is important not to claim too much. Contrary to Walter Brueggemann's assertion, it is not that "God's withdrawal has caused fertility to end and exposes the land...to chaos." The issue of agency is rather more complex; God neither initiates this action, nor acts alone. It is better to say that the already devastating effects of the people's wickedness are thereby brought to completion in the moral order that God mediates. Moreover, to assert that "Yahweh has withdrawn fidelity" goes beyond any textual claim. Such a statement suggests that God can be *unfaithful* or that God is not faithful in judgment. In fact, judgment may be the only way in which God can be faithful to promises made in this particular situation.

Walter Brueggemann, *A Commentary on Jeremiah: Exile and Homecoming* (Grand Rapids: Eerdmans, 1998), 121-22.

vulnerability, for God opens the divine self up to hurt should things go wrong—and we hear that hurt expressed here in anguished tones.

God's lament begins with a virtual refrain regarding what God has done with respect to the land and people. God has forsaken (9:2; 25:38), but this is not a divine initiative; God has forsaken because the people have forsaken God (2:13, 17, 19; 5:7, 19). God has abandoned (7:29; 23:33, 39), but (again) because the people have abandoned God (15:6). God has given them over to their enemies (as in 21:7) because of their wickedness. Notice the passive language in v. 7; God gives them over to the effects of their own sins (see Isa 54:7-8; 64:7). [Brueggemann on God's Actions]

Does God Not Make Things Worse?

The sensitive reader will ask whether just the Israelites and foreign armies are to blame for what has happened. Why is God lamenting? Is not God also to blame? After all, God has forsaken and abandoned; God has hated; God has commanded the "animals" to gather over the corpse that is Israel. And now (v. 12), it is *God's* sword that devours the people from one end of the land to the other and no one is safe. As v. 13 puts it, the "fierce anger of the Lord" has been a key factor in what has occurred.

Readers, who are apt to focus on the effects of these judgments on people, should ponder the sheer force of all of these agents arrayed against the land! The land doesn't stand a chance and becomes prey. In this respect, the land is like the people, but is more like God. Like God! Land and God are both undeserving of what has happened to them. The land shares with God the status of "prey." Land and God are also alike in that both mourn. But, while there is this mutuality in mourning over what has happened, there is a deep inequality as well: the land mourns *to* God (v. 11), for God is able to marshal resources for this moment that may lead to healing that the land cannot.

But Jeremiah's (and the readers'!) questions in v. 4 now return, only at a higher decibel. What kinds of resources does God bring? Does God not make things even worse for the land? *God's* sword-wielding anger across the length and breadth of the land has resulted in a land that is more devastated and desolate (v. 12). How long will the land mourn?! Jeremiah had asked God to pull the people out of the land for the sake of the land (vv. 3-4). God's response in vv. 7-13 is that the resolution of Jeremiah's lament is more complicated than Jeremiah (and often readers) think.

Yes, Jeremiah is right; the people must be uprooted from the land for the sake of the land, but that end cannot be accomplished with a divine flick of the wrist. The enemies of God and land cannot be dealt with in a moment—with no collateral damage. God's sword does not cut clean, for God has chosen to relate to the world through means that are available—and only violent means may be available—rather than do things "all by himself." And God does not perfect people before working through them, including armies led by "my servant" Nebuchadrezzar (25:9; 27:6; see 25:12-14). And so, God responds to the mourning of Jeremiah and the land, but it will take a complex series of often violent events to bring about a "land of peace" once again.

This divine move may sound suspect, but we are helped in thinking about it by the other dimension of God's response to the situation, namely, grief. The personal, emotional, and repetitious language shows how much this is a genuine loss for God. Given the divine commitment to people and land and the centuries-long relationship with them, God cannot (!) respond indifferently. God is truly caught up in what has happened here and mourns the loss. [Heschel on Divine Abandonment]

Heschel on Divine Abandonment

Abraham Heschel captures this thought well: "With Israel's distress came the affliction of God, His displacement, His homelessness in the land, in the world . . . Should Israel cease to be home, then God, we might say, would be without a home in the world." Yes, God forsakes and abandons and gives over the land with its people, but at tremendous loss for God. Yet, divine suffering is the only way into a future for the land (see 31:20; Isa 54:7-8). This divine agony is necessary for the sake of a future for the land, and vv. 14-17 begin to address that issue.

Abraham Heschel, *The Prophets* (New York: Haper, 1962), 112.

Again, it is important to think carefully about matters of agency in these texts. A complex understanding of agency is at work here, involving Israel, God, and the Babylonian armies. God is active in mediating judgment on the Israelites, but the mediator (the Babylonian armies) is not a puppet in the hands of God, and Israel's own wickedness is the primary factor in bringing about these effects. When the text speaks of the sword of the Lord, then, it is not as if God is personally wielding the sword. The

Babylonians wield the sword, but because they mediate the *divine* judgment, God and sword are inextricably linked (see **Introduction**). That the very next verses (12:14-17) will speak of judgment on the invaders themselves shows that God is not micromanaging their activities (see also 25:12-14; 51; Isa 47:6-11).

NOTES

[1] See especially Kathleen O'Connor, *The Confessions of Jeremiah: Their Interpretation and Role in Chapters 1–25* (Atlanta: Scholars Press, 1988); A. R. Diamond, *The Confessions of Jeremiah in Context: Scenes of a Prophetic Drama* (Sheffield: Academic Press, 1987); W. Baumgartner, *Jeremiah's Poems of Lament* (Sheffield: Almond, 1988); Robert Carroll, *Jeremiah* (Philadephia: Westminster, 1986) 275-79; see also the summary discussion of Walter Brueggemann, *A Commentary on Jeremiah: Exile and Homecoming* (Grand Rapids: Eerdmans, 1998), 114-15, and Samuel Balentine, *Prayer in the Hebrew Bible: The Drama of the Divine-Human Dialogue* (Minneapolis: Fortress, 1993), 150-68.

[2] On this understanding, see Terence Fretheim, *The Suffering of God: An Old Testament Perspective* (Philadelphia: Fortress, 1984), 156-59.

[3] For a fuller development of these arguments, see Terence Fretheim, "The Earth Story in Jeremiah 12," in *Reading the Bible from the Perspective of the Earth*, ed. N. Habel (Sheffield: Academic Press, 2000).

SYMBOLIC ACTIONS
AND VIOLENT WORDS

13:1-27

This chapter consists of these segments: a narrative report of the first of several symbolic actions of Jeremiah (vv. 1-11); a speech that focuses on a specific object as a centering symbol for the point being made (vv. 12-14; see also ch. 18); and a series of judgment oracles (vv. 15-17, 18-19, 20-27) that are linked, with each other and with what precedes, by elements of lament and various catchwords.

COMMENTARY

The Linen Loincloth, 13:1-11

This narrative of a symbolic act, with Jeremiah as narrator, begins with a series of divine commands to which Jeremiah responds positively (vv. 1-7); God's second and third commands (vv. 3-4, 6) are made possible only by Jeremiah's obedience. This series of events is followed by a divine interpretation of the meaning of the commands, but it is given only to the prophet (vv. 8-11); no word to the people is commanded or given. The loincloth functions essentially as a metaphor for the people of God. [Symbolic Acts]

God's initial request (v. 1) seems bizarre, probably as much to ancient audiences as to modern. God tells Jeremiah to buy a new change of linen underwear (=loincloth), to put it on, but not to dip it in water before doing so (apparently to assure its newness). A loincloth was an undergarment—a *personal* piece of clothing—that was wrapped around the middle of the body. Linen was a valuable, if common material used for clothing, household accompaniments (e.g., curtains), and various rituals (e.g., burial shrouds).

After Jeremiah does so (v. 2), God tells him to go the Euphrates river (a major Babylonian artery) and to hide the loincloth in the cleft of a rock. Because it seems unlikely that Jeremiah would travel the great distance to Babylon twice (it would take 3–4 months), some scholars have read the Hebrew (*pĕrāt*) as a reference to the village of

Symbolic Acts

This is the first of several symbolic acts of Jeremiah. It is uncertain how many of his acts should be so considered, for the possible texts are not structured in any conventional way. The following texts have been considered narratives of symbolic acts by one or another commentator: 16:1-9; 18:1-11; 19:1-15; 25:15-29; 27-28; 32:1-15; 43:8-13; 51:59-64 (they are also common in Ezekiel, e.g., 4:1-17). These actions are called "symbolic" because they point beyond themselves to another level of reality. These symbolic acts may serve graphically to illustrate a particular point in the prophetic message, yet the people seldom view these actions. In such cases, their illustrative purpose would be lost to any immediate audience. In this text no audience sees what Jeremiah does, nor does God commission him to pass the interpretation along to an audience (some scholars think that v. 12a belongs with this text rather than the one that follows).

The value of the symbolic action seems to be reserved for later readers, though the act may also be said to have been a revelatory word for the prophet's own understanding of these events. Exilic readers of this text are the only certain "audience" for this symbolic act of the prophet; they would be able to put the prophetic action and divine interpretation together. They would thus be able to interpret their history with God in these terms (especially since they now lived on the Euphrates river; 51:59-64 may be considered a kind of reversal of this act). Such symbolic actions are often thought to have an efficacy in their very happening; that is, they set in motion that future which they portray. Yet, it is not clear that the symbolic acts do this in a way that would not be true of other actions in at least some sense. The actions are not understood in some magical sense (though they may have their roots in such practices) nor are they regarded as inevitably shaping a certain future. This particular symbolic action, for example, bespeaks the past (v. 11) as much as the future (vv. 9-10).

Parah, about five miles northeast of Jerusalem (some translations, e.g., NAB, REB, simply transliterate the Hebrew, "the Perath"). But, if this is a reference to the village, then it symbolized the Euphrates for Jeremiah.

Given the exilic audience for this material, the river Euphrates (whether actual or symbolic) would have carried still further significance; they were exiled as a ruined people in the very place that Jeremiah was asked to hide his loincloth. Some scholars think that Jeremiah undertook no literal journey at all, and that the entire narrative is to be symbolically interpreted (as, say, vision, dream, or street theater). Yet, the relatively straightforward sequence of commands and obedient responses, and the absence of any language associated with dreams or visions, suggests a greater degree of realism.

Jeremiah does as God commanded (v. 5). He hides his loincloth at Perath (or, near the Euphrates river); we learn from v. 7 that he had buried it in the ground. After many days (however long it takes for a buried loincloth to become ruined), God commands Jeremiah (v. 6) to go back to the spot where he had hidden the loincloth and take it away from that place (back to Jerusalem?). Jeremiah once more does as God had commanded (v. 7). After digging it out from the ground where he had buried it, he found that it was not good for the purpose for which it was made or for any other purpose; the linen had rotted. Importantly, we are not told what he did with the loincloth. It is often assumed that he simply discarded it, but that is not stated, nor is it necessarily implied in the following interpretation. The issue at stake is the effect of the judgment on Israel, which is stated in terms of the ruin of Israel's "pride" (the content of which is given in v. 11), not the rejection of Israel as God's people (v. 9).[1]

God proceeds to give Jeremiah an interpretation of this series of events (vv. 8-11), which included both divine commands and human obedience. Because there is no audience, God's interpretation is intended for the illumination of the prophet himself and, at some unknown point, exilic readers. It has been well observed[2] that God's interpretation starts with the end of the story and works back to the beginning. At the same time, this observation does not say enough; to return at the *end* of the explanation to the theme of Israel clinging to God is to suggest that God's purposes for this people remain intact, namely, "that they might be for me a people, a name, a praise, and a glory."

The main points of God's interpretation are these. Just as the loincloth had been ruined, and is good for nothing, so God will ruin the pride of Judah and the great pride of Jerusalem (v. 9; see vv. 15, 17; Isa 2:6-22; Prov 16:18). The explanation follows in v. 10. These people are "evil" (*ra*ʿ); they refuse to heed the word of God; they are stubborn and persistently follow their own will rather than God's will (see 7:24; see **Connections**, ch. 5). The focus of this evil, resistance, and stubbornness is their continued worship of gods other than Yahweh. The judgmental effects are that they (exiled readers!), like the loincloth, reside in Babylon as a ruined and shamed people (a theme in vv. 20-27).

Verse 11 steps back from this vivid word of judgment and recalls the divine decision originally to enter into a binding relationship with Israel. Just as the loincloth is purchased new and clings to Jeremiah's loins (hence the reason Jeremiah was to wear it), so God long ago elected Israel and bound himself to this "unsoiled" people (see 2:2-3; both North and South are in view here). [Loincloth] God entered into this relationship so that they might be God's own people (see Exod 19:5-6). Using the language of Deuteronomy 26:19, God has set them "high above all nations that he has made, in praise and in fame and in honor." But, even with all of these benefits, the people rejected the relationship and refused to listen to

Loincloth

The loincloth was a male undergarment made of either linen or leather that extended from the waist to the thighs. It was most likely loosened at night, while sleeping, but there is no indication that it was changed daily. As with the degrees of wealth in any culture, the poor owned very few if even enough clothes while the rich possessed an ostentatious wardrobe. The common man, however, would have been intimately familiar with the fit and purpose of a loincloth, making the symbolism of this passage in Jeremiah accessible to the Israelite audience.

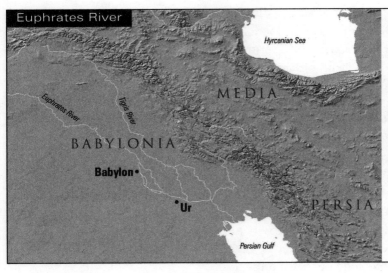

Euphrates River

The Euphrates River is the largest river in western Asia. The river is mentioned by name many times in the Bible, and referenced as "the river" in several other places. Jeremiah's mention of the Euphrates River in his prophecy indicates the significance the river played in ancient biblical life, both literally and symbolically.

God's word and will for them (exilic readers would recall their earlier responses to God and prophet). [A People of Honor]

The Metaphor of the Wine Jars, 13:12-14

This brief prose speech develops a metaphor as a vivid and concrete way of announcing divine judgment on Israel. The metaphor was probably drawn from an everyday proverb: "every wine jar should [is meant to] be filled with wine [not anything else]." In terms of this metaphor, the people of Israel are the wine jars that should be filled with wine, that is, filled with what they were intended to be filled, namely, the blessings that a faithful relationship to God brings. Instead, they will be filled with drunkenness, that is, the wrath of God (see at 25:15-16, 27). [Wine Jar] Another possible interpretation considers this image to be a play on words, with the Hebrew word for "jar" (*nēbel*) playing on the word for "fool" (*nābāl*); hence, all Israelites are fools who are about to drink the wine of God's wrath.

Unlike vv. 1-11, God commands Jeremiah to speak the proverb to Israel (v. 12). Predictably, God says, the people will claim to have this knowledge and so the words will be thrown back at the prophet. Two options for interpreting their verbal comeback seem possible. One, they will see the saying as a mouthing of

A People of Honor

Verse 11 contains such remarkable language for God to use for human beings! In view of God's binding himself with them, the people would receive an honorable name and other peoples would honor them for what they had become within this relationship with God (see Deut 4:6). For exilic readers, the description of God's people in v. 11 would also be understood as a future possibility beyond the shame of exile. Even though they, like the loincloth, have been ruined, God's original purpose for them had not been abrogated; it remained intact through all the death and devastation. At the same time, these words of honor are not simply descriptive of the people, they are also descriptive of the God of these people. In becoming God's people and being faithful in relationship, other peoples would also praise and honor the God in whom they believed.

Wine

Viticulture was a common industry in Israel and its wines were renowned throughout the ancient Near East. Because of its considerable economic and social value, wine became a joyful symbol of God's blessing (Deut 7:13), including the time immediately after the fall of Jerusalem (40:10-12) and eventual restoration to the land (31:5, 12). While a cup of wine could be a cup of blessing (Ps 16:5; 23:5; cf. 1 Cor 10:16) or a cup of consolation (see 16:7), it could also be a cup of wrath as it was related to drunkenness because of too much wine (25:15-28; 49:12; see [The Cup of Wrath]).

the obvious—a truism. In other words, they will interpret the image literally and will not perceive its deeper application to their lives. Or, alternatively, they will understand the saying metaphorically, as the prophet intended, but expect that God would fill them with life's blessings. Though the people have voiced several times that they have not experienced God's blessings (see 3:5; 4:8; 8:20), this appears to have been their expectation.

When the people have replied in this way, the prophet is to speak a word of judgment that builds on this image of wine jars that are empty but should be full (vv. 13-14). The people of Israel are the wine jars, but God will not fill them with the blessings of wine and the associated gladness and joy. Rather, God will fill the jars with drunkenness (not wine!), that is, mediate the *effects* of their own sinful actions; this is another way of speaking of curses or the divine wrath—being at the mercy of what has been drunk. The linkage between *drunkenness* and wrath is important, for it shows that God does not introduce anything new into the judgmental situation, but mediates the effects of the people's unfaithfulness (see 6:19; 21:14).

The symbol of drunkenness evinces matters such as public shame, disorientation in thinking and moving, even madness, and hence greater vulnerability (see Deut 28: 27-28). The imaging of dashing/smashing the people together (v. 14), even within the same household, may be an extension of the image of drunkenness and the physical

Wine Jar

Contrary to the common assumption of the parallel between sobriety and religious conviction, Jewish tradition readily endorses the use of wine. It was described as the symbol of joy and was the essential element of all festivals. When Jeremiah speaks of filling-up the wine jars with wine, and then with drunkenness, he uses the common vessel of the wine jar as the analogy for the impending judgment to come upon the house of Judah.

Rhodian oenochos (wine jar) with animal decor, deer and swans. 7th C. BC. Louvre. Paris, France. (Credit: Erich Lessing/Art Resource, NY)

abusiveness that often occurs in such situations (see 9:3-6). This image is developed in terms of the cup of God's wrath in 25:15-29, where Babylon is the mediator (see [The Cup of Wrath]; cf. 51:7; Ps 75:8; Isa 51:17; Lam 4:21; Hab 2:15-16; on the drinking of poison, see Jer 8:14; 9:15; 23:15).

The audience for this word is remarkably inclusive; it covers all the leaders (Davidic kings, priests, and prophets) and the entire population of Jerusalem, including parents and children. The brief object lesson ends with a harsh statement, particularly when children have just been mentioned (as if to sharpen the point, it is newly introduced by the word of God; see **Connections**, ch. 6). In the destruction—a strong word—that is about to occur (it has been made clear that God will not relent, 4:28), God will show no pity or compassion (three essentially synonymous words are piled up here for maximum effect). This is an especially severe word and can only be properly understood if it is correlated with 21:7, where exactly the same language is used for Nebuchadrezzar (see **Introduction**) (see **Connections: God Will Not Pity or Spare or Have Compassion, 13:14**).

Another Chance before Exile?, 13:15-17

This segment begins by urging the people of Israel not to be haughty (cf. "pride" in vv. 9, 18), but to give glory to God (see 9:23-24). Jeremiah is usually considered to be the speaker, though the last designation of speaker is God (vv. 12, 14). Some interpreters understand v. 15b to designate God as the speaker for what follows (vv. 16-17) rather than what precedes (vv. 12-14); v. 18 is almost certainly a command of God to Jeremiah. Keeping vv. 12-14 and vv. 15-27 together, the divine command to Jeremiah to speak "this word" to Israel (v. 12) could cover the rest of the chapter. While that seems likely, the voices of God and prophet are often impossible to sort out, as has been evident in several texts (e.g., 8:18–9:3).

These verses stand in no little tension with v. 14 and vv. 18-27. God has just announced the destruction to be wrought by the Babylonians in unequivocal terms, and the description of judgment in vv. 20-27 leaves little, if any hope (v. 27b?). What would a call to repentance mean in this context? It is common to suggest that vv. 15-17 are a last call before the deluge; perhaps a last-minute escape would be possible.

A somewhat differently nuanced interpretation is more likely. The call of vv. 15-17 comes when the Babylonian destruction is inevitable. The call to repentance is not to hold back the deluge; no words hold that out as a possibility (cf. 3:12-14). Rather, the call is given in the hope that at least some people, perhaps only a remnant, might move through this horrendous time clinging to their faith in God. Those who would listen are urged "to give glory to the Lord your God." This uncommon phrase, if interpreted in the light of its usage in Josh 7:16-21, would be a call to the party guilty of a crime (as Israel corporately was) to give praise to God, who is worthy of worship even in the midst of judgment, regardless of what happens. The people are urged to do this before all hell breaks loose, not in order to stop its occurrence, but to give them strength and hope for the difficult days to come. God had called Israel to repentance, *even when such an act would not stop the deluge.* God had hung in there with them to the end, urging response. In exile it would be possible to so respond, and hence this call has a special significance for exilic readers. But, when the day of judgment does arrive, and that is now inevitable, gloom and darkness will fill their lives, with all the dangers that darkness brings. [Darkness]

Darkness

ΑΩ Images of darkness are commonly used in judgment texts (Isa 5:30; 8:22; Lam 3:2, 6; Joel 2:2; Amos 5:18-20; 8:9; Zeph 1:15). Such images would call forth remembrances of various traditions. They suggest a pre-creational state of darkness, when there was as yet no light (see 4:23; Isa 8:20-22; Amos 5:8). These images are also used metaphorically in laments and could refer to a time of deep suffering (see Job 3:1-6; 10:21-22; Ps 44:19), not least the experience of being a prisoner (Ps 107:10-16). These images also recall the wilderness wanderings (see Jer 2:6) and, in a kind of pilgrimage in reverse, the journey to exile in Babylon. The journey stumbling across "mountains of twilight" could have reference to just such a difficult journey, filled with pain and remorse. This language would in turn link up to themes of light and darkness used by exilic prophets for the return from exile (e.g., Isa 42:7, 16; 60:1-3).

The focus of the conditional statement in v. 17 is striking. If the people will not respond to this call, then Jeremiah/God will weep; indeed, the language for weeping is very intense (see 9:1, 17-18; 14:17). One might expect the condition to read: if you do not respond, then you will be destroyed (as in 4:3-4). Rather, the focus is on the effect that the captivity of Israel will have on Jeremiah/God! That Israel is here named "the Lord's flock" shows that the focus is not on the flock but on the shepherd, God. God is deeply affected by how Israel does or does not respond. Note, too, that the flock does not cease to be God's flock after it has been taken captive! [A Word on God's Grief for Exilic Readers]

A Word on God's Grief for Exilic Readers

This is an important word for the exiles. They have been taken captive, but they are still the Lord's flock, and even more, God's response to what has happened is grief so profound that only an accumulation of weeping language can convey the effect on God/Jeremiah. The readers are thus not left with the harsh words of v. 14, as if God were left untouched by these events. Rather, Israel can see that the horrendous experience through which it has gone has had a deep effect on the divine life. Israel's weeping has been accompanied by the weeping of God. The uncertain phrase, "in secret," may refer to the unseen depths of grief that are the internal side of wrath, and that Jeremiah here reveals to the readers.

No Hope for Royalty, 13:18-19

Jeremiah is commanded by God to speak to the king and queen mother (the imperative is masculine singular). The linkage with what proceeds may revolve around the matter of haughtiness (v. 15), perhaps associated with the Davidic royalty. The identity of the king and queen mother remains uncertain, but a general point is being made in any case: the end of the monarchy! It could be Jehoiachin and his mother Nehushta; they are the most likely candidates in view of the attention given them in 22:24-27 (see also 2 Kgs 24:8-17; Jer 52:31-34). It could also be Zedekiah and Hamutal (see 2 Kgs 24:18-20). If the addressee is Jehoiachin, he need not have actually heard the word; it might have been considered important for the exiles (which included Jehoiachin and his mother) to know that God had spoken such a word.

The word of God to the king and his mother is an announcement regarding the end of his reign and the end of the political power exercised by the king and the queen mother (a common phenomenon, e.g., 2 Kgs 11:1-3). This ending is symbolized by the removal of the crowns from their heads (so NAB; NRSV reads singular) and taking a lowly seat (compared to the throne). In effect, they are humiliated (as the people are in vv. 20-27). The disaster has a democratizing effect. Verse 19 specifies the reasons for the end of the reign. The villages of the Negeb (the southern part of Judah, and hence the last towns to be taken) symbolize all the towns in Judah that provided some protection for Jerusalem from invaders; they have been irretrievably captured. And all Judah—the entire country, including royalty—has been taken into exile.

Jerusalem's Shame, 13:20-27

The imperatives in v. 20 (and the "you" throughout) are feminine singular, and the vocative in v. 27b indicates that the mother city of Jerusalem is addressed in this unit (as some versions do in v. 20). The linkage with the prior verses may well center on the theme of pride; here God announces a judgment that centers on images of humiliation.

This segment is best characterized as an announcement of judgment integrating an indictment and cast largely in the language of a lament. The prominence of questions is to be noted in particular. The entire segment has been prompted by the people's question in v. 22, "Why have these things come upon me?" The question "Why?!"—so common in the lament psalms (e.g., 22:1)—was often voiced by the people in the wake of the devastation of

Jerusalem (e.g., 5:19; 9:12; 14:19; 16:10; 22:8; Lam 5:20; Deut 29:24; 1 Kgs 9:8; see **Introduction**). This question is matched again and again by a "why?" question from both Jeremiah (e.g., 15:18) and God (e.g., 2:29-31). In this segment, God addresses Israel with a series of questions, finishing with a question of wonderment, "How long?" (v. 27).

This unit begins with a call to Jerusalem to observe the foe that comes from the north (a theme prominent in chs. 4–10). Using sheep/shepherd imagery, God asks the leaders of Jerusalem (with an implicit link back to vv. 18-19) what has happened to those placed in their charge. God's descriptive phrase for the people, "your beautiful flock," is moving in its pathos (see 12:7). Though the translation of v. 21a is uncertain, it probably refers to new leaders placed over Israel who are not from their own people, but whom Israel has courted as allies. This may well refer to the situation of exilic readers, given the "Why?!" question asked in v. 22. When Israel has lost its own shepherds and is ruled by outsiders, God asks, will they not experience great pain like unto that of a woman giving birth? The suffering of the people corresponds to the suffering of God/prophet in v. 17.

God answers the people's question in terms comparable to earlier responses (v. 22; see 5:19; 9:12-16). Only this time the sexual imagery used for Israel's infidelity and its disastrous effects is blatant and repulsive (see **Connections: The Sexual Imagery**). Israel's great iniquity ("great sin/guilt" is the type of language used for adultery in some contexts, see Gen 20:9; 39:9) has led to a great judgment, expressed in terms of sexual violence. While this imagery could reflect the public shaming of an unfaithful wife, it more likely has reference to the victimization of women in time of war; the imagery of rape would be associated with a common treatment of women in time of war (see Lam 5:11). The violent language of exposure and violation has reference to the actions on the part of the foe from the north (v. 20). Interestingly, the same image of exposure is used with God as subject in v. 26, but the image of violation is not repeated (see **Introduction** for the common language used for God and for God's instrument of judgment, Babylon).

Verse 23 states the issue in a proverbial way through God's use of a rhetorical question. The proverb probably has reference to any situation that cannot be changed. Can Ethiopians (a black people from Cush, south of Egypt) change the color of their skin? Can leopards remove their spots? The answer is obvious, but to be sure that the point is not lost, v. 23b makes it clear (though the NRSV translation is somewhat ambiguous, making it sound like the answer to the prior question is "yes"!). If they could (and they cannot) then you who are so accustomed (learned) in doing evil could do good (see REB, "No more can you do good, you who are schooled in evil"). This is not a general statement about human sinfulness or the futility of repentance or the inability of human beings to do any good at all. This is a statement about Israel in this time and place, so stubborn and resistant to God's word (see v. 10; **Connections**, ch. 5). [A Leopard and Its Spots]

A Leopard and Its Spots

"Shall the leopard then change spots at will?
   Shall you,
evil your wont and will,
beyond custom, become
virtuous on the moment?"

The diagnosis is merciless. Jeremiah sees his culture steeped in a "state of sin" . . . . He sees as well the consequences of this "sin become of nature," the morally abnormal normalized. He sees catastrophe in the offing.

Daniel Berrigan, *Jeremiah: The World, the Wound of God* (Minneapolis: Fortress, 1999), 66.

In v. 24, God moves to an agricultural image to speak of Israel's judgment (it is uncertain why the object of the verb is "them" in Hebrew rather than "you"; see NRSV footnote). God will scatter them like chaff. That the chaff is driven by a wind from the desert intensifies the image by including the heat of that wind and its common velocity. The image is also especially suitable for being driven away from the land into exile (a theme struck already in vv. 17, 19).

Verse 25 begins by reiterating the essential point of the judgment and concludes with the reason for it. The language of "lot" is commonly used for the distribution of the land of promise (e.g., Num 26:55-56). God is now going to measure out a different portion for them, namely, being driven away from the land of promise and placed in the landlessness of exile. Once again, the reason is unfaithfulness to the relationship with God. They have trusted in lies, especially the lies of the false prophets (e.g., 14:14; 23:25-32), and have forgotten the identity of their proper spouse. The forgetting is linked to the activities of the false prophets in 23:27 (see also 2:32; 3:21; 18:15)

Verses 26-27 return to the sexual imagery (see v. 22), stating first the judgment (v. 26) and then the reason for it (v. 27a). The imagery of adultery and prostitution has been prominently used heretofore (e.g., 3:1-5), as has the language of abomination (see 4:1; 7:30; cf. 7:10). The image of the neighing of lusty stallions was used earlier for unfaithfulness within the marriage relationship (5:7-8). Here that image is extended to refer to unfaithfulness to God on the hills of the countryside where the Baal shrines were commonly located (see 2:20) (see **Connections: The Sexual Imagery**).

This unit concludes with a "woe oracle" and a lament. The woe oracle is a succinct statement of the judgment visited on Jerusalem. The concluding "how long" question, similar to that found in laments (see Ps 13:1-2), demonstrates that the God who has spoken this harsh and judgmental language is a God full of pathos over what has happened. The phrase, literally "how long (until)?" actually occurs at the very end of the verse, and so the unit ends on this note. This language could also suggest a certain divine hopefulness regarding the future, that the answer is something other than "never." And if the text speaks to exilic readers, then the "how long" could speak of the time of exile, and the time necessary for Israel to be cleansed of its sins and their disastrous effects.

CONNECTIONS

God Will Not Pity or Spare or Have Compassion, 13:14

In seeking to understand God's harsh words in v. 9 ("I will ruin") and v. 14 ("I will not pity or spare or have compassion"), important texts to consider are 36:29 and 21:7. In 36:29 (and 51:25) Babylon is the subject of the verb "to ruin, destroy." In 21:7, exactly the same three verbs are used as in v. 14 to describe what king Nebuchadrezzar will do when the Babylonian armies move in to destroy Jerusalem (see **Introduction** on the correlation of language for God and God's agent). The same correlation of language is used for Babylon in 13:22 and for God in 13:26.

In view of these precise parallels, several issues come to the fore. For one, God is not the sole agent in this situation; God acts in and through the agency of the Babylonian king and his armies.[3] For another, God does not micromanage the actions of the Babylonians; they will act just as kings and armies in that world have historically been known to act. That is predictable and God (as well as other observers) knows this from experience with conquerors such as these. And so, God in judgment will not spare, pity, or have compassion, because that is what the Babylonians, the instruments of divine judgment, will not do. And so this is a kind of extreme realism regarding what is about to happen to the people. And exilic readers will have experienced what it feels like for God not to have pity or to spare or to have compassion. A significant community does survive the onslaught, however, and with them God will begin again. God's love has been everlasting after all and through it all (31:3). From another angle, God severely judges the

Babylonians for over-extending their destructive actions (25:12-13; 50–51).

The Sexual Imagery

Verses 20-27 use strong sexual imagery to refer to the sin of Israel (v. 27) and the correlative judgment experienced (vv. 22, 26). Notably, there is no subject of the exposing and violating in v. 22 (the word for "violated" is used only here in the OT); rather, the language of act-consequence is used and the violation is understood to be mediated by the foe from the north (v. 20). This "what goes around, comes around" understanding is reinforced by the imagery used for Israel's sin in v. 27 (and often heretofore, e.g., 3:1-5). Israel's sin is sexual (unfaithfulness imaged in terms of adultery and prostitution) and hence the judgment is sexual. The rape of women would have been a common way in which those defeated in war were treated (see 38:23; Lam 5:11; both then and in more recent times!). [Carroll on the Sexual Imagery]

Carroll on the Sexual Imagery

Robert Carroll describes this graphic situation well. These images "are metaphors of the city's humiliation and defeat, but they are drawn from the real world of horrendous aggression directed against women in time of war and invasion….Metaphors and reality combine to portray a sickening picture of battered sexuality and torn flesh, an image of a culture invaded, raped, and devastated." It comes as no little surprise that, in v. 26, the subject is made specific, namely, God. God, working in and through the Babylonian armies, lifts up Israel's skirts and exposes her shame. This multiple agency is similar to that which we have seen above in connection with v. 14 (with 21:7); language that would be descriptive of the violating effects of war upon a defeated Israel is used both for God and God's instruments.

Robert Carroll, *Jeremiah* (Philadelphia: Westminster, 1986), 304.

For modern readers (at least), the language used in this unit is remarkably harsh and demeaning in its use of female imagery. We are helped some in noting that the language of lament was powerfully stated in v. 17 and now continues in this segment in various ways. The God who speaks here is once again the God who has experienced infidelity on the part of the spouse, and responds with all the anger, sorrow, frustration, and pain that accompanies the breakdown of intimate relationships (see 3:1-5).[4]

Yet, the interpreter must ask not only whether the effects of this kind of language have contributed to a second-class role for women through the years, indeed allowed for the perpetuation of violence against women. It needs also to be asked whether such texts can continue to be used in any way, given our modern sensitivities. At the same time, it also should be wondered whether the use of such language was appropriate in the first place. Granted, one takes the ancient context into account, but that does not excuse the use of this language. Nor does this contextual reality mean that evaluative comment regarding the use of such violent images is placed off limits just because it is in the Bible. And placed in the mouth of God no less![5]

NOTES

[1] Contrary to Leo Perdue, *The Collapse of History: Reconstructing Old Testament Theology* (OBT; Minneapolis: Fortress, 1994), 214-15.

[2] Walter Brueggemann, *A Commentary on Jeremiah: Exile and Homecoming* (Grand Rapids: Eerdmans, 1998), 127-28.

[3] Contrary to Robert Carroll, *Jeremiah* (Philadelphia: Westminster, 1986), 294, on 13:9, "Yahweh does the destroying rather than Babylon."

[4] See Renita J. Weems, *Battered Love: Marriage, Sex, and Violence in the Hebrew Prophets* (Minneapolis: Fortress, 1995), 52-58.

[5] For further reflections on this kind of issue, see Terence Fretheim, "Is the Biblical Portrayal of God Always Trustworthy?" in T. Fretheim and K. Froehlich, eds., *The Bible as Word of God* (Eugene OR: Wipf & Stock, 2002), 97-111.

IT IS TOO LATE!

14:1–15:9

The unit is fundamentally dialogical in character, with contributions from people (vv. 7-9, 17-19), prophet (v. 13), and God (vv. 1-6, 10-12, 14-18; 15:1-9; see **Connections**, ch. 2). It is dominated by laments—from the people, both indirect (vv. 1-6) and direct (vv. 7-9, 19-22), from the prophet (v. 13), and from God (vv. 1-6 [in effect], 17-18; 15:5-9). The laments of people (especially) and prophet are matched by the laments of God. The people voice questions (vv. 8-9, 19, 22) to which God responds, if not in ways that the people would like (vv. 10-12; 15:1-9).

In terms of overall structure, parallel poetic materials bracket prose speeches in vv. 11-16—divine description of the situation (vv. 1-6, 17-18), communal lament (vv. 7-9, 19-22), and divine response (v. 10; 5:1-9). Verses 11-16 may be said to extend the divine response in v. 10. This interactive character and the communal laments give the whole a certain liturgical character; a "counter-liturgy" designation has been proposed (cf. Amos 4:4-5), namely, a vehicle for the announcement of judgment rather than salvation (cf. Joel 1-2 for a communal lament that leads to an announcement of salvation).

Notably, Jeremiah stands in the background in this segment; only in the prose segment (vv. 11-16) does he play a role beyond that of being the recipient of a word from God. The force of these verses is that nothing can stop the destruction of Israel, not religious or political leaders, not sacrificial acts, or intercessions, or confessions of sin, or professions of faith, not even sincere lamentation. It is too late! (On the theological issues regarding the people's repentance and God's response, see **Connections: Judgment in Spite of [Sincere] Prayers**).

COMMENTARY

The Drought and Its Effects, 14:1-6

The word of God regarding Israel's experience of a devastating drought comes to Jeremiah (for this introduction, see 46:1; 47:1; 49:34). With no indication that this word should be passed on to the people, the reader may wonder why God would convey this matter to Jeremiah. Basically, God informs the prophet of the dismay that has taken hold of the people because of the drought's destructive effects on land and animals. As such, the people's lament has become God's lament (and is parallel to the divine lament in vv. 17-18). Notably, God uses *totally nonreligious language* to convey the grim realities of the situation and is remarkably observant regarding the plight of both people and animals.

But certainly this word of God constitutes more than the transmission of data. God sees the difficulties that the people have to endure and gives voice to their lament. This devastation has its roots in the people's iniquity (v. 7), but their suffering situation matters to God and prompts a lament (also in vv. 17-18). [For Exilic Readers]

The effects of this prolonged drought are vividly portrayed. All of Judah mourns and the normally bustling gates of the city are lifeless (v. 2; see Isa 3:26). While the people sink down in gloom, their cry goes up to God. Even the wealthy nobles are having difficulty coping in the face of this drought (v. 3). They send their servants on searches for water that prove to be fruitless; all the cisterns are dry. In the face of this dilemma, they cover their heads as a sign of shame and despair. The farmers do so as well because the ground is hardened and "cracked," yielding no crops (v. 4). More literally, the ground "is dismayed" (NAB, "stricken"; see 12:4, 11, where the land "mourns" to God) and so is caught up in a chorus of dismay with the human populace. Both nobles and farmers respond not simply out of a general malaise, but because they understand that the drought is to be linked to their own behaviors (see v. 7; Deut 11:13-17; 28:23-24).

Notably, it is not only land and people who suffer; the animals do so as well (vv. 5-6). The deer forsake their newborn because there is no grass on which to feed. The wild asses gather on the trails (or the hills), perhaps looking for food from passing caravans.

For Exilic Readers

At another level, this word of God is being passed on to the exilic readers of this text. And so the exiles can look back on these ruinous events and be given a glimpse of how God had responded to their distressful situation. To see how their God had lamentfully responded would help shape their continuing understanding of the kind of God with whom they have to do. Divine judgment is accompanied by grief; such devastation was not what God had wanted for the people (or for the land and the animals!).

They are close to death and gasp for breath (just like the jackals do?); their eyes fail because there is no vegetation to sustain their health and strength. [On the Drought]

A Penitential Lament and Divine Response, 14:7-10

The lament-filled divine description of the drought-filled situation moves into a lament from the people in their shame and despair. Though it is common to claim that Jeremiah is the intermediary in these verses, there is no textual marker to indicate this (note the first person plural, as in vv. 19-22; see 8:14-15). Given the absence of an introduction, these words are likely still a part of the word spoken by God to Jeremiah as with vv. 1-6. That God quotes the people's prayers is a witness that God has indeed heard them and passes them on to the prophet. That God receives the prayers of people in distress would be an important word for exilic readers to hear (see [For Exilic Readers]). This prayer and that in vv. 19-22 have much in common; the rhetoric is somewhat softened in the latter compared to the pointed images that are used for God in vv. 8-9.

The juxtaposition of vv. 1-6 and the confession of sin in v. 7 (and in v. 20) link the drought and the iniquities of the people. Their confession of sin is a public testimony that they are the problem, whether sincere or not (see **Connections: Judgment in Spite of [Sincere] Prayers**). The threefold repetition of the confession of sin in v. 7—using three different words for sin/apostasy—yields a remarkably intense and direct penitential lament (see Dan 9:4-19 for a fuller confession). This confession surrounds the people's petition to God to act on behalf of the community (vv. 7a, 9c). The people ask God to act, not on the basis of anything they bring to this moment of prayer ("although"), but only that God would act for the sake of his name (see Isa 43:25). That is, they plead for God to act on their behalf for the effect that this action

On the Drought

Walter Brueggemann describes the situation well: "The devastation caused by the drought is sounded in a ringing repetition: 'no water' (Jer 14:3), 'no rain' (v. 4), 'no grass' (v. 5), 'no herbage' (v. 6)....The drought causes the social processes of the community to come to a halt, because now nobles, farmers, cows, asses, and jackals all have something in common. Life is under threat for all of them." Suffering is a great leveler.

Walter Brueggemann, *A Commentary on Jeremiah: Exile and Homecoming* (Grand Rapids: Eerdmans, 1998), 135.

Drought

As seen in this picture of the land surrounding Damascus, not a living thing could grow without the refreshing waters of the heavens, leaving the ground cracked and almost impenetrable.
(Credit: Brewton-Parker College)

might have on the divine reputation, indeed the divine self, given the divine commitments God has made to Israel. Would not God's name be enhanced among the Israelites (and even a broader audience) if God acted to relieve the devastation wrought by the drought?

The invocation "O hope of Israel" in v. 8 is added to the "O Lord" in vv. 7 and 9 (they are brought together in 17:13). To the confession of sin is added this strong confession of faith in a savior God (typical for laments; e.g., Ps 17:7). The address to God as "hope" is linked to God as one who has a history of saving people in a time of trouble. God is called "hope" precisely because God has shown himself to be savior of Israel over the course of their life together. With this kind of God, troubles need not be the end of the story. There are future possibilities with this God that move in salutary ways beyond the present debacle. Notably, the people do not explicitly ask God to forgive their sin, though God has a history of responding to repentance in this way. The people focus on deliverance from calamities that in the rest of the chapter (and beyond) go by the name of "sword, famine, and pestilence." The language of salvation is used here and elsewhere in the Old Testament in a comprehensive sense of divine action that issues in life and total well being.

After the confession of sin and the confession of faith the people address several "why?!" questions to God (vv. 8b-9). This language, reproachful as it is, should not suggest insincerity or disrespect. This is typical language for communal laments (e.g., Psalm 44:23-26; 74; 79; Lam 5:20)—cries from people who are suffering adversity of one kind or another. They wonder why God is like a stranger to them, like a person traveling through the land who stops only for a night. God is present in the country so rarely that no one would recognize him, and his commitments run no deeper than those of a passing stranger. In addition, the people wonder why God is like a confused or disoriented person, as if God did not recognize where and when he is needed. Or, why is God like a helpless giant, a warrior who is not able to deliver on his reputation?

These questions are surprisingly modern in their content and apparent tone, and are comparable to the theodicy questions raised by Jeremiah in 12:1 (see Isa 63:18-19). The complaints turn once again to a confession of trust in God (v. 9b); for all the contrary images, God *is* confessed to be in their midst. Even more, they are called by the name of the Lord (see Deut 28:10; that would be

Michelangelo's Jeremiah

Michelangelo completed this fresco of Jeremiah during his mammoth project on the ceilings of the Sistine Chapel. Michelangelo was commissioned by Pope Julius II to adorn the ceiling of the chapel, and the project was finished in the years between 1508–1512. The frescos of the chapel represent the *praeparatio evangelica*, depicting a sequence of scenes beginning with the Creation of the world through temptation and sin, to the Prophets of the Old Testament, and the Sibyls of the Gentiles.

Michelangelo (1475–1564). *Prophet Jeremiah*. 16th C. Sistine Chapel, Vatican Palace. Rome, Italy (Credit: Scala/Art Resource, NY).

comparable to being called Christians). Finally, the people once again (cf. v. 7) petition God not to abandon them to their troubles.

In v. 10, God responds to the people's lament (cf. 12:5-17), but with a word of judgment not, as might be expected from the lament form, salvation. Again, it is spoken only to Jeremiah, though as a written text it would be read by exiles who would remember the distressful situation. It is as though God were deaf to the people's lament. God's response is a succinct combination of indictment and announcement of judgment (cf. Hos 8:13; 9:9). The indictment is framed in terms of a metaphor of a wanderer who does not care about the effect of the wandering on his life (cf. the image of God as traveler in v. 8). God refers to their wandering as a lifestyle that has brought them to this point. Even if the prayers are sincere, given this history it is too late for prayers to do any good; God will not accept them, let alone their prayers (v. 10; see Isa 1:15; 59:1-2). God will remember their sin and "visit" their sins upon them (NRSV "punish" says too much; see **Introduction**; note the reversal in 31:34). The die is cast.

Interaction between God and Jeremiah, 14:11-16

This announcement of judgment (v. 10) flows into the directive given to Jeremiah not to pray for the welfare of this people (v. 11; see 7:16; 11:14; 15:1; [Do Not Intercede for Them!]). In effect, God reinforces earlier commands that Jeremiah be conformed to God's decision for judgment (yet, see v. 13). God will not listen to Israel's prayers (v. 12); by implication God will not listen to *Jeremiah's* prayers for them, even though they are accompanied by the right liturgical moves, including fasting and various offerings. Apparently, the people are engaged in acts of worship that are appropriate according to formal criteria (at least) and perhaps on any sincerity barometer (see **Connections: Judgment in Spite of [Sincere] Prayers**). But God will not accept them.

We know from texts such as Joel 2:12-20 that these very rituals can serve as vehicles in and through which God acts salvifically on behalf of the worshiping community. But not now; it is too late! A many-sided judgment—sword, famine, and disease—is already in process, mediated by God through the armies from the north. The people will be consumed (see 9:16). The language of "sword and famine" is a refrain in the verses that follow (14:13, 15, 16, 18; 15:2; see **Introduction**). This phrase probably picks up on both natural and historical dimensions of the disaster; though famine may be associated with army sieges, the references to drought are too dominant in the text to this point to ignore.

At this point in the dialogue, Jeremiah intervenes on behalf of the people (on his "ah, Lord God," see 1:6). In the face of God's command not to pray for this people (see Moses in Exod 32:10-14), he claims that the (false) prophets are really to blame for the people's apostasy (v. 13). They have been promising no famine, among other things, and the community is looking famine and invasion in the face. God responds, not by excusing the people, but by indicting the prophets (again). This prophetic word promising peace, indeed true/genuine peace, has been a common theme heretofore (see 4:9-10; 5:12; 6:13-15; 8:10-12).

God indicts the prophets for the lies they proclaim, and proclaim "in my name." These prophets either understand themselves to be true Yahwistic prophets (such as Hananiah in ch. 28) or they are consciously false; it is not always possible to tell. If Jeremiah thinks that God is responsible for deceiving these prophets (see 4:9-10), God closes off that possibility. God has not sent them, commanded them, or spoken to them.

Balancing that threefold denial are three divine evaluations of their prophecies—lying visions, worthless divination, deception—all products of their own imaginations. If they are receiving visions, they are false; divination is worthless in any case. If they are sincere, they have deceived themselves. [Berrigan on the Prophets]

This indictment of the prophets is followed by an announcement of judgment on them (v. 15). The extensive introduction gathers up the basic points of the previous verses and announces that they will receive the same judgment as the people: sword and famine (see v. 12; 23:9-20). Or, put in terms of a "what goes around, comes around" way of thinking, the prophets have claimed that the people would not see sword and famine (vv. 13, 15) and that is precisely what they will experience. In v. 16 God specifies in a vivid, even gross fashion what "sword and famine" will mean. So many people (and prophets) will die of sword and famine and their dead bodies will accumulate so quickly in public places that they will not be buried (a matter of great shame, see 7:33–8:3; 19:7; see **Introduction**). This judgment will be inclusive—men and women, adults and children (on children, see **Connections**, ch. 6). This devastating description is no doubt informed by the actual experience (as is v. 18 and 15:2-3).

Berrigan on the Prophets

Daniel Berrigan describes the false prophets very well: "a tawdry band of hallucinators buzz about, deceiving and disorienting the people. They offer no critique of political realities, no reproof, no urge to repent. Instead, they busily shore up the corrupt, unjust system on which they have staked all. Talk about acculturated religion!"

Daniel Berrigan, *Jeremiah: The World, the Wound of God* (Minneapolis: Fortress, 1999), 69.

This announcement of judgment concludes with a succinct understanding regarding the relationship between wickedness and judgment (v. 16c). God will pour out *their* wickedness upon them. Judgment is the effect of Israel's own wickedness, not something that God newly introduces as a penalty or punishment (see 2:19; 6:19; 21:14). God "pours out" (as with "wrath" in 10:25), but the content is shaped by the people's own sin. God sees to the moral order, mediating sin's own consequences (see **Introduction**).

God and People Lament, 14:17-22

Verses 17-18 introduce another divine lament over the people of Israel (see 9:1, 17-18; 12:7-13; 13:17), a lament that speaks of God's tear-filled eyes over what has happened to the people in these destructive events. While perhaps set in the midst of Babylon's final onslaught (see vv. 17-18), the text also fits well in the post-destruction era. God's continued use of the metaphor, "virgin daughter," and "my people" implies Israel is still considered the people of God. God explicitly commands Jeremiah to convey this lament to these people. The insight that the prophet has received into the inner life of God is to be made public so that all can observe it, especially exilic readers.

The common translation of the verb in v. 17a as a jussive ("let my eyes run down with tears") can carry the sense of certainty—my eyes will do so. God not only weeps over what has happened to the people (see 9:1; 13:17), but weeps day and night; indeed, this is an ongoing weeping over their experience—a crushing blow (at the hands of the Babylon) that has caused a grievous wound. Wherever God looks—in the fields and in the city—he is confronted with death and devastation caused by both sword and famine. God again voices a key reason for the catastrophe: like traveling salesmen, the leaders of the people—prophet and priest—have gone about plying their wares. And they don't know what they are talking about! They have no true knowledge of God (see v. 14; 13:17). Or, better, the prophet and priest are not exempt from this catastrophe. They have been reduced to the status of traveling salesmen, seeking to peddle wares wherever they can, but without having any special knowledge to give to anyone (probably a reference back to vv. 13-14). [A God Who Judges and Weeps]

A God Who Judges and Weeps

The reason for this revelation of the divine emotions is to give readers a glimpse of the inner-divine side of wrath. The God who judges is also the God who weeps. This God is not punitive or uncaring with respect to what the people have had to endure. Such a portrayal of God is important in any interpretation of these events. Exilic readers of this material are reminded that this is the kind of God with whom they are related. This God is genuinely caught up in what has happened and mourns over the disasters experienced by this "virgin daughter," responding like any good parent would. There is hope for the future with this kind of God (see the images of 31:20).

The people respond to God's lament, conveyed to them by Jeremiah (v. 17a), with their own lament (vv. 19-22). Again, there is no good reason to suppose that Jeremiah speaks this lament (note the first person plural and see v. 11). Their lament includes invocations ("*our* God," v. 22), reproachful questions, confessions of sin and of faith, and petitions for deliverance from a God in whom they hope (vv. 19-22; cf. the discussion of vv. 7-9). As noted above, all of these elements are typical for Israel's laments.

The people's lament begins with questions this time (v. 19), in language similar to that of Lamentations 5:20-22 (and hence a link to exilic readers). In the face of the tragedy that has struck their community, their questioning moves in several directions; all the questions assume that God is responsible for what has happened. First, they wonder whether God has completely rejected them. Second, they wonder whether God finds them loathsome. Finally, they question why God has struck them down with such severity that no healing is available. The last lines of v. 19 are picked up from an earlier lament of the people (8:15). In the midst of the devastation, they have looked for peace and healing, but everything only gets worse; no goodness can be found anywhere.

The people move from their questions and resignation to a three-fold confession of sin in language similar to v. 7 (v. 20; see 3:25). This time they recall ancestral sins as well as their own (see Ps 106:6). Their petitions in v. 21 only implicitly request deliverance and healing, and they do not plead for forgiveness. The petitions assume that God has not yet spurned them, not yet disdained or dishonored "your glorious throne" (=Jerusalem, as in 3:17; or more likely, the temple and its ark, as in 17:12), not yet broken the covenant with Israel (presumably the Abrahamic/Davidic covenant, see 33:14-26). The people apparently consider these effects to be a lively possibility; yet, one must consider their rhetorical strategy to get God's attention in this matter. Generally, laments cannot be pressed for their theological precision (e.g., Ps 44:23).

The lament concludes (v. 22) with a confession of faith. Three rhetorical questions make these points (note the drought, v. 1): idols do not bring rain; the heavens (astral deities are in mind) do not decide to send showers; Israel's God alone does these things, a reference to divine providence (see 5:24; 10:12-13). Hence, the people will set their hope in Yahweh alone. This conclusion assumes an absence of syncretism; other gods have no power with respect to matters such as weather (the particular province of Baal; see [Ancient Israelite Creeds]). In other words, the people's prayers to

God are shaped by a confession in Yahweh alone as their God. But it is too late!

God's Response to the People's Lament, 15:1-9

In response to the people's lament, God speaks to Jeremiah regarding this people. They have prayed their lament, but God will not listen (cf. 14:10-12); God's heart has turned away from them. Jeremiah was commanded not to pray for this people in 14:11; the prayers would not be effective because it was too late. God reinforces this point: even if two of the greatest intercessors in the tradition (Moses and Samuel), whose prayers were instrumental in averting catastrophe for Israel in earlier emergency situations (Exod 32:7-14; 1 Sam 12:17-18), were to pray on behalf of these people it would do no good. It is too late. [Israel's Intercessors]

Israel's Intercessors

Moses' intercessions can be studied in Exod 32:11-14, 30-34; Num 14:13-19; Deut 9:6-29. For Samuel's intercessions, see 1 Sam 7:5-11; 8:1-22; 12:17-23. See Ps 99:6 for a witness to their intercessions—they had become proverbial. See also the roles given Noah, Daniel, and Job in Ezek 14:14, 16. These texts assume an understanding of prayer wherein the human party is able to engage God about the shape of the future. God is shown to be the kind of God—a genuinely relational God—who will consider such human participation and can be persuaded by human pleas to take a different course. At the same time, God's ways into the future may be circumscribed by earthly realities because of creational commitments.

God commands Jeremiah to send the people away from the divine presence and "let them go." The same language is used for sending the Israelites out of Egypt (see Exod 3:10-12; 5:1); Jeremiah is given a role comparable to Moses, only this time in an anti-exodus move. In speaking this word, Jeremiah is thereby made the subject of an action commonly ascribed elsewhere to God (see the anti-exodus language in 15:6; 44) or to Babylon or both (cf. 25:15). Anticipating the people's question regarding where they should go (that is, to whom should they now turn?), God tells Jeremiah to speak of four destinations (developed in v. 3): pestilence, sword, famine, and exile (see 14:12; comparably, Ezek 5:12; 14:21; see Rev 6:1-8; 13:9-10). The language of exile, not included at 14:12 (but at 43:11), connects well with earlier references to God's judgment making less than a "full end" (e.g., 4:27).

The NRSV translation "destined" could be misleading (v. 2); actually no Hebrew verb is used at this point. A more common verb used is "marked" (e.g., NAB). The sense is that everyone will experience some kind of hardship, at least some of which would lead to death; whatever it is, that is the answer to the question: "Where shall we go?"

God goes on to speak of Israel in the third person in vv. 3-9, except vv. 5-6 (perhaps a quotation of an earlier word of God). Though pre-fall Jerusalem would not have heard this conversation between God and Jeremiah, exilic readers would hear themselves addressed, especially in the use of the word "captivity/exile" (v. 2) and the direct address ("you") of vv. 5-6.

Verse 3 develops the fourfold theme of v. 2. The opening verb is *pāqad,* "visit" (NRSV, "appoint over"; NAB, "decreed"); it carries the same sense as in 14:10; 21:14 (NRSV, "punish"; see **Introduction**): God will mediate the effects of the people's own sins upon them. Four different agents are used by God in these ravaging events: soldiers wielding swords; dogs dragging away the bodies thrown into the streets (14:16); and birds and wild animals picking at the bodies (as in 7:33; 12:9; 16:4; 19:7). The images are gruesome and correspond to what actually happened in the fall of Jerusalem (see Lam 5:9-13; **Introduction**). This language constitutes a "what goes around, comes around" understanding. Because the people's sins have had a devastating effect upon birds and wild animals, the latter will act against them (4:25; 9:10; 12:4).

In this horrendous judgment, God will make Israel a "horror" (=an object of horror) to *all* the nations (v. 4; see 24:9; 29:18; 34:17; Deut 28:37; 1 Kgs 9:7; also used for other nations such as Edom [49:13-17] and Babylon [50:23; 51:37-43]). A remarkable range of language is used in these other texts to speak of devastated Israel: disgrace, byword, object of hissing and cursing, shame, derision, taunt (see **Introduction**; in 24:9, this language is used for the "bad figs").

When anyone anywhere thinks about Israel, they will be horrified at the appalling levels of death and destruction. At one level, the nations will be "gapers" at the scene of a massacre, having difficulty averting their eyes. At another level, God's judgment will be a matter of disgrace; what did the people do that their own God would do this to them? It must have been a shameful thing (and King Manasseh is cited). [King Manasseh] Moreover, these devastating effects would become a matter of derision—that Israel could think that they would be protected from such disasters! Even more, these events would constitute a kind of witness to Israel's God, a God who would enter into judgment against his own chosen ones. What kind of God must this be? Is it possible that people would be attracted to a God who would be so just that even God's own children must be disciplined, and even harshly so (see Amos 3:2)?

God now speaks another lament (vv. 5-9). The lament character of these verses is signaled by the last phrase of v. 6, "I am weary of relenting" (see 20:9) (see **Connections: The Weariness of God**). God opens with rhetorical questions that seem to call for a negative reply (see Isa 51:19 for comparable questions). No one will have

King Manasseh

King Manasseh, Davidic ruler over Judah for forty-five years (687–642 BC), is mentioned only here in Jeremiah (v. 4). Yet, his promotional zeal of idolatrous ways in Jerusalem probably provides the near background for much of Jeremiah's strong language regarding Israel's fidelity. He is more explicitly named the villain in 2 Kings 21:1-20; 23:12, 26 and especially 24:3, "Surely this [the Babylonian invasion] came upon Judah at the command of the LORD, to remove them out of his sight, for the sins of Manasseh, for all that he had committed, and also for the innocent blood that he had shed; for he had filled Jerusalem with innocent blood, and the LORD was not willing to pardon." While Jeremiah spreads the responsibility for Israel's situation into every corner of Israel's society, certain persons, because of their standing in the community, are especially responsible for failures of leadership (kings, prophets, priests, and the wise). The reference to Manasseh also makes clear that the fall of Jerusalem has been long in coming; the boat was set to go over the falls a century earlier and nothing that Israel, or its religious leaders (including Jeremiah), accomplished could finally do anything about such an eventuality.

---

pity/compassion on you, O Jerusalem (not even God, 13:14; cf. 21:7). No one will go into mourning for you (even Jeremiah is commanded not to do so, 16:5). No one will stop and ask about your well-being (*šalom*), for God has taken it away (16:5) and the people realize it (14:19). The sense might be put like this: Who will mourn for *you*? Given what you have done! I cannot imagine it; and you cannot imagine it either! [No Simple Rhetorical Questions]

God has often ameliorated the effects of your sins and sought alternative ways into the future, but that strategy is no longer possible. It is too late—not only because of the cumulative effects of your sins, but because of my own weariness in taking this course. I

No Simple Rhetorical Questions

The questions in v. 5 are probably to be called rhetorical, yet 9:17-19 (and other weeping texts, e.g., 9:1; 14:17) suggests that the response to God's questions is not a simple negative. A divine ambivalence is present in these questions and in the revelation regarding divine weariness (v. 6). Who will have pity on you? Oh, that there were someone! Who will mourn for you? O that there may be a time when the mourning women weep over you! Who will take the time to care for you? I wish there were someone to do so, but you have rejected me and turned your back on me (v. 6) and hence I am not welcome among you for such a purpose.

am worn out! And so I have, in effect, reversed the exodus. You will recall that time when I stretched out my hand on your behalf and delivered you from the Egyptians. Now I stretch out my hand against you and visit destruction upon you. There is finality evident in these words.

In vv. 7-9 God returns to the third person in his talk about Israel. The net effect of these words is to confirm and further specify the divine decision to bring judgment. Yet, for all the harshness of God's language, these are still "my people" (v. 7) and the anguish of the people, especially the women, is voiced. Though the reader cannot hear the tone God uses, this language suggests that the lament of vv. 5-6 continues into these verses.

Several metaphors are used to speak of the destruction of Judah/Jerusalem (not prior disciplinary measures). Like a farmer at the city gates (where this task was commonly done), God uses a winnowing fork to remove the chaff from the grain and the wind scatters it (see Isa 41:16). This metaphor suggests that judgment is not total (note that in 4:11, God said he would not come to winnow!). [Winnowing Fork] Another metaphor relates to family life and death. God has bereaved Israel, that is, God has so destroyed them that they have lost their capability of assuring their own future. The allusion to the promise of Abraham (v. 8a; "numerous"; "sand of the sea," see Gen 22:17) is especially notable. While this language does not claim that the Abrahamic promise has been cancelled, certainly the effects of the judgment have brought the people back to the point where they are but a small clan, as they were at the beginning.

So many men, both fathers and their male children, have been killed in battle, that every house seems populated by a widow and a mourning mother. These women (and the effects on women are especially noted) are filled with anguish and terror over what has happened to their families, and the more so because it has happened so quickly (see 6:26). The mother who has borne seven children (a symbolic number for a family so blessed with children that their future is assured, see 1 Sam 2:5; Ruth 4:15) gasps for breath in the face of the tragedy. For many of these women the sun was still high in the sky; they were in the prime of their lives. Now their night has fallen before its time, and with that comes shame and dismay. And, to put the final nail in the coffin: if there are any who are still alive, God will give them over to be killed (see 6:9). This sounds final and stands in tension with the earlier "less than a full end" texts (e.g., 4:27). Yet, the reference to exile in this context (v. 2) suggests that this is a type of hyperbolic speaking for effect (and for exilic readers, the destruction no doubt did seem final). Moreover, the referent for "the rest of them" (v. 9) is not entirely clear, not least because the shamed mothers are apparently still living. Parenthetically, as if to make sure the reason behind the divine action is never lost from sight (v. 7c), they did not repent.

Winnowing Fork

A winnowing fork was a tool used by farmers to separate grain from the straw chaff by tossing the mixture of grain and chaff into the air, allowing the chaff to blow away and the grain to return to the floor for collection. The winnowing fork had tines placed close enough together to hold the semi-clean grain. The winnowing fork served as a symbol for the enacting of divine judgment.

CONNECTIONS

Judgment in Spite of (Sincere) Prayers

This chapter has occasioned no little difficulty for interpreters. The people engage in penitential lament, openly confessing their sins to God (vv. 7, 20). Yet, God continues to announce judgment, after both confessions (14:10; 15:1-9), and takes even further initiative by refusing to allow Jeremiah to pray for their welfare (14:11; 15:1) and by rejecting any form of worship (14:12). Jeremiah seeks to deflect some of the blame from the people by accusing the (false) prophets of deceiving them (v. 13). But this effort does not deter God from the course of judgment. God responds with a condemnation of both prophets and people (vv. 14-16), though agonizing over the matter (vv. 17-18).

Some interpreters have sought to resolve the issue by suggesting that the people's prayers and worship were insincere. But there is no specific evidence for this approach. A more helpful way of understanding the chapter is to recognize that, *whether the people's prayers were sincere or not*, they were too late, just as the prophet's prayers would be. The effects of the people's sins, both historical and natural (14:1-6, 12, 15-16, 18; 15:2-3), had been so pervasive that the situation could not be turned around. It was too late! The judgment had to fall. The only future for this people was on the far side of natural and historical devastation. This segment may be concerned with the exiles' question of "Why!?" the fall had taken place in spite of the many prayers that had been offered. [Clements on the People's Prayers]

The experience of judgment was the very situation faced by the exilic readers of this material, and for them this material takes on a

---

Clements on the People's Prayers

Another unhelpful direction to take with this text is that Jeremiah's intercessions would "represent an impossible affront to God" because "their sins were so severe." To be consistent, would not the interpreter also have to so interpret Moses' prayers after God's command prohibiting him not to do so (Exod 32:10)? In these events, God is not out to protect himself! Clements also claims that "Israel's sins had become too deeply ingrained and too immense in their scale for God to forgive them." Are we to say that God can forgive sins only if their scale is not so immense? That God can respond to prayers of repentance only if the sins are not "so severe"? If God's forgiveness is so calculated, no one can be forgiven! The issue for God is not simply the severity of Israel's sins, but the devastating *effects* that their sins have had on every aspect of life over an extended period of time. Clements goes on to speak of those whose experience of the horrors of these events may have evoked "the reply that the punishment far exceeded the demands of righteousness. However the prophetic insistence is that this cannot have been so." Yet, the book of Jeremiah insists that it was so! The Babylonians overreached in mediating the divine judgment, and God turns against them for precisely this reason (25:12-14; 50:29; 51:24, 49; see Isa 47:5-7). The judgment did exceed "the demands of righteousness"!

Ronald E. Clements, *Jeremiah* (IBC; Atlanta: John Knox, 1988), 92-94.

renewed significance. The prayers of the people in this chapter could serve as models for them; in fact, the description of the people's plight before the fall of Jerusalem is not unlike the exilic situation (cf., e.g., 14:19-21 with Lam 5:1-22). At the same time, this material would be a reminder that prayers to God, even sincere prayers, are not necessarily efficacious.

The people of God may think that their prayers are offered in isolation from other factors at work in a given situation (social, medical, individual and communal history), as if God had only to take into account the prayers in and of themselves in moving into a future. But prayers are spoken and received in a context shaped by a vast array of factors, and those factors will shape the efficacy of the prayers offered. Even the sincerity (or insincerity) of those who pray, while not to be discounted, may often not count in any decisive way toward the resolution of a difficult situation about which the prayers are offered. It may even be that God wills that the prayers of the people be answered positively, but that God is not able to do so in view of the relationships God has established with people and world. God's will for the world often does not always get done, as people's resistance to that will (whether Israel's sins or Babylonian excesses) demonstrates. It may be too late, even for God!

The Freedom of God

One basic distinction between true and false prophecy lifted up in this text (14:13-16) and elsewhere in Jeremiah (e.g., 6:14=8:11; 23:9-22; 28) has to do with the preaching of peace and judgment. The false prophets brought only a word of peace and assurance to the people in the face of their infidelity; Jeremiah and other prophets (e.g., Amos 3:2) understood that God would stand in judgment, even over the chosen people.

One of the ways in which this distinction has been articulated theologically is in terms of the freedom of God. For example, Brueggemann asserts that "The tradition of Jeremiah asserts God's freedom, even from God's partner.... To judge Jeremiah to be true is a theological verdict which allows for something wild, dangerous, unfettered, and free in the character of Yahweh."[1] It *is* very important to affirm, with Brueggemann, that God is free to enter into judgment of God's own people. At the same time, it is important to stress that God's freedom cannot be maintained in an unqualified way.

To speak of God's promises (e.g., the covenants with Noah, Abraham, David) is to speak of a God who has chosen not to remain unfettered. Indeed, to speak of God's election of Israel and God's promise to be their God places a decisive limitation on any talk about divine freedom. God has exercised freedom in making such promises in the first place, but having freely made the promises, thereafter God's freedom is truly limited by those promises. God will do what God says God will do; God will be faithful to God's own promises. One might also speak more generally of God's relationship with people and world; God will be true to those relationships.

Even for God to enter into judgment is not fundamentally an exercise in freedom, though it may evidence an element of that. God's judgment is always informed by God's will and purpose for people and world, and so that very judgment may be *necessary* if God is going to be true to that will and purpose. Judgment may be the only way in which God can do justice to relationships and to a purpose to which God is committed.

Moreover, the immense agony and suffering of God witnessed to in the book of Jeremiah is a demonstration that God is not truly free of this relationship with Israel. If God had "radical, unquestionable freedom"[2] (a theme common in the literature), then God would not agonize, either over the breakdown in the relationship or over judgment passed on the other party. God would just exercise freedom, slice their throats, and walk away. God agonizes because God is in a committed relationship with a people whom God loves. So, we would be wise in speaking of divine freedom in a qualified way.

The Weariness of God

What does it mean for God to be weary (15:6), not least in view of the witness of Isa 40:28 that God is one who "does not faint or grow weary"? The context of the Isaiah passage, with its reference to the weariness of human beings, suggests that its claim about God pertains to stamina. But Jeremiah 15:6 does not refer to divine tiredness (physical, emotional, or mental) or even what we would call "being sick and tired." This reference is not isolated; several texts testify to a divine weariness (Isa 1:14; 7:13; 43:24; Ezek 24:12; Mal 2:17), and Jeremiah himself will speak of being weary, that is, being conformed to the weariness of God (6:11; 20:9).

I have suggested elsewhere[3] that such texts refer to the expending of the divine life; God's life is in some sense being spent because of the people's unfaithfulness. By bearing the sins of the people over a long period of time, God suffers; such divine forbearance is costly to God. By holding back the judgment they deserve (see Isa 42:14; 48:9; 57:11; Ezek 20:21-22; Ps 78:38; see Rom 2:4; 3:25), by carrying their sins on the divine shoulders (Isa 43:23-24), by repenting of announcements of judgment (see at ch. 18), God chooses to suffer their infidelity in patience. Such continued divine restraint in the face of continued rejection must have meant for an intensification of suffering for God. Weariness entails a self-giving for the sake of the continuing relationship. The old word, "long-suffering," a refusal to deal with the people on strictly legal or contractual terms, may capture some of what this has cost God. The result of this divine suffering, of course, has meant a continued life for an unfaithful people. But there is a limit to the divine patience and an end to the holding back of the forces that make for death and destruction. [A Divine Pattern]

A Divine Pattern

In speaking of a divine weariness, there may be an intimation that God is the kind of God whose suffering on behalf of the people's continuing life will someday take a further step (cf. also Mal 2:17). God will take their sins into the divine life and bear them there (see Isa 43:23-25; Hos 11:8-9) and, even more, bodily assume the form of a servant to suffering death on a cross (Phil 2:6-8; see John 4:6). Jeremiah conforms to the weariness of God; Jesus does as well, in an unsurpassable way.

NOTES

[1] Walter Brueggemann, *A Commentary on Jeremiah: Exile and Homecoming* (Grand Rapids: Eerdmans, 1998), 138.

[2] The phrase is that of Leo Perdue, *The Collapse of History: Reconstructing Old Testament Theology* (Minneapolis: Fortress, 1994), 216.

[3] Terence Fretheim, *The Suffering of God: An Old Testament Perspective* (Philadelphia: Fortress, 1984), 141.

MORE LAMENTS
FROM JEREMIAH

15:10-21

This unit consists of two laments by Jeremiah (vv. 10, 15-18; though he is not identified explicitly as the speaker), each followed by a divine response (vv. 11-14 , 19-21). That dialogical pattern was characteristic of Jeremiah's laments in 11:18-23; 12:1-6 (see introduction to 11:18–12:17; on the lament pattern, see [The Lament Psalms]) (see **Connections: Appropriation of Jeremiah's Laments**).

COMMENTARY

Jeremiah's Lament and God's Response, 15:10-14

This segment is in prose (cf. God's response in 11:21-23). Jeremiah, in a unique address to his mother (links up with the mothers of vv. 8-9; a few understand "mother" here to be a reference to Jerusalem), expresses regret that he was ever born (he does so more intensely in 20:14-18; see Job 3:3-4). Recall that Jeremiah was called to be a prophet in his mother's womb (1:5), and hence this is a wish that he had not been born to carry out that role.

This lament reveals a crisis of call for Jeremiah in view of his experience of exercising that call. He has acquired an unhappy reputation among the people as a contentious individual; he speaks sharply critical words of the populace and stirs up strife wherever he goes. And though Jeremiah has been called to speak these words, he is dismayed that people are so critical of him. Everyone is out to get him! Everyone curses him, treating him with contempt! Even his own family and friends (11:21-23). Indeed, he is persecuted and brought to trial (see chs. 26; 36–38). The proverbial statement that he has not been either a borrower or a lender (activities that tended to generate quarrels; see Job 6:22) is meant as evidence that he has not sought conflict (see **Connections: Jeremiah's Laments and His Call**).

God responds to Jeremiah with words of assurance, though within a context of continuing conflict and judgment, so that the news is

---

Jeremiah 15:11-14 and 17:1-4

📖 Jeremiah 15:11-14 are textually difficult, and have evoked a variety of scholarly opinions, not least because of their similarity to 17:1-4. The latter is clearly a word of judgment addressed to an unfaithful people, and it has been difficult for interpreters to see comparable words addressed to Jeremiah (see NAB, e.g., which omits vv. 12-14 as a dittography of 17:1, 3-4; NEB omits vv. 13-14). Some interpreters, following the LXX, consider vv. 11-14 to be a continuation of Jeremiah's lament (see NAB; RSV; JB), sometimes with vv. 13-14 seen as Jeremiah's quotation of God's words. Without much evidence to go on, it seems best to interpret vv. 11-14 as God's response to Jeremiah (e.g., NRSV; NIV). Important differences from the judgment oracle in 17:1-4 exist (e.g., the "you" is singular throughout vv. 11-14 except for a final phrase; see the discussion in William Holladay, *Jeremiah 1* [Philadelphia: Fortress, 1989], 116-17, 255-57). Only a general sense of these verses can be given.

---

not simply good (vv. 11-14; comparably vv. 19-21 and 12:5-6). [Jeremiah 15:11-14 and 17:1-4] Translations of v. 11 differ and no certainty is possible. One translation has God speaking in entirely positive language: God will intervene on Jeremiah's behalf in his times of trouble and distress and bring his enemies under his feet (see NEB, NIV). In other translations (NRSV; cf. REB), God speaks of acting in Jeremiah's life for good but at the same time recognizes that God's word has created enemies for him as well. If the latter sense is correct, which seems likely, then Jeremiah's experience of God has generated both blessing and bane for him, a typical reality for prophets and other individuals called to such a critical leadership role.

Various interpretations of v. 12 are possible, depending on the translation (which varies, cf., e.g., NRSV; NIV; REB). I prefer the translation "Can iron break iron from the north and bronze."[1] The first reference to "iron" could refer to the stubborn people Jeremiah faces (as in 6:28); hence, they will not be able to break "iron from the north" (that is, Babylon). This would support the thrust of Jeremiah's message. The "bronze" could refer to Jeremiah (as in v. 20; cf. 1:18). Hence Jeremiah's God-given strength in the face of opposition from the people will be reinforced by the strength of Babylon. The iron-willed people will not be able to break either Babylon (iron) or Jeremiah (bronze). Understanding the expression as a word of assurance to Jeremiah is probably best.

If the singular "you" is retained in vv. 13-14a, it probably refers to the prophet (many commentators read a plural with 17:3 or suggest a singular reference to Israel or Jeremiah's enemies). Though God has been with Jeremiah through his difficulties, his future will not be a bed of roses. His wealth and other belongings will become spoil for the Babylonians, for which they will pay nothing (as will be the case for other Israelites, throughout all the territory of Israel, see 17:3). But (letting the "not" govern "sins" as well as "price") this looting will *not* be because of his sins (in contrast to his enemies, 17:3).[2] Alternatively, "your sins" could refer to Jeremiah's own sins; in some sense, albeit attenuated, he participates in the larger communal problem.

Verse 14 continues God's response to Jeremiah's having to suffer the antagonism of his enemies. The verb in Hebrew should be kept, "But [or, and] I will send your [Jeremiah's] enemies into a land that you do not know," that is, exile. (On the first clause of v. 14, the NRSV, in correspondence with the corporate reference of 17:4, follows the LXX, "I will make you serve your enemies.") God's response concludes with a metaphor for judgment that will envelop everyone, including Jeremiah (the Hebrew text reads, "over/against you [plural]," at the end of v. 14; it is amended in NRSV to "forever"; cf. NIV; REB). Finally, Jeremiah will suffer the disaster the people suffer.

Once Again, Jeremiah's Lament and God's Response, 15:15-21

The exchange between Jeremiah and God in vv. 11-14 is followed by another (vv. 15-21). Jeremiah's continuing lament (vv. 15-18), perhaps in at least partial response to God's word in vv. 11-14, again receives a response from God (vv. 19-21). Jeremiah's lament moves from petition (v. 15ab) to protestation of faithfulness as motivation for divine action (vv. 15c-17) to complaint (v. 18).

Beginning with an acknowledgment that God knows him and his situation (v. 15a), Jeremiah continues his complaint anyway, as if to make sure that God takes these reflections into account. He petitions God to remember him during this time of oppression and to visit him with a specific action—bringing judgment down on those who persecute him (on the NRSV translation, "retribution," see at 5:9). This is a request Jeremiah has previously voiced (see 11:20; 12:3). As noted in that discussion, while this petition has a personal dimension, it must also be related to the prophet's being conformed to the wrath of God (see at v. 17c).

Jeremiah quickly shifts away from the fate of his persecutors to the shape of his own future (though they remain linked). In view of the verbal abuse he has undergone because of God's call (cf. Ps 69:7-8), he pleads that God would be patient and "not take me away" (v. 15). This refers either to being exiled along with the rest of the people or to his own death (see v. 14). It stands in some tension with v. 10 and the wish never to have been born; but, having been born, life is precious.

Jeremiah proceeds to give God reasons to act on his behalf (vv. 15c-17). Pursuing with God the idea that his suffering has been "on your account," he recalls a key element in his call (v. 16; see 1:9). In effect, God is responsible for putting him in this situation and that entails a divine commitment to him. By being lenient to his persecutors (see 12:1), God is prolonging his suffering. The phrase "your words were found" (v. 16) is best understood in the sense of, "your words were offered/presented" (as with the call of Ezekiel, 3:1). Having been presented with God's words (note the repeated "*your* words"), Jeremiah did not reject the offer; he ingested them, that is, took them into his very self (see 1:9, and **Connections** there; Ezek 2:8–3:3). [A New Identity]

Jeremiah continues to give God a rationale for his plea. Over the course of his life, Jeremiah has been faithful to his calling (v. 17; cf. the protestation of innocence in the lament psalms, e.g., 17:3-5; 26:3-5). Given the nature of the word he was given to proclaim, heavily weighted on the side of judgment (see 1:10), Jeremiah's public mien was not that of a merrymaker (see 30:19; 31:4). That is, he did not participate in those special occasions in his community that called for celebration (it does not mean that he walked around all day with a sour face!). His daily life was shaped in such a way as to correlate with the message he spoke (for more detail, see 16:1-13). [On Living with a Call from God]

God's "hand" was the pressure that God's word fostered in the prophet (see Isa 8:11; Ezek 1:3; 3:14). That it was a heavy hand meant, not that he was forced into this posture, but that the message he was called to bring was one of divine anger and wrath issuing in devastation for Israel. The weight of this kind of message meant that Jeremiah became isolated within his community. This

A New Identity

The words God had placed in Jeremiah's mouth had become an integral part of his identity; he was now an embodied word of God. He now bore the name of Yahweh in his very self! This statement is more than a play on his name (which means "Yahweh exalts"); it is a claim regarding a new identity. He is now called by the name of Yahweh (v. 16; see Isa 43:5-7 for comparable language for the exiles). God's word has so shaped his life that the call was not simply a joyful occasion, but a self-defining moment.

On Living with a Call from God

While Jeremiah's calling was a joy and a delight for him (v. 16) it was not a matter of public celebration. The calling itself was a delight; the effects of the calling were something else again. Jeremiah's language of delight stands in some tension with his complaints that follow, but this is not unusual; anyone who has received such a call has experienced this tension. Living with a call from God is always marked by a certain amount of ambivalence, including moments of joy and delight as well as moments of doubt and questioning. In living with such a call, acceptance and reluctance come together time and time again.

William Holladay, *Jeremiah 1* (Philadelphia: Fortress, 1986), 412-13.

way of being in the community was fundamentally because, having eaten the word of God, he was filled with divine wrath (as in 6:11; see [Full of Wrath]). His life was shaped in such a way as to conform to the shape of the life of God toward Israel at this particular moment (see **Introduction**; this observation suggests that the complaint proper does not start until v. 18). Another way to think about this protestation would be to note that Jeremiah has committed no sin that should lead to this type of suffering. As often in the Old Testament (rooted in Israel's suffering in Egypt), people suffer because of other people's sins and not because of their own sin (cf. the arguments of Job).

Jeremiah proceeds to pour out his "Why!?" questions to God (v. 18). That God is called to account does not mean that God is believed to be the sole factor in his suffering (as shown by v. 10; see 11:19). The issue is framed in terms of God's not bringing that suffering to its proper end. Given his complaint that enemies are "out to get him," it is striking that Jeremiah speaks not only of unceasing pain but also of wounds that will not heal (this language is used for the exiles, 30:12; see 8:15; 14:19 for the use in communal laments). Jeremiah will also use the language of healing in 17:14. Though Jeremiah's complaint may be physical or psychological in orientation (see chs. 36–38), this language seems to refer to the effects of his troubles on his entire person. That his antagonists persecute him and even seek to kill him, and relationships with his own friends and family are severely ruptured, causes a deep, ongoing pain; no resolution to his persecution and isolation seems possible. [A Poem of Bonhoeffer]

At the same time, Jeremiah's language must be related to vv. 16-17; Jeremiah's pain and suffering participate in the suffering of God. Just as he is filled with the divine wrath, so also is he filled with the *divine* pain and woundedness over what has happened to the relationship (see 8:18–9:1, 10; 13:17; 14:17). One might also link his sufferings with those of the people (see 8:15; 14:19; 30:12-15) and his reproachful questions with theirs (14:9, 19). Jeremiah stands between God and people, asks the questions of both, and bears the sufferings of both (see **Connections: Jeremiah's Laments and His Call**).

In view of this seemingly endless suffering, Jeremiah reproaches God (v. 18). Why is God like a deceitful brook, like waters that fail? This metaphor recalls the experience of a sojourner in the desert who sees the outlines of a streambed in the distance, which prompts the hope that thirst will be quenched. But, upon arrival, he finds the stream dry. Jeremiah likens God to this kind of water

A Poem of Bonhoeffer

At least some of the poetry of Dietrich Bonhoeffer in his *Letters and Papers from Prison* appear to have been influenced by these laments of Jeremiah.

Who am I? They often tell me
I would step from my cell's confinement
calmly, cheerfully, firmly,
like a squire from his country house.

Who am I? They often tell me
I would talk to my warders
freely and friendly and clearly,
as though it were mine to command.

Who am I? They also tell me
I would bear the days of misfortune
equably, smilingly, proudly,
like one accustomed to win.

Am I then really all that which other men tell of?
Or am I only what I know of myself,
restless and longing and sick, like a bird in a cage,
struggling for breath, as though hands were compressing my throat,
yearning for colors, for flowers, for the voices of birds,
thirsting for words of kindness, for neighborliness,
trembling with anger at despotisms and petty humiliation,
tossing in expectation of great events,
powerlessly trembling for friends at an infinite distance,
weary and empty at praying, at thinking, at making,
faint, and ready to say farewell to it all?

Who am I? This or the other?
Am I one person today, and tomorrow another?
Am I both at once? A hypocrite before others,
and before myself a contemptibly woebegone weakling?
Or is something within me still like a beaten army,
fleeing in disorder from victory already achieved?

Who am I? They mock me, these lonely questions of mine.
Whoever I am, thou knowest, O God, I am thine.

Dietrich Bonhoeffer (New York: Macmillan, 1971), 347-48. Quoted in William Holladay, *Jeremiah 1* (Philadelphia: Fortress, 1986), 472-73.

Dietrich Bonhoeffer

As a modern-day prophet, Dietrich Bonhoeffer stood against the Third Reich of the Nazi regime during the Second World War. Endorsing the ecumenical movement, Bonhoeffer sided with the Confessing Christians against the German Christians; he signed the Barmen Declaration in 1934. He returned to Germany from America at the outbreak of the war to join his brothers and sisters in the resistance against the Nazis. In 1943, he was arrested and imprisoned for his opposition to the Nazi government. In 1945, he was hanged by the Gestapo.

supply; God raises hopes but doesn't satisfy needs. God had claimed to be a fountain of living waters (2:13) in contrast to other sources of water (2:18); God had also denied being a wilderness to Israel (2:31). In effect, Jeremiah calls God to account. Is God all that God claims to be? Where is God when Jeremiah needs relief? Is God reliable, especially when the needs are the greatest?

God's reply (vv. 19-21) has occasioned differing interpretations. Several scholars think that, in reproaching God, Jeremiah has abandoned his prophetic task, and is here being disciplined by God. The repetition of the verb *šûb* ("turn, turn back") in v. 19a is thought to be a call to repentance (see 3:12-14), and the call to stand before God suggests Jeremiah's need to stand in readiness before God to do what he is commanded to do, regardless of the consequences. From this perspective, God's repeated "if" is a divine condition regarding Jeremiah's status as a prophet. Only if he speaks in words other than those he has just uttered can he continue to be a prophet of God.[3]

A preferable interpretation understands God's response in somewhat different terms.[4] Working from within the lament tradition, it is not at all unusual that those in a faithful relationship with God reproach the deity or seek to hold God accountable (e.g., Ps 22:1-2). Jeremiah has experienced a loss of focus, his call is in some kind of crisis, and he is dispirited in the face of all the opposition. God's speaking has the purpose of seeking to restore his focus by speaking words that could jolt him out of the crisis and give him a new lease on his calling. But Jeremiah has not sinned in what he has had to say and is in no need of repentance for it. Notably, Jeremiah does not respond to this word from God with repentance or any acknowledgment of wrongdoing (more generally, of course, as a sinner Jeremiah would need to repent).

The basic force of God's response in v. 19 is "Get on with it!" or "Face up to it!" The repeated "if" has to do with what it will take for Jeremiah to get back on course regarding the ministry to which he is called. The conditions are matter-of-fact conditions (such as, "if you go out in the rain, you will get wet"). If Jeremiah returns to focus, then God will welcome him and he will stand before God (see 23:18) as one ready to get on with his call. If Jeremiah utters words that are valuable/noble and not frivolous/worthless (this word has a general reference and does not refer back to Jeremiah's lament), then he will indeed speak God's word ("serve as my mouth" has links to the Mosaic tradition; see Exod 4:16; 7:1). It is not that there is nothing at stake in the faithfulness of the prophet; there is. God's purposes in this time and place are at stake; God

Salvation for Jeremiah?

The list of key words for salvation used in vv. 20-21 for God's actions toward Jeremiah is remarkable ("save"; "deliver" [twice]; "redeem"). At least two issues arise in this connection. The first arises in connection with a common understanding of salvation among Bible readers. Salvation is often understood in a narrowly spiritual sense, with a focus on an individual's personal relationship with God and often on salvation in the life to come. But, remarkably, none of these words has a narrowly spiritual sense, either more generally or in Jeremiah's case. For example, God's deliverance of Israel from the hand of the Egyptians is described in terms of salvation (e.g., Exod 14:30; 15:2), redemption (e.g., Deut 7:8) and deliverance (e.g., Exod 6:6). Or, the psalmists speak of deliverance of both individuals and the community from persecutors and enemies with a comparable range of language (e.g., Pss 7:1; 78:42). The effects of God's saving activity in these cases pertains to the establishment of personal and communal well-being in every aspect of life. More generally, salvation in these cases relates to Israel's being delivered from the ill effects *of the sins of others, not salvation from their own sins* (the latter may be the case in certain contexts, e.g., Ps. 130:8).

With respect to Jeremiah, the issue is to be delivered from oppression and death at the hands of his persecutors. But this raises the second issue: Did God follow through on this promise to Jeremiah? While his (later?) persecutions (e.g., ch. 26) stand in some tension with these divine promises, Jeremiah's deliverance takes place to some degree in individual situations (e.g., 26:24; 36:26; 38:7-13) and one might also speak of the removal of many of his persecutors in the fall of Jerusalem. New forms of persecution will come his way in post-fall Judah (43–44), and his future beyond exile in Egypt is left unstated. And so Jeremiah does experience deliverance from his persecutors, but not in any absolute sense.

---

risks that the prophet will be faithful. And so God seeks to keep the prophet on track for the sake of God and God's own purposes. In another play on the verb *šûb*, the people about whom he is so troubled are the ones who need to turn to him and to the word he speaks; he is not to turn back toward them and back off from the word he is called to speak.

In v. 20 God recalls for Jeremiah the basic promises made in his original call (see at 1:8, 18-19). Verse 21 expands upon those original words, with an even sharper indictment of those who oppose Jeremiah ("wicked"; "ruthless"). These are words of reassurance and reaffirmation. As such, they are in some sense a reply to Jeremiah's voiced concerns. God will make him resistant to their oppressive behaviors toward him ("a fortified wall of bronze") and they will not be able to overcome him. God will be with him to deliver him from their attempts to kill him. [Salvation for Jeremiah?]

CONNECTIONS

Appropriation of Jeremiah's Laments

Exilic readers of this material could discern something basic from this prophet-God exchange about the nature of the God-Israel relationship more generally. From one perspective,[5] Jeremiah's experience could be understood as paradigmatic of those who suffer and lament. His laments could become theirs, as could the divine response of assurance and deliverance to their situation as both individuals and community. They might even be able to understand Jeremiah's calling as in some sense their own.

Yet, there are sharp limits to such an approach to these texts. Jeremiah's protestations of innocence (vv. 15c-17) could not easily become those of exilic readers (the indictment of Israel was universal, "every one of you," 16:12). Most if not all of the exiles would understand themselves to be directly or indirectly responsible for the persecution of the prophet that was the primary occasion for Jeremiah's laments in the first place. From this perspective, these laments serve to confront readers with their own past and the profoundly negative effects their words and deeds have had on God's own prophet (and leaders in every age!). Let readers not be too quick to make these laments their own! That appropriating move may be a subtle way of avoiding the indictment the prophet speaks.

Jeremiah's Laments and His Call

These laments of Jeremiah are similar to the others in that they reveal that the prophet is stuck between a rock and a hard place, between a hardened people and a God who persists in meeting that obstinacy with a hard word of judgment. Jeremiah lives in a pressure cooker. On the one hand, he has been called to speak the word of God, a strong word of indictment and an even harsher word of judgment. God's word has filled him with indignation and he has been faithful in showing forth that divine indignation in his word to the people (v. 17). But the prophet is never comfortable in doing so. He is despondent and despairing over the harsh message he is called to bring—even though it comes from God. Jeremiah feels the unending pressure from God to be true to his calling, though God does not overpower him (see ch. 20). This is shown by the fact that the prophet retains a capacity to react sharply to this extraordinarily difficult calling and that he is able to voice these laments. Moreover, when Jeremiah is even forbidden, repeatedly, to intercede on behalf of this people before God, he increasingly senses that he stands alone with God against the world.

On the other hand, Jeremiah is confronted with the opposition of the people at every turn. However much the word he speaks is like a hammer that breaks the rock in pieces (23:29), that word could be resisted and usually was. The people not only resist the word of God, they resist the one who speaks that word. They not only reject the God whose word was being spoken, they bear down on the prophet himself. They apparently make no distinction between the word and the person. Jeremiah is rejected as much as is God. He is opposed by the powerful and common, by kings and peasants. Because he is not a figure of power in his own right, he could put up little resistance in return. As a result, the prophet often suffers at the hands of others, even to the point that his life is put in danger (see 26:10-24). Moreover, the prophet has no favorites who are immune to the word of judgment he brings; his word does not pertain to "outsiders," while those who think like he does can escape from the force of the word. Everyone—including the prophet himself! (15:14)—will get caught up in the effects of the word of judgment. [Is the Prophet Successful?]

From still another perspective, issues of discernment faced by the prophet occasion suffering. How does he know for certain that the word he hears is the word of God that is to be spoken? Jeremiah stands virtually alone among prophets that were active during his time (an exception is Uriah, 26:20-23) He knows that he holds a decidedly minority opinion; scads of prophets discern that God has another word to speak (see at chs. 23; 27–29). Can all of them be wrong and he alone be right? It is one thing to stand isolated among the people; it is another thing to stand isolated among other prophets. For all of God's assurances, the prophet cannot finally be relieved of the sense that he may be wrong. But, actually, living with such a note of uncertainty is important for the prophet; it keeps him alert and open to new possibilities. He recognizes that God's word is dynamic and on the move, always integrally related to the shifting nature of the situation into which it is addressed. That reality means that he can never settle in with what he now knows; he must always be questioning himself, God, and others.

Is the Prophet Successful?

The people of Israel do not repent; does this mean that the prophet is not successful in what he has been called to do? Jeremiah's personal suffering is not only occasioned by overt persecution. He suffers because of the apparent lack of success that his word has among the people. I say "apparent" because, in the absence of a positive response from the people, the word of God is successful in another respect: the word of judgment goes forth and does accomplish its purpose. In response to his message the unfaithful people become even more hardened in their rejection of the Word of God and it is this continued resistance that finally brings the word of judgment to fruition.

And so the people's refusal to repent constitutes a form of success! Neither God nor prophet are desirous of this fulfillment (see 26:2-3; 36:2-3), and both agonize over the prospect that the judgmental word entails. It is entirely natural that it would take longer for the prophet to become oriented to this kind of "success," not least because of the horrendous toll it takes on his emotional and physical life, let alone on the community to which he belongs. But what happens to Israel demonstrates the efficacy of the word that Jeremiah spoke. Measuring one's success as a preacher or prophet gets to be a very subtle matter; success may in fact entail resistance, rejection, and "failure."

It is no wonder that it is difficult for any individual to be a bearer of the word of God. It is no wonder that many of those who are called to speak that word err on the side of bringing only or mostly words of peace and affirmation. It is not difficult for such individuals to understand why the false prophets spoke only a word of peace; it is much easier that way. They no longer stand betwixt and between; at least they do not alienate their human counterparts, and that is a more comfortable place to stand. Or, at least it seems so; the pressure that God brings may not be so obvious, or is more resistible, at least to all appearances.

More commonly, perhaps, many "prophets" feel called to find a way in between—to speak a word of peace to some people and a word of judgment to others (the latter often consist of those who think or act differently from the preacher on one or another matter). As if some people, such as "insiders," might come to believe that they are excused from the judgmental word of God! Every prophet will be called to bring such a word at some time or another, whether against individuals or groups or entire nations. But, in every such case, Jeremiah provides a model in showing that no bearer of such a word can do so with integrity without at least some personal discomfort and sorrow. If the prophet seems only to be delighted in bringing such a sharp word of judgment, then the reader/hearer should beware.

NOTES

[1] See Kathleen O'Connor, *The Confessions of Jeremiah: Their Interpretation and Role in Chapters 1–25* (Atlanta: Scholar's Press, 1988), 27.

[2] With William Holladay, *Jeremiah 1* (Philadelphia: Fortress, 1986).

[3] See Walter Brueggemann, *A Commentary on Jeremiah: Exile and Homecoming* (Grand Rapids: Eerdmans, 1998), 148.

[4] The discussion of Samuel Balentine, *Prayer in the Hebrew Bible: The Drama of the Divine-Human Dialogue* (Minneapolis: Fortress, 1993), 160-61, moves in this direction.

[5] See E. Gerstenberger, "Jeremiah's Complaints: Observations on Jer. 15:10-21," *JBL* 82 (1963): 393-408.

THE SHAPE OF THE LIFE
OF A PROPHET

16:1-21

This chapter begins with a series of prose commands regarding Jeremiah's personal life as embodied word of God (vv. 1-9). Whatever their original form, these commands are now cast in the form of a sermon (the "you" in v. 9 is plural) in view of the people's questions, probably exilic readers (v. 10; see 5:19; 9:12; 14:19). Verses 1-9 lead to a word of indictment (vv. 11-12) and judgment (v. 13). Verses 16-18, 21 are commonly included as elements of that word of judgment, but they have been "interrupted" by a restoration oracle (vv. 14-15) and a poetic fragment of thanksgiving (vv. 19-20). But, if vv. 16-18, 21 were words of judgment on Israel in some earlier form, the verses that now "interrupt" them have occasioned a shift in their meaning. Judgment is not the last word for this people, and exilic readers are especially in view.

COMMENTARY

An Embodied Word of Judgment, 16:1-13

The focus on Jeremiah's personal life may be placed at this point in view of the prior references to several dimensions of his call (links to 15:2-3, 8-9 have also been noted). These prohibited dimensions of Jeremiah's common life help to explain 15:17 in particular; because of the nature of the word Jeremiah is called to speak (the end of šālôm, v. 5), Jeremiah's personal life cannot proceed in any way that would suggest normalcy. To this end God commands Jeremiah not to marry or to have a family; nor is he to mourn for the people. [Prophetic Biography?]

God's commands to Jeremiah are intended to convey a word of God to the people *in person* (see v. 10a; cf. Hosea 1-3; Ezek 24:15-27 for other divine "interruptions" in prophetic marriages). Given the importance of children in that culture, this prohibition would have been startling to both prophet and people (see 9:20-22; on the

Prophetic Biography?

This text only incidentally serves as biographical information; these prophetic actions are symbolic acts related to the word of God, not a divine advocacy for the ascetic life per se (see [Symbolic Acts]). Jeremiah's personal life constitutes a word of God to the people. Just as *God* had forsaken and abandoned people and land (12:7), so Jeremiah was to remove himself from the normal rounds of their daily life. Once again, he is to be conformed to the life of God (see 14:11-12; 15:17). Jeremiah thus conveys the word of God not simply by what he says but also by who he is and what he does. The prophet is an embodied word of God; by looking at the prophet's life the people could see how God was relating to them.

children, see **Connections**, ch. 6). Regarding marriage, no Old Testament text speaks of a bachelor, so such a life is at least unusual, if not socially isolating.

These actions do not constitute a warning, however, but a statement that Israel's situation has already deteriorated to such a point that Jeremiah is a living image of the future Israel faces. The message inherent in these acts is that Israelite parents and their children who are born in the land of Canaan will experience great devastation. They will die of various causes (disease, sword, and famine; see 14:12; 15:2-3), they will not be lamented, and their bodies will not be buried, but thrown out on the ground to become food for birds and wild animals (see 7:33; 12:9; 15:3; see **Introduction**).

The repeated point that this word pertains (only) to children born "in this place/land" (vv. 2-3, 6) may be a special word for exilic readers; they need not worry that this word pertains to children born to them in exile (for them assurances are stated in 29:6). This command would also add to the reassuring words of God to Jeremiah in 15:19-21; his celibacy would protect him from the grief that other parents would suffer at the horrible deaths of their children.

God picks up on elements of the word spoken in v. 4 and extends the command to Jeremiah even further (vv. 5, 8; see Ezek 24:15-18). When these deaths of both "great and small" occur in the land, Jeremiah is not to express sorrow, offer sympathy in any form, or participate in any mourning rites (should any occur). God's peace, mercy, and steadfast love are going to be taken away and Jeremiah should follow suit (see **Connections: Peace, Mercy, and Steadfast Love Taken Away**). Verses 6-7 could be understood to be an extension of this command to everyone, though it more likely refers to what will in fact occur (see v. 9). The events will be so devastating (God will "banish/silence" in this way) that the people will not participate in normal funerary customs, nor will any joyful community events occur, such as weddings (as also 7:34; 25:10; for their restoration, see 33:11). Life as people know it will disappear

Edvard Munch. *The Death Chamber.* 1892. Munch Museum. Oslo, Norway. [Credit: © 2002 The Munch Museum / The Munch-Ellingsen Group / Artists Rights Society (ARS), NY]

House of Mourning and Feasting

The "house of mourning" (vv. 5, 8) refers to a room in any house where the community would gather for mutual comfort and consolation that included eating and drinking (v. 7; see Amos 6:7). The gashing and shaving of the head were also mourning practices (see 41:4-5; 47:5), often associated with pagan worship; they were forbidden by Israelite law (see Lev 19:27-28; 21:5; Deut 14:1-2). The phrase "house of feasting" is often understood to have reference to weddings (see v. 9). The point may be not simply to focus on funerals and weddings, but on any social gatherings. The normal run of everyday life with its joys and sorrows will be abruptly ended. In McKane's words, Jeremiah "is no longer able to weep with those who weep and to rejoice with those who rejoice." This is not only disaster for this (or any) community, it is catastrophe.

William McKane, *A Critical and Exegetical Commentary on Jeremiah* (2 vols.; ICC; Edinburgh: T. & T. Clark, 1986), 368.

altogether. Jeremiah will live to see these events take place (v. 9; see 15:5; 22:10). The reference to mourning in 8:21 refers to personal anguish; God's calls to mourning over the death of the city in 6:26; 9:17-18, probably refer to post-destruction rituals. If they have reference to pre-destruction activities, Jeremiah is not to participate in them. [House of Mourning and Feasting]

In vv. 10-13 God anticipates questions the people will ask when they have heard Jeremiah convey these words. Their questions focus on causes for the disaster (not mentioned in vv. 1-9), not on Jeremiah's personal life, for his address had ended with a sharp statement of judgment directed against the people (v. 9, the "you" is plural). The question and answer format has been common in Jeremiah, particularly in the prose sections, and focuses primarily on "Why!?" questions regarding the destruction of Judah/Jerusalem and exile (see 5:19; 9:12; 22:8-9). In their present form (at least) they are questions asked by exilic readers, perhaps echoing earlier questions they had asked.

Here the question of "Why!?" is focused not so much on the destruction per se as on God's announcement of judgment. The people ask that God name the sin for them! In the context of the *book* this question is almost comical; this issue has been addressed in a regular drumbeat in the preceding chapters. Given this context, this exchange may be considered testimony to the incredible stubbornness of the people, perhaps in the tradition of their denial at 2:35.

The divine response recalls the litany of Israel's history of sin and stubbornness at 7:24-26 and 9:13-14 (see also 5:23; 6:28; 13:10; 17:23; 19:15). The present generation—"every one of you!"—has learned idolatry from its ancestors, but has outdistanced them in infidelity. While idolatry is the focus, general wicked behaviors contrary to the Law are also cited, such as not listening to God (through the prophets).

This direct and blunt list of reasons is followed by "therefore," introducing the typical announcement of judgment. The judgment centers on exile in a land no Israelite has known (see 15:14; 17:4; cf. 10:18; 13:17, 19), obviously Babylon from the perspective of exiled readers. The metaphor used for God's exiling activity is similar to that at 10:18; God will throw them out of the land as a warrior throws a spear (this image is used because Babylonians using spears will be agents of the divine judgment; see **Introduction**). The additional note that they will serve other gods extends the theme of serving strange peoples at 5:19 (see Deut 28:64). This is best understood in terms of the moral order: "what goes around, comes around." They worshipped that which was worthless, and which offered no help or mercy (see 2:8, 11, 13, 18, 28), and ironically, they will get their wish. These gods will show no mercy and neither will Yahweh!

"Therefore" (16:14)

AΩ The opening word of v. 14 (*lākēn*), usually translated "therefore," is difficult in that it suggests a close relationship with what precedes (though NIV and NAB translate "However"; JB has "See, then"). If "therefore" is the correct translation, with its usual force, the prior verses could be understood as the necessary judgment before restoration. Contrary to William McKane, "further threats" would not have to follow for this point to be made. The disaster itself could be understood as a refining fire that, in view of God's *salvific* purposes, in fact shapes the possibility of a new future.

William McKane, *A Critical and Exegetical Commentary on Jeremiah* (2 vols.; ICC; Edinburgh: T. & T. Clark, 1986), 373.

Restoration of Israel and the Nations, 16:14-21

It is commonplace to understand vv. 14-15 as a later addition (adapted from 23:5-6) that interrupt the sermon continued in v. 16. ["Therefore" (16:14)] Whatever may be the case editorially, for exilic readers who hear the words in vv. 10-13 (especially) about God hurling them into exile, this restoration oracle qualifies the preceding verses in some ways and would be important for the faith and hope of that community. This qualification does not set aside the word of judgment or the harshness of the word about death and exile; the new confession assumes that to have been the case (v. 15). But it shows that the word of judgment is not God's last word with respect to this people. This rhythm of people's questions followed by reasons, which in turn are followed by a word of restoration, is also found in Deuteronomy 29:24-29; 30:1-10. This oracle regarding return to their own land would make clear to exilic readers that the declaration that Yahweh would show no mercy, love, and favor (vv. 5, 13) has temporal limits. That it takes the form of a repeated divine oath ("As the Lord lives") makes the promise as certain as God's own life.

This segment proclaims to exiles that the days are surely coming when God will again show favor and return Israel from exile (="the land of the north") to their ancestral land (see 12:15; 24:6; 29:10-14). This new divine action is explicitly represented as a reversal of God's driving them away into exile. Indeed, this saving act of God in restoring Israel to their own land will center a new confession of faith for them (to be used in a variety of contexts, including oaths). This restoration, a *salvific* event, would be so important that it would be newly constitutive for the community of faith, with the result that the prior constitutive event—the exodus—would be reduced in its confessional importance. The importance of this point is evident in that this same text is repeated at 23:7-8 at the conclusion of other restoration oracles.

Verses 16-18 may have originally continued the sermon "interrupted" at v. 13, but we cannot be certain of that. In any case the "interruption" of vv. 14-15 has changed the contextual reality for these verses (note that the "you" of v. 13 has become "them" in vv. 16-18, 21, as in v. 15). Verses 16-18 (or at least vv. 16-17) are formally an announcement of judgment. The fishermen and hunters could conceivably be identified, respectively, with Egypt (see Isa 19:5-10) and Babylon (Lam 4:18-19), instruments of the divine hunt to capture Israel and send it into exile (though exile is not explicitly mentioned).[1] Coming after v. 15, however, a report of this kind of activity on the part of God and the nations suggests that these verses are to be read in hopeful ways. How one translates v. 18 will affect one's reading of this segment; it seems best to follow the Hebrew and see a contrast between vv. 16-17 and v. 18.

[The Translation of Verse 18]

The Translation of Verse 18

AΩ The Hebrew reads "I will *first* repay…" at the beginning of v. 18 (so NEB; NRSV footnote). This suggests that the prior verses (vv. 16-17) pertain to a different reality from the judgment on Israel in v. 18. Verses 16-17 could thus be interpreted in hopeful ways following upon vv. 14-15. That God will "doubly" repay Israel for its iniquity is unique in Jeremiah, though it is probably to be connected to the "double" of 17:18. Although it seems to make the judgment even more severe than vv. 1-13, it may have reference to "totality and inescapability." The word "doubly" could also be interpreted in terms of two experiences of judgment (597 and 587 BC).

William McKane, *A Critical and Exegetical Commentary on Jeremiah* (2 vols., ICC; Edinburgh: T. & T. Clark, 1986), 377.

If God uses fishermen and hunters to seek people out for judgment, surely this kind of God is capable of using agents to seek dispersed people out from the nooks and crannies of the countries into which they have been thrown. If God's eyes are on all the ways of the people when they are sinning (v. 17; see 23:24), surely the exiles are not hidden from God in their captivity (see 32:19; Job 34:21).

Then v. 18 follows, "but first" judgment must fall. Verse 18 could even be read as containing an implicit reversal. If God doubly repays Israel's iniquity and sin—a wish Jeremiah also has for his persecutors (17:18)—because they have polluted the land with idol carcasses and other such religious abominations (v. 18; see Lev 26:30), then God can also redeem them doubly (so Isa 40:2; 61:7; Zech 9:12; see Job 42:10). To speak of the carcasses of detestable idols is satirical; the idols were never alive in the first place, so they were never anything other than carcasses, and comparably polluting of the land (see v. 20; 10:1-16, especially v. 15). The emphasis on the pollution of the land (=inheritance) is a theme struck earlier in Jeremiah (see 3:1-2, 9; 12:1-17); the relationship between religious infidelity and environmental degradation seems close at hand.

Verses 16-18 could also be read in terms of God's judgment on *Babylon*. Jeremiah has asked God to pour out his wrath on the nations that do not know the LORD and have devastated people and land (10:25). God later speaks of judging the nations for their iniquity and for "making the land an everlasting waste" (25:12). This reading could in turn link up with vv. 19-21, where the idolatries of v. 18 refer, not to the practices of Israel, but to these of the nations (see 50:2).

Verses 19-20 are Jeremiah's response to God's words in vv. 1-18 and reach back to God's promises to him in 15:20-21. God will be his refuge and strength, a very present help in trouble (see 17:17), themes echoing numerous psalms (e.g., Pss 46:1; 27:1; 37:39-40) and the people's confession in 14:8. The gods of the idolaters are no gods at all (see 14:22); only Yahweh is God, and Jeremiah can rest back in that reality. [Jeremiah Comforts Yahweh]

Jeremiah takes the response in an unexpected direction by speaking of the *nations* (see 12:14-17), yet the transition would not

Jeremiah Comforts Yahweh

Daniel Berrigan's reflections on vv. 19-21 are striking: "Thus Jeremiah has a prophecy of his own, offered to comfort Yahweh: one day, the idolatries of all the ages will come to a halt. And more: the devotees will confess and repent and arrive at a better heart, converted to true God: 'Nations will come to you from the ends of the earth.' We might have expected such words, but proceeding only from Yahweh. No, they are Jeremiah's, his daring. In a Godlike moment of clairvoyance (and tact!), he takes visionary words to himself. It is exactly what needs saying—exactly, one thinks, what Yahweh longs to hear....And to all intents, Yahweh agrees. One imagines the Deific One nodding approval. And growing calm, in the assurance of Jeremiah; Yahweh remains, despite all pretenders to the throne, Yahweh. 'I am going to make them know my strength and might.'"

Daniel Berrigan, *Jeremiah: The World, the Wound of God* (Minneapolis: Fortress, 1999), 78.

be so abrupt if vv. 16-17 (18) referred to the nations. The nations shall come to Zion (a theme struck in 3:17; see Isa 2:3=Mic 4:2; Zech 8:20-23; 14:16-19) and make confession concerning *their* ancestors who have inherited lies and worthless things (=idols, as in 2:8, 11). This kind of confession on the part of the nations is rare in the Old Testament (see Isa 2:3=Mic 4:2), though their turning to Yahweh is present elsewhere (see Isa 19:19-25; 45:22; 49:6; and the vision of certain psalms, e.g., 67; 96). Importantly, this kind of claim for the destiny of the nations is characteristic of the lament in Psalm 22:27-28 and could be seen as parallel to the affirmation of Jeremiah in these verses following his lament.[2] Human beings cannot make gods for themselves; idols are not gods, and the nations will come to recognize this (see 10:1-16)!

Though v. 21 is commonly considered a reference to Israel, concluding the sermon from v. 18, the present context interprets "them" as the nations, and could constitute a divine response to vv. 19-20. When the nations see God's power at work in these events, they will be taught by God (see 12:16; 4:2; Isa 2:3; Mic 4:2) and they shall know Yahweh is LORD (see Ezek 36:23; 37:28; 39:7; Isa 45:6; 49:26). Israel may well be included among these nations who know the LORD (see 31:34). The return of the nations links back to the return of Israel from exile in vv. 14-15. The last phrase in the chapter reveals that God's purpose in these events is not simply negative; God's judgment is not for the sake of judgment. God's purpose in judgment reaches beyond judgment to the knowledge of the LORD that will be taught to all the nations of the world.

CONNECTIONS

Peace, Mercy, and Steadfast Love Taken Away

The announcement of God in v. 5b is especially problematic (see also the discussion of 13:14). In this great devastation for people and land, God will take away peace (*šālôm*; see 12:12, the absence of peace in the land), steadfast love (*ḥesed*), and mercy (*raḥămîm*; "grace, favor" [*ḥănînāh*] is added in v. 13). *Šālôm* seems to be defined as the *effect* of God's exercise of steadfast love and mercy (see 9:24 for a general statement about God's practicing steadfast love, justice, and righteousness "in the earth"). [Is God Unfaithful?]

While readers (then and now) can understand that these events would mean the end of peace, and even the end of divine mercy (that is, no more relenting, 15:6), the removal of steadfast love is

---

Is God Unfaithful?

Walter Brueggemann claims that this indicates that "The covenant relation is now over." God's "most fundamental commitments" are now "exhausted and terminated." And, "In the tradition of covenant, even Yahweh's gracious *inclination* [emphasis mine] depends finally on some appropriate response" (one wonders then how it can be called "grace"!). In view of Israel's nonresponse, God retracts earlier commitments (2 Sam 7:14-15 is cited). Though the promises are unconditional, God did not foresee this kind of infidelity. And so, Brueggemann goes on to speak of a "complete absence of fidelity on God's part." But, what might it mean to make the claim that God is unfaithful, or at least is no longer so? What does faithfulness mean if it can be turned off and on like a faucet? But, more to the point, what kind of definition of faithfulness is being used, if it is absent in any sharp statement of judgment? Why is judgment an act of unfaithfulness? I would claim that judgment is *always* in the service of God's loving and gracious purposes.

Walter Brueggemann, *A Commentary on Jeremiah: Exile and Homecoming* (Grand Rapids: Eerdmans, 1998), 151-52.

---

harder to understand (so also for king Saul, 2 Sam 7:15, in which context God promises *never* to remove *ḥesed* from David). Elsewhere Jeremiah will speak of God's steadfast love enduring forever (33:11; see also 31:3; 32:18; Ps 136:1). In these events, are the people cut off altogether from the love of God? Can God decide one moment to love and the next moment not to love?

It seems that this phrase does not challenge the affirmation that "God is love," but accents particular actions that are in fact *grounded* in that love. Isaiah 54:7-8 may help us understand. Just as the divine forsaking does not mean a suspension of divine presence (omnipresence would be a general Old Testament claim for God), so also the removal of steadfast love does not mean a suspension of love, but a suspension of the *exercise* of that love in the particular situation. It is helpful to note that the restoration of mercy could take place through the king of Babylon (42:11-12). The taking away of peace and mercy is thus related to the agency of Nebuchadrezzar, and links this divine action to the particular mediation of the king of Babylon (as in 21:7; see **Introduction**).

NOTES

1 See the discussion in William Holladay, *Jeremiah 1* (Philadelphia: Fortress, 1986), 478-79.

2 Ibid., 480-81.

IN WHOM DO YOU TRUST?

Jeremiah 17:1-27

This chapter consists of a montage of various types of literature, including a judgment oracle (17:1-4), several wisdom sayings (vv. 5-11), a hymn fragment (vv. 12-13), another lament from Jeremiah (vv. 14-18), and a sermon regarding Sabbath obedience (vv. 19-27). The speaker is uncertainly specified; the text shifts from God in vv. 1-8 (see vv. 3-5) to Jeremiah in v. 9 (possibly) to God in vv. 10-11 to the community (vv. 12-13) to Jeremiah (vv. 14-18) and back to God (vv. 19-27). It is difficult to discern the rationale for the organization of these disparate pieces. Yet, the contrast between the righteous and the wicked (a prominent theme in vv. 5-13) provide basic assumptions for Jeremiah's lament in vv. 14-18 and set up the "either-or" framework of the sermon on the Sabbath in vv. 17-29.

COMMENTARY

An Oracle of Judgment, 17:1-4

This prose sermon, which assumes the exile (see v. 4), consists of an indictment (vv. 1-3a) and announcement of judgment (v. 3b-4; cf. 15:13-14; see [Jeremiah 15:11-14 and 17:1-4]). The immediate center of attention is "the sin of Judah." The basic point of the complex imagery that follows is that Judah's sin is so blatant and so pervasive in its effects that it will be long remembered. Given the witness of Jeremiah and other texts, this has proved to be the case. An iron pen (see Job 24:19) would be used on very durable material such as stone or metal. An engraving instrument with a point made of a hard stone (such as emery) would impress the matter on tablets of stone that would last for a long period of time (cf. the Decalogue; Exod 31:18). [Written on the Heart (17:1 and 31:33)]

To engrave "sin" on the horns of the altar is a difficult image. Altars commonly had four horns, a projection on each corner (see Exod 27:2; some stone horns have been unearthed); the horns were either a symbol of God (see Num 23:22) or of the animals offered on the

---

Written on the Heart (17:1 and 31:33)

📖 Engraving the "sin of Judah" on the "tablets of their hearts" (17:1) extends the image still further. In 31:33, God speaks of writing the Law upon the hearts of those involved in the new covenant; that suggests not only indelibility but also new identity (see the new heart in 24:7; 32:39; Ezek 36:26). To work back to the image in the present text, to write "sin" on Israel's heart is to put a certain *identity* for this people in place (see v. 9). Then, to reconnect with 31:33, the only way for Israel to move beyond such an identity is for God to make a new covenant with them and give them a new heart.

---

altar. The image may refer primarily to the altars of the children in v. 2. It could then speak of parental sins being carried through the generations and finding expression in idolatrous altars and sacred poles at Baal shrines near trees and on hills. [Sacred Poles] While sexually immoral rituals were practiced at these shrines, the primary force of the biblical condemnation was the idolatry involved, namely, unfaithfulness to Yahweh. Their worship practices at such altars were thereby named "the sin of Judah."

The horns of the altar could also be a reference to sacrificial acts and the placing of atoning blood on the four horns (Exod 29:12; Lev 4:7). This would suggest that the offerings at these altars no longer had atoning value. Indeed, by having their sins carved on the altar, it would mean that *they* would be forever before God (note Deut 27:5 and the prohibition of the use of iron on an altar). Or, the horns could refer to the altar as a place of refuge or sanctuary for those who had committed inadvertent sins (but not willful sins; see 1 Kgs 1:50-51; 2:28-34). This use of the image could suggest that Israel's sins were willful and hence they could find no sanctuary at the horns of the altar from those who would exact judgment.

Sacred Poles

🏛 Sacred poles (*'ašērîm*) were actual trees or wooden poles (see 2:27; Judg 6:25; Deut 16:21) that represented the goddess Asherah. They were set up near Canaanite altars, commonly erected on "high hills" and "under every green tree" (see 2:20; 3:14), and associated especially with rain and fertility. Asherah was the consort of Baal in Canaanite worship practice and together they became key figures in Israelite idolatrous practice (see 1 Kgs 15:13; 18:19; 2 Kgs 21:7; 23:4; see [Baal and Canaanite Religion]).

Verses 3-4 (cf. 15:13-14; 5:19) specify that the people will lose their wealth and property; it will become spoils for Babylon in the devastation of Jerusalem. This loss of wealth—this judgment—is named as the "price" for their sins. They will lose their God-given heritage (=land) and be exiled to be enslaved to strangers in a foreign land. The NRSV translation, "by your own act," or by your own hand, though not entirely clear, suggests that the people have no one to blame but themselves for what happens. Their actions have provoked the divine anger, likened to a fire that will burn forever (or a long, long time, matching the memory of Israel's sins). The word about such a length of time links back to the engraved tablet in v. 1. The effects of this judgment will not pass away quickly. God's anger will burn "forever," that is, a long, long time (see 42:10).

In Whom Do You Trust?, 17:5-11

As a collection of wisdom sayings, these verses bear a family resemblance to the books of Job, Proverbs, and Ecclesiastes, and certain psalms (for other wisdom pieces in Jeremiah, see 9:23-24; 10:12-16, 23-24; 13:23). The use of images from the nonhuman world (vv. 6, 8, 11, 13) makes the point that God's historical action is in tune with the very structures of the creation. Perhaps the presence of wisdom teachers among the exiles made the incorporation of such sayings into this prophetic corpus important. The use of this language became a way of integrating prophetic thought with that of the wisdom school, perhaps as a way of showing that their concerns are fundamentally compatible.

These sayings seem designed to speak especially to exilic readers. In their contrast of the righteous and the wicked, their purpose is to give direction for a shape that the people's life should take in the aftermath of the judgment just described. The basic issue is put in these terms: In whom do you trust? Unlike those who have chosen the way of trust in other gods (vv. 1-4), their daily walk is to be marked by trust in Yahweh. Most basically, the issue at stake is not one of intellectual error, but of lack of trust in God. The call to trust in the Lord rather than in human beings (and not just human wisdom, see Ps 146:3-4) becomes the key instruction for maximal well-being.

The first unit (vv. 5-8) is a wisdom poem that resembles other texts, especially Psalm 1 (cf. Pss 52:8; 92:12-14). Both texts sketch the two basic ways in which life in the community of faith can be shaped: the way of the righteous and the way of the wicked. Both texts use natural imagery (a tree and chaff/shrub) in contrasting these two ways (see also 11:16). Yet, whereas Psalm 1 centers on the Law and the reader's delight in it, the Jeremiah text focuses on the reader's trust in the LORD (v. 7). In this respect, it connects well with another wisdom theme: the fear of the LORD is the beginning of wisdom (Prov 1:7) and "trust in the LORD with all your heart" (see Prov 3:5-8).

Those who turn away from God and put their trust in human beings (including their wisdom and strength; see Isa 31:1-3) are cursed, that is, their lives are marked by judgment—the divinely mediated negative effects of such misplaced trust. They are likened to a desert shrub (perhaps a juniper) that lives in the parched and

Berrigan on Jeremiah 17:5-8

Thus Yahweh:
    cursed the one
whose trust
stops short of Me,
    lodged
foolish, futile
in humankind,
who Me
belittle, of Me
make near nothing!

Rootless, blind,
weightless, sterile,
    that one—
a tumbleweed
by vagrant winds
buffeted
hither and yon.

Not that one!
blessed the one
whose hope takes root
deep, deep in Me.

A waterfall, soft
as ghost's footfall
rewards the root
planted firm, ever green—

Hope on, hope on,
in due time, yes
plenteous My harvest!

Daniel Berrigan, *Jeremiah: The World, the Wound of God* (Minneapolis: Fortress, 1999), 79-80.

salt-filled lands of the wilderness. They will not experience the seasonal changes that bring life-giving water on a regular basis and will shrivel up in the heat and drought (a reference back to the image of fire in v. 4). At the same time, such shrubs commonly do stay alive in the desert, so the metaphor is inexact. This word is a reminder to exilic readers regarding the negative effects of a lack of trust in the LORD. [Berrigan on Jeremiah 17:5-8]

On the other hand, those who trust in the LORD (note the repetition in v. 7) are blessed, that is, their lives will be marked by bounty and well-being. They will be like a tree that is planted near a steady supply of water so that its roots can depend on this regular source of nourishment. When heat or drought do come, and come they will, its leaves will stay green and it will continue to bear fruit. In the context of judgment, this means that those who are faithful to the LORD will survive the heat of the LORD's anger, or any other adversity, and continue to thrive (v. 4). [Exilic Readers and Desert Plants]

Verses 9-11 consist of three wisdom sayings that illustrate the need to be vigilant regarding the relationship with God. Verse 9 essentially generalizes on the point of 13:23, that "*the* heart" (=will), that is, *everyone's* heart (cf. Gen 6:5), is devious/deceitful, not upright. To connect this point with v. 1, "sin" is written on the heart with an iron pen. The issue is both deception in relationships with others and self-deception. As if to make sure the point is not lost, the heart is said to be perverse/willful, "beyond cure" (so NIV). The emphasis in Jeremiah on Israel's stubbornness and its will to resist God lies in the background (see **Connections**, ch. 5). Who can fathom the depths of this human reality (cf. Ps 64:6)? Certainly no human being can, and the questions of God in Jeremiah suggest that, while God knows the human heart, *even God* cannot fully understand it (e.g., 2:5, 31; 8:5).

Jeremiah may speak the question in v. 9 and, though it is rhetorical, God does make a response (v. 10). God does search the mind and try the human heart (lit., "kidneys") (see **Connections: Testing**). This is a common theme in Jeremiah and elsewhere (9:7; 11:20; 12:3; 20:12; 32:19; cf. also Pss 7:9; 17:3; 139:23). God's knowledge of human beings is not confined to external appearances (see 1 Sam 16:7); God can look on the human heart and can discern motives, drives, and the presence or absence of faithfulness. God's discernment is the basis for judgment—the issue in the

Exilic Readers and Desert Plants

To exilic readers this word about plants in the wilderness connects well with their present life situation. This wisdom word is both sound counsel regarding the importance of faithfulness and an assurance that, in spite of all the hardships they are having to endure, their trust in the Lord will see them through (see the promissory language of Isa 58:11). Such a word about blessing may seem less applicable to Jeremiah's own life of rejection and isolation. Yet, blessing does not eliminate suffering, as the reference to drought indicates. Even for those who undergo deep suffering, including the wilderness experience of exile, the image of the tree well rooted and grounded, with access to springs of water, can still apply in remarkable ways to how that wilderness experience will affect the flow of energy and life (see 29:5-7).

The tamarisk tree is most likely the reference of v. 6 because of its tolerance of sandy and saline soils, as well as its ability to live in either desert or fertile climates. The tamarisk tree has widespread branches with small, flat leaves, enhancing its water retention. The tree is both a rare shade in the desert and a sacred burial spot. The tree is mentioned in two other places in the Old Testament. In Genesis 21:33, Abraham planted a tamarisk tree in the place where he prayed to "Yahweh, the Everlasting God." First Samuel 31:11-13 reports the account of the rescue of Saul and Jonathan's defiled bodies from the walls of Bethshan, after which their bones were buried under a tamarisk tree.

(Credit: James L. Reveal)

larger context of Jeremiah. God mediates the effects of human actions in terms of the moral order (see Jer 6:19; 21:14; Ezek 7:27; see **Introduction**). God does not bring anything new into a judgmental situation, but "gives" or mediates the consequences of the deeds committed (cf. *nātan*, "give, put," in Ezek 7:3-4, unfortunately translated "punish" in NRSV) (see **Connections: The Imprecision of Judgment**).

This kind of general, but imprecise truth is illustrated by the image of v. 11. As the partridge hatches the eggs of other birds and raises the young as her own, so are those affluent citizens who have amassed their wealth on the backs of their laborers (see 22:13). But their wealth is not forever; it is fleeting and will leave them before death (as the partridge will lose many eggs and/or young to predators; see Luke 12:13-21). In the context of the judgment on Israel, this proved to be the case with many wealthy landowners that built their wealth in unjust ways (see **Connections: Wealth and Blessing**).

A Hymnic Interlude, 17:12-13

This unit is a fragment of a hymn, "a doxology of judgment," that both exalts the "glorious throne" and announces judgment on those who forsake the rule of God (cf. Amos 5:8-13; 9:5-10). The speaker could be Jeremiah (who speaks vv. 14-18) and it has been thought to function as part of the invocation for the lament. More likely, it is a hymnic interlude drawn from the liturgical heritage (see "our") inserted editorially to continue the contrast between the righteous and the wicked and to keep the praise of God in the forefront.

God's throne has been understood in several ways, as the city of Jerusalem (3:17; 14:21), the temple and its ark (Ezek 43:7), God's throne in heaven (Ps 11:4; Isa 66:1), and more generally the rule of God (Lam 5:19). The last understanding seems likely in this text, and may play off the usage for Jerusalem in 14:21, now destroyed for exilic readers. The glorious throne is a metaphor for God, emphasizing the rule of God, which is from the beginning and endures forever (as in Ps 93:2; Lam 5:19). The throne of God as Jerusalem is destroyed and the promise is that Jerusalem will become the throne of God again (3:17). Between these two times, God himself is the people's only sanctuary (see Ezek 11:16). "O glorious throne" and "O place/shrine of our sanctuary" are best treated as vocatives, emphasizing divine rule and presence, and as parallel to "O hope of Israel, O LORD" in v. 13 (see also the vocative in Jeremiah's address in 16:19).

God as the hope of Israel was hymned by the people in 14:8 (see 50:7), and would be an important theme not only for Jeremiah (who is again assured regarding his enemies, 15:21) but also for exiles. Forsaking the LORD is not only a matter of past history; it is also an issue for readers who might be tempted to turn away from the LORD. The note about forsaking and turning away from God, the fountain of living waters (see 2:13), links back to themes in vv. 5-8. Together they speak of water as crucial for life and the disastrous consequences of shame and disgrace (see 2:26, 36; 9:19; 13:26; 15:9) that forsaking the water of life brings. The NRSV, "recorded in the underworld," suggests Sheol, the abode of the dead, but this status has no association with punishment. The preferred translation is "in the earth/dust" (NIV; REB; NRSV footnote). In contrast to Israel's sin being written with an iron pen (v. 1), their names will be written in dust, easily erased from memory.[1]

Jeremiah's Lament, 17:14-18

Jeremiah continues his lamenting (see [The Lament Psalms] for the common structure of laments); he is still concerned about his persecutors. As with the Psalms, the "I" of the prophet calls upon God ("you") with regard to "they, them" (the enemy). The contrast between the righteous and the wicked in vv. 5-13 prepares well for the concern Jeremiah voices; as noted, these verses articulate some basic assumptions that inform his lament. Unlike his earlier prayers, God does not respond specifically to this lament (as is usual in the psalms). Yet, no conclusions should be drawn regarding a divine silence, for *in the text* God immediately speaks to Jeremiah (vv. 19-27).[2] In terms of content, it might be suggested that 18:1-12 is also part of a divine reply.

Jeremiah's prayer for healing draws from the lament tradition (Pss 6:2; 30:2; 41:3-4) and Israel's confession about God generally (Exod 15:26). God earlier promised to heal a repentant Israel (3:22) and healing is a leading theme in the oracles of restoration (30:7-17; 33:6). The petition to be saved is also typical for laments, particularly salvation from enemies (Pss 7:1; 54:1). Healing and saving are essentially synonymous, though the latter may be more oriented to external deliverance and the former to inward healing. The prophet calls upon God for relief from both personal anguish and external threats (see 26:7-19); this petition in v. 14 follows from God's promise to Jeremiah (15:20). Jeremiah shows his confidence in God's acting by the parallel clauses that he *will* be healed and *will* be saved. He also gives a rationale for his petition ("for"); God is "my praise," that is, God is the one to whom he witnesses in word and deed and that constitutes a reason for God to act on his behalf (typical of laments, Pss 22:25; 71:6; 109:1; see 51:15).

Jeremiah again recalls ways in which his persecutors torment him (v. 15). They challenge his claim to be God's spokesman: if you speak the word of God, then let it be fulfilled! Fulfillment is necessary for them to believe that he speaks the word of the Lord (see Isa 5:19; 2 Pet 3:4). Yet, Jeremiah has not buckled under these pressures (v. 16; see 1:17-18). The meaning of the first line of v. 16 is uncertain, but may use the image of a shepherd who did not run away from difficult tasks (so NRSV); or it may be parallel to the second line (so NAB, "Yet I did not press you to send calamity"). In either case, in order for Jeremiah to demonstrate to his persecutors the truth of his words, he might have urged God to fulfill his words immediately. But he did not do this; he did not press for this day of disaster (the day of the Lord) to arrive so that he might be proved right. He was not overly eager, though he will still call upon God to act (v. 18). God had given him this word to speak and he was faithful in doing so in spite of external pressures and his own feelings. God knows that Jeremiah has been faithful in speaking God's words; they were right "in God's face," so to speak, and God has that discerning capacity to know of his integrity (v. 16b; see v. 10).

Jeremiah returns to petitioning God in vv. 17-18. He asks that God not be a (source of) terror to him (see 1:17), as God can be, such as the foe from the north was for Israel (cf. 6:25; 8:15 and God's promise to exiles regarding such terrors, Isa 54:14). He repeats his confession of God as a refuge in the day of disaster (*rāʿāh*; see 16:19). He prays that he (and his word) will be vindicated, that the announced day will come on his persecutors (as in 15:15; and even more extensively in 18:19-23; this is also an element in the lament psalms, 31:17-18; 35:4-5). He prays that he not be shamed or dismayed, but that his oppressors will be! He asks God to destroy them—twice (see "doubly" in 16:18)!

It is often noted that this expressed desire stands in some tension with v. 16, where Jeremiah states that he has not pressed God that this day arrive. Though some have sought to distinguish between a day of disaster for all Israel in v. 16 and a day for only his persecutors in v. 18, they are almost certainly the same "day." Jeremiah has the destruction of Judah/Jerusalem in mind in both cases, namely, the day of wrath (see Zeph 1:14-18). This day was not something that he has longed for or pressed for (v. 16) but, given his assumption of the task to which he has been called and his own anguish associated with it, God should act (v. 18). Jeremiah asks that he might be brought through it all without being terrorized, shamed or destroyed (see 15:11-14). This interpretation would link the wrath of God (17:4) and the wrath of Jeremiah (see 15:17; see **Introduction**). The petition in v. 18 is not evidence of the crankiness of a vindictive individual. Rather, Jeremiah's wrath against his persecutors is conformed to the wrath of God. At the same time, the exercise of wrath is left up to God alone; Jeremiah will not take the matter into his own hands (see **Connections**, ch. 18).

Hallow the Sabbath Day, 17:19-27

This prose sermon on the importance of keeping Sabbath has an uncertain relationship to its context. Generally, it seems to be one more illustration of the wickedness of the people of Israel (v. 23), yet that note is missing in vv. 24-27, except as a potential future. At the same time, it speaks in hopeful tones of a future wherein judgment is not inevitable and that normal life might be restored, even the monarchy (see vv. 25-26). This positive note in a larger context filled with judgment suggests that exilic readers are in view (see below). This text is one of several "either-or" sermons in Jeremiah and elsewhere (e.g., 12:14-17; 22:1-5), in connection with which the people's decisions regarding a matter (Sabbath-keeping here) do in fact shape their future. These options for the future also link up with the righteous/wicked contrasts in vv. 5-18.

God seems to be genuinely open to differing futures for the people (for those who listen or do not listen), and the future itself is somewhat open-ended in this passage (see discussion at 22:1-5). Such a future possibility does not jibe very well with many texts in Jeremiah up to this point (e.g., 4:28). The command to Jeremiah to speak to "kings" (plural, v. 20; 19:3) suggests a more generalized context. The virtual absence of words about an imminent fall (cf. v. 27) also suggests a different time and place. Special post-exilic interests in Sabbath-keeping have been noted (see Neh 13:15-22), but the concern to develop distinctive religious practices is probably already current among the exiles. In view of such opinions, the text is commonly thought to be exilic or post-exilic and to reflect that later time (see Isa 56:1-8; 58:13-14; Ezek 46:1-8).

From the standpoint of exilic readers, vv. 19-23 may reflect the time before the fall of Jerusalem, with a focus on their ancestors' stubbornness and disobedience of the Law (vv. 22b-23). Jeremiah has made reference to the Decalogue (7:5-10; cf. 16:11) and so Sabbath-keeping would not be out of place and the people's disobedience of Sabbath law could be ironically related to the importance they have given the temple. On the other hand, the either-or in vv. 24-27 seems to pertain to Israel's anticipated time of return to Jerusalem, with a somewhat idealistic image of that future time (especially vv. 25-26). Whatever the original setting of this material, it is likely that exilic readers would interpret the "you" of vv. 24, 27 as pertaining to them.

God commands Jeremiah to stand in the People's Gate (see 20:2; 7:2; a central gate of the city/temple) and speak this word. Indeed, the prophet is commanded to go to all the gates of Jerusalem and do so. Unusual is God's command to speak this word both to people and to kings (see 22:2): the Sabbath is to be kept holy as God had commanded Israel's ancestors (see Exod 20:9-11; 23:12; 31:12-17; Deut 5:12-15).

The Sabbath law has to do, not fundamentally with worship (though see v. 26), but with work and rest. The people are to take care not to bear burdens on the Sabbath, either to bring that burden in by the city gates or to carry that burden out of their houses. Nor are they to do any work. The rationale for the commandment is clearly stated: "for the sake of your lives" (v. 21; see Deut 5:33). But the "ancestors" did not listen to the word of God (vv. 22b-23). They stiffened their necks, that is, they were stubborn (see 5:3; 7:24; 16:11; see **Connections**, ch. 5) and would not receive instruction (Neh 13:15-18 remembers this disobedience and its disastrous consequences).

Having reported the disobedience of the Sabbath commandment on the part of Israel's ancestors, the issue is newly put before the readers ("you"). The either-or formulation is straightforward (vv. 24-27):

1. If you carry no burdens on the Sabbath (only the gates of the city are mentioned this time, not the houses), do no work on it, and keep the day holy, *then* your future will be bright. Kings from the Davidic line, officials, and all the people will *enter* the gates of the city, and the city will be inhabited forever. It is important that there is no statement about going in and out of the gates (as in v. 19), only entering them. This sounds like a time of restoration to the city, combined with a promise regarding the eternal habitation of the city (as in 3:17; see Ezek 48:35). Moreover, the list of persons in v. 26 (from all over the land) will come to the city to centralized worship at the temple; this list of places in 32:44 and 33:13 clearly refers to the time when God "will restore their fortunes." [Details in Verse 26] The various offerings and sacrifices are here understood to be pleasing to God once again (contrast 6:20; and will be a part of the restoration, 33:18). Thank offerings (thanksgiving for salvation experienced) are mentioned only one other time of Jeremiah and that in association with the restoration (33:11). The call for obedience in v. 24 would thus seem to pertain to the exiles, wherever they may be, even in the ruins of Jerusalem.

Details in Verse 26

AΩ The Shephelah refers to the low hills that run up and down the country between the Mediterranean coastal plain and the "hill country" (see 32:44; 33:13). The "land of Benjamin" is to be paired with "Judah" as those tribal units comprising the (former) southern kingdom. The Negeb is the wilderness area in the southern part of Judah. The references to the various offerings and frankincense are mentioned in 6:20; 7:21-22; and 14:21 as those worship practices with which God is not pleased; here they are regarded as appropriate and important.

2. If you do carry burdens on the Sabbath day through the gates of the city, then God will judge the city in fire and it will consume Jerusalem's palaces; and that fire will not be quenched. The same images used for the destruction of Jerusalem earlier (see 15:14; 17:4; cf. Amos 1–2) seem here to be used for still another possible destruction of Jerusalem. This corporate judgment may be an

Sabbath-Keeping and Legalism

It is remarkable that the future of Israel hangs on Sabbath-keeping, particularly given all the emphasis on idolatry (and other sins) in the prior chapters. How can one sin issue in such a disastrous future? This perspective has often called forth a charge of legalism and a sign of degeneration in Israel's ethical reflection. Yet, the larger context of Jeremiah suggests that Sabbath-keeping in this text has taken on symbolic value; it is a sign of whether the relationship with God is in good order. Sabbath-*breaking* is seen here, not as an isolated matter, but as one more indication of the people's stubbornness (v. 23). Sabbath-*keeping*, on the other hand, would be an indication that Israel is no longer stiffening its neck and resisting the will of God for its life.

In Walter Brueggemann's words, "Everything hangs on the Sabbath, because the Sabbath is the most dramatic sign that the will of God is honored and the life-giving power of God is trusted. To break Sabbath means to violate God's will and to distrust God's gifts." Moreover, "the Sabbath becomes the identifying mark for the covenant community….In the purview of covenant, the stability of political life (v. 25) and the effectiveness of worship (v. 26) depend on Sabbath, an act that hands life back to God in trusting obedience. If life is not handed back to God regularly, with discipline and intentionality, then the entire political-religious system will end in destruction."

The larger context of Jeremiah and the prophetic literature (e.g., Isa 1:10-15; Amos 5:21-24), however, makes clear that Sabbath-keeping in and of itself is no *sure* sign of faithfulness. Perhaps it is best to say that, while Sabbath-breaking is a sign of unfaithfulness, Sabbath-keeping will need to be supported by other signs that the relationship with God is in good order.

See Walter Brueggemann, *A Commentary on Jeremiah: Exile and Homecoming* (Grand Rapids: Eerdmans, 1998), 166-67.

---

extension of the more individual judgment announced for Sabbath-breaking in Exod 31:14; 35:2 (cf. Num 15:32-36). [Sabbath-Keeping and Legalism]

What does it mean for God to lay out two such futures with integrity (see the discussion at 22:1-5)? Brueggemann's language is helpful: "God's rule is not a mechanical management by fiat, nor a despotic absolutism. The prophets do not entertain such a naïve supernaturalism. They know there is slippage, anguish, ambiguity, and human initiative."[3] There is an open-endedness in God's way of ruling that entails a certain risk and an understanding that the future is shaped in significant part by what people say and do.

CONNECTIONS

Testing

Testing must be understood relationally, not legalistically. Life in relationship, with God or other human beings, will inevitably bring tests. Individuals in such relationships will often find themselves in situations where their loyalty is tested. What constitutes testing will be determined by the nature of the relationship and the expectations the parties have for it. As a relationship matures and trust levels are built up, faithful responses to the testing of the relational bond will tend to become second nature. Yet, even in a mature relationship, sharp moments of testing may present themselves. God's testing is not designed to trip people up or to trap them in some kind of sting operation (even in Job). Testing is an integral part of the life of any relationship of consequence.

Wealth and Blessing

The proverb in v. 11 is linked with the word about blessing in vv. 7-8. It has too often been thought that the amassing of material possessions or having general well-being in life is a sign of God's blessing. But, importantly, just because a person is wealthy does not necessarily mean that that individual is blessed. Wealth gained on the backs of others is no blessing; it is stealing, pure and simple. Such wealth may look like a blessing to outsiders, but in fact it is ill-gotten gain. This point in turn relates to the divine discernment in v. 10; God is able to see how a person's wealth has been obtained. It also connects to v. 18; while Jeremiah's persecutors (like those who amass wealth unjustly) may be getting away scot-free right now, their end will come.

The Imprecision of Judgment

The moral order does not function in a precise way. The agents of God's judgment can execute judgment in ways too severe (see 25:12-14; 51:24), and so the *experience* of judgment may go beyond any simple correspondence of the relationship between deed and consequence. Hence, while God's discernment may be accurate, God does not have absolute control of the agents that "give to all according to their ways." The traditional wisdom saying in v. 10 thus connects well with prophetic reflections on judgment, but states the matter in a way that is *generally* true rather than mathematically or inevitably so. This imprecision may help explain how it is that Jeremiah, a person who trusts in the Lord, is visited with the experiences of antagonism and persecution that occasion his laments. From the perspective of the lament in vv. 14-18, this divine discerning capacity is an assumption that lies behind v. 16; the God who "knows" the human heart will know that Jeremiah has been faithful in his calling.

NOTES

[1] So William McKane, *A Critical and Exegetical Commentary on Jeremiah* (2 vols.; ICC; Edinburgh: T. & T. Clark, 1986), 407.

[2] Contrary to Walter Brueggemann, *A Commentary on Jeremiah: Exile and Homecoming* (Grand Rapids: Eerdmans, 1998), 165.

[3] Ibid., 158.

THE POTTER AND THE PLOTS

18:1-23

Commentators usually divide this chapter into three or more units (e.g., vv. 1-12, 13-17, 18-23). Yet, whatever history these materials may have had before they achieved their present form, a basic unity can now be discerned. Verses 1-6 are a narrative of a symbolic act, though unlike 13:1-14 *Jeremiah's* actions do not constitute the sign. A general statement regarding God's ways with all peoples, including Israel, follows (vv. 7-10). God commands Jeremiah (v. 11) to tell Israel that God the potter is shaping disaster (=*rā'āh*; inconsistently, NRSV translates this word "disaster" in v. 8 and "evil" in v. 11) and urges Israel to repent, which Israel refuses to do (v. 12). God responds with an announcement of judgment (vv. 13-17), integrating still further indictments. Verses 18-23 report the persecution of Jeremiah (v. 18), followed by his lament (vv. 19-23). Verses 12-17 and 18-23 are parallel passages, each beginning with a statement regarding the people's "plans/plots" (vv. 12, 18), followed by similar responses by God and Jeremiah.[1]

COMMENTARY

The Potter and the Clay, 18:1-11

First of all, we consider the potter (God). The potter initiates all stages of work with the clay. [Pottery Making] To make the vessel is the potter's will as is the decision to rework it when it turns out badly. The potter certainly wants to make the best vessel possible with the materials with which he has to work, and will work perseveringly to that end. At the same time, this potter is faced with a problem; his work now and then turns out badly. The story does not assume an ideal situation in which the potter's work always turns out well. Given the analogy that the potter is God, it can be assumed that God is not the reason for the inferior results; it is the clay/people that are corrupt. The issue for the potter, then, is to make the best pottery out of the situation that he possibly can.

Pottery Making

Pottery making was a significant industry in the ancient world and so knowledge regarding the process would have been readily available to readers. Various methods of making pottery existed, but the wheel was the most common. As the wheel was turned (either by hand or foot) the potter shaped the clay with his hands; the resultant product was dried and then fired in a kiln for hardening, after which it was smoothed and polished. While the potter was able to work with the clay and use his imagination in the shaping of the vessel, the quality of the clay did have some effect on the ability of the potter to do what he wished; that in turn would affect the quality of the product. For an ancient description of pottery making, see Sirach 38:29-30.

Two Potters at the Kiln. Painted wood and stucco. Middle Kingdom. Egyptian Museum. Cairo, Egypt. (Credit: Borromeo/Art Resource, NY)

Second, we consider the clay (Israel). It is often wondered whether the clay/people analogy really works. Clay is inanimate and people are living, and the range of response possible for people is barely analogous to the clay's responsiveness to the potter. Yet, knowledge of pottery making suggests that the clay can adversely affect the potter's work, depending upon the quality of the clay and the centrifugal forces at work on the pottery wheel. This is sufficient to make the analogy work with respect to people who are not passive and whose future is not absolutely predetermined. We are presented with a dynamic situation in which God is faced with the task of working with positive and negative factors in order to shape Israel into the best vessel possible. The focus is not on God's power and control over the people, but on God's initiative, creativity, patience, and responsiveness in relation to the possibilities inherent in the situation.

Verses 4-6 have proved to be the most difficult to interpret. Most scholars translate the verse as a general, iterative reference to the potter's activity rather than a one-time event. NEB puts this well: "Now and then a vessel he was making out of the clay would be spoilt in his hands, and then he would start again and mould it into another vessel to his liking." Scholars differ as to how the potter's activity is to be interpreted with respect to God's word regarding Israel in v. 6. Some find a (potentially) positive word: just as the potter takes clay that turns out badly on the wheel and starts over again *with the same clay,* so God will take unfaithful Israel and work with it until it becomes the vessel God intends it to be.[2]

Others find a negative word: just as the potter takes the clay that turns out badly and replaces it with *other clay*, so God will replace corrupt Israel with another vessel.[3]

While the first option is preferable in view of exilic readers (they would understand themselves to be "the same clay"), a variation on that option should be considered wherein the shape of Israel's future remains somewhat open for Israel regarding the shape of its future. That is, just as the potter recreates a vessel that seems good to him in view of the possibilities inherent in the clay, so God will take corrupt Israel and work with the possibilities inherent in the human situation. Integral to that situation is the way in which Israel responds to God's continuing work; God will work with what is available, yet with God's good purposes always in mind. This interpretation coheres with the openness of the future implicit in vv. 7-10 and the call to repentance in v. 11. It also coheres with an understanding that a period of time passed between God's planning judgment (v. 11) and God's execution of it (vv. 13-17), which has become a certain future for Israel at this point. That distinction would be important for exilic readers and their understanding of God, whose patience and provision of opportunities before the fall occurred open up present possibilities for their future. God is still engaged in pottery work, shaping this people for a future beyond judgment (see **Connections: God the Potter**).

This interpretation also correlates well with the openness of the possibilities outlined in the generalized statements of vv. 7-10; the future is shaped at least in part by the human response to God's word. The nations of the world (including Israel) can respond to God's declared word in two different ways. They can repent of their evil and turn to God or they can turn away from God, not listening to God's voice. By their response the people have the God-given capacity to shape God's own response, though only in a limited way. Certain human actions will lead to specified divine responses, as they seem "good to the potter to do." Still, the direction of God's reshaping activity will depend to some degree on what God has to work with in this situation, including the people's own response (see ch. 26 for divine repentance). It should be noted that *God* is the subject of the verbs in vv. 7 and 9 (pluck up, plant, etc.), always the case in Jeremiah, except in the prophet's call narrative (1:10). [God Repents of a Promised Good?]

Unlike vv. 6 and 11, vv. 7-10 speak not of Israel but of "nations and kingdoms." Israel's particular history is placed within the context of the wider creation. This theme stands in continuity with the use of the "natural" image of God the Creator as a potter. The way in which God acts toward Israel is not unique among the nations of

God Repents of a Promised Good?

📖 We pursue the topic of divine repentance more generally at ch. 26, but note here the unusual theme that God will change his mind with respect to a promised *good*. This kind of divine action is rare in the Old Testament, having links to two other texts. At the outset of the flood story God repents of having made the good creation (Gen 6:5) and at the beginning of the monarchy God repents of having made Saul king (1 Sam 15:35). At the same time, these two instances are unusual in that God turns around and offers unconditional promises, both to the creation as a whole (see Gen 8:21-22; 9:8-17) and to the Davidic line (1 Sam 15:28-29; 2 Sam 7). In the Jeremiah text a promised "good" is also opened up to the possibility of divine repentance. Rather varied promised "goods" seem to be in view (cf. 12:15-17; 27:1-11).

It is important not to confuse such specific promises to Israel (or any other *corporate* entity, "nation or kingdom") with God's salvific purposes for Israel, indeed the entire creation, that are unchangeable (given the promises noted above; see [Israel's Election Nullified?]). God's good purposes for Israel may be relied upon absolutely, but neither Israel nor any other "nation or kingdom" can be *guaranteed* participation in the reality of fulfillment irrespective of their response. God will remain true to God's promises, but not in some universalistic sense. Those who reject God's declared word will not participate in the promised good (cf. Amos 5:18-20). At the same time, the promises of God will never be made null and void and will always be available for the faithful to cling to or return to.

the world (so also 12:14-17; 16:16-21; 17:5-11; 27:1-11). Whether it is Israel or any other people, God will turn away from a judgment word upon human repentance, just as God will turn away from a promised blessing upon rejection of a divine word. The use of this creational motif relates to Israel's questions to God regarding fair treatment (2:35; 5:19; 9:12-16; 16:10-13; 31:27-30). Given the consistent worldwide pattern of God's ways of working, Israel cannot bring God into court claiming unjust treatment. [A Universal Pattern in God's Ways of Working]

Verse 11 applies this general principle to Israel. God immediately announces that Israel's situation is so evil (*rā'āh*) that God is shaping (*yṣr*, the same root as "potter") judgment (*rā'āh*) against them. This word does not yet announce that he will *bring* evil; that awaits a later moment (v. 17; cf. 19:3). God makes plans, just as the people do against both God (v. 12) and Jeremiah (v. 18). In other words, v. 11 announces that God's declaration of judgment just noted in v. 7 has been made; but the execution of that judgment awaits developments. Verse 8 indicates that upon such a declaration of judgment, the future is still somewhat open, awaiting a repentant response (offered to Israel in v. 11). Yet, God in making the declaration of judgment is moving decisively in a certain direction. In terms of the exilic readers of Jeremiah, this dimension of the image would be a rehearsal of the possibilities inherent

A Universal Pattern in God's Ways of Working

📖 In alerting Israel that God's basic ways of acting with Israel are not different from God's ways of working with nations and kingdoms, God speaks of a *universal pattern*. God's responses outlined in vv 7-10 are not to be conceived in terms of, say, a daily fluctuating divine response to every instance of human obedience/disobedience. The divine patience would still be in view, and God enters into relationships that are not precisely programmed. The focus on *national* rather than individual response in these verses makes clear that the concern is with pervasive tendencies among a people (as is the case with Israel more generally in Jeremiah and other prophets).

in Israel's situation at a point before the judgment became inevitable (now stated in the following verses).

The People's Plots against God and God's Response, 18:12-17

Verse 12 immediately informs readers of this response. It is probably best to see Jeremiah as the speaker of this verse, though not specifically introduced (as at v. 19 and often). Jeremiah states that the people keep saying (the sense is iterative) that they will not repent, that they will follow their own plans, shaped by the stubbornness of their evil will and a resistance to God's word heretofore. That Jeremiah represents the people as admitting that they are acting "according to the stubbornness of our evil will" and that "It is no use!" is striking; they are addicted to idolatry (see 2:25 for a comparable admission, see [Baal and Canaanite Religion]; **Connections**, ch. 5). In reporting this, Jeremiah in effect rejects God's command to him to speak (v. 11); given who these people are, it is no use to lay out this option. If v. 11 constitutes a divine openness to a last-ditch effort to salvage the situation (see at 13:15-17), Jeremiah's report in v. 12 puts the kibosh on it. In effect Jeremiah has arrived at an assessment of the people correspondent to earlier divine decisions (e.g., 4:28); vv. 14-18 then, in effect, urge God to get on with the task. [Israel's Election Nullified?] At the same time, exilic readers would learn about a God who had been

---

Israel's Election Nullified?

The effect of God's response in vv. 13-17 is that the potential divine repentance that was announced in vv. 7-8, 11 is no longer possible. In Walter Brueggemann's words, "resistance to God practiced so long eventually nullifies the capacity to choose life." God's options for the future of this people in view of this response is limited to plucking up and breaking down and destroying (v. 7), and so God moves to the announcement of judgment (vv. 13-17). The potter must start all over with the clay. The potter's intent to make a good vessel remains, but the possibilities have narrowed even further and any future that the people might have with God now lies through judgment.

At the same time, the text does not claim that "the clay has no future" (Brueggemann). Rather, any future it has lies through and beyond judgment and is dependent on God's new actions on its behalf (a situation in which the exiles find themselves). Nor does the text understand judgment to mean "the abrogation and revocation of [Israel's] elect status" or "the *forfeiture* of Israel's election" (Stulman). To

interpret judgment in these terms neglects the "less than full end" texts (e.g., 4:27), the witness to God's commitment to Israel being as firm as the fixed orders of creation (31:35-37; 33:14-26), and God's "everlasting love" for Israel (31:3). God is not free from such promises and commitments; God has bound himself to Israel in such a way that God cannot move to "unchoose" this *community* (see [God as the Portion of Jacob]). But individuals within this community may reject God and suffer the consequences of self-removal from the sphere of the promise, a move that God will honor. Wrongful forms of reliance upon election by Israelites, recognized as a problem by the prophets (e.g., Amos; perhaps evident in Jer 7:1-10), raises a somewhat different issue and may or may not be linked with, say, idolatry. But to wrongly rely on God's election does not in and of itself invalidate the election.

Walter Brueggemann, *A Commentary on Jeremiah: Exile and Homecoming* (Grand Rapids: Eerdmans, 1998), 169.

L. Stulman, *Order Amid Chaos: Jeremiah as Symbolic Tapestry* (Sheffield: Sheffield Academic Press, 1998), 47.

remarkably open to futures other than the one that eventuated and would also hear a call to repentance in their own time and place.

The divine response (vv. 13-17) is an announcement of judgment that integrates elements of the indictment of the people (e.g., 5:6-9; 8:10; 9:7-9). Some have thought the announcement begins only with v. 17, the only verse with a divine subject.[4] Yet, this combination of divine rhetorical questions and God's having been rejected/forgotten is typical of divine laments (see 2:29-32; 3:19-21; 8:4-7; 13:20-27; 15:5-9). One can name this a divine lament and consider it parallel with the lament of Jeremiah in vv. 19-23.

These verses begin with a reference to the "nations," placing Israel once again in the larger world of creation (linking up "nations" in vv. 7, 9). The nations are asked to make an assessment of Israel's rejection of God (comparable to 2:10-11; see 22:8-9; Deut 29:24-25). In their experience, have they ever heard the likes of the horrible things Israel has done (see 5:30)? The nations are asked to do this, not in terms of anything revealed uniquely to Israel (e.g., Sinaitic Law), but in terms of *natural* relationships (as also in 8:7). The snow can be seen on Mt. Hermon all year round and water rushes down the mountain streams without ceasing. The rhetorical questions of v. 14, which assume the constancy of snow and flowing water, highlight fidelity within relationship. Just as it is unnatural for the snow and water to disappear, so it is unnatural for Israel to forget Yahweh and turn to idols that are worthless, indeed nonexistent. It is also unnatural for travelers to leave the main roads of the tradition (see 6:16) and wander about aimlessly on side roads. It is likely (with NIV; REB; NRSV footnote) that the idols have made them stumble and so caused them to wander (yet, the unnaturalness of this is still the point).

Anyone who passes by, seeing the desolation wrought on the land (see ch. 12), will immediately recognize the issue and be horrified, hissing and shaking their heads (v. 16; see 19:8; 22:8-9; Lev 26:32; 1 Kgs 9:8). Notably, this is a response to Israel's forgetting Yahweh; elsewhere the reaction is to Israel's destruction (19:8; 25:9, 18; 29:18). There is a consistent, if not mechanistic creation-wide moral order to God's ways that is known by the nations (an assumption of the oracles against the nations, chs. 46–51); God's ways with Israel are God's ways with all. The nations will recognize that what God does with Israel is just; Israel has violated basic human norms for relationships and must suffer the effects. The latter are imaged in terms of another creational image in v. 17—a hot wind (the sirocco; see 4:11; 13:24; Hos 13:15). This wind from the east, the direction from which Babylon comes, will scatter and disperse them across the landscape. These agents are the mediators of God's judgmental work, imaged as God's turning his back on the people and forsaking them, not hearing their cries (see 12:7). This is not a declaration of divine absence, but of divine presence in wrath (God "shows" his back; cf. Exod 33:22).

The People's Plots against Jeremiah and His Response, 18:18-23

The lament of Jeremiah in vv. 19-23 is linked by v. 18 to plots by his persecutors (cf. 11:18-23; 12:1-4; 15:10-21; 17:14-18). The ringleaders, who name Jeremiah for the first time, are probably to be identified with the leaders noted. The entire religious establishment (note the absence of kings) is arrayed against him. They conspire to bring charges, using his own words to condemn him to death. At the same time, they are representatives of the entire community in the plot (see vv. 11-12; 26:7-19 makes some distinctions among people and leaders for at least that situation).[5] The people as a whole are given the status of adversary. [Rejection of God for Religious Reasons]

> ### Rejection of God for Religious Reasons
>
> In v. 18 all the major *religious* leaders cite *religious* reasons for their conspiracy against God and Jeremiah! As with Israel, so with other religious communities, most prophetic voices coming from within or from without are silenced for such reasons, especially when the religious establishment is challenged. Their common claim is that they want to preserve the tradition: the Torah (priestly instruction), the counsel of the wise, and the word of the prophet. In general terms, their motives seem to be excellent, and they are probably sincere about the words they spoke (see Hananiah, ch. 28). They understand Jeremiah's confrontational words to be contrary to the best that Israel's religious tradition has to offer. What faithful Israelite would not want to preserve the tradition! But, as so often in such cases, their understanding of the tradition seems to be closed in upon itself; *their* interpretations of "texts" allow for no variation or exception and no outside voices or contrary points of view are allowed to get through for careful consideration. These are texts for self-examination on the part of any religious community, not least the leaders of such communities.

This opposition to Jeremiah (and Jeremiah's response) has fundamentally to do with the word he speaks, but his opponents do not finally distinguish between the word and its mediator. They attack him because he applies the indictment and announcement of calamitous judgment directly to them. The plots against God (v. 12) and the plots against the prophet (v. 18) finally flow together. And Jeremiah's response pertains to both. The enemies of God and of Jeremiah are one and the same.

Jeremiah responds to these plots with another lament to God (vv. 19-23; this example of lament is dominated by petitions; cf. 15:15-18). Again, the "I" of Jeremiah confronts the "you" (God) about "them" (the enemy); notably, no charges are brought against God (cf. 12:1; 15:18). He begins with a petition for God to listen, both to him and to what his adversaries are saying (some think Jeremiah quotes what they say in the first line of v. 20). God already knows what they seek to do (v. 23a), but by this plea he wants God to focus on their scheming. They have dug a pit, that is, devised ways to entrap him in what he says (this image is developed further in v. 22; see Pss 57:6; 119:85; 140:1-5). Will all the good that he has done on behalf of his adversaries be rewarded with evil (*rā'āh*, v. 20a; see Ps 35:12)? He pleads with God to remember (see 15:15) all the good he has done on their behalf, standing before God (see 15:19) and interceding that God's wrath be turned away (mostly not preserved, but see 4:10; 14:13). Jeremiah follows with his own "therefore" (!), asking that God assume his own words of judgment as God's own and begin the previously announced judgment forthwith (see 11:20; 12:3; 17:16; 20:12).

His words are very harsh, though they are typical for laments in cases of unjust treatment by enemies (e.g., Pss 35:4-6; 58:6-11; 109:9-11). The extent to which Jeremiah appropriates God's own language in speaking of judgment is striking (see the listing in the **Introduction**). The introductory "therefore" is typical of God's oracles (e.g., 18:13). Verses 21-22a describe the effects that a Babylonian invasion would have (famine, sword, pestilence), language used earlier by *God* (14:12; 15:2). The images of the death of the old and young male warriors, with wives becoming widows and mothers childless, is also language used earlier by God (6:11b-12; 15:7-9), including the word "suddenly." It is *God* who has mentioned their "cries" in distress, cries that he will not answer (11:11-12). In conclusion (v. 23), beginning with the familiar confession regarding God's intimate knowledge of the situation (see 12:3; 15:15), he asks God not to forgive their sins (just as God would not hear their confessions of sin, 14:7, 20). Rather, he asks God to deal with them in the "time" of the divine anger (on this use of "time" see 6:15; 10:15; 11:12, 14). The "day of their calamity" (v. 17) is the "time" of *God's* anger. As at 17:18, Jeremiah gives these matters over to God; he plans no personal strikes, yet his words contribute to that end.

In understanding Jeremiah's outbursts properly, these parallels between Jeremiah and God are important. Interpreters who speak of Jeremiah's identity with the people have difficulty with this text; Jeremiah here stands together not with them but against them and with God. The plotters' schemes against Jeremiah are correspondent to their plans against God (v. 12). To oppose one is to oppose the other. As noted, Jeremiah's words of judgment are God's words of judgment (14:12; 15:2, 8). Also, he will no longer intercede with God on their behalf (v. 20), as God has commanded him to do (11:14; 14:11). These parallels show that Jeremiah's strong language against his adversaries is precisely correspondent to God's announcement of judgment. What might seem to be a very personal vendetta is, in fact, a conformation of the prophet's words to the message of the wrath of God.[6] God's experience has become the prophet's experience. The people's failure to repent and their plots against both God and prophet are followed by the judgments of both. The prophet's words reinforce those of God; they agree on what needs to happen. At the same time, Jeremiah's words urge God, whose patience has just been reported (see at vv. 11-12), to delay no longer (see **Connections: Jeremiah's Use of God's Language**).

As with the lament in 17:14-18, God does not respond directly. But God continues the conversation! And 19:1-13 may be God's reply (see at ch. 19).

CONNECTIONS

God the Potter

The story of the potter is often thought to illustrate the absolute sovereignty of God. Just as a potter can shape what he wills with clay, so God can do what God wills with Israel. [God as Potter in Other Texts] For some commentators, the potter "retains complete mastery over the material he uses"; he "completely controls the clay" and, following the analogy, Israel is "completely in the control of Yahweh."[7] Inconsistently, these authors go on to speak of relationship; but it is difficult to understand how one can speak of relationship in any significant sense if God is in total control. Moreover, if God is completely in control then the problem lies with God the potter rather than Israel the clay. That is to say, if God had this kind of control, the clay (=Israel) would be spoiled only if God wanted it to be spoiled; an all-determining God could have prevented that from happening. If we would speak of "Yahweh's complete sovereignty" then, given how unruly Israel is, we would have to score God a crashing management failure or consider Israel's sin the will of God. To go on to speak of Yahweh's "responsive sovereignty," as Walter

God as Potter in Other Texts

References to the image of God as potter in other texts is thought to reinforce this interpretation (Isa 29:15-16; 45:9-13; 64:8). This argumentation is problematic, however, for the potter image in each of these texts (and more generally) is primarily associated with God as Creator and human beings as creatures (see 10:16=51:19; for the potter image in the creation story, see Gen 2:7; cf. Isa 45:7, 18; Ps 95:5). In Isaiah 29 and 45 the Creator's prerogative and knowledge is affirmed in response to the creature's questioning the propriety of God's actions (cf. Jer 27:5). The nature of the human activity in these texts indicates that the issue is divine right/knowledge not divine rule/control. God may be confessed as sovereign, but human activity is a powerful force in these texts. The clay is not considered passive; God's rule is not absolute.

Berrigan on Jeremiah's Language

One way to respond to Jeremiah's language is that promoted by Daniel Berrigan, whose reflections on Jeremiah are often helpful, not least on the use of the word of judgment in our own time. Yet, listen to his reflections on this text: "Who is this God anyway, the God of Jeremiah, what of his moral physiognomy? Do such oracles as are here recorded, with their summons to violent reprisal (a call taken seriously, more, initiated again and again by Yahweh), offer sound insight into God, our God as well as Jeremiah's? Insight into God's hope for ourselves? Into crime (ours) and punishment (God's)—an ineluctable hyphenation, a logic of terrifying consequence? Why does the God of Jeremiah never once counsel—forgiveness? For this we are forced to turn in another direction than Jeremiah, to a later time, another seer—maligned as he is, put to scorn, murdered. And amid the infamy, a far different response is offered to his persecutors; a prayer on their behalf, an intercession (Luke 23:24). Jeremiah, we confess in confusion of heart, much resembles ourselves. And Jesus much resembles God. But not the God of Jeremiah, the God of Jesus." But is it so simple? Is this not a return to that old saw about Jesus coming to deliver us from the angry, abusive God of the Old Testament? Does Jesus mean that there is no place anymore for harsh, unforgiving rhetoric? Should a situation ever arise in our own culture that is comparable to that of Israel, should not such language again have a place?

Daniel Berrigan, *Jeremiah: The World, the Wound of God* (Minneapolis: Fortress, 1999), 84.

Brueggemann helpfully does, is to pull back from the original claim for God's "complete" sovereignty.[8]

More must be said about our claim that God is not free from promises made (see [Rejection of God for Religious Reasons]). Such a claim does not eliminate divine freedom from the discussion altogether (see **Connections**, ch. 14). In the declaring of God's word (vv. 7, 9) God takes the initiative in freedom. God freely makes promises to bind God's self, freely determines that these will be the divine responses to human responses to the declared word. The phrases "at one moment . . . at another moment" may seem overly binding on God, as if God's response to human response is mechanical in nature. Yet, these phrases serve to guard against any suggestion of capriciousness on God's part. On the one hand, God can be depended upon to react in consonance with the divine will to save by responding positively to human repentance. On the other hand, God will allow people to say what Israel says in v. 12 and to suffer the consequences.

That God will repent in both ways noted (vv. 8, 10) should impress upon exilic (and other) readers the remarkably patient and open ways of their God as well as the seriousness with which they should shape their own lives into the future.

Jeremiah's Use of God's Language

The extent to which Jeremiah's language conforms to God's own language raises certain ethical issues (see **Introduction**).[9] To put it in other terms, the character of God has shaped the character of Jeremiah, and the results as seen in vv. 19-23 are at least questionable with respect to their harshness and unforgiving nature. Jeremiah has learned to use such acrimonious and merciless language from God! However much Jeremiah's language might be said to correspond to laments of imprecation in the Psalter (and it does, as noted), it cannot simply be ascribed to outbursts over his own suffering and pain at the hands of his enemies. His language conforms to that used by God. And is one not thereby being asked by the text to think that this is a good thing for Jeremiah to do?

But is it? Many interpreters have had difficulty with this language of Jeremiah and have sought to explain it (away) in various ways, usually in terms of Jeremiah's humanity. This is a human being in deep anguish. But these texts want to say more, namely, that Jeremiah's language, however human it may be, is not simply to be evaluated in these terms: "he's only human." Because, clearly, God has taught Jeremiah how to talk like this! It is striking that those interpreters who seek to explain Jeremiah's language in terms of his humanity or who otherwise pass judgment on it, do not make a comparable judgment of the language of God; God usually gets home scot-free. [Berrigan on Jeremiah's Language]

But, if we do not take Berrigan's route (and many have), do we simply move over to the ditch on the other side of the road and accept this language without evaluation? If the Bible has God using such language, and one of God's own revered prophets as well, then that language is beyond scrutiny, or so it is argued. Even more, even if it is not said in so many terms, that biblical usage places an imprimatur on the use, perhaps even the indiscriminate use, of such language on the part of those who learn how to speak and act from such a God. And, in my experience, this is not to speak only of certain stereotypical preachers of fire and brimstone.

One might try to find a middle way here and raise the issue of the nature of the situation into which such a word might be spoken. Upon careful discernment of a given situation of, say, the horrific abuse of human beings, one might be called upon to speak such a harsh word. And so this language of God and Jeremiah would be placed in the same rare-use category as the psalms of imprecation, and then used only by those whose personal experience calls for such rhetoric, or by those who stand in solidarity with them.

But, however important it is to have this language available for such moments, the issue with the God of Jeremiah seems more complex. It is one thing to set a half-dozen psalms on the back burner for potential use; it is another thing to have the unrelenting harsh imagery of a major biblical book such as Jeremiah drummed into our consciousness on a regular basis. Will we not, as readers and hearers of this word, learn all too well how to speak and act from this portrayal of God? And often without the quality of discernment of which God is capable?

NOTES

[1] For detail, see Terence Fretheim, "The Repentance of God: A Study of Jeremiah 18:7-10," *HAR* 11 (1987): 81-92.

[2] See William Holladay, *Jeremiah 1* (Philadelphia: Fortress, 1986), 514-15.

[3] See William McKane, *A Critical and Exegetical Commentary on Jeremiah* (2 vols.; ICC; Edinburgh: T. & T. Clark, 1986), 422-23.

[4] See Holladay, *Jeremiah 1,* 520-21.

[5] See McKane, 440.

[6] See Terence Fretheim, *The Suffering of God: An Old Testament Perspective* (Philadelphia: Fortress, 1984), 158.

[7] Ronald E. Clements, *Jeremiah* (IBC; Atlanta: John Knox, 1988), 112; Walter Brueggemann, *A Commentary on Jeremiah: Exile and Homecoming* (Grand Rapids: Eerdmans, 1998), 167.

[8] Brueggemann, ibid., 168.

[9] See Terence Fretheim, "The Character of God in Jeremiah," forthcoming.

A BROKEN JUG
AND ITS EFFECTS

19:1–20:6

This prose narrative is a report of a symbolic act (see 13:1-14) accompanied by three announcements of judgment (19:1-15), in view of which Jeremiah is persecuted by Pashhur, a temple official (20:1-6). The text is commonly considered composite (with vv. 2b-9, 11b-13 "interrupting" the story). The narrative continues themes struck in chapter 18, especially the image of a potter (cf. vv. 1, 10-11 with 18:1-6, 11; here the focus is on a finished jug), a link to the "plans/plots" of the people (cf. v. 7 with 18:12, 18, 23), and the passers-by horrified at the severity of the judgment (cf. v. 8 with 18:16). Moreover, the command of God in v. 1 may be a response to Jeremiah's lament in 18:19-23; God will void the plans of Jeremiah's (and God's) enemies (v. 7) and visit judgment upon them, as Jeremiah had requested. Jeremiah does not act in the narrative until v. 14, at which point it is assumed that Jeremiah has done what God commanded in vv. 1-2, 11-12. [The Text and Exilic Readers]

The Text and Exilic Readers

The first announcement of judgment (vv. 3-9) is to be addressed to the kings (plural, see vv. 4, 13; 17:20) of Judah and the people of Jerusalem. From the perspective of exilic readers, the general reference to "kings" would make the text cross-generational in its significance. In other words, the purpose of this narrative is not to report a one-time event in the life of Jeremiah or Jerusalem, but to illustrate how a specific event gathers up the generations and depicts what has been an ongoing reality regarding the relationship between God and an unfaithful Israel.

COMMENTARY

The Breaking of the Jug, 19:1-15

God commands Jeremiah both to act and to speak in the presence of some priests and elders (vv. 1-2, 10). Jeremiah is to purchase a potter's earthenware jug or flask and to journey with these community leaders to the valley of the son of Hinnom (the later Gehenna; see 7:31), near the entrance to the Potsherd Gate (see Neh 2:13;

The Valley and the Gate

The valley is thought to be located just south of the walls of Jerusalem (see at 7:31). The Potsherd gate, probably in the south wall of Jerusalem, is thought to be the exit through which broken pottery and other refuse is carried to the city dump, as the name implies. That the flask was to be broken in the city dump and disposed of there is probably intended as an analogy for the fate of Judah and Jerusalem. The whole place will become a dump, strewn with the bodies of the people of Israel.

3:13-14). [The Valley and the Gate] No question is raised whether these leaders will accompany him; unbeknownst to them, they will function as witnesses, though they may think they can entrap him.

Jeremiah is commanded to give three related announcements of judgment. The first is to follow upon completion of this short trip (vv. 3-9). The second is to accompany the breaking of the jug in the presence of the leaders of city and temple (vv. 10-13). The third occurs when Jeremiah has returned from the valley and speaks to *all* the people in the temple court (vv. 14-15). The symbolic import of this trip is complex; it is related to the journey to the city dump and the taking of an *unbroken* potter's vessel to that site, the breaking of it there in the presence of witnesses, and the return to the temple precincts.

The first word of judgment (vv. 3-9) immediately announces a "disaster" that God is going to bring upon Jerusalem. Again, as often in Jeremiah, God is the subject of the verb, but does not act alone (v. 7) (see **Connections: God's Action Is Mediated**). God acts through means other than God, namely, the Babylonian armies and the birds and animals. Moreover, the result of this action by multiple agents is named *rāʿāh* (vv. 3, 15), which links up with the people's wickedness (=*rāʿāh*, see 1:14-16; **Introduction**). God does not introduce anything new into the situation, but tends to the moral order in mediating the effects of the people's own sins. When people, whether from Israel or other nations, hear of these events, the news will be so disastrous that they will feel their ears tingling or ringing (see 18:13-17; 2 Kgs 21:12).

Verses 4-5 give the reasons for the disaster; vv. 6-9 return to the announcement of judgment ("therefore") with greater specificity (similarly, 7:30-34). The *specific* focus of the idolatry is the sacrifice of children, which is symptomatic of the more basic issue of infidelity. The people "have forsaken me" and worshiped alien gods (this recalls the marriage imagery, e.g., 1:16 and often), profaning "this place" (=city and temple), so that it is no longer a holy place (v. 4). Indeed, they have been creative in their infidelity, worshiping gods unknown to their ancestors and even to the kings of Judah! Because their relationship with God is not in good order, all sorts of evil practices are generated and tolerated. The "innocent blood" refers, not to children who have been sacrificed, but to the oppression of the underprivileged (see 2:34; 5:26-28; 7:6; 22:3; cf. the

practices of Manasseh in 2 Kgs 21:16; 24:4). Notably, God again
(see 7:31; 14:14; 32:35) states that such practices were not commanded by God, or even considered (suggesting that the idolaters
associated them with Yahweh in syncretistic fashion). This doubly
made point makes clear that God has not been
involved in any way in this practice; it is totally
against the will of God. To put this point in
other terms: the will of God is resistible and
God here testifies to this very fact.

> **A Play on Words**
>
> AΩ The verb translated "make void" (v. 7, NRSV; *baqqôtî*) is a word-play on the word for "flask" (*baqbuq*) and has suggested to some that the flask (whose contents would be the "plans" of the people) was to be poured out in the dump as part of the symbolic act.

The judgment God announces in vv. 6-9 is
introduced by a typical prophetic formulation
regarding the "coming days" (cf. 7:32; 9:25;
16:14; 23:7). The force of this announcement responds to the previously announced "plans" of the people (18:12, 18, 23), which
divinely mediated events will soon make null and void. [A Play on
Words]

The effects are gruesome. Changing the name of the valley to the
Valley of Slaughter reflects what will happen to Israel (see 7:32;
12:3): they will fall by a slashing sword wielded by their enemies.
They seek Jeremiah's life (18:20); their enemies will seek their life.
What goes around comes around. God's involvement in giving
their bodies for food to birds and animals is made more sharply
clear here compared to 7:33. Once again (see 18:16), the effect on
Jerusalem will be so horrific that even strangers will take note,
exclaim, and catch their breath (see also 17:13-17; 25:9, 18; 29:18;
also used for Edom and Babylon, 49:17; 50:13). God will even
make them eat the flesh of their children and neighbors! We know
from other texts that the eating of children occurred when food
supplies failed during times of famine and siege (see 2 Kgs 6:24-31;
Lam 2:20; 4:10), so this language is not hyperbolic. The correspondence between the people offering their children as sacrifices
to Baal and their eating of their own children is notable. Giving up
their children to sacrifice has the effect of losing even more of their
children (see **Connections** regarding the children at ch. 6).

The second announcement of judgment is to accompany the
breaking of the jug in the valley of Hinnom in the presence of witnesses (vv. 10-13). The breaking of a potter's vessel is a symbol of
destruction (see Ps 2:9); as the pottery is broken, so God will break
both city and people. [The Breaking of the Pot] The breaking would be
both sudden (see 18:22) and final. One particular effect of the pot
being broken is stated; "it can never be mended" (the Hebrew verb
is *rāpā'*, translated elsewhere as "heal," e.g., 6:14; 30:17). Unlike

The Breaking of the Pot

The image of breaking the potter's vessel (see Ps 2:9) may have been prompted by the Near Eastern practice of inscribing the names of the king's enemies on the pottery and smashing it while uttering curses against them, thereby bringing about what has been dramatized (a form of sympathetic magic). Whatever the roots of the prophetic symbolic acts, they have to do with the provision of a vivid image and accompanying rhetoric not the predetermination or the explanation of an event. Brueggemann says it well: "the dramatic act opened up a field of fertile imagination filled with dread and fresh discernment." The symbolic act does not make the event of judgment inevitable (contrary to William McKane, *A Critical and Exegetical Commentary on Jeremiah* [2 vols,; ICC: Edinburgh: T. & T. Clark, 1986], 458); that inevitability is already in place and has been verbalized in several ways (e.g., 4:28). This action adds to that word and portrays more concretely what is to happen. Action and word together participate in that swirling drive toward judgment and are descriptive of what will happen to Israel. Notably, Jeremiah's symbolic act does not substitute for God's own involvement in the bringing of the disaster (vv. 12, 15; see also ch. 13). It should also be noted, importantly, that if the symbolic act were understood to be so crucial for the *occurrence* of the historical event, then it is strange that the text does not even report that the symbolic act itself took place. The act must not have been so crucial.

Amphora. AD 400. (Credit: Scott Nash)

Walter Brueggemann, *A Commentary on Jeremiah: Exile and Homecoming* (Grand Rapids: Eerdmans, 1998), 177.

the clay at the potter's wheel in 18:1-6, the clay has hardened and, once broken, could no longer function as a pot.

This dimension of the analogy may have two levels of significance. One, no repentant (or other) act on the part of the people will be able to bring about a new future—death and judgment is certain. Two, any future for this people will have to come from a new creative act of God (30:17; 33:6; see 3:22; the new heart in 24:7; 32:39; cf. 31:31-34). The false prophets had healed the wound of this people lightly (6:14–8:11). The only way in which this people could be healed was through judgment and death. But the testimony of Jeremiah (from the "build and plant" of 1:10 and the episodic promissory oracles, e.g., 3:15-18) is that God remembers Israel through this valley of death and will raise it to new life. The death is a real death for Israel, but it is not God's final word for them.

The burying in Topheth (or the valley of slaughter) until there is no more room recalls 7:32 (see [A Word for Exilic Readers]). Making Jerusalem, including its houses and palaces, like Topheth means that the city, too, will be filled with corpses. The city will become a cemetery, only the bodies will not be buried. Moreover, recalling

2 Kings 23:10, where King Josiah destroys Topheth during his reformation, v. 12 could refer to destruction generally, not just corpses specifically. This understanding is also suggested by v. 13, which speaks of the defilement of the houses of both kings and populace in Jerusalem. The houses especially chosen for destruction are those where idolatrous sacrifices have been made to the "whole host of heaven," that is, every god under the sun (see v. 4), and where drink offerings have been made to these gods (see also 32:29). The entire place has been profaned and hence has been made inhospitable as a dwelling place for God.

The third announcement of judgment occurs upon Jeremiah's return to Jerusalem (vv. 14-15). The narrative assumes that he has done all that God commanded him in vv. 1-2, 11-12. He speaks in the temple court (as in 7:2; 26:2) to "all the people" and summarizes the message that he spoke to the political and religious leaders in the valley of Hinnom. God is going to act on the words that have been spoken, namely, to bring disaster (=*rā'āh*) upon Jerusalem and all the towns of Judah. Note that God does not understand that the prophetic word/act alone will work this destruction; God will now act to bring this judgment about. The reason given: the people have been stubborn and have refused to listen to the word of God (see 7:26).

Jeremiah Persecuted Publicly, 20:1-6

This addendum to the previous narrative illustrates how Jeremiah the *prophet* (stressed in vv. 1-2 and 19:14) has been persecuted and how the highest *religious* authorities were involved in a calculated way (see 18:18; [Rejection of God for Religious Reasons]). This context is the first specific reference to Jeremiah as prophet since 1:5 (19:14; 20:1-2), and the first time his antagonists are named (and Babylon, vv. 4-6). The specificity may be a point of clarity needed by the exilic readers.

The prophet's persecution occurs at the hands of a temple official named Pashhur (the Pashhur in 21:1; 38:1 is a different person). Note that it is when the word is delivered in the temple courts that the authorities take action (cf. ch. 26)! Pashhur is concerned about good order in these precincts; in effect he is a member of the temple police (see their function at 29:26). Ironically, the effect of God's word is that *disorder* will reign in this well-ordered place. Pashhur, having heard Jeremiah preach, apprehends him, beats him, and makes him a public spectacle by putting him in stocks for one day. Jeremiah becomes a *religious* prisoner! The stocks were near the Benjamin gate, one of the gates of the temple; it was apparently close to where Jeremiah had been speaking (19:14).

From reports such as this, it is clear that Jeremiah's laments are not based on an overactive imagination (cf. the confrontation of Amos with king Amaziah in Amos 7:10-17).

When Jeremiah is released after a day's time in the stocks, he does not back away from his disturbing message. In fact, he particularizes it. He speaks a word of judgment not only regarding Israel but also about Pashhur and his household. Apparently it was a private word to him, but with great public consequences. First, he gives Pashhur a new name (v. 3); he speaks in the Lord's name, though there is no indication that God told him to do this. [Pashhur's New Name] The last phrase in v. 6 suggests that Pashhur had a prophetic role in the community. Yet, there is no other reference to such a role; perhaps his "prophesying" is the message his name falsely conveyed to the community.

Next, in vv. 4-6 Jeremiah explains the various dimensions of the meaning of the new name. The situation with which all the people are faced (v. 10; 6:25) has now become Pashhur's personal fate (and that of his friends and family) and he himself will be terrorized by what is happening ("a terror to yourself"). As he had been a terror to Jeremiah, so he will now be a terror to his friends as well, as they will be killed while he looks on. Jeremiah is not one to shy away from sharp indictments of individual leaders (prophets, kings); he does not "hide" behind general castigation of the people as a whole (e.g., 22:10-30; 28:15-16).

These terrors will be inflicted by Babylon, which is named here for the first time (vv. 4-6). The Israelites will be given into the hands of the king of Babylon (Nebuchadrezzar is named for the first time in 21:2); they will be exiled to that country, and many will be killed. The language of exile assumes that not all will be killed, though the current generation will all die and be buried in captivity. In the process the Babylonian armies will plunder Jerusalem and the royal treasuries, taking "all it has toiled for and holds dear" (NAB; see 2 Kgs 20:17; 24:13-14) and transport it to Babylon. Pashhur and his family and friends will be among the exiles, and they shall die and be buried in Babylon.

Pashhur's New Name

AΩ As with names generally, Pashhur's name bespeaks not only *his* new life situation (cf. the renaming of Jacob as Israel in Gen 32:22-32), but he becomes a *public* sign of what will happen to "all Judah" (cf. the names of Hosea's children, Hos 1:1-9). This makes clear that Jeremiah is not just insulting Pashhur, but using the occasion to deliver a larger message. His old name, Pashhur (perhaps meaning "Fruitful [or Joy]-all-around"; see William Holladay, *Jeremiah I* [Philadelphia: Fortress, 1986], 543-44) is changed to Magor-Missabib, perhaps meaning "Terror-all-around" (on the use of this phrase, see v. 10; 6:25; 46:5; 49:29).

CONNECTIONS

God's Judgment Is Mediated

To have God as subject of the verbs in vv. 7-9 is especially startling. Alongside this witness is the first explicit mention of the Babylonians (20:4-6); they are the "enemies" of 19:7. The reader must not back away from God's involvement in this disaster (see **Introduction** for the conformation of the actions of God and Babylon). The image, however, is not that of a God who will in some unmediated way[1] coerce the people to be cannibals or specifically see to it that birds and animals eat their dead bodies as food. The Babylonians are effective agents in this situation; they are the "enemies" who wield "the sword" and whose "hand" seeks the life of Israelites (language from 19:7 repeated in 20:4-6). They will afflict them in such a way that they are full of distress, and kill people so that their bodies are strewn about in the open. Once these armies are let loose into this situation, they will wreak havoc in a devastating, but somewhat predictable way, given patterns of warfare in that world. That they will proceed without pity or compassion seems inevitable (cf. 13:14 and 21:7). The involvement of the birds and animals is also to be noted (they are named as Nebuchadrezzar's servants in 27:6). [The Devastation of Israel and Deuteronomy 28]

Another agent of which the interpreter must speak in this situation is the created moral order. God works in this situation in and through the existing moral order; generally, the Old Testament will not speak of this order in deistic ways. God will see to the moral order so that sin and evil do not go unchecked in the life of the world. The people's *rā'āh* will issue in their *rā'āh* (see **Introduction**). At the same time, this divine involvement must not

---

The Devastation of Israel and Deuteronomy 28

These effects on Jerusalem and its populace are sketched in the curses of Deuteronomy 28 in no little detail. Parallels to these curses have been found in ancient Near Eastern treaties; hence, they may be linked here as the consequences of the breaking of covenant (see 11:1-17). They include the following: becoming an object of horror (Deut 28:25, 37), having their bodies serve as food for birds and animals (v. 26), and even the cannibalistic practices (vv. 53-57; see Lev 26:29). These effects are considered a curse for infidelity, but it is important to note the two different formulations for such curses in Deut 28. On the one hand, the curses are seen in more impersonal terms as "coming upon" the people, "pursuing and overtaking" them (vv. 15, 22, 45). On the other hand, God is the subject of the mediated judgment (vv. 20-28, 35-36, 47-49, 59-64). Both dimensions of this reality must be affirmed; God is agent and God uses various nondivine agents to mediate these effects.

be conceived in terms of micromanagement, as God's later judgment on the Babylonians for their overkill makes clear (see 25:12-13; 50–51).

NOTE

[1] Contrary to Walter Brueggemann, *A Commentary on Jeremiah: Exile and Homecoming* (Grand Rapids: Eerdmans, 1998), 176.

JEREMIAH'S FINAL LAMENT

20:7-18

This textual segment is commonly thought to consist of two laments of Jeremiah (vv. 7-12 [13], 14-18); they conclude his laments, begun at 11:18 with earlier antecedents. Verse 13, a call to praise, is often considered interruptive; its plural imperatives have suggested dependence on a communal use of the lament. Yet, praise language and the certainty of a hearing is often found in laments, both within the psalm (see 35:9-10; 144:9) and as concluding words (see 13:6; 59:16-17; 109:30-31).[1] The call to praise in Psalm 22:23 (in the middle of the psalm) and Psalm 31:24 (cf. 27:14) at the end are important parallels.

In addition, it is sometimes suggested (as here) that vv. 14-18 belong together with vv. 7-13.[2] Concluding sharp laments and questions after a strong confession of faith are attested elsewhere (e.g., Lam 5:20-22 after 5:19 and 3:22-33; cf. Ps 89). One is given to wonder whether the common division of the text is informed by a preconceived sense of the lament. Verses 7-18 stand together editorially, whatever their original function. It is best to understand vv. 7-18 as a single lament that includes elements of complaint, confession of trust, petition, certainty of being heard, and thanksgiving, concluding on a sharp note of questioning (see [The Lament Psalms]). In this lament, Jeremiah brings together several themes that he has previously lifted up, including complaints for hardships endured in carrying out his commission (cf. v. 7 with 15:15-18) and calls for judgment against his persecutors (cf. vv. 10-12 with 17:14-18; 18:19-23).

It is commonly thought that this, the last lament of Jeremiah, is so filled with anguish because the prophet has a deep sympathy with the people in their now certain death and destruction. But, if so, the text does not say much about this, if anything. In fact, because Jeremiah's antagonists can be identified with the people (e.g., 18:20b), he expresses no sympathy for them; rather, he fervently prays that God's judgment be quickly forthcoming on the whole lot. The anguish is better related to the nature of his calling and his sense of being torn between God and people. If there is some sympathetic anguish on Jeremiah's part, it is more closely linked to the anguish of *God* over

As for how exiles would read this lament, it is unlikely that they could identify their anguish with the anguish of the prophet (or of God). The prophet's grief could not become their grief (contrary to Clements, *Jeremiah*, 123). After all, they had been (and perhaps still were) the *problem* to which Jeremiah speaks. At best, reading this text might engender some sense of remorse for their behaviors, perhaps even repentance, as they observe the anguish through which they put both prophet and God. Look at what it took—such personal cost—for the prophet to speak the word of God to them. In short, the text would function as *proclamation*. The word of God is proclaimed to them once again, this time through a suffering prophet that is textually embodied (see **Connections**, ch. 12).

the broken relationship. As such, this particularly intense and final lament may bring the lament-filled chapters 11–20 to a climax. [Jeremiah's Lament and Exilic Readers]

This lament of Jeremiah follows upon his persecution at the hands of Pashhur (vv. 1-6), with both differences and similarities from the others he has spoken. It is similar in that the rhetoric against his persecutors is as sharp as ever. It is different in that Jeremiah's accusations of God are not as sharp as in 15:18 (though many consider them comparable) and his statements about his own life reach a new level of intensity in vv. 14-18. It is worth remarking that Jeremiah, though complaining that God has deceived him, never suggests that the *word* that God has called him to proclaim is false. Nor is a question raised about God's faithfulness, as vv. 11-13 make clear; the divine deception does not become grounds for challenging basic divine attributes.

COMMENTARY

Jeremiah's Complaint, 20:7-13

This lament is remarkable for the strength of its images; they have even been called blasphemous (especially v. 7). Jeremiah begins by sharply addressing God (v. 7), The nuance given to the verbs can

What Does God Do to Jeremiah in 20:7?

The verb *pātāh* ("entice," NRSV; "deceive," NIV; "dupe," NEB/REB, NAB; "seduce," JB) is difficult to translate. It can have the sense of seduce (see Exod 22:16, a virgin is seduced); allure, entice (God allures Israel in the wilderness, Hos 2:14; Prov 1:10); persuade (Prov 25:15); most commonly, deceive (God deceives a prophet, 1 Kgs 22:20-22; Ezek 14:9) or dupe/make a fool of (Job 5:2). Although the verb is somewhat ambiguous in this text, it seems best to link its usage to the other prophetic references.

The next verb (*ḥāzaq*) is also important in thinking through the meaning of the verse; it can have the sense of "overpower" (NRSV; NIV; JB) or, somewhat softer, "be

strong" (cf. NAB; NRSV in 1 Kgs 20:23-25); NEB/REB translates "outwit," hence, *mental* strength. The verb may be used in a military sense (1 Kgs 20:25) or in a physical sense, e.g., for rape (2 Sam 13:14; Deut 22:25-27). It can also refer to the effect of *words spoken* (e.g., 2 Sam 24:4); this is an important sense in view of the use of this verb in v. 9 ("I can[not]"); God's prevailing has fundamentally to do with God's *word*. Whatever the divine means of showing strength, Jeremiah acknowledges that God has "prevailed" (*yākal*). The latter is also used in vv. 10-11 regarding the attempt of Jeremiah's persecutors to "prevail" over him, as well as in God's assurances to Jeremiah in his call that they will not "prevail" (1:18), which Jeremiah may recall in 20:11.

affect interpretation greatly, and no consensus exists regarding their translation. [What Does God Do to Jeremiah in 20:7?]

The initial verb (*pātāh*; NRSV "entice") is used twice in v. 7 and then again in v. 10 with Jeremiah's persecutors as subject. It is difficult to believe that his antagonists are trying to "persuade" him or commit a sexual act (yet the metaphor is multivocal, so such a connotation may occur to readers). The translations "harass" or "take advantage of"[3] could sharpen the point, but "deceive" carries the basic idea well, not least because of its use in other prophetic texts (1 Kgs 22:20-22; Ezek 14:9).

The sense of the verb *ḥāzāq* (NRSV, "overpower") is also difficult. Whatever God did, Jeremiah acknowledges that God has "prevailed" (*yākal*). Inasmuch as Jeremiah uses the same verb for "prevail" in v. 9 (I "can[not]" hold the word in; NRSV), that usage may inform its sense in v. 7, that is, God's *word* has prevailed in Jeremiah's life. This is not a question of God's power in a general way,[4] as if this were a test of sheer strength, which would be no contest (in which case, God would not need to deceive). The power with which Jeremiah has to do is the power of the word that he hears or that wells up within him. The issue for God is to overcome Jeremiah's silence and his resistance to speak the word he has been called to speak and in fact has already often spoken.

It also seems best to consider the meaning of v. 7 in light of v. 10, since *pātāh* and *yākal* ("prevail," NRSV) are also used there. These repeated verbs frame the issue for Jeremiah; he is beset by the word of God on the one hand and beleaguered by persecutors on the other. Jeremiah believes, not that God's *word* is deceitful (see v. 11), but that God has called him into a vocation wherein he feels trapped between an insistent God with an overpowering message and a resistant people (1:17-18 would have given him some sense of this). Generally, he did not fully realize what he was "getting into," and he laments regarding the two basic parties responsible for his personal quandary.

An associated dimension of this accusation of deception immediately follows (vv. 8-9). Jeremiah bemoans his inability to stop speaking the word of God—so compelling is it. He "must" speak it, even the language about violence and destruction. The latter has a double reference: the violence perpetrated by the people, which in turn flows into its violent consequence, that is, the judgment of God (v. 8; this could include his own experience of violence at their hands). Because of this word of God he has become a reproach and is derided. In other words, because he embodies the word of God

McKane on Compulsion

For this theme of compulsion, see 23:9; Amos 3:8; 1 Cor 9:16. Jeremiah finally does not speak against his will, as though he were forced to do so; what he says is really what *he* says and not the word of God in some unmediated way. He remains a genuine human mediator of the word. McKane says it well, the inner conflict of the prophet over whether to speak "is not to be interpreted as rebellion and guilt or reduced to human frailty." Even more, if Jeremiah

> Speaks against his will, his freedom is overwhelmed by a force which he cannot resist, and his utterance is no more his than that of a man whose integrity has been destroyed by violence or torture or drugs . . . . The most that can be made of "compulsion" is that what we are loath to utter and can only utter after overcoming inner resistance is not so subject to the dangers of willfulness, self-assertiveness or self-deception as those utterances which we have a natural inclination to make. The thoughts which are congenial to us and which we are inclined to embrace, or the attitudes which are agreeable with our desire for security are more liable to error than those which force themselves on us because they have a truth which we cannot ultimately evade and to which we must give expression, even if we fear or shrink from the consequences of so speaking.

These sentences are worthy of careful reflection.

William McKane, *A Critical and Exegetical Commentary on Jeremiah* (2 vols.; ICC; Edinburgh: T. & T. Clark, 1986), 474.

---

regarding violence he suffers what the word suffers at the hand of others.

When he resolves not to speak God's word (following REB, v. 9a is a reference to "it," the word of God, rather than "him," NRSV; see Deut 18:19-22) because of all the "guff" he receives, he is not able to maintain that stance. Yet, the word so burns within him that he "cannot" (*yākāl*, as in God's "prevailing" in v. 7) but speak it. He suffers if he speaks and he suffers if he does not, and the God who called him from the womb is ultimately responsible for *both* realities. *Therein lies the essence of the deception* (see **Connections: God and the Deception of Jeremiah**).

Trying to hold back the judgment word of God produces a profound weariness (as in 6:11). Notably, God also experiences such weariness (see 15:6). God is weary from holding back the judgment on an unrepentant people. So Jeremiah, in being unable to hold back the word, is conformed to the very word of God he embodies. His weariness and God's are of one and the same piece; as it is with God, so is it with Jeremiah. Hence, this inability should not be interpreted as a clinical compulsion, but as a theological and vocational one. [McKane on Compulsion] He finally speaks because he comes to the point where he believes that is what he must do. The continuing divine pressure on him to speak words of judgment is real and Jeremiah recognizes that he cannot be true to himself or to his calling by being silent. If it were not for God, he would not be in this predicament. Even more, if it were not for his persecutors, his dilemma would be different.

The most basic personal effect of this divine commission is that Jeremiah has been made to look the fool ("a fool for God"?), a laughingstock to "everyone" (v. 7). His speaking this word means that people ridicule him, subjecting him to rebuke and censure. Their mocking of him for his claim to be speaking a word of God has become a daily experience, indeed "all day long." From their perspective, Jeremiah is a disgrace (v. 8, see v. 18). Moreover (v. 10), they engage in a "whispering campaign," and Jeremiah quotes them twice in v. 10 (see quotation marks in NRSV). They sarcastically repeat his message that "terror is all around" (see v. 3; [Pashur's New Name]; Ps 31:13; alternatively, this expression is Jeremiah's cry *about* his persecutors), when to all external appearances that is not the case (this reflects a time before the fall). They conspire among themselves to "get him." Even his close friends and neighbors are on the watch (vv. 7, 10; see 11:21), for they are in a position to observe him closely, hoping that he will make a misstep so that they can obtain a firmer basis on which to silence him. Indeed, they hope to trick him into making a blunder (see Luke 20:20); then they can get rid of him and his accusing words, making him suffer the very end he has been predicting for them ("revenge"; see also at v. 12).

For all of Jeremiah's complaining about God and the situation into which God has called him, he expresses great confidence that God will provide a "way out" for him (v. 11). His God is a "great warrior" (NRSV) or "mighty champion" (NAB), words normally used of enemies (but of God in Ps 78:65-66); in effect, God will turn the tables on his behalf. As God had doubly promised in his call (see 1:8, 18), and repeated after an earlier lament (15:20-21), God would be with him to deliver him. Though his persecutors fought against him, they would "stumble" rather than he; they would be shamed rather than he. God would prove to be the stronger and would prevail against them rather than they against him. Indeed, he is confident that they will be discredited; great dishonor will be brought upon them and their shame will be remembered through all generations. It is they, not he, who will be a "disgrace" (NRSV, "dishonor") just as they so judged the word of God and the prophet in v. 8 (NRSV, "reproach"). For God to visit them with God's "vengeance" (NIV and most translations; NRSV's "retribution" is too forensic a notion; see at 5:9) has reference to the "revenge" planned by them against Jeremiah ("what goes around comes around").

Verse 12 virtually repeats the words of 11:20; it is often thought to provide an inclusio for Jeremiah's laments. He commits his cause to God, trusting that God will see that his persecutors are judged appropriately (see also 17:18; 18:23). As has been noted in the latter texts, this language is not a personal vendetta, but reveals that his stance toward these unfaithful people now conforms to that of God (see **Connections**, ch. 18). Jeremiah's wrath matches the wrath of God. But he will not personally execute this wrath; he will leave that up to God.

The language of testing (v. 12a; see 17:16) is a personal reflection on Jeremiah's own situation with respect to God. In effect, he moves to the point of responding to his own initial complaint. The negative effects on his life and person wrought by attending faithfully to the call of God constitute a test for him. Testing is inherent to all relationships of consequence (see **Connections**, ch. 17): will those involved remain faithful to the relationship in the face of every circumstance? Jeremiah understands his situation to constitute such a test, but he also proceeds to call upon *God* to be true to the relationship by delivering him from his persecutors.

Then, in v. 13 Jeremiah voices praise to God (and invites exilic *readers* to do the same) in the certainty that God will hear his lament and deliver him from his enemies (see Ps 70); he returns to God's assurance in his call (1:8, 18). The reference to himself as "needy" does not refer to his social status, but to his need of help, falling back on traditional formulations common to the Psalter (e.g., 72:12). [Berrigan on 20:7-18]

Jeremiah's Cry of the Heart, 20:14-18

These verses have occasioned much discussion, and have often been interpreted as a sign of Jeremiah's deep despair. The search for language to describe the speaker has ranged widely, including self-hatred or self-loathing and self-curse. Links with Job 3:3-26 and 10:18-19 have suggested the latter to many scholars. That is, these verses are not addressed to God, and hence should not be considered a prayer; rather, they are self-directed. But in fact Jeremiah does not direct the curses toward *himself*, but to the day of his birth and to the messenger who announced it. A key question for readers: is the word "cursed" a call for his birthday (and the messenger) to be cursed or is it a declaration that they are in fact cursed. The latter seems much more likely.[5]

Berrigan on 20:7-18

Daniel Berrigan's recasting of Jeremiah's last lament is remarkable in the way in which it gathers new images to make it sing once again. But note that he has changed the order of the verses; v. 13 is placed at the end. This move, of course, changes the rhetorical character of the poem, and it now stands more like many a lament in the Psalter. At least the book of Jeremiah does not want to leave it like this for the reader.

Yahweh, you trickster,
with a flick of your finger
you whirl me about—
this way, that, a weather—
vane in your wild weathers,
whim, tornado, mood.

Never shall I countenance
this mad charade of yours!

You wound me, spur my flanks—
I must
under your whip
a cowering beast
neigh, whinny, roar—
"Root up, Tear down!"
On every side
ridicule greets me,
disdain, scorn.

In corners they gather,
like whispering spiders
weaving rumors—
"Malcontent, he sees
through a glass, darkness only."

Friends grown sly,
weave their spells—
"Only wait,
await his downfall!"

My soul beleaguered
whispers;
Peace, poor soul, peace—
let pass this awful
behest of His
in sweet forgetting!

Then
I swear it
your word erupts—
a fire shut in my bones
smolders there, consuming—
I cannot contain, endure it!

Cursed, thrice cursed
be the ill-starred
night of my birth,
a mother's womb my tomb!
Cursed the gladdening word—
"A child is born, a son!"

Good news?
No. A plague—
sorrow, disgrace my lot.

Nevertheless,
You
cloud of unknowing,
of undoing—
I cling to You, fiery pillar cling to You, burn of you
and I sing, I raise
a song against the night;
my Scandal
my Love—
stand with me in the breach!

Daniel Berrigan, *Jeremiah: The World, the Wound of God* (Minneapolis: Fortress, 1999), 86-88.

To curse something/someone is to call down death or destruction on them; it is the opposite of blessing, which is directed toward life, fertility, and well-being. But the day and the messenger lie in the past, irretrievable except to memory; Jeremiah cannot get at them

On the Translation of Verses 14-16

ΑΩ The verbs beginning the two halves of v. 16 are often translated as jussives ["let..."], following the LXX rather than the Hebrew. They are probably better translated as simple future [NEB], present, or even past (see William Holladay, *Jeremiah 1* [Philadelphia: Fortress, 1986], 560; Peter C. Craigie, Page Kelley, and Joel F. Drinkard Jr. *Jeremiah 1–25* [WBC 26; Dallas: Word Books, 1991], 278). As for the last line in v. 14, it can be translated, "it could never be blessed," or similar. These translations would support the understanding that Jeremiah's use of the word "cursed" (in vv. 14-15) is a declaration, not a petition or desire.

with a retroactive curse. But, as a *personal* declaration that these realities are in fact cursed, this is a sharp statement of what Jeremiah believes their (*ongoing*) status to have been. [The Translation of Verses 14-16] As such, these realities associated with his birth signify to him that, in view of God's choosing him in the womb (about which he could do nothing), he has personally embodied death and destruction from that point on (see 1:5). This is who he is and it is not pretty! He then expresses the desire that he would have been killed in the womb (v. 17) so as not to have *become* what he became in the womb and has been since he came forth from the womb (v. 18). It is, in essence, a wish that he had not become a prophet, or at least a prophet called to speak this kind of word; but because he was chosen from the womb, his cry becomes a more global wish that he had not been born at all.

Verses 14-18 are not specifically addressed to God (but neither is 15:10-11), and there is no petition here (if curse is interpreted as above). Yet, if vv. 7-18 belong together, the address to God is probably implicit. A sharp cry in the night ending in a sharp question is one way of thinking about the lament. As noted, laments could end with deep questioning even after statements of trust and confidence (notably, there is no curse of God in this lament, see Job 2:9) (see **Connections: A Crisis of Faith or Vocation?**).

The wish that he would not have been born but killed in the womb (see 15:10 for related motifs) is not a reference to abortion but to his becoming a dead fetus in his mother's womb ("my grave"), a fetus which his mother would have carried to her grave. Inasmuch as he was called from the womb (1:5, a possible *inclusio* with this chapter), this strongly expressed language is, in effect, a fervent wish that he had not been called to this kind of vocation and to be put in this position.

Even more, Jeremiah *declares as cursed* (see above) the man who delivered what would have been good and joyful news about the birth of a son to his father rather than killing him in the womb (vv. 15-17). Most commentators consider the phrase, "like the cities that the Lord overthrew" to be a reference to Sodom and Gomorrah, also the object of divine judgment (see Gen 19:25). Yet, these cities are *named* elsewhere in Jeremiah (23:14; 49:18; 50:40) and the phrase, "without pity," is not used of those cities. Exilic readers (at least) would probably see in this a reference to the cities of *Judah* that God overthrew without pity (v. 16a; for the pitiless theme, see 4:28; 16:7; 13:14; 21:14; for Babylon, see Isa 13:19). They would have remembered that during that time they had voiced the "outcry" and heard the "alarm" (see 4:19; 11:11; 18:22).

But why would this messenger be singled out for such a fate? The role of the messenger has been linked to other reports of bad news (e.g., 6:22-26; 30:5-6; 49:23; 50:43) to which Jeremiah or others respond in anguish. The messenger who brought the news about Jeremiah's birth announced it as good news, but in fact Jeremiah's birth was not good news, for himself, his family, or his community. And so that man, who should have brought bad news, will *himself* be caught up in the devastation that Jeremiah announces. If he had instead killed Jeremiah in the womb he would have saved not only himself but also an entire people from death and destruction. Alternatively, one could consider the subject of the first line of v. 17 to be, not the messenger, but indefinite and translate something like REB, "since death did not claim me before birth."[6]

Jeremiah's final question encapsulates the basic point of the prior verses (the "why?" questions of Gen 25:2; 27:46 have been noted; the questions in Lam 5:20-22 are important). Why did he come forth from the womb to be a prophet and suffer so? From the womb he has been the embodiment of the God's word, a word decisively shaped by the message of sword, famine, and death. As a consequence he has had to live a life of great hardship and anguish (cf. Baruch in 45:3), having to spend every day dishonored by his compatriots and friends (see his petition regarding "shame" in 17:18). Why?! [Is God Silent?]

Is God Silent?

The issue of the apparent lack of a divine response to vv. 14-18 is often noted. But does God respond with silence? As for the *textual* Jeremiah (we do not know about the experience of the *actual* Jeremiah), it is important to note that God does *not* respond with silence. Jeremiah speaks his words of complaint and curse, and God is right there with another word to speak (21:1). It is not a word of commiseration or assurance, as many readers might like, but it is, in effect, a word to continue doing what he has been called to do (not unlike 12:5-6; 15:19-20). As if to provide an immediate illustration of Jeremiah's point in 20:8-9, God insists that he keep speaking no matter how he feels. At least from the text's perspective, God does not allow Jeremiah to linger in his despair; God keeps the pressure on. Such is the life of a prophet.

CONNECTIONS

God and the Deception of Jeremiah

Wherein does God's deception of Jeremiah lie? It is not made entirely clear. It surely has something to do with his call, but in what sense? Some think that Jeremiah's sense of being deceived relates to the lack of fulfillment of his prophecies of doom and the derision to which he was subjected because of that. God has failed to deliver on the word he was called to proclaim. Yet, while Jeremiah may well be impatient for the word to be fulfilled (see 17:14-18; 18:19-23), the timing issue is not specifically raised and we cannot be certain when this outburst was forthcoming. Others think the deception is related to the absence of a positive response from the people; he expected that his word would bring about repentance, and it did not.[7] Yet, the unrelenting way in which Jeremiah announces that judgment will be forthcoming, and the stubbornness of the people which is often a part of his indictment, suggests that he was not naïve in this regard. The expression of personal failure seems at best to be on the edge of his laments; the issue seems to be more related to his "success" in saying what had to be said.

Another direction for thinking about the deception is preferable, namely, his sense of entrapment between an overpowering word from an insistent God and a stubborn and derisive people. He has been deceived and overpowered by God (v. 7) and the people are trying to do the same thing to him (v. 10). As has been pointed out regarding this lament, there is an interweaving of Jeremiah's focus on God (vv. 7a, 8a, 9) and on his persecutors (vv. 7b, 8b, 12).[8] At the same time, there appears to be a difference in his approach to the "you" and the "them." Though God is sharply addressed, it is doubtful that the language is properly designated as accusatory (as it usually is). God duped him, but he immediately recognizes that action for what it was and he has done what he was called to do in the full knowledge of the deception. *Deception recognized* changes the equation. Jeremiah complains that he was deceived but he also acknowledges that that divine action was in the service of a compelling truth; he never intimates that God's word was a false word. God's call has *overpowered* him, but at the same time he recognizes (several times) the *overpowering* truth of the word that God has called him to speak.

And so Jeremiah's complaint does not stay focused on God; it immediately (and again and again) moves to the response that God's word has engendered (v. 7b). God's call has placed him directly in the line of fire and he finds that to be oppressive, but he recognizes that this would not be the case if it were not for his antagonists' failure to acknowledge the truth of the word he speaks. His real complaints are about his persecutors, and his *only* petition relates to them (v. 12). He does not ask God to take the call back, and expresses confidence that God will deliver him (vv. 11-13; this expressed confidence is a move beyond the accusation of deception in 15:18 and picks up the assuring language of God's response in 15:20-21). Jeremiah complains about God duping him and prevailing over him, but he finally is concerned more about his antagonist's duping him and prevailing over him and the word he is called to speak (vv. 10-11). His last sharp complaint in vv. 14-18 expresses in strong terms a wish that he had not been placed in this position; but there is not a hint of concern that the word that God has called him to speak is false. Jeremiah's anguish is as severe as it is because he recognizes the *truth* of the word he has spoken and the conflict it has engendered.

That the language of deception is used (approvingly) for God in other prophetic texts (noted above) means that Jeremiah is not being innovative, let alone rebellious or blasphemous. In view of this prophetic tradition, to use this verb as evidence for Jeremiah accusing God "of having broken the relation which he had initiated" is unacceptable.[9] Or, to claim that Jeremiah had a "love-hate relation" with God is much too global in its assessment.[10] People with deep and genuine faith can use accusatory language—if that's what this is—in prayer to God (e.g., Ps 44:22-23) and raise sharp questions with God (e.g., Gen 18:25). This is the type of honest interaction that God encourages in relationships, and the text often gives evidence for this kind of relationship with Jeremiah. [Genre and Theological Formulation]

Genre and Theological Formulation

Recognition of genre (and "point of view") is important in any theological assessment of this material. Jeremiah is expressing with some exasperation what this experience with God (and his persecutors) has felt like to him. It seems unlikely that he is giving a carefully reasoned statement; yet, this candid assessment of his experience carries its own weight and conveys its own truthfulness. He stands in the middle between these two parties that have quite different agendas, of course, and he feels squeezed by this experience. God's commission is the primary reality for him; it is God's word that has set all of these difficulties into motion in the first place, and Jeremiah's exasperated cry conveys this in its own way. At the same time, if the people had listened and not made life so difficult for him! It is impossible to know whether others (or God) would have theologically assessed the interaction in terms comparable to those Jeremiah expresses. At the least, interpreters should be careful to assess what difference it makes that this is a lament and not a carefully crafted theological statement. What prayers say about God in their screams in the night they may not want integrated into a creedal statement. Yet, that such language is used to address God directly does say something very important about the nature of the relationship between them, which in turn should affect how one speaks of God more generally.

A Crisis of Faith or Vocation?

Keeping vv. 14-18 together with what precedes, and adopting the above sense of curse, probably makes Jeremiah somewhat less despairing than is commonly thought and makes the issue less a psychological problem. Words like self-pity and self-hatred do not capture the point (as an initial reading might suggest). If this cry is *vocationally* oriented, then it is less that his life has no value, than that his life as prophet is so caught between God and people that it has not been worth the trouble. This is *not* a crisis of faith in the sense that if he had a stronger faith in God he would not go through such times. Persons of rich faith in God and sharp insight often have such moments, as a survey of the lives of faithful people through the centuries will show. God is part of the problem, but that is commonly voiced in the Old Testament.

This is a crisis of vocation. It is an issue for Jeremiah of having to *be(!)* a certain kind of person, namely, a prophet. Jeremiah has expressed certainty that God would deliver him from his persecutors, but he still feels squeezed between an insistent God with an overpowering word and a resistant people with a derisive word. He has had to voice violence and destruction and he has had to deal with a people who have done violence to him for doing just that. He is caught in the middle—the story of many a prophet and preacher. This focus on the particular obligations of his call links vv. 7-20 together. Readers are left with an image of a prophet in anguish, but the point for exilic (and other) readers is not to arouse sympathy for the prophet (poor Jeremiah!) but repentance at what human recalcitrance and violent words can do (see introduction above).

NOTES

[1] See Kathleen O'Connor, *The Confessions of Jeremiah*; D. J. A. Clines and D. Gunn, "Form, Occasion, and Redaction in Jeremiah 20," *ZAW* 88 (1976): 390-409.

[2] See J. G. Janzen, "Jeremiah 20:7-18," *Interpretation* 37 (1983): 179-83.

[3] See Walter Brueggemann, *A Commentary on Jeremiah: Exile and Homecoming* (Grand Rapids: Eerdmans, 1998), 181.

[4] So ibid. and William Holladay, *Jeremiah 1* (Philadelphia: Fortress, 1986), 553, "brute force."

[5] See Holladay, ibid., 560-61.

[6] See William McKane, *A Critical and Exegetical Commentary on Jeremiah* (2 vols.; ICC; Edinburgh: T. & T. Clark, 1986), 488.

[7] So Ronald E. Clements, *Jeremiah* (IBC; Atlanta: John Knox, 1988), 122.

[8] Clines and Gunn, 390-409.

[9] Holladay, *Jeremiah 1,* 522.

[10] Ibid., 559.

ORACLES TO KINGS AND PEOPLE

21:1-14

Indictment of Israel's Leadership, 21:1–23:40

Jeremiah 21–24 is commonly considered an appendix to the previous chapters. It consists of prose pieces and poetic oracles regarding several Davidic kings (and the dynasty) and Jerusalem, the religious and political capital of the Davidic kingdom (21:1–23:8), followed by materials focused on the (false) prophets (23:9-40). Together these sections are a crushing indictment of Israel's leadership during this tumultuous time. At the same time, neither God nor Jeremiah is represented as opposed to the Davidic line in principle (see 23:1-6; 33:14-26), any more than they are antagonistic to prophets as such.

Jeremiah 21 is distinguished from what precedes by its specific references to kings (and others) and to events associated with the fall of Jerusalem (anticipated by 20:1-6 and its first specific reference to Babylon; King Nebuchadrezzar is first mentioned in 21:2). [Nebuchadrezzar] Earlier chapters were undated; now specific names and events come to the fore and the historical context is more clearly visible. So, for example, the first text (21:1-7) is dated during the siege of Jerusalem by the Babylonians in 588–587 BC. This kind of specificity will be common in subsequent chapters. At the same time, these texts are not placed in chronological order (cf. 21:1; 24:1; 25:1). This combination of dated and undated materials accomplishes two things; it grounds the ministry of Jeremiah in a particular historical period but at the same time opens up the material to more general usage and application.

In the sections that follow the introductory segment (21:1-7), general oracles about Jerusalem and its people (21:8-10; 22:8-9, 20-23; possibly 21:13-14) are interwoven with those concerning the Davidic kingship more generally (21:11–22:7). These segments in turn introduce oracles against specific kings in chronological order (22:10-30): Jehoahaz or Shallum (22:10-12); Jehoiakim (22:13-19); Jehoiachin or Coniah (22:24-30). That the initial segment (21:1-7) focuses on the last king, Zedekiah, serves to complete the list of the last kings of Israel. Oracles of promise regarding the Davidic line and the gathering of the exiles conclude the oracles regarding kingship (23:1-8).

Nebuchadrezzar

Nebuchadrezzar II was king of Babylon from 605 to 562 BC and was the "Napoleon" of his time in that part of the world. He was also famous for his various building projects in Babylon itself and elsewhere (the Hanging Gardens are commonly thought to be one such project). A variant spelling of his name (Nebuchadnezzar) occurs elsewhere (e.g., 27:6-20; 28:11; 29:3). His Akkadian name means, "May Nabu [a Babylonian deity] protect the boundary [or my son]." He gained control of his larger world by defeating Pharaoh Neco of Egypt (and his allies) at Carchemish in 605 BC (referred to in Jer 46:2). Following up that victory, he conquered the Philistine city of Ashkelon in 604 BC (probably referenced in Jer 47:5-7). He first conquered Jerusalem in 597 BC (on March 16 according to the Babylonian Chronicle), removed King Jehoiachin of Judah who had reigned for only three months (see 2 Kgs 24:17), exacted tribute, and placed his brother Zedekiah on the throne. When Zedekiah rebelled, Nebuchadrezzar came against Jerusalem and after a siege of one and one-half years destroyed it in 587 BC (see 39:1-10; 52:4-16).

The Hanging Gardens of Babylon—one of the seven ancient wonders of the world—were built by King Nebuchadnezzar II for his homesick wife, Amyitis, in the late seventh century BC. The gardens are speculated to have been 100 to 400 feet wide, 150 to 400 feet long, and at least 80 feet high. This artificial mound created on the plains of Mesopotamia, though absent from mention in Scriptures, stood as a testament to the power and decadence of the Babylonian regime, at least as much as the Trade Center Towers of New York exemplify(ied) American capitalistic achievement.

unmuseum.mus.pa.us/hangg.htm. 1/7/02. Lee Krystek, 1998.

Maarten van Heemskerck. *The Hanging Gardens of Babylon.* 16th C. Brown ink on paper. Louvre. Paris, France. (Credit: Réunion des Musées Nationaux/Art Resource, NY)

COMMENTARY

Jeremiah 21:1-10 is usually separated from 21:11–23:8. Yet, it seems best to honor the placement of the oracle to Zedekiah (21:1-7) as the lens through which the other oracles regarding kings and kingship are to be interpreted. This segment shows that royal strategies, however clothed in traditional religious expressions (21:2), are doomed to failure; the devastation of Jerusalem by Babylon under Nebuchadrezzar is certain. The segment 20:1-6, where Jeremiah is persecuted by Pashhur, is a mirror image of 21:1-7 (with its reference to another Pashhur); here the tables are turned and officials are coming to *Jeremiah* for counsel!

This chapter consists of three oracles to King Zedekiah (vv. 1-7), the people of Jerusalem (vv. 8-10), and "the house of the king of Judah" (vv. 11-14). Whatever the origins of these texts, they are now tied together. In this reading, vv. 1-7 highlight the royal appeals that are doomed to failure; vv. 8-10 provide the basic options the people have in the face of certain devastation; vv. 11-14 focus on the royal house (and the associated Zion theology) and its utter failure to uphold the royal ideal.

The original setting of these oracles may be 588–587 BC, after Zedekiah had rebelled against Babylonian rule. [Zedekiah] Some scholars have seen parallels between this text and the events reported in 52:4-16. Whatever the setting, the concern of the present text is to recall for exilic readers the nature of God's involvement during the years just before the destruction of Jerusalem. The oracles demonstrate that, though divine judgment on Israel was inevitable at this late stage (both in history and in the book), God remained concerned about a "way of life" (v. 8) for the people of God.

Zedekiah

Zedekiah, a son of King Josiah (see at 3:6) and member of the Davidic line, reigned from 597 to 587 BC. He was placed on the throne by King Nebuchadrezzar after the subjugation of Jerusalem in 597 BC and the first exile of the populace to Babylon. Zedekiah functioned subserviently as Nebuchadrezzar's puppet for nearly a decade. Finally, however, in spite of repeated warnings from Jeremiah, Zedekiah rebelled against Babylonian rule in 588 BC. This shortsighted action led to the destruction of Jerusalem in 587 BC and the second exile of Judeans to Babylon. Zedekiah was blinded by Nebuchadrezzar and taken into exile.

Oracles against Zedekiah and Jerusalem, 21:1-10

Verses 1-2 report the inquiry that Zedekiah brings to Jeremiah through two emissaries, the royal prince Pashhur and the priest Zephaniah. [Pashhur and Zephaniah] These key leaders from both political and religious spheres are called upon to make this appeal. Apparently they also have differing sympathies with respect to Jeremiah's activity. Zedekiah makes such an inquiry three other times in the book, once through a delegation that includes Zephaniah again (37:3-10) and twice on his own (37:17-21; 38:14-28; see Jeremiah's confrontation of Zedekiah in 34:1-7). For kings to "inquire of the LORD" is a common tradition in Israel (see, e.g., 1 Kgs 22:5). Such an inquiry entails the consultation of

Pashhur and Zephaniah

Pashhur is identified as the son of Malchiah, otherwise mentioned as a prince (possibly a son of Zedekiah) who owned the cistern in which Jeremiah was incarcerated for a time (38:6). Pashhur, not to be confused with the temple official of 20:1-6, is a royal prince and is identified as an opponent of Jeremiah in 38:1-4. One of his descendants was a priest in the time of Nehemiah (Neh 11:12).

The priest Zephaniah, identified as the son of Maaseiah (see 35:4; 37:3), is otherwise known from 29:24-32; 37:3; 52:24-27. During the Babylonian siege of 597 BC he was rebuked by the prophet Shemaiah for not opposing Jeremiah's prophecy regarding the length of the exile (see 29:24-32). He (along with others) was executed by Nebuchadrezzar himself at Riblah after the fall of Jerusalem (587 BC; see 52:24-27).

God's prophet for a word from God regarding a crisis; Jeremiah earlier condemns the kings for not so inquiring (10:21).

In the face of the Babylonian invasion, Zedekiah asks Jeremiah to inquire whether God might act to deliver Israel from this threat "as he has often done" on behalf of Israel in the past (v. 2). Zedekiah appeals to the tradition of God's "wonderful deeds," or "mighty acts," such as the exodus and land settlement (see Exod 3:20; Ps 26:7). The "perhaps" shows some theological sophistication, as in the "who knows?" of David (2 Sam 12:22), Joel 2:14, and Jonah 3:9. Yet, while it is difficult to assess sincerity, it is likely that they seek to use Jeremiah for their own advantage. [The Motivations of Israel's Leadership]

God's reply to this royal appeal is sharply negative (vv. 3-7). Jeremiah is to announce this divine decision directly to the king, using traditional language from the very "mighty acts" tradition that Zedekiah cited. In stark contrast to God's oft-cited actions on behalf of Israel in the past, including the "holy wars" in Israel's early years, in this war God will take the side of the *Babylonians* (=Chaldeans). God will be *against* Israel this time, not for Israel (see **Connections: Was Jeremiah Pro-Babylonian?**).

In boomerang fashion, God will turn Israel's own weapons back on Jerusalem itself instead of directing them toward the approaching Babylonian armies, who in turn shall occupy the city (v. 4). In other words, Israel with its weapons will be in retreat, absolutely ineffective against the Babylonians. In fact, they will be so ineffective that it will seem like Israel is fighting against itself "together" with the Babylonians! Though ambiguous, the last line in v. 4 may mean that both Israel's weapons and Babylon's armies will "occupy" the city. This, of course, is precisely the story of Israel's history. Israel has set itself up for the fall; by virtue of its infidelity, Israel has become an active agent in it own destruction (see **Connections: A Religion against Itself**).

But God is also an active agent in this matter (vv. 5-7). Israel not only has to battle against the effects of its own wickedness and the Babylonian armies, it also has to contend with God. Notably, the metaphors used to speak of God battling *against* Israel are those commonly used in the tradition for God's acts on behalf of Israel. Hence, just as God fought for Israel against the Egyptians (e.g., Exod 14:14, 25; Josh 10:14) so now God will "fight" (*lāḥam*) against Israel. *Israel* is now the enemy of God (see Lam 2:4-5; Isa

---

The Motivations of Israel's Leadership

Daniel Berrigan sees only ulterior motives in Zedekiah's inquiry, and his language is worth pondering. "The episode reeks with the self-interest of altitudinous noses, sniffing the winds of chance. Which is to say, now and again it accrues to the advantage of those in power to make use of the likes of Jeremiah . . . . Hardly to be thought of single mind, or devoted to the words of the prophet or the God he invokes, such eminences seek to bend the prophet to their advantage."

Daniel Berrigan, *Jeremiah: The World, the Wound of God* (Minneapolis: Fortress, 1999), 90.

63:10)! Just as God has used "outstretched hand and mighty arm" for Israel (see 32:21; Deut 26:8), so now they will be used against Israel. Just as God struck down the Egyptians (Exod 12:12-13, 29) so now God will "strike" (*nākah*) the Israelites (v. 6; as Jeremiah had requested in 18:21!). God will strike them with a "pestilence" such as Egypt experienced (see 16:4; see Exod 9:15; about which Israel was warned, see Lev 26:25; Deut 28:21). Note also that both human beings and animals are adversely affected by this invasion (v. 6; see 7:20; 12:1-11). The piling up of words for anger in v. 5 is remarkable: anger, fury, great wrath (similarly 31:37; Deut 29:28; see **Connections**, ch. 4). The usage of three words strung together is also characteristic of four groups of words in v. 7. [A Reversal of the Exodus]

In v. 7 a specific, if repetitive word is directed to King Zedekiah himself, his officials, and the survivors of the events described in v. 6 (see 24:8-10). They will be given into the hands of others, also named in three ways: King Nebuchadrezzar, their enemies, and those who have sought to kill them. It is an especially sharp blow that the Davidic king, about whom God has made such key promises (see 2 Sam 7:14-16), will be taken into exile (texts such as Psalm 89 struggle theologically with this reality). Jeremiah will assure exilic readers in no uncertain terms that God will not renege on these promises (e.g., 23:1-6; 30:9; 33:14-26).

> **A Reversal of the Exodus**
>
> The total effect of this "traditional" rhetoric in vv. 5-6 is that God's actions in the fall of Jerusalem are understood to reverse the divine actions in Egypt and the settlement in the land (see also 22:7). Israel is still the people of God, but it is thrown back into its pre-exodus days, in effect, and thus stands in need of a new exodus and land settlement. Therefore, these disastrous events have created the need for a new confession at the time when God's new constitutive acts occur, which God says are surely coming to pass (see at 16:14-16 = 23:7-8).

The last sentence of v. 7 summarizes the actions of Nebuchadrezzar, the mediator of divine judgment, against Israel. For striking down the Israelites, three terms are used that were earlier ascribed to God (see at 13:14): he will not pity or spare or have compassion. That such startling language is used for both God and Nebuchadrezzar is testimony to God's use of others to mediate the divine will and work (on mediation, see **Connections** in chs. 13, 19; **Introduction**). Verse 7 seems to announce the annihilation of everyone, but that is certainly a rhetorical convention (strategy?) in view of other texts (including vv. 8-10) and the experience of those who wrote and read these words. The fate of Zedekiah probably cannot finally be reconciled with that presented in 34:2-7 or 39:4-7 (52:4-11).

Verses 8-10 turn from the king to the entire community. God commissions Jeremiah to address the *people* of Israel. Zedekiah seems to be excluded, yet in 38:17-18 a comparable offer is made

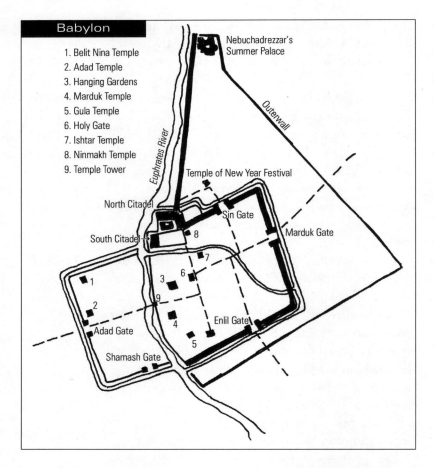

to him. The time and place of these verses are not specified (the prior verses suggest the time of Zedekiah) but the fall of Jerusalem is certain. God sets a choice before the people in language found elsewhere in Deuteronomy 30:15, 19 (cf. Prov 4:10-19), "I am setting before you the way of life and the way of death." Unlike the Deuteronomy passage, however, the issue here is not obedience to basic covenant requirements or choosing whether to remain a member of the people of God (cf. Josh 24:15). This "either-or" formula (see also 22:1-5) presents the people with these stark options: stay in the city and die; leave the city to surrender to Babylon and live (also in 38:2). That these options are not understood in an absolutistic sense is shown by 39:9-10 and 52:12-16, where this distinction is not precisely followed.

The people who surrender will not have any spoils ("prize") as a result of such an action, except their own lives (see 38:2; 39:18; 45:5). Even if it means surrendering their freedom to the Babylonians (again, in a kind of reverse exodus), to have life is no little prize! Even in the midst of great judgment, when God has set his face against Jerusalem for disaster (*rāʿāh*; NRSV, "evil") rather than goodness or blessing, God puts a "way of life" before this people. Even when it is clear that the city will be given into the hands of Babylon to burn and destroy, God remains concerned about this people's future. This would be a particularly important word for the exiles to hear. Even in the midst of death God wants life for as many of these people as possible. The destruction of Jerusalem does not mean the end of God's purposes in and through Israel.

In offering these options to Israel, God takes sides in this conflict. In this text and several others (e.g., 27:1-5; 38:17-18), God's will for Israel is *surrender* to the Babylonians rather than resistance and the resultant devastation. Because Jeremiah voices this conviction, he is considered a traitor by some and his life is threatened (see 37:11-15). These treasonous-sounding words are no doubt one key factor behind the energetic efforts of his persecutors to put him away (see **Connections: Was Jeremiah Pro-Babylonian?**).

General Oracles against King and City, 21:11-14

While vv. 8-10 are to be addressed to the people, vv. 11-14 are to be addressed to the "house" (=dynasty) of the king of Judah (cf. 23:9, "concerning the prophets"). These verses, with their concern for justice, are often thought to introduce the following oracles about the kingship (22:1-30). With their royal focus they also look back to vv. 1-7 and the references to judgment by fire (vv. 12, 14) recall vv. 8-10.

In context the audience for this oracle is probably thought to be Zedekiah. Yet, because the oracle is generalized in its address, all Davidic kings come up for review. In view of this generalized address, it is likely that no escape from the threatened judgment is envisaged (or in 22:1-5). Rather, these options represent those that kings (indeed all Israelites, Exod 22:23-24) have had through the years. Verse 12 sets the principle in place: Execute justice. The considerations regarding the kings that now follow illustrate how that principle has been violated (see 22:3, 13-17). This same theme will provide the basic charge for the ideal king of the future (23:5-6).

Though v. 12 is commonly separated out from vv. 13-14, both segments have to do with the kings of the house of David and the royal city of Jerusalem. Verse 12 is parallel to vv. 13-14 in other respects. Both segments end with a statement about Israel's evil doings as the cause for the disaster and speak of the wrath of God in terms of fire (see v. 10; 4:4). Verse 12a is linked to v. 13b; the former charges the kings to execute justice and the latter constitutes a (contested) claim that their city is inviolable regardless of what they do. As it turns out, the city is not safe from either Babylon or God.

Verse 12 is a charge and a warning to any and all kings of the house of David. This charge, presented in apodictic or unconditional form, is stated initially in terms of general principle—pursue ("act with") justice—and moves to a particular illustration (see **Connections: The Practice of Justice and Going beyond the Law**). This central concern for the practice of justice is part and parcel of God's charge to the Davidic dynasty from the beginning (see, e.g., Pss 72; 101) as it is of God's Law (e.g., Exod 22:21-28). The import of the king ruling justly is related to order in the social sphere, which in turn affects order in the cosmic sphere (hence, the adverse cosmic effects throughout Jeremiah, e.g., 4:23-26; 9:10; 12:4-13). The absence of justice issues in God's wrath, imaged in terms of an unquenchable fire (see at 4:4). God's wrath is impersonally conceived as a fire breaking out, burning uncontrollably, and devouring everything in its path (see **Introduction**).

The call to execute justice "in the morning" (v. 12a) may refer generally to the haste or regularity with which justice is pursued and, by implication, to the pursuit of this charge as the focus for a typical royal day. Justice is not something to be handled on the side or only late in the day. This text is not satisfied with a statement of principle, but moves quickly to the particular (v. 12b; see 22:3), namely, to see to justice for those who have been oppressed and are the victims of economic injustice.

Verse 13 assumes that justice has not been practiced, for God is "against" the kings of Judah (on God's being "against," see also v. 5; 23:30-32; 50:31; 51:25). The addressee (feminine singular) is Jerusalem, but the focus remains on the kings through metonymy. [Two Ironic Metonyms for the King] The royal self-deception is further specified in the quotation (v. 13b). The kings (the populace would follow) thought that no enemy could be successful against them and enter their place of refuge. But such a misplaced confidence forgets that the threat may come from a God who is "against"

Two Ironic Metonyms for the King

AΩ The two addresses used in v. 13a have as much reference to the king as to the city (cf. the White House as a metonym for the president). And so the "inhabitant [or, one enthroned] of/over the valley," while literally a reference to the city (with its palace complex) surrounded by valleys, actually addresses the kings in their status as head of state. Though the "rock [or plateau] of the plain" is nowhere else applied to Jerusalem, it would be an appropriate characterization; it would be another metonym for the king as one who, to all appearances, is as invulnerable as the city was thought to be. The terms of address reveal a deep irony on God's part, perhaps even derision or sarcasm. These images depict what the kings think they are and the names by which they are called, but they deceive themselves; only in God can security be found. Israel's God cannot and will not be subsumed under a nationalistic banner of "eternal security" with a religious patina.

them. Only God can be considered the enthroned one (see Isa 37:16); only God can be considered the Rock (see Deut 32:18).

If justice is not practiced, the consequences will be devastating (v. 12b; 14b). Once again, it is important to discern the relationship between human wickedness and the wrath of God. The key reason for these devastating events is placed squarely on Israel's "(evil) doings" (vv. 12, 14; "your" is plural; see at 4:4). As commonly in Jeremiah (see **Introduction**), these disastrous events grow out of evil deeds; the judgment is "the fruit of your doings." God does not introduce anything new into the situation; at most, God will provide the spark needed to set the royal buildings and the surrounding city ablaze (v. 14b; the "forest" may refer to the palace made from the cedars of Lebanon, 1 Kgs 7:2; 10:17, 21; Isa 22:8). God is already "against" them (see v. 5; 23:30; 50:31; 51:25) and will mediate the effects of the king's wickedness on the entire people.

CONNECTIONS

Was Jeremiah Pro-Babylonian?

Notably, God has a will with respect to socio-political situations such as the one faced by Israel, and Jeremiah risks speaking and acting in view of this divine will. His conflict with other prophets, priests, and royal officials fundamentally has to do with his discernment of the will of God for the "Babylonian question."

Jeremiah's stance toward Babylon has often been considered problematic. Is he pro-Babylonian? Yes and no. He was certainly regarded as a traitor by some Israelites (see 37:11-21; 38:14-28) and the Babylonians do give him royal treatment after the fall of Jerusalem (39:11-14; 40:1-6). He is pro-Babylonian in the sense that he believes that God is mediating judgment in and through their armies; indeed, Nebuchadrezzar is God's servant (25:9; 27:6). He is pro-Babylonian in the sense that he counsels people to surrender to the invader, for the fall of Jerusalem is certain and this is the only way they can save their lives. In effect Jeremiah issues a call for them to recognize themselves as the recipients of God's judgment and to submit to that future. But it is also to recognize that judgment is not divinely intended to be the full end of the people. God wants to save lives in the midst of judgment (an important word for exiles to hear). Jeremiah is also pro-Babylonian in the sense that he will counsel the exiles to seek the welfare of the

God, Church, and State

The sharp separation between church and state in American society has often obscured God's connection with the "state side" of our life together. Most basically, God's creational work has provided for structures of various sorts—political, economic, social, legal—to order the life of society. But God does not simply provide for these structures and then let them run on their own. God continues to be at work in and through (and beyond!) persons charged with the development of public policies and with their administration, not least with the gift of wisdom (see 1 Kgs 3:9-12, 28). At the same time, because God will not micromanage their work, how such individuals draw on that wisdom and make use of it will make a difference as to how God's ordering of society is promoted and advanced for life-giving purposes.

Babylonians (see 29:5-7). Yet, he chooses to stay in the land (40:1-6; 42:7-22).

But Jeremiah is not pro-Babylonian if that means that he will be on Babylon's side come what may. And so, when the Babylonians overreach and exceed the divine mandate, Jeremiah will proclaim God's judgment on the Babylonians (25:12-14; 50-51). Hence, the nature of the situation shapes Jeremiah's particular word about Babylon (cf. the comparable relationship to Assyria on the part of Isaiah, e.g., Isa 10:5-19).

Generally, these activities of Jeremiah show that there is an explicit and direct link between the public world and God's purposes. God is engaged on behalf of those purposes in every sphere of life, and not just its spiritual and religious dimensions. God will be at work in and through these "secular" structures and their related personnel on behalf of those purposes, which encompass the entire creation. [God, Church, and State]

A Religion against Itself

God's repeated word of being "against" Israel, including specific leaders, is remarkable for what it says about God's relationship to God's own elect people. This relationship is of such a nature that God will not inevitably support the Israelites in what they do and say. In fact, in view of the insight Israel has received into God's will and ways, God will hold them to a higher standard. In the words of Amos 3:2, "You only have I known of all the families of the earth; *therefore* (!) I will visit your iniquities upon you." God will be faithful, but that faithfulness may well manifest itself in being against those whom God loves.

This capacity to be a "religion against itself" sets Israel's theological perspective into a quite uncommon mode in the history of the world's religions, including Christian churches and movements.

The tendency on the part of such institutions is to be protective of the "insiders" and to be suspicious of and rail against the "outsiders," those who do not belong to the particular community or those who are critical of its words and ways. One's suspicions should be raised if a leader or group seldom or never speaks or acts in ways that stand "against" their own "insiders." One's suspicions should be raised if the critical or evaluative work of a community is always directed against "others," often those who think or act differently. One's suspicions should be raised if the God of whom such persons speak is never "in your face"; then sharp questions need to be raised about the adequacy of that understanding of God. Issues do need to be raised regarding *how best* to be God's spokesperson "against" one's own religious community, but this "how" is a matter of strategy and not of fundamental stance or commitment.

Whether Jeremiah can be a model for such critical work in a community is still another issue. Discernment of the needs of the situation is crucial in such decision-making, and Jeremiah's *various* specific situations will not always, perhaps not even often, be our own. But Jeremiah is a profound witness to the fact that God is not only at work "for us"; God is also at work "against us." The role of the leader (especially) is to discern those areas of "divine againstness" in our communal and individual life and to speak boldly about them, even if it means speaking into the teeth of a storm.

The Practice of Justice and Going beyond the Law

While justice can often pertain to fairness in the legal sphere, its more general sense is to act with uprightness and integrity in all dealings with others, especially the less advantaged (e.g., strangers, widows, orphans). Basic to that principle is that it is insufficient to be upright in tending to the details of torah; the practice of justice will often mean going beyond the Law. The call to care for the less advantaged, for example, will often mean acting toward others in compassionate ways that find no specification in any body of law (even Israel's).

If the charge were left at the level of general principle ("execute justice"), it would be all too easy to define justice on one's own terms and to claim that it has been done. Issues of accountability have to be addressed with respect to *specific* situations as well. The particular kind of situation cited in v. 12b is understood both in terms of common thieves and more sophisticated "economic theft," that is, the exploitation of the less advantaged through inadequate wages or land-grabbing. This particular type of oppression should not be understood to *define* justice, but to illustrate what justice would look like in a specific type of circumstance (23:3, 15-16 will give further illustrations). Functioning as an illustration, this particular instance opens up the practice of justice to unlimited application, and faithfulness to the Law will often mean going beyond specific directions given by the Law.

Among all the commandments that might have been cited in these oracles against the kings, repeatedly choosing those that have to do with the exercise of abusive power against the weak and needy is remarkable. We know all too well how easy it is for people in power (and those who evaluate them!) to focus on other concerns and other commandments, and to neglect the needs of the less fortunate among us. These people are of particular concern to God, as is especially evident in the exodus events, but certainly not only in that context. Because the needs of the less fortunate are God's concern they are a prophetic concern and should also be that of the people of God in any age. But in order to do justice to these specific concerns we need to be imaginative in our words and deeds and not be narrowly focused on particular laws.

THE TROUBLE WITH KINGS

22:1–23:8

This segment continues with oracles directed to the kings of Judah (see at 21:1-14). After an opening section addressed to "the king of Judah" regarding the royal palace and the city of Jerusalem (vv. 1-9), specific oracles are directed to three sons of Josiah who reigned from 609 to 598 BC (vv. 10-30), with an intervening oracle regarding Jerusalem (vv. 20-23). [Sons of Josiah] This segment concludes with promises regarding future kings and a return from exile (23:1-8).

Sons of Josiah

1. Jehoahaz (Shallum). Having been installed as king by the people, he reigned for three months after the death of his father Josiah in 609 BC. He was removed from the throne and exiled to Egypt by the pharaoh Neco, who no doubt wanted more control over Israel. He died in Egypt at an unknown date (see 2 Kgs 23:31-34; 2 Chr 36:1-4), but the fact that he continued to live during Jehoiakim's reign probably meant for divided loyalties among the Israelite people.

2. Jehoiakim. This son of Josiah reigned from 609 to 598 BC (see 2 Kgs 23:36–24:6). The superscription of the book (1:3) specifically cites Jehoiakim's reign as a context for Jeremiah's ministry (see also 25:1; 26:1; 35:1; 36:1). But unlike Zedekiah, Jehoiakim is not represented as ever having a direct encounter with Jeremiah. He was placed on the throne by Egyptian Pharaoh Neco in 609 BC, and hence was without popular support (in contrast to Jehoahaz). Jehoiakim was killed in 598 BC after having rebelled against King Nebuchadrezzar (who took control of Israel after defeating Egypt in 605 BC; see [Nebuchadrezzar]).

3. Jehoiachin (Coniah). This son of Josiah succeeded his brother in 598 BC when he was eighteen years old (2 Kgs 24:8-10). He was placed on the throne by his own people after Nebuchadrezzar had deposed and exiled Jehoiakim. He ruled for only three months until Jerusalem fell; he was exiled to Babylon with his family, officials, and many others (see 52:31-34; 2 Kgs 24:8-15). Considerable allegiance continued to be attached to him as a member of the Davidic line, unlike his uncle Zedekiah, who had been placed on the throne by Nebuchadrezzar. Jehoiachin may have been associated with messianic hopes, especially when he was released from prison ca. 560 BC and given certain rights and properties (see 52:31-34). Babylonian texts refer to him as the "King of Judah."

COMMENTARY

Why Jerusalem Was Destroyed, 22:1-9

This section is driven by the question in v. 8, asked in view of the destruction of Jerusalem. Why has God done this to the city, including its palace and temple? This question emerges after Jerusalem has fallen, and so the possibilities for the future laid out in vv. 1-5 have already been decided, at least in the near term. This "Why?" question suggests that vv. 1-7 focus on the city and its buildings, particularly the "house" (palace) of the king (see vv. 1, 4, 5-6). The answer given in v. 9 is familiar to readers (see 5:19; 9:12-16; 16:10-13): because its people have been unfaithful to the God with whom they entered into covenant and have turned to the worship of other gods. It is this relationship with God that proves to be the decisive issue (see also v. 16) (see **Connections: Faithfulness, Justice, and Knowing God**).

God commands Jeremiah to "go down" (from the temple) to the "house" (=the palace) of the king. The text does not tell us if he actually did this. The king of Judah to whom Jeremiah is to speak is left unnamed; in context it likely refers to Zedekiah, but the general reference is important for exilic readers. The lack of a name for the king on "the throne of David" suggests that any king of the Davidic dynasty is in view (see 21:11; [The Text and Exilic Readers]). At the same time, while the king is front and center as the addressee of this word from God, the charge to do justice and righteousness is also placed before his officials and the people of Jerusalem (v. 2).

The commands God makes to king and people are an elaboration of the charge presented in 21:12. The first charge (v. 3a) repeats the sentence in 21:12, but adds "righteousness" to "justice." The upshot of this addition is that more relational language is introduced; to do righteousness is to act faithfully with respect to any and all relationships, whether or not it is "just" or legal (see Gen 38:26). The charges in v. 3b give still further illustrations of what it means to act with justice and righteousness. The concern for the less fortunate in Israel, namely, the alien (a resident foreigner, refugee), the orphan, and the widow, is extraordinarily common. These persons and related themes were introduced in 7:1-6; this phrase is especially frequent in Deuteronomy and related literature (see Deut 10:18-19; 24:17-22; note the curse in Deut 27:19; Exod 22:21-24). Shedding "innocent blood" has primary reference to the abuse of judicial power on the part of the strong against the weak (see also v. 17; 2:34; 5:26-28; 7:6; 19:4 and the curse in Deut 27:25; Jeremiah appeals to this command when his life is threatened, 26:15).

The "either-or" address in vv. 4-5 is common in Jeremiah (see 12:16-17; 17:24-27; 21:8-10; 38:17-18; 42:9-17; see 1 Kgs 9:4-6; Isa 1:19-20) and has significant theological implications (see **Connections: God, the "Either-Or" Address, and Divine Foreknowledge**). God presents two options to any member of the Davidic dynasty, their officials, and the people (v. 2; the "you " in vv. 4-5 is plural). The focus on kings recognizes that they have often led the way in idolatrous practice and the shedding of "innocent blood" (e.g., Manasseh, 2 Kgs 21:16; 24:4).

The options are sharply stated. On the one hand, if they obey this charge from God, then kings will continue to pass through the gates of this "house" (=palace), accompanied by chariots, horses, officials, and people (cf. 17:25, where Sabbath-keeping results in the same future). Perhaps coronation processions are in mind. On the other hand, if they do not heed these words, then this "house" (palace) shall become a ruin (NAB, "rubble"; see 17:27; 25:18). These options do not speak to the future of the Davidic line as such (see below), though that will be deeply affected, but to the future of the palace (=the house, vv. 5-6) in particular, and by extension the city of Jerusalem (note the "gates" in vv. 2, 4). The negative future possibility (v. 5) is introduced with the phrase, "I swear by myself," indicating that, should this future option occur, God can be true to God's self only by acting on what is sworn. [God Swears an Oath]

The theme of v. 5 continues in vv. 6-7, as God speaks another word regarding the palace. But now the negative possibility of v. 5 is realized (no indictment is given, see v. 9), and God swears once again (v. 6), so that the positive future of v. 4 is no longer available. This suggests that the options of vv. 1-5 do not function as real possibilities in their present context (as they once did), but as principled statements (so also 18:1-12) (see **Connections: God, the "Either-Or" Address, and Divine Foreknowledge**). The image of trees for the palace continues (see 21:14; 22:20, 23). God likens the palace to Lebanon and Gilead, both mountainous regions known for their forests, which supplied wood for Jerusalem's buildings (see v. 7b). Gilead is in the Transjordan, north of Moab; Lebanon is northeast of Canaan, extending across Syria.

God Swears an Oath

God's swearing an oath is used with reference to various divine promises—the Noachic (Isa 54:9), the ancestral (e.g., Gen 22:15; Mic 7:20), and the Davidic (e.g., Pss 89:3, 35; 132:11). God also uses this language with respect to future judgments (e.g., Amos 4:2; 6:8) and those associated with the restoration to the land (e.g., Isa 45:23; 62:8). When oaths were taken by human beings, the name of God (or the gods) was invoked as a way of helping to assure truth-telling (see at 4:2). For God to swear by God's own self means that this statement is in effect a divine oath. In other words, God stands behind this word, and will remain as true to it as surely as God is God (see Jer 11:5; 16:14-15; 44:26; 49:13; 51:14).

Though God thinks highly of the palace and, by extension, the city of Jerusalem, God swears (again!) that it will become a desert, if the king and people do not heed the charge to do justice. "Uninhabited cities" (see NRSV footnote) may be a hyperbolic expression for total devastation. Continuing with the image of the palace as a cedar forest, God will prepare a "destroyer" (used in Exod 12:23 for the Passover destroyer; a reversal of the exodus theme common elsewhere, see [A Reversal of the Exodus]), who will come against the palace. With their tools (NAB, "axe") they will cut down their finest cedars (=buildings) and burn them in fire (see 21:10, 12, 14; the Babylonians are described in these terms in Ps 74:4-7).

As noted, this section is driven by the question/answer of vv. 8-9, a question often addressed heretofore (e.g., 9:12), though here it is spoken—and answered!—by the "nations" (as in Deut 29:22-28; 1 Kgs 9:8-9). From the perspective of exilic readers, it is clear why the city and its buildings have been destroyed: Israel has been unfaithful to its God. Even the nations know this (see 17:13-17)! Abandoning "covenant" occurs only here (as in Deut 29:24; Jer 9:12 refers to "law"); usually the reference is to abandoning God (see 16:11; 19:4-8), and hence one might interpret the phrase as abandoning the relationship with God. Though this question-answer form is conventional in that world, the ascription of this question (and answer) to the "nations" should not be emptied of theological content. Genuine insight into what has happened is ascribed to those outside of the community of faith, no doubt to set up a contrast to many of the Israelites themselves (cf. the birds in 8:7!).

Concerning King Jehoahaz, 22:10-12

In the final form of the text, the enigmatic poem in v. 10 is clarified in the prose oracle of vv. 11-12. Verse 10 is a fragment of a divine oracle addressed to the people of Israel regarding two unidentified male individuals; one dead and the other in exile. Verses 11-12 identify the exiled person as King Shallum (Jehoahaz was his royal name; see [Sons of Josiah]); he succeeded his father Josiah, who is implicitly identified as the individual who has died. The people are admonished not to lament for Josiah, who died tragically in battle with the Egyptians at Megiddo in 609 BC. Such an admonition is given to those who are in fact lamenting for him; 2 Chronicles 35:24-25 reports that both the people and the prophet Jeremiah lamented for Josiah, and that this mourning became a custom in

Israel. Josiah's death was particularly traumatic, for it brought an end to dreams regarding freedom from foreign domination and the reunification of the people of Israel. But such dreams would not be realized; that was irrecoverable past history.

Instead, the people are to lament for King Shallum. The oracle states that he would die in exile—never to return to Israel—and so he did (see 2 Kgs 23:30-34). The people are to lament for him because his passing was a sign of dashed hopes for the future of Israel. This king, chosen by the people, would not return as king. Pharaoh Neco replaced him with his brother, Jehoiakim, who becomes the subject of the following oracle (vv. 13-19), where another kind of contrast between father and son is developed.

Concerning King Jehoiakim, 22:13-19

This segment consists of an indictment of King Jehoiakim (see v. 18; [Sons of Josiah]), especially for his unjust practices (vv. 13-17), followed by an announcement of judgment on him (vv. 18-19). The indictment is remarkable for its intensity. He is charged with conspicuous luxury and mistreatment of his people (see 2 Kgs 23:35 for a description; he is linked with King Manasseh in 2 Kgs 24:4).

The announcement of judgment in vv. 18-19 is even fiercer as the king dies in total disrepute; words such as defamatory, vitriolic, and vituperative come to mind. The indictment and announcement of judgment come together in the repeated use of the word "Woe" or "Alas" (vv. 13, 18), a funerary dirge that becomes accusation. Commonly used in oracles of judgment (see Amos 5:16-18; 6:1), this word announces the "funerals" of those addressed. And so, Jeremiah announces the king's funeral in v. 13; but at his death no one will lament his passing (v. 18). One can imagine what the reaction would be today if a prominent preacher said comparable things about, say, a president or governor!

The indictment of Jehoiakim focuses on his "house" (=palace, v. 13), a topic of much interest in chapters 21–22. He has been engaged in major renovations of the palace, many of them going by the name of luxury. Verse 14 gives some details, including roof chambers with spacious rooms, large windows, cedar paneling (continuing Solomon's practice, 1 Kgs 7:7), and ostentatious painting (vermilion is a brilliant red). Two related issues come together: conspicuous luxury and the forced use of uncompensated workers (v. 13; cf. Solomon, 1 Kgs 5:13-18; 12:3-4; cf. Deut 24:14 on the payment of hired laborers). Such a mistreatment of his workers is named for what it is: unrighteousness and injustice; hence it stands in violation of the charge to the Davidic monarch in v. 3 (and 21:12).

The links made to the oppressive rule of Solomon are contrasted with the rule of his father Josiah in vv. 15-17 (see 2 Kgs 23:25). Verses 15-16 drive the point home with several pointed rhetorical questions. Does Jehoiakim think that his ostentatious building projects qualify him for the kingship or demonstrate that he is a royal figure? Did not his father (Josiah) eat and drink (a reference to his daily life) and practice justice and righteousness (see vv. 3, 13)? The focus of Josiah's reign that illustrates this point is similar to the charge of v. 3: he took up the cause of the poor and needy. Because he did these things it was well with him, a point repeated in vv. 15-16. Yet, the reader would have to add this caveat: generally speaking! Josiah's being killed in battle is an obvious indication that not everything went well with him.

The third rhetorical question is somewhat startling: is not this to know me? The antecedent of "this" is the practice of justice on behalf of the poor and needy. Verse 17 caps off the indictment by naming a veritable litany of sins that sets Jehoiakim off from his father Josiah. He sets both eyes and heart (external and internal) on matters that adversely affect the poor and needy: dishonesty in gaining wealth, shedding innocent blood (see v. 3), oppression, and violence. So, then, if the king (or anyone!) avoids these practices and cares for the poor and needy, then he "knows" the Lord (see **Connections: Faithfulness, Justice, and Knowing God**).

The announcement of judgment follows in vv. 18-19. Only at this point do readers certainly know the identity of the king indicted in vv. 13-17, though readers familiar with the temple renovations would have been able to infer his identity. This sharply worded announcement focuses on the death of Jehoiakim. When he dies, no one will lament for him (note the accusatory "woe" of v. 13). The designations of the king as "sister," "brother," "lord," and "his majesty" may reflect symbolic roles that he played in people's lives (see 1 Kgs 13:30). The list reinforces the idea that *nobody* will weep when he dies. Indeed, he will be held in such contempt by everyone that, as with a dead donkey, he will receive no burial at all. His corpse will be dragged outside the city to serve as food for scavengers (so also 7:33; 8:1-3; 16:4-6; 36:30). This fate for the king, a horrible curse (see Deut 28:26), will be comparable to that experienced by other residents of Jerusalem. [Jehoiakim's Fate]

Jehoiakim's Fate

No text reports that the content of Jeremiah's oracle actually proved to be his fate. The end of Jehoiakim announced in 36:30 upon rejection of Jeremiah's scroll corresponds to that described here. On the other hand, 2 Chr 36:6 (cf. 2 Kgs 24:6) relates that Nebuchadrezzar bound him in chains to be taken into exile. This lack of precise correspondence between prophecy and fulfillment is not uncommon in the Old Testament (see, e.g., the qualification of Elijah's announcement regarding the fate of Ahab's dynasty in 1 Kgs 21:27-29; cf. 1 Kgs 19:15-17; 2 Kgs 20:1-7). The prophetic word about the future retains a certain openness to events (e.g., the penitence of Ahab). God remains open to change and adjustment in view of human response; this has been set out in a principled way in Jer 18:7-10 and is illustrated with respect to a prophecy of Micah in Jer 26:18-19. We are not informed of any response on Jehoiakim's part that would have qualified the oracle.

Concerning Jerusalem, 22:20-23

These verses suspend consideration of individual kings and return to the theme of judgment on city and palace (see 21:14; 22:1-9). God is the speaker (see v. 21). This segment also marks a return to the theme of Israel's infidelity with other "lovers" (vv. 20, 22), either other gods (see 2:33; 3:1-5) or, more likely, other nations that Israel has courted for their potential protection (see 4:30; 30:14). God personifies Jerusalem as an adulterous wife and calls her to lament over her approaching death (see **Connections**, chs. 2 and 13). The people of Jerusalem are to pick a mountain (Lebanon, Bashan, and Abarim are mountainous regions, ranging from northeast to southeast of Israel) and climb it, the better to broadcast her lament (see 31:15; cf. Jephthah's daughter in Judg 11:37-38).

In v. 21, God recalls the story of "Jerusalem" as a rebellious child from its youth (so also 3:24-25; 31:19; 32:30; see 2:2 on its initial devotion). Jerusalem has refused to listen to God, even in prosperous times. Or, is it *because* of its prosperity?! Verse 22 refers to three different groups of people: (a) The shepherds are Israel's own leaders, who are condemned in 23:1-2 (see 10:21), but God will raise up new shepherds to replace them (23:4; see 3:15). God's judgment of the shepherds is imaged as a hot wind (see 4:11-12; 13:24; 18:17); they will be tossed about and blown into exile, no longer in control. (b) The lovers are probably other nations (see v. 20), and they will be of no help either, for they will be "crushed" and exiles just as much as Israel. (c) Jerusalem will have her evil ways exposed to the world, and her reaction will be shame and dishonor (on shame, see [Heschel on Justice as Personal]).

In v. 23, God calls to Jerusalem once again, this time returning to the image of Lebanon and its cedars (see 1 Kgs 7:2), material used for palace and temple (see 21:13-14; 22:6-7). Jerusalem is imaged as a bird nesting comfortably among these cedars, but who will comfort her when she experiences pain like unto that of one of the sharpest pains known—childbirth? Verse 20 begins with a call to Israel to lament; v. 23 ends this segment with a glimpse of a God who sorrows over a painful situation for Israel because no comfort will be found when all hell breaks loose on the city of Jerusalem.

Concerning King Jehoiachin, 22:24-30

This segment consists of two oracles (vv. 24-27, 28-30), both of which are announcements of judgment against Jehoiachin (see [Sons of Josiah]). They are directed against hopes among the populace, fostered by false prophets (see 28:4; cf. Ezek 1:2), that Jehoiachin would return from exile and reestablish Davidic rule. The word from God declares this to be a false hope; the future of Israel is not to be associated with his leadership. The first oracle establishes that this was the will of God even before Jehoiachin's exile in 597 BC; the second oracle maintains this stance after the exile has occurred.

The first oracle (vv. 24-27), in prose, is cast in the form of a divine oath ("as I live," see 16:14-15; [God Swears an Oath]); it is thus identified as having a special stature. Apparently set during the three-month reign of Jehoiachin in 597 BC, it establishes for exiles that God's will had already been set for him during his rule. God leaves no doubt about this matter, as especially strong language is used for his rejection. It is not clear why this king who ruled for only three months should be so virulently denounced, for no indictment is cited (contrast Jehoiakim, vv. 13-19). Even if Jehoiachin were a signet ring on *God's* right hand (or, "although" he is; see REB), God would tear the ring off his own finger, deprive him of his authority as king, and give him (and his mother, see 13:18) into the hands of Nebuchadrezzar to be exiled. [The Signet Ring] In fact, God will "hurl" (see v. 28; 16:13) them into a country that is not their own. Though they "long to return" to their own land (note the probable perspective of exilic readers), they will die in exile (see 2 Kgs 25:30; cf. Zedekiah in 21:7; 34:21).

The second oracle (vv. 28-30), in poetry, reinforces the point of vv. 24-27 from the perspective of Jehoiachin in exile. The divine judgment is that Jehoiachin does not rule with God's authority in exile and that will stand into the future. The speaker of the questions in v. 28 is uncertain. It is likely that these are questions voiced by the king's supporters, to which God responds (but does not answer) in vv. 29-30. Verse 28 is a rhetorical question: is Jehoiachin an individual without honor, like a broken pot that nobody wants?

The Signet Ring

The signet ring bore the seal of the owner (in this case, God himself). The seal mounted in the ring was the king's signature and was used to stamp official documents, thereby giving them royal authority (in Hag 2:23, Zerubbabel, a member of the Davidic line, is declared to be like such a signet ring). In this text, Jehoiachin's name would be inscribed in *God's* signet ring. Two translations are possible. "Even if" the king were God's signet ring, his rule would not be stamped with the divine "signature" (blessing). Alternatively, "although" he is God's signet ring, he will be divested of his authority. If the former, this means, in effect, that Jehoiachin ruled Israel without divine authority for three months in 597 BC, and he would be given no such authority in Israel's future. If the latter ("although"), the reference is only to the time after his reign.

Seal of Jeroboam, King of Israel. Copy of lost original. 1000 BC. Reuben & Edith Hecht Collection, Haifa University. Haifa, Israel. (Credit: Erich Lessing/Art Resource, NY)

The implied answer is *negative.* The "Why" questions follows directly; if he is not such a pot, why has he been hurled out of his own land and cast into an unfamiliar land? This verse thus amounts to a lament for him and his fate.

The response from God is addressed to the land, and readers can hear the tones of lament (v. 29, cf. 2:31; the threefold reference to the temple in 7:4). God addresses both the land itself (what might that entail about an understanding of land?) and any people in the land who harbor hopes that Jehoiachin would someday rule with God's authority. Jehoiachin is stripped of any relationship to the land of Israel; he no longer has a homeland. Alternatively, and more likely, the call to the "land" in v. 29 refers back to the "land" of exile in v. 28. If so, this becomes, in effect, a call to the exiles (including King Jehoiachin), hurled out of their own land, to once again hear this word. Possibly the verse is ambiguous, with both lands in view.

God commands the land (and its people) that Jehoiachin, who will not himself return to the throne, be registered as childless or stripped of heirs. This is not to say that he has no children; in fact, the last part of the verse ("his offspring") presupposes that he does (1 Chr 3:17-18 speaks of seven sons). The point is that in terms of the Davidic line (for the record, as it were) not a single one of those children will succeed him to the throne of David. Historically, this proves to be the case, if one understands "offspring" as his own children and/or "the throne of David" literally. [The End of the Davidic Line?]

Return to the Land under Faithful Rulers, 23:1-8

This collection of brief prose oracles begins with the typical rhythm of indictment (v. 1) followed by an announcement of judgment (v. 2). The "woe" of v. 1 continues the form and theme struck in 22:13. Readers are prepared to hear more of the judgments so prevalent over the last chapters. But, in a sudden turn, God breaks into that rhythm with several announcements of salvation (vv. 3-8; cf. the interruptive character of earlier salvation oracles, 3:14b-18; 12:14-15; 16:14-21). The judgment on the shepherds (=kings) also turns out to be good news for exiled readers; they will no longer have to endure such inept and wicked leadership, for God will raise up a shepherd who will rule as God himself would rule. These themes anticipate later oracles of salvation (e.g., 30:2; 31:9-10; 32:42; 33:6-27). That the shepherds are addressed in the plural and in general terms means that they refer to the entire Davidic line, a link back to 21:11; 22:1, 22 (see 10:21).

The End of the Davidic Line?

This oracle (especially v. 30) has been interpreted as a divine declaration of the end of the Davidic dynasty. But, whatever may have been the case historically, the text immediately following makes clear that, at least in this context, this is not understood to be the case. God will one day "raise up for David a righteous Branch" (23:5). For all the discontinuity in the destruction of the monarchy, God will find a way into the future and will raise up a king from the Davidic line (see also 30:9; 33:14-26; 52:31-34). A grandson of Jehoiachin, Zerubbabel, did govern the Judean community for a time after the exile; though neither he nor his offspring is named as king (the monarchy is not reinstated after the exile; see [The Righteous Branch]). But Zerubbabel does continue the line of David that, from a New Testament perspective, leads to the Christ (see the genealogy in Matt 1:12-16).

Verses 1-2 address the shepherds who have destroyed and scattered "the sheep of my pasture" (=Israel) and they bring the prior oracles against individual kings to a collective summary judgment (the "you" of v. 2 is plural). They are condemned for their failure to "visit" (*pāqad*) the people in caring ways (for detail, see Ezek 34:1-6) and are directly blamed for the destruction and exile. They have misled the people, causing them to stray off the paths of righteousness and justice. Prior texts do not relieve the people of responsibility in following the shepherds' lead, but the kings are singled out as bearing a fundamental responsibility for what has happened. If they had been faithful, there may have been a different story to tell. Hence, God will "visit" (*pāqad*; NRSV "attend to") their evil deeds upon them (see 21:12, 14; 22:22; see Ezek 34:7-10). Note the direct correspondence between their wicked deeds and the consequences. Again, God does not introduce anything new into the judgments being made; the kings reap the consequences of their own deeds (see **Introduction**).

With the shepherds having been singled out for a judgmental future, God now attends in a special way to the sheep that have been scattered across the landscape of ancient near Eastern nations ("remnant," vv. 3-4; see 6:9; 8:3). These verses appear to continue the address of vv. 1-2 to the shepherds, and as such this positive language would be a pointed word to them that God will attend to the future of the sheep in a way that they have not.

Not so surprisingly, God is now the one who is said to have driven Israel away (see **Connections: Agency in Jeremiah 23:1-8**). God will gather "my flock" (see 29:14; 31:8, 10; 32:37). Note God's repeated language for the people: "my flock" (vv. 2-3; see 13:17); "my people" (v. 2; over forty times in Jeremiah!); and "the sheep of my pasture" (v. 1; see the divine "my" in 12:7-14). The personalism of these references demonstrates a special relationship between God and people; God claims these people as God's own. Notably, there is continuity in this relationship across the divide of destruction and exile; "my flock" has been scattered and "my flock" will be gathered. At least from the perspective of the remnant of Israel, there has been no time that they have ceased to be God's flock. Note as well the emphasized subject of the activity (v. 3; "I myself"). These divine claims would be a comforting word for exilic readers.

God will gather the remnant from all lands (more than Babylon is in mind) where they have been scattered and bring them back to the fold (=the community of Israel on its own land; see 32:37). God promises that they will be fruitful and multiply there. This promise of fruitfulness, already struck in 3:16 (see 30:19), is given to the exiles in 29:6; it recalls both creational texts (Gen 1:28) and ancestral promises (Gen 17:1-8, 20; 28:3; 48:4). With this dual reference, this promise not only represents the fulfillment of God's commitment to Israel's ancestors, but also realizes God's creational intentions. God's commitment to these promises is made in an especially forceful way in 33:25-26 and is also linked in that context to God's commitment to all creation in the Noachic covenant (33:20, 25; so also 31:35-37). God's action in returning Israel from exile is thus understood to focus on more than the Israelite community; it has cosmic implications (see also Isaiah 35; 40–55).

Verse 4 depicts a divine action that follows upon the completion of the actions of v.3, though the translation is not altogether certain. When (or, before) Israel has been brought back from exile and placed once again on its own land, God will raise up shepherds who will truly shepherd them; presumably a succession of shepherds is in mind not multiple leaders (as in 3:15; see vv. 5-6; Ezek 34:11-24). The people will not be fearful anymore or be dismayed (often the case under Israel's kings and no doubt the rulers of the nations where they have been scattered). A common translation of the last verb of v. 4 is "nor shall any be missing" (NRSV; NAB).

Yet, the sense that every single member of the faithful remnant will be accounted for or will return home is unlikely (though it may be hyperbolic). Another interpretation is preferable (cf. REB, "punishment"). The verb (*pāqad*) has been used twice in v. 2, the second instance of which refers to God "visiting" the kings' wickedness upon them. This may be the sense of the verb in v. 4. That is, the remnant—though not innocent in what led to the exile—will not suffer the fate of the shepherds (see this sense of the verb in Isa 24:22; Prov 19:23). The positive sense of being visited in caring ways is implied, however (in contrast to the kings "not visiting" in v. 2).

Verses 5-6 move from the "shepherds" whom God will raise up (v. 4) to a single leader from the line of David (note the dynastic point) whom God will raise up, whose rule of justice and righteousness (see 21:12; 22:3, 15) will be that of a true shepherd. The verses could be related temporally. That is, upon return from exile, God will raise up shepherds who will rule justly over the returned community, from among whom will be chosen the "righteous Branch," who will rule as God himself would rule. [The Righteous Branch] Alternatively, the "righteous Branch" is a way of speaking of *each* of a *succession* of promised shepherds. The latter seems to be the interpretation of these verses when they are repeated in 33:15-16 (with modifications; see 30:9), for 33:17 speaks of a succession of rulers when it promises that "David shall never lack a man to sit on the throne of Israel."

This future of a community over whom a righteous king rules is made possible only by God's action: God will raise him up; but once raised up, the king himself will rule. The fundamental characteristic of the reign of this future king is that he will rule wisely and with justice and righteousness. He would thus be true to God's calling for the kings in 22:3 (21:12) and stand in the tradition of

---

The Righteous Branch

AΩ This image is used for the Davidic king in both 23:5 and 33:15. The word "branch" is used as a messianic title in Zech 3:8 and 6:12; this image is also employed in Isa 11:1, though a different Hebrew word is used (see also the verb "sprout" for the Davidic dynasty in Ps 132:17). The image of "branch" (and related tree motifs) is also used for the righteous remnant (see Isa 4:2; 6:13; 60:21; 61:3). The attribute "righteous" may be intended as an ironic contrast to King Zedekiah, whose name means "Yahweh is righteousness." It may be, however, that the Branch is described as "rightful, legitimate" rather than "righteous" (see William Holladay, *Jeremiah I* [Philadelphia:

Fortress, 1989], 618). Also to be linked to this image is Zerubbabel (the name means "branch of Babylon"); as noted in [The End of the Davidic Line?], he is a leader of Israel upon its return from exile and is linked to a possible re-establishment of the Davidic kingship during that time (see Hag 2:20-23). The imagery drawn from vegetation suggests fresh growth from dead roots (see Isa 6:13; 11:1); that entails continuity but a newness that is possible only by a creative act of God. The branch image is not used as a messianic title in the New Testament, but it is possible that the image of the vine and branches in John 15:1-8 draws on these roots.

Josiah (22:15). This verse may be linked with other prophetic texts that speak of a coming king who will rule wisely and justly (see Isa 9:5-7; 11:1-5; Ezek 34:23-24, which speaks of this king as a shepherd).

The name given to this king of the Davidic line is "The Lord is our righteousness" (cf. the names given in Isa 7:14; 9:5). That is, he will rule as God himself would rule; God's righteous rule would be exercised in and through this individual. Given his name, it would be God's rule, not the rule of the Branch that would be seen and recognized by the community. This name may be a wordplay on Zedekiah (="Yahweh is righteousness"), the last king of Judah, whose name was given him by Nebuchadrezzar at the time of his appointment (see 2 Kgs 24:17). The point would be, in effect, God is our righteous king, not Zedekiah (though some see a positive reference to Zedekiah here). The decisive effect of the rule of God's righteous branch is that "Judah will be saved (*yāšaʿ*) and Israel will live in safety." Note the reference to both northern and southern kingdoms. Moreover, the force of this salvation language is not narrowly spiritual in nature; salvation encompasses every sphere of life, which will characterized by health, deliverance from their enemies, safety in the face of any threat, and general well-being—back on the "land."

Verses 7-8 are a virtual repetition of 16:14-15 (see discussion there). The phrase, "as the LORD lives," is an oath formula (see 22:5, 24). As such, this text, which assumes the return to the land, reinforces the promissory elements of vv. 1-6. It speaks of a basic change in Israel's confessional orientation when it has returned to the land. No longer will the exodus from Egypt be the center of Israel's confession of faith (see Deut 26:5-9). Rather, this newly re-established community will center its confession in God's gathering of the remnant from all the lands to which they have been scattered and in their restoration to the land of promise (as promised in vv. 3-4; see 24:6). This language of "new exodus" is echoed elsewhere in the major prophets (e.g., Isa 43:15-21; 51:9-11).

CONNECTIONS

Faithfulness, Justice, and Knowing God

The response to the question of v. 8 in v. 9 helps readers understand more clearly what is at stake in vv. 1-5. The practice of righteousness and justice is an issue *from within* the more comprehensive God-Israel relationship. Failure to practice justice is symptomatic of a more comprehensive problem, namely, abandoning their God and worshiping and serving other deities. *Injustice reveals infidelity.* The call for justice not only serves the neighbor but reveals the nature of the relationship with God that exists. Serving God and neighbor go together. The implication is that if Israel's relationship with its God is in good order, their lives will be shaped by righteousness and justice.[1]

Verse 16 returns to this theme: what can it mean that doing justice is to "know" God? Given all the references in Jeremiah to Israel's infidelity and worshiping the gods of other nations (most recently, v. 9), how can it be claimed that one who practices justice "knows" God? The point certainly would not be that one is able to worship other gods as much as one likes so long as one cares for the poor and the needy (see their linkage in 7:5-6)! The point, at least in part, would be that the worship of God can be distinguished but not separated from the concern for the poor and needy. To claim a right relationship with God and then turn around and abuse and neglect the needy is a sign that the relationship with God is not in good order (see Amos 5:21-24). To care for the less fortunate is to do justice to the relationship, that is, to know God and God's ways in the world. At the same time, such behaviors would not be the only means by which to evaluate the rightness of the relationship with God. [Heschel on Justice]

Usually the practice of justice and righteousness will mean life and well-being, but not inevitably (witness the death of the just king Josiah in battle, 2 Kgs 23:28-30). The world is not created to run like a machine; there is room for randomness as well as for what is genuinely new. No theory of retribution can explain how the world works; the righteous will suffer; the wicked will prosper (see 12:1).

Heschel on Justice

Justice is not an ancient custom, a human convention, a value, but a transcendent demand, freighted with divine concern. It is not only a relationship between man and man [sic!], it is an *act* involving God, a divine need. Justice is His line, righteousness His plummet (Isa. 28:17). It is not one of His ways, but in all of His ways. Its validity is not only universal, but also eternal, independent of will and experience. People think that to be just is a virtue, deserving honor and rewards; that in doing righteousness one confers a favor on society. No one expects to receive a reward for the habit of breathing. Justice is as much a necessity as breathing is, and a constant occupation.

Abraham Heschel, *The Prophets* (New York: Haper, 1962), 198-99.

God, the "Either-Or" Address, and Divine Foreknowledge

The "either-or" form of address in 22:1-5 assumes some interesting perspectives regarding the God who makes this offer. Two specific future possibilities are open to the king (and the people, v. 2), depending upon the fulfillment of justice according to the command of the Lord (v. 3). For each of these options to have integrity,

God cannot know for sure what will in fact happen, at least at the time this oracle is delivered. If God knows for certain that the negative future will occur, then for God to offer the positive future would be a deception. Divine deception is a possibility, but in the absence of some indication that this is so (see at 20:7; 1 Kings 22), it seems unlikely. Moreover, all other "either-or" offers would then be open to such an interpretation. That God would engage in so much deception seems unlikely; all of God's words regarding the future would thus be potentially untrustworthy. And so it seems more true to the texts that God offers genuine options to king and people. If the positive future of v. 4b is a genuine possibility for the king, then it must be a possibility, and only a possibility, for God as well. For God to speak in terms of a possibility (or probability) suggests some uncertainty as to what will in fact occur.

Such language shows how deeply God has entered into Israel's situation. God is faced with possibilities as is Israel, with all that such a dilemma means in terms of reflection, planning, and openness to alternative courses of action, depending upon the course of events. Where the divine perspective exceeds the human lies in the ability to delineate all of the possibilities of the future, and the likelihood of their occurrence, in view of the thoroughgoing divine knowledge of the past and present. Yet God, too, moves into a future that is to some extent unknown. [Divine Knowledge and Exilic Readers]

Agency in Jeremiah 23:1-8

Upon reading 23:3 after 23:2, readers may be surprised by the subject that drives away the people. In v. 2 the shepherds are indicted for doing so (*nādaḥ*); in v. 3, *God* claims to have driven (*nādaḥ*) them into exile (also in v. 8 (=16:15); 8:3; 24:9; on this kind of duality, cf. also 13:14 with 21:7). In 50:17, Babylon (and Assyria) are the subject of this verb, making the issue of agency even more complex. A similar complexity is evident in the other scattering verb used in these verses (*pûṣ*). In 23:1-2, the shepherds are twice said to be the ones who have "scattered" the flock of God. In other Jeremiah texts, however, it is *God* who has done the scattering (see 9:16; 13:24; 18:17; 30:11; see **Introduction**).

Divine Knowledge and Exilic Readers

For exilic readers, who would know which of the two options in 22:1-5 did in fact occur, hearing about this offer from God would show them the degree to which God was open to alternative futures at that point in time when both options were still possible. This means that the devastating future that they have experienced was not set for all time in the mind of God. Their experience was not predetermined nor was it a matter of *fate*; there was something that they could have (not) done with respect to their faith and life to make another kind of (positive) future possible. At the same time, hearing about this divine way of moving into the future would enable the exiles to realize that their own future is not somehow set in stone, which given Babylon's hegemony must have seemed the most likely possibility. But the key factors that shaped the options that were originally presented (22:3, "justice and righteousness") would also come into play as they thought of their own future, matters that they would now be urged to take seriously.

Holladay claims that God as the subject of the verb in v. 3 "contradicts the accusation against the shepherds in v. 2."[2] On the contrary, readers are not being asked to choose among these statements, as if only one of them could be correct. Agency is here conceived in a complex sense; shepherds, Babylonians, and God are all active agents in the exiling of the people. At the same time, it is important to discern some priorities here. God and Babylon become subjects of the scattering only because of the prior activity on the part of the shepherds; and, in an even more complex way, the Babylonians become involved because God uses them to mediate the judgment. At the same time, God's use of them does not entail micromanagement of their activities, as is evident in the way they exceed the divine mandate (25:12-14; 50–51).

NOTES

[1] Contrary to Walter Brueggemann, *A Commentary on Jeremiah: Exile and Homecoming* (Grand Rapids: Eerdmans, 1998), 197, who collapses the distinction between theological and ethical.

[2] William Holladay, *Jeremiah 1* (Philadelphia: Fortress, 1986), 615.

TRUE AND FALSE PROPHETS

23:9-40

This section is a collection of various oracles "concerning the prophets" (v. 9), in both poetry (vv. 9-22) and prose (vv. 23-40). The basic concern reflected throughout is prophetic conflict, more particularly, conflict over authority between Jeremiah and other (false) prophets. Who among those who go by the name of prophet speaks the word of God? On what grounds does one make such a decision? Though criteria are not made available in any systematic way, there is a kind of "you will know them by their fruits" (Matt 7:15-16) perspective that shapes much of this material. Just look at the effect the false prophets have had on Israel, its people and its land! In time Israel will fall because so many prophets have failed (see **Connections: False Prophets**).

These oracles may be characterized in the following basic terms: a lament of Jeremiah (v. 9) that gathers up a divine indictment and announcement of judgment (vv. 10-12); another indictment and announcement of judgment (vv. 13-15); a warning to readers about false prophets, whose word is rejected for failure to discern the appropriate word of God (vv. 16-22); a prose section expanding on the failure of the false prophets (vv. 23-32); concluding with a midrash or interpretive commentary on the meaning of the phrase, "the burden of the LORD" (v. 33). No progression of thought is evident across the entire section; rather, various oracles concerning false prophets have been gathered into a kind of collage, which carries its own rhetorical force.

Unlike the previous section where kings were often specifically named and an historical setting discerned, no prophets are named and specifics from the context are very general. That fact seems to say that false prophecy was an ongoing issue for Israel. Such generalizing could be related to the situation of exilic readers, for whom false prophets were a continuing problem (see chs. 27–28). The indictments and condemnations of this text thereby become more generally applicable across the generations, including their own.

COMMENTARY

A General Indictment, 23:9-12

This introductory section focuses on people and land in general terms; it lays out the state of affairs for which the (now to be discussed) prophets have a deep responsibility. Jeremiah is likely the speaker of vv. 9-12, but given the repeated "says the LORD" (vv. 11-12), vv. 10-12 are probably to be identified with the "holy words" cited at the end of v. 9.

Verse 9 harks back to the laments of the prophet in chapters 11–20; they describe the physical and mental state of Jeremiah as he is encountered by the word of the LORD. Jeremiah's self-description—a broken spirit and trembling body, likening himself to a drunkard—sounds like an instance of prophetic ecstasy (see 1 Sam 10:1-13; 19:23-24). If so, Jeremiah thereby makes claims for his own prophetic experience in contrast to that of the other prophets; he had received "holy words" of judgment, which he proceeds to cite in vv. 10-12, not words of peace (cf. 6:14; 14:13). This interpretation would correlate well with the argument that is presented in vv. 16-22. Alternatively, this language describes how the prophet is personally affected at being confronted by the sharp judgmental words of the LORD against the people. We have seen comparable expressions heretofore (see 4:19-22; 15:17-18; 20:7-9). [Heartbroken, I Stand]

That v. 10 begins with the word "for" (*kî*) suggests that what follows are several specific features of the "holy words" that have been revealed to him (or, to which he responds as he does in v. 9). The land is full of adulterers; this refers both to adultery (see v. 14; 5:7-9; 29:23) and spiritual infidelity (as in 9:2; see 3:1-5), given the association with immoral temple practices (v. 11). Both prophetic and priestly wickedness (*rā'āh*) are mentioned (v. 11). Yet, when it comes to infidelity and leading the people to serve other gods (see v. 13), the prophets are the problem; the text speaks of clergy misconduct, not just poor preaching. Their way of life (v. 10; NRSV, "course") is evil (*rā'āh*); this is primarily a reference to oppression of the needy ("might" [NRSV] is used similarly at

Heartbroken, I Stand

Heartbroken I Stand—
Your word, a vagrant bird, southward
speeding from world's winter,
has fled my lips.

That wine, that word
bloodies my life, stains
like a lamb's life
lintel and doorposts, Xs me—
Yours.

What make I
(what make You)
of those others, blathering
fair words in foul weather,
peace for conflict, high noon
for night's blear?

Who sent them, whose
credential?

Never mine—
to set minds awry, the time's
intent
bent like a bow
strung and sprung
straight to self-advantage.
My people they urge
astray, to dead-ends,
to abattoir, to death of soul.

Of Sodom, Gomorrah
(never Jerusalem the holy)—
their reeking tongues, their
gross and
native ground.

Daniel Berrigan, *Jeremiah: The World, the Wound of God* (Minneapolis: Fortress, 1999), 95-96.

22:17). The felicitous phrasing, "their might is not right," says it well; the prophets (and others) use power to preserve their way of life at the expense of the less fortunate. The ungodliness of prophet and priest is a common charge in Jeremiah (e.g., 5:31; 6:13). Such behaviors are perpetrated even in God's own "house" (=temple).

This behavior results in a curse (see 11:3; 17:5; 26:6) that has deeply affected the larger environment (v. 10; see Gen 3:17, "cursed is the ground"): the land mourns and the pastures are dried up. This is a pervasive theme in Jeremiah (see at 3:2-3; 4:23-28; 9:10; 12:4, 10-11; 14:1-6; see **Connections**, chs. 4 and 12). Moral order adversely affects cosmic order; human sin has had a deeply negative effect upon the environment (just the opposite of claims made for Baal worship on the land's fertility).

The "therefore" of v. 12 introduces the announcement of judgment, though it has been anticipated in the references to curse, land, and pasture in v. 10. Judgment shall fall upon everyone, but prophet and priest are especially in view. Their wickedness/evil (the *rā'āh* of vv. 10-11) shall result in disaster (the *rā'āh* of v. 12). Once again, *rā'āh* leads to *rā'āh*; the disaster grows out of human wickedness and God mediates the connection (see **Introduction**). Such divine mediation is what is meant by the "year of *their* punishment [lit., "visitation"]." This use of "visit" language is comparable to that in 21:14 and elsewhere in Jeremiah; God will visit the people's own sins upon them. Images for this personal disaster are presented in the first clauses of v. 12. Their paths/ways (=daily walk) will be both dark and slippery (see Ps 35:6) because their behaviors have been dark and slippery. They will lose their balance and their footing and fall headlong to their ruin; again, God will mediate these consequences, as they are "driven" to this end (see v. 3).

The Prophets Are the Problem, 23:13-15

Verses 13-15 focus on the prophets, with an indictment (vv. 13-14) followed by an announcement of judgment (v. 15). Prophets from both northern kingdom (Samaria, its capital) and southern (Jerusalem) are targeted, though the apostasies of the latter are adjudged to be more shocking (so also in 3:6-11). The prophets from Israel are indicted because they prophesied in the name of Baal rather than Yahweh and, the key point, they thereby led the people astray. These individuals seem not to be Canaanite Baal prophets (see 1 Kgs 18:25-29) but Israelite prophets who have become unfaithfully syncretistic (see 1 Kgs 18:21). This activity is named "disgusting" (NRSV) or "unseemly" (NAB), a difficult word

Sodom and Gomorrah

The story of the destruction of Sodom and Gomorrah is the most often cited Genesis story in the rest of the Bible (Gen 18:16–19:29)—more than twenty times in both Old Testament and New. These cities are referenced primarily because of their great wickedness and the consequent destruction they experienced in an environmental catastrophe (e.g., Deut 29:23; Isa 13:19; Lam 4:6; Amos 4:11). Sometimes the focus is on the sins of Sodom, sometimes on its destruction (as with Jer 23:14; 49:18; 50:40). As such, these cities become a symbol for wickedness at its worst that will, in turn, lead to unmitigated disaster, perhaps even worse than that experienced by Sodom (see Isa 1:9-10; Ezek 16:46-52). Jesus uses the story in comparable ways (see Matt 10:15; 11:23-24; Luke 10:12; 17:29).

The specific sites of the infamous cities are unknown. The numerous references that associate the cities with impending judgment throughout the Old and New Testament, however, suggests the gravity of the analogue to Sodom and Gomorrah in the verses of Jeremiah. In the same way that Sodom and Gomorrah were destroyed for refusing to repent of their sin, God condemns Israel to certain irreversible punishment.

Joseph Mallord William Turner. *The Destruction of Sodom.* 19th c. Tate Gallery. London, England. (Credit: Clore Collection, Tate Gallery/Art Resource, NY)

The cited sins of Sodom cover the waterfront, from the lists of Ezek 16:49-50 to Jesus' focus on inhospitality (Matt 10:15) to sexual activity with angels (Jude 7). Jeremiah's common link between human sin and environmental degradation (e.g., 4:23-26; 12:1-13; see **Connections**, ch. 12) parallels the link made by the Genesis story (see Gen 13:10-13). The emphasis of the Genesis story on God's using of nature as an instrument for judgment has some parallels in Jeremiah in the texts noted, but for the prophet God's agents are primarily historical. (See Terence Fretheim, "Divine Judgment and the Warming of the World," in *God, Evil, and Suffering: Essays in Honor of Paul Sponheim,* ed. by T. Fretheim and C. Thompson. Word and World Supplement Series 4 [2000], 21-32.)

to translate; NRSV seems closer to the mark, for the activity named by God is more than simply inappropriate or fatuous.

The prophets from Jerusalem are adjudged as having been involved in even more horrible behavior (v. 14). They commit adultery (see v. 10), live in lies (both speaking and acting), and take sides with those who do evil, supporting their schemes rather than calling them to account. The result is that the people are not turned from their wicked ways and their wicked behaviors are reinforced (see v. 22; 6:14). From God's perspective they are like Sodom and Gomorrah (Gen 18:16–19:29), so wicked that they are deserving of nothing but condemnation. [Sodom and Gomorrah]

Verse 15 announces God's judgment on these prophets ("therefore"); the prophets of Jerusalem are especially in view. Images of eating and drinking are used to describe God's judgment. The

Grounding for the Charge against the False Prophets

What is the most basic theological grounding that informs the message of the false prophets? The misplaced confidence trumpeted by the false prophets could be rooted in a theological perspective regarding the inviolability of Zion or the Davidic covenant; yet, the text does not say that. The reasons are probably deeper, rooted both in a defective anthropology (see vv. 17, 22) and a distorted understanding of God (see vv. 23-24). The anthropology of the false prophets is evident in the first explicit, twice-stated judgment on their message: they have treated the wound of my people lightly (6:14; 8:11). In other words, they failed to recognize the pervasive and stubborn wickedness of the people and had prescribed an over-the-counter medication when only radical surgery could resolve the matter. Jeremiah is more explicit on this anthropological point in 23:17, 22; a storm of judgment was the only appropriate response (v. 19). Regarding their understanding of God, evident especially in 23:23-24, they thought that God was so far removed from daily life that he would overlook the people's wickedness. Should judgment come, they would certainly find a place to "hide." But this is not the God of the tradition (see **Connections: The World Is Full of God**).

---

disastrous consequences are likened to eating wormwood (a shrub with a bitter taste, see 9:15) and drinking poisoned water (see 8:14). Their activities are named as godless (see v. 11), and the horrible thing is that they have had a profoundly negative influence on the larger community: everyone has taken on *their* godless identity.

The Council of the Lord, 23:16-22

Verses 16-17 are addressed to the people and warn them of the message of the false prophets—"they are deluding you!" The exilic readers would hear this "you" as an address to them, not least because of the issue of false prophecy that was present in the exile community (see ch. 27). These prophets do not get their word from the Lord; their visions are created out of their own minds (as we might say, "it's a figment of their imagination"). Their falseness is demonstrated by the *content* of their message. Though the people to whom they speak despise the word of the Lord, the prophets keep assuring them that all will be well. Though the people's hearts are stubborn and they persist in walking in their wicked ways, the prophets keep telling them that no disaster (*rā'āh*) will fall on them. As Jeremiah has repeatedly noted, they speak, "Peace, peace," when there is no peace (5:12-13; 6:14; 8:11; 16:13-16; see Ezek 13:10; Mic 3:11; Zech 10:2). Hananiah is a prophet who speaks this kind of word (see 28:1-17). The prophets are not only personally corrupt, they encourage wickedness in the people by not calling them to account for what they have done; this fleshes out the point made in v. 14, "no one turns from wickedness" (so also v. 22). [Grounding for the Charge against the False Prophets]

The Council of God

The council of the Lord is usually understood to be a gathering of divine beings, over whom God presides and with whom God consults regarding earthly affairs (see Gen 1:26; 1 Kgs 22:19-23; Job 1-2; 15:8; Ps 82; Isa 6:1-8). As Gen 1:26 and Job 1-2 show, this is a consultative body, not just a group to which God delivers edicts. There is an element of mutuality present in these texts. The prophet was understood to be a participant in these consultations, bringing the word "back" to Israel regarding the word to be announced.

More generally, the council demonstrates that God is not in heaven alone, but that a complex sociality is basic to the divine life. In other words, relationship is integral to the identity of God, independent of God's relationship to the world. In some sense the prophet was invited to participate in this relationship. The boundary between human and divine communities is not seen to be fixed or impenetrable. The human is caught up into the divine life and together they become involved in the becoming of the world. In so doing the prophet retains his individuality, and his humanness is not compromised. Yet, the prophet, in leaving the council table with a word to speak, becomes the embodiment of the word of God in the world. The prophet is a vehicle for divine immanence.

Giulio Romano (1499–1546). *Olympus. Sala dei Giganti.* Fresco. 16th C. Palazzo de Te'. Mantua, Italy. (Credit: Alinari/Art Resource, NY)

Verses 18-22 (probably addressed to Jeremiah; see "their" in v. 22) demonstrate further why the prophets' words are false. Two rhetorical questions introduce the council of the Lord. Who (among these prophets) has been a part of that council to hear and see (!) what God has to say (see Job 15:8)? And, if they have heard that word, who among them has proclaimed it? These prophets have neither stood in the council of the Lord (as Jeremiah has) nor have they proclaimed the word that God has spoken there. The content of that word is given in vv. 19-20; essentially, it is an announcement of judgment (repeated in 30:23-24, where it functions as an oracle of salvation). [The Council of God]

The image of the storm is drawn from the tradition of theophanies of God as warrior, which portray God active in judgment against the wicked (see Hab 3:1-19). Jeremiah often uses this storm imagery (e.g., 4:11-12; 13:24; 18:17; 25:32). The "mind" (*lēb*) of God (v. 20; contrasted with the "minds" of the prophets in v. 16) could also be translated as the "will" of God. Judgment is named as the will of God, but it is important to name it the "circumstantial" will of God, entirely contingent upon, responsive to human wickedness (see **Connections: The Circumstantial Will of God**). Hence, to speak of the anger of God (see 4:8, 26) is not to speak of a divine attribute; if there were no sin, there would be no wrath. [The Wrath of God]

The last phrase in v. 20, "in the latter days you will understand it clearly," continues the "you" of v. 16, and exilic readers would recognize this oracle as a special word for them. They probably understand themselves to be living "in the latter days" and are coming to understand with no little clarity—through books such as Jeremiah—what these momentous events in their history mean. Note that it is clear from chapters 27–29 that false prophets were a continuing problem for exilic readers.

Verses 21-22 expand on the theme of the divine council and the nonparticipation of the false prophets in those counsels (v. 18). God did not send the prophets as divine messengers, yet they "ran" as if they were God's personal emissaries. God did not speak to them, yet they spoke as if they had a divine commission to do so (for Jeremiah as one who is sent to speak, see 1:7). If they had participated in the divine council, they would have been given the right words to speak to "my people."

The argument of v. 22 is not: if they had stood in the council they would have been *successful* in turning people from their evil ways, as if Jeremiah's lack of success would be "evidence" that he

The Wrath of God

AΩ The wrath of God is often imaged in quite impersonal terms: it goes forth, whirls like a tempest, and bursts upon the head of the wicked (v. 19). This language is comparable to Jeremiah's imaging of wrath as a raging fire (see 4:4; 21:12), a cup being poured out (7:20; 10:25; 25:15; 42:18), and weaponry (50:25). This characterization of wrath is true to the understanding of moral order that we have discerned elsewhere in Jeremiah; human wickedness triggers negative effects in the larger social and cosmic order that are then linked to God and named as wrath (see Num 1:53; 16:46; Josh 22:20; see **Introduction**). At the same time, this wrath is named in more personal terms as "the anger of the LORD" (v. 20). This language makes it clear that wrath is not simply to be interpreted in impersonal terms; the effects of human wickedness are mediated by God and God uses them to carry out the divine intentions (see **Connections**, chs. 4 and 25).

was not privy to the words of the divine council.[1] The focus is the nature of the word to be spoken. If they had heard the council deliberations, their words would have been of such a nature as to (potentially) turn the people from their evil ways rather than reinforce them in their wickedness (as in v. 14). The word "it shall be well with you . . . no calamity shall come upon you" (v. 17) had no capacity to effect this result. The jussive translation of v. 22bc (NEB, JB, NJV) is possible, "let them proclaim my words to my people and turn them from their evil course and their evil doings." Yet, the point is that they have already had their chance and have failed to do so; the effect of their falseness is the judgment that is already set to burst upon them (v. 19).

Dreams and Words, 23:23-32

Verses 23-32 approach the issue of false prophecy from several other angles, making clear the extent to which God is "against" these prophets (see the threefold "against" in vv. 30-32; **Connections**, ch. 21). Verses 23-24 are cast in the form of three rhetorical questions. The answer to the first: God is both near and far off.[2] The answer to the second: nobody can hide from God. The answer to the third: yes, God fills heaven and earth; this in turn doubles back and makes the first point clearer: because God fills heaven and earth, God is both near and far. [God Both Near and Far] That God "fills heaven and earth" is a remarkable theological claim; it makes clear that God is both near and far, in touch with every sphere of creation. God cannot be evicted from either individual or communal life! (see **Connections: The World Is Full of God**).

Verses 25-29 focus on the claim of the false prophets that they have had dreams in which the word of God has been revealed to them. The issue addressed is not the means by which God's word comes; dreams may be (and usually are so considered) an appropriate vehicle for divine communication (e.g., Jacob in Gen 28:10-22; Moses in Num 12:6-8). God can use dreams as well as other means to convey the word (e.g., speaking directly into the human mind). The issue is "*lying* dreams" (v. 32), that is, the *content* of the word spoken, which in turn will show whether the

God Both Near and Far

Verses 23-24 may be explained in part with reference to 12:2b which speaks of the wicked as having God "near" to their lips but "far" from their hearts. Two related perceptions by the false prophets are thus brought into play: (a) That because they (think they) make God near in their speaking the word, they forget that God is not thereby under their control. God is "near," but God is not confined to any local times and places; God has revealed God's word, but the revelation in the divine council is "far" from their minds and hearts. (b) That they would be able to escape the judgment word of God and have a sure place to hide from the coming disaster. But God's action in the world is not restricted by human efforts to hide. God is hidden (not fully revealed) from human beings, but human beings are not hidden from God (see 16:17; 32:19). In the coming day of judgment, no matter their hiding place, they will encounter God.

God's Word as Fire and Hammer

Given the linkage of the images of fire and hammer to words of judgment (see 4:4; 5:14; 20:9 for fire; 50:23; 51:20 for hammer) the rhetorical questions in 23:29 may have specific rather than general reference. That is, these images may not be revealing of a general understanding of the word of God, but of the particular word that Jeremiah has been speaking, namely, the devastating word of judgment. Hence, the images of fire and rock-smashing have to do with the kind of word Jeremiah brings and the false prophets should have brought (vv. 14, 17, 22). This interpretation is also suggested by the fact that, if one thinks of the power of the word more generally, the words of the false prophets are also like rocks and hammers; they have the power to lead people astray and indeed have done just that (e.g., v. 14). More generally, it should also be noted that God's word, as powerful as it is, can also be resisted, as is evident throughout Jeremiah (see the specific language of resistance in Ezek 2:7; 3:11).

---

dream is from God. Even more, "legitimate techniques in the hands of people who are false become false themselves."[3] God calls their speech what it is: "lies in my name."

Using speech typical of human lament ("How Long?" see Ps 13:1-2), God laments over the situation presented by these prophets. God agonizes over whether the deceitful hearts of those who prophesy lies will ever turn back to God (the implied answer is negative). These prophets share their dreams with another and, with even greater consequences, they pass them off to the people as the word of God. This amounts to a scheme to make the people forget their Lord, just as their ancestors forgot Yahweh for Baal (see v. 13; 2:8; 7:9; 9:14; see Deut 13:1-6).

In v. 28 God in effect proposes a contest between those who claim to have had a divine revelation in their dreams and those who have received a genuine word from God. Let the one tell the dream and let the other speak God's word faithfully. The result would make it clear whose word is genuine. The claimed means of revelation (=straw, chaff) are nothing compared to the content of the word of God, faithfully spoken (=wheat, food). This contrast is preferable to the view that dreams per se are chaff and God's word per se is wheat, not least because dreams can be the vehicle of word. Moreover, God's word is like fire, an image for judgment (see at 4:4; 5:14); it burns within Jeremiah until it is spoken (20:9). God's word is like a hammer that "smashes" rocks in pieces (see 50:23; 51:20; the verb *pṣṣ* may play on the verb *pûṣ*, "scatter," in vv. 1-2; see Heb 4:12). [God's Word as Fire and Hammer]

God proceeds to speak three sentences that repeat the key point that God is "against" these prophets, though without stating a specific judgment (vv. 30-32; see **Connections**, ch. 21). Verse 30 states that the words they steal from one another are still to be identified as "my words." Given the emphasis God places on "my word" in vv. 28-29, this usage of the plural is puzzling. Some put the phrase in quotes, "my words," thinking that God is quoting the prophets or speaking with sarcasm. Others suggest, more plausibly, that these prophets do at times speak God's word, but that they have stolen the language from true prophets and then proceeded to use it for self-serving purposes (or for a situation no longer applicable).

God is also against the prophets because they claim that their words are the word of God when they speak only for themselves (v. 31). Verse 32 summarizes God's case against these prophets: God did not send them; their dreams are lies and empty boasting; they lead "my people" astray, doing them no good or even worse—generating evil. The repeated use of the phrase, "says the LORD," in vv. 30-32 pounds the point home: these prophets are false and their words are a deception.

The Burden/Oracle of the Lord, 23:33-40

This prose section likely consists of an original verse (v. 33) that has been expanded, perhaps in several stages, in the form of a commentary (midrash) on the phrase, "the burden/oracle of the LORD." The key to this repetitive, even baroque segment is a wordplay involving the dual meaning of the Hebrew word *maśāʾ*, namely, either "burden" or "oracle" (the latter is often used in the prophets, e.g., Hab 1:1). The concern of the passage includes everyone in the community, with prophets and priests singled out for special attention. Verses 33-34 seem to be addressed to Jeremiah (the "you" in v. 33 is singular), whereas vv. 35-40 are addressed to the people/priests/prophets (the "you" is plural except for v. 37, which may acknowledge an individual speaker). God seems to be the speaker throughout.

These verses appear to assume a situation in the community in which various persons claim to have received a word from God (a burden/oracle); the basic concern is to delimit the persons who are authorized to speak that word through prohibition and warning. No one is to use the word "burden/oracle" for any claimed revelation. This material may have emerged at a time when prophetic voices were suspect (postexilic period? see Zech 13:2-6) and a need arose to ground the identity of a word from God in a genuine prophetic voice. Or, more likely, the text is concerned to make claims for the prophecy of Jeremiah (in either oral or written form), especially with respect to its *burdensome* message of "gloom and doom," in the face of critical voices. In either case, the concern is to distinguish between true prophecy and false (and hence its fit in this particular context), but the text is finally less than fully clear as to just how this distinction is to be made.

The commentary on *maśā'* is launched by a question and answer (common in Jeremiah; see 5:19). When Jeremiah is asked for a *maśā'* (that is, oracle) from the LORD by *anyone,* he is to reply "*You* are the *maśā'* (that is, burden)!" Such inquiring (and skeptical) persons are the ones who have become a burden to God (see Isa 43:23-24) and God will cast them off (away from the land, v. 39) as a man would cast a burden off his back. *No one*—including prophets—is to claim to have received an "oracle" from the LORD; if any of them does do so, God will "visit" (NRSV, "punish") that act upon that individual and his/her household (v. 34).

Verses 35-40 expand upon this basic point. The people/priests/prophets may ask among themselves what word from the LORD has been received. But they shall not claim to have received such a word (identifying it as "the burden/oracle of the LORD"), because the words they speak are their own words and God has not spoken to them. Hence, any claim that God has spoken to them would be a perversion of the word of the living God (vv. 35-36). They may also ask "the prophet" (either a known prophet in the community or Jeremiah) the same questions (v. 37; as in v. 35). But in so doing they must not make an assumption that it is a burden/oracle—as the questioner did in v. 33—implying that a word from God has in fact been received and that there is a burden/oracle to speak—apparently one that stands over against those that Jeremiah has already spoken (v. 38). If they do, judgment will follow (note the repetition of the reason, "if," "because"). God will lift them up (or "forget," see NRSV footnote) and cast (or abandon) them—and the city God has given to them and their ancestors—away from God's own presence (vv. 38-39). God will visit such disgrace and shame upon them that it shall never be forgotten (v. 40; see 20:11; note the correspondence with the people "forgetting" Yahweh's name in v. 27).

CONNECTIONS

False Prophets

Conflict among prophets was a common phenomenon in Israel, especially in the decades leading up to the fall of Jerusalem in 587 BC. The sheer number of texts in Jeremiah shows the extent to which this conflict was ongoing: 2:8, 26; 4:9; 5:13, 31; 6:13-15 (=8:10-12); 14:13-18; 18:18; 27:1-22; 28:1-17.[4] Such conflicts have been frequent through the centuries, as various persons and movements have emerged claiming to know and speak the word of God; even Jesus had to contend with them (Matt 7:15-20). Our own time seems to have been visited by a virtual religious cacophony, and members of the community of faith are often hard put to sort out the true from the false.

True prophets such as Jeremiah often have to contend with other voices and other claims, and the text does not hesitate to pronounce those claims as false. Various criteria were apparently used to try to distinguish truth from falsehood, and some of those efforts may be evident in this text. Examples include: their worship of false gods, including Baal; promising good news rather than judgment; false claims to have received a word from God or to have had visions and dreams; immorality; absence from the council of the Lord. Yet, these are not sure-fire criteria, not least because these claims cannot be publicly demonstrated. Even so, issues of discernment regarding the truth or falsehood of a word from God remain important; the community of faith is called to be vigilant and always to "test the spirits to see whether they are from God" (1 John 4:1). But, finally, one is stuck with a "Wait and see" approach to such matters (see also at ch. 28).

The World Is Full of God

Where in the world is God? This question is often asked, especially in times of suffering and death. Jeremiah 23:24 makes some claims about divine presence in the world that are important in thinking about this question.

Most basically, the claim that God "fills heaven and earth" is a claim that God's relationship with the world is comprehensive in its scope. Other Old Testament texts fill out what it means for the world to be filled with God. For example, they speak of the world as being "full of the steadfast love of God" (Pss 33:5; 119:64; cf. 36:5; 48:11; 57:10) and the glory of God (Isa 6:3; Num 21:14; cf. Hab 3:3). God is a part of the map of reality and is relational, indeed lovingly relational to all that is not God. Wherever there is world, there is God.[5]

To say that the world is filled with God means that the world does not cease to be the world—or there would be nothing left for God to fill. The world and its creatures retain their own integrity in the presence of God. To say that the world is filled with the love of

God's Presence, Absence, and Wrath

It should be noted that actual absence is not recognized as a divine possibility in the Old Testament, or the world would no longer be filled with God (nor would God be omnipresent). God's forsaking and abandoning Israel (e.g., 12:7) is not a move to absence, but a move to distance, to a less and less intense presence, with the result that the forces that make for death and destruction will have their way. That divine distance does not mean absence is made clear in the judgment texts, where God's forsaking issues in an especially intense divine presence of wrath. The human cry with respect to divine forsakenness may reflect this experience of distance and wrath (see Lam 5:20-22). In other texts, the reason for such an experience may not be known; yet, the cry is commonly addressed to one who is within hearing range (e.g., Ps 22:1) but whose engagement seems not to address the expressed needs of the one who prays. (For these distinctions, see Samuel Balentine, *The Hidden God. The Hiding of the Face of God in the Old Testament* [Oxford: Clarendon Press, 1983].) The word from Jeremiah 23:23-24 is that, whatever the nature of the experience, God does fill heaven and earth.

God means that God's presence is not static or passive or indifferent. God is not simply here and there; God is always lovingly at work in every nook and cranny of the universe. God's love is a factor to be reckoned with in every occasion. This God is not simply present to Israel and active in the life of the chosen people; God is engaged in the lives of people in every time and place. Hence, everyone everywhere has experienced the loving presence of God, though they may not name their experience in those terms.

There are certainly times and places where God chooses to be present in an especially intense way (e.g., the tabernacle, Exod 40:34-38), but that is not an exclusive move simply for the sake of an elect few. God's initially exclusive move is for the sake of a maximally inclusive end. [God's Presence, Absence, and Wrath]

The Circumstantial Will of God

It is important to make distinctions within the will of God.[6] A key question to be addressed: what does it mean for God to have a will and to be in relationship? Analogies to the human will are helpful. The will of any human being in a relationship of integrity cannot be static, remaining the same in every circumstance of life. Because relationships are always in process, always changing, then what one wills for the relationship is always changing in order to relate appropriately to that new situation. At the same time, if there is not a constancy of will in the relationship (e.g., faithfulness) then one or another party to the relationship is tossed to and fro without any continuity and anchorage.

With respect to God, we must speak of both constancy and change with respect to the divine will. We can speak of constancy when it comes to divine promises or God's will for life and blessing for all. This is testimony to the unconditional will of God, freely exercised at the divine initiative. God is eternally resolute with respect to that will. At the same time, one must speak of the circumstantial will of God, the changing will of God in view of changing circumstances in the lives of those to whom God relates. As people act, speak, and move in one way or another, God's will for the particulars in their lives will change. This can be observed in the various either-or constructions in Jeremiah (see at 22:1-5), wherein God's future action is shaped by the response of human beings. One such possible future is judgment. But this will of God for judgment has not been set for all eternity; it has arisen in view of Israel's infidelity in relationship. At the same time, God's constant, unconditional will is always at work, even in such judgmental moments. And so the community of faith, though experiencing destruction and exile, can be assured that that judgment will not be the final word of God for them.

NOTES

[1] Contrary to Robert Carroll, *Jeremiah* (Philadelphia: Westminster, 1986), 463; see William McKane, *A Critical and Exegetical Commentary on Jeremiah* (2 vols.; ICC; Edinburgh: T. & T. Clark, 1986), 584.

[2] Contrary to Walter Brueggemann, *A Commentary on Jeremiah: Exile and Homecoming* (Grand Rapids: Eerdmans, 1998), 213-15; see W. Lemke, "The Near and the Distant God: A Study of Jer. 23:23-24 in its Biblical Theological Context," *JBL* 100 (1981): 541-55.

[3] So Carroll, *Jeremiah,* 473.

[4] For discussions of the phenomenon of false prophecy, see James Crenshaw, *Prophetic Conflict* (Berlin: de Gruyter, 1971); T. Overholt, *The Threat of Falsehood: A Study in the Theology of the Book of Jeremiah* (London: SCM, 1970).

[5] For detail, see Terence Fretheim, *The Suffering of God: An Old Testament Perspective* (Philadelphia: Fortress, 1984), 60-78.

[6] For detail, see Terence Fretheim, "Will of God in the OT," *ABD,* 6:914-20.

VISION OF THE GOOD
AND THE BAD FIGS

24:1-10

Chapter 24 is often grouped with chapter 25; together they announce the futures of the nations of the world. Chapter 24 announces the future of two groups from the people of Israel (similarly, 21:8-10), chapter 25 the future of Babylon and all other nations (and, implicitly, the future of Israel).

This narrative reports a prophetic vision similar to those associated with Jeremiah's call (see 1:11-18); the building/planting theme also links these chapters (cf. 24:7 with 1:10). The vision may have been prompted by a focus on an actual basket of figs (see Amos 7:7-9; 8:1-3). God does not tell Jeremiah to report this vision to any audience; the vision is apparently for his own enlightenment and, having been written down, that of exilic readers, who would identify themselves with the good figs. The report consists of a description of the vision (vv. 1-2), a dialogue between prophet and God (v. 3), and a divine interpretation of the vision, focusing first on the good figs (vv. 4-7) and then on the bad figs (vv. 8-10).

The vision is set in the period between the first deportation of Judeans to Babylon (597 BC) and the destruction of Jerusalem (587 BC). It draws a distinction between two groups of people: (1) The exiles of 597 BC—including King Jeconiah= Jehoiachin ("good figs"), with whom God will shape a future for Israel. These are the chosen remnant; God will give them a new heart/will, bring them back to the land, and move with them into the future. [The Need for a New Heart] (2) Those who remained behind in the land, King Zedekiah and his

---

The Need for a New Heart

Daniel Berrigan makes the need for a new heart an ever-contemporary concern. "A new heart—Who has not longed for it, knowing all too well the cold, slow beat, the insufficiency, caprice, and selfishness of the old? And who, at the same time, has not felt the spirit shriveling within, how the 'old' cannot fire the soul, how convention and habit and rote and moral boredom seize on and throttle other images—those of clairvoyance, of a frenzied sense of justice, of hope itself? One thing is clear (at least to Yahweh, if not to us): along with the ferocious plundering of the resources of the planet, our spiritual resources also dwindle, all but vanish. Eventually we cannot imagine ourselves as a new people, noncompetitive, compassionate, nonviolent. . . . The word of Yahweh is clear. The One who knows the heart, who sets it beating, weak or heroic, must act, intervene."

Daniel Berrigan, *Jeremiah: The World, the Wound of God* (Minneapolis: Fortress, 1999), 100.

Figs

The fig *(ficus carica)* is referenced more than sixty times in the Bible, where sitting under a fig tree represents peace and security while destroying a fig tree foreshadows national crisis. A fig is a high-fructose fruit that is produced more than once a season. After blooming in the spring, the first fruits are ripe in May, while the second fruits are not ripe until mid August. It was common to eat the fruit fresh off the tree as well as to dry it into a cake for storage.

Giovanna Garzoni (1600–1670). *Plate of Figs.* 17th C. Galleria Palatina. Palazzo Pitti, Florence, Italy. (Credit: Scala/Art Resource, NY)

officials, and those living in Egypt ("bad figs"; see 29:17; Hos 9:10), whom God will disperse and destroy.

While perhaps rooted in a vision of Jeremiah, this text seems to assume the post-fall disposition of the various Israelite groups: exiles in Babylon (v. 5) and in Egypt (v. 8), and those left in the land. Conflict existed among these communities (see chs. 27–29; 41–44) and this vision report grounded the claims of one group (the exiles in Babylon) over against the claims of others.[1] After the exile, the returnees from Babylon (including Zerubbabel, grandson of Jehoiachin) assumed the leadership role for the Jewish community and gave decisive shape to Israel's literature. The torch passed to them and they ran with it. The perspective of this chapter, so favorable to the exiles in Babylon, was no doubt shaped by those very exiles.

COMMENTARY

The Vision, 24:1-3

God shows Jeremiah two baskets of figs that had been placed in front of the temple (v. 1). The temple location is of uncertain import; perhaps God, in the manner of a priest, would determine the acceptability of the offerings "placed before the temple of the LORD." The time of the vision is important to the narrator—after the first deportation in 597 BC but before the destruction of Jerusalem in 587 BC. Those who participated in the exile to Babylon are carefully listed, though only Jehoiachin is named. Also included among these exiles were various officials, artisans, and smiths—professional classes. The figs in one basket were very good, the first picking of the season (fig trees bear two crops a season); the figs in the other basket were rotten and could not be eaten. As in 1:11 and 1:13, God asks Jeremiah what he sees, and Jeremiah names the two baskets of figs for what they are (v. 3).

The Good Figs, 24:4-7

God then provides the interpretation of the vision (as in 1:12 and 1:14-18), a crucial matter given the simple starting point. God first focuses on the good figs (vv. 5-7). Like the good figs, God regards as good those Judeans who were exiled to Babylonia (=Chaldea). God has chosen (=set his eyes upon; cf. Amos 9:4) them as the object of his special blessing ("for good"; contrast Amos 9:4). God will bring them back to their land and give them a new heart/will. [A New Will?]

A New Will?

In view of the emphasis in Jeremiah on the people's stubbornness (e.g., 3:17; 5:23; see **Connections**, ch. 5), the word commonly translated "heart" (*lēb*) probably carries a volitional sense, and hence the translation "will" seems best (cf. NEB/REB, "wit"). This is supported by the fact that the people's "will" has often been described as "evil" up this point (3:17; 7:24; 11:8; 16:12; 18:12; NRSV translates "will" in these texts). What is at stake here is not individual or communal sinful actions, though they were certainly epidemic, but that more basic willful disposition that generated such activity (cf. 13:23; 17:9). It is not that the people had become evil (or essentially evil) so that they ceased to be human beings; in fact, God repeatedly calls

them "good" even as they languish in exile. What a remarkably encouraging word for exiled readers to hear! At the same time, their sad story is that they could not be other than unfaithful in word and deed (see at 2:25; 18:11). And so God must act in such a way that this will not happen again (note the "for all time" in the gift of the new heart in 32:39). Given the exceptional depth and breadth of Jeremiah's indictment of these people up to this point in the book, this decision by God to give these unfaithful ones a new will and "regard" them "as good" in God's sight is remarkable. With this God, who is a God of new beginnings, this people can begin again.

The language used to describe God's actions with respect to these exiles is striking by the way in which it gathers elements from the call of Jeremiah (1:5-10), though now with God as subject. God will plant them in the land, not pluck them up; God will build them up, not tear them down (see also 32:41). These explicit linkages (and others) to the call indicate that, at least for the editors of the book, this vision was that of the prophet himself. From this perspective, then, the negative oracles against Jehoiachin were probably interpreted more in terms of the individual King Jehoiachin (see at 22:24-30 and cf. 52:31-34). But the judgment against him personally did not cut off the promises to the Davidic line (note the juxtaposition of 23:1-8 to the oracle against Jehoiachin in 22:24-30). In this view, the falsehood of Hananiah's prophecy about the return of Jehoiachin and the exiles from Babylon (28:3-4) has to do, not with its content, but with its timing.

Verse 7 highlights certain themes that appear elsewhere in Jeremiah (e.g., 7:23; 11:4; 29:10-14; 30:3, 22; 31:1; 32:38; see also Ezek 11:14-21; 18:31; 36:24-26), anticipating especially the promises of 31:31-34 and 32:37-41. Several of these thematic elements are characteristic of the covenant with Israel's ancestors (see Gen 17:1-8; Lev 26:44-45). To be given a new heart/will is new language, but the exiles are the same people whose ancestors received these old promises, and those promises are still in place, including the promise of a land (see **Connections: A New Heart/Will for the Same People on the Old Land**).

The Bad Figs, 24:8-10

In these verses God interprets that part of the vision concerning the "bad figs," figs so bad they cannot be eaten. Included in this group are King Zedekiah (who ends up with the exiles in Babylon, 39:7!), his officials, the remnant that remains in the land (after the exile in 597 BC), and those who live in Egypt (including King Jehoahaz/Shallum, 2 Kgs 23:34; see chs. 41–44, especially 42:9-17). God is going to treat these people like a person would handle bad figs, namely, throw them away (their future is restated in 29:16-19, with reasons offered). God will make them a horror, an evil thing (*rā'āh*) to all (!) the nations. Wherever they are scattered, these people will be a disgrace and a byword, an object of cursing and the taunt (see 15:4; 19:8; 25:9, 18; 29:18; 42:18; 44:8, 12, 22; Deut 28:37; 1 Kgs 9:7). God will send the now familiar "sword, famine, and pestilence" upon them (14:12-18; 15:2) until they have disappeared from the land of promise (but apparently not annihilated).

This chapter is a two-edged sword. On the one hand, the remnant of Israel whom God sent away into exile in Babylon continues to be God's own people. Across the events of 597 BC, God continues to name these exiles the chosen people and acts on behalf of their life and salvation; they had not been removed from the sphere of God's promises. In fact, God was working to create a new future for them. It might be noted that the "less than a full end" segments of chapters 2–23 probably have the reality of the "good figs" in mind. On the other hand, for those remaining in the land, this vision made it clear that the destruction of Jerusalem and exile (to Babylon, Egypt, and "all the places") was yet before them; they had not escaped from the judgment of God. Even more, the vision suggests that not all members of the original Israel remain among God's chosen, or at least they would not survive into the promised future of God's people.

It is not entirely clear why those who remain in the land (and in Egypt) are judged so harshly, but some signals are given. In view of several texts (Ezek 11:14-15; 33:23-29), this vision report probably sought to cut against the grain of popular notions that those left in the land were the elect of God and could claim the ancestral promises for themselves. This land was their land. Moreover, they had a sense, encouraged by prophets such as Hananiah (28:1-17; see 29:16-19), that the time of Jeremiah's prophecies of judgment had passed (and they had escaped!).

Jeremiah's vision provides an alternative perspective; what appears to be divine abandonment for the exiles in Babylon has turned into a new creation; what appears to be divine deliverance for those remaining in the land is seen to be rejection. The "bad figs" will undergo a second round of disaster and many will be killed (the fall in 587 BC and later events). They are not to be counted among God's elect ones, that is, "the exiles from Judah" (v. 5). If post-587 BC events are taken into account, though Jeremiah's work among those remaining in the land was initially positive, it turned sharply negative (see chs. 40–43). [What of the Post-587 BC Exiles to Babylon?]

What of the Post-587 BC Exiles to Babylon?

It has often been noted that many of these "bad figs" are taken to Babylon in the deportations of 587 BC and later (see 39:9-10; 52:28-30), join the community that is already there, and are among those who later return to the land. Jeremiah's vision, however, at least as it is presently dated (v. 1), ignores these individuals, excluding them from the vision for the good figs. But rather too much can be made of this fact. It is likely that the interpretation of the vision in its present form has been shaped in a time after the destruction (see above). The phrase "the exiles from Judah" (v. 5) would certainly be understood by post-587 BC readers as including everyone in Babylon. In any case, the dichotomy between good figs and bad figs is best regarded as a *generalization*, developed in the service of a situational polemic against the claims of those who remained in the land and in Egypt. As such, the vision may not have been understood in a strictly quantitative sense or in starkly black-and-white terms.

If the setting of the vision in the post-597 BC period is emphasized, the vision was a means by which to encourage the first exiles
in Babylon in their time of hardship (cf. 29:4-7) and to burst any
balloons created by those who remained in the land. As for later
times, the vision would have functioned as a basis upon which the
continuity of the community of Israel and its leadership was to be
determined. According to the vision, the position of the good figs
in the community of exiles in Babylon was grounded in a divine
decision.

CONNECTIONS

A New Heart/Will for the Same People on the Old Land

The promise, "I will give them a heart/will to know that I am the
LORD," is language new to Jeremiah. It is a remarkable text, especially given what has been said about these people up to this point
in the book. God regards these people as "good" (though certainly
no less guilty than others who were not exiled); it sounds like the
sixth day of creation once again. At the same time, while these
exiles may be good figs, they need a new heart/will. God still has
some work to do with these folk, and it is not a minor matter. God
must engage in another creative act, shaping a new heart/will for
good figs.

Moreover, these good figs will need a new place to live to go with
their new heart (v. 6). God does not create in them a new heart and
leave them languishing in exile. Simply giving them a new heart
will not do. The divine action needed for this people must include
both internal and external components—a new heart and a specific
place in which to grow and develop. In other terms, God will not
only forgive these people, God will deliver (=save) them from
Babylon. It is not enough that these people know that God is their
Lord and that they are God's people, as crucial as this divine action
is. They must also be delivered out of the hands of their captors
and established again on their land.

At the same time, these good figs are the people of *Israel.* God is
not destroying one people and starting over with another. Or,
better, however much death and destruction this people will have
experienced, God still determines to work with the same people
and move into the future with them. Across the divide of disaster
and exile, there are important elements of continuity. However
much the "old" heart was spoiled, indeed rotten, the people within

whom that heart was beating are the ones with whom God will work to create this new future. At another level, there is continuity with respect to land. A new land will not be created for them; they will be returned to their own land, to familiar places and spaces, and become established there once again. Even more, God promises not to tear them down or pluck them up out of that land ever again.

This concreteness provided by the land promise is important so as to prevent an over-spiritualization of this text and reduce Israel's faith to an inner spirituality. The promises just articulated in 23:1-8 help fill out this picture, as will also be the case in chapters 30–34. The claim of Clements that "God is not to be found through physical symbols of his presence but through an inner spiritual movement of heart and will," seems far removed from these concerns of Jeremiah.[2] [Is the New Heart a Conditional Promise?]

Is the New Heart a Conditional Promise?

How is this promise of a new heart to be linked to the last clause of v. 7, "for they shall return to me with their whole heart" (see 3:10; Deut 30:10; 1 Kgs 8:48)? Clearly the promises in v. 7 are not conditional upon the people's returning to God. If the *prior* action would be the people's returning to God with "their whole heart," why would they need to be given a "heart" to know God? Also, the other new heart text in Jeremiah (32:37-41) consists solely of unconditional promises. That is also the case in this text (note also the unconditional announcement of judgment in vv. 8-10). God gives them a new heart and this gift enables them to return to God with their whole heart (see William McKane, *A Critical and Exegetical Commentary on Jeremiah* [2 vols.; ICC; Edinburgh: T. & T. Clark, 1986], 609). At the same time, these people with a new heart do not thereby become passive creatures; they are still the *subject* of the verb "return" and the land to which they are returned will need work to bring it back to what it once was.

NOTES

[1] See C. Seitz, *Theology in Conflict: Reactions to the Exile in the Book of Jeremiah* (Berlin: de Gruyter, 1989).

[2] Ronald E. Clements, *Jeremiah* (IBC; Atlanta: John Knox, 1988), 147.

SUMMARY JUDGMENTS AGAINST THE NATIONS

25:1-38

The complexity of this chapter is recognized by all commentators, not least because of the differences of the Hebrew text from that of the Greek (LXX) translation (see **Introduction**). Most basically, the LXX places the oracles against the nations (chs. 46–51 in the Hebrew text) after 25:13a. Scholars commonly consider this to be evidence that an earlier Hebrew text of Jeremiah also placed the oracles against the nations at this point. This is but one indication that the material in this chapter has undergone much revision at the hands of various redactors.

This chapter consists of three sections: a prose sermon summarizing the message of Jeremiah (vv. 1-14) and a narrative of a symbolic action or vision (vv. 15-29) with an accompanying announcement of judgment against the nations (vv. 30-38).

COMMENTARY

Summary Indictment and Judgment, 25:1-14

This summary section is usually understood to be an editorial effort to bring together the major emphases of the message of Jeremiah to this point in the book (often identified with the first scroll, see ch. 36). A certain roughness is evident in the identification of the speaker (Jeremiah clearly in v. 3, God clearly in vv. 6-7; note quotation marks in NRSV around vv. 5-6). It is best to consider vv. 5-7 Jeremiah's recollection of what God said (cf. NIV) and hence the speaker of vv. 3-7. This merging of the divine and prophetic subjects is also evident in vv. 15-17. This section explicitly speaks of the first twenty-three years of Jeremiah's ministry (v. 3) and summarizes the content of his message in the form of a recollection Jeremiah received from God concerning the people of Israel. Unlike many other recitals of Israel's history that emphasized God's saving deeds (e.g., Deut 26:5-9), this recital is unrelenting in its focus on sin and judgment.

The emphasis on "all" the people in vv. 1-2 makes clear that both groups in chapter 24 are included. The essence of the review is an indictment of the people for their infidelity and refusal to repent (vv. 3-7) and a consequent announcement of judgment (vv. 8-14). The latter is unusual in that it includes both Israel (vv. 8-11) and Babylon, for exceeding the divine mandate (vv. 12-14). The latter moves this section beyond a review of the prior chapters and begins to catch up nations other than Israel in the scope of the divine judgment. This theme will provide the focus for the balance of the chapter (vv. 15-38) and for chapters 46–51 (see **Connections** there).

This review covers the time from the thirteenth year of Josiah (627 BC; see 1:2) to the year this message was received (v. 3; "to this day"), the fourth year of Jehoiakim (605 BC), which was also the first year of Nebuchadrezzar's reign. This dating (and basic content) coincides with that of 36:1-2 and the writing of the scroll by Baruch; hence, many have linked this chapter with that scroll in various ways. This time is an ominous moment not only for Israel but also for all the nations of that world; the life of every nation will be deeply and negatively affected by the rise of Babylon. The theological claim of these texts, however, is that these developments cannot simply be understood in political and military terms. God is caught up in the stories of these nations and is working out the divine purposes in and through a variety of agents (see **Connections: Nebuchadrezzar, My Servant**).

Over the course of the twenty-three years of his ministry Jeremiah has spoken persistently to the people of Israel, as have all "his servants the prophets" whom God has "sent" (v. 4; see 7:25-26; 11:7-8; 35:14b-15; 44:4-5). Jeremiah has not been alone in bringing this message (see 26:20-23; 2 Kgs 17:13-15; 2 Chr 36:15-16). The upshot of those years of preaching: the people have not listened. The prophets untiringly proclaimed this word of God to the people (vv. 5-6): repent of your evil (*rāʿāh*) way of life and your wicked (*rōaʿ*) deeds. If you do, you will be able to remain in the land that God has promised to you and to your ancestors "forever" (so 7:6-7; on repentance in Jeremiah, see **Connections** at 3:1–4:4; 18). The land has been promised "forever," and God will not go back on that promise, but the people have chosen to remove themselves from the sphere of the promise—a move that God honors—and they will suffer the consequence of landlessness.

In addition, the prophets had warned the people over the years not to serve other gods and worship "the work of your hands" (vv. 6-7). If they had not done so, God would have done them "no harm" (=brought disaster, *rāʿaʿ*; so also in 25:29; 31:28), that is, mediated the consequences of their own deeds (as often in Jeremiah, *rāʿah* leads to *rāʿah*; see **Introduction**). But the people did not listen and they constructed gods with their own hands; consequently, God was provoked to anger "to your own harm" (*raʿ*, v. 7; so also 7:6; cf. 7:19). Repeated phrases in vv. 6-7 make doubly clear that the people have acted in ways that result in the disaster that God, provoked to anger, mediates. That God's anger is "provoked" by what the people have done is important in showing that anger is not an attribute of God, but a contingent response.

The announcement of judgment on Israel follows in vv. 8-11; the "therefore" makes clear that the disaster is the consequence of the people's own wickedness. These verses continue to reiterate what Jeremiah has spoken over the years (v. 2). This text is the first to explicitly identify the foe from "the north" as the Babylonians under King Nebuchadrezzar (see 20:4-6; 21:7). Especially to be noted is God's identification of Nebuchadrezzar as "my servant" (so also 27:6; 43:10) (see **Connections: Nebuchadrezzar, My Servant**). God will "send for" his armies and allied armies ("all the tribes of the north," see 1:15) against the land of Israel and all of its inhabitants, as well as on Israel's neighbors, "all these nations around" (v. 9; listed in vv. 19-26; detailed in chs. 46–49). God had "sent" his "servants" the prophets (v. 4); in view of their response God now correspondingly "sends" his "servant" Nebuchadrezzar (v. 9).

God then becomes the only subject of the verbs of destruction that follow (vv. 9b-10; on the conformation of language about God with that of God's servant, Nebuchadrezzar, see **Introduction**). God will utterly destroy; God will make Israel (and all its neighbors) an object of horror and ridicule, an everlasting disgrace (though "everlasting" means an indefinite period of time into the future, there is a sense in which the "disgrace" continues). God will banish from among the Israelites the sounds and sights of everyday life, including laughter and gladness, joyous weddings, and people happily going about their daily tasks (see 7:34; 16:9; millstones are used for grinding grain). The lights of house lamps will no longer be seen (see the reapplication of this language in Rev 18:21-24). The entire land will become a ruin, a veritable wasteland, and Israel (and its neighbors) will serve Babylon for seventy years (v. 11). [The Seventy Years]

Verses 12-14 turn from judgment on Israel to judgment on Babylon for exceeding its divine mandate. After the seventy years have passed, God will "visit" the iniquity of Nebuchrezzar and the

The Seventy Years

AΩ This number is difficult to understand (25:11; 29:10), not least because it is not clear whether it is used literally, metaphorically, or as a literary convention. Numerous suggestions have been made. Seventy may be a general number for the span of a life (Ps 90:10), or the dying out of the generation that experienced the fall of Jerusalem, or the traditional time for the ruination of a city/land, or the life of a dynasty (cf. 27:7; Isa 23:15-17), or a time for the land to rest after a lengthy period of infidelity.

Seventy could also be understood more literally in terms of the period of exile. The exile would be sixty-six years if one figures from 605 BC (the dating of this announcement) to 539 BC, when King Cyrus of Persia conquered Babylon and let the exiles return home (Ezra 1:1-4). In Zech 1:12, the seventy years is figured from the destruction of the temple in 587 BC and concludes with its being rebuilt in 515/516 BC. In

Jer 27:7-8, the temporal reference has a different sense: "until the time of his own land comes" (that is, a build-up of iniquity in Babylon, see 25:34). The phrase is reinterpreted in Dan 9:2 in terms of seventy weeks of years (=490 years) and related to Antiochus Epiphanes in the second century BC.

In the context of an expectation on the part of some Israelites that the exile of 597 BC would be short-lived (see 28:3), this number makes it clear that such will not be the case. On the other hand, seventy years is a limited period and hence could be understood as sign of hope for the exiles. God has a future for this people beyond these tragic events—because God is faithful. (For a review of opinion, see G. Keown, P. Scalise, and T. Smothers, *Jeremiah 26–52* [Dallas: Word Books, 1993], 74-75; Walter Brueggemann, *A Commentary on Jeremiah: Exile and Homecoming* [Grand Rapids: Eerdmans, 1998], 278-79).

Babylonians upon them; the iniquity is identified as making the land of *Israel* "an everlasting waste" (note the NAB translation— *Babylon* shall become an everlasting waste, see Isa 13:20-22). Once again, as with Israel in vv. 9b-10, God is the subject of the verbs. In visiting their iniquity upon them, God will bring upon Babylon all the words that God has uttered against it (now found in chs. 50–51). The reference in v. 13 to "that land" has sometimes been thought to refer back to Israel, but in this context (between vv. 12 and 14) this phrase is certainly a reference to Babylon. [Judgment on Babylon]

These words are written in "this book, which Jeremiah prophesied against all the nations" (v. 13; recall that Jeremiah is a "prophet to the nations," 1:5, 10). The "book" probably has reference to the oracles "against all the nations," that is, chapters 46–51. In view of the placement of these oracles at this point in the text of the LXX, they may have followed at this point in an earlier version of the Hebrew text (vv. 15-29 are located after the oracles against the nations in the LXX, 32:1-24). In the present text, however, vv. 12-38 anticipate those later oracles. The "mobile" character of these oracles probably means that they existed in a separate "book" at one point. In v. 14, the Babylonians will themselves become the slaves of conquering nations, as God repays or returns to (*šālôm*) them according to their own iniquitous deeds and the work of their hands (on *šālēm*, in the sense of coming full circle, see 16:18; 18:20; 32:18; 50:29; 51:6, 24, 56).

Judgment on Babylon

Scholars often note that the two-sided character of Jeremiah's oracles about Babylon seem contradictory. On the one hand, Babylon is the instrument of God for the judgment of Israel (and other nations); on the other hand, Babylon is judged for exceeding its divine mandate, going beyond its proper judgmental activities, and committed iniquity itself in making the land an "everlasting waste." (so also chs. 50–51). But, if one understands these two different messages in temporal sequence, this dual message is not contradictory. The relationship of God to Babylon changes in view of Babylon's own conduct as the agent of judgment. When Babylon engages in excessively destructive behaviors, it opens itself up to reaping what it has sown (50:29; 51:24). God turns against God's own agent on the basis of issues of justice; this is a divine pattern also evident with respect to Israel (see Exod 22:21-24). If God were not to change in view of changing circumstances, God would be unfaithful to God's own commitments.

This text is also testimony to the way in which God uses agents; God does not "control" or micromanage their behaviors. These agents are not puppets in the divine hand; they retain the power to make decisions and execute policies. God's agents can act in ways that are contrary to God's own will for the situation; God's will and action in these events is not "irresistible" (as Israel's own sin testifies; contrary to Walter Brueggemann, *A Comentary on Jeremiah: Exile and homecoming* [Grand Rapids: Eerdmanns, 1998], 222).

This risky divine way of working in the world also opens God up to misunderstanding and may besmirch God's own reputation in the world (and often has). This way of working also has negative effects on God's own life. God's grieving, so commonly displayed in Jeremiah, is intensified when human suffering is intensified. This understanding of Babylon's excessiveness also reflects back on issues of divine foreknowledge (see **Connections** at 22:1-5). Though, because God certainly knew of the possibility of Babylon's overreaching conduct, God is not finally "off the hook" regarding what happens. And so Jeremiah will speak of God expressing regret over what has happened, namely, the excessive violence Israel has had to endure (see **Connections** at 42:10).

God's Wrath Poured Out on the Nations, 25:15-38

This prose narrative continues the theme of Jeremiah as a prophet to the nations (1:5, 10). It is commonly thought to report a symbolic action (see 13:1-14 and 19:1-15), yet it differs from other such acts. For Jeremiah to take the cup and make the nations drink from it (v. 17) is not an action that he proceeds to carry out in any literal sense. This action is either a vivid metaphor or, more likely, a vision in which Jeremiah participates. The entire chapter takes place within the vision.

The flow of thought is difficult to follow, however. Verses 18 (17)-26 or vv. 27-29 are commonly considered intrusive in this report; yet, a certain sense can be made of the present text. It may be outlined as follows: God's command to Jeremiah (vv. 15-16); Jeremiah's obedient response, taking the cup and making all the nations listed drink it (vv. 17-26; note the colon at the end of v. 17 in NRSV, NAB, NIV); divine directives to *speak* certain words to the nations (vv. 27-29); the proclamation itself (vv. 30-38).

Drinking the Cup of Wrath, 25:15-29

Verses 15-16 constitute God's command to Jeremiah to make the nations drink the cup of wrath and give a preliminary indication of

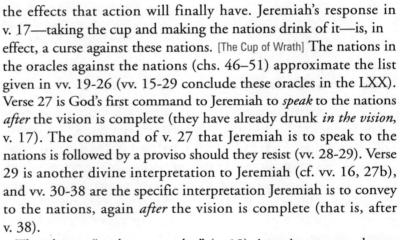

The Cup of Wrath

The image of drinking from a cup is a common image for experiencing the effects of both curse (48:26; 49:12; 51:7; Lam 4:21; Pss 11:6; 75:8; Rev 14:10; 16:19; 17:4; 18:6) and blessing (16:7; Pss 16:5; 23:5; see also Hab 2:16; Ezek 23:32; Isa 51:17-21). Note the parallels with Jer 13:12-14. The contents of the cup determine the effect it has on those who drink from it. Here the cup is filled with "the wine of wrath" (in effect, a kind of poison, see 8:14; 9:15) which, when drunk, results in a suffocating stupor that leads to death (this effect is more than drunkenness). A background for the cup image has been sought in the trial by ordeal in Num 5:11-31; it may be so, but it is important to note that the nations drink from the cup "of wrath" and have already been declared guilty (see vv. 9, 11). Obadiah 15–16 introduces the theme of drinking the cup of wrath with this language, "as you have done, it shall be done to you; your deeds shall return on your own head," understanding wrath in terms of the moral order (see **Introduction**; for a review of opinion, see Walter Brueggemann, *A Commentary on Jeremiah: Exile and homecoming* [Grand Rapids: Eerdmanns, 1998], 278-79).

the effects that action will finally have. Jeremiah's response in v. 17—taking the cup and making the nations drink of it—is, in effect, a curse against these nations. [The Cup of Wrath] The nations in the oracles against the nations (chs. 46–51) approximate the list given in vv. 19-26 (vv. 15-29 conclude these oracles in the LXX). Verse 27 is God's first command to Jeremiah to *speak* to the nations *after* the vision is complete (they have already drunk *in the vision*, v. 17). The command of v. 27 that Jeremiah is to speak to the nations is followed by a proviso should they resist (vv. 28-29). Verse 29 is another divine interpretation to Jeremiah (cf. vv. 16, 27b), and vv. 30-38 are the specific interpretation Jeremiah is to convey to the nations, again *after* the vision is complete (that is, after v. 38).

The phrase, "as they are today" (v. 18), is an important clue to the text. From the perspective of the writer (and exilic readers), Jerusalem has already become "a desolation and a waste, an object of hissing and of cursing." The other nations are to experience what Israel has endured. This suggests that vv. 17-26 are a visionary representation of the words commanded in vv. 27-29 (30-38) and their devastating aftermath. When Jeremiah actually speaks what God commissions him to say to the nations, it is in the wake of that word that the nations to whom he is sent will *actually* drink the cup. It is then that they will become drunk, affected both physically ("stagger") and mentally ("go out of their minds").

At the same time, more than Jeremiah's actions and speaking are involved. Verses 16, 27b and 29 make clear that it is God's use of the sword that will have this effect (this theme is repeated in vv. 31,

38). The cup of wrath is a vivid image of the experience of death by sword and related terrors.[1] Of course, Jeremiah wields no sword, so his action and subsequent word are not efficacious in some magical way. God will use the weapons of the Babylonians to effect this word (see at vv. 8-10). Yet, even more seems to be at stake here, namely, the merging of divine action and human action (see Amos 9:1 for a comparable command). Jeremiah's actions and words are elided with those of the Babylonian armies; in turn these are conformed to the actions of God in this situation.

Jerusalem and all the cities of Judah lead the list of nations (v. 18), as they do in vv. 29 and 30. Those with the grandest religious heritage of all go to the guillotine first! They (kings and officials are specifically mentioned) have drunk the cup of wrath and the city and country has become a wasteland, an object of contempt and ridicule (see 24:9). From the editor's (and exilic readers') vantage point, this has already happened ("as they are today"). After a summary reference to "all the kingdoms of the world that are on the face of the earth," Babylon is finally mentioned (v. 26b), though in cryptic fashion. Sheshach (see also 51:41) is an example of the athbash cipher in which Hebrew letters in reverse alphabetical order are substituted for Babel. All the nations mentioned in vv. 18-25 would drink the cup of the *armies of Babylon* (as in 51:7; see 48:26; 49:12), but finally Babylon itself would drink the cup of God's wrath (anticipated in 25:12-14). [The Nations of 25:19-26]

Then, God commissions Jeremiah to speak and to demand, in the name of the Lord of hosts and the God of *Israel* (note the identity, even in judgment), that the nations drink of the cup of wrath (v. 27). The phrase "the LORD of hosts" brackets vv. 27-29; "hosts" is a reference to armies. These are not heavenly armies, but the army of Babylon used as an instrument of divine judgment. The juxtaposition of Lord of Hosts and God of Israel brings together the universal and particular relationships that this God maintains.

All the nations are to drink until they are so drunk that they vomit and fall, never again to rise. In effect, they are to drink until they are dead. Note again, as in v. 16, it is the sword of conquering armies that will serve as the instrument of divine wrath, not simply Jeremiah's (or God's!) words and deeds. If the nations refuse to drink from the cup upon being commanded to do so (v. 28), Jeremiah is to insist that they drink. This insistence means that the nations no longer have a choice in the matter, as v. 29 further demonstrates. They *must* drink because they *will* drink regardless of what they do (see 49:12)! Given the fact that God is already

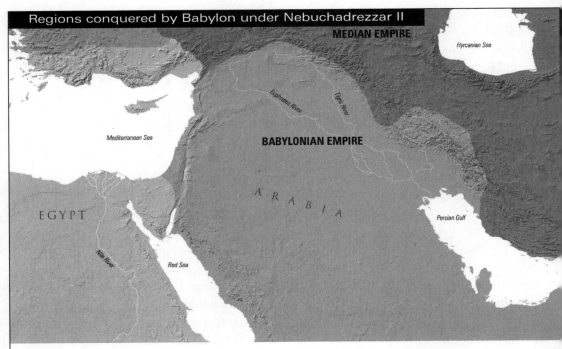

Regions conquered by Babylon under Nebuchadrezzar II

The Nations in 25:19-26

The list of nations includes those that were conquered by Babylon under Nebuchadrezzar in the years after 605 BC. The reason for the order in which they are mentioned is uncertain, but may be geographically oriented. After Israel, Pharaoh and the Egyptians are named (v. 19; see the oracle against them in 46:1-26). Egypt is followed by an uncertain ethnographical and geographical reference: the "mixed people" and the kings of the land of Uz (perhaps various peoples from the desert areas east of Israel). The Philistines, with their cities of Ashkelon, Gaza, Ekron, and Ashdod in the southern coastal plain, are mentioned next; Ashdod is a remnant because the Egyptians destroyed it during the seventh century (see the oracle against them in 47:1-7). Edom, Moab and Ammon are bunched together as Transjordanian nations without further comment (see the oracles against them in 48:1-47; 49:7-22; 49:1-6).

The Phoenicians are represented by the kings of Tyre and Sidon (city-states north of Israel) and the islands and coastal areas of the Mediterranean (where Phoenicians had settled); they are mentioned in the oracles against the nations only in passing (47:4). Among the various Arabian tribes and "mixed peoples" from the desert areas (vv. 23-24), only the tribes of Dedan, Tema, and Buz (unknown, but presumably from this area) are named—only Dedan is mentioned in the oracles against the nations (49:8), though other Arabian tribes are named in 49:28-33. On the religious practice of shaving temples among some Arabian tribes, see 9:26. In v. 26, Elam and Media (and presumably Zimri, though its location is unknown) are east of Babylon—only Elam is mentioned in the oracles against the nations (49:34-39). Verse 26 gathers in a summary way "all the kings of the north," among which would be included presumably Damascus (see 49:23-27). Finally, Babylon is mentioned in the last line of v. 26 with the code name Sheshach.

bringing disaster (*rāʿah*) against the city "called by my name" (=Jerusalem) and that none of the nations are innocent, the cup of wrath can no longer be held back against any of them (vv. 28-29). In other words, the Babylonians (=the sword that "the LORD of hosts" is summoning) are in the process of conquering that world, and no nation will escape from the devastating effects of its invading armies. The reason given is not made explicit (v. 29); this judgment occurs only because, if Israel experiences judgment, other nations are certainly just as guilty.

Jeremiah's Word to the Nations, 25:30-38

This section continues God's commission to Jeremiah to speak judgment against *all* the nations. No explicit indictments are cited (though see v. 12 regarding Babylon), but the nations are "guilty" (v. 31) and God's anger lies behind what happens (vv. 37-38). The result is unremitting devastation.

Two poetic oracles that announce judgment (vv. 30-32) and raise a lament over the devastating effects (vv. 34-38) surround a brief descriptive commentary in prose on the extent of the disaster (v. 33). The "sword" (vv. 31, 38) has reference to Babylonian armies, instruments of God's judgment against these nations.

Verses 30-32 begin with an image of God as a lion roaring *against* the sheep, an image that opens and closes this section (vv. 30, 38; Babylon is the lion in 4:7; 5:6; 51:38). This image of judgment is sometimes used of God, as in this text (49:19; 50:44), and sometimes of conquering armies (see 2:15; 4:7; 5:6; 50:17). Once again, note the way in which the same images are used for God and the instruments in and through which God has chosen to work judgment in this situation (see **Introduction**). God roars from "on high" and "from his holy habitation," probably references God's heavenly dwelling place (see Ps 11:4; cf. Amos 1:2, where God roars from Jerusalem). God will roar like a lion against his "fold." The image of Israel as a flock usually is associated with the image of God as a shepherd who protects them from marauding animals (e.g., Ps 23:1). Here all the nations are included in God's "fold," namely, as God's creatures (as shown by the use of the shepherd/sheep image for all nations in vv. 34-38). In this image God becomes the ravaging lion, with the implication that God is no longer functioning as a protective shepherd.

A second image of God in v. 30 is that of the shouting treader of grapes, though shouting not for joy at the harvest, but shouting as in a victory (see 48:33; 51:14; Isa 63:1-6; on the treading of grain, see 51:33). The object of God's shout is "all the inhabitants of the earth," parallel to "fold." The clamor or tumult from these judgments will be so loud that all the ends of the earth will hear it.

A third image of God is that of judge (v. 31). God has an indictment against, not simply Israel (see Hos 4:1; Mic 6:1-2), but against all nations, and hence is entering into judgment against them. The indictment/announcement of judgment pattern we have seen brought against Israel so often in Jeremiah (e.g., 25:7-11) is seen here to be exactly the same pattern for God's actions among all peoples. The judgment is inevitable and it comes upon "the guilty" (and "all flesh" is guilty), though the means of judgment will never be so clean that the innocent (e.g., children) do not get caught up in it or that the armies do not overdo the killing (see vv. 12-14; see **Connections**, ch. 6). Communal judgments are never precise in sorting out the guilty and the innocent (witness the two World Wars). Once again, the means of judgment is made clear: the sword. And it will be wielded by the Babylonian armies (see vv. 16, 27, 29, 38).

Still another image of God's judgment is that of the tempest (v. 32; see 23:19); it is stirring up and blowing away peoples from the entire earth. Another image of God's judgment might be evident in the "disaster (*rā'āh*)" that is spreading from nation to nation; it sounds almost like an epidemic that spreads across all national boundaries.

The brief prose interlude in v. 33 describes the devastating effects of this judgment. The number of dead is extensive; no nation will be spared. Because the dead will be so numerous, they will not be lamented or buried, but over time serve as dung on the surface of the ground, language also used for God's judgment on Israel (see 8:2; 9:22; 16:4, 6). The text speaks sharply of God as the subject of the verb "slay," indeed those slain by God will extend from one end of the earth to the other. [God the Slayer (25:33)]

As often in Jeremiah, so in vv. 34-38, laments accompany the effects of judgment on the people. In these verses, God calls upon the leaders of Israel (for shepherds, see 3:15) to wail and roll in ashes, a sign of mourning (see 4:8; Joel 1:13). These shepherds, leaders of God's flock, have utterly failed in their leadership (see

---

God the Slayer (25:33)

One of the more difficult images for God in this text (v. 33) is God as a slayer, "Those slain by the LORD on that day shall extend from one end of the earth to the other."

God is made responsible for the deaths of a great many people. But God does not act alone; as God puts it in 27:9, "I have completed its destruction by his [Nebuchadrezzar's] hand." God is the subject of the verb *ḥālal* ("slay") in 25:33, but the larger context makes clear that God is using the "sword" of the Babylonians (vv. 31, 38). Moreover, human instruments are the subject of the same verb in other texts (e.g., 14:18); note also the language of 51:49 and its

similarity to 25:33: "the slain of all the earth have fallen because of *Babylon*." The language used for God's actions in Jeremiah is often conformed to the means that God uses, one effect of which is the ascription to God of an inordinate amount of violence (see the listing in the **Introduction**).

Given God as the subject of the verb "slay" in 25:33, it is of no little interest to recall the divine lament in 9:1: God *weeps* for the "slain [*ḥālal*] of my poor people"! Here is revealed something of the inner life of the God who judges and who uses agents who cannot be divinely controlled (see [Judgment in Babylon]). The God who judges is the God who mourns and who calls for others to mourn (9:17).

23:1-2), and hence they are appointed to the slaughter; changing the image, they shall "be shattered" (so NIV; NRSV, "dispersions," that is, "scattered"), like fine pottery that has fallen (some translations retain the image of slaughter, "fine/choice rams," e.g., NAB; REB). There will be no escape for leaders any more than for the people; they failed their flock and flight shall fail them. The phrase, "the days of your slaughter have come" probably has reference to that time when the build-up of iniquity bursts forth in judgment (see Gen 15:16).

Verses 36-37 report the shepherds' lament: God in his fierce anger is despoiling their pasture (=land) and decimating their flocks (=people). God the lion (returning to the image of v. 30) has left his lair, has been on the prowl, and the land is laid waste. Verses 37b-38 speak clearly to the issue of agency: God in anger and the Babylonians with their cruel sword (as also in vv. 16, 27, 29, 31). Both are engaged in this judgmental act.

CONNECTIONS

Nebuchadrezzar, My Servant

Somewhat surprisingly, the king of Babylon, Nebuchadrezzar, is identified as God's servant. Comparably, at the time of the return from exile, King Cyrus of Persia will be identified as God's "anointed one" (Isa 45:1-7). This divine identification of a foreign king as the servant of God is very important for understanding judgment in Jeremiah. God's judgment is mediated in and through one who is not a member of God's chosen community; as with Cyrus (Isa 45:4), Nebuchadrezzar does not know Yahweh. This coalescence of God's actions and those of Nebuchadrezzar has been made clear several times already (e.g., compare 13:14 with 21:7; see **Introduction**). God will bring the Babylonian armies against Israel and utterly destroy them (and their neighbors).

If God is able to use a "pagan" king such as Nebuchadrezzar for the divine purposes, and even call him a "servant" of God, then readers (then and now) are asked to be discerning with respect to other such agents God may choose to use. For exilic readers, this theological perspective may well prepare them to discern that King Cyrus could be one of God's agents. For readers in every generation, this perspective calls them to be alert as to whether and how God may be using "secular" and "pagan" agents to fulfill the divine purposes in given situations. God works for good in everything and readers should be prepared to be surprised at the means that God chooses.

Notably, upon making it clear that King Nebuchadrezzar is God's servant, God becomes the sole subject of the destroying verbs that follow in vv. 9-10. A surface reading of the text would suggest that God is the sole actor in these events. But the designation of Nebuchadrezzar as servant of God has significant content. God acts in and through the servant's actions, but the Babylonians have their own will and ways.

That God is not the only effective agency in these events is made clear also by the divine judgment on Babylon that follows in vv. 12-14 (see also chs. 50–51; Isa 47:6-7; [Judgment on Babylon]). [God as Creator]

While these texts witness to the work of God as Creator, the references to the seventy-year limitation and the end of Babylonian hegemony also give readers a glimpse of God's salvific activity on behalf of Israel (further amplified in chs. 50–51). The devastating judgments on Israel are not the final word of God for these people. The future "is always left open for God's new and transformative action."[2] The reason for the positive future of the "good figs" developed in 24:3-7 is given in this text; the exiles will have such a future because judgment will be visited upon Babylon. And God will once again use a pagan king (Cyrus) to achieve those salvific purposes.

God as Creator

The understanding of God's involvement in the movements of emperors and armies in ch. 25 is a significant testimony to the work of God as Creator (see **Introduction**). God is not a local god, narrowly confined to Israel's borders. God is a God of all creation, present and active in the lives of all peoples and in every sphere of their life. Israel's testimony is that prophets such as Jeremiah have been given the insight to name that experience for what it is, to see the "something more" that lies in, with, and under these events. The nations may not know that the God whom Israel confesses is active among them, but they have in fact experienced this God. While this chapter testifies to God's wrathful actions among the nations, God's work of blessing is also in evidence. For example, the work of God as Creator is evident in the assumption that the nations such as Babylon should be able to discern that there are certain basic standards for human behavior. Such standards are made available to them in the natural order of things, and they are held accountable to them.

NOTES

[1] Contrary to William McKane, *A Critical and Exegetical Commentary on Jeremiah* (2 vols.; ICC; Edinburgh: T. & T. Clark, 1986), 636.

[2] Ibid., 222.

THE TEMPLE SERMON REVISITED

26:1-24

Jeremiah in Controversy, 26–29

These chapters consist of a series of narratives (the only poetry is a quotation from Mic 3:12 in 26:18) that portray Jeremiah in times of persecution and conflict (some scholars consider the unit to consist of chs. 27–29).[1] [Structure of Chapters 26–52] The specific cause of these difficulties is the nature of the word of God he has been called to proclaim, a word that conflicts with the agenda of both religious and political leaders. At the same time, the *religious* leaders are the special focus of the opposition in these chapters (priests and prophets are often mentioned, e.g., 26:7, 16). King Jehoiakim is hardly active in these settings (only in 26:20-23) and Zedekiah even less so. The "officials" declare Jeremiah innocent (26:16); the elders quote the tradition in support of the prophet (26:17-19); and the persons who saved Jeremiah (26:24) are political leaders. This focus on religious leaders may be ironic given the larger context of Jeremiah; but readers

---

Structure of Chapters 26–52

Chapters 26–51 can be understood as a cohesive unit (ch. 52 is an historical appendix). The oracles against the nations (OAN) conclude this unit (46–51), just as they conclude chs. 1–25 in summary form (25:15-38). Regarding chs. 26–45, divisions are disputed. Some include the entirety of chs. 26–45. Others, largely on formal grounds, break up this segment into chs. 26–36 and chs. 37–45, suggested by the change from the reign of Jehoiakim (26:1) to that of Zedekiah (37:1). This division seems best, with ch. 36 also functioning as a bridge between the two sections.

Chapters 26–45 differ from chs. 1–25 in several ways: the predominance of prose (chs. 30–31 are a notable exception); a focus on incidents from the life and ministry of Jeremiah (though 39:1-10; 40:7-41:18 do not mention him specifically); the presence of named persons, peoples, and events that tie the book more specifically to the time before and after the fall of Jerusalem; a greater number of salvation-oriented oracles (though judgment material is also present, e.g., 32:26-35; 34:8-22; 43–44).

Regarding chs. 26–36, with Robert Carroll (*Jeremiah* [Philadelphia: Westminster, 1986], 510) and others, it seems best to consider ch. 36 the concluding element rather than ch. 35. Chapter 36 closes the discussion of chs. 26–35 in a way comparable to the function of 25:1-14 in relation to chs. 2–24. The word of God in ch. 26 is spoken directly by Jeremiah; it is presented in written form in ch. 36 (cf. 26:3 and 36:3). Both occasions take place in the temple precincts. Jehoiakim, whom Jeremiah never confronts face-to-face in the book, is not present for the events of 26:1-19; he is front and center for the events of ch. 36. Jeremiah, on the other hand, is a lively presence in ch. 26, while largely in the background in ch. 36. Some think that ch. 26 still envisages the possibility of avoiding disaster through repentance (see 26:3, 13), while that future is closed off in ch. 36. To the contrary, the combination of conditional (26:3, 13) and unconditional (26:9) elements is present in a way comparable to that of Jer 7 (see discussion there). It is in fact the *finality* of Jeremiah's message (and Uriah's in vv. 20-23) that generates such deathly opposition.

are here asked to think about these authorities in particular and how they drive the opposition in apparent independence of the political leaders, though no doubt with their tacit support.

The first story (26:1-24) recalls Jeremiah's temple sermon in 7:1-15 and the trials he (and Uriah) underwent in the wake of that

Devastation of the Temple

Jeremiah 26:5-6—In pronouncing the impending destruction of the Temple at Jerusalem, YHWH—through Jeremiah—compares its devastation to that of the desolation of the Tent of Meeting at Shiloh by the Philistines. Because the Temple was the nucleus of Israelite life, this reference was a red flag for the readers of Jeremiah; YHWH, the center of Israelite life, was removing Himself from their midst by removing His tangible sign.

The Babylonians destroyed the Temple in 587 BC by dismantling the ornamentation and sacred objects, carrying them back to Babylon. The objects and structures they did not use were torched, essentially leaving the temple in ruin.

Jeremiah on the Ruins of the Sanctuary. Austro-Hungarian. Eglomise-glass. c. 1800. Judaica Collection Max Berger. Vienna, Austria. (Credit: Erich Lessing/Art Resource, NY)

public statement. The second story (27:1–28:17) portrays Jeremiah in conflict with king (Zedekiah) and prophet (Hananiah). The third story (29:1-32) depicts Jeremiah in communication with the exiles in Babylon and addresses, among other things, the conflict with false prophets among them.

These chapters center the issue in terms of prophets and the truth of their words; specific illustrations of the condemnation of false prophets in 23:9-40 (and other texts in chs. 2–25) are here provided. The issue of false prophecy is raised in these chapters in a cross-generational fashion. That is, false prophecy was an issue that Jeremiah faced before the fall of Jerusalem, but it was also an issue faced by exilic readers. Both settings are picked up in these chapters. The issue of discerning true prophecy from false was an ongoing problem for Israel and continues into New Testament times and our own (see **Connections**, ch. 28).

COMMENTARY

Sermon and Trial, 26:1-19

Chapter 26 apparently recalls Jeremiah's temple sermon of 7:1-15 in abbreviated form (vv. 1-6) and depicts the negative response it got from the community—Jeremiah goes on trial for his life (vv. 7-19). These verses are followed by an illustration that Jeremiah was not alone among the prophets in being persecuted for speaking "in the name of the LORD" (vv. 20-24). At the same time, the situation sketched by this chapter is even more complex. Remarkably, "the officials and all the people" (and the elders, v. 17) are said to recognize that Jeremiah has spoken "in the name of the LORD our God" and does not deserve the death sentence (v. 16). Yet, "the people" are the ones from whom Jeremiah is protected in v. 24, and they are represented as rejecting the word of the Lord throughout the book to this point (and as recently as v. 9). How are readers to understand this "fickleness"? The chapter seems just as incoherent whether approached from a literary or historical perspective.[2]

Temple Sermon Recalled, 26:1-6

This recollection of Jeremiah's temple sermon is set at the beginning of the reign of Jehoiakim (609 BC; see [Sons of Josiah]), probably at some (unknown) public worship occasion when large crowds were present. God commissions Jeremiah to speak a word to this crowd; the message he is to speak is given in abbreviated form in

vv. 4-6. For the only time in the book, God tells him not to hold back a word. Did God think that Jeremiah might hold back on the harsh language in view of a negative reception (see 42:4)? This proviso, which Jeremiah obeys (v. 8), helps prepare the reader for the harsh reaction in vv. 7-19.

God's reason for calling Jeremiah to this task is given in v. 3: it may be that the people will repent of their evil (*rāʿāh*) doings and God could then change his mind about the disaster (*rāʿāh*) that God intended to bring on them for their evil (*rōaʿ*) doings (see 18:7-10; see **Introduction**). This divine statement holds out a positive possibility (delivered only to Jeremiah, who reflects it in v. 13; cf. v. 19); it reveals that the divine purpose in the prophetic preaching (at least at some point) was to turn the people from their wicked ways and to prevent the disaster from occurring. If the people will repent, God will repent. But note God's "it may be" (or "perhaps"; see 36:3 and **Connections** there); God does not finally know what they will do, though the "perhaps" language suggests that God does not think it likely, especially if one takes seriously the reference to "all of them" (see **Connections: Jeremiah 26:3 and the Will of God**).

The message Jeremiah is to proclaim is cast in somewhat different terms from the sermon reported in 7:3-7. Unlike the latter, the actual words to be spoken (26:4-6) are cast only in negative terms ("if you will *not*"); a possible positive future is given only in God's rationale to Jeremiah (v. 3), though Jeremiah does speak from this perspective in his defense in v. 13 (see below; cf. 7:3-5).

A Warning to Exilic Readers

That the prophet had given this warning would be an important word for the recollection of exilic readers. The destruction of city and temple was due not to some divine caprice, but because the people were so set in their ways that they refused to amend their lives. This perspective also makes clear that God and prophet were not somehow opposed to the temple and its worship as such, and hence exilic readers could think through the possibility of a new temple with appropriate worship practices for the future (see Ezekiel 40–48).

The parenthetical phrase in v. 5 ("though you have not heeded") suggests that refusal to listen has become such a way of life for this people that no other future is likely (see **Connections**, ch. 7). [A Warning to Exilic Readers]

Note how God personalizes each of the clauses. If the people do not listen "to me," do not walk in "my" law, and do not give heed to the urgent word of "my" servants the prophets (see 25:4), then "I" (God) will devastate the temple (=house)—as was done to the sanctuary in Shiloh by the Philistines in the eleventh century (see 7:12-15). Thereby the status of Jerusalem was placed on the same level as that of Shiloh, no doubt anathema to those who understood God's commitment to Jerusalem to be unparalleled. Moreover, God ("I") will make Jerusalem an object of cursing and ridicule for all nations (a common theme, e.g., 25:9, 18; note the response of the nations in 22:8-9). All the first person language makes it clear that the people have to do with God himself and not just some official word or external code. The phrase "listen to me" is specified in two ways, walking in the Law (unspecified, but apparently a body of law known to hearers/readers, see 9:13; 16:12; 44:10, 23) and heeding the words of the prophets (see 7:25; 25:4; 29:19; 35:15; 44:4). The latter would focus on indictment and announcement of judgment, but v. 3 makes clear that God's purpose in the preaching of the prophets was, finally, salvation.

Jeremiah's Life Threatened, 26:7-19

Throughout chapters 11–20, readers have heard Jeremiah complain about the opposition he has faced and the persecution he has had to endure at the hands of everyone, including his family and friends. This narrative, anticipated in 20:1-6, is the first major report regarding the range of the opposition Jeremiah faced. The trial reported in vv. 8-16 (19?) is unique in the Old Testament.

Verse 7 makes clear that the people involved in Jeremiah's persecution included both leaders (especially prophets and priests; government officials are not yet mentioned; after v. 1, Jehoiakim is not mentioned in vv. 1-19) and "all the people" (that is, those present were representative of the entire populace). When Jeremiah had finished speaking everything God had commissioned him to say, both leaders and people lay hold of him and speak with one voice: Jeremiah must die (the penalty for false prophecy was death according to Deut 18:20; cf. 28:17)! This immediate conclusion on their part demonstrates that their question of "Why?" to Jeremiah (v. 9) is accusatory and not designed to elicit a response. Jeremiah was treasonous in saying that the temple and the city—considered inviolable and protected by God's own commitments (see Ps 132:11-14)—would be destroyed and emptied of its inhabitants; but, even more, to claim that God had so spoken was a lie and hence blasphemous. Ominously, they crowd around Jeremiah. The last sentence of v. 9 is ironic: the house of the Lord is the place where God's prophet is threatened with his life. [Jeremiah and Jesus]

Jeremiah's accusers claim that his prophecy regarding the destruction of city and temple is spoken with finality; this is their future, no ifs, ands, or buts (v. 9). Is this a misrepresentation of Jeremiah's preaching?[3] Not necessarily. While there is a conditional element in vv. 4-6, no positive possibility has been stated (as it will be in v. 13 and was implied in God's initial statement to the prophet in v. 3). And so, given what Jeremiah actually says, if the people understand

Jeremiah and Jesus

Nicolas of Verdun (1150–1205). *Flagellation of Christ and the Prophet Jeremiah.* 12th C. Cologne, Germany. (Credit: Erich lessing/Art Resouce, NY)

That this chapter, centered as it is on *religious* opposition and placed in a temple setting, begins this long stretch of largely narrative material has recalled for some the words and actions of Jesus regarding the temple. According to John 2:13-25 (esp. v. 19), Jesus' preaching about the destruction of the temple also brought him into conflict with the religious authorities and was a key factor in bringing him to trial (see Matt 26:57-68; 24:2; Mark 14:58). Jesus thereby stands in the tradition of Jeremiah.

that repentance is not in fact possible (see 2:25; 18:12), then they correctly interpret his preaching in terms of unconditional destruction (see **Connections**, ch. 7).

This commotion in the temple is overheard by the palace officials (v. 10); they come to the temple and take their seat in the New Gate (its location is unknown). This action means that they assume a judicial role in this situation and initiate a court proceeding; it is strange that they rather than priests assume jurisdiction in such a matter (see Deut 17:8-13), but they may be present at the behest of Jehoiakim (see 38:4). The prophets and priests assume the position of prosecuting attorney (v. 11), declaring to the officials and to "all" the people that Jeremiah deserves to die for announcing the destruction of Jerusalem. The people who have heard him preach are his accusers in vv. 8-9, but in the judicial proceeding only the priests and prophets bring the charges (v. 11). Their reference to the officials having heard "with your own ears" could be understood in general terms or as a recognition that the palace had its spies in the crowd (the palace and the temple were contiguous buildings). The people may function as witnesses or even as a jury, given their response in v. 16 (the phrase "all the people" occurs eight times in vv. 7-18, apparently with reference to the same "mob").

Jeremiah responds in his own defense, first by restating (and admitting!) the basic message he has been charged with bringing (vv. 12-13) and then by drawing out the implications of their judgment of him personally (vv. 14-15). The claim that God is the one who has "sent" him brackets the speech (vv. 12, 15; so also 1:7); this claim contrasts him with the false prophets (e.g., 23:21, 32). Jeremiah's words against the temple and the city have not originated with him; God has given the words to him. He proceeds to speak of a possible positive future, reflecting God's word to him in v. 3 (but not the public words of vv. 4-6). Their future is in their own hands. He calls upon them to repent and amend their ways and their doings and to obey "the voice of the LORD your God" (cf. 7:5-7). If they do, God will (better, "may," so REB) change his mind and recall the prophesied disaster (*rā'āh*). The translation "may" leaves the future open-ended not only with respect to the people but also with respect to God. It may in fact be too late, but the people should repent in case it is not, "Who knows?" (see Joel 2:14; Jonah 3:9). Alternatively, and more convincingly in view of v. 9 (see above) and chapter 7 (see **Connections** there), Jeremiah is calling upon the people to amend their ways, but knowing full well that they would not do so. Jeremiah thereby makes clear what is at stake in these events.

Jeremiah continues to speak from a personal perspective ("as for me," vv. 14-15). He places himself in the hands of the court to do with him what *they* think is right and good, a move both humble and clever. At the same time, he issues a warning that if they put him to death they will be condemning an innocent man (an appeal to acknowledged Israelite Law, see Deut 19:10-13). In so doing, they will bring innocent blood (bloodguilt) upon themselves and the city (see 2:34; 22:17), because he does not speak his own word, but "*in truth*" speaks the word of the God who had sent him to speak to them. The execution of Uriah in v. 23 in effect refers back to the "innocent blood" of v. 14.

Jeremiah's defense proves to be persuasive to the court and, remarkably, to the people; they inform the priests and prophets that Jeremiah does not deserve to die, for he has spoken in the name of "the LORD *our* God" (v. 16). In so doing, they recognize that Jeremiah has spoken "in truth" and has not spoken in the name of another god or made false claims, which would carry the death penalty (see Deut 13:1-5; 18:15-22). Ironically, then, their claims about Jeremiah's truth-telling recognize the authority of his word rather than that of the false prophets. Notably, however, they also make no reference to the amendment of life called for by Jeremiah in v. 13. The reader might well expect the narrative to end at this point; Jeremiah has been vindicated.

Some scholars think that because v. 16 is not spoken to Jeremiah (cf. v. 11), it may only be meant as a contribution to an ongoing litigious process. Yet, this does appear to be the formal end of the trial; at the same time, the conversation continues. Verse 19c does not suggest that the trial itself continues; rather, it refers back to the larger issues of the community addressed in vv. 3, 13, rather than to Jeremiah personally. Non-repentance will mean disaster. In other words, Jeremiah is vindicated, but that is not really the issue faced by this community. Perhaps they think that by freeing the prophet, and even if he continues to speak, they will be freeing themselves from the judgment he announces. After all, if by killing him they will incur bloodguilt (v. 15), the alternative will certainly be less severe! The elders' entrance onto the scene addresses precisely this point; Jeremiah's acquittal is not the end of the matter.

Unexpectedly, some elders of the people speak up; their function in the community is uncertain, but apparently they had a certain commitment to the tradition and a recognized stature regarding its interpretation (see 19:1 for an earlier appearance in the book). They make their presence known for the first time in this narrative and cite historical precedent, not only to support the verdict but also to bring the real issue to the forefront (vv. 17-19). Micah of Moresheth (some 25 miles southwest of Jerusalem) prophesied a comparable word during the reign of King Hezekiah (715–687 BC). They quote a passage from his prophecy, directed against Jerusalem's leaders (in Mic 3:12), a word similar to that of God in v. 6 (see v. 9). This quotation of an earlier prophet is unique in prophetic literature (though there are many allusions); the citation also indicates that his prophecies had gained some authoritative stature in the community at some (uncertain) point. That they had been collected in written form seems likely, but not certain. If so, then the writing down of Jeremiah's prophecies (see ch. 36) has a significant precedent within Israel. It should also be noted that familiarity with the story of Hezekiah in 2 Kings (or a tradition like it) seems likely (see 2 Kgs 19).

Micah had announced that Jerusalem/Zion would be so devastated that it would become a field that could be cultivated, and the temple mount (=mountain of the house) would be cleared of buildings and reforested. On the basis of this word from the past, they drive their point home through the use of three rhetorical questions, the first implies a negative answer, the next two a positive answer. King Hezekiah had responded positively to Micah's message and Micah had not been put to death. The king feared (=believed) the Lord and interceded with the Lord on behalf of the people and the city. Hezekiah was an exemplary king (2 Kgs 18:5); he offered prayers of repentance that were key to saving the city from the Assyrians (though Kings does not speak of Micah; see 2 Kgs 19:1, 14-19). Hezekiah's prayer proved to be efficacious, and God changed his mind about the disaster (*rāʿāh*) that had been announced as word of God by the prophet Micah (see Isa 36–37; 2 Chr 32:26; **Connections** ch. 18). Micah's message of certain and unconditional judgment is comparable to that of Jonah, whose unremitting message of doom also occasions "repentance" on the part of both God and people (see Jonah 3). Jeremiah's message, however, does not have a comparable effect (see **Connections: The Efficacy of Hezekiah's Prayer and Unfulfilled Prophecy**).

Notably, the *prayer* (no amendment of life is indicated!) of a single individual had this salutary effect on Jerusalem (no mention is made of the *people's* response).[4] That the pray-er was a king demonstrates the importance of the leader, whose behaviors (whether negative or positive) may be decisive in shaping the future of the community. Not all kings are to be condemned; indeed, their practices may even be exemplary (cf. 22:15-16). Hezekiah may well be put forward as a model for the current ruler (Jehoiakim). What if he would respond as Hezekiah did? Might God "change his mind" (as Jeremiah had intimated in v. 13; cf. 18:7-10) and Jerusalem be saved again? But, finally, in this context Hezekiah is contrasted with Jehoiakim, whose sharply negative response is described in what follows (see especially v. 23). Even more, given the fact that Jeremiah's intercessions are forbidden (7:16; 11:14; 14:11), and that God would not listen to the people's prayers (7:16; 11:14; 14:12; 15:1), it appears that Hezekiah's intercessory example is no longer a possibility for Israel (or any individual). Hence, v. 19c is to be interpreted in terms of certain disaster.

The elders' concluding comment (v. 19c) probably is not a formal part of the trial (though the reference to the potential death of Micah in v. 19a suggests that Jeremiah is not yet out of the woods, see v. 24), but extends the point made by vv. 3, 13. Israel is facing a disastrous future in view of the lack of response to Jeremiah's preaching (this assumes that they understand his word to be true).[5] The point seems not to be that by putting Jeremiah to death, they would be responsible for the disaster (*rā'āh*) that followed (see v. 15); the latter would occur because of the lack of repentance, regardless of what happened to the prophet. In terms of exilic readers, this statement from the elders would both remind them of the factors that led to the fall of Jerusalem and call upon them to respond in ways comparable to Hezekiah in thinking about their future. The assumption of the word in v. 19c is that, for pre-fall Israel, it is already too late.

Death for One Prophet, Deliverance for Another, 26:20-24

This brief story reports the activity and consequent fate of an otherwise unknown prophet named Uriah, who spoke "words exactly like those of Jeremiah" (v. 20). He is a genuine martyr, killed for the sake of the word of God that he proclaimed when he could have kept silent. He was silenced, but this text enables his witness to live on. The story follows vv. 1-19 both to illustrate the ruthlessness of the opposition that Jeremiah faced (in contrast to that of Micah under Hezekiah) and to show that Jeremiah was neither alone in announcing judgment on Israel nor unique in not being heeded (see v. 5, illustrated in this text). That Uriah fled in the face of persecution (v. 21) may be intended to highlight Jeremiah's courage, or perhaps that Jeremiah had protective friends (v. 24) that Uriah did not have. But the key factor in the textual placement is that, in contrast to Hezekiah, it demonstrates the prominence of King Jehoiakim in the persecution of the prophets (though he is not mentioned as involved in the trial vv. 1-19). Was the death of Uriah, who received no trial as Jeremiah had, the king's warning to Jeremiah? Jehoiakim will become explicitly involved in opposing Jeremiah in 36:26.

Uriah was a true prophet of the Lord; his roots were in the region of Kiriath-jearim, a few miles west and north of Jerusalem, the place where the ark of the covenant was housed for a time after the destruction of the sanctuary at Shiloh (1 Sam 7:1-2). Like Micah, he was also from outside of Jerusalem. Like Jeremiah (v. 20), he prophesied against the city and the temple. When word of his activities came to the attention of Jehoiakim (and his officials and warriors), he sought to put Uriah to death. Uriah fled to Egypt, but King Jehoiakim sent several men after him, led by Elnathan. They

Elnathan, Ahikam, and Shaphan

Elnathan was the father of Nehushta, the mother of King Jehoiakim (2 Kgs 24:8), and served as a government official (see 36:12). In 36:25, Elnathan was among those who urged King Jehoiakim not to burn Jeremiah's scroll (36:25), but he also led the party that captured the prophet Uriah in Egypt and brought him back to King Jehoiakim (26:22-23).

Ahikam, son of Shaphan, was an officer in the service of King Josiah and helped secure the prophetess Huldah's interpretation of the scroll found in the temple (2 Kgs 22:12, 14). Ahikam was the father of Gedaliah (40:5-6), who was appointed governor of Judah after the fall of Jerusalem in 587 BC (see ch. 40).

Shaphan was Josiah's personal secretary. He received the law book discovered in the temple from the high priest Hilkiah, reported its existence to the Josiah, and read it aloud to him (2 Kgs 22:8-10). Accompanied by his son Ahikam and others, he obeyed Josiah's command to consult a prophet regarding its authenticity and they took it to the prophetess Huldah for interpretation (2 Kgs 22:11-14).

These few references to Ahikam and Shaphan indicate that Jeremiah received significant levels of support from this family. Though Jeremiah often lamented about all his enemies, he had his supporters as well (see 38:7-13; 39:14).

capture him and bring him back to King Jehoiakim in Jerusalem. The king personally kills him with his sword and throws his body into a burial place set aside for common people (a fate comparable to that of Jehoiakim himself, 22:18-19; 36:30). Only an obscure prophet named Zechariah is reported to have met a comparable fate (2 Chr 24:20-22, but see also Jer 2:30 and Jezebel's efforts against Elijah, 1 Kgs 19:2).

Verse 24 provides a note about how Jeremiah fared in the wake of the killing of Uriah. He had followers committed to his ministry; he did not stand alone. Among Jeremiah's supporters was a man named Ahikam, son of Shaphan. [Elnathan, Ahikam, and Shaphan] He provided some kind of refuge for the prophet so that he did not fall into the hands of the people, who were apparently still seeking Jeremiah's death (cf. Obadiah in 1 Kgs 18:13). As in vv. 1-19, nothing is said at this point about the actions of King Jehoiakim. The reference to the people in v. 24 is strange, given their verdict of v. 16. This juxtaposition may be put forward as evidence for the fickleness of this people (we do not know the historical sequence). An ironic point may be most prominent here, however; the people recognize that Jeremiah is indeed one who has spoken "in the name of the LORD our God," but they still seek to find ways to get rid of him. Their unfaithful words and deeds are thus undertaken in the full knowledge that Jeremiah is God's spokesman. This would be another illustration of their stubbornness (see 2:25; 18:12; **Connections**, ch. 5).

CONNECTIONS

Jeremiah 26:3 and the Will of God

Several features of this verse are worthy of special attention:

1. Once again readers meet up with the connection between the people's evil doings and the disaster that God intends to bring (see, e.g., 6:19; 21:14). The *rāʿāh* (disaster) grows out of the *rāʿah/ rōaʿ* (evil doings) of the people. God mediates the consequences of the people's wickedness and that issues in disaster (see **Introduction**).

2. By making this offer to the people, God makes it clear that God prefers repentance, with resultant life and blessing, to disaster. Two understandings of the will of God are present here, one of which takes priority over the other. God does "intend" (*ḥāšab*) that the people experience the consequences of their wickedness (most fundamentally the moral order exists so that sin and evil do not go unchecked in the life of the world). This mediation of sin's consequences might be termed the circumstantial will of God; it is God's will *only* in view of specific circumstances that have developed. That disaster is not the primary will of God for Israel is made clear by God's commission to Jeremiah: God desires the people's repentance so that God can change God's mind regarding the intention to bring disaster. This reveals God's absolute will for the people: God prefers Israel's life to Israel's death; blessing instead of curse; salvation instead of judgment. That this is God's absolute will comes into play again with respect to the promises that punctuate Jeremiah. God's circumstantial will for judgment will in fact come to fruition, but it is not God's final word for Israel. God's absolute will for Israel's life and salvation persists through the fires of judgment and God's absolute will for this people emerges on the far side of the disaster with the offer of new life and blessing.

3. This God uses language that suggests that God does not have absolute foreknowledge of the future. God tells Jeremiah that "it may be" (Heb., *'ûlay*, "perhaps"). [The Divine Perhaps]

4. God is the kind of God who is open to changing his mind about a circumstantial matter, as noted in the next segment (see 18:7-10; **Connections**, ch. 18).

The Divine Perhaps

📖 It seems clear from several Old Testament passages that God is not altogether certain how the people will respond to the prophetic word (e.g., Ezek 12:1-3; cf. Jer 36:3, 7; 51:8; Isa 47:12; Luke 20:13). "God is certainly aware of the various possibilities regarding Israel's response. One might even say that God, given a thoroughgoing knowledge of Israel, knows what its response is likely to be (cf., e.g., Pss 11:4; 33:13; 94:9-11). There will be no surprises for God in the sense of not anticipating what might happen. Yet, in God's own words, God does not finally know….All of this means, of course, that God's future is somewhat…open-ended as well; what God will do at least in part depends upon what Israel does. God's actions are not predetermined. Thus, Israel's response will contribute in a genuine way to the shaping not only of its own future, but to the future of God."

Terence Fretheim, *The Suffering of God: An Old Testament Perspective* (Philadelphia: Fortress, 1984), 45-47.

The Efficacy of Hezekiah's Prayer and Unfulfilled Prophecy

Verse 19 reports that King Hezekiah responded positively to the prophecy of Micah 3:12. He believed the word of the Lord that the prophet had spoken and prayed that God would change his mind about the announced disaster. The text makes a clear point about the efficacy of Hezekiah's prayer; the prophecy did not come to pass (for a similar story about Hezekiah and the prophet Isaiah, see 2 Kgs 20:1-7).

In thinking through the import of the Micah prophecy, it is important to understand that Micah's prophecy is not now, at long last, recognized as coming to fulfillment.[6] The text explicitly claims that in view of Hezekiah's prayers God had changed his mind about the destruction of the city in that time and place (26:19). There is no indication that this divine change of mind was temporary. Micah's prophecy was not fulfilled because God called back that word; thereupon that word was no longer "waiting in the wings" to be fulfilled at some future time. The destruction of Jerusalem in 587 BC was not understood to be a fulfillment of Micah's word at all, but the fulfillment of a new word from God spoken at a new time and place through Jeremiah and others.

The implications of such an understanding are considerable. For one, it shows that God can in fact change God's mind about announcements of judgment made by the prophets, and that that

Unfulfilled Prophecy as Continuing Word of God

📖 The use of Micah's prophecy in 26:18-19 shows that a prophetic word of judgment is (and remains) word of God even if it is not finally fulfilled. Micah's word continues to function as word of God in the community in several other ways.

1. It shows that the destruction of city and temple was understood to be possible in God's good purpose; they were not inviolable Israelite institutions. This understanding would support the reference to Shiloh in 26:6.

2. It shows that God's decision of non-fulfillment at one point in time does not mean that there would never again be a comparable word from God about the same matter. New situations may call for another such word from God.

3. It shows that at least at some point in Jeremiah's prophecy a divine change of mind could have taken place again. Micah's "precedent" was available for new times and places.

4. It revealed to exilic readers that God was a certain kind of God; God was open to new directions in view of changing events, a word that would have brought comfort and hope to a dispirited people.

divine decision is real. For another, it shows that prophetic words of judgment can in fact be cut off. Biblical interpreters should not be looking for the fulfillment of every unfulfilled prophetic word of judgment. [Unfulfilled Prophecy as Continuing Word of God]

NOTES

[1] See G. Keown, P. Scalise, and T. Smothers, *Jeremiah 26–52* (Dallas: Word Books, 1993), 35-38.

[2] Contrary to Robert Carroll, *Jeremiah* (Philadelphia: Westminster, 1986), 514-15.

[3] So Walter Brueggemann, *A Commentary on Jeremiah: Exile and Homecoming* (Grand Rapids: Eerdmans, 1998), 234.

[4] Pace Carroll, 518-20.

[5] Pace Brueggemann, 236.

[6] Contrary to Ronald E. Clements, *Jeremiah* (IBC; Atlanta: John Knox, 1988), 157.

THE YOKE OF SUBMISSION
TO BABYLON

27:1-22

Jeremiah and False Prophecy, 27–28

These two chapters are linked by the reference, "in that same year," in 28:1. The yoke that Jeremiah wears also surfaces in both chapters as does the concern for the temple vessels and the issue of submission to Nebuchadnezzar. These chapters (and ch. 29) are dated shortly after the first subjugation of the city by Babylon in 597 BC and before the devastation of 586 BC. Many of the leaders have been exiled to Babylon (see 52:28), including King Jehoiachin, and Zedekiah has been placed on the throne of David by the Babylonians. One of the basic questions in the community, rooted both in a discernment of God's purposes and political realities, pertains to the length of the exile and continued submission to Babylon (see 27:16; 28:3).

[A Convocation of Nations]

One common thread running through these two chapters is Jeremiah's opposition to the efforts of Zedekiah (and others) to foment rebellion against the Babylonians. For Jeremiah, Judah's only hope in this situation, if one can still speak of hope, was to submit to Babylonian rule and to reject the word of any prophetic voice that advised to the contrary ("do not listen" to them, vv. 9, 14, 16, 17). Jeremiah's indictment of the prophets for prophesying lies is a key theme in each segment (vv. 10, 14, 16) (see **Connections: On Submitting to Babylon and Violence**).

Both chapters have to do with another symbolic act by Jeremiah (see 13:1-14; 16:1-13; 18:1-12; 19:1-15; 24:1-10; cf. Isaiah 20:1-6 for a comparable sign). He wears a yoke that symbolizes (no magic is

---

A Convocation of Nations

Some scholars date these particular chapters to 594/593 BC, a time when emissaries from the surrounding nations of Edom, Moab, Ammon, Tyre, and Sidon met in Jerusalem to make (apparently unrealized) plans for such a rebellion (see 27:2). Such a date for this convocation would have coincided with the accession of a new pharaoh in Egypt (Psammetichus II, 594-589 BC), which probably encouraged pro-Egyptian conspirators in Israel to plan a rebellion. It is difficult to know the extent to which this report corresponds to actual events, but convocations such as these seem likely in view of Babylonian expansionism. Later editors have certainly shaped this material in light of their particular theological perspective and intended audience.

apparent) continued submission (on the part of *every* nation, v. 8!) to Babylon as the only hope for Judah's future. Chapter 27 does not report that Jeremiah actually donned the yoke, though it is presumed that he did; 28:10 indicates that he wore it in that context (note the reference to the "same year" in 28:1; did he wear it for an extended period of time?). The significance of the yoke is extended in Jeremiah's conflict with the prophet Hananiah (28:10-14).

COMMENTARY

Chapter 27 in its entirety consists of words spoken by Jeremiah in the first person (as is 28:1), though divine oracles constitute the bulk of the content. The chapter is structured in terms of three oracles: to foreign kings (vv. 1-11), King Zedekiah (vv. 12-15), and priests and people (vv. 16-22). The first of these segments reports what God said to Jeremiah (his obedience is implied); the second and third segments consist of Jeremiah's personal report (unique in the book) of his conveyance of God's word to the differing audiences (none of whom respond). Each receives essentially the same message regarding submission.

God commands Jeremiah to make and wear a yoke of straps and bars. [The Yoke] God commissions him to speak to the "masters" of various neighboring nations (through their envoys) who are gathered for a convocation to foment intrigue against Babylon (all closely related to or integrated into the Davidic-Solomonic empire). All those little nations who think they can stop Babylon! It would be ludicrous if it were not so pathetic. It is possible that God commissions Jeremiah not only to speak to (the kings of) these nations but also to send yokes to them (see NRSV footnote, v. 3). If so, it is not only Jeremiah's word that is to be conveyed by

---

The Yoke

The yoke is a wooden crossbar (with straps of rope or leather) placed across the necks of two oxen to pull heavy loads; a wooden shaft was fastened to the crossbar and extended back to the cart carrying the load (see 1 Sam 6:7). The yoke became a metaphor for submission or servitude (see 1 Kgs 12:1-11). Inasmuch as the yoke was probably intended for two oxen, one side of the yoke would have been unfilled, perhaps inviting others to submit as he was submitting (see G. Keown, P. Scalise, and T. Smothers, *Jeremiah 26–52* [Dallas: Word Books, 1993], 48).

these emissaries to their respective masters, but also the symbolic act itself is to be transmitted. This material is also to be connected to Jeremiah's call to be a "prophet to that nations" (1:5, 10). Note that the original reference to the five emissaries (v. 3) is extended to include "any nation or kingdom" (v. 8; see 18:7-10 for another use of this language).

Such a strange action for Jeremiah to undertake, assuming the place of a beast of burden under the yoke! Perhaps its very strangeness would jolt a few to pay some attention to the accompanying words. The yoke not only highlights the theme of submission (e.g., 1 Kgs 12:4) — certainly a difficult word for human beings to hear in any situation — it also alludes to the burden of the *message* that Jeremiah brings. Given the reference to the "yoke of the king of Babylon" in v. 8 (see Isa 47:6), the theme of submission carries a dual significance, namely, submit now or submit later (with more lives lost); you have no other choice. Even more, submission to the king of Babylon implies submission to the purpose of God in this particular situation (v. 7). The yoke is thus both God's and Nebuchadnezzar's (see **Connections: On Submitting to Babylon and Violence**).

Word Regarding Coalition against Babylon, 27:1-11

This segment is dated in the reign of Zedekiah after the fall of Jerusalem to Babylon (so also 28:1). [Translation of 27:1] Jeremiah's word begins with a statement about God's sovereignty in the created order (v. 5; on creation themes in Jeremiah, see **Introduction**). This is an appeal (not an indictment) based on an argument from creation; this kind of argument is especially to be linked to the non-Israelite audience. These "outsiders" might be able to connect with such an argument; the more specific reference to God's work in Israel would be too narrow an appeal (see the comparable argument in a similar context by the Apostle Paul in Acts 17:22-31). By God's power and outstretched arm (language also used for God's saving work on behalf of Israel, Deut 26:8), God has created human beings and animals (see 32:17). As the creator of all, God gives it (that is, the earth) to those who are "right in [God's] eyes" ("I see fit," NEB; see 18:4; 34:15; cf. the language for human beings in 26:14; 40:5) and would best serve God's purposes in this time and place.

Translation of 27:1

AΩ Most Hebrew manuscripts of 27:1 begin with the phrase, "In the beginning of the reign of King *Jehoiakim*," an obvious scribal mistake in view of vv. 3, 12 and 28:1 (hence reading Zedekiah; see NRSV footnote).

Until Its Time Comes

This reference to a time when the effect of Babylon's wickedness will have so built up that it bursts forth with devastating effects has numerous parallels (see Gen 15:16; Exod 20:5; Lev 18:4-5; Deut 9:4-5; Joel 3:13; 2 Chr 36:20-21). It takes time for sins to have their full effects. In Gen 15:16, the same idea is conveyed with the phrase, "the iniquity of the Amorites is not yet complete" (or "not yet reached its full measure," NIV; "will not be ripe for punishment until then," NEB). Such a fate for Babylon has been specified before (25:14), where the common translation "repay, requite" is better rendered "bring to completion" (so also 50:29; 51:6, 24, 56).

This end for Babylon is tied to its own wickedness in overextending its divine mandate by its excessive violence in conquering Israel and other nations. In effect, God's choice of Babylon is not a choice in perpetuity. These texts recognize not only that empires rise and fall but that "in a world of moral accountability" (so Walter Brueggemann, *A Commentary on Jeremiah: Exile and Homecoming* [Grand Rapids: Eerdmans, 1998], 244) human sin and evil will not go unchecked forever; in time it will "catch up" with the perpetrators and return on their own heads (Obad 15).

It is with this kind of God that these pretenders have to do, but none of them care a whit for what the word of God might have to say for this moment or for all those innocent children and others who will be swept up in the violence. They will be the "gods" in charge of these matters. Verse 5 makes no general claims about whether God's choices will always be realized (other texts demonstrate that God's will is resistible, e.g., disobedience of the commandments), but in this case Jeremiah is certain of the future work of God of which he speaks.

In this particular case God gives "the earth" to Babylon under Nebuchadnezzar (v. 6). As creator, God has chosen King Nebuchadnezzar as "my servant" for a particular role in carrying out the will of God for this time and place (also 25:9; 43:10; on the spelling of the name, 21:2). To call Nebuchadnezzar God's "servant" does not mean that he is God's "devotee" (see **Connections**, ch. 21).[1] God has given him "all these lands" (mentioned in v. 3) and even the wild animals will serve him (see 28:14; 12:9; this theme may also be related to the common element in the announcements of judgment that animals will feed on the corpses of Israelites, e.g., 7:33).

Moreover, all these nations shall serve Nebuchadnezzar through the time of his own reign as well as those of his son and grandson (v. 7). The phrase, "until the time of his own land comes," refers to the time when the build-up of wickedness in Babylon is so great that the tables are turned and it is conquered and enslaved (under Cyrus of Persia in 539 BC). [Until Its Time Comes] That the time is rather closely specified is testimony to God-given insight into the course of events (even though it may have been written at a time when those events had already happened or were about to do so), though without precision. [The Dynasty of Nebuchadnezzar] This is a word of hope for exilic readers (as is v. 22) tucked into what is otherwise an ominous text regarding the future of the people of Israel.

The either-or form of discourse is used again in vv. 8-11 (see 22:1-5). If any nation or kingdom (see 18:7-10), including Israel, does not submit to King Nebuchadnezzar (=put its neck under the yoke), then God will "visit" (*pāqad*) that nation with sword, famine, and pestilence, typical effects of a marauding army (see 14:12-18; 15:2; 21:7-9; 24:10). This visitation will be sustained until destruction has occurred. Note the final clause of v. 8, "by his hand"; the agency of Nebuchadnezzar is genuine. God "visits" the nations through the agency of that which is other than God (see

Introduction). This being the case, it is urgent that neither kings nor people from any nation listen to those who are counseling rebellion against the policy of submission to the king of Babylon (quite a list!): prophets, diviners, dream(er)s, soothsayers, sorcerers (v. 9; see 29:8-9 for their threat to the exiles). All of these prophet-types from all these nations live by predicting the future and, in counseling nonsubmission to Babylon, they are practicing deception; they are all liars! The result will be that the populace from these nations will be displaced from their land; indeed, God will drive them into exile, and they will perish (v. 10; see 25:8-11). On the other hand, if any of these peoples do submit to the king of Babylon, they will be a subjugated nation, but *God* will leave them on their own land to cultivate its soil and to dwell in its towns and villages (v. 11) (see **Connections: On the Prophets and Politics**). [Bonhoeffer on 27:11 and 29:7]

The Dynasty of Nebuchadnezzar

Verse 7 (missing in the LXX) is a puzzle, particularly for those who think that every word about the future must come to pass just as prophesied. Numerous efforts, usually strained, have been made to clarify the text (see Robert Carroll, *Jeremiah* [Philadelphia: Westminster, 1986], 527-28). The last king of the neo-Babylonian empire was Nabonidus (556-539 BC), the fourth king after Nebuchadnezzar, but not his descendant. The "son and grandson" could be a general reference to three generations or refer to Nabonidus and, his son, Belshazzar (see Dan 5:2, where he is called the son of Nebuchadnezzar). Many biblical texts, however, imply an understanding that prophecies are subject to adjustment and reversal (e.g., 1 Kgs 21:27-29; 2 Kgs 20:1-7). Perhaps it is best simply to understand this verse as an instance of an adjusted or unfulfilled prophecy.

Bonhoeffer on 27:11 and 29:7

In May, 1944, Dietrich Bonhoeffer used these two texts from Jeremiah to help interpret his own situation and that of others: "We may have to face events and changes that take no account of our wishes and our rights. But if so, we shall not give way to embittered and barren pride, but consciously submit to divine judgment, and so prove ourselves worthy to survive by identifying ourselves generously and unselfishly with the life of the community and the sufferings of our fellow-men."

Dietrich Bonhoeffer, *Letters and Papers from Prison* (The Enlarged Edition; New York: Macmillan, 1971), 299.

Word to Zedekiah, 27:12-15

In this oracle Jeremiah delivers essentially the same message to King Zedekiah of Judah (cf. 38:17-18) as he had to the emissaries from other nations (vv. 1-11). Zedekiah was being pulled between pro-Babylonian and anti-Babylonian (or pro-Egyptian) factions. Whatever the military/political arguments or strategies, he is called to ignore them and, obedient to the word of God, subject himself *and his people* (the imperatives in vv. 12 and 14 are plural) to the yoke of Babylon. The only way to life rather than death is to serve the king of Babylon. Why should the king rebel against Babylon (and God!) and thereby ensure that his own people would suffer from famine, sword, and pestilence (see 14:12-18; 15:2; 21:7-9; 24:10)? The king is told to ignore the various prophets that encourage rebellion against Babylon. They are liars, pure and simple; God has not sent them (see 14:13-16). If the king follows their lead, both he and these prophets will be driven from the land and perish (cf. the fate of the prophet Hananiah in 28:17; see 29:31-32). This is in fact what is announced for Zedekiah in no uncertain terms in 24:8-10; apparently, that text is set at a time when the option provided in this chapter is no longer viable.

Word to People and Priests, 27:16-22

The same message is now delivered to the people and the priests, with different nuances given the new audience. The note of restoration is also introduced in this segment (v. 22). The priests become involved because many of the sacred objects of the temple had been taken to Babylon in 597 BC, along with King Jehoiachin (=Jeconiah) and "all the nobles of Judah and Jerusalem," and there had been no little effort made to see that those vessels be returned. Once again, the prophets are the problem. Once again, they are preaching deception. Just as the prophets were advising against submitting to Babylon, they were assuring the priests that the exile would be short-lived and these sacred vessels would soon be returned (v. 16).

An example of such prophetic preaching is presented in the next chapter (see the message of the prophet Hananiah in 28:3). Once again, Jeremiah advises them to submit to Babylon so that they might live, uttering once more the plaintive cry: why make Jerusalem a desolation (see v. 13)? Exilic readers could understand how subversive a claim such as this would be: Serve (*'ābad*) the king of Babylon and live! Serve Yahweh and live, yes; but serve Nebuchadnezzar? That sounds like blasphemy (see **Connections: On Submitting to Babylon and Violence**).

Jeremiah presents a new argument in v. 18: *if* these prophets are true prophets (note the "if"! Jeremiah does not grant the point) with a genuine word from God, then let them intercede with God on behalf of the sacred vessels the Babylonians left behind in the temple and the palace. [The Temple Vessels] Let them speak, not on behalf of the vessels that have been taken, but on behalf of the vessels that have *not* yet been taken. They are to intercede with God, because that would be the only entreaty that could conceivably be effective. Jeremiah knows that God has announced judgment on Jerusalem and Judah and said that the remaining vessels will be taken away to Babylon as well (so v. 22, after the repeated "thus says the Lord" in vv. 19, 21); hence, it is *God* who would have to be persuaded otherwise.

This is, in effect, a challenge thrown to the prophets to demonstrate that they know God's word and will for this situation; let us see if God will respond to their intercessions and they can be shown to be true prophets. But Jeremiah knows that God had commanded Jeremiah not to intercede for this people (11:14; 14:11); the reader may rightly wonder whether Jeremiah issues this challenge knowing full well that it would not be successful. These prophets will thus be shown not only to be wrong about the vessels that have been taken but also incapable of protecting those vessels that are still in place! The only way to assure the latter would be to submit to Babylon.

As it happened, in fulfillment of Jeremiah's word (vv. 19-21), the pillars and sea were broken into pieces and carried along with other vessels to Babylon in the destruction of temple and city in 586 BC (see 52:17-23; 2 Kgs 25:13-17; 2 Chr 36: 7, 10, 18). At the same time, this negative word is not God's final word about the temple vessels (and, by implication, the people of Israel). The rest of the vessels will be carried away, but beyond that devastation, the day will come (v. 22; see v. 7) when God will give renewed attention to these vessels and will restore them to "this place" (=the temple). This return is reported in Ezra 1:7-11. But that future on the far side of great judgment is possible only because God is faithful.

[Temple Vessels as Word of Hope]

The Temple Vessels

The vessels still left in the city included the following (v. 19): two bronze pillars (named Jachin and Boaz) that stood at the entrance to the temple (1 Kgs 7:15-22); the bronze sea, used as a priestly wash basin, also located at the temple entrance (1 Kgs 7:23-26; 2 Chr 4:6); the ornamented bronze stands, upon which the ten wash basins were mounted (1 Kgs 7:27-39); and other miscellaneous vessels. The relationship between this text and 2 Kgs 24:13, where "all" the temple treasures are said to have been carried off in 597 BC, is uncertain. The word "all" may be an exaggeration to make the devastating point (see the reference to "all" the people in ch. 26 or the use of "all" in other traditions, e.g., in Exod 7–10 for the effects of the plagues).

Temple Vessels as Word of Hope

It is remarkable that God would attend to such temple details (yet see the considerable detail directly commanded by God with respect to the building of the tabernacle in Exodus 25–31, 35–40; cf. also 1 Kings 7). A rebuilt temple seems to be in view that has significant continuity with the temple that had been destroyed; the vessels would provide that significant point of continuity between old and new. The vessels are thus understood both literally and as a metaphor for continuity. In a sense the prophets of 27:16 and Hananiah in 28:3 are right about what will happen to these vessels; they just get their timing wrong (Robert Carroll, *Jeremiah* [Philadelphia: Westminster, 1986], 537). But that proves to be a crucial element in the assessment of the truth of their prophecy, especially because it skips over the devastation of 586 BC.

The libation cups pictured here were like those used in the Temple for anointing animal sacrifices with either wine or oil, and only represent a small fraction of the vessels that adorned the Temple. The Temple Vessels were made of gold, silver, copper, bronze, and alabaster. When the vessels were replaced, such as after the destruction of the Temple by the Babylonians, the materials used were of lesser value than the originals. As synagogues were built in the absence of the Temple, it was forbidden to furnish the synagogues with vessels identical to the Temple vessels.

Libation cups. 8th C. BC. Iron Age II. Reuben and Edith Hecht Collection. Haifa, Israel. (Credit: Erich Lessing/Art Resource, NY)

CONNECTIONS

On Submitting to Babylon and Violence

For Jeremiah to call for submission to the Babylonian king and his empire is a strange message from several angles. To use more modern language, Jeremiah counsels nonviolence in the face of those who counsel war. Jeremiah's counsel stands in no little tension with God's language of violence associated with the fall of Jerusalem elsewhere in Jeremiah. It is to be noted that Jerusalem had already suffered considerable violence in the initial conquest of the city (597 BC). The counsel that Jeremiah offers here comes after that fall of the city and before the much more devastating destruction still to come. It is as if a second chance is being given to the city, its leaders and its people. If so, it is a remarkably worded opportunity: take a nonviolent stance or you will experience more devastating violence than you have already experienced! If this word/act seeks to convey a second chance, then, on the far side of the fall of Jerusalem, this would be an important word for exilic readers to hear. God's will was not for violence at all costs; God makes last-ditch efforts to stop the deluge. This would mean that God's future for them does not take the shape of still more violence.

It is possible, of course, that this word is not really a second chance and that Jeremiah (and God) knows that this counsel will be rejected and the devastating violence against the city will take place. Yet, the still further rejection of that call on the part of all of these parties listed in the chapter, from kings to commoners, hastens the end. Such a pervasive rejection of the word from God on the part of all these people creates an even further build-up of the forces that make for disaster (as it will for Babylon, v. 7; [Until Its Time Comes]).

From another perspective, God, in siding with Babylon in this conflict, places a divine imprimatur on the imperialistic policies and campaigns of Nebuchadnezzar. While the end of Babylonian hegemony is finally in view (27:7), at least for a time God takes the side of the imperialists over against the idealistic thinking of nation-states such as Judah. One might simply ascribe this stance to political realism, but it is remarkable that God works in and through a wide variety of political structures and ideologies to accomplish the divine purposes. [God Takes Sides]

God, too, has a stake in Israel's submission to Babylon. God's call for Israel to submit to Babylon is important in thinking through the theme of violence in Jeremiah, not least because much of it is associated with the work of God. If this divine command were to be obeyed, it would reduce the violence. With a kind of political

God Takes Sides

For God to take the side of the imperialistic oppressors is striking, not least given the Exodus tradition, where God takes the side of the oppressed, certainly the dominant testimony of the biblical writings. But even the latter dimension of God's purposes is not to be maintained in an absolutely consistent manner. Notably, what will in fact lead to this turning of the tables are oppressive policies on the part of Israel (see, e.g., Jer 22:13-19). Because Israel has unfaithfully become an oppressor over the course of its long history as a people, its own judgment will correspond to its wicked deeds and it will in turn become the oppressed (see Exod 22:21-24 for a basic statement in the Law). And Babylon is God's vehicle for seeing to this moral order of things.

God as Creator and History

God as creator makes choices among human beings and socio-political realities to carry out God's work in the world (27:5-6; see 50:44). This divine choice does not mean "the power and significance of Babylon are completely nullified" (contrary to Walter Brueggemann, *A Commentary on Jeremiah: Exile and Homecoming* [Grand Rapids: Eerdmans, 1998], 242), not least because Babylon uses its power in inappropriate ways (see v. 7; 25:12-14; 50-51). God makes free choices, but they are constrained by relationships established and are related to the powers that are available in and through which God can work. God connects the divine will for Israel and others with the rise of the Babylonian empire and its expansionist policies. To all external observation, God is not involved in these military and political activities; the claim of this text is that God is at work in and through them on behalf of God's global purposes. Observers cannot factor out just how God is so involved, but the text *confesses* that God's will is somehow at work.

Notably, God's actions in *history* are here grounded in an understanding of God as *Creator*. God's purposes span the globe and God's actions with Israel are interconnected with these creation-wide designs. This formulation is an Old Testament perspective often neglected in the now century-long rush to connect God's activity in the world with historical realities in particular, resulting in a neglect of the work of God as Creator, with no little negative impact on the larger environment.

realism, God's announcement implies that, if Israel would not rebel against Babylon, its future would take a less violent course. In other words, Babylon would function as agent of divine judgment in different ways, depending upon how Israel responded to the call for nonviolence. Israel's own resorting to violence would lead to its experience of even greater violence. Such a positive response on Israel's part would also mean that God's association with violence would be less (for both Israel and for readers!).

And so God has no little stake in such a nonviolent response of Israel; God's reputation is at stake, with all the implications that has for the appeal for the minds and hearts of readers in every generation. And the fact that such pervasive violence turned out to be the order of the day for Israel has in fact negatively affected the divine reputation in the world: Why is such violence associated with the God of the Bible?

On the Prophets and Politics

The prophets of Israel regularly become involved in political matters. This involvement can be observed from the time of Elijah and Elisha through Isaiah to Jeremiah. Some of Jeremiah's sharpest words are directed to the kings and their policies and programs (see ch. 22). In this chapter, the prophetic level of involvement moves beyond indictment of the kings for their infidelity to God and the neglect of issues of social justice. Here Jeremiah is more like Elisha in counseling very specific political/military moves (see 2 Kings 6-9; see also 1 Kgs 20; 22).

The prophet involves himself in political life beyond the traditionally religious sphere. Even more, the prophet (at God's call), engages in specific actions with respect to the internal political affairs of countries other than Israel. The theological grounding for such political activity is the belief that God is the Creator who is caught up in the life of the world and its peoples beyond the boundaries of Israel and pursues the divine will in every time and place. The prophet not only claims *that* God is so involved (an important first step) but also seeks to delineate *how* God is so engaged and to speak and act in ways congruent with that. [God as Creator and History]

The prophet's powers of discernment are key. He interprets what is happening on the world scene in terms of the will of God, and then has the energy, courage, and sheer audacity both to speak and to act in such a way as to bring that will to effect (remembering that the will of God is not irresistible). In the person and work of the prophet more resources can be accessed for interpreting the world's affairs that what political and military leaders conventionally consider to be available. And, typically, Zedekiah refuses to listen.

NOTE

[1] Contrary to Robert Carroll, *Jeremiah* (Philadelphia: Westminster, 1986), 531.

JEREMIAH AND HANANIAH

28:1-17

The narrative in chapter 28 is a parade example of conflict between two prophets, both of whom claim to be speaking the word of God. Prophetic conflict has been a prominent theme in the book to this point (e.g., 14:13-16; 23:9-40; 27), but no false prophets have been named. With the introduction of Hananiah that anonymity changes; here is a specific individual who embodies the falseness of which Jeremiah has spoken so often, most recently in chapter 27. Yet, vv. 13-14 show that Hananiah is presented as more than "a concrete instance" of false prophecy. His prophetic activity becomes the occasion for a delimitation of Israel's (and the other nations) future possibilities; in other words, the options presented in 27:8-11 are no longer available. A genuine advance in Jeremiah's word about Israel's future is occasioned by this confrontation. [Hananiah as Surprise for the Reader]

Hananiah as Surprise for the Reader

Hananiah (otherwise unknown) is something of a surprise for the reader. Jeremiah's sharp and pervasive indictment of the false prophets has suggested that we have to do with charlatans or quacks, prophets who are obviously deceptive. Readers might well wonder how anyone could be taken in by "pretenders" such as Hananiah. The portrayal of Hananiah cuts against such an expectation (and thereby contributes to an understanding of false prophets that the general indictments against them do not).

Hananiah's name means, "Yahweh has been gracious"; he seems to be a model of prophetic propriety; he uses all the right language, including the typical messenger formula ("Thus says the Lord, . . ." v. 2) and the use of the divine "I." He also performs symbolic acts (v. 10). He is given genealogical and geographical identity, comparable to that of Jeremiah himself (cf. v. 1 with 1:1). Moreover, he is identified simply as "the prophet," with no qualification (the LXX identifies him as a "false prophet"). And the historical setting for Hananiah's speaking (v. 1) is similar to that often provided for Jeremiah (e.g., 26:1). Hananiah is presented in terms that suggest that he is a "true" prophet, which makes the task of discerning true prophecy from false all the more difficult.

COMMENTARY

Jeremiah's Word to Hananiah and His Response, 28:1-11a

The opening clause of chapter 28, "in that same year" (see 27:1), links this narrative with the preceding chapter and its reports of

Translation Difficulties in Verse 1

AΩ The NRSV translates the Hebrew text as it stands, though "the beginning of" the reign of Jehoiakim (597 BC) stands in tension with "the fourth year." This is probably a scribal error. The NAB is likely correct in putting the former clause in brackets in view of its omission in the LXX.

prophetic conflict over submission to the king of Babylon and the return of the vessels to the temple. [Translation Difficulties in Verse 1] Hananiah is identified as the son of Azzur (of uncertain identification) from Gibeon, an important sanctuary site, probably located about six miles northwest of Jerusalem (see 1 Kgs 3:3-15). The narrative is initially told from Jeremiah's perspective in terms of a personal confrontation in a public setting (the temple courts, v. 5). As v. 1 puts it, Hananiah spoke "to me" in "the presence of the priests and all the people." (That Jeremiah is referred to in the third person in vv. 5-15 does not speak against the "to me," though most scholars emend the text; mixture of persons is common in Jeremiah, e.g., 8:18–9:3.) The text makes the confrontation sound like a Jerusalem "town meeting," with two individuals engaged in a debate before a live audience.

Hananiah's words are introduced by the messenger formula typical for (true) prophets, "Thus says the LORD of hosts, the God of Israel" (e.g., 7:3, 21). The basic word he speaks is an announcement of salvation, bracketed by the claim that God has broken the yoke of the king of Babylon (vv. 2, 4; see 27:8, 11-12). The result: within two years God will bring back the vessels Nebuchadnezzar took from the temple and carried to Babylon (in 597 BC) and God will also bring back King Jehoiachin (=Jeconiah) and all the other exiles. In other words, according to Hananiah, the events of 587 BC are not in the cards for God or for Israel. One might even say that he interpreted the prophecies of Jeremiah in such as way that the events of 597 BC were the final fulfillment of his word about Jerusalem. The importance attached to the temple vessels should be linked with the importance given them by God in 27:19-22 (see [The Temple Vessels]). The vessels are symbols of continuity and restoration. [Is Hananiah Anti-Babylonian?]

Jeremiah is (still?) wearing the yoke God commissioned him to wear (v. 10; see 27:2), and it becomes a key metaphor for this

---

Is Hananiah Anti-Babylonian?

In terms of the conflict in these chapters, Hananiah would seem to represent an anti-Babylonian stance (in line with the prophets of 27:9, 14-16). Yet, his words reveal a more complex perspective. His prophecy includes a return of King Jehoiachin (v. 4), which presumably entails a reestablishment of the Davidic throne; this certainly would not be good news to Zedekiah and his minions. So, in at least some respects, he sides neither with Jeremiah nor the ruling elite in Jerusalem. His prophecy is risky indeed. (See Robert Carroll, *Jeremiah* [Philadelphia: Westminster, 1986], 549.)

His commitment to God's promises regarding the Davidic throne could be claimed as orthodox in a fundamental way.

confrontation. Jeremiah's wearing of the yoke was a symbolic act, a vivid portrayal of God's will that Israel should submit to the sovereignty of the king of Babylon. Hananiah's claimed word from God—God has broken the yoke of the king of Babylon—thus stands in direct confrontation to that symbolic act. If, however, the clause in v. 2 is translated (as in vv. 4, 11) "I will break the yoke" (so NAB), then, given the two-year specification, the confrontation is less direct, and becomes a matter of timing, initially at least (vv. 3-4). God had specified to Jeremiah how long Israel and the nations should submit to the king of Babylon (27:7); Hananiah cuts that time way back. But in v. 11 Hananiah cuts against Jeremiah's prophecy in another respect; the submission to Babylon of which Hananiah speaks is already a fact, whereas Jeremiah thinks of a more intense future submission as an obligation (27:8, 11-12).[1]

"The prophet" Jeremiah responds to "the prophet" Hananiah in the same setting with the same audience (vv. 5-9). Jeremiah expresses the desire that God would do what Hananiah said God would do (in this chapter it is finally God who discerns true from false and acts upon it). This response is important in making clear that Jeremiah (and God!) would like things to turn out this way; he was not desirous of subjection to the king of Babylon nor did he relish the destruction of Judah and Jerusalem. But he understands that other factors are at work in this situation, and he invites the audience to consider an argument (vv. 8-9). Interestingly, in this first response he does not counter Hananiah's word with a word from God; he does not use the messenger formula, as he will three times in vv. 13-16. In fact, Jeremiah is unusually irenic and considerate in his approach to Hananiah (this may not be typical of his behaviors, but it reveals a complexity in the presentation of his person). At least until vv. 13-16!

Jeremiah's argument is more complex than at first appears. He draws on two factors to be considered in distinguishing true prophecy from false (see **Connections: On Distinguishing True Prophecy from False**). First, he appeals to tradition, the history of prophecy. How does Hananiah's word fit with respect to this long history? The prophets who have spoken heretofore have prophesied war, famine, and pestilence against many nations and great kingdoms, including Jeremiah himself (e.g., 14:12; 27:8; note the connection with Jeremiah's call to be a "prophet to the nations," 1:5, 10). Though Hananiah's prophecy would presumably entail an outbreak of war if the yoke of the king of Babylon were to be broken (v. 2), it is the peace element that provides his focus.

Are God's Promises Good for All Time?

In response to Jeremiah, Hananiah might have cited Isaiah, who had prophesied peace, namely, the deliverance of Jerusalem from the Assyrians (Isa 31:4-5; 37:33-35). He may in fact have had Isaiah's promise of deliverance in mind. Inasmuch as Isaiah, a true prophet, had articulated the promises of God that Jerusalem would be delivered, would not a promise from God be considered valid across the generations? Would not Hananiah have been in the company of true prophets in claiming that Isaiah's prophecy was still in order? Even more, did not God's promises to dynasty and people as articulated by Isaiah make Jerusalem invulnerable to destruction? More generally, given Jeremiah's refusal to honor this point of view, do readers in every generation have to wonder whether God keeps promises?

This probable perception regarding God's promises on the part of Hananiah may well be refuted by Jer 18:9-10. In that text we learn that God may cut off God's own promises regarding specific matters, if any nation or kingdom "does evil in [God's] sight." Jeremiah claims that Israel has in fact done so. So, interpreters need to make some kind of distinction among God's promises, those that will not be set aside by God come what may (see Jer 31:35-37; 33:14-26) and those that are related to a specific historical situation (such as Isa 31:5-6). Hananiah collapsed these promises into a single fabric, believing that the Davidic promise entailed a promise regarding the continued existence of Jerusalem and its temple.

Second, Jeremiah states that if prophets do prophesy peace, as Hananiah has just done, then one will know that God has sent the prophet only if that word comes to pass (see Deut 18:22, which speaks of the fulfillment of all prophecies, not just those of peace).

Readers, who are not told of any response from others present at this confrontation (v. 1), would be able to understand why Hananiah is not convinced by Jeremiah's arguments (vv. 10-11). Jeremiah has in essence argued a "wait and see" approach, and that approach is no different for prophesies of war than for prophesies of peace. The latter may be uncommon, of course, but they have occurred. [Are God's Promises Good for All Time?]

Hananiah chooses a dramatic form of response to Jeremiah, performing a symbolic act of his own, which would probably be thought somehow to nullify Jeremiah's act. This is a conflict not only between words, but also between actions. In full view of the audience, he removes the yoke (or yoke-bar, singular of the word in 27:2) from Jeremiah and breaks it. He then explains the symbolism of his action, using the messenger formula once again. Just as he has broken the yoke, so God will break the yoke of the king of Babylon within two years, not only from Israel, but also from "all nations" (see 27:6-7). As noted above, Hananiah's word assumes that the submission to Babylon has already occurred; Jeremiah's prophecy spoke of a more intense submission that still lay in the future (see 27:8, 11-12).

Jeremiah Responds to Hananiah, 28:11b-17

Jeremiah's initial response to Hananiah's challenge was simply to walk out of the meeting (v. 11). From the perspective of the gathered audience, this was probably read as a concession on Jeremiah's part. Jeremiah is not in fact finished with this confrontation, but he takes an unknown amount of time before he responds further (v. 12). For Jeremiah, the delay in response to Hananiah (see also v. 6) is evidence of the need for careful discernment on his part. The word of a prophet is not simply to be dismissed but is to be thought through with care, awaiting further insight.

Jeremiah responds only when he has heard from the Lord (in private). Assuming that Hananiah is not reporting a word from God, God now speaks for the first time in this chapter. Jeremiah is certain about the falseness of Hananiah only upon hearing from God. The word of the Lord comes to Jeremiah in the form of an oracle to be delivered to Hananiah (vv. 13-16). Notable about this response is the repeated use of the messenger formula (vv. 13, 14, 16). The initial oracle (vv. 13-14) concerns the basic issue about which Hananiah had spoken. Jeremiah then responds personally to Hananiah in v. 15, continuing with a further word from the Lord about him as an individual in v. 16.

God's word to Jeremiah initially counters Hananiah's word through a new use of the yoke symbolism (vv. 13-14; see Jesus' use of the yoke symbolism in Matt 11:28–30). Hananiah has broken the wooden yoke but in the process of doing so has forged an iron yoke, which no human being can break (see 15:12; Deut 28:48 on "iron yoke"). That is, he has made the original word of Jeremiah even more certain and the nations' service of the king of Babylon even more severe (see 27:6; contrary to Walter Brueggemann,[2] Nebuchadnezzar is indeed a "real agent"). Hence, submission it will still be, but now it will be forced on them and be more severe than the earlier option Jeremiah had announced. For, the word of God continues, God has placed an iron yoke on all the nations, that is, all nations shall *certainly* serve the king of Babylon, as will the wild animals. God's original word to the nations through Jeremiah (see 27:6) will be fulfilled—in spades. Hence, Hananiah's prophecy turns out to be more than an illustration of the reality of false prophecy presented in chapter 27; it limits the possibilities of the future in relation to the Babylonians (see 27:8-11).

Jeremiah then addresses Hananiah personally, first in his own words of indictment (v. 15) and then with an announcement of judgment from the Lord (v. 16; "therefore"). It is striking that Jeremiah does not tell Hananiah exactly what God told him to say in vv. 13-14. Might this be an example of a certain prophetic freedom to interpret or expand upon the word received from God? He declares that God has not sent him, but that he has been speaking a lie; Hananiah thus falls into the category of the lying prophets indicted throughout chapter 27 (vv. 9-10, 14-15, 16-18). Because he has spoken falsely he will suffer the consequence specified in the law (see Deut 13:1-11; 18:20). God has not "sent" him as a prophet (v. 15), but God will "send" him off the face of the earth (v. 16). Because he has spoken rebellion against the Lord, he will be dead within the year (comparably for another such prophet, 29:30-32).

Jeremiah's prophecy was fulfilled; Hananiah died in the seventh month of that year (v. 17), that is, within two months (see v. 1). No indication is given as to how he died; remarkably, God is not made the subject of his death. For readers, his death, in light of the Deuteronomic law, would confirm that Hananiah was a false prophet.

CONNECTIONS

On Judgment and Grace

It is important not to distinguish between the prophecies of Jeremiah and Hananiah in terms of judgment and grace. Certainly Hananiah's prophecy is a word of a gracious move made by God on behalf of Israel and its future; one could even consider it a gospel word. At the same time, Jeremiah's word of judgment is not a word against grace (remembering that grace is a more comprehensive term than gospel). Jeremiah's prophecy is a word against this particular manifestation of grace at this moment in time. Even more, Jeremiah's word of judgment must be integrated into the larger fabric of Jeremiah's preaching, namely, that God's word of judgment is finally in the interests of a gracious divine purpose. Given what has happened to the community of Israel, the most gracious way for God to move into the future with this people is through the fires of judgment, as difficult as that is for all concerned, including God. The gracious activity of God moves through judgment; even in judgment God's gracious purposes remain intact.

On Distinguishing True Prophecy from False

This chapter is not explicitly interested in setting out criteria on the basis of which to distinguish between true and false prophets, yet it features this issue in several ways. Jeremiah himself introduces two criteria, namely, the relationship of the prophecy to the received *tradition and whether or not the prophecy has come to pass.*

Regarding the first criterion, the issue is not that their prophetic predecessors have never prophesied peace, but it has been uncommon to do so. And, hence, prophecies of peace have more need of the test of fulfillment to demonstrate their truthfulness. This amounts to a statement of likelihood; given the history of prophecy, it is more likely that Hananiah's word is not a word from God than that it is (events prove that Jeremiah's initial inclination was correct, and his place in the tradition is thereby secured). [On Judgment and Grace]

Regarding the second criterion, the larger context in Jeremiah, and indeed the tradition of prophecy itself, complicates the argument from success. From one angle, even if the prophecy does come to pass, that is no sure sign that the word is from God (as specified in Deut 13:1-5). From another angle, the lack of success is no sure sign either. A prophecy of Micah announcing the devastation of Jerusalem was cited in 26:18, and it did *not* come to pass. Obviously, the conclusion was not drawn that Micah was thereby shown to be a false prophet. One had to take into account other factors, not least how people responded to the message and, then, how God had responded to that response. Hence, for example, God could "repent" or "change his mind" about the word of judgment (as in 26:19, and potentially 26:3, 13; for the general principle, see 18:7-10; **Connections**, ch. 18). It may be that Jeremiah recognizes that this divine change of plans is possible in this case (see 27:18). The only way in which the matter could be resolved is if *God* spoke to the matter (see, e.g., Jonah 3:10 or, without the use of "repentance" language, see 2 Kgs 20:1-7). So Jeremiah bides his time and waits for God to speak to the situation and God does speak to the point (vv. 13-14).

Inasmuch as false prophets continued to work among exilic readers, this story would serve as a concrete instance of the careful discernment needed in assessing prophetic claims. Prophets may have all the traditional credentials for being a prophet; they may conduct themselves in the community in an exemplary way; they may use all the right language; they may claim to have received their message from the Lord; they may even claim to be a prophet

---

Descendants of Hananiah

The phenomenon of false prophecy did not come to an end with Hananiah. False prophets plagued Ezekiel and later prophets (e.g., Ezek 13; Zech 13:2-6; see Sir 36:20-21; 1 Macc 14:41 for the concern about a "trustworthy" prophet). Comparable issues regarding the truth of prophecy were anticipated by Jesus and experienced by the New Testament community. They included the development of various criteria, especially in view of the confession regarding Jesus and matters relating to the end times (see, e.g., Matt 7:15-16; 24:11, 24; Mark 13:22; Acts 13:6; 1 Thess 5:3; 1 John 4:1; 2 Pet 2:1; see Rev 16:13; 19:20; 20:10; Luke 6:26).

So it has been in every age since. There have always been those who have claimed to speak a word from God, and the faithful religious communities have had to struggle with issues of discernment ever anew. The various texts in Jeremiah can be a resource in this ongoing process (perhaps especially, beware of those who speak only words of comfort and peace), but they provide no surefire criteria. A "wait and see" approach will remain a common response. For studies on this issue, see James Crenshaw, *Prophetic Conflict* (Berlin: de Gruyter, 1971); Thomas Overholt, *The Threat of Falsehood* (Naperville IL: A. R. Allenson, 1970).

of Yahweh. Hananiah seems to satisfy each of these criteria. But meeting criteria is insufficient evidence for determining whether the word spoken is indeed true or false.

When readers have finished with this story, with a particular person being portrayed, they can better understand that the dividing line between true and false prophet is very difficult to discern. Before believing what a prophet may say, great care must be taken. Jeremiah's waiting for time to pass and waiting on a word from God were wise responses in the face of such a conflict.

[Descendants of Hananiah]

NOTES

[1] See G. Keown, P. Scalise, and T. Smothers, *Jeremiah 26–52* (Dallas: Word Books, 1993), 56-57.

[2] Walter Brueggemann, *A Commentary on Jeremiah: Exile and Homecoming* (Grand Rapids: Eerdmans, 1998), 255.

JEREMIAH'S LETTERS TO THE EXILES

29:1-32

This chapter reports on three (some think two) letters of Jeremiah (and one of Shemaiah) that address issues that were raised in chapters 26–28, especially false hopes among the exiles. [Another Letter of Jeremiah] Jeremiah's words are introduced as the word of God in typical messenger fashion (see vv. 4, 8, 10, 16, 17, 21, 23, 25, 31, 32). The movement of thought in the chapter is not altogether clear, evident especially in vv. 16-20 (not in the LXX) and in vv. 24-28, where it is difficult to sort out the content of the letters involved. Probably the editors did not have the letters before them in exactly this form (the first is the most complete). Some of the content has been created from memory or reformulated in view of a specific editorial interest (a practice congruent with that of envoys who delivered letters in that culture). While this exchange of letters occurs in the time after 597 BC and before the fall of Jerusalem in 587 BC, in their present form they are addressed to exiles after 587 BC.

The first letter from Jeremiah (vv. 1-23) is sent to the exiles in Babylon, sometime following the deportation in 597 BC (see 2 Kings

---

Another Letter of Jeremiah

Another letter purported to be by Jeremiah is found among the deuterocanonical books included in all Orthodox and Roman Catholic Bibles, namely, A Letter of Jeremiah (the King James Version and the Latin Vulgate print this letter as the sixth chapter of the deuterocanonical book Baruch). While this letter is addressed to exiles in Babylon, it most likely originated sometime during the 4th century. The letter imitates the letter to the exiles in Jeremiah 29, but the bulk of its content expresses the futility of idol worship, developing the theme of Jer 10:1-16. The deuterocanonical book Baruch also takes the form of a letter, this one sent by Baruch to the people of Jerusalem (see ch. 36).

Letter from Hilarion to Alis. (Credit: Victoria University Library, Toronto)

Israelites in Exile

From various texts (e.g., Ezek 3:15; 11:15-16; 17:11-21) it is apparent that the exiles were not enslaved in Babylon, but were allowed to establish enclaves of their own with limited freedom. For reasons not altogether clear, the Babylonians determined that regular contacts between the exiles and those left in the land were important for the stability of the empire. Perhaps they viewed the exiles as hostages, the better to control the government they had put in place in Jerusalem. Certainly those prophets and others (both among the exiles and in Jerusalem) who pursued an anti-Babylonian policy threatened the well-being of the exiles.

Jeremiah's counsel was, in effect: do not make waves! The way to get through this period of time is to be content with your lot; that will be the surest way to conform your lives to the will of God. God does have other plans for the exiles, plans to give them "a future with hope," but it will take time. That Jeremiah writes letters to this exilic community shows that his word to them would be respected, at least on the part of some exiles, unlike the attention his words received from this same community prior to 597 BC.

24:10-16). The basic concern is to address issues faced by these exiles in view of Jeremiah's word that their stay in Babylon will be an extended one, well beyond that suggested by several false prophets. Two of the latter are specifically named (Ahab and Zedekiah); they were fomenting unrest among the exiles and had apparently announced an early return to the land. The basic response is to settle in for the long haul, but know that God will in time restore them to their own land. [Israelites in Exile]

Jeremiah's second letter is addressed to the false prophet Shemaiah who had written a letter in response to Jeremiah's letter (cf. vv. 5 and 28) in an attempt to silence him (vv. 24-28; some think that these verses have been corrupted and refer only to Shemaiah's letter[1]). After Shemaiah's letter is read to Jeremiah, he writes a third letter to the exiles (vv. 29-32). These letters are further illustrations of the difficulties that Jeremiah confronted among the false prophets, and the fate to which they are assigned because they have led the people astray by their lies.

The presence of written material (probably on papyrus) is common in Jeremiah (see 29:1; 30:2; 36:2; 51:60). Such writing is usually considered a sign that prophetic materials are being increasingly understood as authoritative for the faith and life of Israel. This may be particularly evident in the way chapter 29 begins. Readers are informed of Jeremiah's written words, which contain various divine oracles; these are assumed to be just as much the word of God to the readers as would Jeremiah's delivering it in person.

The Legend of the Wandering Jew

According to legend, the Wandering Jew appears at various times and places and describes events that have happened. Jesus. Since the 1600s, many writers have used the legend as the framework for political and social commentary, especially because the character had observed so much of world history. The legend of the Wandering Jew has also been used to promote prejudice against Jews.

It is appropriate for Marc Chagall to depict a fantasy image of the Wandering Jew. So much of his painting is informed and guided by his personal experince growing up in Russia as a Jew. Subliminal images from Jewish folklore abound in his many works. In a childlike simplicity, this subliminal "icon" of the Jewish dispora is shown with an intensity of vision and purpose that clearly is beyond the realm of ordinary life in the city, referenced in the background. Rather, his gait and stare are fixed perhaps upon the invisible but real presence of God. The depiction of a ram at the lower left of the painting, as a dream-like image, may suggest the Ram provided by God in the thicket in Abraham's sacrifice of Isaac. A suggestion of a domed, orthodox church (perhaps associated with his Russian experience) can be seen in the background as the wandering Jew steadfastly proceeds through life.

Marc Chagall (1887–1985). *Ahasver, the Legendary Figure of the Eternally Wandering Jew.* Oil on canvas. c 1900. Petit Palais, Musee d'Art Moderne. Geneva, Switzerland. [© 2002 Artists Rights Society (ARS). New York / ADAGP, Paris]

Contributor: Richard R. Ring, Ph.D., Collection Development Librarian, University of Kansas.

COMMENTARY

Jeremiah's First Letter, 29:1-23

The first letter from Jeremiah is addressed to all the exiles, with special attention to the elders, priests, and prophets among them. Interestingly, though Jehoiachin (=Jeconiah) and the queen mother (=Nehushta) are among the exiles, they are not specifically addressed (v. 2; see 28:4; 22:24-30). The letter was delivered (and read aloud?) by Elasah and Gemariah whom King Zedekiah had sent as emissaries to King Nebuchadnezzar for purposes unknown (payment of tribute?). [Elasah and Gemariah]

Elasah and Gemariah

Elasah son of Shaphan was probably a brother of Ahikam son of Shaphan, both of whom had been involved in the reform of Josiah (see at 26:24). Gemariah was the son of Hilkiah, probably to be identified with the high priest who had participated in the discovery and interpretation of the book of the law found in the temple during the reform of Josiah (see 2 Kngs 22–23). If these identifications are correct, then Jeremiah was supported by two prominent families from both royal and priestly circles that had been involved in reforming activities over the course of the last generation.

The content of the letter is represented as a word from "the LORD of hosts, the God of Israel" (the same formula used by Hananiah in 28:2). God's address is made to the exiles generally (v. 4; unlike v. 1, no leaders are specified). God is the only agent named who had sent them into exile in vv. 4, 7, 14, but the king of Babylon is the only agent noted in v. 1 (and elsewhere). As is common in Jeremiah, both God and Nebuchadnezzar are agents (see **Connections**, ch. 20).

The letter is an admixture of exhortation to the exiles and announcements of judgment pertinent to their evaluation of the prophetic voices among them. The structure of the letter consists of the following elements: exhortations to the exiles to build their homes in Babylon and live peacefully there (vv. 5-7); exhortations to ignore the false prophets who dream of an early restoration (vv. 8-9); assurances that God has their welfare in mind and when the seventy years (see at 25:11-12) have been completed they will be restored to the land (vv. 10-14); an announcement of the coming judgment on the city of Jerusalem and its inhabitants in view of the exiles' misplaced confidence on prophetic voices among them (vv. 15-19); an announcement of judgment on two of the prophets who have been misleading the exiles (vv. 20-23).

The basic force of the hortatory words to the exiles (vv. 5-7) is that they should settle down in Babylon for the long haul; it will be seventy years before God will act to deliver them. As signs of their acceptance of this divine strategy, and their trust in ancient divine promises, they should build houses and plant gardens (note the links to Jeremiah's call, 1:10), marry and have children, and plan for the marriages of their children (see Deut 20:5-10). They will even have grandchildren born in exile! (Actually, many Jews remained in Babylon long after the several returns, indeed to the present day.) The exhortation to multiply (*rābāh*) and not decrease brings to mind prior divine promises and assurances (see 3:16; 23:3; see 30:19; 33:22; note also the links to creational charges and ancestral promises, Gen 1:28; Exod 1:7). The assumption in this hortatory language is that God will be present and active in their daily lives even in this foreign land and among people they could name as their enemies (see **Connections: The Exiles and God's Work as Creator**).

Even more, the divine exhortation to the exiles concerns not only their own life and their community's future. Remarkably, the letter also focuses on the people among whom they live (v. 7). God exhorts the exiles to seek (NAB, "promote") the well-being of Babylon and, even more, to pray for it (their enemies!; cf. Deut 20:10; Prov 25:21; see Matt 5:44; 1 Tim 2:1-2 for a comparable New Testament perspective). The word commonly translated "welfare" is *šālôm*, used three times in this verse (and again in v. 11, specifically for the exiles) for a comprehensive sense of well-being that touches every aspect of their lives. God is concerned about the welfare of a "pagan" city, which would include its individual inhabitants and the community as a whole. The effects of this combination of work and prayer on the part of the exiles would affect their own lives in a positive way, but they would also reverberate out to contribute to the welfare of Babylonians and all those with whom they came into contact (see **Connections: Seek the Welfare of the City**).

Verses 8-9 consist of exhortations to beware of false prophets. The exhortation to seek Babylon's welfare stands over against the word of the false prophets (included among the deportees, but see v. 15). They have been at work among the exiles; in light of the larger context (see 27:14-16), though not explicit at this point in the text, they have been predicting an early return to the promised land. These prophets would probably be anti-Babylonian in their perspective, encouraging the exiles to stand over against Babylon (see chs. 27–28). That the exiles have been attracted to these prophecies is clear; some among them have even claimed that God himself has raised up these prophets in exile (v. 15). God warns the exiles about the message of these prophets, given in the name of Yahweh, and the dreams they claim to have had (see 23:23-32); they are deceivers and liars, for God did not send them. They have the wrong word for this time and place in the life of the community of faith.

Verses 10-14 consist of assurances regarding a future salvation, with implications for the present situation of the exiles. These words of hope (a shorter version of which is found in the LXX) provide a transition to the Book of Consolation in chapters 30–33. These verses are closely linked to Deuteronomy 4:29-31 (v. 13 is a paraphrase of Deut 4:29). Deuteronomy 4:29 refers to a distressful exilic experience, when Israel will seek the Lord "from there," that is, from exile in Babylon. This phrase constitutes one hint regarding how Jeremiah 29:12-14a is to be interpreted; these verses

Present and Future in 29:10-14

Verses 10 and 14bc bracket this segment and their temporal relationship to vv. 11-14a is not altogether clear. Do vv. 12-14a take place after the return (so v. 10 seems to imply) or before the return (so the placement of v. 14bc seems to imply)? It seems best to adopt the latter interpretation and consider v. 10 to be a summary announcement of future salvation, with v. 11 being a reference to these divine "plans" of restoration for the "future." When, and only when, the seventy years have been completed (see at 25:11-12), will God act on these plans and bring the exiles back home. Given the length of time (seventy years), the "you" of the text in effect pertains to several generations of exiles and speaks to their situation in exile.

The NRSV and NIV begin v. 12 with the translation, "then," which make vv. 10-14 entirely a future matter. NEB and NAB, however, do not translate a "then" and the effect is to give vv. 12-14a a present sense (supported by Deut 4:29). Verses 11-14 belong together as a fuller statement of God's *ongoing* promised relationship to the exiles (note the linkage between the prayers and "welfare" of v. 7 and vv. 11-13), climaxing in the deliverance of v. 14bc (which includes exiles in Babylon and elsewhere). It should be said that these words of hope do not call into question Jeremiah's word of vv. 5-7 that the exiles should settle into their Babylonian situation; indeed, such words of hope are a powerful motivation for the interim strategy (contrary to William McKane, *A Critical and Exegetical Commentary on Jeremiah* [2 vols.; ICC; Edinburgh: T. & T. Clark, 1986], 737-38).

---

refer to a promised experience for the exiles *while still in Babylon* and not just afterwards. [Present and Future in 29:10-14]

Three strong statements of the divine initiative in this announcement of salvation are important in assessing what follows (v. 10). First, God will "visit" the exiles; the verb is *pāqad,* a verb often used in Jeremiah for God's visiting the people in judgment (often translated "punish" in the NRSV, e.g., 21:14). So, this divine action is an explicit reversal of the judgment that the people have experienced. Second, God will fulfill "my promise" to the exiles. Given the next clause about returning to the land, this promise may refer to texts such as 23:3, 5-8; 24:6; 27:22; it is probably also a more general reference to the ancestral promises regarding land (see 30:3; 33:26; cf. 14:21). Third, God will act to bring the exiles back to their own land, a promise that opens and closes this section (see v. 14bc; 24:6; see Nebuchadnezzar as the subject of this verb in 42:12). Any interpretation of the people's response in vv. 12-14a must take into account this many-sided statement of the divine initiative. The people are able to respond positively because God has already taken the initiative and given them promises upon which they can count.

God surely "knows" (v. 11; the expression is emphatic, also in v. 23) what plans God "intends" (*ḥāšab,* NRSV, "have"; see God's intending *rāʿāh* for Israel in 26:3) with respect to Israel's future, and hence Israel can rest back in that divine knowledge and intention (no special foreknowledge is needed for "plans"). God's "plans" (mentioned three times here) are God's designs for this people in view of God's promises (see Isa 46:10). Those plans for Israel are plans for its welfare (*šālôm*), and while still in exile (see its threefold use in v. 7 for the "welfare" of both Israel and Babylon), and not for its harm (*rāʿāh*). The word *rāʿāh* has commonly been used in Jeremiah for the disaster experienced by Israel as a consequence of its own wickedness (e.g., this word defined God's "*plans*" for Israel in 18:11). As far as the exiles are concerned, they no longer have to worry about disaster (*rāʿāh*), even though their plans had been evil (see 18:12, 18); God intends that they have a future filled with hope. God seeks to assure the exiles that their past wickedness does not shape their future. God has new plans for them, characterized by a comprehensive peace, well-being, and stability on their own land.

Because God has these kinds of plans for Israel (while they are still in exile!), the exiles can be assured that God will hear them *now* when they call upon God and come before God in prayer—not only on behalf of Babylon (see v. 7), but also regarding their own concerns (v. 12). In the past, God had commanded Jeremiah not to pray for the welfare of this people (7:16; 11:14; 14:11); now the people will encounter a new moment in the life of God, and that will affect the prayers of both people and prophet (see **Connections: Exile and Spirituality**).

When the exiles seek God (or draw near to God) in prayer (the only ritual called for!), they will not have to conduct a search for God as if God were hiding or unavailable. God will be able to be found by the seeker (that is, God is accessible), for God has turned the divine face toward the people. God is no longer hidden in judgment (see 33:3-5) and God no longer has forsaken Israel (7:29; 12:7; see Isa 54:7-8). When they turn to God, God will be there. When they seek God they will encounter God, when (or, if) they seek God with all their heart (v. 13 is a paraphrase of Deut 4:29). [Repentance in 29:12-13?]

God will be newly present and active among the people (v. 14; NRSV, "I will let you find me"; NAB, "you will find me with you"), and God would then change their lot from being exiles to being a restored people. God will gather exiles from all the nations where they had been scattered and reestablish them in their own land with all of its attendant blessings (see 23:3, 8; 24:6). The God who

Repentance in 29:12-13?

Despite the claims of Walter Brueggemann (*A Commentary on Jeremiah: Exile and Homecoming* [Grand Rapids: Eerdmans, 1998], 259), there is no word in vv. 12-13 about repentance, except as it may be included as a type of prayer among other prayers. The point is not that "life is made newly possible" for the exiles *when* they demonstrate that they are "an utterly devoted people." That would be no "assertion of the gospel"; the gospel word has been sharply conditioned in such a formulation (see **Connections: Exiles and Spirituality**).

had scattered would now gather. The people who had been dispersed would now be brought together into one family.

Verses 15-19 are an announcement of judgment. [The Coherence of 29:15-19] Because at least some exiles, like those remaining in Jerusalem, have been attracted to the message of the false prophets,

thinking that God has raised them up (v. 15; see Deut 18:15-18), the letter turns to counter that claim. It does so in two ways. One, it refers to those remaining in Jerusalem (vv. 16-19), among whom the exiles were recently numbered as not listening to the true prophets (v. 19; their record is not so good on recognizing prophets!). Two, it refers to the exiles more particularly (vv. 20-23). These prophets have been declared deceivers in vv. 8-9 (see 27:9-10, 14-16; 14:13-16). Verses 16-19 now counter their deceptions with a word about what God is in fact going to do, initially focusing on the fate of those who are still in Jerusalem—the Davidic king and "your kinsfolk who did not go out with you into exile" (v. 16). But, this is the fate of Jerusalem also because the *exiles* were among those who did not listen (v. 19)! They contributed to the shape of Jerusalem's future. Moreover, these verses could serve as a warning to exiles more generally; they link up with other announcements of judgment in Jeremiah, indicating how such words could still be applicable to them.[2]

Interpreters have often noted that this order of hope for the exiles (vv. 10-14) and judgment on those remaining in Jerusalem (vv. 16-19) is similar to the announcements regarding the "good figs" in 24:4-7 and the "bad figs" in 24:8-10 (see the reference to "bad figs" in 29:17). Yet, the "you" in v. 19 makes the presentation more complex in this chapter; the exiles are not so sharply separated out from those remaining in Jerusalem.[3] The community of exiles is rather more complex than 24:8-10 implies.

The announcement of judgment picks up on themes common in previous oracles, especially the language of judgment used in 24:8-10. Typically, God is the subject of this action, mediated in and through the "sword" of the Babylonian armies and the resultant famine and pestilence. The NRSV translation of "let loose" (*pi'el* of *šālaḥ*) is helpful here; God will let the forces of destruction have their way. Notably, they will be *made* "bad figs" because of the devastating effects of the judgment. The reason for this judgment is clearly stated (as it is not in 24:7-10, but commonly elsewhere, e.g., 7:24-26; 25:4; 26:5; see 35:14-15; 44:4-5); they would not heed the word of God, though God had persistently sent the prophets to turn them from their evil way (v. 19).

Verses 20-23 are an announcement of judgment on two false prophets. The conclusion of Jeremiah's letter to the exiles is a sharp condemnation of two false prophets in the name of "the Lord of hosts, the God of Israel" (they are specific instances of the prophets of vv. 8-9). Their names are Ahab and Zechariah, otherwise unknown. They will be given over to King Nebuchadrezzar, who will execute them "in the fire" (see Dan 3:6 for such a practice, also attested in ancient Near Eastern annals) in a public setting ("before your eyes"). This fiery fate, which anticipates that of Jerusalem (see 17:27; 52:13), suggests that their activity had subversive political implications relative to Babylonian authority. They had made deceptive prophecies "in my name"—offering a futile hope (vv. 21, 23), had committed adultery with their neighbors' wives (see 23:14; Deut 22:22 for the law involved), and by these means had "perpetrated outrage in Israel." In effect, they are common criminals and had made the exiles their prey in both word and deed. God himself knows of this outrage and by their execution bears witness to their infidelities. Because of what these two men have done their names will be used in curses by the exiles, "may God make you like Zedekiah and Ahab." At the same time, it should be recalled that, as with Hananiah but unlike Jeremiah, these prophets risked their lives in promoting an anti-Babylonian perspective.[4]

The reference to God as one who bears witness (v. 23; see 32:12) means that God is understood to be a signer (or cosigner) of this letter. This gives to the letter a divine level of authority. What has been presented is not just Jeremiah's opinion.

Two More Letters from Jeremiah, 29:24-32

This segment continues the theme of vv. 21-23 in addressing the issue of false prophets among the exiles, though the transition is abrupt and not altogether clear. There also appears to be some textual confusion in these verses (both the LXX and the Syriac have different readings of vv. 24-25), though it is likely that two letters of Jeremiah are reported. In the first case (vv. 24-28), v. 24 is likely a word from God to Jeremiah telling him to speak (via letter) to the false prophet Shemaiah (not otherwise known). This first command of God to Jeremiah in the chapter is likely in response to a letter that Shemaiah had sent to Jerusalem from exile—in his own name and hence under his own authority (see NAB). The occasion for Shemaiah's letter had been to respond to Jeremiah's earlier letter to the exiles (quoted in part in v. 28, though Jeremiah is not mentioned by name; cf. v. 5). It is possible that this letter to Jeremiah has been broken off, for Jeremiah only reports to him what he has written, and without condemnation (e.g., see the ellipsis in NAB at the end of v. 28; other solutions have been suggested).[5] Verses 29-32, which constitute another letter to the exiles, appear to be a second response from Jeremiah to Shemaiah's letter, after Zephaniah had read it to him.

In Jeremiah's first response to Shemaiah's letter, he immediately gets to the point by quoting from it (vv. 26-28). While Shemaiah's letter is sent to the attention of the people, the priest Zephaniah, and all the other priests in Jerusalem, the letter specifically addresses the priest Zephaniah (the "you" is singular). Readers have encountered Zephaniah before in a situation hostile to Jeremiah (21:1; see also 37:3; 52:24-27). Shemaiah claims that *God* has made Zephaniah high priest instead of Jehoiada in order to control (through police officers) "any madman who plays the prophet," that is, poses as one (on the prophets as madmen, see 2 Kgs 9:11; Hos 9:7). Such individuals are to be placed in the stocks (a wooden framework with holes for head and hands), which would expose him to public ridicule and contempt (Pashhur had so subjected him, 20:1-3). Shemaiah demands to know why Zephaniah has not followed up on his responsibilities by making a public spectacle of Jeremiah, who "plays the prophet" (v. 27). Shemaiah both summarizes ("it will be a long time," cf. v. 10) and quotes from Jeremiah's letter to the exiles (cf. v. 28 with v. 5). He is obviously distressed at Jeremiah's word that the exile would last a long time and that the exiles should settle in for the long haul.

Verse 29 reports that the priest Zephaniah read Shemaiah's letter to Jeremiah (though he apparently does not put him in the stocks). This would have to be an event earlier than that reported in vv. 24-28, which assume that Jeremiah knows of the letter. Having heard the letter, Jeremiah now sends a letter to "all the exiles," conveying a word from the Lord about Shemaiah (vv. 30-32). While Shemaiah has prophesied among the exiles, God did not send him to do so (as many exiles believed, see v. 15). He has misled the exiles, getting them to "trust in a lie" (see 28:15), giving them false confidence in an early return from exile. Jeremiah then announces a word of divine judgment on Shemaiah (v. 32, "therefore"). He has spoken rebellion against the Lord, and so God will "visit" (*pāqad*) this deed upon him and upon his descendants: No one from his family will live to experience God's action of deliverance of God's people from exile (see vv. 10-14).

CONNECTIONS

The Exiles and God's Work as Creator

The assumption of Jeremiah's exhortations is that the foreign context, even living among people whom the exiles would name their enemies, is conducive to life and growth. This language recalls the realities of Israel's life in Egypt (Exod 1:7), where the people were fruitful and multiplied in a foreign country, in a world outside the promised land. A hospitable setting can be provided by people who have experienced (if not known) God's work as creator. How significant a work is here carried out by the "non-chosen" to provide life and blessing for the chosen. How often this has been the case over the centuries since. How seldom it has been acknowledged by the chosen people!

The theological assumption here is that God is not absent from life in exile, from the worst situations God's people may have to endure. God is present and active for good among those who had experienced the sharpest of divine judgments. This word is testimony to God's ongoing work of creation and blessing, that flowing, rhythmic, non-dramatic divine activity. God's work in this respect will be unobtrusive; the exiles will not be able to claim divine activity in any obvious way. But God's intentions in creation (Gen 1:28; 9:1, 7) continue to be realized among these displaced people. This word to the exiles also links up with God's promises to their ancestors (see Gen 17:2-6; 48:4), promises to which God has long been faithful; they *will be* fruitful and multiply. For the exiles to attend to this exhortation is for them to choose to remain within the sphere of those ancestral promises.

This creative work of God is an important time of preparation for God's eventual work of redemption. When God's redemptive activity does occur, and the exiles are promised that it will, it will not occur in a vacuum. God's creational activity among the exiles is a crucial ingredient for what happens in redemption. Only in and through the growth of this people will God have anyone to redeem! God's work in creation is the basis for God's work in redemption. God's work in redemption will fulfill God's work in creation (and hence the powerful creation language of Isa 40–55 as well as in Jer, e.g., 31:35-37; 33:14-26). The effect of God's redemptive work, finally, is a new creation (see Isa 65:17-25; 2 Cor 5:17; Rev 21–22).

This creational work of God among the exiles lays an important groundwork for their confidence in God's promises of restoration.

If God is still at work among them to fulfill creational intentions and ancestral promises, then there is hope that other divine promises will be fulfilled, not least a restoration to the land. Because God is a God of life and blessing, God will do redemptive work should those creational gifts ever be endangered or diminished.

Seek the Welfare of the City

On one level, readers might treat the exhortation in v. 7 with some cynicism. Inasmuch as the exiles' welfare is dependent on Babylon's welfare, their motivation could be interpreted as self-centered (tough enlightened self-interest might be better language to use). On another level, there are theological issues at stake. The exiles are not only to seek the well-being of Babylon, they are to pray to God on behalf of the city. Such prayers assume that God desires to be present and active in a focused way in the lives of the exiles and in the lives of the Babylonians. This is the image of a Creator God who is active in the world even in the lives of people who do not acknowledge him as Lord. God's work will be effective among them for good, even though they may not realize that God is so involved. And these positive results will redound to the benefit of the Babylonians themselves, and not just to the Israelites among them. And so, even if the motivation is enlightened self-interest, the benefits that would accrue to the Babylonians will multiply across the entire society, and through the Babylonians to other cultures.

At the same time, there is no sense given in this text that God will be micromanaging their lives. After all, the people are encouraged to pray for their welfare; this assumes that prayers would make a difference, that God can be effective in the city because of their prayers in ways that would not otherwise be possible. Abraham's intercessory advocacy on behalf of Sodom and Gomorrah may well be informed by such an understanding (see Gen 18:16–19:29). [On Living in a Pluralistic World]

On Living in a Pluralistic World

John Bracke helpfully reflects on Jeremiah 29:5-7 as follows: "Perhaps a comparison for us is how we relate to persons or groups from whom we feel estrangement, other racial or social groups, for instance. One way of relating is to accept out of necessity that we now live in a pluralistic world where we must inevitably relate to people we do not particularly like. Another way of relating is to see those who are different from us as a gift from God who enrich us, and so to embrace and welcome diversity and relationships with others as for our 'welfare' and the welfare of God's creation. Jeremiah calls on those already exiled in Babylon not merely to accept their plight but to embrace it as a gift from God for their welfare."

John Bracke, *Jeremiah 1–29* (Louisville: Westminster John Knox, 2000), 223.

Exile and Spirituality

Ronald Clements thinks that the language in which God's promise of a return to Judah is couched reveals "an intense inwardness of religion."[6] Texts such as 29:13 point to the exile as "years of spiritual discipline." The larger context of chapter 29, however, does not permit such a stress on inwardness. God has plans for the people's "welfare" (*šālôm*, v. 11), which certainly entails more than spirituality. Jeremiah has expressly lifted up attention to the building of houses, the planting of gardens, and the various dimensions of life that marriage entails (vv. 5-6). To be concerned about the welfare of Babylon is in the best interests of Israel's own welfare (v. 7), which certainly encompasses the gamut of life. To separate out these aspects of life from the consideration of vv. 12-13 is an improper exercise in compartmentalization.

In addition, Clements speaks of a certain temporal ordering of the content of these verses. Only when "the time of discipline" had been accomplished (seventy years?) could Israel "truly seek God 'with a whole heart'; only then could a return to the homeland become a genuine possibility, because only then could it become spiritually meaningful."[7] Apparently this means that the time of discipline must be completed before Israel could "truly seek God" (how does that sequencing work?) and "only then" would return from exile be possible. In effect, the return from exile is entirely dependent upon Israel's reaching a certain level of spiritual maturity. Any initiative God has, it would seem, must await Israel's development (cf. Isaiah 40–55!). One wonders how that would be timed to occur when the seventy years are up! Even more, life in exile was "to provide the essentials for an interim relationship with

---

On Seeking and Finding God

Care must be used in sorting out the issues in vv. 13-14. The word for Israel is not: Try as hard as you can and then you can find God. If this were the case, then Israel's relationship with God would be a perpetual game of hide-and-seek. Israel would forever be stuck wondering whether it is trying hard enough or, in other terms, whether it has achieved the proper spiritual temperature. The issue is God's new accessibility and Israel's heart, not Israel's searching capacities. Israel had earlier sought out other gods (2:33; 8:2); Israel had given its heart to other lovers. Israel had not repented with its whole heart (3:10); it has had a stubborn and rebellious heart (5:23-24; 9:14). The issue for Israel is having a faithful heart; such a heart will find a home in God, a God who is newly accessible to those who have passed through the vale of judgment.

Jeremiah speaks in still another way about Israel's heart, only this time set in a time after the return. God's promise is that Israel would be given a heart to know the Lord and "they shall return to me with their whole heart" (24:7; see 31:33; 32:39-40). At that time, Israel would no longer stubbornly follow its own heart (3:17), for it will have a new heart and would not even have to seek the Lord (see discussion at 31:31-34). Another sense of Israel's seeking God is stated in 50:4-5; the exiles in returning from Babylon will come to Zion, weeping as they seek the Lord in that place. The seeking of the Lord in v. 13 assumes a time before the new heart and the new covenant is given, when seeking is no longer necessary. This is another factor in recognizing vv. 12-14a as applicable to the exiles prior to their return to the land.

God; it would be less than full communion, a reality that would become possible only when Israel" returned from exile. What is entailed in such an "interim relationship"; in what respects is it less than "full communion"? It is striking that in such a formulation the "intense *inwardness*" is apparently possible only when Israel has returned to the *land!* [On Seeking and Finding God]

NOTES

[1] See William McKane, *A Critical and Exegetical Commentary on Jeremiah* (2 vols.; ICC; Edinburgh: T. & T. Clark, 1986), 731-33.

[2] See G. Keown, P. Scalise, and T. Smothers, *Jeremiah 26–52* (Dallas: Word Books, 1993), 81.

[3] Ibid., 67.

[4] See Robert Carroll, *Jeremiah* (Philadelphia: Westminster, 1986), 562.

[5] See William Holladay, *Jeremiah 2*, (Philadelphia: Fortress, 1989), ad loc.

[6] Ronald E. Clements, *Jeremiah* (IBC; Atlanta: John Knox, 1988), 173.

[7] Ibid.

PROMISED RESTORATION
FOR ISRAEL AND JUDAH

30:1-24

The Book of Consolation, 30:1–33:26

Chapters 30–33 (or chs. 30–31, according to some scholars) are commonly referred to as The Book of Consolation. Mostly in poetic form, these oracles announce God's future restoration of Israel. This promised future is the prevailing theme throughout. Why these chapters are included at this point in Jeremiah is something of a mystery, but may be related to the idea that, before Jerusalem finally was destroyed (ch. 39), this salvific work of God was seen to be already at work in the midst of judgment.[1] That Israel was in exile was the judgmental work of God mediated in and through the Babylonians, but *even before that happened* God's promises had been articulated. This time of destruction and its exilic aftermath was not barren, either for God or for Israel. It is from within this cauldron of fire that Israel is refined and prepared for the new day that God has always— even in the midst of the most horrendous devastation—had in mind for God's own people.

Most segments in these chapters are considered oracles of salvation. Some depiction of the present suffering situation for exiles is helpfully juxtaposed with assurances and promises of God's saving work, not least to show that God's salvation always is directed to specific needs. The oracles are often introduced and/or concluded with the messenger formula (Thus says the Lord), thus indicating that God himself stands behind these promises; this is no human word in which the exiles are asked to place their trust. Moreover, these oracles are usually placed in the second person direct address. As such, they become a very personal word from God to this suffering people. The poetic form is a superb vehicle for the content. This is an exuberant "gospel" word that breaks the bounds of normal speech patterns; it can only be concluded by an exclamation point. The prose that follows (chs. 32–33) is a concrete symbolization of these new possibilities for Israel, together with still further interpretations of that material.[2] [Links to the Abrahamic Covenant]

There is much debate regarding the authorship of these oracles, and no clear consensus has emerged. Commonly, the essence of this

---

Links to the Abrahamic Covenant

That the promise of land to the ancestors stands at the beginning of the Book of Consolation (v. 3) suggests that the entire unit should be read in terms of the covenant with Abraham (see 7:7 for a statement about the land being given "forever"). The repeated use of the "covenant formula" in 30:22; 31:1, 33; 32:38 (see 24:7) recalls the covenant with Abraham (see Gen 17:7-8, reiterated at Sinai, 11:4), as do the repeated themes of land and posterity (e.g., 30:19; 31:5, 8, 12; 32:37, 41; 33:10-13). The language of possession/inheritance also links up with the land promise in Genesis (see 15:7-8; 28:4). Jeremiah's purchase of a field (32:1-25) may be linked to Abraham's purchase of land in Genesis 23, seen not least in the language of "inheritance" (32:8). The reference to the ancestors in 33:26 may provide an inclusio for these chapters, linking back to 30:3 (see Biddle, "The Literary Frame").

This centering of the Abrahamic covenant may have the same function as Moses' use of it in Exod 32:13 in the wake of the golden calf debacle (an argument that God accepts, Exod 32:14). That is to say, even Israel's idolatry does not break off the relationship between God and Israel (see Jer 31:35-37). In fact, the divine judgment serves a specific purpose within the larger scope of God's relationship with Israel; God's judgment is not an end in itself, but a refining means to carry the relationship with Israel forward into the future.

---

material may be rooted in the prophet's message, with later editors giving them their present shape. Moreover, there is no agreement as to when Jeremiah may have uttered such oracles of salvation. They are commonly dated either early in his ministry or late, after the fall to Babylon in 597 BC and/or after the destruction of Jerusalem in 587 BC. The latter view is more likely; the chapters seem to be set at a time before the end of the exile (see 30:11-17, 23-24; 31:27-28). Chapter 32 is set in 587 BC (32:1) and may be intended to provide a setting for chapters 30–33; Jeremiah's buying of the field at Israel's darkest moment becomes a concrete symbol that God still has a future for this people. The exiles are the primary audience of these edited materials in their present form, whoever composed them and whenever they were composed.

Scholars commonly understand that many of these oracles were originally addressed to the exiles of the northern kingdom, but the present form of the context has both North and South in view (30:3). The reference to "all the families of Israel" in 31:1 is another way of making the same point. The reference in 30:3 to the land given to the ancestors suggests that the whole land is in view, which assumes both North and South.

Chapters 30–31 are ordered along the following lines, characteristic of which is a moving back and forth between Israel's present fear and hurt and God's future salvation.[3] The effect of this rhythm is that God's salvation is directed to very specific situations of need in the life of the exiles. The outline is complex: a general introduction (30:1-4); a lament over the effects of God's judgment upon the people, followed by an announcement of salvation in prose and poetry (30:5-11); a description of the deep suffering of Israel with an oracle of salvation (30:12-17), followed by still another oracle of

salvation, including an announcement of judgment against the
nations, and hence salvation for Israel (30:18–31:1); several oracles
of salvation (31:2-6, 7-14), the last integrated with a depiction of
Israel's joyful return from exile; a portrayal of the suffering of the
people integrated with an announcement of salvation (31:15-22); a
description of the restoration of Israel and life upon return to the
land (vv. 23-30); an announcement of the new covenant (31:31-
34); the divine commitment to Israel's future (31:35-37); the
rebuilding of the city of Jerusalem (31:38-40).

As is apparent from this outline, there is no careful logic used in
the ordering of this material. It is as if God's restoration of Israel
were a gem and, as that gem is turned in the light, various angles of
vision on this new world for Israel are made available for viewing
(see Isa 62:3 for this image). Straightforward logic and careful
coherence would not be able to convey the astounding character of
what God is doing for Israel; its reality confounds human sensibili-
ties and can only be grasped in impressionistic terms.

COMMENTARY

Introduction to Book of Consolation, 30:1-3

The editorial introduction to the Book of Consolation (vv. 1-3)
speaks specifically of a "book" that God commissions Jeremiah to
write (see also 29:1; 30:2; 36:2; 51:60). He is told to write "all the
words" that God has spoken to him, identified with what follows
(see v. 4, "these are the words"). According to v. 3, the reason for
the book is the announcement of a change in the fortunes for both
Israel and Judah (see 29:10-14). Readers would interpret the indefinite "days are coming" (see also 31:27, 31, 38) in terms of the
previously announced seventy years (e.g., 29:10-14).

God is the subject of the key verbs in this text. Israel's restoration
will be God's work, and no conditions are attached (e.g., repentance). But, again, God acts through means; while the agent is not
explicitly mentioned (cf. Isa 45:1-4), v.16 makes clear that Babylon
will experience at the hands of its enemy something comparable to
what Israel experienced (chs. 50–51 will speak of foreign armies).
These changed fortunes will encompass all aspects of Israel's life,
internal and external. It is one-sided to speak of "the essentially
inward and spiritual nature of hope."[4] Hope and salvation are
broadly conceived in these chapters. Indeed, central to the articulation of this hope is that God's people will be restored to the land

that their ancestors possessed centuries ago. On this link back to the ancestral promises, see [Links to the Abrahamic Covenant]. The direct address in much of chapter 30 (vv. 8, 10-17, 22) personalizes this promissory word to exilic readers.

It is deemed important to get these oracles in writing for reasons that are not altogether clear. Perhaps this step was deemed important in order to preserve the oracles in an unsettled time and make them available through coming generations. Writing may also have enabled the exiles to have these promises and assurances readily accessible for consolation during the years of captivity yet remaining. The readerly audience would understand this book as the written word of God, and as such it was able to achieve a level of independence beyond the person of the prophet and his followers (see discussion at ch. 36).

God's Lament at Israel's Fear with Announcements of Salvation, 30:4-11

God is identified as the speaker of these verses, and hence the "we" of v. 5 probably refers to the divine council (see 23:18, 22; cf. Isa 6:8, which combines both singular and plural pronouns for the Godhead, as here; see v. 6). The cries of God's people who have been caught up in the destruction of Jerusalem and its aftermath have come up to God (see Exod 2:23-25; 3:7-8). They are the cries of panic and terror; God's own people have no peace on the far side of destruction and exile. God's response is lament and mourning ("Why?"; "Alas"), voiced in part in three questions (God voices the lament in vv. 12-17 as well). The questions are rhetorical and existential, voiced within the divine council. These questions are not a divine wonderment at the distress the people are voicing; the reason is known (v. 7). These questions show that the great distress endured by the people of God has entered into the divine life; God has taken up the people's questions and made them God's own (for the divine lament, see **Introduction** and **Connections**, chs. 3, 8–9)

How can it be that men are experiencing the kind of pain usually associated with childbirth? God uses an image voiced earlier (4:31; 13:21) and even by the people themselves (6:24; see also 49:24; 50:43), though here it is focused on the males of the community. God's repeated "Why?" suggests that even God is taken aback at the severity of the suffering of the people (cf. 42:10; on God's questions as existential questions, see 2:29-31; 8:5, 19, 22; 44:7-8). Why such pain? Why so many pale faces? At one level, the answer is simple: it is because the "day" of judgment has been so severe and filled with distress (v. 7); this answer would then be comparable to the relationship between v. 15a and v. 15b (cf. 13:22). But the improbable metaphor of men in labor (rather than women) may carry a deeper point, in a way not unrelated to birthing images in Isaiah, where the pains of exile are likened to labor pains (see 49:19-21; 66:7-9). The people in themselves (where no women are in labor) are not able to make their own future possible; only God is able to bring a new generation of people to birth. [Berrigan on Birthing in Jeremiah 30:1-9]

It becomes clear in these chapters that God enters into the people's suffering, voices it within the divine council, and seeks to deliver and to heal Israel (see, e.g., 31:20). God's "Alas!" mirrors the "Alas!" of the people; their mourning has become God's. There has never been a "day" like this in the distress experienced by Jacob (=all Israel). Yet, God, having entered deeply into their suffering, has not been reduced to powerlessness. For God to take that suffering into the divine life means that suffering will not have the last word. God has determined to redeem the people from their captivity. However much the people deserve these consequences for their infidelities (see vv. 14-15), God will not leave them to wallow in them, but will move on to a new "day" and extricate them from the effects of their own sin.

Verses 8-9 begin to specify what kind of divine action will be needed for this rescue; the images used are political/military, probably to meet the issue of fear and the need for security. The first oracle of salvation (vv. 8-9) in prose (so NRSV; NIV renders it poetry) recalls the symbolic act of chapter 27 and the conflict over the yoke between Jeremiah and Hananiah in chapter 28 (see 27:8, 11-12; 28:11). God, with no motivation stated (see 31:3), announces that a "day" will come (see v. 3) when God will break the yoke of the king of Babylon on Israel's neck (see Ezek 34:27) and burst its chains. The effect: God's people will no longer be slaves to strangers (Babylon and any other oppressor). [The Day of the LORD]

God's action means Israel's freedom from slavery; this divine move is like that of the exodus from Egypt (see 23:7-8, where the parallel is specifically drawn). Some translations change the

---

Berrigan on Birthing in Jeremiah 30:1-9

See what I see, My people—
strange epiphanies,
reversals in nature—
men fainting in their tracks,
white of face, terrified
like women come to term—

changes, sea changes, as though
in nature's violation, men
grew pregnant, nine months gone.

My day, come to term!
See, I loose the bonds,
loose the newborn
squalling in the world!

Exiles, slaves,
indentured ones, come forth!

Daniel Berrigan, *Jeremiah: The World, the Wound of God* (Minneapolis: Fortress, 1999), 126.

The Day of the LORD

AΩ The word "day" occurs in vv. 7-8 in two different senses. In v. 7, the "day" refers to the day of judgment; Jeremiah has used the word "day" in this sense from time to time as shorthand for "the day of the LORD" (see 17:16-18; Isa 2:12-21; Amos 5:18-20; Zeph 1:14-18). This phrase has reference, not to a single day on the calendar, but to several different days of judgment. Yet, it came to have reference primarily to the "day" that the Assyrians destroyed the North and the Babylonians the South. In v. 8, the "day" also refers to the "day of the LORD," but this day will be a "day" of salvation. Israel lives through the terror of God's day of judgment and they will be raised by God to see the light of a new day.

Hebrew "your" to "his" in v. 8 (see NRSV footnote), but the second person direct address should be retained (as in vv. 10-11), even though it entails some roughness (see NAB, which places the first half of v. 8 in quotes). The parallels with Israel's exodus experience continue in v. 9. Just as Israel moved from servitude to the pharaoh in Egypt to the service of Yahweh at the tabernacle (see Exod 40:34-38), so God here promises that Israel will move from servitude to the king of Babylon to the service of Yahweh. This language links up with the reference to Israel as the servant of God in v. 10.

Even more, the people will serve the kings of the Davidic line whom God will raise up to rule over a unified people of God (see v. 21; 23:5-6; 33:14-26; Hos 3:5; Amos 9:11; Ezek 34:23-24; 37:24-25). This is a remarkable claim, and is often thought to stand over against Jeremiah's basic message (see his oracles against the kings in 21:11–22:30). The language of serving the Davidic king is an especially sharp departure! Jeremiah is certainly sharply critical of the Davidic monarchy, but it is apparent that the Davidic king whom God will raise up "will execute righteousness and justice in the land," under the aegis of Yahweh (23:5; 32:15). And so, as with the people who will receive a new heart, the king will indeed rule as God himself would rule. Whatever may have been true of Jeremiah himself, this perspective is characteristic of the book that goes by his name.

The poetic oracle of salvation in vv. 10-11 is virtually duplicated in 46:27-28, in the context of the oracles against the nations. The rhetoric recalls that of Second Isaiah, a prophet who also addressed such oracles to the exiles (see Isa 41:8-14; 43:1-5), not least the reference to Israel/Jacob as the servant of God, developing the point of v. 9 (see Isa 44:1-2, 21; see also Jeremiah's call, 1:8). [Israel as God's Servant]

Into the midst of Israel's fear and panic (as noted by God in vv. 5-7) comes this gospel word in direct address: have no fear, do not be dismayed, for I, God, am with you (cf. 1:8, 19) and am going to save (*yāšaʿ*) you—a repeated theme in vv. 10-11. The salvation that God brings has both internal and external aspects. God's salvation entails deliverance both from fear and dismay (this theme brackets v. 10) and from lands/nations far away, where the people were scattered and have been suffering in captivity. The people of Israel will return to their own land and remain there in quietness and rest; the violence and fear of recent decades will no longer be characteristic of their life together. In a remarkably global word of assurance, the nations that have visited such violence and panic on Israel will come to an end (note that more than Babylon is in view) and will no longer threaten Israel's future (see at vv. 16, 23-24; on "end" see Amos 8:2; Ezek 7:2). But, unlike these other nations, God will not put an end to Israel—a promise repeated several times already (4:27; 5:10, 18). The normal run of world affairs is turned topsy-turvy; the weak, enslaved peoples are lifted up and the oppressive empires disappear.

Israel as God's Servant

That God addresses the Israelite people in exile as "my servant" is a remarkable claim, especially given their sorry history (cf. Nebuchadrezzar, 27:9). God does not say to the exiles: someday you will be my servant again. They *are* God's servant where they are, in the midst of exile, not yet a people delivered from bondage, not yet a recipient of God's act of deliverance. God understands the relationship with Israel to be in place. God simply names the people for who they are apart from anything they have done to be so named, and in spite of their long history of failure in the role of a servant.

The reference to chastisement or discipline (see also 10:23-25; 31:18), coming as it does after a reference to less than a full end, is likely a reference to the present captivity through which the exiles are suffering (less likely, it refers to Israel's future in the land, where discipline will still be needed in view of continued sinfulness). This time of discipline is necessary, for sin will not go unvisited (see Exod 34:6-7, where God's graciousness and forgiveness is also in view), but it is not an end in itself; discipline is finally only a means that serves God's purposes to refine and restore Israel.

Israel's Suffering and God's Healing, 30:12-17

The image of healing in relation to repeated references to pain and hurt provides the focus for this segment; the healing has reference to both internal and external dimensions of Israel's wounded life. While the image is communal in orientation (the "you" is feminine singular, a personification of Zion, v. 17), individuals would take heart from these promises. The verses are bracketed by references to Israel's wounds as unhealable (by any known non-divine agent) and yet healable by God (vv. 12, 17). Initially, these verses return to a description of Israel's present situation of pain and hurt and then, once again, the lament is voiced by God (as in vv. 5-7). It is as though Israel has lost its voice, and God takes up the lament on its behalf. But these words do not "maintain a harsh and unrelenting message of threat and condemnation,"[5] except for other nations (v. 16). Rather, in rhythm with the pattern of this chapter, these words recall the desperate straits in which Israel finds itself due to sin. Such a recollection is important for the hearing of the good news that follows, this time using the language of God the healer (v. 17) (see **Connections: Healing for Israel**). [6]

A variety of metaphors are used to drive the point home. No court will take up Israel's "lost cause." No medicine will cure its diseases. No physician can close up its wounds (v. 13; see 8:22). No lovers are left to remember or care (v. 14; see v. 17b where the enemies taunt Israel because of this reality; cf. Hos 5:13)—probably a reference to Israel's allies who failed miserably when Babylon advanced (37:5; Lam 1:19) and would go into exile along with them (22:20-22). No human source or creational resource can bring healing to this devastated people. The only resources that will enable Israel's healing must come from God.

The divine healing of Israel has been anticipated (3:22) and is here taken up in strong words of promise and assurance (v. 17; see 33:6). God will remember (31:20) when all others have forgotten. The healing can only come from God because God has been the judge, striking Israel with a judgment because of its many sins and great guilt, a point that is repeated word for word in vv. 14-15 (the word translated "guilt" in the NRSV is *ʿāwôn*, commonly translated "iniquity"). This repeated point stresses that the devastation experienced by the exiles is rooted in their own sin, not divine caprice. Hope is truly possible only when this reality is fully acknowledged. God is the subject of the judgment ("I have done these things to you"), but God is not the only agent. God has mediated this judgment in and through the blows of a merciless enemy (the word "merciless, cruel" is used for the foe from the north in 6:23; see 50:42; see **Introduction**), the effects of which have been internal and external, communal and individual.

The word translated "punished" in NRSV in v. 14 is the same verb translated "chastise" in v. 11; the latter translation is more pertinent in this context. This theme provides testimony to the *intent* of God in the judgment, even though chastisement proved fruitless before (see 2:30; 5:3; 7:28; 17:23). It is striking that God's "admission" ("I have done these things to you") is spoken by the same God who voices these promises. God's "Why?" question in v. 15 is similar to the questions in v. 6, but in v. 15b God more closely specifies that the exiles have only to look to themselves as the

A Change in God?

Walter Brueggemann contends that this text presents a positive future for Israel only because of a change in God: "Everything…has changed about God. Between v. 15 and v. 16 there is a radical alteration in God's attitude, perspective, and inclination. The indignant One has become the compassionate One…Yahweh found depths of love for Israel about which God did not heretofore know" (*A Commentary on Jeremiah: Exile and Homecoming* [Grand Rapids: Eerdmans, 1998], 277). To the contrary, God's love and salvific will for this people has been constant throughout (the claim of 31:3), indeed, this saving divine will is rooted in the call of Jeremiah (1:10).

But judgment becomes necessary—a means—to bring this people to the point where salvation is possible. That point for Israel's salvation has now arrived. The people are deep in exile and unable to heal themselves; they have no power remaining to generate their own future. Because they are in such straits, Israel is now prepared to receive God's saving deed. Israel's only hope is that God's salvific will for them *remains constant* and that God will act in view of what Israel has become in the depths of exile.

---

reason for their incurable situation; they have no one else to blame. They knew what the consequences might well be when they did what they did. Verse 15a is a legitimate question with the answer given in v. 15b. This is comparable to the question and answer of 13:22, except that in this text God articulates the lament of the people. Why do they cry out over their hurt and over their incurable pain? The answer is clear: they have sinned and God and has visited them with judgment.

Verses 16-17 are an oracle of salvation in response to this grievous situation in which Israel finds itself. The "therefore" at the beginning of v. 16 carries a force different from its usual function of introducing an announcement of judgment (cf. 16:14; 32:36; 35:19; Hos 2:14). The fact that Israel has suffered the effects of its sins and has no strength or resources to raise itself up gives room for the delivering work of God (see Deut 32:36, "the Lord will vindicate his people, have compassion on his servants, when he sees that their power is gone"). Israel can do nothing to bring about the divine deliverance; even their cries are considered of no account (v. 15a). God's work of judgment is the necessary preparation for the word of salvation, hence "therefore"; the word of life comes in the midst of death. [A Change in God?]

The taunt of the exiles by their enemies (v. 17b) is also linked to the divine saving action ("because"). God is motivated to act on their behalf because of this treatment (see God's motivation in Ezek 36:22-32). This experience of taunting is one more indication of the vulnerability of Israel. In his laments, Jeremiah appeals to God for deliverance because of what his enemies have to say against him (11:19-20; 18:19-20; 20:8-10) and his appeal with respect to such

Samaria

When speaking of the "city rebuilt upon its mound," the reference is either to the city of Samaria or Jerusalem. The city of Samaria, pictured above, was built in the early ninth century and defensively sat atop a 300ft. hill, with valleys to the north, south, and west as well as a sloping ridge to the east. Samaria served as the northern capital of Israel, and because of its strategic location, gave access to numerous important cities and areas in Israel, including Jerusalem, Meggido, and the Jezreel Valley. (Credit: Brewton-Parker College)

taunts is specifically linked to God's healing in 17:14-15 (Jeremiah's laments have parallels in the Psalms, e.g., 35:24-25).

God's saving work is stated in negative and positive terms. First, it means judgment on Israel's enemies (v. 16; see 25:12-14). These judgments are expressed in a series of four actions that illustrate the adage, "what goes around comes around." The nations who devoured Israel shall themselves be devoured (see 2:3; 5:17-18; 10:25); those who sent Israel into captivity shall themselves be made captive (see 15:2; 22:22); those who plundered Israel shall themselves be plundered; and all those who despoiled Israel shall themselves become spoil (see 20:5). Israel will not simply be removed from being captive to its enemies; its enemies will experience a judgment comparable to that experienced by Israel.

Then, God's saving work is expressed in positive terms (v. 17). The healing that was formerly not available (8:22) will now surely be made available by God; the wounds that were formerly not healable (v. 12) will now surely be healed. Israel has been called an outcast, with no one to care for them (as stated in v. 14). But now, with God's act of deliverance on behalf of the exiles, that situation has all been changed: God will care for Israel. That care is then specified in the following oracle of salvation.

An Oracle of Salvation, 30:18-22

God continues the promises of restoration in vv. 18-22, with a shift to the third person (v. 22 returns to the second person direct address), with images focused on a restoration of all that is needed for a healthy community life. The restoration of Israel's "fortunes" refers not simply to the *recovery* of everything that has been lost, but also issues in something genuinely new. This will be a new day, not just the old day revived. Verse 18 focuses on the reconstruction of homes (tents, dwellings) and cities with their citadels (these words are literal and yet also metonyms for the people of Israel). God's compassion (see 31:20; 33:26), formerly withheld (13:14, 21:7; **Connections**, ch. 16), will be evident in the provision of homes (tents and dwellings) and cities in which the returned exiles can dwell. God will not leave this people without a place they can call home.

God's restoration of the fortunes of Israel's dwelling places means, in effect, that destroyed homes and cities—including Jerusalem—will be rebuilt (presumably by human agents!) on their traditional sites (see 29:14; 30:3; 33:7). When people reside in these rebuilt homes, then songs of thanksgiving (perhaps including temple worship, see 33:11) and the joyful sounds of merrymakers, taken away in the destruction of the city (7:34; 16:9; 25:10; cf. 15:17), will be heard once again on the streets (see 31:13; 33:10; Isa 35:10; 51:11). Moreover, God will act so that the people will be fruitful and multiply, as promised in 23:3 (cf. 29:6; a continuing fulfillment of the ancestral promises, cf. Gen 17:2; Exod 1:7; note that v. 22 has links to Gen 17:7-8). In addition, their shame, so much in evidence heretofore (see 9:19; 29:18), will be turned into honor (v. 19). This passage may be intended as "a reaffirmation of the covenant with Abraham";[7] the reference in v. 3 to the land given to the ancestors sets that context for the entire Book of Consolation (see [Links to the Abrahamic Covenant]). [Berrigan on Salvation]

Berrigan on Salvation

And this to follow:
restoration, joy!
ringaround of sons and daughters,
dwellings, cities rising—
a second springtime!

On eyes that welled,
lips that spelled
all the lamentable years
dirge, reproach only
life's endless sigh—
farewell, farewell.

Hear instead
songs of praise, laughter
like icy streams
under noon sun benignant
temperate, flowing free!

And grave, majestic, equable
the promise I hand over
deed and warranty—
   your own
lands, possessions, flocks
fig tree, vine exuberant—
your bloodline owning
no increment to tyrants.

I your God—
approach, and live!

Daniel Berrigan, *Jeremiah: The World, the Wound of God* (Minneapolis: Fortress, 1999), 127-28.

I Will Be Your God

The last verse in this oracle of salvation (v. 22) consists of the typical covenant formula, repeating 24:7 (see 7:23; 11:4). The formula functions as a kind of summary of this new situation for Israel and anticipates the new covenant passage in 31:31-34 (see [Intensification of Dialogue]): Israel will be God's people; and God promises to be their God with all the blessings that entails. This promise, so fundamental to the more specific promises outlined in these verses, is repeated at key points in the chapters that follow (31:1, 33; 32:38). This first occurrence of the formula in the Book of Consolation is, however, different from the other texts in that it is direct address to the people, and as such returns to the form of address begun in vv. 10-17.

God will restore Israel's "children" (see 31:15) "as of old" (v. 20); this probably has reference to the reestablishment of both northern and southern kingdoms (see v. 3) as a single community or "congregation" (see 31:1). No oppressors shall abuse Israel anymore, for God will "visit" their oppression upon them (anticipating vv. 23-24, recalling vv. 8, 16). Their prince/ruler ("king" is not used here, but see v. 9) shall be an Israelite, one of their own (as specified in Deut 17:15), who will see to the good order of the community. By implication God's promises mean that Israel will no more be in subjection to foreign rulers. The prince will even be able to approach God in an intimate way (on the piety of kings, see Deut 17:14-20). This passage may not have reference to approaching God in the sanctuary, normally a priestly prerogative (though see 33:11; the role of the prince in Ezek 46:2; 37:26-28), but more generally. The last clause in v. 21 is difficult, but may refer back to *God's* bringing the prince near to God; if God did not take this action, who would risk their lives to make such an approach? [I Will Be Your God]

God's Wrath as Salvation for Israel, 30:23-24

These two verses are a repetition of 23:19-20. In that context, however, God's wrath, likened to a windstorm, is the word that the prophet (who has participated in the divine council) is to speak to the people of *Israel.* From the perspective of the present context, Israel has already experienced the wrath of God, and so the repetition of this text in this salvation-oriented context must relate God's wrath to the enemies of Israel. The nations with whom God in wrath enters into judgment are identified as "wicked, guilty" in 25:31 also. Moreover, the "until" (v. 24) picks up on the "until" references to Babylon in 27:7, 22. God's accomplishing the "intents of his mind" relates to God's salvific purposes, which become possible only when the oppressor's power has been destroyed (see "plans" in 29:10-14). Interpreted in this way, these two verses ground the deliverance materials that are present in vv. 8, 11a, 16, 17b, and 20b. Israel's situation has changed and God's promise of judgment on Israel's oppressors is hereby claimed to be as certain as God's visitation of wrath upon Israel had been.

"In the latter days you will understand." These "days" link up with the "days" in vv. 3 and 8. It is probably not very clear to Israel, fearful and dispirited, how these divine purposes are all going to work out. The prophet speaks clearly, and with great insight, but this kind of future seems impossible in the midst of exile, with a powerful overlord such as Babylon. Some day it will become clear to all concerned; for now, they can only sit back, watching and waiting, and trusting that God will see to these salvific purposes that will change their lives forever. In effect God says: Trust me.

CONNECTIONS

Healing for Israel and God

The theme of healing is available in the tradition in varying contexts (see Exod 15:26; 2 Kgs 20:5; Pss 30:2; 103:3; Isa 30:26; Hos 6:1; 11:3; 14:4) and is also used by Second Isaiah in the midst of the exile (Isa 53:5; 57:18-19). God has described Israel in terms such as these before in Jeremiah (6:7; 14:17) and Jeremiah has described himself in a comparable way in view of his vocation (15:18; cf. 8:18; 17:14). The people have also used such language to describe themselves (8:15; 10:19; 14:19). The false prophets have certainly not been helpful; their words have only "healed the wound of my people lightly" (6:14; 8:11). Even God has drawn on language from this semantic field to describe God's own pain (see 8:18-22); Israel's hurt has entered deeply into the divine life. Israel is inflicted with a hurt that is incurable and a wound that is unhealable (v. 12), at least in terms of any human cure or human healing (also descriptive of Egypt and Babylon, 46:11; 51:8-9). And how will healing become a reality for God? God will be healed only when Israel has been healed.

It is important not to be reductionistic in thinking about God's healing of Israel. God's healing is as comprehensive as is God's salvation: it is individual and communal; present and future; spiritual and psychical/bodily; religious and social/economic/political. Healing would include both forgiveness of sins and deliverance from the effects of sins—both the sins of Israel and the sins of others. Indeed, the healing of all creation is in view.

NOTES

[1] Cf. Brevard Childs, *An Introduction to the Old Testament as Scripture,* 351.

[2] See Mark Biddle, "The Literary Frame Surrounding Jeremiah 30,1–33:26," ZAW 100 (1988): 409-13. B. Bozak, *Life "Anew": A Literary-Theological Study of Jer. 30–31* (Rome: Pontifical Biblical Institute, 1991). R. M. Hals, "Some Aspects of the Exegesis of Jer 31:31-34," in *When Jews and Christians Meet,* ed. J. Petuchowski (Albany: State University of New York Press, 1988), 87-97. R. Rendtorff, "What is New in the New Covenant," in *Canon and Theology: Overtures to an Old Testament Theology* (Minneapolis: Fortress, 1993), 196-206.

[3] See G. Keown, P. Scalise, and T. Smothers, *Jeremiah 26–52* (Dallas: Word Books, 1993), 86-87; Bozak, 18-32.

[4] So Ronald E. Clements, *Jeremiah* (IBC; Atlanta: John Knox, 1988), 179.

[5] Ibid., 182.

[6] For an analysis of this segment, see Walter Brueggemann, "The 'Uncared For' Now Cared For (Jer 30:12-17): A Methodological Consideration," JBL 104 (1985): 419-28.

[7] So William Holladay, *Jeremiah 2* (Philadelphia: Fortress, 1989), 168.

RESTORATION AND NEW COVENANT

31:1-40

This chapter continues the Book of Consolation, begun at 30:1. It may be outlined as follows: several oracles of salvation (31:2-6, 7-9, 10-14); the people respond to God's word with weeping, to which God responds in turn with oracles of salvation (31:15-26); an oracle regarding life back in the land of promise (31:27-30); an oracle of salvation focused on the new covenant (31:31-34); divine assurance that Israel will continue to be God's people (31:35-37); oracle on the rebuilding of Jerusalem and the purification of desecrated areas (31:38-40). [Images in Chapter 31]

> **Images in Chapter 31**
>
> The images used throughout this section are predominantly familial rather than political or military. Feminine images, especially as associated with birth and new life, are prominent. The return to the everyday life of the village, with its familiar tasks and joys, are given special attention. God is imaged as a loving, nurturing parent (both as father and mother), comforting those who sorrow and caring for the needs of a bruised community. It is as if God is finally able to get back to doing what God has always wanted to do for this people.

COMMENTARY

With an Everlasting Love, 31:1-6

These verses pertain to "all the families of Israel" and hence have in view an Israel reunified by God (31:1; this verse is linked to what precedes by "at that time" and the repetition of 30:22). These verses contain several translation issues, and NRSV generally captures the sense well. Verses 2-3a may, however, be God's own introduction to the divine oracle in the first person of vv. 3b-6 (see NIV, which puts quotation marks around the latter). Lending support to such a view, Israel is referred to in the third person in vv. 2-3a and then, in direct address, in the second feminine in vv. 3b-6 ("virgin Israel"). Surprisingly, the virgin that God once took as a bride (see 2:2-3) is once again called a virgin (and in v. 21)—after all the indictments for Israel's infidelities!

Parallels Between Exile and Exodus

These parallels are drawn between Israel's exodus experience and God's anticipated act of salvation on behalf of the exiles (see vv. 1-6):

- Israel survived the sword of foreign armies just as did its ancestors (see Exod 14–15).
- Israel has experienced divine favor in its present wilderness trek just as it did after a period of oppression in Egypt (Exod 15–18).
- The exiles seek rest in the land of promise, just as Israel wandering in the wilderness once sought rest there (Exod 33:14; a reversal of Deut 28:65).
- Once again Israel will plant vineyards in the land of promise, and they will enjoy the fruits of their labor (see v. 12; Isa 65:21; Amos 9:14), just as Israel did upon entrance into the land (though it found vineyards already planted there, e.g., Josh 24:13).
- God will appear to the exiles and act on their behalf, as God appeared to Israel in the wilderness at Sinai from far away (see Deut 33:1-2; or "in the past," so NIV; cf. NRSV fn.).
- Once again, it will be time for the exiles to make music, so long silenced (e.g., 7:34; 16:9; 25:10). The redeemed will go forth with tambourines and dancing (30:19; 31:13), just as Miriam and "all the women" went forth from the sea crossing (Exod 15:20-21).
- The people of Israel will go up to the house of the Lord again (cf. Isa 2:3) as they used to "go up to Zion" (see Exod 15:18; 40:34-38; Ps 122:1). The exiles will be called by sentinels to go up to Zion, no longer uncared for (see 30:17), to worship the Lord (v. 6; see v. 12; so also Isa 27:13), with a focus on thanksgiving (see 30:19; 33:11).
- Once again, the people of Israel will be a united people, when those in both North and South will be brought back together as in those early years.

This introduction makes clear that the addressees are all exiles from both North and South, though the specifically northern references in vv. 2-22 (Israel; Samaria; Ephraim) have suggested an originally northern provenance (see 3:6-14). But all Israel is now in view (see Zion in vv. 6, 12). Verses 2-3a could be an historical reference to Israel's post-exodus experience (see NRSV) or, less likely, a future reference (see NIV). The people of Israel survived the sword (of the Egyptians) and, though wandering in the "wilderness," experienced God's favor (see 2:2) as they sought rest in the land of promise, and God appeared (at Sinai especially) to them in that wilderness setting. The "wilderness" becomes a metaphor for exile, for the present experience of readers.

Parallels between present experience and past history are drawn out (see the threefold "again" in vv. 4-5). Exiled readers are invited to think of this present time in terms of that ancient journey. [Parallels between Exile and Exodus] In effect, all dimensions of their physical and spiritual life are reversals of their recent experience and will be ordered as they had been in the past. Though this is a somewhat idyllic view of the past, no simple cyclical perspective is being claimed, for genuine newness is announced in the passage as a whole. Both continuity and discontinuity are claimed (see introduction to chs. 30–33). The most fundamental continuity for

Israel is to be found in God, whose commitments span the divide of destruction and exile.

The word that God spoke to Israel in the past still pertains to Israel now. God's love for Israel in that ancient time (see Deut 7:8; 10:15; Isa 63:9; Hos 11:1) persists into this present time of exile (see Isa 43:4; 48:14; 54:8). God's love for Israel, imaged as a virgin bride (v. 4), is an everlasting love and God has continued that steadfast love (*hesed*; NRSV "faithfulness"; the only occurrence with God as subject in Jeremiah) for Israel throughout the generations, even through the recent devastating judgment. There has been no point at which God's love of Israel ceased; it is "everlasting" (Isa 54:7-8 has a comparable understanding).

This piling up of words of God's love for Israel (v. 3) is used to ground God's promises to the exiles. Simply put: God will act in salvific ways on Israel's behalf because God loves Israel. It is not that "God's freshly offered love" to Israel "issues in faithfulness,"[1] as if God's judgment meant that God's love for Israel had ceased and God's fidelity had been withdrawn. Rather, God's love remained steadfast through thick and thin, God's faithfulness remained intact through Israel's infidelity and the consequent judgment, and was now at work to recreate Israel out of the rubble of exile. As often in the Bible, God works death in order to bring about new life.

In this appeal to Israel's historical experience with its Lord and God's continuing love for Israel, the divine promises for the future of Israel are now stated (vv. 4-14). To put it in other terms, Israel brings no words or deeds to this relationship that motivate God to make these promises of salvation. But Israel is a people loved by God, not simply in spite of who they are but also *because* of who they are, and because of the continuity in that love for these particular people, God makes promises to them that fit into the long-standing divine plans for Israel.

At this crucial juncture in the book, the text returns to the key verbs of Jeremiah's call, which now have God as the subject (see 1:10): God has pulled down and overthrown, plucked up and destroyed; God will now build and plant (vv. 4-5). This redemptive action of God is introduced by a threefold "again": building, dancing, planting (see v. 12; Ezek 36:35-36, where the image of the Garden of Eden is used; see also Isa 58:11-12). God will redeem Israel as God once before redeemed Israel (see 23:7-8 for the juxtaposition of these redemptive events).

As before, God will build; this is a creational image, for the building up of a family (see Ruth 4:11; and a possible reference to the "building" of the woman in Gen 2:22). God will plant as well

(v. 28), but Israel also becomes the subject of this verb (v. 5), as was Jeremiah in his call (1:10). God's salvific action does not reduce Israel to passivity, as the people also get caught up in seeing to this new life in the land. The assumption in v. 6 is that Jerusalem and the temple will be rebuilt (see 30:18-19; 31:23; 33:11) and become the center for Israel's life of worship once again. At the same time, going up to Zion may be a call to leave Babylon (as in 50:8, 28; 51:6, 45, 50), and vv. 7-14 specify some aspects of that journey back home.

Turning Mourning into Joy, 31:7-14

These verses continue the oracles of salvation; they often remind the reader of the lyrical cadences of Isaiah 35 and 40–55. The language is not that of precise or literal description (the actual event will be described in more literal ways, and without the God language, e.g., Ezra 1). Rather, these oracles are a lyrical, hymnic celebration of the anticipated return of the exiles to Jerusalem; they contrast with the fearful language of 30:5-7. Many such words are gathered in v. 7 (also common in psalms of praise and thanksgiving): sing, shout, proclaim, and praise. Note that the call is to sing and shout "for" Israel, "for" "the chief of the nations" (that is, God's elect) of the world. It is not altogether clear to whom these imperatives are addressed, though the nations are explicitly mentioned in v. 10; perhaps we are to think of all creation (see 6:19, where it hears of disaster; cf. Isa 44:23). More likely, the addressees are the exiles themselves (see Isa 12:3-6; 48:20; 54:1).

The Translation of Verse 7

AΩ The people are to call upon God to save "your people, the remnant of Israel" (so NRSV, following the Hebrew) or testify, "The Lord has delivered his people, the remnant of Israel" (so NAB and most, following the LXX). The latter, which finds a parallel in v. 11, seems more appropriate in view of the fact that the petition to save is normally a part of the lament, not the oracle of salvation (yet, see the weeping in v. 9; cf. v. 15). Notice again the language of "remnant" (v. 7; see 23:3); this designation recognizes two realities, namely, that not all of the exiles will return home to Israel (for a variety of reasons) and many people were in fact killed in the fall of Jerusalem.

Whatever their identity, God calls them to sing and shout in anticipation of God's deliverance of his people. What they are to sing out is stated in v. 7c (cf. the word to be spoken in v. 10b). [The Translation of Verse 7] Verses 8-9 state the reason for the praise of v. 7: God is going to bring the remnant of Israel back from Babylon ("the land of the north"; see Isa 43:6), gathering them (so also v. 10) from all the other lands to which they have been scattered—even those lands farthest from Israel (see 3:18; 23: 3-8). The trek back from exile follows the route of the invaders from the North (see 6:22). God once brought judgment from those quarters, but now God will bring Israel deliverance along that same itinerary.[2] God had once brought an army of great strength and speed (4:13;

5:15-17), but now God will bring along that route the weak and disabled. God had once brought death along that route, but now God would bring new life (that may account for the presence of feminine images throughout this chapter as well as the reference to God as Father in v. 9). Notably, the leaders and the affluent are not lifted up for special attention; though they would doubtlessly be included, the point here is a kind of democratization in the experience of deliverance (see v. 34, from the least to the greatest). The returnees will include the blind and the lame (as in Isa 35:5-6; Mic 4:6-8; Zeph 3:19-20), the pregnant and those about to give birth—all of them together. It will be a great company of people— a throng!—who will return to the land of promise. It is precisely all of these "weak" ones who are declared to be God's valued firstborn, members of the family of God (v. 9).

The return will be a time of joy and gladness, but it will also be a time of weeping (v. 9; see vv. 15-20; 3:21; NAB, however, places this clause in the past tense). It is unlikely that this refers to joyous weeping or to repentance (see v. 19). Rather, weeping would be normal for people able to return to their homes but unaccompanied by so many friends and family who had been killed in the onslaught (see v. 15)—joy and weeping often do go together at such times. But God, who will personally lead them back, will comfort them with words of consolation and, according to v. 13, turn their weeping into joy and their sorrow into gladness. God will lead them by streams of water (cf. Ps 23:2) and along straight paths so that they do not stumble (cf. Isa 40:3).

The last clauses of v. 9, as with vv. 2-6, provide continuity with Israel's past relationship with God (the specific linkage here is with Exod 4:22 and perhaps to Gen 48:8-20, where Ephraim is declared the firstborn). Explicit parental metaphors for God are not particularly common in Jeremiah (see 3:19; 4:3; Hos 11:1), but they appear sharply in v. 9 (and v. 20). A key question for the exiles would be: whose child are we, given the debacle? Are we still the children of the God of Israel? God's claim is that Israel=Ephraim is "my firstborn" (as in Exod 4:22; cf. 2 Sam 7:14), not the child of any other sovereign. Israel is the elect one, the adopted child, brought into close relationship with God, with all the intimacy that a parent-child relationship implies. They are God's family with all of the blessings of being a part of this household. Given the sharp experience of suffering, God as parent enters into the suffering of the children (see v. 20) and claims them for life and for freedom. Moreover, as God's "firstborn," Israel is the one who receives a double share of the father's estate and the paternal blessing.

In v. 10, all the nations (cf. 6:18, where they hear of disaster) are called upon to listen to this new word from God regarding God's child. Even more, they are called upon to proclaim it on distant coasts, so that the word might spread abroad and everyone be able to hear of the salvation of God (see Isa 48:20). This is not something that they "have to" do;[3] they will be so astounded by what they see that they will change their observations regarding Israel (on the earlier insight of the nations, see 22:8-9; Deut 29:24-28). The word that is to be proclaimed follows in v. 10b, while v. 11 introduces the reason for this testimony ("for"). The God who scattered Israel is the same God (!) who will now gather them (as in 23:3) and keep them as a shepherd keeps his flock (the pastoral images dominate in vv. 9-14). The foreign armies had been likened to shepherds that would invade Israel (6:3). Israel's own leaders had been likened to shepherds that cared not for their flock and the sheep were scattered (10:21; 13:20; 23:2-3; 25:34-38). But God as shepherd will gather the flock (see Ezek 34:15; Ps 23:1-2), keep them as a good shepherd would, and, in turn, raise up human shepherds who would care for them as God himself would (so 3:15; 23:4; see 30:21).

The reason for the testimony is that God has ransomed Jacob/Israel and redeemed the exiles from those who were stronger (v. 11). It appears that Israel's redemption has occurred even before the deliverance from Babylon (vv. 12-14). [The Language of Deliverance] Whereas v. 9 spoke of the people weeping as they return, in vv. 12-13 they come rejoicing and dancing (see v. 7; 30:19). They will sing again as they climb the heights of Jerusalem/Zion (see the Psalms of Ascent, Pss 121–134) and "be radiant (with joy)" (see NRSV) over the source of divine blessings (an alternative translation for "be radiant" is "stream," so NAB; see Isa 2:2). They will be joyful over the gifts of grain, wine, oil, and the young of flock and herd (similarly, Isa 60:5-7). The mourning land (see 12:4-13;

The Language of Deliverance

AΩ Verses 7-14 are ringing words of deliverance, with various verbs used to make the point doubly clear. The verbs in v. 11 have been loosened from their metaphoric roots (*pādāh*; *gōʾēl*); they are essentially synonymous with the verb, *yāšaʿ*, "save," used in v. 7 and 30:10-11. An array of deliverance language is drawn upon to declare what God has done. God's "ransom" of the firstborn (v. 9) in Exod 13:14-16 (see Isa 51:10-11) is specifically linked to God's deliverance from Egypt (language used in Deut, e.g., 7:8; 9:26). Exodus 6:6; 15:15 speaks of the same event with the word "redeem" (language common in Isaiah, e.g., 43:1; 44:22). These words are combined also in Isa 35:9-10. Deliverance from Egypt and deliverance from Babylon are linked by this vocabulary, though now the latter takes precedence over the former as the constitutive event for the continued life of Israel (16:14-15=23:7-8).

14:1-6) will once again be productive and provide sustenance for both people and animals (as in the prior entry into the land, Deut 7:13; 8:7-10). Their lives will become like a watered garden, flourishing and fruitful, and they will never (!) languish again (similarly, Ezek 36:35; Isa 58:11).

Notably, the language of creation is drawn into this hymnic response; salvation for Israel is salvation also for the land and all of its creatures. This action of God is not simply a people-oriented salvation; all God's creatures that were so adversely affected by the devastation (e.g., 9:10) will experience the salvation of God. The rejoicing of the returnees is especially associated with the pilgrimage to Zion (v. 12, see v. 6) and so a transformation of Israel's worship is envisaged. Another dimension of Israel's worship is picked up in v. 14, as the priests are promised their fill of the choice portions of the sacrificial animals that are offered to God—the thanksgiving theme would be natural in this context (as in 30:19; 33:11).

In a remarkably inclusive text (v. 13), the young and the old will rejoice, and young women and young men shall dance and make merry. The God who turned their joy into mourning (6:26; 14:2) now turns their mourning into joy; the God who turned their gladness into sorrow now turns their sorrow into gladness (similarly, Ps 30:11; Hos 6:1). God will comfort sorrowing Israel (see Isa 40:1; 49:13; 51:3, 12), in effect reversing the earlier command not to comfort (16:7). In v. 15 readers will encounter a "mother" who refuses to be comforted, but God will speak to comfort her (vv. 16-20). The herds and flocks will be so plentiful that the priests will have no worries about their livelihood (v. 14). Generally speaking, the people of God will be sated with the bounty of the Lord.

God is Moved by Israel's Suffering, 31:15-22

These verses return to the theme of weeping (see v. 9). The human response to the devastating judgment is presented by Rachel (v. 15) and by Ephraim (vv. 18-19), to each of which God responds (vv. 16-17, 20-22).

Verses 15-17 serve to illustrate God's intention to turn Israel's mourning into joy (v. 13; see 9:17 on women as mourners). God initially describes the situation of the exiles, personified as Rachel (v. 15), before proceeding with direct speech in response (vv. 16-17). God describes what God has heard in Ramah (see [Images in Chapter 31]): bitter weeping, moaning, lamentation. [Ramah and Rachel] Perhaps readers would recall not only their own experience as

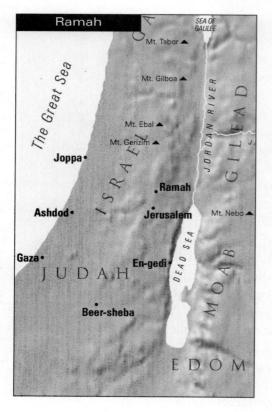

refugees, but also the common refugee experience in that world (and, it might be noted, in ours). That God is the one who voices this lamentful language indicates that God is deeply alert to this suffering. Even more, human suffering has entered into the divine life and shapes the divine speaking and acting (see v. 20).

The image presented in v. 15 is not that of a dead Rachel weeping in her grave, but Rachel as the personification of all of Israel's mothers. They are weeping over all their children who have been killed and taken away from the land (note v. 16, "they shall come back," which indicates that the phrase "they are no more" refers to loss in various ways, not just death). So many children taken away, so many children lost! One can understand why the weeping would never finally stop. Yet, v. 17 suggests that the issue is not simply the loss of children as such; the sorrow also catches up the loss of a future embodied in those children. Without children Israel has no future. And so God's comfort addresses both past loss and future hope (see 29:11; on God as the hope of Israel, see 14:8; 17:13). [Berrigan on 31:15-20]

The God of comfort (see v. 13) does not leave Rachel to her own resources. The God who voices the lament also responds to that lament (vv. 16-17). Recognizing her weeping and her tears, God seeks to comfort her with a word of unconditional promise, completely without motivation or rationale. Note the repetition of "says the LORD" in this reply, as if to assure Rachel that God means

Ramah and Rachel

Ramah is located five miles north of Jerusalem, it may have been the place from which exiles were sent to Babylon (40:1-4) and Jeremiah released (40:6); it is also near the burial place of Rachel, according to one tradition (1 Sam 10:2).

Rachel was the favored wife of Jacob (=Israel), who is mentioned in 30:10, and the figurative mother of Israel (=Ephraim). Her son is Joseph and his sons are Ephraim (vv. 6, 9, 18, 20) and Manasseh; so in terms of the Genesis story (Gen 30:22-24; 48), Rachel was Ephraim's

grandmother. Her sorrow is expressly mentioned at the birth of Benjamin in Gen 35:18; her last words before she dies in childbirth are filled with sorrow, which is probably the link to the image of weeping here. Ephraim was chief among the northern tribes, and some have linked this material at some stage to Northern tribes. But Rachel is certainly presented as the mother of all Israel in this text. This text is quoted in Matt 2:18 in connection with the slaughter of the innocents by King Herod; Rachel remains a strong symbol for the suffering which the Hebrew people undergo.

what God says. God promises that Rachel will have a future, a future of hope rather than despair. In concrete terms, God will raise up children for Rachel and, repeated for the sake of emphasis, they shall "come back" from the land of the enemy (=Babylon) and settle again in their homeland. [Reward, Wages]

Verses 18-19 move from Rachel to Ephraim (Rachel's grandson through Joseph); he would personify the children of Rachel/Israel (see v. 20). Rachel's children do continue to live and they are here given a voice. The focus on a return to the land in vv. 16-17 is now accompanied by an inner return to God. Ephraim is lamenting; the image is that of a person shaking or rocking back and forth in grief over what has happened. The focus for him is the behavior that led to their loss and what it might take to restore the fractured relationship. He speaks of the experience of destruction and exile as a divine discipline (see 30:11, 14). He was like an undisciplined calf (cf. Hos 10:11), refusing to accept correction (e.g., 2:30; 5:3); and he now understands himself as one who was appropriately disciplined. With that self-understanding he makes a plea to God, whom he confesses to be "the Lord my God." Repentance is the primary issue in view, and the language of "turn, return" also relates to vv. 16-17 (the verb appears nine times in this segment). The return from exile and the return to faithfulness in relationship with God go together (see Deut 30:1-10 for similar formulations) (see **Connections: Turning and Returning**).

Verse 20 constitutes God's remarkable response to Ephraim's request to God to bring him back. The force of the verse is similar to that of Hosea 11:1-11, wherein God's love persists through Israel's childhood rebellion and, though judgment is experienced, God finally takes the divine wrath into God's own self, and the exiles are allowed to return home. The verse opens with two

---

📖 Berrigan on 31:15-20

Rachel, mourn no longer
I, mother Yahweh
large in loss,
assuage your tears.
    Even as you
comfort me.

That son, the prodigal—
My heart stirs, I must
like Rachel
    run headlong,
make of him—
    (recusant,
slow returning,
against all chance
    renewed)
firstborn of My love.

Daniel Berrigan, *Jeremiah: The World, the Wound of God* (Minneapolis: Fortress, 1999), 129-30.

Reward, Wages

AΩ The language of "reward, recompense" in 31:16 should be understood in terms of such texts in Isaiah 40:10; 62:11 (see 49:22), and the imagery of the story of Rachel and Jacob in Genesis (see Genesis 29–33). Jacob (Israel) and Rachel will return from exile (that is, their years working under Laban in the far country) with all their children with them, understood as their "wages" for all their efforts (this language is used to name the child Issachar in Gen 30:18). In the words of Isa 62: "Say to daughter Zion, 'See,

your salvation comes; his (God's) reward is with him, and his recompense before him'." All of the children born to "Rachel" in exile are her "wages" for her time in Babylon; these children will come back from Babylon to Canaan. And so, given all these children, there is hope for the future of Rachel and Jacob (see 29:10-14). The reader cannot help but wonder, however, whether lost children, perhaps especially those lost in violent situations, can ever be "replaced" by others; there is an inner weeping that never ends, at least for the lives of those directly involved.

rhetorical questions. Is Ephraim my dear son? Yes! Is Ephraim the child that God delights in? Yes! God's response begins with a claim that reinforces v. 9: Ephraim has not ceased to be God's child. The parental image of God is stunning in its recognition that, in spite of all (!) that has happened, Ephraim remains a child in whom God delights (see Isa 5:7; Prov 8:30-31). God's parental love for the child Ephraim (v. 3) has persisted through thick and thin, through all of Ephraim's infidelities.

Though God has often spoken against him (recall the indictments throughout the book), God has not forgotten that Ephraim is his child. Indeed, God *remembers* him (unlike those who forget, 30:14)! And for God to remember (see Exod 2:24) is for God to act on behalf of the one remembered. God's remembering issues in a "therefore," but in a sense quite different from its common use in Jeremiah as an introduction to an announcement of judgment (cf. 30:16 and texts noted there). God's memory means two things here: God's being deeply moved for Ephraim's suffering in exile (see 4:19 for a deeply moved heart) and God's self-commitment ("surely," an infinitive absolute) to have mercy (or compassion, *rāḥam*; cf. 30:18; contrast 13:14) on him. This verse carries an emotional force that informs Israel's understanding of a God that is caught up in its life in ways that affect God himself in a deeply personal way (see **Connections**). From within that culture this may help explain the use of the maternal metaphors.

It has been argued convincingly that the meaning of this verb, the root of *reḥem*, "womb," can best be conveyed in a phrase such as "motherly compassion."[4] This same combination of words (being deeply moved issuing in mercy) is found in Isa 63:15, wherein Israel complains that God's yearning and compassion have been withheld. In this context we have seen Rachel weeping for her children (v. 15). In v. 20, God takes up the role of the mother of the child Ephraim and reinforces the resources that Rachel brings to this moment. As Rachel remembers her children, so now God remembers. Yet, a difference is seen in that, while Rachel seems incapacitated by her mourning (v. 15), it is different with God. God will turn their mourning into joy, and give them gladness for sorrow (v. 13). This emphasis on divine compassion and divine remembering recalls Isa 49:15. It has been claimed that this imagery grounds the story of the Prodigal Son, with its image of the father welcoming the son back home (Luke 15:11-32). [Images in 31:20]

Verses 21-22 continue God's response to Ephraim. These verses may be an inclusio with 30:5-7, with the people in desperate straits

Images in 31:20

Phyllis Trible puts it this way: "In summary, strophe four [31:20] is the voice of Yahweh the mother. Parallels between Rachel and Yahweh occur in each of its three sections. The rhetorical question calling Ephraim a 'darling child' suggests that God identifies with Rachel's caring for her children. The motivational clause recalls Rachel remembering her lost sons with tenderness. And the conclusion makes explicit the maternal metaphor for God. As Rachel mourns the loss of the fruit of her womb, so Yahweh, from the divine womb, mourns the same child. Yet there is a difference. The human mother refuses consolation; the divine mother changes grief into grace. As a result, the poem has moved from the desolate lamentation of Rachel to the redemptive compassion of God. Female imagery surrounds Ephraim; words of a mother embrace her son."

Ronald Clements puts it this way: "By blending together these domestic images of a home broken and disturbed by the loss and departure of children and the rejoicing at their return, the prophet portrays the intensity and nature of God's love for his people. If human beings behave in such a fashion when lost children return to their home, how much more must this be true of God who has created these human beings to be capable of loving in this way."

Phyllis Trible, *God and the Rhetoric of Sexuality* (Philadelphia: Fortress, 1978), 45.

Ronald E. Clements, *Jeremiah* (IBC; Atlanta: John Knox, 1988), 186-87.

---

with no future. Now God's promise of return from exile is about to be realized. In symbolic language, Israel (feminine address) is to set out highway signs ("road makers"; "guideposts") along the roads it will travel on its way back to the land (see v. 9). It may be that this language is meant to refer to "the ancient paths" of the tradition, both law and prophets (6:16) as well as paths that lead from Babylon back home. God calls upon "virgin Israel" (as in v. 4) to take to that road and return home, both to God and to its cities in the land of promise. In seeming contradiction, God's question in v. 22 is addressed to the "faithless daughter." This reference assumes that the exiles have a history of wavering and faithlessness, not necessarily that that is the situation at this point. Alternatively, they are vacillating (many do not actually return) and their faithlessness (see 3:14, 22) is evident once again in this hesitation to return. Why should they waver, because ("for") God is at work creating a new thing for them? The use of "create" with God as subject (the only subject of this verb in the Old Testament) here connects best with Isa 65:18, where God creates Jerusalem a delight and a joy. The word "new" appears in a substantive sense elsewhere in Jeremiah only in v. 31; could this new thing be an introductory reference to that covenant? The word "earth" (NRSV; NIV) is better translated "land" in view of all the promises associated with return to the land (see 30:3).

The last half of v. 22 has occasioned much discussion, not least because the translation of the final verb is uncertain (see NRSV footnote). Translations suggested include: a woman encompasses a man (NRSV); the woman must encompass the man with devotion

Other Possible Interpretations of 31:22

Other interpretations include interpreting the "man" as a child, who is now being born again and whom the mother embraces; or, it could mean a reversal of traditional roles for male and female, so that the woman will protect the man. That is, Israel will be so secure in its own land that men will no longer have to assume traditional roles with respect to women (e.g., protection; sexual initiative; support), but there can be greater mutuality, wherein the woman can take the lead in these and other areas. The text may well loop back to the images of Rachel and God (especially in v. 20); the motherly compassion and nurture will take priority over the more patriarchal, physical, and often militaristic propensities of the male (in that culture). The proverb could also be a general expression for a situation that has been completely reversed; what God is now doing is entirely at odds with what one would expect—God creates that which is genuinely new.

(NAB); a female shall encompass a hero; a woman protects, embraces, or woos a man; a woman sets out to find her husband again.

The phrase seems to be a proverbial expression, but the substance of it is quite uncertain. Also unclear is the identification of the woman and the man. Given the references to virgin and daughter in the prior lines, the woman would seem to be a reference to Israel, and hence the "man" could be a reference to God. And so the "new thing" that God is creating is a new relationship between Israel and God (now to be developed further in vv. 31-34). Or, more likely, if the loss of children for which Rachel weeps in v. 15 is in mind (cf. 30:6), then God's new thing is the creation of children through the embrace of man and woman. This would assure Israel's future (cf. Isa 40–66 for the barrenness of the exiles and new creation language). Some such reference to the repopulation of Israel seems most likely and would link up with emphases throughout this passage. [Other Possible Interpretations of 31:22]

The Restoration of Judah, 31:23-26

In vv. 23-40, Israel is consistently referred to in the third person, and God commonly uses the first person. These verses seem to be originally separate snippets that have been combined to speak of the restoration of the people in their land. Judah is the focus of concern in this segment, following upon the use of predominantly Northern names in vv. 1-22, but Israel and Judah are mentioned together in vv. 27 and 31.

When Israel has returned from exile and its fortunes are restored (see 30:3), the people shall once again ask God's blessings on the city of Jerusalem and, apparently, its temple (v. 23; see Ps 122:6-9). The words of blessing assume that city and temple will have been restored and worship returned to its normal rhythms ("once again"; see v. 6; 33:11; cf. 3:16-17). All the inhabitants of Judah and its towns will live together in peace, with a specific word of assurance for the farmers and the shepherds (often at odds with one another). The strength of the weary (see 6:11; 20:9; cf. 45:3; see 15:6, where even God is weary) returnees from exile will be renewed and all their needs, both physical and spiritual, will be satisfied (similarly,

Isa 40:29-31). Once again, the exiles will be at home, content with the good fortunes that their God has supplied.

The difficult v. 26 is often considered an editorially placed word from Jeremiah indicating that the prior words of consolation and restoration had been revealed to him in a dream (see discussion of dreams at ch. 23; 30:1). More likely, as with v. 23, it is spoken by the exiles in response to these salvation oracles from God, particularly v. 25.[5] They now awaken from the sleep of weariness and death. For such weary ones, it was a God-given pleasant sleep indeed, almost too good to be true!

Still Another Look at Restoration, 31:27-30

The phrase, "the days are surely coming," which introduced the Book of Consolation (30:3), is returned to for the first time and punctuates several of the following sections (vv. 27, 31, 38; 33:14). Verses 27-28 look at the time of restoration of both Israel and Judah on the land from the perspective of Jeremiah's call (see 1:10). Verses 29-30 respond to a proverb that was no doubt common among the exiles.

Verse 27 picks up on an earlier theme of repopulation (see 3:16; 23:3; 29:6; 30:19) but speaks not only of the growth of the human community, but of the animals as well, so adversely affected in the Babylonian devastation (see 9:10; 12:4). Once again (see v. 12) all God's creatures will participate in God's salvific deed. God's salvation will catch up the entire created order.

The image used in v. 27 (planting the seed) is drawn from Jeremiah's call (1:10) and more precisely recalled in v. 28. Over the course of the previous chapters, God has been certainly "watching" (see the vision in 1:11-12) to pluck up and break down, to overthrow and destroy. All of these verbs are summarized in the phrase, "bring disaster [*rāʿāh*]," that is, the effects of Israel's own wickedness (*rāʿāh*; see the linkage in the call narrative, 1:14, 16; **Introduction**). But just as God has brought judgment, so God will now watch over the people to build and to plant (see also 30:4-5). The deliverance will be as certain as the judgment has already been. In other words, the announced future is as certain as a past event. God worked judgment, yes, but that is past history, and now God will work life; indeed, God's work of judgment was finally for the sake of life. Of this future the readers need not doubt or despair. The implication is that Israel does not have the capacity to restore itself, either in terms of the human or animal population. Only

God can enable new life to emerge again in this devastated community and that is a sure thing (see Isa 49:19-21).

The relationship of vv. 29-30 to what precedes is uncertain. The reference to bringing disaster is probably the key to their placement here. God's activity in judgment in v. 28 was a communal reality, experienced by all the people of Israel. The saying in v. 29 (similarly Ezek 18:2; Lam 5:7) was a proverbial way in which the exiles spoke of a kind of fatalism. It matters not what we do, they thought; the sins of previous generations (=eaten sour grapes) have set the course for the judgment we have experienced (=teeth set on edge), and our future seems to be set in these terms.

The theme of the unfaithfulness of the ancestors and its negative cumulative impact on the community has been raised at various points (e.g., 2:5; 3:24-25; 7:25-26). The experience of judgment raised issues of fairness: the exiles had borne the effects of the sins of multiple generations, a long history of failure; the effects were unfairly distributed; earlier generations had escaped such effects and the load had been "dumped" on this generation. What hope can there be for our future, given this history of treatment at the hands of God?

The experience of death and destruction had also engendered feelings of despair and hopelessness: the exiles were but the inheritors of an ineluctable fate (and those earlier generations escaped from the full effects of their own sins!). There is nothing they could do about the future, good or evil. Will this judgment be the end of the consequences of all these sins, or will we continue to suffer in perpetuity, continually passing on the effects of the sins of one generation to the next? The response is that this proverb will no longer apply in this new day that God is bringing into being.

Verses 29-30 state that "in those days" people will suffer and die for their own sins, not for the sins of others (note that sin is still part of the picture for "those days"). It is not that judgment in the future will be more individualistic (v. 30 is still communal in orientation); this stipulation is not the application of a new law (such as Deut 24:16). Rather, each generation will suffer the consequences of their own sins (that is, those who eat sour grapes will have their own teeth set on edge). The proverb may have captured a legitimate point with respect to past judgments, but the promise for "those days" is that it will not be possible to so speak. The sins of the past will not continue to apply to this or future generations; such a past will not dictate the shape of the future of the readers. One special force of this new situation is that the exiles will not continue to have the sins of the past hang over their heads. God is one who can forget the past (v. 34) and begin again. [Has the Promise of Verse 30 Been Fulfilled?]

The New Covenant, 31:31-34

This is a classic text. It is picked up in several New Testament texts (e.g., Luke 22:20; 1 Cor 11:25; 2 Cor 3:5-14; Heb 8:8-12 [the longest OT text quoted in the NT]; 10:16-17) and has often shaped more general theological reflection through the centuries. The passage is commonly considered prose, though NIV prints the text as poetry in its entirety. The text stands in a climactic position relative to what has preceded in the Book of Consolation. God's salvific act of bringing the exiles back home, which now becomes the new constitutive event in Israel's history (so 16:14-15=23:7-8), has been strongly emphasized heretofore. That new act of salvation now issues in a new covenant (see below).

This text has generated various interpretations, not always positive. Some have thought that the text, with its references to the law, fosters a kind of legalism. Others have interpreted it in supersessionist terms, as if Israel here predicts its own demise, with Christians in time becoming the sole people of the new covenant (and Heb 8:13 is often appealed to, see below). Still others reject such interpretations and consider the text to be a theological high point in Jeremiah, if not the Old Testament. The discussion below will tend toward the latter interpretation.

As part of a series of oracles introduced by "the days are surely coming," it is important not to isolate this text from its context. The new covenant is to be accompanied by a repopulation of the land (vv. 27-28) and a rebuilding of Jerusalem (vv. 38-40). The context is earthly, not heavenly; it is historical, not beyond this world. Notably, this covenant is given to *Israel*, not to some new people that God will create in the future. Indeed, God will make a new covenant with *all* Israel; people from both the Northern and Southern kingdoms are specifically included. The text claims a fundamental continuity in the identity of the people with whom God will make this new covenant, and in the identity of God as the God of this people ("my people").

The promise is given to a people who are in exile because of pervasive unfaithfulness to Yahweh (11:1-7 spells this out in covenantal terms). This promise is a word from God given to a defeated and dispirited people, who wonder whether God may in

Has the Promise of Verse 30 Been Fulfilled?

As with the following verses (vv. 31–34) "those days" have not *finally* arrived. Children have continued to suffer for the sins of the parents from that day forward and communities have suffered the effects of the sins of previous generations as well. The moral order has continued to function in an inexact way and hence does not cut clean with regard to the effects that sins will have. Individuals and communities will not suffer only for their own sins (except in a narrow judicial sense regarding individuals).

fact have rejected them (see on v. 37 below). Unless the new covenant is God's promise for the sake of the future of this very specific group of people, it is a promise for no one else. And, certainly, those responsible for transmitting this promise understand the new covenant to be a promise God has given to this people, a people who will *never* be rejected by God (vv. 35-37). The promise of a new covenant is thus given to a particular people within a specific geographical locale; to interpret this text in individualistic, universalistic, or narrowly spiritual terms violates its context (see **Connections: Old Covenant and New Covenant**).

This context also makes clear that sin and death will be realities in this new day (v. 30; so also Isaiah's vision of the new heaven and earth, 65:20). The proper distribution of the effects of sin seems to be the concern of vv. 29-30, and that reality will make for a different earthly order. The forgiveness promised in 31:34 also seems to imply continuing sinfulness, unless the divine action refers specifically and only to forgiveness of Israel's sin that led to destruction and exile (see 33:8; Isa 40:2; 43:25). It is important to note that the act of forgiveness (*sālāh*) always has God as its subject in the OT (in Jeremiah, see 5:1, 7; 33:8; 36:3; 50:20).

This is the only Old Testament passage where "new" modifies "covenant," though other modifiers are used that imply newness (cf. "everlasting" in 32:40; 50:5). What is "new" about this covenant is a disputed issue. The only other substantive use of the word "new" in Jeremiah is in v. 22 (see the new heart and new spirit in Ezek 36:26 and the "new things" of Isa 42:9; 43:19). This new covenant is explicitly said *not* to be like the one that God made with a redeemed-from-Egypt Israel at Mt. Sinai. This reference to the exodus should be connected to the call for a change of confession in 16:14-16=23:7-8, also introduced by "the days are surely coming." The new covenant will be linked neither to Mt. Sinai nor to the exodus! The return from exile is a newly *constitutive* event for the people of Israel and the new covenant is an accompaniment integral to that event. Given the pattern in the book of Exodus, it is appropriate that a new covenant with Israel follow upon this newly constitutive salvific event. This new covenant will be made by God "after those days" (v. 33), that is, after Israel's return from exile.

What this constitutive event positively entails for Israel has been spelled out in 24:6-7; God will build them and plant them and "give them a heart to know that I am the LORD" (more closely defined in 32:39; probably reflecting on Deut 30:1-14; see also Ezek 11:19-20; 36:26-27). This new heart will replace the "evil will/heart" so characteristic of Israel's life before exile (see 13:10; 18:12; 23:17). This will be a new "exodus" in terms of the more basic themes, but so different in other ways (see **Connections**). The old covenant formula of relationship still applies, "I will be their God, and they shall be my people" (v. 33; 24:7; a theme struck in the immediately prior sections, 30:22; 31:1), but Israel will now be constituted as the people of God in a new way. God will give them a new heart so that they will know the Lord, indeed *all* of the people will know the Lord (contrast 5:4-5; 8:7; cf. 9:24 and especially 22:15-16, where the knowledge of the Lord and justice concerns coalesce). God will still be their "husband" (*ba'al*, v. 32; a reference to Israel's seeking other lovers among the Baals), evident in the phrase, "know me" (v. 34), but what that knowledge means for Israel will change (see 32:38-41).

The law remains a key point of continuity between the old and the new; but the law will no longer be an external code; it will be written upon the heart. In view of this promise, many commentators speak of the interiorization of this covenant compared to other covenants. Yet, the language of texts such as Deuteronomy 30:6 and 30:14 speak of a similar internal reality for older covenantal understandings. The difference seems only to be that such people will no longer need to be taught via the written Torah. This new reality helps to explain 3:16-17; the ark of the covenant, where the tablets of the law were placed, will be needed no more. [Is the Law on the Heart the Same as Sinai Law?]

The repeated "for" in v. 34 gives two reasons as to why teaching the people of God will no longer be needed: "for" they shall all know God and "for" God will forgive their iniquity. A relational

---

Is the Law on the Heart the Same as Sinai Law?

It is common to claim that, "There is no indication that the content of the law, God's will revealed in commandment, statute, and ordinance, will be altered in the new covenant." But such a claim seems to violate the understanding of law in the Penateuch. Inasmuch as pentateuchal law was never understood as a fixed entity for Israel (witness the changes between Exod and Deut, for example), to confine the law on the heart to existing laws is much too static a view of law and the new heart (see Terence Fretheim, "Law in the Service of Life: The Dynamic Sense of Law in Deuteronomy," forthcoming). It is also much too static a view of life, as if the law existing at the time of this text were the entirety of God's will for the life of everyone at every future time. Rather, the law refers to the will of God for life in more general terms (as the law was defined in some other texts, such as Ps 119). The law here is as dynamic as the new relationship between God and people of which this text speaks in terms of knowing the Lord. The knowledge of God does not have a narrow understanding of the law; it has to do with all of God's ways and the totality of God's will for God's people.

G. Keown, P. Scalise, and T. Smothers, *Jeremiah 26–52* (Dallas: Word Books, 1993), 134.; Walter Brueggemann also speaks of "the same commandments as at Sinai" (*A Commentary on Jeremiah: Exile and Homecoming* [Grand Rapids: Eerdmans, 1998], 293.)

knowledge of the Lord and a unilateral, unconditional divine for-giveness are the heart and soul of this new covenant; they enable an ongoing life in relationship with God and provide its ongoing grounding. Israel's past becomes truly past, never more to hang over the people; never again need they wonder whether God would remember their sins again. In the phrase, "from the least of them to the greatest," a democratization of the people is in view. No person will have special access to the knowledge of God or the forgiveness of sin. Everyone, from whatever class or status, from priest to peasant, from king to commoner, from child to adult, will know the Lord (see Jer 6:11-13; cf. 5:3-5; see **Connections**).

God's Faithful Commitment to Israel, 31:35-37

This statement is not a promise of something new, but a promise of continuity with that which is firmly in place; indeed, the promises of something new are grounded in this promise that the "old" will be maintained in perpetuity. In what is probably an effort to reas-sure a dispirited community in the face of a devastating judgment, God's purposes for and commitment to Israel are shown to be intact. "God's love for Israel is as sure and durable and credible as God's governance of the world itself."[6] Psalm 136:7-9 also links these orders of creation with God's faithful love. The focus of this text is not on God's power in cre-ating or on God's ruling (see 32:17),[7] but on the *fixed* orders of creation that God long ago estab-lished and that God continues to regard as fixed. The point is not God's creational power relative to Israel's future, but on God's creational *com-mitments*; pointedly, the repeated reference is to Israel's "offspring." This text thinks ahead to all coming generations of Israelites.

The conditions stated are impossible con-ditions; the "if" is stated to show in fact just how permanent is this God-people linkage. The first "condition" speaks of the perpetuity of Israel; the second refers to the permanence of God's choice of Israel. God had "rejected," yes (6:30; 7:29; 33:24; cf. the people's question of rejection in 14:19; this text in effect answers that question; see also Lam 5:20-22), but it was a prior generation, not "all the offspring" of Israel (see also 33:24-25). [Salvation for Exilic Readers]

Salvation for Exilic Readers

This oracle of salvation is remarkable in its witness to the depth and breadth of God's commitment to Israel. This point is stressed by the fourfold "says the LORD." It may be important that these verses are unlike the others in these chapters in that they envisage no reversal of a past situation. This divine commitment has always been in place and always will be. This divine loyalty to Israel undergirds not only the promissory elements that have just been articulated but also the judgment of Israel's recent experience. Both promise and judgment may be (and have been) necessary in order for God to remain true to this commitment. This word would function to subvert any claims, from within Israel or without (including more modern claims!), that place the eternal divine commitment to Israel in question. This word would also counter any doubts on the part of a dispirited exilic community about the divine constancy regarding their future as God's people.

The oracle combines hymnic and promissory elements. The oracle begins with the former—language praising God for certain elements of the created order: the sun that gives light by day, the ordinances (NRSV, "fixed order") of the moon and stars that give light by night, and the roaring of the sea and the raging of its waves. This God is the God of hosts—a probable reference to this divine heavenly and earthly army, created by God and upheld by God's continuing care. No astrological competition among the gods is evident here. For a comparable use of creational materials to ground God's commitment to the Davidic kingship, the levitical priesthood, and "the offspring of Jacob," see 31:27 ("seed") and 33:14-26. Second Isaiah also draws out the divine commitment to Israel in terms of creational realities (e.g., Isa 40:12, 26; 45:18). In fact, Isa 54:10 will take the point a step further than Jeremiah in claiming that God's love would not depart from Israel even if the creation ceased to be what it was created to be!

Initially, the reader is not certain what direction this opening witness to God the creator will take. The images brought to mind upon reading v. 35 include order (ordinances) and an unruly sea; light and darkness; day and night; sun and moon; quietness (of the stars in their courses) and noise (cf. Gen 1:14-18; 8:22). Verse 35 immediately draws on the image of the ordinances (NRSV, "fixed order"; NAB, "natural laws") and applies it to *everything* that precedes—including the unruly sea! Even the unruly, noisy sea has a consistency and order to it (the sea here is creature, not the powers of chaos), that is, you can count on it to be the creature God created to be (for the image, see Ps 89:9). All of these orders of creation function as the creatures they are in the presence of God ("my presence"). That is, they do not exist independently of the continuing divine care and upholding of the creation; at the same time, God does not micromanage their ways of functioning in the life of creation. The point is that they will continue to be what they were created to be.

Having sketched these broad orders of creation, God proceeds to make the point. If these orders of creation were ever to cease being what they were created to be, and they will not (and the covenant promises in Gen 8:22 and 9:8-17 are certainly in mind, as Jer 33:20, 25 suggest), then Israel's descendants would cease to be a people in the presence of God for all time. Hence, positively, Israel can be assured of the divine commitment to its continued existence; indeed, the "before me" (parallel to the "my presence" with the orders of creation) testifies to God's ongoing presence and activity among them.

Verse 37 makes a related point in somewhat different terms, though still grounding the divine commitment in creational realities (cf. Isa 40:12). If the heavens could be measured and the earth fully explored, and they cannot be (see Job 28; this is even true with modern science!), then God would reject the descendants of Israel because of all they have done (see 33:26). The last phrase brings the point home in an especially sharp way, and is probably designed to address questions the exiles have (see 14:19, "have you utterly rejected Judah?"; Lam 5:20-22; Isa 54:6) or claims other peoples might make (see 33:24).

Given Israel's infidelities, rehearsed in such detail over the prior chapters, one would have expected God to reject these people. Readers may even get the impression from the uncompromising indictments of those chapters that God has indeed rejected them. In fact, some texts state the matter directly (e.g., 6:30, "The LORD has rejected them," that is, the wicked; 7:29 also speaks this language, though it qualifies the rejection in speaking of "the generation that provoked his wrath"). This text claims that the earlier language of rejection was not absolute. At the same time, it was a rejection; God deems it necessary for this people to die in order to be raised up as God's people again (see Isa 54:6-8). In spite of what the people have done, God's commitment to them as God's people (a communal reference) remains intact for all time.

These claims do not stand over against the "breaking" of the covenant in v. 32.[8] Israel's election by God and God's commitments to Israel remained intact even through Israel's infidelities and the resultant judgment. Israel broke the covenant from its side, but that human unfaithfulness did not finally define God's relationship to this people.

Jerusalem Rebuilt and Enlarged, 31:38-40

Once again, God promises that "the days are surely coming." Unlike the previous texts, where the focus is on Israel's relationship with God, this text centers on a specific space within the land of promise, namely, the city of Jerusalem. The city shall be rebuilt and enlarged in very specific terms. A reversal of the devastation experienced by the city is here promised (see 7:30–8:3).

While this text may seem to shift from theology to geography, theology remains basic. According to this text, Jerusalem is to be rebuilt, not for the returning exiles (except implicitly), but for God! This city itself (no temple is mentioned, but see 33:11) will be God's dwelling place among the people (see 3:16-17; Ezek 48:35, where the name of Jerusalem will be "the Lord is there"; cf. Ps 132:13-14). The promise is that God will not remain aloof or otherwise removed from this redeemed people, but will take up residence in their very midst. So that these spaces will be "sacred to the Lord," the whole area will be purified, especially where dead bodies and their ashes had been scattered (see, e.g., 7:31–8:2; 19:6-7; 33:5).

The promise regarding Jerusalem is very strong: never again will it be uprooted or overthrown (recalling again the images of Jeremiah's call, 1:10). Jerusalem is promised a perduring existence—forever (see Isa 65:17-25)! The question immediately arises as to whether this promise has been fulfilled (for similar promises, see Joel 3:20; Zech 14:10-11). In terms of these passages, one might claim that the city has remained inhabited through the centuries; but the promise that it will never be uprooted or overthrown seems to have fallen short of fulfillment. This is not unusual for Hebrew prophecy, not least because changing situations regularly occasion adjustments of one kind or another (see **Connections**, ch. 26).

Notably, the map of this rebuilt Jerusalem will include the valleys around Jerusalem as well as the high areas; yet, the city will still be safe. [The Dimensions of the New Jerusalem]

> **The Dimensions of the New Jerusalem**
>
> The new boundaries given the city are seen in terms of certain material and natural landmarks (cf. Neh 12:38-39). From the tower of Hananel (Neh 3:1) to the Corner Gate (2 Kgs 14:13) measures the city moving from northeast to northwest. The Horse Gate is in the eastern city wall. The valley of corpses and ashes is the valley of Hinnom (7:32; 19:6), which is in the south and joins the Wadi Kidron (2 Kgs 23:4, 6) at the southeast of the city, where the Horse Gate is located (Neh 3:28). Gareb and Goah are unknown locations.

CONNECTIONS

Turning and Returning

Ephraim's formulation in v. 18b is important, and is best translated as follows (the verb is the same, *šûb*): bring me back and I will (with emphasis) come back. God's action is recognized as primary here; if he is to come back, God must bring him back (so NRSV; NAB, "if you allow me," is too weak). At the same time, the second action has human energy and will in the formulation (so NAB; NRSV, "let me come back," takes the edge off God's bringing back). When Ephraim says he will come back, that is a genuine yielding to God's bringing back. Or, negatively framed, Ephraim will not resist God's action of returning him, both to the land of Canaan and to a proper relationship with God. But, he cannot bring himself back—in either case! Repentance is not represented as a condition for the return,[9] but one could resist the divine action in not returning. This formulation assumes that repentance has occurred among the exiles, but it is not represented in conditional terms in this text.

The translation of the first verb in v. 19 (*šûb*) is also difficult; does it mean repent, re(turn) (so NAB), turn away (so NRSV), or does it have more than one sense? The second verb (*niḥam*) is difficult to translate as well, though "repent" is common (NAB; NRSV). The opening "for" in v. 19 provides some motivation for the request to God to bring him back in v. 18. Perhaps the sense runs something like this: after Ephraim had turned away into exile, he repented; after he was brought to realize what he had done, he struck his thigh (a gesture of remorse). He was ashamed and dismayed because he bore the disgrace (being exiled) of his sin (what he had done as a youth).

Old Covenant and New Covenant

A key question arises in connection with 31:31-34. Inasmuch as the people broke the old covenant, what enabled the community to survive across the divide between old and new? When this divide emerged in connection with the people's infidelities at Mt. Sinai (the golden calf), Moses appealed to God on the basis of the ancestral covenant (Exod 32:13), an appeal that God honored. From this Mosaic intercession we learn that the Sinai covenant was not the event that constituted Israel as the people of God; they were "my [God's] people" throughout the early chapters of Exodus (see Exod 2:24; 6:2-8). The Sinai covenant was "under the umbrella" of the ancestral covenant; elsewhere I have referred to the former as a vocational covenant.[10] Even though the people had broken the Sinai covenant, the ancestral covenant persisted through that brokenness so that Israel as God's chosen people and God's promises continued to be a reality even in their sinfulness. Hence, when Jeremiah refers to the Sinai covenant as having been broken, this in itself does not entail the end of the God-Israel relationship, at least from the side of God. God has made unconditional promises to this people independent of the covenant at Sinai.

Jeremiah nowhere refers explicitly to this ancestral "covenant" (though see 14:21) but it is implicit in several texts, and this in two ways (cf. Isa 29:22; 41:8; 51:2; Mic 7:20; 2 Kgs 13:23). One reference is 33:26, which frames the Book of Consolation with 30:3. It has the only prophetic reference to "Abraham, Isaac, and Jacob" (in the former prophets, only at 1 Kgs 18:36; 2 Kgs 13:23); the heart of the promise in 33:13-26 has to do with the offspring of Abraham, Isaac, and Jacob. Also to be noted in 33:26 is the reference to "the offspring of Jacob," perhaps shorthand for the longer phrase. That the occurrences of the name "Jacob" in Jeremiah are centered in the promissory chapters may signal an effort to link up with the ancestral promises (30:7, 10 [bis], 18; 31:7, 11; 33:26 [bis]; cf. 46:27-28). The people may refer to the ancestral covenant in 14:21. Given the connections between Abrahamic and Davidic covenants, it is notable that the latter is considered by God to be inviolable (33:14-26; see 23:5-6). But Jeremiah's appeal to the promises of God is grounded even more deeply in the covenant with Noah (33:14-26; see 31:35-37). The upshot of these links is that God's promises to Israel are considered as firm as God's covenant with the entire creation (see [Links to the Abrahamic Covenant]).

Another link between the time of the old covenant and new covenant is forgiveness. It was in the wake of the golden calf debacle that forgiveness emerged as new reality for the people of God, in and through Moses' continued intercession (see Exod 34:6-7). When Moses pleads for forgiveness for the people, God responds with the making of a covenant (34:9-10). Here forgiveness is made integral to the covenant and is obviously something that Israel continued to experience over the course of its history. Similarly, in the new covenant, God's forgiveness is made the *ground* for the new covenant (v. 34; "for"). God's unilateral act of the forgiveness of Israel ("for my own sake," Isa 43:25) is the basis upon which this new covenant is established. [Differences between Old Covenant and New]

Another issue raised by this text is the question of its fulfillment. Does the Epistle to the Hebrews present a supersessionist view so that it is to be identified as "a distorted reading"?[11] Having used the word "obsolete" for the old covenant (Heb 8:13), however, Hebrews seems not to draw any negative conclusions regarding the relationship of the Jewish people to God. In fact, the references to the promises to Abraham in Hebrews 6:13-20 probably mean that the promises made to Abraham (and David?) are "unchangeable," concerning which "it is impossible that God would prove false" (Heb 6:18). Hence, those who have been recipients of this Abrahamic promise remain the people of God.

The relationship between these promises to Abraham and the "obsolete" Sinai covenant could be understood in terms not unlike that stated above regarding Exodus 32:13. That is, even though the Sinai covenant is broken or obsolete, God's promises to Abraham remain, and to those promises the faithful (see Heb 11) could

Differences between Old Covenant and New

How is this new covenant *not* like the old covenant? The more important differences include:

- The new covenant is grounded in a newly constitutive salvific event, namely, the return from exile, described in almost lyrical detail in chs. 30–31, and given confessional standing 16:14-15 and 23:7-8. Following the pattern set by the book of Exodus, the new covenant follows upon God's new constitutive salvific event. This new reality may be a more decisive factor for understanding the new covenant than is commonly recognized.

- The new covenant cannot be broken. The *people* broke the old covenant (through their infidelities, see 11:10; 22:9), though it is not clear whether they broke it in a habitual or in a final way. In any case, God did not break the covenant. Implicit in the text's promise is the understanding that neither people nor God can break the new covenant, for it is *everlasting* (32:40; 50:5).

- The new covenant has a unilateral character. The promise of the new covenant is sheer promise, initiated and "made" solely by God; it is nowhere stated that this covenant is something to which the people must agree (unlike the old covenant, Exod 24:3, 7).

- Everyone will know the Lord, that is, every member of the community, from the least to the greatest, will be in a right relationship with their God.

- Sin will continue to characterize their lives, but with the gift of a new heart they will not have an "evil will" ever again, for God's forgiveness will regularly take hold in their lives and the past shall not be remembered. God's forgiveness is certainly *not* a new reality for Israel (see Exod 34:6-7), but the promise here suggests that this is God's unilateral act independent of human repentance (see Isa 43:25).

---

cling. In this light, the formulation in Hebrews regarding the new covenant might mean that Christians are now drawn into the new relationship with God of which Jeremiah speaks, not unlike the manner in which Paul speaks of being grafted into the vine (Rom 11). In another formulation (Gal 3:17-18; cf. Rom 9:4) Paul will claim that the giving of the law does not make the promises to Abraham null and void.

Even from a Christian perspective this text cannot be said to have been fully fulfilled. We are not yet a point where we no longer need teachers or evangelists who will encourage others to "know the Lord." We are not yet at the point where we can claim that "all know me, from the least of them to the greatest." This remains a promise for the future, which is also recognized by the Epistle to the Hebrews.

NOTES

[1] Walter Brueggemann, *A Commentary on Jeremiah: Exile and Homecoming* (Grand Rapids: Eerdmans, 1998), 283.

[2] See Robert Carroll, *Jeremiah* (Philadelphia: Westminster, 1986), 591.

[3] Contrary to G. Keown, P. Scalise, and T. Smothers, *Jeremiah 26–52* (Dallas: Word Books, 1993), 115.

[4] See Phyllis Trible, *God and the Rhetoric of Sexuality* (Philadelphia: Fortress, 1978), 38-53.

[5] See Keown, 128-29.

[6] See Brueggemann, *Jeremiah,* 296.

[7] Contrary to Brueggemann, *Jeremiah,* 296.

[8] Contrary to Brueggemann, *Jeremiah,* 297.

[9] Contrary to Carroll, *Jeremiah,* 600, this text is not at odds with the context that so stresses God's unconditional action.

[10] See Terence Fretheim, *Exodus* (IBC; Louisville: Westminster John Knox, 1991), 208-14.

[11] So Brueggemann, *Jeremiah,* 295.

IS ANYTHING TOO HARD
FOR THE LORD? YES!

32:1-44

Signs and Promises of Restoration, 32:1-33:26

Though the Book of Consolation is commonly confined to the predominantly poetic oracles of chapters 30–31, its themes of promise and restoration extend through the prose of chapters 32–33. In the present form of the book, the latter may be considered a part of the Book of Consolation. Chapters 30–31 center on various words regarding the future of the exiles (30:2); chapters 32–33, however, are more concrete in that they focus on land as a sign of the restoration of Israel's fortunes in a specific place. Moreover, chapter 32, particularly as seen in Jeremiah's prayer (vv. 16-25) and God's response (vv. 26-44), finally has to do with a question of timing and God's possibilities related to the restoration of the land (see below).

Chapters 32–33 are explicitly set during a specific time in Jeremiah's ministry, just before the fall of Jerusalem in 587 BC, when he is confined to King Hezekiah's "court of the guard" (32:2; 33:1). In other words, in one of the darkest moments in Israel's history, during the final days of the Babylonian siege of Jerusalem (32:2), a word of promise regarding Israel's future is announced. These words of promise, however, are not words of deliverance from the siege itself (contrast Isa 31:4-5), but of deliverance on the far side of destruction and exile. [Promise Before the Fall]

Promise Before the Fall

The specific historical placement of these words shortly before the fall of Jerusalem (32:1) is important for interpreting the judgment that is about to occur. To set these words of God at this time may have been considered theologically important for exilic readers. These readers could link any announcements of salvation during the exilic period back to God's purposes that had been in place *prior to* the final destruction. God's commitment to their future has long been in place. God's salvific purposes were at work even in judgment, even in this dark moment of Israel's life! But salvation would come only in and through the valley of death.

However sharp the break in Israel's own story, a future for Israel can be seen in the continuing place that Israel has in the "heart and soul" of God (see 32:41). God's love for Israel and God's faithfulness to promises given to Israel are in place before, during, and after the fall of Jerusalem (see 31:3). Exilic readers would hear in these words that their restoration was not because God had "second thoughts" after the experience of judgment; the judgment was never intended to be God's final word for Israel. But, in order to get to that restoration and hope, Israel must go through a refiner's fire. And so the balance of ch. 32 is, in effect, a response to Zedekiah's "Why?" question (vv. 3-5).

COMMENTARY

This narrative is set in the year 588 BC (the tenth year of King Zedekiah) during the Babylonian siege of Jerusalem that was to result in the destruction of city and temple within a year. The entire story takes place in the palace area of "the court of the guard" where Jeremiah has been confined by Zedekiah (vv. 2-3, 8, 12). The focus of the narrative is Jeremiah's purchase of a field in his hometown of Anathoth "in accordance with the word of the LORD" (vv. 6-8). Verses 6-15 are a first-person account, unusual in Jeremiah (see 11:5-17; 13:1-11; 14:11-16; 17:19-27; 27:2-22; cf. 16:1).

The chapter has a rather straightforward outline. It begins with an announcement of God's word to Jeremiah with respect to a specific situation, described in vv. 1-5 (the actual word is introduced by Jeremiah in vv. 6-7). Zedekiah's "Why?" question—regarding a prior word of the Lord from Jeremiah with respect to the Babylonian siege and his own fate—constitutes the heart of the situation (vv. 3-5). The balance of the chapter is presented as Jeremiah's response to this question (v. 26, which refers to Jeremiah in the third person, may suggest otherwise, but see also 27:1-2). Jeremiah's initial response to the king includes a report of the land purchase (vv. 6-15). That report includes God's prior statements to him about the purchase (especially vv. 14-15), about which Jeremiah prays to God (vv. 16-25). God's reply (vv. 26-44) includes not only a response to this prayer, but also a reply to Zedekiah's "Why?" question of vv. 3-5.

Each of the major segments of the chapter concludes with a reference to the land purchase. King Zedekiah's accusation of Jeremiah for treason (vv. 3-5) concludes with a report of God's word regarding the purchase (vv. 6-8). Jeremiah's actual purchase of the land (vv. 9-12) concludes with a report of God's word that this is a sign that "houses and fields and vineyards shall again be bought in this land" (v. 15). Jeremiah's prayer, which recalls the story of God's work of salvation and judgment in Israel up to the moment of the prayer (vv. 16-24), concludes with the "yet" that the land purchase signifies for the future of Israel in spite of present destruction (v. 25). God's response to Jeremiah's prayer (vv. 26-44) is a review of the reasons for the destruction of the city and the exile in terms of Israel's infidelities (vv. 28-35) and a unilateral promise of salvation (vv. 36-44); its climactic verses repeat the theme of the future land purchase (vv. 43-44). This repeated word about the land is a clear sign regarding Israel's future on that very land.

This purchase of land is another symbolic act of the prophet (see 13:1-14; 16:1-13; 19:1-15). Once again, something concrete and tangible becomes a sign of God's work; the purchase of a plot of land is a sign that this family, as representative of the people of God, will use this land in the future restoration. Beyond destruction, the people of Israel will once again sign deeds and purchase fields in the land (vv. 15, 25, 43-44). This symbolic act of Jeremiah is to be linked to Genesis 23, where a comparable act by Abraham is a sign of God's gift of land to the chosen family. Other references to the story of Abraham are to be found throughout these chapters. We have noted that the gift of land brackets the entire Book of Consolation (30:3; 33:26), and is integral to Jeremiah's prayer (vv. 22-23; see [Links to the Abrahamic Covenant] and [Old Covenant and New Covenant]).

Jeremiah Buys a Field, 32:1-15

As noted in [Promise before the Fall], the narrator takes pains to set this word of God into a very specific situation (588 BC): the tenth year of Zedekiah and the eighteenth year of Nebuchadrezzar. The Babylonian armies are besieging Jerusalem. The prophet Jeremiah was being forcibly confined to "the court of the guard" in the palace of Judah's king.

The story associated with Jeremiah's confinement in the house of the guard is not altogether clear. It seems to be related to the incident reported in 37:11-21: Jeremiah is arrested for desertion when, during a lull in the siege, he attempts to leave Jerusalem—into enemy territory!—to take care of family business regarding property in the land of Benjamin (Anathoth?). Zedekiah (finally) confines Jeremiah in the court of the guard (37:21). This confinement is apparently of such a nature that some freedom is allowed. It seems that 32:6-15 reports how Jeremiah proceeds to deal with this family property issue from prison through his associates (perhaps during a break in the fighting, see 37:5). But before Jeremiah does this, an encounter between him and King Zedekiah is reported (vv. 3-5). This is the first of several encounters (see 34:1-7; 37:1-21; 38:1-6, 14-28 for others; cf. 21:1-7). These texts are somewhat ambiguous regarding the fate of Zedekiah (see 38:17-18, where he would be delivered if he would only surrender; cf. 21:8-12).

Zedekiah accuses Jeremiah of treason for what he has been prophesying; the charge is presented in the form of a lengthy accusatory question (vv. 3-5; see 34:2-3 for God's command to speak comparable words to the king). Why does Jeremiah claim what he does, namely, that the Lord has said that Jerusalem will fall to the Babylonians (=Chaldeans) and that the king will have a face-to-face encounter with the king of Babylon and be sent into exile? Why does Jeremiah claim that, though Zedekiah fights against the Babylonians, he will not succeed (see also 37:6-10)?

Readers should note the complex understanding of agency in this reported word from the Lord. *God* will give the city into the hand of the king of Babylon, but *Nebuchadrezzar* is the one who will take it (v. 3; similarly, 34:2). Zedekiah will fall into the hands of the *Chaldeans* and be given to the king of Babylon (v. 4; similarly, 34:3; cf. 38:18, 23), who will send him into exile until *God* changes his fortunes (39:4-7 reports in somewhat more detail the capture and exile of Zedekiah; cf. 52:8-11).

This question of the fate of Zedekiah seems to be left hanging in the air, as he is not mentioned again in this chapter. Yet, as noted, the redaction represents the balance of the chapter as a response to the king. At one level, Jeremiah's explanation regarding the family property in vv. 6-8 can only be understood in view of the reasons for Jeremiah's confinement, clearly evident only in 37:11-21. But at a more profound level, Zedekiah's "Why?" question is considered and answered: Judgment must fall upon Jerusalem, because it is only through that refining fire that any hope for the future of the people of God becomes possible. Life can come only through death.

Jeremiah reports in v. 6 that he received a word from the Lord regarding the disposition of family property in Anathoth. Jeremiah's cousin Hanamel, son of his uncle Shallum (both persons are mentioned only in this context), will come to him and ask him to buy a field that was the "inheritance" of the family. Hanamel will do so apparently because the family property had been sold (to some unknown person) in view of some financial or other difficulty (see Lev 25:25-28 for the family *obligation*, but the links with this text are not precise). This "right of (possession and) redemption" by a family member was a means to keep the property in the family. This "right" is Jeremiah's rather than that of some other member of the family probably because he was the closest relative. The language of "possession" links Jeremiah's purchase to God's original giving of the land for "possession" (vv. 22-23), suggesting that God's original ancestral promise is still intact (see 30:3 for God's promise of land).

In "accordance with the word of the LORD," Hanamel does come to Jeremiah and present the offer of land purchase (v. 8).

Jeremiah 36:4—Baruch Writing Jeremiah's Prophecies

Gustave Doré. *Baruch Writing Jeremiah's Prophecies* from the *Illustrated Bible*. 19th C. Engraving. (Credit: Dover Pictorial Archive Series)

When this happens, Jeremiah "knows" that the word spoken was from the Lord (see **Connections: Theological Issues in 32:6-8**). According to v. 25, Jeremiah understands that this land purchase is a direct command from the Lord. It has been suggested that this encounter between Jeremiah and members of his family in Anathoth is evidence for reconciliation with members of his family, a relationship ruptured because of the nature of Jeremiah's word (see 11:18-23; 12:6). This may also be a sign of a new day about to dawn, but if so, the text is remarkably silent about it.

Baruch

This is the first reference to Baruch in the book of Jeremiah; the first chronological reference, however, is in 36:4 (dated some eighteen years earlier, about 605 BC). So the relationship between Jeremiah and his secretary was long-standing. His brother Seraiah in mentioned in 51:59; they may have been members of a prominent Jerusalem family. Baruch was Jeremiah's secretary (amanuensis; see 36:26, 32) and accompanied him on various pursuits, including his exile in Egypt (43:6). In this text he becomes the custodian of the land purchase documents, and thereby he symbolically embodies the transition from the old era to the new. Much more will be said of Baruch in chs. 36–45. His name, as well as that of his father (Neriah), appear on a recently discovered seal-stamp, dating from the seventh century; it likely refers to this person, given that the name Neriah is otherwise rarely attested.

Verses 9-15 provide detail regarding Jeremiah's land purchase and the *divine* interpretation of its meaning. The seventeen shekels of silver that Jeremiah pays for the field is a reference to weight (v. 10; about seven ounces) and not to coins (which were apparently not used until the Persian period in the late sixth century BC). Jeremiah signs the deed in the presence of (two?) witnesses (who also sign it, v. 12; see v. 25), rolls up the scroll, and seals that copy of the deed. This was the official copy, but there was also an "open copy," apparently rolled around the sealed deed, for easy public reference.

Jeremiah gives both copies of the deed to Baruch in the presence of Hanamel, the witnesses, and the Judeans who were present in the court where Jeremiah was confined (vv. 12-13). [Baruch] These various witnesses indicate that this is a genuine legal procedure and also assure that adequate memory of this transaction will survive the devastation. Such a written document will also constitute a verification of the truth of Jeremiah's word on the far side of these disastrous events for the land.

In giving the deed to Baruch, Jeremiah charges him with a word from the Lord (apparently received earlier) regarding the secure disposition of the deed (v. 14). Is it because of the uncertain future of Jeremiah that Baruch is given this role? Baruch is to take both deeds and preserve them for future usage in an earthenware jar (the kind of jar in which the first of the Dead Sea Scrolls were found), for the day will certainly come when houses and fields and vineyards will again be purchased in the land. The symbolism associated with the act includes houses and vineyards, and commercial activity related thereto, so that the field is but a sign of a much more comprehensive future reality (v. 15; see 31:5, 12).

This word of God that Jeremiah conveys to Baruch (vv. 14-15) is a divine *interpretation* of this purchase as a sign of a certain future life that the people will have in the land. Note that these properties are to be purchased, even though they may have belonged originally to the families involved (vv. 15, 43-44). In other terms, this future constitutes no new conquest of the land, but a peaceful reappropriation of property. [Bonhoeffer on 32:15]

Bonhoeffer on 32:15

Three months before his arrest, Bonhoeffer wrote that there "remains for us only the very narrow way, often extremely difficult to find, of living every day as if it were our last, and yet living in faith and responsibility as though there were to be a great future: 'Houses and fields and vineyards will again be bought in this land' proclaims Jeremiah (32:15), in paradoxical contrast to his prophecies of woe, just before the destruction of the holy city. It is a sign from God and a pledge of a fresh start and a great future, just when all seems black. Thinking and acting for the sake of the coming generation, but being ready any day to go without fear or anxiety—that, in practice, is the spirit in which we are forced to live. It is not easy to be brave and keep that spirit alive, but it is imperative."

While in prison, Bonhoeffer wrote to his fiancee Maria: "When Jeremiah said, in his people's hour of direst need, that 'houses and fields and [vineyards] shall again be bought in this land,' it was a token of confidence in the future. That requires faith, and may God grant us it daily. I don't mean the faith that flees the world, but the faith that endures in the world and loves and remains true to the world in spite of all the hardships it brings us. Our marriage must be a 'yes' to God's earth. It must strengthen our resolve to do and accomplish something on earth. I fear that Christians who venture to stand on earth on only one leg will stand in heaven on only one leg too."

Bonhoeffer's cell in Tegel. (Credit: Christian Kaiser Verlag)

Dietrich Bonhoeffer, *Letters and Papers from Prison* (Enlarged Edition; London: SCM Press, 1971), 14-15.

Dietrich Bonhoeffer and M. von Wedemeyer, *Love Letters from Cell 92*, 1943–45 (ed. Ruth-Alice von Bismarck and U. Kabitz; London: Harper Collins, 1994), 48-49.

Jeremiah Prays for Wisdom, 32:16-25

These verses are specifically identified as a prayer, the only time in the book that Jeremiah prays for personal guidance (v. 16; the only other time that Jeremiah "prays" is 42:4, where he prays for others). The explicit reference back to the deed of purchase (v. 16), and the prayer's ending (v. 25), indicates that this prayer is Jeremiah's response to the events of vv. 6-15, particularly the word of God in vv. 14-15. [The Point of Jeremiah's Prayer]

The canonical placement of chapter 32 after the salvation oracles of chapters 30–31 has always been something of a puzzle. It might be resolved if chapter 32 finally has to do with a question of timing and God's possibilities related thereto. The word from God regarding the land purchase (vv. 6-15) sounds like God will do something on behalf of the city *before* the destruction (as God did earlier with the Assyrians; see Isa 31:4-5). Jeremiah in effect says that all things are possible for God. But this deferential opening to

---

The Point of Jeremiah's Prayer

The point of Jeremiah's prayer seems basically to be an expression of wonderment that, given the catastrophe now at Judah's doorstep, God would encourage Jeremiah to purchase land. Jeremiah had completed the transaction in obedience to God's word, but now expresses his puzzlement about it. The initial "Ah Lord God!" (used elsewhere at 1:6; 4:10; 14:13) refers to an expression of uncertainty or puzzlement (not dismay or accusation) that Jeremiah raises about the land purchase. In a time of war and devastation, this peaceful, everyday, care-for-the-land act seems so incongruous! This prayer is not a sign of a crisis in the life of Jeremiah, but a matter of Jeremiah's *understanding* about what God is about in the matter of land purchase. In response to Jeremiah's questioning, God reveals more clearly what God is about in this situation (vv. 26-44). This divine response is a revelatory event for a questioning Jeremiah (cf. the interaction between God and Moses in Exodus 3–7).

---

his prayer contains an implicit question to God: is not the disaster too far along even for God (!) to turn the situation around?

Jeremiah's prayer both recalls the wondrous things that God has done in the past and testifies to what God is doing at the very moment—as if to make sure that God is up-to-date ("See!" v. 24). His witness to the greatness and strength of God is reiterated in various ways, but he begins with a confession regarding creation (as does Hezekiah in 2 Kgs 19:15; so also the creedal formulations in Neh 9:6; Pss 135–136). He uses language more common to the exodus tradition to do so (as in v. 21; see Exod 6:6; Deut 4:34; 26:8). This testimony regarding creation grounds all that follows (see especially vv. 19-20), as demonstrated by the immediate placement of the word about nothing being too wonder-full for God. The word about God's other wondrous deeds (*pālēʾ*) is rooted in the wonder of God's creational deed. It is because God is the creator, and has shown therein the kind of God that Israel's Lord is, that God accomplishes all that is done in the historical sphere. God will agree with this creational premise in v. 27.

But then Jeremiah states a second premise, namely, nothing is too hard for God. God will raise a question with respect to this premise in v. 27 (see below). Given the prayer that now follows, Jeremiah's declaration is in effect a question: let us grant the point that nothing is too hard for God, but I do not understand how God can simply intervene at this juncture and stop the deserved and impending disaster. I need an explanation for the land purchase, especially given all of God's words of inevitable disaster up to this point. [Is Anything Too Hard for God?]

Moving from the base of creation and nothing being too hard for God, Jeremiah expresses this witness to God by drawing on two major types of creedal formulations used by Israelites. The

Is Anything too Hard for God?

The nuance of the verb *pālēʾ* is difficult to discern (vv. 17, 27; NRSV, "hard"; see Gen 18:14 for a comparable phrasing). Is the emphasis on the difficulty of what God does, or on the wondrous nature of the divine deeds? The use of the word in this context for divine actions in both creation and history corresponds with its usage elsewhere for the wondrous deeds of God (e.g., Exod 3:20; 15:11). The claim regarding divine possibilities might also refer back to the story of Abraham and Sarah regarding the birth of a child in their old age (Gen 18:14), not least given other Abrahamic allusions in these chapters (see Walter Brueggemann, *A Commentary on Jeremiah: Exile and Homecoming* [Grand Rapids: Eerdmans, 1998], 303). The word appears to lift up the work of God as extraordinary, wonder-full, marvelous, even surprising or astonishing. The theme of strength is certainly present, but it is implicit in what is a more comprehensive testimony to the work of God.

Some New Testament texts also use such language (e.g., Mark 10:27; Luke 1:37), but it is difficult to generalize regarding meaning. In any thorough investigation, readers would have to take into account texts such as Matt 17:20, where nothing is impossible for *human beings*! Also to be considered are Matt 26:39, where Jesus' "if it is possible" prayer to God raises questions of divine self-limitation, and not unlike the limitations of which God speaks in this Jeremiah text; the nature of God's purposes and promises places certain possibilities off limits for God. Note also Mark 6:5, where Jesus' healing powers are limited by the dynamics of the situation that he faces.

Issues of divine possibility must be considered from within an understanding of the God-human relationship. Because God honors the relationship and honors the commitments that God has made within that covenant (for example, God will be faithful to promises made), God is not able to act in ways that would be unfaithful to the relationship. Relationships of integrity involve matters of constraint and restraint. The marriage relationship, used in the Old Testament in various ways for the God-Israel relationship, might be a helpful analogy: either party to the relationship *is able* to violate the wedding vows, but they *cannot* do so and still be faithful. They are able, but they cannot. Something like that is also true for God within relationships established.

---

movement within the two types of confession (see below) is the same as the movement within this passage: from the God of steadfast love to the God of judgment (vv. 18-19) and from the God of saving actions to the God of judging actions (vv. 20-24). The God who is "for Israel" can also be "against Israel." This understanding would also be characteristic of any human relationship of consequence (e.g., parents and children).

Regarding the first creedal reference, Jeremiah recalls the confession that focuses on the nature and character of God (most directly gathered in Exod 34:6-7), with an emphasis on how those divine characteristics manifest themselves in particular activities. God shows steadfast love (*ḥesed*) to the thousandth generation (see 9:24), but God also has the wisdom, strength, and acuity to see to it that sin and evil do not go unchecked in the life of the world (vv. 18-19). The thousand generations of God's steadfast love, however, is not suddenly cut off at the moment that God's judgment kicks in (see 31:3). In every such activity God sees everything (eyes that are open to all, see Job 34:21; Ps 33:13), has the wisdom to know how to respond, and the strength to do so appropriately.

God as clear-sighted judge is the more dominant theme in this context and the point is expressed in two ways in vv. 18-19. First, using language similar to Exodus 20:5/Deuteronomy 5:9, Jeremiah speaks of God completing (*šālôm*; NRSV, "repay"; *pāqad* is used in Exod/Deut) the iniquity of the parents upon the (laps of) the children, that is, seeing that the moral order comes full circle in terms of sin's effects (see Isa 65:6-7). On *šālêm* in this sense of correspondence between deed and consequence in Jeremiah, see 50:29, "repay her according to her deeds; just as she has done, do to her" (cf. 16:18; 25:14).

Second, essentially the same point is made in v. 19; God gives (*nātan*; NRSV, "rewarding"; for this sense see Ezek 7:3-4, where NRSV translates "punish") to each according to their ways and the fruit of their doings ("what goes around comes around," see **Connections**, ch. 1; **Introduction**). Notably, this claim covers all human beings, whatever their relationship to Israel; Israel is being treated no differently in this judgment than is the case with every other people on earth. Israel cannot claim that God is being unfair or capricious. Jeremiah uses the image of fruit in this sense also in 6:19; 17:10; 21:14. The image of judgment used is nonretributive; it is the flowering of the deed (see Ezek 7:10), with the consequences corresponding to the deed. Jeremiah's point is that God sees to this moral order among all peoples, not only Israel.

Regarding the second creedal reference, Jeremiah recalls the confession that recites the various wondrous deeds of God in the past (e.g., Deut 26:5-9). Here he refers primarily to the complex of divine acts associated with the exodus from Egypt and the settlement in the land, a land that God had promised to the ancestors (vv. 20-23; also in 30:3; 11:3-5; see 3:18; 7:7). This reference to land possession recalls God's promises to the ancestors and Abraham's purchase of land (Gen 15:18; 17:8; 23:1-20). But Jeremiah also wraps into this traditional confession a repeated update: "to this day" and "to this very day" (v. 20). That is, these "signs and wonders" do not belong simply to the distant past (see Pss 78:43; 105:27); they have been experienced by Israel all along its journey, even up to the present time. Indeed, these deeds have been seen by "all humankind" and have made God's name great among them all (as in Isa 63:12-14), even to this day (Neh 9:10). The divine reputation has spread out and about in the larger world (in modern terms, this is a kind of "mission" statement). But, then, in view of human sin—persistently doing *nothing* to obey God's voice or follow God's law (v. 23b), God's actions have turned from salvation to judgment ("therefore," vv. 23c-24).

But judgment is the fundamental concern of this moment of prayer for Jeremiah. The present situation is one of disaster (*rā'āh*; used for the people's "evil" in vv. 30, 32), which God let happen

(Hi. *qārē'*; NRSV, "made…come"; on this more passive sense of the verb, see 13:22; 44:23) to them. Jeremiah's language becomes very vivid at this point. Siege ramps—virtually personified—have been erected to scale the walls of the city and are in place to take it; Jerusalem is faced with sword, famine, and pestilence (a triad used in 14:12 and often). The Chaldeans are fighting against the city and are poised to subjugate it (note the real human agency; see also v. 29; 33:4-5). What God has said would happen is happening. God can see for himself!

Jeremiah's prayer ends with a great "Yet!" The NAB captures the sense of v. 25 very well: "and yet you tell me, O LORD God: Buy the field with money, call in witnesses. But the city has already been handed over to the Chaldeans!" In other words, Jeremiah is not yet able to see the sense of the land purchase, given God's ways with the world, just rehearsed, and the present disastrous situation, which God can obviously see. Jeremiah apparently interprets God's word about the land purchase (v. 15) to mean that houses and fields and vineyards would be purchased in the face of the destruction. His vision does not yet properly link the destruction and that new day of which the land purchase is a sign. And so God's response (vv. 26-44) has to fill in the picture for Jeremiah in a clarifying way.

God's Response Regarding Israel's Future Beyond Disaster, 32:26-44

God responds directly to Jeremiah's prayer (note the "See," v. 26; cf. v. 24). The essential point of the response is to clarify for Jeremiah the sequence of events that are so difficult to perceive in the maelstrom of the moment, and which God has complicated with the command to purchase land. This divine word is also a response to the "Why?" question placed by King Zedekiah in vv. 3-5. In order for the people of Israel to move into a hopeful future, they must go through the fires of judgment. This point is portrayed through parallel texts, each introduced by "therefore," of indictment/announcement of judgment (vv. 28-35) and salvation (vv. 36-44)

God initially picks up on the opening elements in Jeremiah's prayer (v. 17). Referencing the creation motif, Israel's God is indeed the God of "all flesh," that is, humankind (referring especially to the "all" in vv. 19-20; see 25:31; for a similar phrase, see Num 16:22; 27:16). Jeremiah is correct on that point. But, then, God restates Jeremiah's "nothing is too hard for you" in question form: is anything too hard for me? Scholars consider the question rhetorical (with a "no" answer implied) and hence in essential agreement with Jeremiah's declaration in v. 17. But it is more likely that the answer to God's question is "yes"!

A Question for Exilic Readers

We pause to note that the question of divine possibility was certainly a question raised by the exiles. Given who God is, why could not God have made possible a different future for us? Are not all things possible for God? Why could not God have restored us without going through the mess of violence and destruction? In this context in Jeremiah, this "Why?" question is put into the mouth of Zedekiah (vv. 3–5). The upshot of the reply is that the premise (nothing is impossible for God) is flawed. Jeremiah senses that this is the case in asking God for an explanation. And this entire narrative is an effort to challenge the questions and their premise regarding God's limitless possibilities that had been raised by exilic readers. God's reply in effect is: given the nature of the situation of this people of God, no shortcuts are possible, even for God.

Recall that Jeremiah's declaration was in effect a question. Nothing is too hard for God, but how can God simply intervene at this juncture and stop the impending disaster? Jeremiah needs an explanation for the land purchase. God offers such an explanation, but not by granting Jeremiah's premise that nothing is too hard for the LORD. From God's perspective, what is at stake in this situation are God's promises and Israel's future, and one approach to this dilemma is in fact impossible. God is not able (!) to take a shortcut into that future and still be faithful to the relationship. What follows is an explanation ("therefore") of this *impossibility* for God (see [Is Anything Too Hard for God?]). [A Question for Exilic Readers]

God's "therefore" (v. 28) introduces the divine argument. In effect: let me explain why it is not possible. Verses 28-29 reiterate themes that have been struck heretofore in Jeremiah (see 21:10, 14; 19:12-13; see also 37:8-10). The city will be given into the hands of the Babylonians, and *they* (note the agent) will burn it down; there is no question that this is Jerusalem's future. This announcement is reiterated in v. 36, providing an inclusio for the indictment in vv. 30-35.

This indictment states the reasons for the judgment ("for"), which is a gathering of earlier indictment themes (vv. 30-35; see 7:24-31; 19:4-5), anticipated by the description of the idolatrous houses to be burned in v. 29b. The provocation/arousal of the divine anger becomes a virtual refrain in vv. 29-32 (picked up again in v. 37). Note also the emphasis on the *personal* character of this anger (the first person is used over ten times in vv. 29-35). God's anger is real, but contingent; God is not eternally angry; if there were no sin, there would be no wrath.

God's anger has been provoked by the evil, indeed "*nothing* but evil" of the people. The range of the evil is all-encompassing: both Israel and Judah ("house of Israel" in v. 30 refers to the North and then to Israel as a whole), the city and rural areas, as well as kings, priests, and prophets ("evil" is repeated in vv. 30, 32). The focus of the divine anger, and the essential definition of "evil" in this context, is the worship of other gods (see also 44:8), "the work of their hands," "the abominations in the house that bears my name" (=the temple). And they have "built the high places of Baal...to offer up sons and daughters," that is, to sacrifice their children (note the identification of Baal and Molech; see 7:31; 19:5; on Molech see Lev 18:21; 20:2-5; 1 Kgs 11:7; 2 Kgs 23:10). In essence, "they have turned their backs on me," and their faces toward other gods. God stresses the long period of time of having to endure this "evil" ("from their youth"; from the day Jerusalem "was built until this day," a unique reference); the implication: God has been incredibly patient, having persistently sent prophets to teach and correct them (v. 33).

The stress on the divine mind in v. 35 (see 7:31; 19:5) shows clearly that the sin of offering up sons and daughters ("causing Judah to sin") is not due to something that God has done. This sin, perhaps especially this sin, was a clear resistance of God's intentions for the people (on their stubbornness, see **Connections**, ch. 5). God had never even thought of such a possibility! It may be that some among the readers claimed that these offerings were commanded by God (see Exod 13:1-2; 22:29; cf. Ezek 20:26) and hence the emphasis that is placed on the point.

Following the extensive indictment comes language typical for the announcement of judgment (v. 36; "therefore"), with which this segment had begun (vv. 28-29). But, while the people's own words (quoted in v. 36) are in effect such an announcement, God makes then makes a surprising turn: the judgment is only a prelude to a quite different future (vv. 37-44). This announcement of judgment in direct address (the "you" in v. 36 is plural, as in v. 43; 33:10) is unusual in that God quotes the people (which the exiles would read as themselves), or less likely Jeremiah and Zedekiah (see vv. 3-4, 24). To use a quotation at this point is God's way of saying that this word of judgment that people, including both Zedekiah and Jeremiah, have been repeating is exactly the right word for this time and place. This is what is going to take place (see vv. 3-5) or, possibly, has already taken place (as in vv. 42-43). But even more importantly, God may use such a quotation as a way of stressing that this is the only future that is possible for them to contemplate at this moment.

In the surprising announcement of salvation (introduced by "See," cf. vv. 24, 27), God sketches out a remarkable future for "them," that is, the unfaithful people of vv. 32-35 who will have experienced such great devastation (the "you" of vv. 36, 43 is probably the same as "them," but seen from the perspective of the exiles). The promise in v. 37 is similar to that given to the exiles of 597 BC (29:14) and hence now includes exiles from the deportation in 586 BC (contrast 24:8-10). This devastation is their future, but it is not their final future. This devastation is a *necessary* refining fire in view of the people's infidelities, but God will be working within the judgment itself to bring about a new day for this people. This wonder-full future is made possible by God within a context in which the people have no possibilities left to offer. Even more, the death of the old heart is necessary for a new heart to be given. The judgment thus does lead to another kind of understanding of the "therefore" of v. 36; given death, therefore life (for this kind of argument, see Deut 32:36).

The features of this new future are sketched in terms that gather themes from previous sections in Jeremiah, especially chapters 30–31, but also bring in several new elements. The theme of God's gathering the exiles from the many lands and bringing them back to the promised land in safety (v. 37) is strongly represented in earlier chapters (e.g., 23:3; 29:14; 30:10; 31:8-14; see also Isa 11:12; Ezek 11:17; 36:24). This is also true of the covenant formula in 32:38 (see 24:7; 30:22; 31:1, 33; Ezek 36:28; Zech 8:8). Stressed throughout is the divine initiative in the creation of this new reality; nothing whatsoever depends upon human response (as also in 31:31-34).

Somewhat different formulations appear in vv. 39-41, but they are essentially continuous with the theme of the new covenant (31:31-34), here called the "everlasting covenant" (v. 40; as in Isa 55:3; 61:8; Ezek 16:60; 37:26), matched by the people's fear of the Lord "for all time" of v. 39. Implicit in the new covenant, wherein the law is written on the heart and everyone will know the Lord, is the gift of "one heart and one way" (the latter phrase may be a reference to the law). The use of the singular "one" for the plural "them" may testify to the communal character of this new reality in which every individual participates.[1]

In view of the creation of this new reality all will fear the Lord (see the development of these themes in Ezek 11:19-20; 36:26-27); the call for obedience is no longer necessary. The "one heart" and the fear of God are brought together in v. 40 in the formulation, "I will put the fear of me in their hearts" (cf. the law in 31:33). The parallel between knowing the Lord in 31:34 and fearing the Lord (32:39-40) is important to observe. They are essentially the same reality viewed from different angles; knowing stresses the closeness of the relationship with all that that entails, while fearing (in the sense of awe) makes clear that the relationship is asymmetrical

(God remains God and humans remain human). The language of trust used in 17:7-8 nicely captures both of these dimensions of the relationship (see **Connections: On the Fulfillment of the Promise of a New Heart**).

Just as God implants a new heart in this people so God will plant them again in the land of promise (v. 41; note the call of Jeremiah, 1:10). The newness that God promises thus has both internal and external elements, and it is important not to lose sight of either. The spiritual dimensions of this new covenant are of crucial importance; they show that the restoration is not simply the result of a political realignment. At the same time, the promise is not a matter of disembodied spirituality. The land purchase theme, so central to this chapter, insists on keeping the life with God down to earth. And it is this theme that finally rounds out the chapter (vv. 42-44).

The people will be returned to their land and be planted there, and they will be like the tree that has been described in 17:7-8. And there they will be "safe" (v. 37; so also 23:6; 33:16), such an important theme in view of the adverse psychical and bodily effects suffered at the hands of the Babylonian armies. Upon returning to the land they will experience only "good" (a repeated theme, vv. 39-42), a good that will extend down through the generations (v. 39); indeed, God will not draw back from doing good and will rejoice in doing good to them (v. 41). This language of goodness hearkens back to the refrains of the creation story in Genesis 1 (see vv. 17, 27); God's creation of a new people is considered to be parallel to God's creation in the beginning, which occurred entirely at the divine initiative and with the same "good" results. It is as if God will once again look out over what has been newly created and pronounce it "very good." [A New Day for God, Too]

> **A New Day for God, Too**
>
> An important insight in vv. 37-41 is the witness made to the very life of God. The oracle of restoration begins with God's strong and personalized statement of "my anger and my wrath and in great indignation" (v. 37) that had driven Israel into exile (picking up on the anger themes in vv. 29-32). Given the fact that Israel will be given a new heart and that they will never again turn from God entails the end of anger for God forever. No more human sin, and hence no more divine anger. This is not only a time of new creation for the people; it is also a new day for God! God will never again draw back from doing good to the people; even more, to put the point positively, God will *rejoice* in doing good to them (see Zeph 3:17; Deut 30:9; Isa 62:5; 65:19).

The divine move to planting the people back in their own land is described in stunning terms (v. 41): This divine action is done in faithfulness (*'emet*; see Zech 8:8) with all of God's heart (*lēb*) and all of God's soul (*nepeš*)! God does this because God is faithful to promises that have been made; God swore to the ancestors that God would give them the land (v. 22; see 30:3; 3:18; 7:7; 11:3-5). And God is a keeper of promises. Moreover, this is no half-hearted move for God, as if God were not really finished with all the anger and is faithful with jaw set and teeth clenched. God does this with all of the divine heart and soul; God rejoices in doing this. The God who had commanded Israel to love the Lord with all their heart and soul (see Deut 6:5) not only sees that that will certainly be the case for the people in the future but also that this is the divine stance toward God's people forever.

The final verses in the chapter (vv. 42-44) return to the theme of the land purchase and make the connection between present disaster and future restoration clear for Jeremiah. Just as certainly as God brought the disaster (*rāʿāh*) so God will bring the good that is now promised. The people's future salvation is as sure as the judgment they have already experienced. Indeed, the latter proves to be the means by which that future is brought into being. God agrees with the people (the "you" in v. 43 is plural and echoes their saying in v. 36) that the land is now desolate, without human or animal life (practically, though not literally the case; expanded upon in 33:10-14), in the wake of the Babylonian onslaught.

But, in the future that God here promises, all this will be changed. And the sign of that future is Jeremiah's purchase of land. His purchase is a sure sign that fields will be purchased in the future and deeds will be signed and sealed within a society that will have returned to its normal pace (note the detail with which his purchase anticipates the future). And, as if to make sure that the land is not some small spot in the region, the promise is associated with all the geographical areas that have been identified with Israel in the past (see 33:13; 17:26; Benjamin, where Jeremiah's land was located, could be a reference to the northern kingdom, though the emphasis is surely on the various southern regions). A final "says the LORD" grounds the promise of restored fortunes (see 33:7); it is a promise that can absolutely be relied upon.

CONNECTIONS

Theological Issues in 32:6-8

An intriguing element in vv. 6-8 is that Jeremiah apparently does not immediately conclude that the word he had received (v. 7) was from God. Only in the light of unfolding events does he "know" (*yādaʿ*) that it was from the Lord (v. 8c). This suggests that Jeremiah is alert to the possibility that "voices" he hears—especially this command!—may not be from God, and that subsequent events are important for authentication of a word as the word of God. On the other hand, perhaps Jeremiah's "knowing" is only a recognition that the events of which the Lord was speaking have now occurred. In either case, given this unusual formulation, it is difficult to know whether this sequence of reflection is typical for Jeremiah.

These verses also raise questions regarding divine omniscience and foreknowledge. Hanamel does come to Jeremiah as God had said he would and makes *essentially* the speech God said he would make. Perhaps God has been active in Hanamel's life, inspiring him to make this kind of move. God apparently foreknows that Hanamel will follow through on this inspired move in view of God's knowledge of Hanamel's present life situation. But, notably, only the substance of Hanamel's speech is represented as being foreknown and not the exact words that he ends up speaking. In any case, Jeremiah's draws the conclusion he does on the basis of significant (if not exact) continuities between God's word and the visit of Hanamel (on divine foreknowledge, see **Connections**, chs. 22 and 26).

Also of interest in these verses is God's use of a third party to convey the word to Jeremiah. Why not just command Jeremiah directly and skip the middleman? This use of a third party is apparently a way to stress that this act is grounded in quite everyday sorts of transactions, which reinforces the idea of a return to normalcy. Moreover, Hanamel functions as a (God-inspired) witness to this transaction; this is not something that has its origins in Jeremiah's own mind.

A still further theological issue raised in this text pertains to the use of an actual event, apparently necessitated by a family issue, as a symbolic act. Usually, the symbolic act is "created" for the situation (see 13:1-11); here an actual event is *interpreted* as foreshadowing the future. Jeremiah apparently had the option of not signing the deed in view of the deteriorating situation; that he did so is a sign that he *interprets* God's word to mean that his people still have a future in the land. This text is the only report of a symbolic act that portends a *positive* future.

[Berrigan on the Land Purchase]

> **Berrigan on the Land Purchase**
>
> One would be hard put to exhaust the symbolic riches of the field. The field collapses time; it symbolizes promise, amplitude, gift, avatar, ardor, an entire land restored. Is the land blood-ridden and desolate? It shall be "a land flowing with milk and honey."
>
> Daniel Berrigan, *Jeremiah: The World, the Wound of God* (Minneapolis: Fortress, 1999), 141.

The Fulfillment of the Promise of a New Heart

One further dimension of the gift of a new heart needs attention (also present in 31:31-34). This new heart is radically different from the old heart in the sense that the people will not turn from

God again, indeed they *cannot* turn from God. This new heart will enable them to fear God "for all time" so that they will never again be unfaithful or "turn from me." The original creation of humankind resulted in human beings who were "able not to sin" (but proceeded to do so). This new creation of human beings seems to yield individuals who will "not be able to sin" (also characteristic of "heaven" in typical Christian eschatology). At the same time, we have seen that texts such as 31:30 assume the presence of sin and death "in those days," and this also seems to be the assumption in 31:34 (as also in texts such as Isa 65:20). Perhaps sin is understood in such a way that it does not entail a turning away from God or sin is act as distinguished from sin as a condition of the heart. In any case, human beings will not have an "evil will" again.

In speaking about the fulfillment of such texts, it is clear that this promise has not yet come to pass in any full sense. Some dimensions of fulfillment can be observed in terms of the return to the land of promise, and perhaps even some signs of a new divine strategy with human beings. But Christians certainly cannot claim that the new covenant constituted with human beings in and through the work of Jesus Christ has brought such inevitably faithful humans into being. Christians, for all their status as saints because of what God has done for them in Jesus Christ, remain sinners (and sheer empirical evidence establishes the point). Nor can this text be appropriated to say that Christians have been given a new heart, and that it is getting better and better, whether steadily or sporadically; the new heart in this text is a gift that enables full faithfulness from the moment of "implantation." This text will be fully fulfilled, it would seem, only in the new heaven and the new earth. At least one implication of this understanding of the text may be suggested. Expectations for Christian faith and life on the basis of this text should not be set out in such an ideal way that life is reduced to striving, to a preoccupation with one's spiritual temperature, or to setting people up for certain failure or discouragement. The new heart will be a gift from God in God's own good time.

NOTE

[1] See G. Keown, P. Scalise, and T. Smothers, *Jeremiah 26–52* (Dallas: Word Books, 1993), 160.

RESTORATION AND
SECURE PROMISES

33:1-26

This chapter is closely linked to chapter 32 by its reference to a second word from the Lord received by Jeremiah while he was confined in the court of the guard (see 32:2) and Babylon's armies threatened the city of Jerusalem (about 588 BC). At the same time, these two chapters bear witness to a time subsequent to the destruction of Jerusalem (32:43; 33:10, 12). Hence, the time of the exilic readers has been integrated into a time before the fall of Jerusalem. Both chapters are thus to be read in light of the fall and exile. [A Future for Exilic Readers]

This chapter is also linked to chapters 30–31 as it describes in greater detail the restoration of the people to a renewed land. The links between 31:31-37 are especially evident in the themes of forgiveness of sin (cf. 31:34 with 33:8) and the appeal to the covenant with Noah (cf. 31:35-37 with 33:19-26). Even if not an original part of the Book of Consolation (30:2), this placement integrates the chapter into that orbit in the present form of the text.

The chapter is usually divided into two segments, vv. 1-13 and vv. 14-26.

A Future for Exilic Readers

Set as they are during Jeremiah's imprisonment, chs. 32–33 reveal a fundamental irony; God's words about freedom and spaciousness are voiced in the midst of restriction and confinement. Jeremiah's life situation thus symbolizes that of the exilic readers. They will hear these promises of freedom and new life in comparably restrictive circumstances. This word is thus not unlike that which Moses brings to the Israelites in Egypt, except that the exiles are themselves responsible for their predicament. Such a promise about freedom, if it would be truly life changing, will need to include a word about forgiveness if they would be truly free (see 33:8). This material bears witness to a positive future for the Israelites *within God* even as they were going through all the terrors of the fall of Jerusalem and its aftermath. God's plans for their future was thus not some "second thought" on God's part on the far side of that event; *God had this future in place before the fall had even occurred.* God's promises thus span these events and they carry the people through this valley of death and exile when they had no resources to assure their own future.

The first focuses on the people and their re-created life setting. The second focuses on their leaders, members of the levitical priesthood and of the Davidic line. The latter segment is not found in the LXX, the longest such continuous passage in Jeremiah (see **Introduction**). This may suggest its secondary status in terms of the formation of the book; yet, it has an important place in the present form of Jeremiah.

Unlike chapter 32, Jeremiah plays no personal role in this chapter, except as a recipient of the word of the Lord (vv. 1, 19, 23).

COMMENTARY

Forgiveness and Restoration, 33:1-13

These verses consist of several related divine oracles filling out the content of the restoration of Israel to its own land. One concern focuses on the specific spaces—homes, streets, towns, pasture-lands—which a restored Israel will occupy upon its return. The portrayal is sketched in terms of a recreation of that which is orderly, secure, abundant, good, and even green. As with 32:17, 27, this future is grounded in the activity of God as Creator. At the same time, this divine re-creative activity is not confined to external spaces. An internal healing will also occur as God forgives Israel's sin; this healing will show itself in the return of the normal rhythms of life and worship.

The meaning of the Hebrew of vv. 2-5 is somewhat uncertain (see NRSV footnotes). The translation "earth" in v. 2 (following the LXX) connects well to what precedes (31:35-37; 32:17, 19-20, 27) and to what follows (especially 33:20, 25; see also Amos 9:5-6). God identifies himself in v. 2 as the creator of the earth, the one who "gave it form and firmness" (so NAB). The verbs "make" and "form" are both used in the Genesis creation stories (e.g., 1:26; 2:7). This divine self-identification as the one who establishes the earth connects well to the content of vv. 1-13, which speak of the rebuilding of Jerusalem and the re-creation of the desolate land without inhabitant, human or animal. [God the Creator]

God the Creator

God's work in the restoration of Israel on its renewed land is made parallel to God's creative work in Genesis 1, which moves from desolateness to a green and inhabited earth/land. Though the devastation wrought by the Babylonians would appear to undo the creative work of God, the uninhabited wasteland that they effected (v. 10) is only a temporary state of affairs. God remains the Creator and, in the face of Israelite sin and Babylonian power, God will heal its creatures and restore their living spaces. The salvation that God will effect is not an end in itself, but stands in the service of a new creation!

God invites Jeremiah to ask God (!) for further revelation regarding the matters under consideration (v. 3), and God will reveal to him things that had been heretofore hidden or inaccessible to him (so also Isa 48:6; see Gen 18:17-19; Amos 3:7; John 16:12-15). Note that what God is about to do for Israel is not dependent on Jeremiah's (or Israel's) acceptance of the invitation; God's impending actions on behalf of Israel are not conditional. This invitation relates to gaining the *knowledge* of God and God's ways; it is not a call to faith in order to participate in God's salvific deeds. That the word "inaccessible" can also be translated "fortified" nicely connects this invitation to the subject of building a secure Jerusalem that follows. This invitation to Jeremiah is remarkable from several perspectives, not least that God proceeds to declare the divine intentions quite apart from Jeremiah's taking up the call (see **Connections: On Gaining Further Knowledge of God**).

The details of vv. 4-5 are unclear in Hebrew, though the basic point is evident; they describe the devastating experience from which God will deliver Israel and its common life. Initially, the focus is on the homes and palaces that have been destroyed in an effort to protect the city. This point is recognized in the NRSV by the colon at the end of v. 4 (the NIV placement of the colon at the end of the first clause of v. 5, "in the fight with the Babylonians," is even clearer). The elements in vv. 4-5 are used to explain why housing was such an important issue to be addressed on behalf of returning exiles. The destruction of Israelite houses and even palaces was necessary to get materials to mount the walls and defend against the siege (see 21:3-4; 32:24).

Moreover, these destroyed houses were defiled by the dead bodies of defenders; they were left where they fell (in view of the loss of access to burial sites). As v. 10 notes, Jerusalem and other towns are an utter wasteland, without inhabitant. [A Comprehensive Healing]

The other element in vv. 4-5 that sets up the following verses is the portrayal of Israel's God. In language comparable to 32:29-32, the wrath of God because of Israel's wickedness stands front and center (v. 5); at the same time, God's "striking" is mediated by the Babylonians. Notably, the reference to "anger and wrath" is followed by a phrase unique in Jeremiah, "for I have hidden my face from this city" (Isa 54:8; 64:6; note the theme of hiddenness in v. 3, though a different Hebrew word is used). The *hiding* of God's face leads to anger and wrath.

A Comprehensive Healing

Given the extent of the death and devastation, what kind of future would be possible? The images of vv. 4-5 serve to set off the wonder of the promises that follow in vv. 6-9; the cities will once again be teeming with people and animals, and life in its everyday normalcy will be reinstated. These promises relate to the "healing" of the destroyed city and its houses as well as those who dwell in them. Healing or salvation is thus understood in a comprehensive sense; it encompasses all of life, and not just bodily, psychical, or spiritual healing. The future thus envisaged relates to concrete, everyday life, not some apocalyptic vision of that which lies beyond earthly times and places. The promised future does not consist of a life discontinuous with the past; the future is sketched in terms of a return to normal life as they have known it at its best.

There is thus a certain indirection with respect to the divine anger; the anger is manifest not because of an intensification of divine presence (as we normally think of human anger) but because of a less intense divine presence. It is when God removes himself from the scene (though never fully or actually absent) that the anger is manifest (on anger and wrath, see **Connections**, ch. 25).

The New City in the New Testament

The new city in these Jeremiah texts becomes a New Testament theme, though there recast in apocalyptic terms (see Rev 3:12; 21; Heb 11:10; 12:22; Gal 4:26; cf. Ezek 40–48). In these texts the city is understood in terms that are more than simply a rebuilding of old ruins, that is, a new city on the same site; a genuinely new creation is in view that exceeds all earthly expectations and bursts its old boundaries. Yet, even in these texts the language speaks of a new heaven and a new earth, and hence something other than an otherworldly vision is in view. The new city remains an earthly reality, not a heavenly one, for it comes down from heaven as a divine gift. It is remarkable that this new creation is no simple return to the Garden of Eden. The new creation differs from the original creation in Gen 1–2 in several ways, not least that human designs and constructions give shape to the vision. In that regard, the new city promised in Jeremiah provides a decisive point of continuity with the New Testament vision.

In vv. 6-13, the promises of God pour forth with respect to the future of the exiles and their dwelling places. Some of these promises refer specifically to the destroyed buildings and city (the "it" and "them" in v. 6 refer to the city and its houses), but in context they take on a comprehensive meaning for the people more generally (e.g., the building metaphor in v. 7). That is, just as in 32:36-44, both internal and external dimensions of the future of the exiles are portrayed. The language of the restoration of fortunes is comparably broad (vv. 7, 11, 26; see 29:14; 30:3, 18; 31:23; 32:44). A remarkably holistic conception of restoration pervades these texts; this perspective is set by the introductory creation language and highlights a view that often stands over against certain spiritualized understandings of salvation present in the Christian community.

Many of the key themes from previous chapters are gathered here and applied to both people and their cities/houses. One important metaphor is (re)building (v. 7), drawn from the call of Jeremiah (1:10) and from the earlier oracles of restoration referring to both people and buildings (30:18; 31:4, 28, 38). Both the people and their city and its devastated houses are to be restored (see Ezek 48:30-35; Isa 65:17-19). [The New City in the New Testament]

Another metaphor used in this text is healing; though applied to the city and its houses in v. 6, it has a broader meaning, related as it is to prior oracles (30:17; see also 3:22) and earlier cries for healing (8:15, 22; 15:18; 17:14; 30:13). The move from dead bodies and defilement to healing and cleansing is a remarkable leap into the future. The word translated "recovery" (NRSV, v. 6) is translated "health" in 30:17 and again refers to both personal healing (see 8:22; Isa 58:8) and to (re)building (see Neh 4:1; 2 Chr 24:13; see [A Comprehensive Healing]).

The phrase "reveal to them abundance of prosperity and security" (NRSV) contains several key words (the word translated "abundance" is of uncertain meaning). The verb *gālāh* ("reveal") can also mean "to go into exile"; this is probably a play on words, having the sense of "recover" of that which was lost in the exile. The words for "prosperity" and "security" are, respectively, *šālôm* (peace, welfare; see v. 9; 29:11; 30:5) and *'emet* (in this context, a synonym for *betah*, "security," 23:6; 32:37; this word is used for divine faithfulness in 32:41). For a people in exile who had lost everything and who had not known safety or security in recent years, these words speak directly to their most pressing needs and desires. The false prophets had promised *šālôm* (6:14; 8:11; 23:17) but such a "peace" would become available to the people only on the far side of destruction and exile.

Still another theme used in this text is forgiveness; v. 8 seems almost overloaded with its emphasis on this work of God. This theme expands upon the theme of the new and everlasting covenant in 31:31-34 and 32:39-40 (cf. 24:7); the new heart will have continuity with the "old" heart, for forgiveness assumes continuity between old and new. The three key Hebrew words for guilt/sin/rebellion are used here five times (*'āwôn*; *hāta'*; *pāša'*), as if to make sure that every transgression is covered by God's forgiving action! Even those just listed in 32:29-35. The verbs to cleanse and forgive are both used, perhaps to look at God's action from both priestly and prophetic perspectives (see Ezek 36:25-27). The theme of forgiveness is central to the oracle of the new covenant (31:34; see also 50:20). It is also used in earlier divine laments (5:1, 7; cf. 36:3), as was the theme of cleansing (13:27), when God himself wonders when Israel would be made clean. That is all now about to change. [Here Comes Joy!]

Verse 9 describes the changed situation of the city *for God* on the far side of the divine restoration of Israel. The issue here is not so much the change in the city itself as to what effect its restoration will have on the divine reputation among the nations (see the arguments of Moses in Exod 32:12; Num 14:13-19). The name of the city (see v. 16) will reflect the joy, praise, and glory of God out to *all* these nations (see 32:20 and the comparable sense in God's having "made yourself a name"; 13:11; Deut 26:19; Ezek 36:22-23). Earlier the city was abhorred by the nations because it had been devastated in judgment (22:8-9;

Here Comes Joy!

God will do for Israel and Judah what they cannot do for themselves: make them qualified for God's good gifts and powerful presence…The outcome of God's resolve and God's action is the rehabilitation of Jerusalem. The city had become a place of grief and wretchedness, and now comes joy! It had become a place of shame and humiliation, and now comes glory and splendor! The action of God makes an utterly new Jerusalem.

Walter Brueggemann, *A Commentary on Jeremiah: Exile and Homecoming* (Grand Rapids: Eerdmans, 1998), 314-15.

Bonhoeffer's Use of 33:9

Dating from May, 1944, Dietrich Bonhoeffer's "Thoughts on the Day of the Baptism of Dietrich Wilhelm Rudiger Bethge" contain several references to Jeremiah, including 33:9: "It is not for us to prophesy the day (though the day will come) when men will once more be called so to utter the word of God that the world will be changed and renewed by it. It will be a new language, perhaps quite non-religious, but liberating and redeeming—as was Jesus' language; it will shock people and yet overcome them by its power; it will be the language of a new righteousness and truth. 'They shall fear and tremble because of all the good and all the prosperity I provide for it' (Jer. 33:9). Till then the Christian cause will be a silent and hidden affair, but there will be those who pray and to write and wait for God's own time."

Dietrich Bonhoeffer, *Letters and Papers from Prison* (London: SCM, 1971), 300.

25:9; 30:17). But now, when they hear of "all the good" and "all the good and prosperity" (on the creational theme of goodness, see at 32:39-42) that God will do on behalf of the city, they will fear and tremble. When Israel's restoration takes place, the nations will gain a new perspective on Israel's God. Given the context of joy and praise, the fear and trembling may be out of joy (see 31:9; Isa 60:5) rather than out of terror. Though in view of texts that speak of judgment on the nations (30:11, 23-24), the latter may be correct (see Isa 64:2). Perhaps both meanings are in view. [Bonhoeffer's Use of 33:9]

Verses 10-13 are somewhat repetitive, but this may be explained in part by the structure of the passage. The content of God's quotation of the people in v. 10a (already quoted in 32:43) regarding the devastation in Jerusalem (in effect, "this place is desolate compared to what it used to be") is affirmed by God by being repeated in v. 10b. The repeated "without" (five times in Hebrew!) stresses that the city is utterly bereft of any living thing.

This same point regarding "without" is repeated in v. 12, but has a different focus. The quotation of the people in v. 10a refers to two devastated realities, namely, humans and animals. Verses 10c-11 pick up on the restoration of *human* activity in Jerusalem and elsewhere; vv. 12-13 focus on the *animal* world and speak of its restoration and of the pasture on which to feed.

In both of these cases, the geographical reference is important. It is specifically noted that the people will be restored to familiar city streets and rural towns. At the same time, the animals will be restored to all the familiar pasture lands and placed under the care of responsible shepherds who will keep track of each one of them (v. 13; cf. 32:44 for the list of places, which is intended to refer to the entire land). Given the imagery of the shepherd for Israel's leaders (see 23:1-4), the image here may move beyond specific reference to the animal world to include human beings (see Ps 23:1;

Ezek 34:1-31; the New Testament picks up on this theme in Luke 15:3-7; John 10:1-18). The cities and lands that are entirely "without" living things will once again become places that are alive with creatures, both animal and human, and they will live under the leadership of shepherds who truly are concerned for those under their care.

The restoration of human activity stresses joy, singing, and thankfulness (vv. 10-11; see 31:4, 13). The divine judgment included the banishment of the everyday activities that made for gladness in the community, not least the weddings (so 7:34; 16:9; 25:10). Now all those joyful voices and the songs of thanksgiving will "once more" be heard ("as at the first," vv. 7, 11). This renewed joyful singing will occur both in common life and in religious life; the psalms of lament will become psalms of praise. Moreover, people will bring their thank-offerings to a restored temple (see 17:26; Lev 7:11-18), no doubt in gratitude for all the renewed blessings they will receive. In doing so, they will a sing a song of thanksgiving (a quotation from Pss 107:1; 136:1) that praises God for all of God's goodness and steadfast love. In Ezra 3:11 the returned exiles do in fact sing this song.

Israel Lives with Secure Promises, 33:14-26

These related oracles of salvation begin (vv. 14-16) with a virtual repetition of the oracle in 23:5-6; vv. 17-26 may be considered a later expansion of that oracle for a specific situation (exile?). Because this entire segment is missing in the LXX, it is often considered a late addition to the book and inauthentic to the basic character of Jeremiah's prophecy (see Introduction). But the editors who included these verses obviously thought otherwise. The upshot of these oracles is that God honors the covenants made with Israel's royal and priestly leadership and, as promised long before, will do so forever. Note that both socio-political and socio-religious leaders are treated together as part and parcel of a holistic community. The king will execute "justice and righteousness" (v. 15) and the priest will minister "in my presence" with the appropriate offerings (including sin offerings presumably, see 31:30).

Verse 14 refers back to the promise made to Israel and Judah (in 23:5-6), stating that God will fulfill that promise (lit. "the good word"). Then the promise is restated with some changes in detail (see Introduction for repetitions in Jeremiah). God will raise up a righteous branch (see at 23:5) for David who, unlike the kings throughout Israel's sorry history, will execute justice and righteousness (see 30:9; the similar language in Isa 11:1-5; the phrase "and he shall reign as king and deal wisely" in 23:5 is omitted here). Then, while "Judah will be saved" is retained, it is Jerusalem rather than Israel that will "live in safety." Moreover, while the Davidic king is named "the LORD is our righteousness" in 23:6, in v. 16 it is the city of Jerusalem that will be so named (as in Ezek 48:35). These changes suggest that the restoration of Jerusalem is the primary concern in this text (as in vv. 1-13), and the question of the future of Israel (the northern kingdom) is taken care of by the opening reference to the fulfillment of the former promise to Israel (23:5-6). It is not clear whether the name change for Jerusalem is now a substitute for the name change for the Davidic king, or whether both are in view given the opening word in v. 14 about the fulfillment of the former promise.

The expansion of the opening oracle comes in three parts, each introduced by a formulaic word from the Lord (vv. 17-18, 19-22, 23-26). Each of these parts in their own way makes the same point: God is bound to the covenants with David and with the Levites and God will not back away from those commitments, come what may. [Covenants in Relationship]

Covenants in Relationship

Just how these perpetual covenants to David and the Levites are to be related to the new covenant of 31:31-34 or the everlasting covenant of 32:40 is not altogether clear. But, at the least, the covenants with Abraham (see ch. 30), David, and the Levites are statements that affirm the continuity in the divine commitment to Israel through the fall of Jerusalem and the exile. And so the new, everlasting covenant does not set these other covenants aside; that shift pertains only to the Sinai covenant. This text thus signals a new way that the people of the new covenant are to understand themselves within the framework of these continuing, promissory covenants.

Verses 17-18 introduce the promise in general terms regarding the royal and priestly lines (on the dual priestly and royal families in the post-exilic period, see Zech 4:11-13; 6:9-13). First of all, a member of the Davidic line will always be available to occupy the throne of "Israel," which at this point must refer to a united land (the same language is used for the Davidic king in 1 Kgs 2:4; 8:25; 9:5, but without the conditional clauses). This understanding makes a temporal point that was not clear in the promise of v. 15, namely, the Davidic kingship will stand forever (as was stated in the original covenant promises in 2 Sam 7:14-16; see 1 Sam 23:3; Ps 89:3-4).

Second, a member of the levitical line will be available "for all time" to present the various offerings and sacrifices (see v. 11). The phrase "in my presence" seems to assume the rebuilding of the temple as the dwelling place of God among the people (see v. 11). While a perpetual priesthood has not been previously promised to all Levites (see Deut 18:1-18), a perpetual covenant was promised to the priests of the house of Aaron within the levitical family

(Num 25:10-13; see also Exod 29:9; 40:15). That may account for the phrase "levitical priests," yet Ezekiel's specific reference to the Zadokite family as the "levitical priests" may be mind here (Ezek 40:46; 43:19; 44:15; 48:11).

The second segment (vv. 19-22) grounds the covenant promises to David and the Levites in God's covenant with Noah that "day and night shall not cease" (Gen 8:21-22; see 9:8-17). If anyone could break that covenant, and that is impossible because it is an unconditional covenant to which (only) God is bound, then God would break the covenants with David and with the Levites (or house of Aaron). In other words, with God these promises are a sure thing. Then a second, related promise is made to David and the Levites, namely, that their offspring will increase. This promise, too, is grounded in creational realities (see 31:35-37). This promise is just as certain as it is impossible to number the stars or measure the sands of the sea (see Gen 15:5; 22:17; 32:12 and the link back to the promises to Abraham, Isaac, and Jacob in v. 26; see also 30:3; 32:22). The point is not that their offspring will be as numerous as the sand/stars, but that the increase of their offspring is as certain as the impossibility of counting the sand/stars.

The third segment (vv. 23-26) continues the linkage between the promise and creational realities, only this time the context is polemical. God asks Jeremiah to observe how certain people are making disparaging comments about Israel, and this in two respects. On the one hand, they claim that God has rejected the "two families" (probably royal and priestly families given the context, though some interpreters consider this a reference to Israel and Judah). On the other hand, they hold "my people" in contempt and without national stature because their God has rejected them and driven them into exile and landlessness. The future of leaders and people are tied together. "These people" are unidentified but they are probably other nations (see v. 9) or the Babylonians among whom the people of God were exiled (see 22:8-9 for the sophisticated assessment on the part of the nations); the words are general enough to fit any situation.

In the face of this contempt, God reiterates the promises. This time, however, the Levites are left aside, and the entire people of Israel ("offspring of Jacob"; "the offspring of Abraham, Isaac, and Jacob") join the members of the Davidic line as the recipient of God's sure and certain promises. The promissory reference to the entire people refers back to the promises of 31:35-37. Yet, the promises to the pre-Sinai "ancestors" may also be in mind given the triad Abraham, Isaac, and Jacob; this is the only such reference in

Jeremiah (yet, see the reference to the "ancestors" in 11:5; 30:3; 32:22 and the images in v. 22). This time the grounding of the promise in creation is somewhat more expansive. The sure and certain creational realities are no longer simply the covenant with "day and night" (see v. 20), but also the covenant with "the ordinances of heaven and earth." In view of 31:35-37 (see also Ps 89:36-37) these "ordinances" may refer to all the other orders of creation (Gen 1). In the face of those who would claim that Israel's election has been forfeited (v. 24), these ongoing promises are articulated. Destruction and exile are external signs that may suggest to observers that Israel is no longer the chosen of God; but external realities in fact mask God's continuing commitments to this people. The offspring of Israel from every future generation can count on these promises come what may, even something as horrid as another destruction and exile.

It is interesting to note that God refers to David as "my servant" three times in this section (vv. 21-22, 26). Notably, God also refers to King Nebuchadrezzar as "my servant" (25:9; 27:6; 43:10), as well the prophets (25:4; 26:5; 29:19; 35:15; 44:4) and the people as a whole (30:10; 46:27-28). The Levites, on the other hand, are referred to as "my ministers" (at the altar). To use the language of servanthood for the members of the Davidic line keeps their place clear in relationship to other servants of God, including a pagan king. The Davidic kings are God's servants as are many others, and they must not elevate themselves to a place above those whom they are called to serve (see Deut 17:14-20; on the ideal kingship, see Ps 72).

The final note in the chapter reiterates the familiar refrain about God's restoring Israel's fortunes (e.g., v. 11). But this time, a note is added, "I will have mercy upon them" (as at 31:20). This added note links up with the reiteration of the promises. That is, God's promises are not just associated with a reversal of political fortunes and the restoration to the land; they have to do with the extended future of this people which will marked by an ongoing experience of the mercy of God.

CONNECTIONS

On Gaining Further Knowledge of God

In v. 3 God invites Jeremiah to ask for more light to be shed on these matters related to the restoration. In other words, God desires to reveal more to the prophet, even "great and hidden things." God does not want to keep people ignorant of God's ways in the world. Yet, God will not force that word on people; the further revelation is said to be dependent upon the human initiative of asking for it. And Jeremiah has not been particularly reticent in God's presence!

Such an invitation calls for participation in a conversation; it calls for a genuine interest in further knowledge; it calls for human boldness before God rather than self-effacement. The people of God who want to know more about what God is about in the world are invited to ask. [Moses as Pray-er] That this invitation is generally applicable for future reference seems evident in that God proceeds to speak without waiting for Jeremiah to ask at this particular moment (see John 16:13 for the Holy Spirit being given to lead God's people into all the truth). God's reference to hiding his face in wrath (v. 5) is a statement about the past; God will now reveal that which has been hidden because of the people's wickedness.

Moses as Pray-er

The book of Exodus provides a comparable word about divine revelation, especially in the dialogues between Moses and God. Moses' ongoing interaction with God is remarkable in that his persistence "occasions a greater fullness in the divine revelation. Human questions find an openness in God and lead to fuller knowledge. God thus reveals himself, not simply at the divine initiative, but in interaction with a questioning human party. Simple deference or passivity in the presence of God would close down the revelatory possibilities . . . . God has so entered into relationship with him that God is not the only one who has something important to say." God does not demand a self-effacing Moses, but draws him out and interacts with him for the sake of fuller knowledge about God and God's ways.

Terence Fretheim, *Exodus* (IBC; Louisville: Westminster/John Knox, 1991), 52-53

ANNOUNCEMENTS OF JUDGMENT TO ZEDEKIAH AND ISRAEL

34:1-22

The chapter begins with an oracle of judgment against King Zedekiah (vv. 1-7) and concludes with an oracle of judgment against Jerusalem for breaking the covenant made regarding the release of their slaves (vv. 8-22).

This chapter is something of a jolt for the reader who has been bathed in oracles of salvation through much of the previous four chapters. This chapter is a "back to reality" sketch. It is a sharp reminder once again (see ch. 32) that the announced restoration will occur only after destruction and exile. Still further reasons are given here as to why king and people must pass through this judgment prior to that promised future. True to form, they are not even able to follow through on their own good intentions, seen in their reversal of their initial covenant to release slaves according to the law (vv. 8-11).

This chapter may have been placed at this point because it is set during the final stages of Nebuchadrezzar's conquest of Israel (vv. 1, 7), as were chapters 32–33, though this chapter probably reflects an earlier time (34:21 speaks of a temporary Babylonian withdrawal; see 37:5; 52:4).

The reader will also notice considerable similarity between 32:1-5 and 34:1-7 (see also 21:1-10); both sections speak of a confrontation between Jeremiah and Zedekiah in which his fate and that of Jerusalem are announced in comparable terms. In 32:1-5, however, Zedekiah confronts Jeremiah with a prophecy that had been reported to him; in 34:1-7 Jeremiah gives him such a word directly (v. 6) after having been commanded by God to do so. This is the only time that God takes the initiative to communicate with the king (vv. 2-5). It seems likely that 34:1-7 (when Jeremiah is not yet imprisoned) occurred before 32:1-5 and that the latter is Zedekiah's confrontation of Jeremiah regarding the announcement reported here (and for which Jeremiah may have been imprisoned). The additional word regarding Zedekiah's death in peace and a suitable burial (34:4-5) is not reported by Zedekiah in 32:1-5.

COMMENTARY

Judgment Pronounced Against Zedekiah, 34:1-7

The chapter begins on an ominous note. The attack against Jerusalem and "all" Israel's cities is being undertaken not simply by "all" the Babylonian armies and "all" the peoples under their control, but "all" the "kingdoms of the earth" (v. 1; cf. the "all" in 27:6-7)! At first glance, this seems to have reference to all the nations that were a part of the Babylonian empire, but the language used is more global (all the kingdoms of the earth). Hyperbolically speaking, the entire world is arrayed against Israel! In such a situation, of course, Israel's resistance would be futile, and that seems to be the basic point being made. Given this rhetoric, v. 7 is not contradictory; it simply speaks of the military situation in more specific and realistic terms, where "all the cities" of v. 1 have been narrowed down to two that are still standing. [Lachish and Azekah (34:7)]

Into this situation God commands Jeremiah to announce a word of judgment against Zedekiah; all other encounters with the king are initiated by an inquiry from Zedekiah (32:2-5; 37:3-10, 17-21; 38:14-28; cf. 21:1-7). As noted above, vv. 2-3 essentially repeat

Lachish and Azekah (34:7)

Lachish was a walled, fortified city about thirty miles southwest of Jerusalem. Azekah was also a fortified city, northeast of Lachish. Among the ruins of Lachish were found several letters written on pottery fragments that are dated shortly before the fall of Jerusalem. In one letter, a sentinel outside of Lachish writes to its military commander: "We are looking for the signals of Lachish, according to all the indications my lord has given, because we do not see Azekah." This suggests that Azekah has already been taken by the Babylonians and that the sentinel wonders about the fate of Lachish.

Tower with Defenders. Assyrians attack the Jewish fortified town of Lachish (701 BC). Detail of a relief from the palace of Sennacherib at Ninevah, Mesopotamia. British Museum, London. (Credit: Erich Lessing/Art Resource, NY)

A Siege Ramp at Work

This low relief from an Assyrian king's palace reveals a siege ramp raised against the Israelite city of Lachish. Depth is conveyed through the "piling" of objects above the siege, indicating that they are to the left of the object. These reliefs frequently decorated the exterior walls of the palace to indicate the king's prowess and successes against formidable foes.

(Right) Detail of the Assyrian conquest of Lachish. Palace of Sennacherib at Niniveh, Mesopotamia. British Museum, London. (Credit: Erich Lessing/Art Resource, NY)

Siege ramp at Lachish. (Credit: Mitchell G. Reddish)

32:3-5a, adding the note about the city being burned with fire (so also v. 22; a theme present elsewhere, e.g., 21:10, and reported in 52:13). That Zedekiah does meet the king of Babylon "eye-to-eye" is reported in 39:5-7, with the ironic result that, having seen his sons killed, his eyes are put out (cf. 21:7).

Verses 4-5 abruptly add a more positive note about Zedekiah's death and burial that stands in no little tension with vv. 2-3 (which presents an unconditional fate for Jerusalem and Zedekiah). This more positive fate seems not to be conditioned by anything he does. The "yet, but, only" and the command to "hear" at the beginning of v. 4 has suggested to some scholars that a condition may be present (and would then bring these verses into conformity with the condition stated in 38:17-18 and probably 21:7-10). Yet, the word he is commanded to hear in vv. 4-5 is a promise (and nothing is required of him in vv. 2-3), and the conditional element, if it is assumed, is not certainly presented in a straightforward way.

Zedekiah is promised that he will die in peace and will be given a proper burial with spices as with earlier kings (2 Chr 16:14; though Jeremiah's disparaging remarks about Jehoiakim's burial in 22:18-19 suggest that at least he is not counted among these "earlier kings"). When his time comes, however, Zedekiah is blinded and exiled to Babylon, where he dies in prison (see 39:5-7; 52:8-11), a less than literal fulfillment of this word. But this is not unusual in Hebrew prophecy (e.g., cf. 2 Kgs 22:20 with 23:29 on the fulfillment of the prophetic word about King Josiah). Even so, the promise made to Zedekiah stands out for its uneven relationship to other words about him.

Jeremiah follows through on God's command and speaks these words to King Zedekiah. Verse 7 notes that he did this when the Babylonians were putting a great deal of pressure on the cities near Jerusalem; only two of "all the cities" (see v. 1) were still standing. This provides a setting of no little urgency for Jeremiah's visit. The word about Zedekiah in vv. 2-3 is picked up again in v. 21 in connection with the violation of the covenant to liberate slaves; but it should be noted that vv. 8-22 nowhere speak of Zedekiah as in violation of the covenant that he himself made with the people.

Judgment on Israel for Mistreatment of Slaves, 34:8-22

The relationship between this segment and the prior verses is not altogether clear. No activity on the part of Zedekiah in this segment would reflect poorly on him (even though the judgment of vv. 2-3 is picked up in part in v. 21). This text may be yet another "case study" of Israel's unfaithfulness, perhaps contrasted with the fidelity of the Rechabites in chapter 35.[1] The people's violation of a specific sworn covenant (with King Zedekiah!) is one more symptom of their inability to keep their covenant with *God* (cf. 17:19-27 and the announcement of judgment for the breaking of Sabbath laws). In relationship to the preceding Book of Consolation, 34:8-22 demonstrates that God's covenantal commitment in those salvation oracles, marked by the return of a genuinely free people, is guaranteed in a way that Israel's covenantal commitments have not been throughout their history (see 33:14-26). But even more seems to be at stake (see **Connections: Slavery and Exodus**).

This word of God to Jeremiah, though announced in v. 8, is not actually begun until v. 13 and then, having been reintroduced

(v. 12), continues to the end of the chapter (cf. the similar strategy in 32:1-6). And, even then, Jeremiah is not commanded to speak these words to anyone, though the direct address ("you") in vv. 13-17 (vv. 18-22 are in third person) implies that they were meant to be spoken to the people. Before God's words are given to Jeremiah, the situation to which this word of God pertains is sketched (vv. 8-11). The word of God, typically, is shaped specifically for this particular moment in the life of the people. God's word reviews these actions on the part of the people from a somewhat different perspective in vv. 15-16.

King Zedekiah had made a covenant with "all" the people of Jerusalem (in the temple, v. 15; cf. the making of a covenant by King Josiah in 2 Kgs 23:3). Notably, God's making covenant with Israel's ancestors (v. 13) is set alongside Zedekiah's making covenant (v. 8), which God in turn refers to as "my covenant" in v. 18. That Zedekiah initiated this covenant suggests that he was motivated by a concern to obey God's covenant and in magnanimous terms (might he even have been motivated by Jeremiah's positive word to him in vv. 4-5?).

The terms of the covenant to which "all the people in Jerusalem" agreed (even if they were not slave-owners!) was that "all" officials and people would liberate their male and female Hebrew slaves— no exceptions!—and, making a key point, would never enslave them again. The inclusion of every slave may be an allusion to the exodus when all Israel was freed from slavery. Readers are informed in v. 16 that the slaves desired their freedom and God calls the slaves "neighbors and friends" in v. 17, which is in line with the word of the covenant in v. 9 that "no one should hold another Judean in slavery." Remarkably, given the history of disobedience, every slave-owner agrees and they set all their (Hebrew) slaves free (vv. 8-10).

The people's obedience, however, is short-lived, and this may well be one of the key points made. They "turn around" (vv. 11, 16; *šûb*) from their "recent repentance" (v. 15; *šûb*) and "take back" (vv. 11, 16; hiph. of *šûb*) their slaves. This play on the word *šûb* suggests that the problem fundamentally pertains to the issue of repentance (the verb *šûb* is used again in v. 22, where God will "bring back" the Babylonians because the slave-owners had "taken back"). The slaves are being "jerked around" by this fickle people; they are liberated one minute only to be re-enslaved in the next (the text betrays no interest in the logistical issue of how all those slaves could have been located and returned to slavery). In this action, the people prove unfaithful to the covenants of both God

On Slavery and Modern Culture

"We have seen it repeatedly. Nothing is more straitly insisted on in Jeremiah (or, for that matter, in the prophets across the board) than the connection between moral irresponsibility and the collapse of a culture. Including a religion absorbed by the culture." At the same time, at least regarding the institution of slavery, it might be said that the attitudes and practices of the larger culture have had no little positive impact on our thinking about the enslavement of human beings. It must not be forgotten, however, that racism continues to be a reality deeply embedded in our societies. Even more, it must be admitted that the lack of a clear biblical witness against slavery (and the not uncommon use of the Bible to ground the practice) has had no little part to play in reinforcing racist perspectives.

Daniel Berrigan, *Jeremiah: The World, the Wound of God* (Minneapolis: Fortress, 1999), 151.

Earl Wilton Richardson (1768–1848). *Employment of Negros in Agriculture*. 1934. Oil on canvas. 32"x48". Smithsonian American Art Museum. Washington DC. (Credit: Smithsonian American Art Museum/Art Resource, NY)

and Zedekiah; unfaithfulness to the latter is a sign of Israel's infidelity to the former. [On Slavery and Modern Culture]

Verse 14 is not a direct quotation from any of the slave laws (cf. Exod 21:1-11; Lev 25:39-46; Deut 15:1, 12-18), but its formulation is closest to Deuteronomy 15:12. The law states that all *Hebrew* slaves that had been purchased for reasons of debt and had served for six years were to be liberated. Yet, v. 9 indicates that a covenant was made to free all slaves, not just those who had been slaves for six years. One effect of this release would be a cancellation of the debts that occasioned their enslavement in the first place. These various elements have suggested to some scholars that the sabbatical year release of debts in Deuteronomy 15:1-11 has influenced the law. As such, it would function like the law of the jubilee year, which called for the emancipation of all indentured slaves (see Lev 25:10, where the word "release, liberty" is used as in vv. 8, 15, 17; cf. Ezek 46:17). Inasmuch as a special covenant was initiated by Zedekiah for this purpose, it appears that the law quoted in v. 14 had not been obeyed as a matter of course, implied in the note regarding ancestral history in v. 14b and the act of repentance in v. 15. This covenant then would be an effort to "catch up" on a long neglected practice and it may have been thought that a fair and magnanimous way to proceed would be to declare a general release.

No specific motivations are given as to why the people were unanimous in agreeing to the covenant other than that stated in v. 9. Yet, the sorry history of this people (recognized in v. 14) has made many readers of this text suspicious of their covenantal agreement. Some scholars have suggested that the law is being obeyed out of self-interest in view of the peril facing Jerusalem. Perhaps king and people thought they could placate the divine anger through obedience and repentance. It is possible to infer from v. 21 that the slave-owners take their slaves back when the Babylonians temporarily withdraw, which would raise questions about their initial sincerity in releasing them.

Yet, this direction of reflection seems to be off target, for it is *God* himself who recognizes the sincerity of this covenant; the people repented and "did what was right" (v. 15). This reference would suggest that the people's obedience was not a sham. It seems better to say that this story illustrates the inability of the people to stay with a covenant to which they have committed themselves. Some "fits and starts" of obedience are evident, but the people's infidelity is so ingrown that they again and again fall into disobedient life patterns. This is a sign of the stubbornness that has been so much a part of Jeremiah's message (see **Connections**, ch. 5).

In view of the people's violation of this covenant regarding the liberation of slaves, subjecting them again to bondage, God indicts them (v.16) and announces their judgment (vv. 17-22, "therefore"). God's announcement is prefaced by a reference to both the exodus and the covenant at Mt. Sinai (vv. 13-14), which included the law regarding liberation of slaves (see above). The virtual repetition of the indictment of the people's re-enslavement of those who had been liberated (vv. 11, 16) brackets this historical reference. As noted, this reference makes it clear that this particular breaking of covenant goes to the heart of God's saving work on Israel's behalf. Notably, God understands this act of reenslavement to be a profanation of the divine name (v. 16). By this act Israel has violated both its own history and God's own name. That is, God's name has been publicly identified with the liberation of slaves (both in the exodus and in the commitment made here); when the lives of God's people do not cohere with that identity, then they bring the name of their God into disrepute.

God's announcement in vv. 17-18 bespeaks the judgment in correspondence terms. As they have *not* done, so it shall be done to them. Because the people have not granted their slaves a release (*dᵉrôr*), they will be granted a release (*dᵉrôr*) to a familiar Jeremianic triad: sword, pestilence, and famine. Moreover, those who transgressed (lit., "passed over," '*br*) the covenant will become like those who "passed" ('*br*) through the animals in the covenant rite.[2] All the nations of the earth will regard them as a horror when this judgment takes effect (see 25:9). Notably, in this announcement God refers to the slaves as "your neighbors and friends" (lit., "brothers," as also in Lev 25:39; Deut 15:12); this designation befits the rationale given in v. 9.

The announcement of judgment is also characterized in terms of the details of the covenant rite, which functions as a metaphor, whether or not it was actually used in Zedekiah's covenant making (vv. 18-20). [Cutting a Covenant] The people who agreed to the covenant and its terms, symbolized by passing between the two parts of the calf, will themselves become like the calf. They will be killed when their city is handed over to their enemies, and they shall not receive a proper burial; rather, their bodies shall be strewn about to become food for birds and wild animals (as also in 7:33; 16:4; 19:7). Zedekiah and his officials shall also be handed over to those who want to kill them.

Cutting a Covenant

Ratification of covenants or treaties between human parties commonly involved an accompanying ritual in which the parties promised to keep the terms of the agreement. The phrase, "to make a covenant," is literally, "to cut a covenant" (so also 31:33), involved the sacrifice of animals and cutting their carcasses into two halves. Then followed an elaborate rite in which the parties to the covenant walked between the two parts of the slaughtered animal(s). In walking through the divided parts of the animal, the parties invoked on themselves a fate similar to that of the slaughtered beast(s) if they should fail to keep their word.

Gen 15:7-21 describes this covenant rite in some detail, only the covenant is unilateral. God alone walks between the spliced parts of the animal and commits himself to the covenant (=promise) regarding the gift of land to Abraham and his descendants.

Notice is given, almost offhandedly, that the Babylonians have temporarily withdrawn from the city (v. 21), perhaps because of the movement of Egyptian armies under Pharaoh Hophra (see 37:5). But at God's command they will be brought back (*šûb*); they will fight against the city, conquer it, and burn it with fire (see vv. 2-3; 32:3-4; 37:6-11). Moreover, all the towns of Judah will be devastated along with Jerusalem and will become uninhabited.

CONNECTIONS

Slavery and Exodus

The reason that the law regarding the release of slaves (see Deut 15:12-18) is used to illustrate the people's sinfulness may be

The Irony of Israel's Slave Laws

That Israelites kept slaves at all is something of an irony given their own continuing appeal to God's deliverance when they were slaves in Egypt (e.g., Deut 24:22). Given that confession, why did Israel not abandon slavery altogether? Apparently, slavery was so much a part of their larger culture, it was impossible to make such a radical move; Israel, it seems, could only make the institution more humane.

Nor did the New Testament ever get to the point where slavery was condemned (see 1 Tim 6:1-2; Titus 2:9-10), though humane treatment was encouraged (Phlm 15–16). A significant breakthrough regarding the practice of slavery has only come as recent as the 19th century, based in part on the slow but certain impact of enlightened individuals, both within and without the religious community, and leveling texts such as Gen 1:26-27 and Gal 3:28-29 (cf. Deut 5:14-15). Bible readers should not overlook that these post-biblical developments regarding slavery have proved to be more just and enlightened than was the biblical witness. Theologically, this development is a testimony to the continued work of the Spirit of God in human societies, both within and without the church.

---

evident in the explicit reference to the exodus from Egypt and God's liberation of Israel from its slavery (v. 13). By not attending to this law in particular the people are violating their own history with God. God ("I myself") had made it possible for Israel to be freed from slavery in Egypt and had made a covenant with them, which entailed a law regarding freedom for their slaves after a six-year period. This law was specifically motivated by the call to "remember that you were a slave in the land of Egypt" (Deut 15:15). Disobedience of this law on the part of the Israelites demonstrates that the exodus—God's act of freeing them when they were slaves—no longer motivates their action or shapes their lives.

This linkage to the exodus suggests that disobedience of this law regarding the treatment of slaves is *not* just one illustration among others that could have been used, as if to say that to break one law is to break them all. This law and Israel's specific covenantal commitment regarding its enforcement goes to the heart of their identity as the people of God: they were once slaves and God did not renege on a personal commitment to deliver them from slavery. Their violation of this law, together with their fickle commitment to covenants made, also demonstrates the need for a new saving act of God (see 16:14-16=23:7-8), promised in no little detail in the immediately preceding chapters. [The Irony of Israel's Slave Laws]

NOTES

[1] So Walter Brueggemann, *A Commentary on Jeremiah: Exile and Homecoming* (Grand Rapids: Eerdmans, 1998), 325.

[2] On these issues, see Patrick Miller, *Sin and Judgment in the Prophets* (Chico CA: Scholars Press, 1982).

COMMENDATION
OF THE RECHABITES

35:1-19

After several chapters set in the reign of King Zedekiah, chapter 35 reverts to the reign of King Jehoiakim (609–598 BC), some ten years earlier. Its fundamental concern is to depict the faithfulness of the Rechabites to their tradition, and is probably placed at this point to provide a contrast with the faithlessness of the citizenry of Jerusalem shown in chapter 34. Indeed, the commitment of the Rechabites is held out as a model for other Israelites (see v. 13). [The Rechabites]

The chapter is structured into two segments: (1) God's command to Jeremiah regarding the Rechabites and his execution thereof, with their response (vv. 1-11); (2) The word of God comparing the Israelites and the Rechabites, with implications drawn regarding their respective futures (vv. 12-18). This action of Jeremiah has been called

---

☐The Rechabites

Our knowledge of the Rechabites is largely based on this text and there is much uncertainty as to their identity. They are probably a small, conservative sectarian group within the larger community of faithful Yahwists. Modern readers might liken them to the Shakers or Amish. They are named after their apparent founder J(eh)onadab, son of Rechab, who lived during the reign of the northern King Jehu (842–815 BC) and supported that king's zealous reform measures (see 2 Kgs 10:15-23). He and his group advocated a radical separation from Canaanite culture and a return to the conditions of

Amish horse cart. (Credit: Photo Disc)

the wilderness wanderings (though not a "nomadic ideal") or possibly to that of the sojourning ancestors in Genesis (NRSV "reside" in v. 7 is "sojourn," used for the early ancestors, Exod 6:4).

The Rechabite concern regarding Canaanite culture was probably related to the close link that obtained between an agrarian economy and associated features of the fertility religion of Baal. They believed that to stay clear of the latter they must not become entangled in the former. This commitment included no cultivation of land, no making and drinking of wine, and no building of houses in which to live. It appears from this text, however, that in the face of the Babylonian threat they did compromise on the latter and lived in houses in Jerusalem, though they did not build them (v. 11; see "house" in v. 2).

a symbolic act. Yet, it seems not to carry any symbolic value, serving only to elicit the fidelity of the Rechabites to their tradition, which in turn serves to demonstrate the infidelity of the Israelites to their God.

COMMENTARY

God's Word Regarding the Rechabites, 35:1-11

God commissions Jeremiah to go the "house" (=household, v. 3; it refers to a dwelling in v. 2) of the Rechabites, to speak with them, to invite them to the temple, and there to offer them some wine to drink (v. 2). Jeremiah proceeds to do so and brings the entire family of Rechabites to the temple. They must have been a small group given these room arrangements. Jeremiah ushers them into the chamber of the "sons of Hanan"; this chamber is identified in relationship to the rooms of various officials, but these spaces are not otherwise known. [The Names in 35:3-4] This close specification of the room is either a witness to the authenticity of this occasion or an effort to stress the privacy that they would have in making the decision to be set before them. That this takes place in the temple emphasizes the seriousness of the occasion. Their decision would be made before the Lord.

The purpose of Jeremiah's visit is to test the faithfulness of the Rechabites to their vows not to drink wine. That this test is not gratuitous, an unwarranted intrusion into their life, may be explained by v. 11. The Rechabites had apparently compromised on one of the charges put before them by their founder, Jonadab; they were living in a house (referred to in v. 2) in Jerusalem in view of the extraordinary situation occasioned by the Babylonian threat. Hence, the test undertaken with respect to wine was to see if they had compromised in other respects (God makes reference only to wine in v. 14). [Were the Rechabites Fully Faithful?]

Jeremiah places before the Rechabites pitchers full of wine and, apparently, cups for each individual present, and invites them to have some wine. They refuse, citing the charge of the founder of their group (vv. 6b-7; Jonadab, son of Rechab): no member of this

The Names in 35:3-4

AΩ Jaazaniah, Jeremiah (not the prophet), and Habazziniah are not mentioned elsewhere (though other persons have the first two names). It is usually assumed that Jaazaniah was the head of this group. The "sons of Hanan, son of Igdaliah, man of God." The word "sons" may refer to the disciples of the otherwise unknown Hanan, "man of God" (=prophet). This phrase, commonly used of earlier prophets (cf. 1 Kgs 13:1-10), occurs only here in Jeremiah. Maaseiah may be the father of the priest Zephaniah (29:25; 37:3). Shallum is not the king (22:11), but a priestly figure. The "keeper of the threshold" (see 52:24) was probably a priestly responsibility to control entrance to the temple areas.

Were the Rechabites Fully Faithful?

The reference to the Rechabites' obedience of "all" the precepts of Jonadab in v. 18 initially sounds like a contradiction that spoils the contrast made with the Israelites. After all, they were now living in houses in Jerusalem. Yet, the point made should be recognized for what it is, namely, that life's circumstances (such as Babylonian invasions) may occasion adjustment in what it means to be obedient. In this move to live in houses, it becomes clear that the Rechabites value their lives more than an absolutely strict adherence to an external code. In view of such changed circumstances of life, the "all" stands as an appropriate statement. Beyond the dangers of invasion, the Rechabites would no doubt go back to their former style of life (we are never informed). At the same time, their apparent expansions on their leader's initial commands (vv. 6-7) suggest that there may have been some general openness with respect to the shape of their daily life.

---

family is to drink wine, build a house, plant seed or a vineyard (or even own one); rather, they are to live in tents all their days. They are to do these things in order that they may live long on the land (see [The Rechabites]).

The Rechabites proceed to make clear to Jeremiah that they have always been true to the tenets of their ancestors in every respect (vv. 8-11). At the same time, note that, while Jonadab's original command concerned only "you and your children," they expand the charge. They specify wives, sons, and daughters (note that only males are mentioned in v. 3) but add "field" to the list of prohibitions. While not conclusive, these additions suggest that they have been interpreting the meaning of Jonadab's original command in more expansive ways, even before their move to Jerusalem.

Then comes the exception, with the reason (v. 11); because of the threat of the Babylonians (and their allies, the Aramaeans) they have moved to the relatively greater safety of the city of Jerusalem. "That is why" they are living in Jerusalem. Obviously, they could not pitch tents in the city, and so they are living in houses (even then, they remain true to the command not to "build" houses). It is not unimportant that they are considered faithful even in the face of such compromises. The language of their obeying/listening (*šamaʿ*) is stressed (vv. 8, 10, 14) and becomes a key point of contrast with Jeremiah's audience, where this word is used five times to stress infidelity (vv. 13, 14, 15, 16, 17; cf. 34:14, 17) (see **Connections: On Rechabite Faithfulness and Israelite Faithlessness**).

Israelites and Rechabites Compared, 35:12-18

Having concluded the test, Jeremiah is commanded by God to speak to the citizenry of Jerusalem. Could they not learn from the Rechabites regarding what it means to be obedient to God? They have been obedient (regarding wine) to the commands of their ancestor (a human being), but Israel has not been obedient to the commands of *God*. The obedience of the Rechabites is repeatedly contrasted with the disobedience of the people (three times in vv. 14-16; see also v. 17). Even though God has been persistent in speaking to them through the prophets, urging them to repent of their evil (*ra'āh*) ways, amend their lives, and turn from the worship of other gods, they have refused (see 7:13, 24-25; 11:7-8; 18:11; 25:3-7; 29:19; 32:33).

The question addressed to the audience in v. 13 could suggest that, if they learned the lesson of the Rechabites, the announced disaster could be avoided. But the repeated reference to Israel's not heeding the word of God (vv. 14, 15, 16, 17) strongly suggests that the die is cast. The call to repentance in v. 15 (reminiscent of 7:3-5; 18:11; 26:13) is stated only in terms of this past history; it is not presented as an option to the present hearers. The question thus implies that they cannot learn the lesson after all, given the deep-seated effects of a long history of infidelity. The question in v. 13 thus becomes a new question for exilic readers. It may be possible for them to learn from this example.

This repeated indictment issues in an announcement of judgment (v. 17; "therefore"). Most basically, the people's "evil" (*ra'āh*) will issue in "disaster" (*ra'āh*).

Every "disaster" that has been announced will take place. Once again, the indictment is sounded: I have spoken, they have not listened; I have called, they have not answered (see Isa 65:1-2 for a remarkable image of this divine calling!). The Rechabites have been obedient even apart from the kind of persistent speaking and calling in which God has been involved with the Israelites. The Israelites cannot lay the blame for these disasters back on God; God has warned them again and again.

Finally, a special word from Jeremiah is given to the Rechabites (v. 18; the use of the name Jeremiah in the introduction is unusual). Because they have been obedient to "all" the precepts of their ancestor Jonadab, the Rechabites will have a descendant that stands before the Lord "for all time." We know from various sources that this group continued to exist into the post-exilic period (see also 1 Chr 2:55), but no specific information is available. Notice that the word "therefore" (v. 19), which normally introduces the announcement of judgment (see v. 17), here introduces an announcement of continued blessing—because they have obeyed/listened (v. 18). Normally, this language of standing "before the LORD" is used for priestly prerogatives in worship, but the

Rechabites were not priests. Priestly language has been appropriated to speak of the important ministry their devotion and zeal has in the service of the Lord. This commendation may reflect a concern for the place of just such a group in the exilic (or post-exilic) community of faith. That the Rechabites shall not "lack a descendant" is similar to the promise given the Davidic and priestly families in 33:17-18. [On Divine Consistency]

On Divine Consistency

Robert Carroll notes the irony that the Rechabites are given this promise for remaining faithful, while the Davidic and priestly families are given essentially the same promise even though they had been unfaithful. At the same time, it should be noted that the Rechabites no doubt also experienced all the terrors of the fall of Jerusalem (they are not mentioned again in Jeremiah); neither God's promise nor their own fidelity insulated them from the disastrous effects of this communal judgment. Faithful and unfaithful Israelites alike were caught up in these events. God's promises to the Rechabites were understood to persist in and through the experience of judgment. And so were God's promises to all Israel!

Robert Carroll, *Jeremiah* (Philadelphia: Westminster, 1986), 665.

CONNECTIONS

On Rechabite Faithfulness and Israelite Faithlessness

While the issue of fidelity is certainly front and center in this text (especially in vv. 14, 16), the faithfulness involved is of a different order than that presented in chapter 34 (and elsewhere in Jeremiah). The text emphasizes that the Rechabites have been faithful to that which has been commanded *by their ancestor Jonadab*. In fact, this point is stated *seven times*, including thrice in the word of God (vv. 6, 8, 10, 14 [twice], 16, 18)!

The Rechabites make no mention of their faithfulness to God or of obedience to the Torah, nor does God so speak in the word of contrast and commendation (vv. 13-19). The specific lack of parallel is probably intended to make the point even sharper than would a straight parallel regarding faithfulness to God. That is, if the Rechabites can be faithful in this way to the voice of another human being, how much more should Israel have listened to the voice of the Lord. They have obeyed the commands of a human being, how much more important is it for Israel to obey the commands of God. The point, finally, focuses on the honoring of commitments made, whether to other human beings or to God, and the contrast between Rechabites and Israelites in this regard. [Is the Rechabite Way of Life Commended to Readers?]

Is the Rechabite Way of Life Commended to Readers?

From the evidence we have, neither the prophet nor the book of Jeremiah espouses the Rechabites' particular way of life. That they do not do so may be an indirect argument that a life of faithfulness does not necessarily entail removing oneself from the culture of which one is a part. The chapter does not even suggest that if Israel had removed itself from the trappings of Canaanite culture in a comparable way that it might have been able to be more faithful to its God. Israel could model the faithfulness of this small community without adopting its particular "against culture" perspective.

THE SCROLLS OF JEREMIAH

36:1-32

This narrative is set in the fourth year of King Jehoiakim (v. 1; 605 BC). This was the year that King Nebuchadrezzar of Babylon defeated the Egyptians at Carchemish and threatened Israel. By 604 BC his armies had invaded the region around Jerusalem (this threat may have occasioned the fast mentioned in v. 9, but Jehoiakim seems remarkably unconcerned). The public reading of the scroll (v. 9) is dated in the ninth month of the fifth year of Jehoiakim (December, 604 BC), approximately the time that Babylon conquered Ashkelon, fifty miles from Jerusalem.

Just how this chapter is related to the overall structure of the book of Jeremiah has been much debated. Scholars have noted the similarities with chapter 26 (cf. 26:3 with 36:3). Both chapters are set in the reign of Jehoiakim and in both Jeremiah is threatened; some have concluded that they provide an inclusio for the segment chapters 26–36. Other interpreters see chapter 36 as introducing a narrative about Jeremiah's life of suffering (through ch. 45). Still others think of chapter 36 as more of a "bridge" chapter,[1] both concluding chapters 26–35 and introducing chapters 37–45. The last noted perspective is probably the better way to proceed.

This chapter has often been mined for clues to the composition of the book of Jeremiah, centered in the scrolls inscribed by Baruch (see **Introduction**). [Baruch and Jeremiah] The description of the production of the scroll is unique in the Old Testament and may give some insight into the development of other prophetic books. Though the historical basis of the chapter should not be pressed in its detail, it probably reflects some features of the origins of the book. That Deuteronomic editors have played a role in the formation of the chapter is commonly recognized (see the more formalized statements in vv. 3, 7, 29, 31), not least because of correspondences with 2 Kings 22. Similarities include the use of a written document to proclaim a word of the Lord, with the use of the formula, "Thus says the LORD" (cf. the use of *rā'āh*, "wickedness, evil"). Josiah "tears" his garments as a sign of mourning; Jehoiakim "tears" the scroll. Josiah "burns" the pagan altars, Jehoiakim "burns" the scroll. Josiah "listens" to the word of the Lord, while Jehoiakim does not. On the other hand, Josiah's

Baruch and Jeremiah

This is the first chronological reference to Baruch in the book of Jeremiah (see at 32:12-13). Baruch is usually identified as both a secretary and a companion to Jeremiah, though their precise relationship is left undefined. He was a member of a prominent Jerusalem family (his brother Seraiah was an official under Zedekiah, 51:59) and was employed as a royal scribe. The names of the two brothers appear on seals excavated near Jerusalem (see [Jeremiah and Baruch]). It is often claimed that Baruch is responsible for producing a kind of memoir of Jeremiah and the last days of Jerusalem (and beyond), yet there is no explicit indication that Baruch is responsible for writing this extensive narrative (for details, see Robert Carroll, *Jeremiah* [Philedelphia: Westminster, 1986], 665.)

Melozzo da Forli (1438–1494). *Prophet Baruch*. Detail of ceiling in sacresty. Fresco, c. 1477. Santuario della Santa Casa. Loreto, Italy. (Credit: Alinari/Art Resource, NY)

reform is not finally successful and judgment falls, as is the case with Jehoiakim's rejection of the word.[2]

Two scrolls of Baruch are mentioned in the chapter (vv. 2, 32), the second written after the first was destroyed by the king. Following God's command to Jeremiah (vv. 1-2), the first scroll is to contain oracles spoken from "the days of Josiah" (probably his call in 627 BC; the thirteenth year of Josiah according to 1:2; 25:3) to the time noted in v. 1 (605 BC). The second scroll contained "all the words" of the first scroll and added "many similar words" (36:32), which included at least the words against Jehoiakim and the certain judgment on Israel in vv. 29-31 (might it also have included this story?). The text does not state where or when Baruch completed this task.

The most fundamental point of this chapter, however, is not to specify the means by which the book of Jeremiah began to be produced (see **Connections: Spoken Word and Written Word**). Rather, its concern centers on the response to the (written) word of God on the part of the king and his officials (especially); the people's response is only incidentally portrayed (see v. 31). King

Jehoiakim rejects that word, not simply in an internal or verbal way, but through a graphic destruction of the scroll on which it was written. Destruction of a book speaks much more loudly than rejection of a word spoken. The entire self becomes involved. In relating vv. 3 and 7 (with their openness to the future) to v. 31, it would appear that it is the response of king and people to the written word that closes off the possibility that Judah and Jerusalem will be spared. Hence, one key purpose of the chapter is to show how it was that, because no one listened to this word, Israel's future was now set. The writing down of the word in a book carries with it a finality of the word therein written. [Brueggemann on the Scroll]

Yet, some positive response is reported in the chapter. The response of the king's officials is more mixed. Most of those who are named in the chapter voice their alarm and concern, urge the king to give the scroll his careful attention, and take steps to protect Jeremiah (vv. 11-19, 25). Their motivations cannot easily be discerned, but at the least they take steps that could lead to a more receptive response to the scroll. On the other hand, those individuals mentioned in v. 26 and "his servants" (v. 24, 31) side with the king in his rejection (the "servants" who are not alarmed in v. 24 seem to be distinguished from the "officials" in v. 16, though see "officials" in v. 21).

Perhaps for the sake of exilic readers, it was important to name the principals involved in this event, not least to show that Jeremiah does receive significant support. Remarkably, the announcement of judgment in the chapter focuses on the king, his offspring, and his servants because they "have dared to burn this scroll" (vv. 29-31). The people are mentioned almost incidentally in v. 31, but their fate is sealed. The king is represented as the problem and the whole populace has been dragged down with him, though without finally excusing their nonlistening response.

Though various outlines of the chapter have been suggested, it seems best to divide the chapter in these terms: vv. 1-8 (the commission

Brueggemann on the Scroll

The scroll text so dramatically actualized in Jeremiah 36 is an utterance that keeps uttering, wherever the text is made available. It is now clear that written utterance has a kind of freedom from context that spoken utterance does not. And this written utterance explodes always again in odd, energetic, and transformative ways. Such texted reality is a great and relentless enemy of silence. The community of this text has learned, many times over, that enforced silence kills (see Ps 39:1-3). All of this is evident in actual practice, without appeal to any special theory of authority for this text. The text authorizes the mute to speak, and to know what to say, in the face of life-canceling power.

Walter Brueggemann, "Texts that Linger, Words that Explode," *Theology Today* 54 (1997): 189.

Bronze scrolls. (Credit: Palestine Archeological Museum)

and writing of the scroll); vv. 9-26 (the three readings of the scroll and their aftermath); vv. 27-32 (God's response to the king's treatment of the scroll).

COMMENTARY

The Writing of the Scroll, 36:1-8

At God's command, Jeremiah requests Baruch to take a scroll and write on it all the words that he has spoken to him from the days of Josiah on. This seems to imply that Baruch has been with Jeremiah throughout this period of ministry and has heard him speak (and written the oracles down?). In v. 4 Jeremiah apparently recalls all these words for Baruch, who writes them down (probably on papyrus). Notably, it is God who wants this book written; the will of God for this moment in Israel's life is that the word of God mediated by Jeremiah is to be preserved for posterity. It is this book with its word of God that has an impact upon its readers and hearers over the course of this chapter.

According to the description in vv. 2-3, the first scroll contained oracles "spoken against Israel and Judah and all the nations" (notice that both North and South are mentioned), certainly words of indictment and announcements of judgment for the most part (though not necessarily exclusively so). These oracles are probably to be identified with those described in a general way in 25:1-14, which refers to a "book" (v. 13), which is likely to be identified with the second scroll (the first having been destroyed). Hence, a common conclusion is that this (second) scroll contained the bulk of chapters 1–25.

At the same time, v. 3 is something of a problem for those who would identify this scroll too closely with chapters 1–25, at least in a form approximating the present text. According to v. 3, the purpose for making the preaching of Jeremiah available in written form is for the sake of a more positive future for Judah (note the narrower audience from v. 2, probably recognizing that the South alone remained). Apparently, the future is still open, for God says "it may be" (lit., "perhaps"). The disaster may be averted if the people repent (that would not be true of chapters 1–25 in their present form). Inasmuch as this is God's own language, even God is not completely certain what the effect of this word might be (see **Connections**, chs. 18 and 26).

These verses seem to reveal what is at the heart of the message of Jeremiah, at least in 605 BC (the date of this writing), however unrelenting it will finally become (and that finality is announced in v. 31). God here announces "disasters" (*rā'āh*), but God's purpose in doing so is to urge the people to repent of their "evil" (*rā'āh*) ways and so prevent the disasters from occurring (for a comparable word, see 26:2-3). In other words, God does not want the "disasters" to occur. God's basic will is that the people repent so that "I may forgive their iniquity and their sin"; were judgment to fall, that would still be what God "intends," but it would not be the primary divine intention (see **Connections**, ch. 26).

When Baruch has completed the writing task, Jeremiah requests that Baruch do a public reading of the scroll, for he himself was barred from the temple area (vv. 5-7; perhaps for earlier preaching, such as is reported in chs. 7; 26).

Baruch is to read the scroll publicly, on a fast day. [Fast Days] Such a reading would be parallel to the public reading of the book of the law by Josiah in 2 Kings 23:1-3; perhaps this reading will have a comparable effect (see above on the several connections with 2 Kgs 22–23). The strategy is shrewd; Baruch is to read the scroll when great crowds will be milling about, buzzing over rumors of war. He is to speak to all those gathered in the temple as well as to the crowds from the rural areas that would assemble in the temple area.

In v. 7 Jeremiah expresses the same hope that God had articulated earlier (in v. 3). In view of God's great wrath (external signs of which were apparent, especially from Babylon), "perhaps" the people would lay their supplications before the Lord (so NAB) and turn from their evil ways. A fast day would be an appropriate time for such lamentations and sacrifices. But, as with God (v. 3), he is quite uncertain what the outcome of such a reading might be (v. 7). His "may be" matches God's "may be" (see **Connections**, ch. 26). This may also be linked with the designation of these words as both God's (v. 8, 11) and Jeremiah's (v. 10); the prophet's words are understood to be the words of God. Certainly Jeremiah knows that this strategy is a risky move; Jehoiakim had not been afraid to dispatch the prophet Uriah with the sword (26:20-23).

Baruch does as Jeremiah had commissioned him to do, as Jeremiah had obeyed God's command (v. 8); the emergence of this book is dependent on the obedience of two key persons. Note that

Various Officials in 36:10-14

It is not possible to identify all the officials named in these verses. Gemariah is the son of Shaphan, whose family was supportive of Jeremiah (see 26:24). Shaphan was the royal secretary who was instrumental in the discovery and promulgation of "the book of the law" in the temple at the time of King Josiah (2 Kgs 22:8-10). His involvement in that public reading probably was a factor in the public reading strategy pursued here. Ironically, in contrast to the negative response of Jehoiakim to the reading of the Jeremiah scroll, Shaphan's reading of the book of the law to Josiah had met a favorable royal response. Micaiah, the grandson of Shaphan (v. 11), upon hearing the Jeremiah scroll, conveys the news to the officials in the palace. One of those officials was Elnathan; he was the father of Nehushta, the mother of Jehoiachin (2 Kgs 24:8). King Jehoiakim had sent him to Egypt to capture the prophet Uriah and bring him back to Jerusalem for execution (26:22-23). It is striking that he urges the king not to burn the scroll (a change of heart?). Jehudi is a key messenger and reader in this text, but is otherwise not known, nor are the members of his family (v. 14) otherwise identifiable.

---

it is Jeremiah, not God, who asks Baruch to read the scroll to a public gathering (from 2 Kgs 23:1-3, it may be inferred that such public readings were not unusual). At first glance, it appears that Baruch read the scroll twice; v. 8 could note the first reading, while vv. 9-10 could describe a second reading in the following year (the fifth year of Jehoiakim, the ninth month). More likely, however, v. 8 states generally that Baruch did what Jeremiah had requested, while vv. 9-10 describe the actual reading of the scroll on the fast day (NAB transposes v. 9 to stand before v. 5 in an effort to smooth this issue out). Such an interpretation is still difficult, however, for the reading called for by Jeremiah would be long delayed (perhaps the writing took some time).

Readings of the Scroll, 36:9-26

Three readings of the scroll now take place. The first reading of the scroll by Baruch took place in the chamber of Gamariah son of Shaphan the secretary. [Various Officials in 36:10-14] Inasmuch as the reading was heard by the people (vv. 10, 13-14), this chamber probably had a window that overlooked the court of the temple. The people's response is not recorded, though v. 31 indicates that they did not listen any more than did the king and his officials. This reading by Baruch may have coincided with Babylon's conquest of Ashkelon (in the Philistine plain). These ominous events apparently prompted the fast day (vv. 6, 9); soon thereafter Jehoiakim swears allegiance to Nebuchadrezzar.

When Micaiah, grandson of Shaphan and a member of a family supportive of Jeremiah (see 26:4), heard Jeremiah's words, he reported them to a group officials gathered in the chamber of

Elishama the royal secretary (vv. 11-13; the distance between Gemariah's chamber, where the scroll was read, and the chamber of Elishama is not known). These officials, obviously impressed by what they have heard, yet uncertain about its import, send a messenger (Jehudi) to Baruch and ask that the scroll be brought to them. Note that the scroll finds its way into settings to which the prophet himself would probably not be invited! Baruch appears before them and, at their request, reads the scroll a second time (vv. 14-15).

The officials are alarmed at what they have heard and consider it important enough to report these developments to King Jehoiakim (v. 16). Apparently, the contents of the scroll are understood to have significant implications for the way in which the king is "running the country" at this time and place. Whether these officials want to influence the policies of the king, using the scroll as leverage, is uncertain. Given their sympathies for Jeremiah (v. 19), however, it may be that they are sympathetic to the words of the scroll and want to pursue their own political/religious agenda about relationships with Babylon.[3] The scroll gives them an opportunity to get to the king without risking their own standing with him.

Before the officials report to the king, however, they inquire of Baruch how the scroll came to be written. They apparently want to be sure that the scroll was dictated by Jeremiah and was not just Baruch's own thinking about these matters (v. 17). The implication is that the author of the scroll is of no small importance as they assess its import. Baruch assures them that this is the case, and that he wrote down exactly what Jeremiah had dictated to him (v. 18; note the explicit reference to "ink"). God is not mentioned in this conversation; perhaps it would be assumed that Jeremiah was God's spokesperson. The officials realize that, given the content of the scroll, this is a dangerous moment for Jeremiah and Baruch; they assume that the king will not be pleased with what is written. Their evident sympathy for Jeremiah and his secretary, and for the contents of the scroll, is shown by telling Baruch to go into hiding with Jeremiah and inform no one—even them!—of their whereabouts (v. 19; cf. v. 26) (see **Connections: "The Lord Hid Them" [v. 26]**).

The officials, leaving the scroll behind in the secretary's chamber, go and report to Jehoiakim (though his name is not used in vv. 20-27) what they have heard. The king sends Jehudi to retrieve the scroll and the messenger reads it to the king in the presence of all the officials (v. 21; the third reading!). The scroll has an impact; it makes its way, quite apart from its authors, ever more deeply into the lives of the powers-that-be—the king's own private chambers! The narrator notes that it was the ninth month (v. 22; see v. 9) and that the king was in his winter apartment (a room in the palace)

Berrigan on the Burning of the Scroll

Willy-nilly, the king who would destroy scripture is herewith included in scripture—as fact and parable. He has earned his dubious eminence—by burning scripture-in-the-making. And lo! Despite his wintry fires and hot furies—we have in hand the scripture he sought to destroy. And ours, alleluia, is an emendated, more complete version than the one he set afire! . . . The king's winter fire is long extinguished. In that fire, in a vain gesture, he sought immunity from judgment. Like his fire, like his vain assault on the word of God, the king too is all but extinguished—a near nobody, a petty tyrant, raving, wreaking, tempestuous. His fretful, childish gesture, futilely standing against God's word, is a case in vain against the winds of truth. Pity him.

Daniel Berrigan, *Jeremiah: The World, the Wound of God* (Minneapolis: Fortress, 1999), 155-56.

with a fire burning in the brazier; the context of a burning fire may be linked to Jeremiah's word about the fate of Jerusalem (see 34:22). As Jehudi reads the scroll, the king interrupts him every three or four columns, and he (or Jehudi at his behest, see NRSV footnote) cuts that portion of the scroll off and throws it into the fire, the equivalent of the more modern paper shredder. Book burning has a long history. [Berrigan on the Burning of the Scroll]

Apparently Jehoiakim thought that Jeremiah's word in written form presented more of a threat to his power than just his speaking did.[4] By burning the scroll the king may have thought he could symbolically counteract the word it contained. Or, perhaps he responds out of contempt or cynicism, symptoms not of disbelief but of unbelief. The scroll has the effect of making the king even more stubborn in his rejection of the word of God. The power of the written word is sharply evident. This pattern is followed until the entire scroll has been destroyed, even though several of the officials urge him not to do so (vv. 23-25).

There is something both horrendous and humorous about these actions (my students commonly laugh when this text is read), as if the king thought he could stop the words from having an effect by destroying the scroll on which they were written (but see below). Unlike the officials (see v. 16) and unlike his father Josiah upon hearing the book of the law (2 Kgs 22:11), neither the king nor his servants are alarmed nor do they tear their garments (a gesture of mourning). Indeed, when three of the officials urge him to preserve the scroll, he refuses to "listen" to their pleas. Instead, the king commands his son Jerahmeel (note the direct familial involvement) and Seraiah (apparently a servant) to arrest Baruch and Jeremiah. Note that the king does not believe that his destruction of the scroll is sufficient to counteract the word it contains; he must go after those who have written this word and silence them. But he fails, at this moment at least, for God hides them (v. 26; see v. 19).

A Final Word of Judgment and a New Scroll, 36:27-32

Sometime after the king had burned the scroll, the word of the Lord comes to Jeremiah and commands that another scroll be written. This scroll is to include "all the former words" that were in the first scroll (vv. 27-28; cf. Exod 34:1 and the preparation of a second set of tablets for the Decalogue). Verse 32 reports that this command was carried out, with Baruch once again functioning as the secretary. But, then, a final clause is added, "and many similar words were added to them" (that is, to the words on the first scroll). A strict reading of this verse could suggest the addition of these words was a disobedient act (God had told him what to write in v. 28). Yet, the narrator passes no judgment on what he does. [Dictation and Interpretation]

Included in God's command to prepare another scroll was a specific word regarding King Jehoiakim (now mentioned by name!), probably not to be spoken to him directly, but integrated into the new scroll (vv. 29-31). First, the indictment is stated (v. 29): he has burned the scroll and has accused Jeremiah of writing that the king of Babylon (note that Jehoiakim identifies the enemy) will lay waste the land and remove its animals and people (cf. 35:17).

Dictation and Interpretation

The additions that Baruch introduced into the scroll reveal an important understanding of word of God. Baruch, and perhaps Jeremiah, apparently understands that God's word (through the prophet) leaves room for human interpretation, and that the addition of these words would not be a violation of the original word of God (or perhaps even of Jeremiah's dictation, see v. 28). Such an understanding seems to have been integral to the transmission of the words of the prophets (and probably of other important traditions as well). In the light of history, readers should be thankful that the king burned the first edition! Certainly the second scroll made life more difficult for Jehoiakim than he had planned.

Then follows the announcement of judgment (vv. 30-31; "therefore"). Note that this addition to the scroll goes beyond the earlier "may be" (vv. 3, 7) and announces a certain judgment on king and his people. Over the course of the chapter, in view of the response, the judgment has become final. First of all, none of his offspring shall occupy the throne of David (though Jehoiachin did rule for three months, about whom a comparable word is spoken in 22:30). Moreover, he will not receive a proper burial; his corpse will be left exposed to the elements (comparable to the judgment announced in 22:18-19). Note that 2 Kings 24:5-6 suggests that he did receive a proper burial, but it is not at all unusual for such imprecision in the fulfillment of prophetic announcements. Second, he, his offspring, and his servants will be "visited" (*pāqad*; NRSV, "punish"; see **Introduction**) for their iniquity; all of the announced disasters (*rā'āh*, as in v. 3) will be brought upon them and on all the inhabitants of Jerusalem. The reason for the judgment is made clear: "they would not listen" to the word of God, a word that had been both spoken and written by Jeremiah.

CONNECTIONS

Spoken Word and Written Word

The importance of writing down Jeremiah's words cannot be over-
estimated. It gives readers a glimpse into a process by which the
spoken word of prophecy becomes the written word, and the special significance of the latter. To have Jeremiah's words in written
form means that they will live on in the community beyond the
prophet's lifetime. Spoken words disappear in time; written words
endure. The spoken words have been rejected; written words will
persist through time and will have either a judgmental or a salutary
effect on subsequent generations.

This chapter would be especially important for exilic readers,
who would know from personal experience that Jeremiah was on
target with the announced word of judgment and King Jehoiakim
was a key culprit in the events leading to the fall of Jerusalem.
Generally, the written word of Jeremiah would come to have a high
status among the exiles and serve for them as an ongoing word of
God.

That Jeremiah himself is not present for the three readings of the
scroll is a narrative way of indicating that his words have a life
beyond his personal presence. This ongoing life for the word is evident as the scroll makes its way from a public reading through the
hands of the officials into the very personal rooms of a king who is
deeply opposed to it. Jeremiah's words are read aloud and, in turn,
the people, officials, and king hear and respond to the reading of
the word. The response to the reading of the word of God has the
same effect as the response to the personally delivered word of the
prophet! (Note that prophets and priests are not specifically
mentioned here, unlike ch. 26; the false prophets cannot be blamed
for everything; the king makes personal decisions without
consultation).

No matter what happens to the prophet, or to his spokesperson
Baruch (both are absent in the third reading of the scroll), and,
even more, no matter what happens to a given copy of his words,
his words can be copied and recopied and take on a life of their
own in the community. In this case, the response of the various
audiences issues in judgment—finally an irrevocable judgment
(v. 31). The burning of the scroll is a sign of the burning of the city.
At the same time, the positive response to these words on the part
of a few is a sign that a remnant of faithful individuals will live on.
In the chapters that follow, those two different futures will be

played out, though the future of irrevocable judgment will be the focus of attention.

The record this chapter provides will show future generations what was really at stake in this time and place. Whose reputation will be sullied as those words are poured over by future generations? No wonder the king and his officials are so concerned about this scroll! Destroy it and put the prophet away so that he does not try to put this "interpretation" on public record again. Let the "official record" stand! But the scroll does get rewritten and has been passed down through the generations for all to see and judge for themselves.[5] [Reflections on Jehoiakim and the Scroll]

Reflections on Jehoiakim and the Scroll

The mortal clash between politics and verity, between an immanent homeland and the space of the transcendent, is spelt out in Jeremiah 36–39. King Jehoiakim seizes the scroll dictated by God's clerk and bookkeeper. He cuts out the offending columns and casts the entire text into the consuming flame (governments, political censors, patriotic vigilantes burn books). God instructs the prophet: "Take thee again another scroll and write on it all the words that were written on the first." The truth will out. Somewhere there is a pencil-stub, a mimeograph machine, a hand-press which the king's men have overlooked. "So Jeremiah abode in the court of the prison till the day that Jerusalem was taken; and he was *there* when Jerusalem was taken." The formulaic specification is magnificent in meaning. The royal city, the nation are laid waste; the text and its transmitter endure, *there* and *now*. The Temple may be destroyed; the texts which it housed sing in the winds that scatter them.

George Steiner, *No Passion Spent. Essays 1978–1995* (New Haven: Yale University Press, 1996), 323.

In this story of a prophetic act the irony lies in the fact that it is the king himself who releases the fatal word rather than the prophet. Jeremiah delegates his authority to Baruch, but the king brings down upon himself and his people the destruction of the nation at the hands of the king of Babylon. The king may have been opposing the power of the spoken word with his undoubted power in the community, but the point of the story is that such royal power is inferior to the prophetic word. Against Yahweh's word there is no effective power, not even that of a prophet-killing king.

Robert Carroll, *Jeremiah* (Philadelphia: Westminster, 1986), 663.

"The Lord hid them" (v. 26)

The narrator pauses in v. 26 to make a brief theological comment: "But the Lord hid them." What is one to make of this claim? In v. 19, the officials had told Baruch that he and Jeremiah should hide and tell no one where they were. At the least, one should claim that God did not act alone, for nondivine agents were involved in the hiding. The officials had initially thought of the importance of hiding; they had urged Baruch to go to Jeremiah and that they together should go into hiding. Their agency in this matter is crucial.

Moreover, Baruch obviously does what they tell him to do; in effect, that is what v. 26 reports. He reports this matter of urgency to Jeremiah and together they go into hiding. And so Baruch's agency is important as well, as is Jeremiah's in acceding to his urging. And so when the text claims that "the Lord hid them," no claim is being made that God acted alone or forced this move on these individuals. This is a confession that God was working in and through various human agencies in order to protect Jeremiah and Baruch, and in the end that divine work was considered the decisive factor, though without overriding actual human decisions and activities.

NOTES

[1] See L. Stulman, *Order Amid Chaos: Jeremiah as Symbolic Tapestry* (Sheffield: Sheffield Academic Press, 1998), 84-88.

[2] For details, see Robert Carroll, *Jeremiah* (Philadelphia: Westminster, 1986), 663-65.

[3] See Walter Brueggemann, *A Commentary on Jeremiah: Exile and Homecoming* (Grand Rapids: Eerdmans, 1998), 349.

[4] See William McKane, *A Critical and Exegetical Commentary on Jeremiah* (2 vols.; ICC; Edinburgh: T. & T. Clark, 1986), 919.

[5] For a powerful retelling of this story, see Daniel Berrigan, *Jeremiah: The World, the Wound of God* (Minneapolis: Fortress, 1999), 151-56.

ENCOUNTERS BETWEEN JEREMIAH AND HEZEKIAH

37:1-21

The "Baruch Narrative," 37:1–45:5

This long prose narrative (the only poetry is 38:22b) chronicles the ministry of Jeremiah during the last days before the destruction of Jerusalem and during its immediate aftermath. While chapters 37–44 are often the recognized unit of material, the inclusion of ch. 45 and its special promise to Baruch is not uncommon and should be followed (sometimes ch. 36, with the role given to Baruch, is included in the unit and provides an inclusio with ch. 45). The announcement of God's salvation, so prominent in chapters 30–33, moves into the background in these chapters. Words of hope are found only in 39:15-18; 40:7-12; 42:9-12; 45:5.

Sometimes this extended narrative is called the "Baruch Narrative" because Baruch is commonly suggested as its author. Though this idea is only an educated guess, it makes a certain sense in view of the nature of the account and Baruch's presence with Jeremiah throughout. The issue as to whether the prophet or the word of the prophet is the chief subject of this segment of Jeremiah presents a choice that does not need to be made. The rejection of word and prophet in these chapters takes shape particularly in terms of an internal conflict regarding Israel's submission to Babylon—between those who counsel submission to Babylon and those who counsel rebellion (see **Connections: Prophet or Word of the Prophet**).

COMMENTARY

Chapters 37–38 narrate three encounters between Jeremiah and King Zedekiah in the course of which Jeremiah's life is endangered and the city of Jerusalem threatened. The chapters are set during the Babylonian siege of Jerusalem in 588–587 BC (as were chs. 21; 32–34), the end of which is reported in chapter 39 (cf. ch. 52). After the introduction (vv. 1-2), chapter 37 may be outlined as follows: Zedekiah's inquiry of Jeremiah and the prophet's reception of a word of God for the king (vv. 3-10); Jeremiah's attempt to leave the city and his imprisonment (vv. 11-16); Zedekiah's second inquiry of Jeremiah, the prophet's response, and an amelioration of his confinement (vv. 17-21).

Zedekiah Pleads in Vain, 37:1-10

In thinking through this chapter, readers must remember that the times are as desperate as Israel's leaders. The Babylonians are threatening Jerusalem. The end is near. King Zedekiah is flailing about, trying to find some way of coping in the face of the onslaught. The king's consultations with Jeremiah are to be interpreted in light of the opening assessment of him by the narrator in v. 2: the king has not listened to the words of the Lord mediated by Jeremiah. In other words, do not trust the motives of the king; he is as unfaithful as ever. Verses 1-2 seem best understood as a bridge between chapters 36 and 37, designed to show that the pattern of not listening evident in 36:25, 31 is followed by Jehoiakim's successors (v. 2; note the similarity between vv. 1-2 and 2 Kgs 24:17-19). (On the relationship between chs. 37 and 38, see the introduction to ch. 38.)

This chapter begins with a notice of royal succession, though not in the usual sense (see Introduction). Nebuchadrezzar had deposed Coniah (=Jehoiachin) son of Jehoiakim after three months and installed Zedekiah, the *brother* of Jehoiakim and son of Josiah, on the throne (see 52:1; 2 Kgs 24:17). These developments are the probable force of the word of the Lord regarding Jehoiakim's succession in 36:30. The opening description of Zedekiah's reign (v. 2)—that neither he nor his servants nor the people listened to the word of the Lord—also places this time in explicit continuity with the reign of Jehoiakim (36:31, "they would not listen"). Jeremiah, however, is no longer in hiding (see 36:19, 26) and is "going in and out among the people," though his future time in prison is ominously anticipated (37:4; see also 32:2; 33:1, where Jeremiah has been confined; chs. 32–34 are set at a time subsequent to the present text).

The explicit summary judgment that Zedekiah did not listen to the words of the Lord (v. 2) is ironically juxtaposed with his request of Jeremiah, through the couriers J(eh)ucal (see 38:1) and the priest Zephaniah (see 21:1; 29:24-32; 52:24-27), that the prophet "please pray for us to the LORD our God" (v. 3; as in 42:2, 20; cf. Hezekiah's request of Isaiah in 2 Kgs 19:4). The explicit reference to "our" God probably shows that Zedekiah understands himself to

The Agonies of Zedekiah

Zedekiah, though a son of King Josiah, ruled at the discretion of the Babylonians. They put him on the throne, and so his future was closely tied to their perceptions of his leadership. Jeremiah (at the behest of his God, see 38:17) and other pro-Babylonians encouraged the king to maintain these ties and so prevent a bloodbath. At the same time, 38:19, 24-27 make it clear that the king had to deal with local patriots who rebelled against the idea of submission to Babylon (and encouraged Egyptian support). The latter group prevailed with Zedekiah after what was probably an agonizing decision-making process. Yet, the word of God had been clearly presented and this decision rejected that word spoken by Jeremiah.

Zedekiah proves to be an indecisive individual, pushed and pulled around by these advisers. His consultations with Jeremiah may have a semblance of sincerity, but by and large the judgment that stands at the head of the narrative (37:2, "he did not listen to the words of the Lord"; a prominent theme in ch. 36) is the primary guide for the interpreter. Some scholars think that Zedekiah is portrayed in more ambiguous terms—seemingly open to words from Jeremiah and yet indecisive as to how to respond to what he hears. Perhaps he is correctly called a "tragic" figure, caught up in the maelstrom of events beyond his control. Yet, though he at times voices anxiety and concern regarding his own situation and that of Jeremiah, these are finally judged to be the plaints and flailings of one whose future has been set by his own stubborn refusal to "listen to the words of the LORD" (37:2).

---

be a faithful Yahweh worshiper; listening or not listening to Jeremiah is for him a matter of discernment (which could be considered commendable for any listener of prophetic speech!).

From what follows Zedekiah apparently does value the counsel of Jeremiah (vv. 17-21), but he is not sensitive enough to discern that Jeremiah's word is the word of the Lord. As noted, the narrator's opening remark (v. 2) makes suspect any subsequent move by Zedekiah, especially theological moves. His request for prayers (v. 3), therefore, should make readers suspicious; this may be an attempt on his part to manipulate Jeremiah or God or both; piety is often so used. Even when Zedekiah responds positively to Jeremiah's request to be imprisoned in more comfortable quarters (v. 21), the reader is given to wonder whether this action will be in Jeremiah's best interest after all. [The Agonies of Zedekiah]

Zedekiah's request for prayers from the prophet is similar to that portrayed in 21:1-10 (where Zephaniah is an emissary), except there the Egyptians are not explicitly in view; it is difficult to know how the two texts are related.[1] Both visits may pertain to new military developments, namely, the advance of Egyptian armies toward Canaan and the (temporary) Babylonian (=Chaldean) withdrawal (v. 5; see the comparable notice in 34:21; this is commonly dated to the summer of 588 BC). Zedekiah does not tell Jeremiah what to pray for, though v. 7 suggests that this is more a request for divine guidance in this time of Babylonian withdrawal than for deliverance from their threat; yet, the latter would certainly be in view (as it was for Zedekiah in 21:2). In any case, Jeremiah does not respond with a prayer (the command of God prohibiting intercession may be in place, see 7:16; 11:14; 14:11). Instead, Jeremiah responds with a word *from* God that provides no guidance or salutary word whatsoever; it simply announces doom.

The Egyptian pharaoh of v. 5 is Hophra (589–570 BC), explicitly included in an announcement of judgment in 44:30. Zedekiah had rebelled against Babylon in concluding an alliance with Egypt in 589 BC. The Egyptian advance was apparently in response to the stipulations of that alliance. It may be that Zedekiah was hoping for a word from the prophet similar to that given by Isaiah a century earlier that resulted in the deliverance of Jerusalem from the Assyrians (see 2 Kgs 18–19; Isa 36–39). Perhaps the temporary lifting of the Babylonian siege was a sign of such a divine deliverance. The repossession of released slaves in 34:8-22 could be related to such an event and the optimism associated with it. But the Egyptians were quickly driven back (see v. 7), confirming that Jeremiah's words about a Babylonian conquest were still on target.

God gives Jeremiah a response for the two emissaries (Jehucal and Zephaniah) to transmit to Zedekiah (vv. 7-10), not unlike that in 21:1-10. Pharaoh's army cannot be relied upon for help against Babylon (see Ezek 17:15-17); it will pull back into Egypt and Babylon will return in force, take the city, and burn it with fire (as in 34:22; but 38:17 still sees some openness for a different future). Zedekiah and his officials are deceiving themselves if they think that Babylon will now disappear from their screen. In fact, to make the point even more sharply through the use of hyperbole (see 2 Sam 5:6), even if they defeated the Babylonian armies and left them with only wounded men, they would find a way to burn the city (v. 10)! In other words, there is no use to seek help for the defense of the city and country; the die is cast. [The Absence of God Language]

Jeremiah Imprisoned, 37:11-21

At the time of the Egyptian advance toward Jerusalem, and the consequent (temporary) Babylonian withdrawal, Jeremiah takes advantage of the lull in the fighting to make a personal journey. He goes to the land of Benjamin to receive his share of family property (probably the same property that is referred to in chapter 32, but the transaction there occurs after he has been imprisoned and hence after the events of this chapter). In the midst of war, Jeremiah pursues an activity that anticipates a future for his family (and hence for Israel). He is, however, detained at the Benjamin Gate of the city (see Zech 14:10) by a sentinel named Irijah and accused of deserting to the Babylonians. Given Jeremiah's words (see 21:8-10), and the desertions of others to Babylon (see 38:19; 52:15), the authorities would be suspicious of his movements. Jeremiah denies the charge, but Irijah does not "listen" (see v. 2) to his protestations and arrests him. Irijah brings him to the authorities; they vent their anger at him, brutalize him, and throw him into a prison (formerly the house of an otherwise unknown secretary named Jonathan, perhaps a "maximum security prison"). In some dungeon-like section of the house (the specific site is uncertain) he remained for many days. Sometime after Jeremiah's imprisonment, the matter of the family property is brought again to his attention by God (see 32:1-2), which occasions the events of chapter 32.

Zedekiah once again makes an effort to consult with Jeremiah, only this time in secret, in the king's own rooms (vv. 17-21). What prompts the visit, given the unequivocal judgment of vv. 7-10, is uncertain. Perhaps the failure of the Egyptian armies was now clear and the siege had been resumed. Perhaps Zedekiah hoped for a miracle (as he had in 21:2), perhaps thinking that Jeremiah might have some information that could be useful to him. That he sought a clandestine meeting with Jeremiah may be explained by 38:19, 24-27 and his fear of opponents to his policies (it might be noted that his change of Jeremiah's prison conditions would also be risky). [An Ironic Visit of King to Prophet]

Zedekiah's query, "Is there any word from the LORD?" has the appearance of genuine inquiry (see v. 3; 21:2), though the narrator has predisposed the reader to be suspicious of his motives (v. 2). Still, Jeremiah's word in 34:4-5 had enough of a positive cast that Zedekiah (and the reader) may be forgiven for wondering what the latest word from God might be. In any case, Jeremiah initially responds as if Zedekiah were a

An Ironic Visit of King to Prophet

That the narrator highlights this visit of the king to Jeremiah may be a way of testifying to the power of the prophet and the word that he brings. The one who rules the country seeks out one who is accused of sedition regarding the future of the country. Kings come to the prophet for advice and counsel; in spite of the non-listening response they make, they are attracted to this individual for what he has said and done. Though the king will not "listen," he somehow still has a need to hear from this prophet, perhaps hoping for a word about a change in the divine mind. Zedekiah, filled with fear and foreboding, visits with an imprisoned prophet, who, ironically, has a kind of freedom of which the king could not begin to dream. This feature of the story is a witness to the power of the prophet and not just to the word he speaks.

genuine seeker, but gives him an ambiguous reply ("There is!"). And then, replying as if the king were asking about his personal fate (not part of his reply in vv. 6-10), he turns the knife: the king will be handed over to another king, the king of Babylon! And Jeremiah states that word in terms that Zedekiah (or at least the reader!) has heard before, directly or indirectly (see 21:7; 34:3, 21; the hopeful word for Zedekiah in 32:4-5 occurs later, but the reader will have already heard it).

Having given the briefest of replies, Jeremiah turns the tables and directs two questions back to the king (vv. 18-19). What wrong has he done to anyone—king, servants, people—that the king (!) has thrown him into prison (similarly, 26:15)? His next question implies that, given the turn of events, he alone among the prophets has been shown to speak the hard truth about Babylon to the king, so why should he be the one who is punished. Where are "your" (the reference is plural, embracing the king and all Israel apparently) prophets who prophesied that the king of Babylon would not come against king and land? Having made his point in such a way that no verbal reply was called for, he pleads in deferential language (please; my lord king; be good enough) that he not be returned to the prison in which he has been held (v. 15). He also may be appealing to Zedekiah's sensitivities with his explicit reference to death (v. 20; for an earlier death threat under King Jehoiakim, see 26:10-19; cf. 36:26).

Zedekiah responds positively to Jeremiah's plea (also in 38:10) and has him committed to the court of the guard, an apparently more comfortable confinement (as noted in 32:2; 33:1). No real justice is evident in the king's reply, understand; but at least Jeremiah receives some positive response, though the motives are certainly ambiguous. Perhaps the king is thinking that he will be treated better if he softens the punishment; at the least, the king acknowledges what the prophet has requested and is moved to respond positively. Jeremiah is given a daily bread allowance until the bread is gone, that is, until the Babylonian siege is so severe that bread was no longer available (see the famine in 52:6). Jeremiah remains in this confinement until the day the Babylonians take Jerusalem (38:28). Sometime before that happens, another encounter between Jeremiah and Zedekiah takes place (see 32:1-7).

CONNECTIONS

Prophet or Word of the Prophet

Interpreters have in the past commonly understood these chapters in terms of a "via dolorosa" or "passion narrative" of the prophet. [Von Rad on Jeremiah's Passion Narrative] Most scholars now think of these chapters more in terms of the story of the word that Jeremiah proclaims. This shift is in part due to the lack of a sustained interest in the prophet; indeed, the prophet disappears from the narrative at several key points (39:1-10; 40:7–41:18). Yet, the narrative at these points is concerned to move the story line along, and Jeremiah is in fact an unheralded participant in the events these texts report. And so he experiences the suffering entailed in such experiences along with other Israelites. It is important to note that the word of God is not always front and center in these texts either

A more satisfactory way of thinking of these chapters is in terms of both prophet and word of God; prophet and word cannot be separated. While Holladay may be overstating the matter, he is not far wrong to call these chapters "an example par excellence of prophetic biography," though not in a modern sense.[2] Better, perhaps, would be a designation that brought the prophet together with the word that he bears. It is the prophet and not the scroll that remains the bearer of the word of God in these chapters (to speak of Jeremiah as "simply the instrument of the divine word" is to diminish the crucial role of prophetic agency).[3] The opening verses of the narrative make this point clear (37:2).

These chapters detail the conflict that God's word generated for the prophet, among the king and his officials in particular. It is best to think of these texts as the story of the rejection of both the word and the prophet who announced that word. The word that Jeremiah brings cannot be reduced to a spoken word. The word of God in and through Jeremiah is an embodied word. The word is both heard and seen by the prophet's audience; he

Von Rad on Jeremiah's Passion Narrative

For Gerhard von Rad, "just as the confessions are confined to the development of the prophet's inner life, so the Baruch narrative is only concerned with describing the outward circumstances of this *via dolorosa* [von Rad also refers to "the stations of Jeremiah's cross"!]. Although it does sometimes contain oracles spoken by the prophet, the accounts here given are not to be understood . . . as no more than the narrative framework for the oracles; no, the subject described here is the dramatic events in which the prophet was involved and which brought him into greater and greater dangers. . . .

Jeremiah's sufferings are described with a grim realism, and the picture is unrelieved by any divine word of comfort or any miracle. The narrator has nothing to say about any guiding hand of God; no ravens feed the prophet in his hunger, no angel stops the lion's mouth. In his abandonment to his enemies Jeremiah is completely powerless—neither by his words nor his sufferings does he make any impression on them. What is particularly sad is the absence of any good or promising issue . . . . Jeremiah's path disappears in misery, and this without any dramatic accompaniments. It would be completely wrong to assume that the story was intended to glorify Jeremiah and his endurance. To the man who described these events neither the suffering itself nor the manner in which it was borne had any positive value, and least of all a heroic value . . . . "

Gerhard von Rad, *Old Testament Theology* (2 vols.; New York: Harper & Row, 1962), 206-08.

conveys the word of God not simply by what he says but also by who he is and the way in which he bears himself in this community (witness the symbolic actions, e.g., ch. 13). Exilic readers would certainly see this narrative in terms of both word and prophet; both have been vindicated by the events that occurred.

NOTES

[1] For a review of the options, see William McKane, *A Critical and Exegetical Commentary on Jeremiah* (2 vols.; ICC; Edinburgh: T. & T. Clark, 1986), 940-45.

[2] William Holladay, *Jeremiah 2* (Philadelphia: Fortress, 1986), 282, 286.

[3] Contrary to Robert Carroll, *Jeremiah* (Philadelphia: Westminster, 1986), 669.

JEREMIAH AMONG FOES AND FRIENDS

38:1-28

This chapter continues the narrative of chapter 37. Its two major sections center on Jeremiah's encounters with those who support an Egyptian alliance (vv. 1-13) and, one last time, with King Zedekiah (vv. 14-28). This chapter is commonly considered a divergent account of the events of chapter 37 (not unlike the relationship of chs. 7 and 26), but with many different details. The difference in detail may be due to different paths in the oral retelling of these events. The reference to Jeremiah's speaking to "all the people" in 38:1 would be most unlikely from prison; it probably assumes a situation like that stated in 37:4. So, both chapters start from the same point.

Among the parallels in 37:15-21, especially to be noted are Jeremiah's arrest by governmental officials and his being charged with treason, followed by imprisonment and a secret encounter with Zedekiah, who ameliorates his punishment by having him confined in the court of the guard. If 37:17-21 is a divergent account of 38:14-28, then what Zedekiah tells Jeremiah to report to the princes (in 38:26) is not a lie, for 37:20 in fact reports that as a topic of their conversation.

COMMENTARY

Jeremiah in the Mud, 38:1-6

The narrative begins with the naming of four opponents of Jeremiah in the battle for the soul of the city of Jerusalem. [The Persons Named in 38:1] Apparently, Jeremiah had enough freedom in the court of the guard to get an audience (v. 1; cf. 32:6-15). These four individuals had heard Jeremiah speak to "all the people" (a reference back to a time before his imprisonment?) advocating surrender to Babylon (vv. 2-3; v. 2 is almost identical to 21:9). Those who continued the rebellion and stayed in the city would die (again, the triad of sword,

Cistern

Like the cistern into which Jeremiah was placed, this large cistern was carved from the limestone bedrock and then covered with waterproof cement. (Credit: Scott Nash)

famine, pestilence; see 14:12). But those who go out to the Babylonians "with their hands up" would live and "have their lives as a prize of war" (see 21:9; 39:18; 45:5). The city is certainly going to be handed over to the king of Babylon, that future is not in doubt; but this avenue of approach allows for the possibility of life rather than death. The issue for God is life (see **Connections: The Issue Is Life**).

In response, these four opponents go to King Zedekiah and complain (v. 4; cf. 29:24-28 for other complaints of Jeremiah's attitude toward Babylon). In effect, they claim that Jeremiah is collaborating with the enemy—a capital crime in their eyes. He is discouraging (or demoralizing; the same expression is used in letter six of the Lachish letters, see 34:7) the soldiers and the people by this kind of talk and should be put to death (as in 26:11-19). It is not enough for these antagonists that Jeremiah is in prison; that is an insufficient penalty for one who counsels sedition. It is possible that they are reacting to Zedekiah's amelioration of Jeremiah's prison conditions (37:21). In a remarkable and ironic use of earlier language in the book, these antagonists claim that Jeremiah is seeking the harm (*rā'āh*) of the city and not its welfare (*šālôm*) (see **Connections: Peace and Not Harm**).

Zedekiah acquiesces to their demands, claiming that he is powerless in the face of their opposition (v. 5). Given their demands and the charge of treason, he can only agree (cf. the king's action in 32:3). In such a situation, they are strong and he is weak. A remarkable claim for a king! But he can also thereby wash his hands of any direct responsibility for what happens to Jeremiah. [A Word on Kingship for Exilic Readers]

The result is that Jeremiah's four opponents seize him and let him down by ropes into the waterless, but muddy cistern of Malchiah, the royal prince, who will be executed by Nebuchadrezzar (39:6). The cistern, probably carved out of limestone rock and shaped like a pitcher, is located in the same area of Jeremiah's imprisonment, away from public scrutiny. A crafty form of punishment, indeed! Without food and water, and exposed to the elements, he will die a slow death, without a mark on his body (cf. v. 9). Letting him down by ropes assures such a fate. A striking phrase describes Jeremiah's newly desperate situation: "Jeremiah sank in the mud" (38:6).

> **A Word on Kingship for Exilic Readers**
>
> Exilic readers would probably infer from the admission of powerlessness on the part of King Zedekiah (v. 5) that these disastrous events were not simply the fault of the king; pro-Egyptian officials had gained de facto control of governmental power and policies. One effect of this presentation is to prevent any simple blaming of the king. He had a great deal of help for these policies, and these officials were probably beyond his own control. And Zedekiah is imaged as wavering, stuck between a prophetic word of God and the word of his own advisors. So, exilic readers could conceivably conclude: if it had not been for his advisers there might have been a different future. This portrayal could also set up an understanding of kingship that prepares the way for a new member of the Davidic line to assume the throne of Israel.

Ebed-melech Rescues Jeremiah, 38:8-13

Jeremiah is not without friends and supporters. One such person is Ebed-melech, an Ethiopian (and hence a black person and a foreigner) whose name, ironically, means "servant of the king"; he was a royal servant or official. When he heard of Jeremiah's plight he brought the prophet's case before the king, who happened to be accessible at the Benjamin Gate of the city (for unstated reasons;

inspecting defenses? attending a public assembly?). Ebed-melech charges that "these men" acted wickedly in throwing Jeremiah into the cistern; he might die of hunger during the food shortage in the city (vv. 7-9). The king was certainly aware that his officials had placed Jeremiah in some kind of life-threatening position; perhaps his indecisiveness is showing once again, especially when confronted by the knowledge that Jeremiah's pro-Babylonian supporters had heard what had been done to the prophet. The phrase, "for there is no bread left in the city," is awkward; perhaps he could not forage for scraps of food in this condition (see 52:6 for a later time when this was the case). This reference could tie into Zedekiah's command in 37:21—knowledge that would have been available to servants like Ebed-melech—that Jeremiah be given a daily supply of bread. [Ebed-melech, a Servant Who Makes a Difference]

The king is now confronted with a contrary point of view regarding the fate of Jeremiah. What will he do? Vacillating as always (cf. vv. 4-5), the king responds positively to Jeremiah's situation and commands that Ebed-melech take thirty men with him and pull the prophet up from the cistern (v. 10; NRSV reads "three" on slim manuscript evidence, but probably correctly; if "thirty" is correct, then opposition to such a move may have been expected). Ebed-melech proceeds to make preparations for the rescue, obeying the king's command to take three men with him (the king even does the planning for the rescue!). Ebed-melech takes some rags and scraps of clothing from a storeroom in the palace (to ease his extrication), lets them down the cistern by ropes (both would be needed), and instructs Jeremiah to place the pieces of cloth between his armpits and the ropes to protect his skin. When Jeremiah has done so, Ebed-melech and the other men pull him from the cistern and house him in the court of the guard (vv. 11-13). He is rescued from certain death, but remains a prisoner. Ebed-melech will later receive a word of promise from God that he would survive the devastation of the city (39:15-18).

Jeremiah and Zedekiah One Last Time, 38:14-28

King Zedekiah commands that Jeremiah be brought to the "third entrance of the temple" (the precise location is unknown) and

---

Ebed-melech, a Servant Who Makes a Difference

A single individual, from the lower ranks of palace officials, persuades the king to reverse the punishment. Ebed-melech's reasoning focuses both on the wickedness of the officials and on keeping Jeremiah alive (v. 9). One level of importance regarding this individual move is to show that, in spite of all the official condemnation of Jeremiah and the public pressures to conform, an individual could break out of the crowd and act in gracious ways that are attuned to the will of God (see 26:16, 24; 36:19 for indications that others were supportive of Jeremiah). Ebed-melech's decisiveness, his risk-taking, and his trust in God (as we learn from 39:18) may be deliberately set over against that of Zedekiah. What might have happened if Zedekiah had been more like Ebed-melech?

again consults with him (v. 14). Of all their encounters, this is the last as well as the most extensive and the most dialogical. The king begins by saying that he has something to tell the prophet, but it is not clear that he ever gets it said, given Jeremiah's response (it could be the information in v. 19). Remarkably, the king, pushed and pulled around by persons in opposing camps and unable to decide between them, consults with (!) the prisoner. No doubt he is hoping against hope that Jeremiah (and God!) will change their tune and promise a brighter future, both for himself personally and for his policies. Who's in charge here? In some sense the king recognizes that the imprisoned Jeremiah still has power, that what he thinks and says counts. And Jeremiah is not afraid to speak directly and bluntly to the king, not only with respect to the political situation, but also regarding his personal situation. When the king asks that the prophet not keep secrets from him, Jeremiah pointedly responds: if I tell you the truth, will you not have me executed? Besides, what good would the truth do, for you will not listen to me anyway (v. 15)?

But Zedekiah responds only to the first of Jeremiah's questions. The king swears an oath (note the use of appropriate language for God as creator and giver of life; see at 4:2) to Jeremiah "in secret" (cf. 38:24; 37:17 for another secret meeting): As the Lord lives, who gave us the breath of life, I will not put you to death or give you to "these men" who seek your life (v. 16). The "men" are probably to be identified with those who threw him into the cistern, and given their power over the king evident on that occasion, Zedekiah's promise would have a flimsy basis (vv. 4-6). Note that Zedekiah does not respond to Jeremiah's point that his counsel has been ignored; this suggests that the king has no intention of listening to him (see 37:2).

The prophet, not giving an inch in the face of continued royal pestering (see 1:18), responds with a word from the Lord (vv. 17-18). This is another "either-or" formulation (see 21:8-10; 22:1-5; 42:9-17). If he surrenders to the king of Babylon, his life will be spared, his "house" (=dynasty) will continue, and the city will be delivered. But if he does not do so, he will not escape and the city will be burned. The only way into a positive future is for the king to back off from the rebellion, quit the warmongering, and submit to the king of Babylon. God's will is that there be no war (see **Connections**)! But, if there is no compliance on this point on the king's part, war there will be. But such an eventuality will not be the result of divine caprice; submission is the only realistic expectation when dealing with powers such as the Babylonians and, given

Options for Interpreting 38:17-18

Four interpretative options seem to be available for interpreting 38:17-18:

One, vv. 17-18 are simply a repetition of vv. 2-3, that is, the city will be handed over to the king of Babylon; that is not in doubt. But surrender rather than resistance would allow for the possibility of life rather than death for many individuals; and the city would not be destroyed. Because this option values life more than rebellion and resistance does, this is God's will for the situation, even if it means surrender to the king of Babylon. In other words, God sides with those who are pro-Babylonian and against those who are pro-Egyptian and resistant to Babylonian submission. But the basic reason given is that "you shall live" (repeated in vv. 2, 17, 20). God wants life for as many as possible, and hence this word of God is appropriate for this moment in Israel's history (see **Connections**).

Two, these are not genuine options. Rather, they constitute just one final effort on Jeremiah's part to demonstrate Zedekiah's failure to listen; recall that Zedekiah

does not respond to Jeremiah's claim that he would not listen anyway (vv. 15-16).

Three, if these are genuine options at this late stage in Babylon's siege then they are testimony to the openness of the (earlier) prophetic word to ongoing developments. This interpretation would cohere with other presentations of the contingency of prophetic words of judgment (e.g., 26:1-5; 36:2-3); yet, 36:29-31 seems to claim that the positive future possibility has been closed off (as do the oracles in chs. 1–25).

Four, given the royal stubbornness and the obduracy of the people, it seems that vv. 17-18 do not in fact state genuine options at this stage. At the same time, the point of stating them as options at this juncture is to reveal what the divine will for this life-threatening situation has in fact been all along. The effect would be to reveal some of the factors involved in the rejection of this word and perhaps, given that rejection, to drive the foregone conclusion even more sharply toward its completion.

the much less disastrous effect that will have, it is the divine will for Israel.

The careful reader may well ask whether Zedekiah does in fact have these options, given earlier statements of Jeremiah about his fate and the fate of the city (32:1-5; 34:1-7; 37:7-10, 17; cf. 21:1-10). A comparable either-or was given to Zedekiah in 27:12-13; it is that word which is given in 38:2-3, reported by the officials as the summary word of the prophet. Yet, most of Jeremiah's words have painted only a negative future. How to interpret these verses is not altogether clear, though the first of the options noted seems most likely. [Options for Interpreting 38:17-18]

Zedekiah responds with a statement of his personal fears (v. 19), namely, that if he were to surrender to the king of Babylon, those Judeans who had already deserted to the Chaldeans would mistreat him (this implies that Jeremiah's counsel had had some effect). It is striking that Zedekiah's most immediate concern is for his own personal safety. Yet, these unnamed persons would, of course, be sympathetic to the kind of message that Jeremiah has just announced. So, if the king follows Jeremiah's advice and surrenders to Babylon, then such an action would be favorably received by these very people! So, what is he worried about?

Apparently he thinks that, whatever decision he makes as a vassal-king, he would be punished by the Babylonians (and their supporters); he has started this rebellion and is responsible for the dilemma in which Israel now finds itself and hence believes that he will be punished. His only chance to escape personally is to continue to resist. He is also certainly fearful of the pro-Egyptian factions who have been counseling against submission to Babylon, as vv. 25-26 suggest (see v. 5). And so, if he surrenders, he would be personally punished more severely, for *both* parties to the conflict would have reason to do so. Even with Jeremiah's assurances, he cannot believe otherwise. What he wants from Jeremiah apparently is a word from God that would cut what he perceives to be this Gordian knot. That is, God could intervene on behalf of Israel and that would mean he would not have to make this decision at all (as in 21:2)!

Jeremiah assures him that he would not be abused by those sympathetic to the Babylonian cause (the prophet would have persuasive access to the folks sympathetic to his perspective), and then proceeds to lay out the options of vv. 17-18 one more time (vv. 20-23). On the one hand, the king only needs to obey the word of the Lord (surrender to the Babylonians) and his life would be spared (v. 20; see 34:4-5). On the other hand, if he does not surrender, God has shown Jeremiah what would happen (vv. 21-22, NRSV "vision" is possible; "insight" is better, for this option is presented only as a possibility).

This "vision, insight," addressed to Zedekiah, focuses on the personal effects of his refusal to surrender, namely, what will happen to "all your wives and your children" (v. 23). This word especially envisages what will happen to his wives (harem?) when they are led out to the officials of the king of Babylon (to do with as they please). Their song, containing elements of both mocking and lament, centers on Zedekiah's betrayal by his erstwhile friends (and is essentially identical to Obad 7). The city has fallen and his trusted friends have betrayed and outmaneuvered him. He is now stuck in the mud (like Jeremiah, v. 6; what goes around comes around!), that is, his fair-weather friends will have all deserted him in the end and the women will suffer greatly (see Job 6:15-17). This poetic snippet may have been taken from a ditty heard on the streets of Jerusalem. Jeremiah interprets this "vision" as follows (v. 23): the king of Babylon will seize the city and burn it with fire, and Zedekiah will be led out of the city with his family to suffer at the hands of the Babylonians (see the fate of his sons in 39:6).

Zedekiah replies to Jeremiah one more time (vv. 24-26). Jeremiah does not respond to the king explicitly, though he does so implicitly according to the narrative that follows (v. 27). Zedekiah's response is again focused on personal fears. He orders Jeremiah to keep this conversation a secret under threat of death (probably at the hands of the officials, not the king), and proceeds to cover any future contingencies. This planning seems devised to protect Zedekiah from any complicity in Jeremiah's death, lest he suffer the consequences from such an eventuality (from God? Nebuchadrezzar?).

If the officials (presumably the pro-Egyptian officials, see vv. 1-5) should hear that king and prophet have spoken to each other, and demand to know what was said (again, under threat of death), then Jeremiah is to have a set reply. He is to tell them that he has been pleading with the king not to imprison him in the house of Jonathan and leave him to die there (see 17:15), using the language of his earlier plea (17:20). So, while a lie, it is softened somewhat because it corresponds with an earlier conversation. This action on the part of the king is thus designed to protect both king and prophet, and ironically Zedekiah thereby places his own future in the hands of Jeremiah! No effort should be made to deny that Jeremiah lies or to find extraordinary ethical reasons for him to have done so; as 37:18-20 and 38:15 indicate, Jeremiah is a human being who would rather live than die!

As Zedekiah had feared, the officials did come and question Jeremiah; Jeremiah did exactly as the king had commanded him to do. Caught between two threats to his life, he chose to equivocate. Another effect of his lying, of course, is that Jeremiah protects Zedekiah from his hostile officials. In view of the fact that the conversation had not been overheard, the officials are satisfied with the explanation (surprisingly in view of v. 4) and stop their questioning. Jeremiah survives the threats and remains in the more comfortable prison until Jerusalem is taken by the Babylonians (v. 28; see 39:14).

CONNECTIONS

The Issue Is Life

It is important to state clearly what is at stake for God in these events, which in turn informs the nature of the prophetic word. The issue for God is not obedience for the sake of obedience; the issue is life for as many people as possible. The specific language of "life" occurs in two primary contexts in Jeremiah, namely 21:8-10 and 38:2, 17, 20. The recurring phrase, "You shall have your (their) lives (life) as a prize of war," occurs in these texts (as well as with reference to two individuals, 39:12; 45:5).

God's objective in this situation is not some capricious divine concern that Zedekiah and the people obey the prophetic word for its own sake. The concern for obedience is grounded in the fact that it serves the life and well being of the people; because of this reality God deems it important to take this stand. This divine strategy may also be considered politically realistic, but realism becomes the divine will because it serves life. The issue is not even pro-Babylonian in a narrow sense; the issue is life for as many as possible. That this divine concern for life continues to be stated in the face of continued obduracy indicates something of the force of the concern. [Life Beyond Disaster]

Life Beyond Disaster

In the description of the Book of Consolation, God's new work with the exiles on the far side of disaster will be effective in bringing new life; "their life shall become like a watered garden" (31:12). God will in time make such a life possible, for these are God's objectives in every life situation. But now, in view of human obduracy, that future filled with life will come to pass only on the far side of much death and destruction.

Peace and Not Harm

The complaint of Jeremiah's antagonists in 38:4 echoes several other texts in the book. This complaint was made earlier among the people about *God* (8:15; 14:19; 30:5); from their perspective, God has taken the peace away (16:5). So the officials do have their finger on the pulse of the situation in the city. There is another sense in which the accusation is right on target; Jeremiah's word of judgment will in fact mean great harm (*rāʿāh*) for the city and its people! And Jeremiah's word and the God from whom he received it are at least indirectly implicated in this reality, however much the problem may be said to lie with the people. At a somewhat different level, this is also the issue that is framed in Jeremiah's contest with Hananiah (28:9) and the false prophets who were proclaiming "peace, peace (*šālôm*)" when there was no peace (6:14; 8:11; 14:13; 23:17). The officials would be echoing the litany of the false prophets in some respects, only the accusation pertains to what Jeremiah was seeking for the city, not what the situation actually was.

When, in 29:11, God announces welfare (=peace) rather than harm for the exiles, this would come only on the far side of great harm done to the city and its people. At that point, the counsel for the exiles is to seek the welfare (=peace) of the *Babylonians* among whom they live (29:7). Even in such an interim arrangement, God is concerned about life and peace for this people. According to 33:6, 9, true peace will come to Israel only on the far side of disaster, but God will finally see to its coming.

THE FALL OF JERUSALEM
AND JEREMIAH'S FATE

39:1-18

This brief chapter describes the fall of Jerusalem to the Babylonians in 587 BC (vv. 1-10) and concludes with notices regarding Jeremiah's release from prison (vv. 11-14) and an oracle of deliverance for Ebedmelech, who had rescued Jeremiah from the cistern (vv. 15-18; see 38:7-13). This chapter is a climactic point in the book, especially in its description of the fall of Jerusalem (it has probably been drawn into this context from 52:4-16; cf. 2 Kgs 25:1-12; these accounts do not mention the name of Jeremiah; 2 Chr 35:21 does mention the prophet in this connection).

Much of the book that precedes this account either gives reasons for the fall (especially infidelity) or announces its occurrence as the judgment of Yahweh. This event has been experienced by many of the first readers of this material, who would read everything in the book in light of this horrendous experience. All readers know from the notice in 1:3 that this disastrous event shapes the form and content of the entire book (see **Connections: God and the Fall of Jerusalem**).

The passage presents several textual problems that are not easily resolved (vv. 4-13 are not found in the LXX). It seems likely that vv. 1-2, 4-10 have been drawn from 52:4-16 and incorporated here so that this story follows upon the prophecy of Jeremiah. The names of the Babylonian officials in vv. 3, 13 are also somewhat uncertain (v. 3 is the one verse in vv. 1-10 that has no parallel in 52:4-16 or 2 Kgs 25:1-12). The placement of vv. 15-18 has the sense of a flashback to 38:7-13.

COMMENTARY

The Destruction of Jerusalem, 39:1-10

In summary fashion the first two verses place the fall of Jerusalem in specific relation to the final years of the reign of Zedekiah, who had

The Babylonian Officials (39:3, 13)

The officials named in v. 3 are not entirely clear, but can be sorted out as follows: Nergal-sharezer was the Samgar-nebo (Simmagir was a Babylonian title or district, though NRSV considers it a fourth name in the list); Sarsechim (=Nebushazban, v. 13) was the Rabsaris, a chief official of the court. A second person named Nergal-sharezer (=Nergalsharursur or Neriglissar) was the Rabmag (another Babylonian title); this name may refer to the same person as the first name on the list (only one person with this name is listed in v. 13). The last named was Nebuchadrezzar's son-in-law; he later was the king of Babylon (560–556 BC). Two of these persons are mentioned in v. 13, where still another name occurs (as well as in vv. 9-10): Nebuzaradan, the captain of the guard (the meanings given to the titles are educated guesses).

---

rebelled against Babylonian rule. After a eighteen-month siege, beginning in early January, 588 BC, the city falls in July, 587 BC. After the city has been taken (v. 3a; a phrase commonly thought to be transposed here from 38:28; see NRSV footnote), key Babylonian officials come and take their place in the middle gate of the city wall (to exercise their authority over what remained of the city). [The Babylonian Officials (39:3, 13)]

At the sight of this entourage of Babylonian officialdom, Zedekiah and "all" the soldiers flee by night out through the king's garden and through another (but unknown) gate (cf. 52:7-11). They head for the Arabah, probably with the intent of crossing the Jordan and gaining the protection of the Ammonites (see 41:15). The Babylonian army, however, pursues them and captures them near Jericho. They bring Zedekiah to King Nebuchadrezzar, encamped at Riblah, who passes sentence upon him for his betrayal, that is, breaking the oath of allegiance to the king of Babylon (v. 5). [Geographical References in vv. 4-6]

Nebuchadrezzar executes the sons of Zedekiah in his presence (his last sight!) as well as all the nobles of Judah. He then puts out Zedekiah's eyes and takes him to Babylon in chains (vv. 6-7; see Jeremiah's reference to Zedekiah's eyes meeting those of the king of Babylon in 34:3). A most pathetic picture of the last king of Israel! In the king's ongoing wavering between opposing factions, the time finally came when the decision was made for him. The Babylonians would not be stopped and Zedekiah and those allied with him suffer the consequences (he joins another Davidic king, already in Babylon, Jehoiachin; see 52:31-34). A month later (according to 2 Kgs 25:8) the Babylonians proceed to burn down the palace and other houses in the city

Geographical References in vv. 4-6

The royal garden was in the Kidron valley, to the south and east of the city. The Arabah was an arid region south of the Dead Sea, but the term could also designate the Jordan Valley (?). Jericho was a city in the Jordan Valley, north of the Dead Sea. Riblah was a city in Lebanon/Syria (referred to here as the "land of Hamath" for the key city of this area) in the Beqaa Valley that served as an important military base during this time, guarding a key trade route between Egypt and Mesopotamia. It had also been used by the Egyptians (see 2 Kgs 23:33).

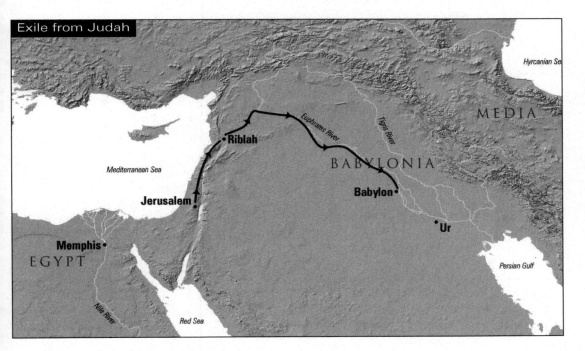

Exile from Judah

and break down the walls of Jerusalem (v. 8; cf. 52:13-14; often anticipated in the prior narrative, e.g., 34:2).

The captain of the guard (Nebuzaradan, who also plays a role in 40:1-6) dispatches into exile many of those who are left in the city (see 21:9-10; 38:2, which states that those who remain in the city shall die; it is apparently understood as a general statement rather than an annihilation). Those who had deserted to the Babylonians were also sent into exile as Jeremiah had promised (38:2; 52:29 specifies that 832 persons were taken into exile). He leaves behind some of the poor people, who were given vineyards and fields (vv. 9-10; cf. 52:15-16; 2 Kgs 25:11-12). Verse 14 indicates that several leading citizens were also left behind (see also 41:10), consisting apparently of those who had been supportive of Jeremiah and Babylon.

Nebuchadrezzar's Treatment of Jeremiah, 39:11-14

A somewhat different account of Jeremiah's release is given in 40:1-6 (see there); that account and these verses are probably to be understood as variants of the same series of events (rather than two events, which is often improbably explained as Jeremiah being released and then arrested a second time).

The king of Babylon commands his captain of the guard to treat Jeremiah well. He is to look after him and not mistreat him (the word used is *ra*ᶜ; hence he does not experience the full brunt of what most in Israel experience); they are even to respond positively to his requests. No doubt for members of the "pro-Egyptian" faction this Babylonian action would be ample evidence that their charge of treason was on target! And so the captain of the guard and several other leading Babylonian officials (see [The Babylonian Officials (39:3, 13)]) release Jeremiah from the court of the guard and entrust him to the care of Gedaliah, later to be appointed governor of Judah by Nebuchadrezzar (see 40:5-7; different from the Gedaliah of 38:1).

Gedaliah brings Jeremiah home (to Anathoth presumably). The named members of Gedaliah's family (v. 14) had earlier seen to the care of Jeremiah (26:24; see 2 Kings 22 for the links to King Josiah). And so Jeremiah is not sent off to exile, but he stays among his own family and friends and is free to move about (40:4-5 indicates that Jeremiah was given a choice as to whether to go or stay behind). That Jeremiah is "with his own people" is an important motif in this section of the book (see 37:4; 40:6). This may be a signal that Jeremiah's word, however harsh and uncompromising, was finally in the best interests of these people. The juxtaposition of this section with the foregoing lifts up the contrasting fates of Jeremiah and Zedekiah (vv. 6-7).
[Jeremiah, Friend of Babylon]

Jeremiah, Friend of Babylon

That Nebuchadrezzar takes such good care of Jeremiah is not surprising given Jeremiah's counsel that Zedekiah and the Judean populace should surrender to the Babylonians; that would certainly be public information. It is surely ironic that Jeremiah, so mistreated by God's chosen people, is so well treated by the "pagan" Babylonians! This reality may be somewhat disconcerting to readers, both ancient and modern: one of God's great prophets has such a positive relationship with one of Israel's greatest enemies! Yet, it should be remembered that Nebuchadrezzar is named a servant of God (25:9; 27:6; 43:10) and hence it would have been natural for the narrator to link Jeremiah and the king of Babylon in this way. Moreover, God had become an enemy of Israel, given its infidelities, and the Babylonians were instruments of God's judgment against Israel. At the same time, it will be recalled that God becomes an enemy of the Babylonians as well (see 25:12-14; 50–51).

God's Promise to Ebed-melech, 39:15-18

This somewhat delayed account is set at a time when Jeremiah is still confined in the court of the guard (v. 15; NIV puts this segment in the pluperfect). It would be only during that time that Ebed-melech would have had to fear his opponents (v. 17; see 38:9; alternatively, it refers to the Babylonian armies, as in v. 18) and that the promise of his deliverance would have been particularly relevant. This segment may have been included here because this was the time the promise had been fulfilled. In addition, it may be included at this point in the text because it is bracketed by two reports of the deliverance of Jeremiah (39:11-14; 40:1-6). It is Ebed-melech's act in the deliverance of Jeremiah from the cistern that enables this latest deliverance of the prophet. Significantly, his deliverance is set in the midst of the basic point of Jeremiah's preaching, namely, the destruction of the city (v. 16).

From another perspective, the focus in these verses is on Ebed-melech's trust in the Lord (v. 18), not his deliverance of the prophet (which is not even mentioned). It is Ebed-melech's relationship to *God* that accounts for his deliverance, not his rescue efforts on behalf of Jeremiah. They are not unrelated, of course, for it is his trust in God that leads to his actions on behalf of the prophet; but this text in effect grounds Ebed-melech's actions in 38:7-13 in a prior trust in God.

The reader will recall that Ebed-melech was the Ethiopian servant of Zedekiah who had rescued Jeremiah from death in the cistern (38:7-13). God gives a special word to Jeremiah to "go and speak" to Ebed-melech regarding his future (that he could "go" while in prison may be a reference to sending a message). Ebed-melech will be a witness to the destruction of the city as a fulfillment of God's words spoken by Jeremiah; it will be a time of evil (*rāʿāh*) for Jerusalem rather than good (see 21:10). But that will not be his fate; that is not the only kind of activity in which God is engaged at this moment. In language that is repeated for emphasis (note also the infinitive absolute, "surely," v. 18), God is the subject of two salvation verbs (vv. 17-18; see **Connections**). Ebed-melech will be delivered on that terrible day for Jerusalem. He will not be handed over to his enemies or be killed; he will have his life "as a prize of war" (on this theme, see 21:9; 38:2 and **Connections** there; 45:5). Once again, as was sharply emphasized in chapter 38, God's will is for the life of these people, not their death.

CONNECTIONS

God and the Fall of Jerusalem

In view of the content of the book as a whole the reader can introduce God language in speaking of what happens in vv. 1-10. But it is important to note that God is never mentioned in this narrative of Jerusalem's fall (or in vv. 11-14 and 52:4-16, though the introduction to the latter text does speak of God's anger in 52:3). Somewhat strangely, neither Jeremiah nor the fulfillment of the word of God he announced is mentioned either (contrast the Deuteronomic History).

The absence of God language in this text (see also at 37:6-10) corresponds to the use of both God and the Babylonians as the subject of various verbs of destruction and exile throughout the book. The language used for God's judgment conforms to the language used for the Babylonians (see **Introduction** for a list of the parallel expressions). The latter are the instrument God uses to accomplish a judgmental purpose and so the kind of political/military activity engaged in by the Babylonians becomes associated with God. God does not act alone, but through means. That God does not control the Babylonians is evident in the fact that they are judged for exceeding their mandate (25:12-14; 50–51).

At the same time, the chapter speaks of more than judgment. Alongside the judgmental activity are two accounts of saving activity, of Jeremiah (vv. 11-14) and of Ebed-melech (vv. 15-18). Notably, the first does not mention God either (Babylon is the medium for acts of deliverance as well, as potentially in 42:12). But the second account does speak of God and shapes the interpretation of the first. [Salvation in the Midst of Judgment]

Salvation in the Midst of Judgment

The combination of texts in 39:11–40:6 relates to God's deliverance of two faithful followers. Amid all the chaos of the destruction of Jerusalem, and all the faithlessness of the Israelites, God is still at work in saving ways (39:17-18). Judgment is not the only action of God at this disastrous moment in Israel's history; indeed, in and through the fires of judgment God's will to save is still very much in view. Judgment is not understood to be God's final word with respect to Israel. In and through the fires of judgment God continues to be at work in saving ways, even with respect to the lives of individuals and that gives hope for Israel's future. Jeremiah and Ebed-melech are signs for exilic readers of that more hopeful future.

GEDALIAH AND
POST-FALL JUDAH

40:1–41:18

These two chapters, set in the aftermath of the fall of Jerusalem, narrate various features of the governorship of Gedaliah and the anarchy that followed his assassination. Groups still aligned with or against pro-Babylonian policies continue to exist among those left in the land; their rivalry and conflict create havoc during the months and years, through no fault of the Babylonians (who are treated positively throughout; see 40:9-12; 42:11). These chapters show how first the one group and then the other (which went to Egypt) were eliminated as possible remnants for a new beginning for Israel. The only hope for Israel lies with those are exiled in Babylon (for Jeremiah's word about their relationship to the Babylonians, see 24:4-7; 29:5-7).

Nebuchadrezzar appointed Gedaliah governor in 587 BC (see 2 Kgs 25:22-26 for another account). [Gedaliah] This narrative is prefaced by a second account of Jeremiah's release (vv. 1-6). Several factors may account for its placement (see discussion in ch. 39), not least the important role given to non-Israelites in helping to preserve Jeremiah's life (Ebed-melech the Ethiopian; Nebuzaradan the Babylonian; and, of course, Nebuchadrezzar).

But the repeated linkage of Jeremiah to Gedaliah may be especially important (40:5-6; cf. 39:14). In each of these texts Gedaliah's familial heritage is given (and twelve times in the subsequent

---

Gedaliah

Some general information about Gedaliah's governorship is in order. After Jerusalem had fallen to the Babylonians, Judah became a province within the Babylonian empire. With the death and exile of most of Israel's leadership, the country was left largely in the hands of poorer classes of people (39:10), though clearly persons from leadership positions were also still available, including Gedaliah (see 40:8 for others). Gedaliah was appointed as governor of the province by Nebuchadrezzar and hence viewed as a person who could be trusted. Gedaliah understands himself to have a good relationship with the Babylonians so that he could serve as an effective advocate for his people with his Babylonian contacts (40:9-

10). To do this well, he must have had some standing in the Judean community, though his assassination at the hands of those opposed to Babylonian rule shows no little opposition to his policies. He was a member of a reform-minded family that was supportive of Jeremiah (see 26:24; 39:14) and his lineage could be tracked back to Shaphan, King Josiah's secretary (see 2 Kgs 22:8-14). The length of Gedaliah's governorship is uncertain, but he was assassinated no later than 582 BC, when a third group of Israelites were taken into exile (52:30).

Gedaliah's death at the hands of Ishmael became an annual fast-day for the Jews, observed on the third day of the month of Tishri (see Zech 7:5; 8:19).

narrative), as if to stress the importance of this reform-minded family which had special links to Jeremiah (26:24; 39:14) and extended back to the time of Josiah. This repetition may be a way in which the reader's sympathies are tilted toward Gedaliah in the narrative that follows. His policies sound like a hopeful beginning for a new Israel. Jeremiah is linked to Gedaliah and his fledgling enterprise and not to Ishmael and others who continue the rebellion against the Babylonians.

The reader may wonder about the relationship of these texts to the negative evaluation of the "bad figs," those left in the land in 24:8-10. That evaluation may have to do with the period between 597–587 and those such as Zedekiah who are therein named. Yet, Ezek 33:23-29 considers all the survivors left in the land to be idolatrous (and hence linked to the assessment of the "bad figs"). It may be that Jeremiah chooses to remain with those in the land and to continue his ministry among them as one who announces judgment (cf. ch. 44) (see **Connections: The "Absence" of Jeremiah and God**).

COMMENTARY

The Release of Jeremiah, 40:1-6

Just how this account of Jeremiah's release is to be related to that of 39:11-14 is not altogether clear. Some interpreters think that Jeremiah was arrested again after 39:14 and then freed once again in 40:1-6, but this seems a strained understanding. It is better to view 39:11-14 and 40:1-6 as variants of the same events, each text giving readers information from a differing perspective. In the present form of the text, the two passages regarding the liberation of Jeremiah enclose the promise to Ebed-melech (39:15-18), as if to show that their promised futures are interdependent.

If an effort were made to relate 40:1-6 coherently to 39:11-14, 40:1-5 would best fit after 39:14a, the point where Nebuzaradan took Jeremiah from the court of the guard. Verses 39:14b and 40:6 are virtually identical, and now serve as the concluding comment of two differing presentations of the liberation of Jeremiah. Notably, Jeremiah does not speak in either segment, though he acts on the choice given him by the Babylonians. Why Jeremiah chooses to stay in the land rather than go into exile is not certain; he may be thinking of his plot of land and the promise of God associated with it for houses, fields, and vineyards for all Israel (32:15). Early signs of such a promising future seem to be evident in 40:12. Perhaps Jeremiah understands his calling to be related specifically to this group that remains in the land.

Jeremiah was bound in chains and brought to Ramah (about five miles north of Jerusalem) to be included in a caravan of exiles bound for Babylon (v. 1). It may be important for *readers* to see that Jeremiah was included "along with all the captives . . . who were being exiled to Babylon." This places Jeremiah within this particular group of people, with whom Jeremiah has identified himself and of whose future he has spoken (see 24:5-7). He is taken from this group of exiles and freed, but his identity with them remains textually established. Moreover, by now casting his lot with the people left in the land (40:5-6) he establishes an identity with that Judean community. It is as though Jeremiah is to be linked with all the people, whether in exile or in the land. He must understand that his ministry is now to focus on this group in the land. But just how he will do so remains uncertain at this point in the text. Do these Judeans have some future in God's purpose, which would stand in no little tension with 24:8-10? Or, might he understand himself in relation to this group only as one who announces the judgment of God (sharply stated in ch. 44)?

A difficulty in understanding this text pertains to the reference in v. 1 to a word that came from the Lord to Jeremiah; the next explicit word of God, however, does not occur until 42:7-22. It seems best to identify this word of God with the following words of *Nebuzaradan* in vv. 2-5b; this oracle is a means by which the word of God comes to Jeremiah in this anxiety-filled situation (the words in vv. 2-3 are similar to those Jeremiah has spoken before). [God Speaks through Nebuzaradan]

God had announced a disaster (*rāʿāh*) on the city of Jerusalem, and God has followed through on what was spoken (vv. 2-3). The reason is clear: "you" (sing. in v. 2; plur. in v. 3, including Jeremiah!) sinned against the Lord and then you did not listen to God's voice (through the prophets, e.g., 7:25-26). The captain announces that Jeremiah (given his support of Babylon) is being freed from his fetters and that he is free to go where he chooses. Like Zedekiah, Jeremiah is faced with choices, but, ironically, either choice results

God Speaks through Nebuzaradan

The phrase in v. 1a, "The word that came to Jeremiah from the LORD," could be a title for what follows, but it seems best to identify this word of God with those words that the captain Nebuzaradan speaks to Jeremiah in vv. 2-5b. This mediated word of God comes into a situation of no little uncertainty for Jeremiah and is a truly gracious word, a word of freedom spoken within the context of recognized judgment.

The knowledgeable theological perspective of this Babylonian official is important to note (cf. the comparable theological assessment of the devastation of Jerusalem by the nations in 22:8-9). Even non-chosen "outsiders" understand what God has been about in the fall of Jerusalem! When coupled with the salutary activity of Ebed-melech (39:15-18; 38:7-13) and the actions of Nebuchadrezzar, these texts show that God's use of non-Israelites to fulfill the divine purposes is given a significant place (as they will later in, say, King Cyrus of Persia).

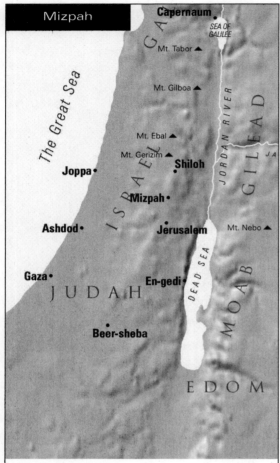

Mizpah

The location of Mizpah is much debated, with sites located five and eight miles north of Jerusalem suggested. In any case, it is near the border of Judah and Benjamin (where Israel chose its first king, 1 Sam 10:17-24). It is established as the center for Gedaliah's government, probably because Jerusalem had been so devastated.

in his freedom. If he wants to go to Babylon that is fine, and he can be assured that the captain will take good care of him. If he does not wish to go into exile, that's fine as well; the entire land of Canaan is open to him and he can go where he thinks it is good and right to go (note the repetition of this point in vv. 4-5). But before he turns to go (so NIV; see NRSV footnote), the captain makes a specific suggestion, to which Jeremiah agrees: that he return to the newly appointed governor Gedaliah and stay with him (see 39:14). The captain then generously gives him a supply of food and an unnamed present and lets him go. Jeremiah, a prophet who has been vindicated by the course of events, stays with Gedaliah at Mizpah among the people left in the land (cf. 39:10, 14). [Mizpah]

Gedaliah's Rule in Mizpah, 40:7-16

This text concerns initial efforts on the part of the Judean community (that did not go into exile) to reestablish themselves in the wake of the debacle. When Nebuchadrezzar appointed Gedaliah (see [Gedaliah]) governor of the province of Judah, he placed him in charge of all the people in the land—men, women, children—that had not been exiled to Babylon (see the parallels in 2 Kgs 25:23-24). Gedaliah was no doubt trusted by the Babylonians and his relationship with the Babylonian regime seems to be exactly what Jeremiah had been calling for in the years before the fall occurred. Now he must make the best of a difficult situation, not least because the Judeans are not united in their relationship to the issue of submission to Babylon. Given such differences among his own people, Gedaliah is faced with a situation not unlike that Zedekiah faced.

Ishmael, Johanan, and Others

In 40:8 Ishmael and several other leaders (of various remaining Judean forces) are mentioned. Some of these individuals remain opposed to submission to Babylon, are not accepting of Gedaliah's rule, and find ways to rebel. Ishmael is especially to be noted. Readers do not learn until 41:1 that he is a member of the Davidic line and one of the chief officers of the deposed King Zedekiah. As such, he clearly represents those who had opposed accommodation to the Babylonians both before and after the fall of Jerusalem. Given his royal lineage, it may be that he had intentions of reestablishing the monarchy in post-fall Judah.

Among these same leaders is Johanan, who is sympathetic to Gedaliah's leadership. Otherwise unknown are Seraiah, the sons of Ephai, and Jezaniah (probably the same as Jaazaniah in 2 Kgs 25:23; a seal ring with this name was discovered at Mizpah in 1932, but its link to this person is uncertain).

When several remaining Judean army units and their leaders hear of Gedaliah's appointment they go to the new governor for a consultation (note that some leading citizens remain in the land). [Ishmael, Johanan, and Others] Gedaliah's leadership seems exemplary in the way he lays out the situation (vv. 9-10). The people respond positively to his initial overtures, which also inspire confidence among exiles in nearby countries (vv. 11-12). He takes an oath in assuring these people that they need not be afraid of Babylon; it will go well with them if they stay in the land and serve the king of Babylon (v. 9; see the earlier assurances of Jeremiah, 27:12). As for himself, he will stay on as governor at Mizpah to represent them in any developing relationships with Babylon (v. 10). As for them, they should settle down in the towns they have occupied, gather in the various crops, and make and store wine and oil (v. 10; similar to Jeremiah's advice to exiles in 29:4-7). With the decimation of the population, there was an abundance of crops for those remaining to harvest and store. When other Judeans who had scattered among the various surrounding nations—Moab, Ammon, Edom, and elsewhere—hear of Gedaliah's appointment over the "remnant of Judah," they return to their own land and rally around Gedaliah at Mizpah. All of them gather an abundant harvest of wines and fruits (vv. 11-12). [The "Remnant in Judah"]

One of the leaders who had earlier come to Mizpah (Johanan, v. 8) returned with his troops to Gedaliah and asked whether he had heard that a conspiracy against him was in the works (v. 13). Johanan claims that a plot is being fomented by Baalis, the king of the neighboring Ammonites, and that he has enlisted Ishmael, a member of the Davidic line (41:1; see below), to assassinate Gedaliah (v. 14). Unfortunately, Gedaliah does not believe him. Johanan refuses to accept this reply and secretly asks Gedaliah for permission to kill Ishmael, assuring him that no one will come to

The "Remnant in Judah"

The use of the language "remnant [in/of Judah]" in vv. 11, 15 (and often in chs. 42–44) is somewhat ambiguous. The word is used Jeremiah in connection with the recipients of both promises (see 23:3; 31:7) and condemnations (24:8). How should the reader assess theologically the "remnant in Judah," the return of scattered ones (40:12; cf. v. 15; 43:5), and the abundance of the land they experience?

The description of the community in v. 12 corresponds in several ways to Jeremiah's earlier promises of salvation (chs. 30–31). From all appearances these promises now seem to be in the process of fulfillment and the future of

God's people in the land is underway. It seems that the Judeans left in the land were given every chance to succeed. This rhetoric may be designed to set up the reader for the soon-to-follow disintegration of this community (of which exilic readers would have had personal knowledge), but the integrity of this remnant's situation should be granted initially. A genuinely positive future is possible for them. While 24:8-10 promotes a perspective that the people left in the land are not the recipient of God's promises, this visionary word was related to the first deportation in 597 BC and times can change things, even visions from the Lord (see 18:7-10).

know who has been involved. His reasoning is clear: Gedaliah is a key person; many scattered Judeans have allied around him and have begun to settle back into the land. If he were killed, then the positive developments in the small community that remained in the land would be jeopardized (as it turns out, a prescient observation).

But Gedaliah again refuses to believe Johanan, accusing him of telling a lie. While Gedaliah would have benefited from listening to Johanan in view of Ishmael's later actions against him (41:2), his instincts regarding Johanan are on target, given Johanan's later rebellion against the word of Jeremiah (43:1-7). At the same time, Gedaliah, for all his gifts in re-establishing the community, is insufficiently discerning regarding threats to his own life. That lack of discernment, so common among Israel's leaders (including Zedekiah), once again becomes a key factor in the disintegration of the Judean community.

Ishmael Leads an Insurrection, 41:1-10

This section is dated in the seventh month; this is apparently some three months after the fall of Jerusalem, though some interpreters think a longer time has elapsed (in view of the deportation in 582 BC). The chapter begins with a more complete identification of Ishmael than had been given in 40:13 (see [Ishmael, Johanan, and Others]).

Ishmael comes to Mizpah with ten men and appears before Gedaliah; the latter's suspicions are apparently not raised, for they sit down and eat a meal together (v. 1). It seems likely that this was a kind of "summit" meeting to sort out differences among Judeans regarding the direction of this new government. That extraordinary precautions were not taken for such a meeting, let alone having the meeting at all, may be testimony again to Gedaliah's lack of discernment.

During the meal Ishmael and his ten men kill Gedaliah with the sword (note again his family credentials). The reason now becomes clear for the first time: Gedaliah is serving at the behest of the king of Babylon, and they believe that to be treason (v. 2; cf. v. 10; 40:14). They will resist Babylonian rule and any Judeans who support these interim measures (the conflict within the community before the fall of Jerusalem thus continues). In addition, in a remarkable feat for only eleven men, Ishmael and his troop kill "all" the Judeans who had rallied around Gedaliah at Mizpah as well as the Babylonian soldiers who were stationed there (v. 3). Verse 10 indicates that many people in Mizpah were not killed, including Jeremiah presumably (see 40:6), so "all the Judeans" may have reference to the armed force protecting the governor or be a hyperbolic statement.

Such an approach to the Babylonians, of course, flies in the face of Jeremiah's counsel at several points, whether to the exiles (29:4-8) or more generally before the fall of Jerusalem (e.g., 27:12; 38:17). Babylon will not sit idly by in the face of such an insurrection. With the assassination of Gedaliah, the idyllic beginning of this Judean community begins to disintegrate; whatever hopes its members may have had to re-establish themselves in the wake of the fall of Jerusalem grow dim.

But Ishmael is not satisfied with just these killings of key leaders. Before the word of his killings gets around, eighty men come to Mizpah from former worship centers of the old northern kingdom (Shechem; Shiloh; Samaria) with offerings to be presented "at the temple of the Lord" (v. 5). Apparently, though the temple had been destroyed, pilgrims came to the site with their offerings. That these Northerners, with apparently honorable if naive intentions, were drawn to the place of the temple in a city in ruins may be a sign of new possibilities for North–South relationships and Gedaliah's new government. This small group may constitute a sign of hope for a united Israel worshiping at the temple once again. But now those hopes will be dashed, at least in this time and place. Their appearance—shaved beards, torn clothes, and gashed bodies—suggests they were engaged in rituals of lamentation over recent disastrous events (no evaluation is given of their rituals, though Deut 14:1 forbids them). The dating in the seventh month (41:1) would coincide with the time of the fall festivals, including the Day of Atonement (see Lev 16:29).

Ishmael's (feigned) weeping and welcome of them would suggest to the visitors that he is sympathetic with their purpose (v. 6). But once the men enter the city, Ishmael and his men turn on the visitors, ruthlessly slaughter many of them, and throw them into a cistern. It is uncertain why Ishmael would be so bloodthirsty; perhaps he thought them to be Gedaliah sympathizers, perhaps even giving homage to one who was, for Ishmael, an illegitimate Babylonian puppet. Ironically, they may have been more sympathetic to Ishmael given their interest in worship at the temple site and its royal connections.

The reason for the precise identification of the cistern into which they were thrown is unknown; perhaps it recalls a comparably difficult time in Israel's life (v. 9). It is the large one constructed by the Southern king Asa (913–873 BC) to defend against the Northern king Baasha (900–877 BC; on this war, see 1 Kgs 15:16-24; recall that the eighty men were Northerners). Ten members of the group do manage to make a case for their survival. They had stores of food hidden in the fields (either near the cities from which they have come, or perhaps hidden in the area in view of perceived threats) and it would be in Ishmael's best interests to be able to access those supplies (v. 8). These ten persons do not appear again in the narrative.

Ishmael is not finished with his insurrection. He captures all the rest of the people in Mizpah who are sympathetic to Gedaliah (including the daughters of the deposed King Zedekiah, see 43:6; cf. 38:23) and who had been committed to Gedaliah by the Babylonian captain Nebuzaradan (v. 10; see 40:5-6). Then Ishmael and his men set out with these hostages (perhaps eyewitnesses to his murders?) to go to Ammon, whose king had sponsored Ishmael's escapades (40:14). The route of their journey is uncertain in that Gibeon (v. 12) is thought to be southwest of Mizpah and not in the direction of Ammon; such a circuitous route may have been demanded by unknown circumstances.

Johanan's Response, 41:11-18

When Johanan, who was opposed to Ishmael's designs (but who had an ambivalent relationship to Gedaliah, 40:16), hears of what Ishmael and his men have done, he and the leaders with him intercept them on their way to Ammon (vv. 11-12; where Johanan's group had been located is not specified; why had he not been close at hand given his knowledge of Ishmael's plot?). He meets them at the great pool of Gibeon, a city about six miles northwest of

Jerusalem. The pool, a deep and circular cavity carved in the rock, was part of the city's water system and a well-known landmark (see 2 Sam 2:13). When "all" the people whom Ishmael had forced to go with him to Ammon see Johanan, they welcome him and joyfully join his forces (vv. 13-14). But Ishmael escapes with eight men to Ammon (v. 15). He is never heard from again, but he has been successful in inflicting a decisive disruption on this fledgling community.

Then Johanan takes charge of "all" the rest of Ishmael's captives—soldiers, women, children, eunuchs (to protect the princesses?)—and sets out from Gibeon to go to Egypt, stopping at an unknown place (Geruth Chimham, see 2 Sam 19:37-38) near Bethlehem (vv. 16-17). Their reason for not returning to Mizpah, but heading to Egypt stems from a fear of Babylonian reprisals for Ishmael's assassination of their appointed governor Gedaliah and their failure to protect him (v. 18). That their fear was not unfounded can be seen from 52:30, which reports that the Babylonians exiled a third group of people (in 582 BC), though Jeremiah will indicate that they need not be afraid of the king of Babylon (42:11).

CONNECTIONS

The "Absence" of God and Jeremiah

The absence of God language in the story of Gedaliah is often noted, but care must be used in drawing conclusions as if, say, God were not present and active in these events. God language is not used in the two descriptions of the fall of Jerusalem either (39:1-10; 52:4-16), but the reader of Jeremiah would certainly conclude that God was involved in that event. The absence of God language shows that the human engagement in these events is effective and can serve God's purposes. The careful and repeated linkage of Gedaliah to Jeremiah is apparently deemed sufficient to provide guidance for the reader in evaluating his rule and the insurrection of Ishmael. At the same time, the lack of any appeal to God on the part of the characters could strike an ominous note.

Jeremiah is also not mentioned in this segment of the text; he is present at the beginning (40:5-6) but does not return until 42:1-2. This could be explained in terms of the insertion of material from a different tradition (Jeremiah is not present in 2 Kgs 25:22-26 either), but that Jeremiah has not been incorporated into this material by editors of the book at some stage still calls for explanation. The prophet is thereby not represented as being present during the time this community falls apart; v. 6 would place him with Gedaliah in Mizpah, a center of the action that follows (he would thus be a marked man from the perspective of the rebels). At the same time, this community at no time in this segment of the narrative calls upon the prophet or God for help in the crisis. That both God and Jeremiah slip into the background during this time could suggest that God's future purposes with Israel are not to be associated with this group of people (see 24:8-10). Jeremiah reappears on the scene only when this group is on its way to Egypt and his role among them is finally that of one whose counsel is rejected and who announces God's judgment on them (ch. 44). [A Return to Egypt]

A Return to Egypt

It is often noted that Jeremiah's journey from the cistern in Canaan to the land of Egypt is parallel to that of Joseph (cf. Gen 37:22-24, 36) and reverses the exodus journey. The reticence to use God language in the Joseph story, especially language regarding God's appearances and action, is another similar parallel. Moreover, Jeremiah and Moses are parallel in their active dialogical relationship with God and in the fact that the people listen to neither of them. The net effect is that this remnant of Israel is returned to slavery in Egypt, but this time they experience only the judgment of God, have no exodus to anticipate and are in time absorbed into the Egyptian community.

JEREMIAH AND THE "REMNANT OF JUDAH"

42:1-22

This chapter continues the narrative of the previous chapters. The basic issue addressed is whether this "remnant" gathered "near Bethlehem" should proceed to Egypt or stay in the land. Jeremiah's response is that staying in the land is God's will for them; in effect, this response is consonant with Jeremiah's previous word that calls for submission to Babylon. [The Remnant of Judah]

The bulk of this chapter consists of speeches, climaxing in God's word to "the remnant of Judah" (vv. 9-22); the latter may consist of two oracles (vv. 9-17, 18-22). This word is a response to the remnant's request of Jeremiah for a word of God regarding their future (vv. 1-3). There follows an exchange in which Jeremiah promises to speak the truth and the people promise to obey whatever word they receive (vv. 4-6). They do obey Jeremiah's summons to hear that word (vv. 7-8), but they reject the word of God (reported in 43:1-7).

COMMENTARY

The Request of the Remnant, 42:1-8

Initially, all the army leaders, with Johanan and Azariah (so NRSV on the basis of the names in 43:2), and "all" the people (including children, "the least," presumably those who were with Johanan on the flight into Egypt, 41:16-18) approach "the prophet" Jeremiah (vv. 1-2). The entire community is said to be behind this request. Jeremiah is clearly recognized as an authoritative prophet, whose access to the word of God is assumed. Yet, he takes no initiative in this situation; the people come to him. In the wake of the death and failure of other leaders, they may be seeking divine approval for their intention to go to Egypt. It is not made clear how it is that Jeremiah is among this group near Bethlehem and he will make no reference to the events of 40:7–41:18 (the assassination of Gedaliah is not even mentioned).

The Remnant of Judah

This text implicitly recognizes that there are two "remnants" that continue to exist in the wake of the fall of Jerusalem. One remnant has been taken to Babylon; the other remains in the land of Canaan, but voices its intention to leave for Egypt. The language of "remnant" used for the latter does not imply that this is the only group with whom God is now concerned. On the other hand, the language of rejection in 24:8-10 for those who stay in the land ought not be used to suggest that *only* the remnant in Babylon is now in God's promised future and that this remnant still in the land is of no account to God (note that 24:8-10 is dated at the time of the first subjugation of Jerusalem, some ten years earlier). After all, they are given promises, albeit conditional

ones, regarding a positive future. It is not unimportant to note that God's command to Jeremiah not to pray for this people (11:14; 14:11) no longer applies in this situation, given recent events. That Jeremiah does pray for this remnant would imply that it has a standing with God that the people before the fall of Jerusalem did not have.

Exilic readers, already in submission to Babylon (see 29:5-7), will understand from this chapter why it developed that a remnant of their number went to Egypt and why they are excluded from the future that God has promised to them and to Israel more generally. In the end, except for some stragglers from Egypt and elsewhere (see 44:14), only the remnant in Babylon will be left.

The people plead with Jeremiah to pray to the Lord "your" God (as does Zedekiah in 37:3, with similar results) for this threatened "remnant of Judah" (see vv. 15, 19; 40:11, 15). They twice call attention to the fact that not many of them are left (v. 2), and they ask Jeremiah to discern what God would like them to do (v. 3). Jeremiah agrees to pray for them to the Lord "your" God (the "your" is used by both parties in this conversation, signaling a mutuality in believing), and whatever the Lord tells him, he will keep nothing back from them (v. 4).

This "remnant" responds to Jeremiah in turn (vv. 5-6). They understand that God is a faithful and true witness (note the emphasis) to what they now agree to do as well as how they act upon their agreement; this language makes their response an oath. They promise to obey *whatever* word (that is, "good or bad") God speaks to them through Jeremiah. The emphatic nature of their promise contrasts sharply with their later failure (the reason for such exaggerated language is uncertain; it is almost as if they themselves needed to be convinced). God is expected to "send" (see vv. 9, 21; 43:1) Jeremiah a word for them and they recognize that to obey the word of God will affect whether it goes well with them or not.

Interestingly, it takes ten days for the word of God to come to Jeremiah (v. 7; cf. 28:12 for an unspecified delay). Notably, Jeremiah does not have a ready reply. [Time for Prophetic Discernment] At the same time, the ten days signals a considerable

Time for Prophetic Discernment

The notice of the time it takes for Jeremiah to receive a word from God (42:7) should probably be understood in the sense that it takes Jeremiah ten days to discern the nature of the word of God for this particular situation. At the same time, this period should *not* be understood in such a way that Jeremiah's own time of reflection is discounted, as if the prophet were somehow disengaged and waiting only for lightning to strike. That is, Jeremiah is engaged with God regarding this matter (by responding to the request for prayer) and it takes time for him to gain enough insight to sort out the issues properly. It is difficult to know how typical this time for reflection has been for Jeremiah or other prophets, but in view also of 28:12 (an unspecified time of delay), it was probably more common than infrequent.

Flight to Egypt

length of time for the remnant to cool their heels waiting for some word from God. They intended to go to Egypt (41:17) and so, even with their expression of openness (42:5-6), that destination would certainly continue to be the direction of their thinking and planning. See below on how this decisiveness shapes Jeremiah's reply, which is especially heavy on the "if not" side of the oracle.

To convey this word, Jeremiah does not convey the matter to just the leaders; he speaks the word to everyone in this remnant, including the children (v. 8). It is unusual that Jeremiah actually delivers this word to the audience; usually he receives the word from God without any report regarding his deliverance of the word. Everyone knows what the word of God for this community now is and what they will need to do to respond faithfully.

God's Word to the Remnant, 42:9-22

The balance of the chapter (vv. 9-22) consists of this word of God. It is shaped in terms of "if-then" constructions, common in Jeremiah (e.g., 22:1-5; 38:17-18, 21-23). The first "if-then" states the positive effects of remaining in the land (vv. 10-12), the second "if-then" spells out in greater detail the negative effects of going to Egypt (vv. 13-17; note that the "if" is stated twice for emphasis, vv. 13, 15). In a continuation of the "then" of vv. 16-17, vv. 18-22 expand upon these negative effects.

The essence of the word of God to this remnant is that they should stay in the land and seek to rebuild it; in effect, they are to do what Gedaliah had set out to do (40:9-10). That is, Gedaliah's word regarding the unnecessary fear of Babylon and the salutary effect of staying in the land here becomes God's word through Jeremiah! God's initial word to them has a very positive tone and outlook (vv. 10-12); indeed, the theological language used is remarkably rich and telling. Themes from Jeremiah's call are here drawn upon to convey the word (see 1:10). If they will remain in the land, then God will build and plant them, not pluck them up or pull them down (note that this judgmental activity of God is not exhausted in the fall of Jerusalem).

God's reason that informs this word is startling: God is sorry for bringing the disaster (*rāʿāh*) upon them, that is, the fall of Jerusalem! (see **Connections: Is God Sorry?**). It should be noted that the language of planting and building is used in the earlier salvation oracles (24:6; 31:28; 32:41) as simple promise, without conditions; here those verbs are used in a conditional clause ("if you remain in the land"). The reasons for this difference are not altogether clear, but one factor may be that, unlike the unconditional promise to exiles regarding their return to the land, this remnant is already in the land and is contemplating leaving the land.

This remnant should not "be afraid" (note the repetition, as in Jeremiah's call, 1:9, 18) of Nebuchadrezzar, for God is with them, and God will save (*yāšāʿ*) them and rescue (*nāṣal*) them from his power. It is not entirely clear what this action entails, but it may be a reference to the ultimate defeat of Babylon (see chs. 50–51). As for now, Babylon is disposed to act mercifully. God will grant them mercy (*raḥᵃmîm*) and Nebuchadrezzar (!) will grant them mercy (*rāḥam*) and restore them to their land. It is rare to find such a string of key words for divine presence, for salvation, and for mercy, long central to Israel's confessions of its experience with this God (see **Connections: Nebuchadrezzar Will Have Mercy!**).

While an "if not" will next be used (v. 13), and will be stated in very strong language, it is important to give high standing to the integrity of the positive declaration. Given this rich theological vocabulary, it seems highly unlikely that it is given with the full knowledge that it will not come to pass (though that is certainly the perspective of the readers). If the positive future were not a genuine possibility, even if remote, then stating matters in this way is deeply deceptive (and one would need some textual warrants to suggest that God is here purposely deceiving them). (For other either-or formulations, see 21:8-10; 22:1-5 [see **Connections** there]; 38:17-18.)

The "if not" in the divine response to Jeremiah's prayer is also stated with clarity; the repetition in vv. 13-17 drives the point home. It is made clear that, if this proves to be their future, they have no one to blame but themselves. As noted above, the length of the "if not" statement is certainly related to a decisive direction in their decision-making (a comparable balance of positive and negative possibilities for the future is present in the curses and blessings of Deut 28). Thinking through this reply is difficult, for by the time the reader gets to v. 22, a positive future seems to be precluded, given certain features of Jeremiah's response.

The predisposition of the remnant to go to Egypt (noted above) seems to be powerfully in evidence in the response of God/Jeremiah; these words seek to overcome decisions of the remnant that, given the passing of ten days, have certainly become more certain. The response of Jeremiah in vv. 13-14 includes specific quotations from the remnant that suggest a certain settledness in their thinking: "we will not stay in this land"; "No, we will go to the land of Egypt...and there we will stay." Certain phrases in Jeremiah's response that seem to address a late stage in decision-making include, "if you continue to say [or, keep saying]" (v. 13); "if you are determined [lit., have set your faces] to enter Egypt and go to settle there" (in both v. 15 and v. 17).

If this remnant insists on leaving the land, thereby disobeying God's voice (which they had just sworn not to do, vv. 5-6), and if they go to Egypt so as not

The Alabaster Sphinx

Alabaster sphinx from the Temple of Ptah in Memphis. C. 1400 BC. (Credit: Brewton-Parker College)

The Alabaster Sphinx is 4.5 m high and 8 m long and weighing some 90 tons. It was found near the entrance of the Temple dedicated to Ptah, the principle god of Memphis. The sphinx may have been built under the rule of Amenhotep II during the New Kingdom, 18th dynasty.

Perhaps the sphinx functioned as an eternal guardian (a surrogate pharoah) to protect the temple of the god, Ptah. The sphinx communicates an eternal vigilance, facing the Nile River—witnessing the annual rising and subsiding of the eternal waters of life. More specifically, it may have functioned in a funerary context as a spiritual surrogate of the pharaoh in order to provide the Ka, spirit of afterlife, a permanent replica of pharoah spirit in case his mummified remains were disturbed.

Projecting an image of power was important. Here, pharoah's power is communicated through the traditional royal costume as seen with the linen headress along with the uraeus,(the cobra symbol of Ra) and the false beard symbolic of kingship. Such symbols of the pharoah's divinity, power and eternal stability had been prevalent in Egyptian art since c. 3000 BC. Ironically, this alabaster sphinx is but a remnant, perhaps reflecting some of the vestiges of defeat by the Persians in 525 BC.

to experience war or the call to war (the trumpet) or hunger, then they must hear a different word (vv. 13-14). The desire to escape from war and its effects seems quite reasonable, but Jeremiah states that their fears are unfounded. In fact, it will be worse for them in Egypt than if they stay in the land. This assessment seems to represent a careful analysis of actual realities, not a "set piece" that has been in place all along (the ten days would be irrelevant in such a case). Life under the Egyptians will actually be worse than life under the Babylonians. The only reasons given are positive, namely, that life under the Babylonians will go very well. Setting this over against life in Egypt probably has in mind the negative potential of a Babylonian invasion of Egypt (foreseen in 43:8-13). In other words, Jeremiah takes the arguments of the remnant for not staying in the land seriously (v. 14) and claims that their analysis is incorrect; it will be much better for them to stay in the land. The announcement of *potential* judgment is then addressed to the "remnant of Judah" (also used in v. 19; 40:15; 43:5; 44:7, 12, 14, 28). If they go to settle in Egypt, then the sword and the famine from which they are fearfully seeking to escape will follow them there and overtake them. In Egypt they will die (vv. 15-16). Then, repeating the point (v. 17), the familiar triad of "sword, famine, and pestilence" (see 14:12) will pursue them all the way to Egypt.

God, who was sorry about bringing the disaster (*rā'āh*) of the fall of Jerusalem and Judah upon them (v. 10), will bring that disaster (*rā'āh*) on them again, and this time there will be no survivors. This remnant will be no more. This is an expression of the strong convictions of the prophet regarding the implications of the move back to Egypt and leaving the land of promise. Theological reasons are added to political realities; this would be a reversal of the exodus (see the divine command about not returning to Egypt in Deut 17:16) and a fulfillment of the curses of Deuteronomy 28:68. Verse 18 draws the conclusion even more sharply, namely, that in going to Egypt, and given the socio-political experience that that will entail, they will experience a judgment just as sharp and decisive as the judgment on Jerusalem (see [A Return to Egypt]). The language used for the latter (wrath; horror; object of cursing and ridicule; e.g., 25:9, 18; 29:18) is here employed to demonstrate the correspondence (see also 44:12; on the wrath of God, so emphasized in v. 18, see **Connections,** ch. 25).

Verses 19-22 repeat the command not to go to Egypt and expand upon the announcement of potential judgment. But here the difficulties mount; they seem to assume that the remnant has already chosen to reject Jeremiah's counsel ("you have made a fatal mistake," v. 20). Some scholars seek to resolve the issue by transferring these verses after 43:1-3, where the remnant does explicitly reject the word of God,[1] but this move is too easy and without textual justification. It seems better to understand these verses as strong argumentation on Jeremiah's part in the face of what appears to be an irreversible decision to go to Egypt (see above). One could translate several verbs as present rather than past; they could thus have the sense: Do not go to Egypt, for if you do, "know for certain that you are deceiving Yahweh and putting your lives at risk."[2] Alternatively, the phrase "you have made a fatal mistake" could also be understood as a sharp and specific response to their announced and apparently continuing intention to go to Egypt. If they follow through on that mistaken decision, that would be fatal. The phrase in v. 21, "you have not obeyed," could be understood in the sense of NIV, "you have still not obeyed." Jeremiah remonstrates with the remnant, reminding them that they were the ones who sought the counsel in the first place, and that they promised to obey the word Jeremiah brought to them. From Jeremiah's perspective, they are still set on going to Egypt. But, he repeats one more time (cf. vv. 17, 22) that, if they do, they will die.

CONNECTIONS

Is God Sorry?

For God to say, "I am sorry," is a striking admission (v. 10). [The Translation of the verb *niham*] Does this phrase mean that God regrets that the judgment has occurred at all? Or, is the point softer, namely, that God is sorry about all the pain that this community has had to experience? Or, does it mean that the past stance of God toward this people that led to judgment has now changed in view of events; God is now open to a future for this people other than judgment? McKane thinks in these terms: "My present attitude to you is benevolent and is not the one which prevailed when I executed judgment against you."[3] It is important to note that the divine "regret" is not prompted by anything that the people have done; this divine move is made entirely at the divine initiative.

It seems to me that this statement of God carries with it the sense of genuine regret, in the sense that the judgment and its painful

The Translation of the Verb niham

AΩ The translation of the verb *niham* in 42:10 is difficult (NRSV, "be sorry"; NAB, "regret"; NIV, "grieve"). This word has been used often in Jeremiah up to this point (e.g., 18:7-10; 26:3, 13, 19), where it has carried the sense of God reversing a direction taken in view of human response (see **Connections**, ch. 18). The NIV translation "grieved over" may be guided by an effort to avoid the more difficult idea of divine regret, as may other translations (NEB, "I grieve for the disaster which I brought upon you"; Daniel Berrigan, "The destruction I caused you has brought me great sorrow"). For this verb with the sense of genuine regret, adopted here, see Gen 6:5-6.

Daniel Berrigan, *Jeremiah, The World, the Wound of God* (Minneapolis: Fortress, 1999), 131 effects proved to be more severe than God had imagined and certainly had intended. This direction of interpretation seems especially apt in view of the fact that Babylon far exceeded their mandate of judgment and made the land and people a waste (see 25:12-14; 50–51; see especially Zech 1:15, "while I was only a little angry; they made the disaster worse"). God does not remove the divine self from responsibility for the choice of means that resulted in an imperfect execution of the mandate. God, who does not foreknow absolutely just what and how the means chosen will speak and act (see **Connections**, ch. 22), accepts responsibility for what happened at least in part (Babylon will also bear its responsibility).

Nebuchadrezzar Will Have Mercy!

It is striking that Nebuchadrezzar is the subject of the verb *rḥm*, "to have mercy." As with the language of judgment throughout Jeremiah (see parallel columns in the Introduction), so here the merciful actions of God and the merciful actions of Babylon come together. The Babylonian treatment of their subjects will be the means in and through which God exercises mercy. God does not override the destructive Babylonian policies that have taken place (though judgment will come for Babylon as well), but will work in and through potential enlightened ones. The people may well have good reason to be fearful, but in the face of such possibilities, God's mercy and Babylon's mercy will prove to be the decisive feature of that future. They will experience no mercy in Egypt and no salvation from Egypt, no exodus "one more time." Their salvation is to be found where they now are, in the land of promise. Their future is here, not there. Exodus this time around will entail a coming out of *Babylon* (see 16:14-15=23:7-8), not a coming out of Egypt.

This unusual use of language is to be linked back to 13:14 and 21:7, where both God and Nebuchadrezzar are the subject of the verb *rḥm*, only in negative terms. Neither God nor Babylonian king would have mercy before; now they will *both* have mercy! And "the remnant of Judah" will be the recipient of this compassion. Moreover, the language used for Nebuchadrezzar restoring them to their land (hiphil of *šûb*) is elsewhere used of God (e.g., 30:3). The strong language of grace, mercy, and salvation seems designed to draw a very reluctant and fearful remnant toward the blessings of staying the land (might it also serve as anticipation for the exiles?). Note the repeated effort to speak to their fears of Babylon in v. 11 (no doubt prompted for the most part by their anticipation of a response to Gedaliah's assassination), and the strong theological language used for the actions of the king of Babylon. The unusual language of divine regret in v. 10 may also be integral to such an appeal. It may be that the divine regret is also related to the announcement in 21:8-10, where the fate for those who remain in the land is exactly the opposite of that offered here. The word for these people that was applicable back then is no longer the word of the future for them.

The relationship between this positive statement regarding the potential future of "the remnant of Judah" and the earlier promises of restoration (chs. 30–33) is not altogether clear. The latter promises are directed to the exiles in Babylon and the promises to this remnant seem designed to draw them into a future like unto that promised the exiles in Babylon. The similarity in motif and language suggests such a relationship, but the point is difficult to discern, not least given the length of time anticipated for the exiles time in Babylon (29:4-7). The suggestion that the remnant of Judah is an "advance guard" or a "down payment" of the grand restoration to come is as close as one can come to a discernment of the connection.

NOTES

[1] See William Holladay, *Jeremiah 2* (Philadelphia: Fortress, 1989), 274-75.

[2] William McKane, *A Critical and Exegetical Commentary on Jeremiah* (2 vols.; ICC; Edinburgh: T. & T. Clark, 1986), 1030, 1044.

[3] Ibid., 1033.

JEREMIAH IN EGYPT

43:1–44:30

The opening verses of chapter 43 (vv. 1-7) continue the narrative from the prior chapters; the "remnant" responds to Jeremiah's word about staying in the land. They refuse to listen to the word of God and their entire company sets out for Egypt. They apparently force Jeremiah and Baruch to go with them, though the text is remarkably silent about the matter. The balance of these chapters (43:8–44:30) report on several interactions between Jeremiah and those among whom he lived in Egypt.

COMMENTARY

The "Remnant of Judah" Rejects the Word of God, 43:1-7

When Jeremiah finishes speaking the word from God that the "remnant of Judah" had themselves requested and promised to obey (42:2-6), their leaders accuse him of "telling a lie"; ironically, this is the accusation commonly brought by Jeremiah against false prophets and others (23:14, 25-26; 27:10; 28:15; 29:21). By such a judgment, they make a counter-claim: God's will is for them to go to Egypt and hence they are to be identified with the people of God.

There is no certain way to demonstrate that this remnant's assessment of Jeremiah's word is correct; the narrative, however, makes that determination for readers by the way in which God's will and word is set against such a judgment of Jeremiah. Johanan and Azariah and "all" the other insolent men (narrower than "all the people" of v.1; yet this phrase returns in v. 4) claim that *God* did not send Jeremiah to tell them that they were not to go down to Egypt and settle. Even more, Jeremiah's word is part of a conspiracy, and it is *Baruch* who has put him up to it (but this still makes Jeremiah a liar as far as they are concerned). Jeremiah's secretary, not mentioned since chapter 36, was so closely allied with the prophet regarding this issue that to accuse him is to make a judgment on both of them. Baruch's counsel, they claim, is actually a ruse so that the Babylonians can either

The Emphasis on "All"

AΩ In 43:1-7 the stress is placed on the involvement of everyone. Johanan and "all" the commanders take "all" the remnant of Judah from "all" the nations down to Egypt—men, women, children, princesses (see 41:10), "everyone" whom the Babylonian captain Nebuzaradan had entrusted to Gedaliah (see 40:5-6, 11-12; 41:10). An ironic point may be made in v. 5 in that those who had returned to the land (in view of Gedaliah's policies, see 40:11-12) are now leaving it again. It may be that these exiles are understood to return to the land too soon; a longer exile had been specified (29:10).

This sweeping "all" seems best understood as hyperbolic (the land was not emptied of every inhabitant, see 52:30). This emphasis on the involvement of everyone may address a concern of the Babylonian exiles: a distinction is made between exiled groups regarding their standing as recipients of the promises of God. These exiles did not need to worry about another group being identified as the object of God's saving work (see chs. 30–31); they were the only group left to be the inheritors of God's promises.

---

execute or exile this remnant, perhaps in retaliation for the killing of Gedaliah (v. 3; cf. 42:14). It is unclear why Baruch receives the brunt of the blame here, for Jeremiah's perspective on this matter has long been a public stance. In any case, they believe these reasons (lies and conspiracy) are sufficient justification for them to violate their promise (42:5-6).

The upshot of this accusation is stated in vv. 4-7; these verses are bracketed by the phrase, "did not obey the voice of the LORD." This refusal to listen to the word of God is key to what they do. The narrative proceeds to stress that there are no exceptions to this response. *Everyone* (from "all" the commanders to "all" the people, v. 4) refuses to stay in the land of Judah. Verse 5 continues the journey begun in 41:16-17. [The Emphasis on "All"] Jeremiah and Baruch are apparently forced to go with them. Yet, notably, this is not explicitly stated; the narrative point may be that Jeremiah's word of judgment follows them all the way to their destination and completes its work. At the same time, the narrative's surprising recall (also 41:10) of the Babylonian captain and Gedaliah indicates that they are held in high regard and that their work in the land of promise is here being undermined by the trip to Egypt.

The remnant settles in the Egyptian city of Tahpanhes (see at 2:16). This was their destination, of course, and by rejecting Jeremiah's word they understand this to be God's will for them. [A Defeat for God]

A Defeat for God

Walter Brueggemann states it well: The remnant of Judah "ended up where the story of Israel had begun, back in Egypt, back in a bondage they misread as freedom . . . . The end result is not only a defeat for Jeremiah. It is an awesome defeat for the God whose work had begun in an escape from Egypt." In properly naming these developments as a "defeat" for God, of course, implies that God is not "in control" of this people. God had wanted a different future for this people, but they would have none of it. Finally, they could only blame themselves, not some predetermined divine decision.

Walter Brueggemann, *A Commentary on Jeremiah: Exile and Homecoming* (Grand Rapids: Eerdmans, 1998), 399.

A Final Symbolic Act by Jeremiah, 43:8-13

This narrative is commonly set sometime after 582 BC. It anticipates the oracle against Egypt in 46:13-26; once again,
Nebuchadrezzar is depicted as the one who reduces Egyptian
dominion to nothing. The word of the Lord and its reception by a
prophet, which know no national boundaries, comes to Jeremiah
in Egypt.

The narrative begins with another symbolic act that God commands Jeremiah to perform; as with the act in 13:1-11, objects of
no apparent religious import are used to symbolize a divine activity
(see **Connections**, ch. 13). Jeremiah's obedience of the command is
not reported, which shows that the action itself was not believed to
have magical or sacramental properties. Jeremiah's action does not
make Babylonian dominion possible or trigger its happening. Its
power lies in the combination of visual and verbal elements. Its
power as a visual symbol was significant enough that God's command includes the requirement that "the Judeans *see* you do it." Its
verbal aspect brings the specific word of God to bear in interpreting its significance.

Jeremiah is to take some large stones and embed (but not completely bury)[1] them in the clay pavement (or, mortar) in front of
the house of Pharaoh. This is probably not the main palace, which
would be in the capital city of Sais at this time; yet, the narrator
may not have had this information available and the point is somewhat softened if it is not the actual palace. Jeremiah is to let the
Judeans see him do this (it would be difficult to accomplish
secretly, in any case), and then announce to them a word of the
Lord, symbolized by this action.

The provision of a specific foundation for the throne of
Nebuchadrezzar is then given verbal expression. God is going to
send "my servant" Nebuchadrezzar into Egypt (on this theme, see
25:9; 27:6; 46:13-26; Ezek 29:19-20; 30:10). He will ravage the
land and he will set (see NRSV footnote) his throne and royal
canopy over the stones that Jeremiah has just embedded. (Note
that the first "I" in this oracle is God and the second "I" seems to
be Jeremiah, but, given that this is a divine oracle, it is probably to
be understood as God acting through the agency of Jeremiah).[2]
The stones that Jeremiah has set in the pavement before pharaoh's
palace will provide the foundation for the dominion of
Nebuchadrezzar over Egypt in the very place of the Pharaoh's
dominion. Once again, in exodus-like fashion, the Egyptian
pharaoh will be bested by powers in and through which Israel's
God is at work. And all the religious symbols that were thought to

establish the throne of pharaoh (temples and idols) will be destroyed or carted away.

The brief poem in v. 11, formerly applied to the devastation of Jerusalem (15:2), is here applied to the destruction of Egypt (anticipated in 42:17, 22). Though the Judeans are not explicitly mentioned as the object of the Babylonian invasion, they are explicitly made witnesses to the sign, and the language of the threat to them in 42:17 is picked up in 43:11. That this segment of the narrative is sandwiched between the Judean's rejection of the word of the Lord (43:1-7) and their apostasy in chapter 44 certainly means that the invasion of Egypt by Nebuchadrezzar has something to do with them. They have now settled among the Egyptians and are included within their population. Hence, ironically, they too will experience at the hands of Nebuchadrezzar what they thought to escape by leaving the land! In effect, it will be an experience of the fall of Jerusalem all over again for them. Once again, they will "die by the sword, by famine, and by pestilence" (42:22). In both cases, they will suffer disaster as a community and Babylonian dominion over them will be established.

The verbs in v. 12 have an interesting feature in that the first ("kindle a fire") has God as subject (see NRSV footnote) and the others have Nebuchadrezzar as subject. As is often the case in Jeremiah, God and the king of Babylon (or the Babylonians) are often the subject of the same words of (usually) judgment (see **Introduction**). Consistently, God works in and through that which is not God to accomplish the divine purposes. *God* will kindle a fire in the temples of the gods in Egypt (see Amos 1:14; Ezek 30:13), and *Nebuchadrezzar* will burn the temples and carry the gods (idols) off into exile (cf. Isa 46:1-2 for such a practice). The image of him picking the land of Egypt clean as a shepherd delouses his garments (so NRSV) is an uncertain translation. The image of Nebuchadrezzar wrapping up Egypt and carrying its spoil away as a shepherd wraps his garment around him and moves on may be more likely.[3] And when he is through devastating the place, he will safely leave. In other words, he will not even be touched! Finally, he will break down the obelisks of Heliopolis and destroy the temples of the gods with fire (apparently, if the present text is correct, this

On the Egyptian Setting

The reference to the "house" or palace of the pharaoh in v. 9 is probably a reference to a royal building or secondary house of Pharaoh, for the capital of Egypt during his time was in Sais. Yet, the narrator may have had less than accurate knowledge about Egypt; the point is much sharper if the actual palace is in view.

Heliopolis (also called On, see Gen 41:45) is the NRSV translation of the Hebrew name Bethshemesh, "house [that is, temple] of the sun" (so translated by NAB; NIV; JB). But the place in mind is not certain. If Heliopolis is correct, it was a city near Cairo and the center for the worship of the sun god Re. It was renowned for its obelisks—free-standing granite pillars with four sides and a pyramidal top.

will complete the job begun in v. 12, though some translators transpose portions of v. 12 and v. 13). [On the Egyptian Setting]

The relationship between this divine oracle and an actual Babylonian invasion of Egypt in 568 BC is difficult because of limited knowledge regarding the latter. It is generally agreed that Babylon did not conquer Egypt, but exacted a punitive strike against it and then withdrew.

Jeremiah's Words to Judeans in Egypt, 44:1-30

Chronologically, these are Jeremiah's last recorded public oracles. Both the prophet and his message continue to be rejected by the people. The time and place of Jeremiah's death are not known; according to tradition, he is murdered in Egypt by fellow Judeans. Textually, however, Jeremiah's oracles against the nations follow (chs. 46–51), which finally promise deliverance for the exiles from their Babylonian overlords.

This chapter consists of three statements by Jeremiah to assembled Judeans in Egypt (vv. 1-14, 20-23, 24-30). The Judeans react to the first statement (vv. 15-19) and Jeremiah's final two oracles respond to this reaction. [Interpretation across the Generations]

An interesting intermixing of audiences has to do with the males and females among the Judeans. In v. 9 the reference to "your own crimes and those of your wives" indicates that the oracle is primarily addressed to the males, but that the females are singled out in a special way (see also v. 15 for the inclusion of both; see below on vv. 15-19). It is possible that the women are specifically mentioned to make clear that, even in a patriarchal culture, they have been as much involved with idolatry as have the men.

Interpretation across the Generations

Remarkable in this chapter is the admixture of references to "they" (the populace of Judah and Jerusalem as a whole at the time of the fall, as well as their ancestors) and "you" (the present Judean audience in Egypt). Essentially, this elision of past and present means that the Judeans in Egypt have followed in the ways of their ancestors that led to the fall of Jerusalem; consequently, they will suffer the same effects. This application of an earlier message to a later generation provides a hermeneutic for all later generations' use of this and other material in Jeremiah. If the situation of the hearers is comparable, then an earlier word of God is considered applicable in a similar way.

From another perspective, the language of indictment and judgment is often similar to that announced before the fall of Jerusalem (cf. the judgment language of 29:18-19 and 32:29-35 with vv. 11-14). But with respect to this Judean community these indictments and announcements of judgment carry a kind of finality that is not the case for pre-fall Jerusalem. It is as though they were given a second chance (noted above) and, having failed in that, their future in the community of faith is forfeited. Exilic readers might be prompted to reflect on the seriousness of their own response in view of this finality.

Indictment and Announcement of Judgment, 44:1-14

The initial word of God (vv. 2-14) consists of a review of Israel's sorry history (vv. 2-6), followed by an indictment (vv. 7-10) and an announcement of judgment (vv. 11-14); each segment is introduced by the full designation, "the Lord of hosts, the God of Israel." These words are spoken specifically to the Judeans who are living in a remarkable number of Egyptian settings (v. 1). [Egyptian Sites] This dispersion of the Judeans across Egypt suggests that some time had elapsed between their migration and the material of this chapter. That Jeremiah would have been able to address all of them is unlikely, but it may be understood that those assembled (v. 15) represented the entire community in Egypt.

Egyptian Sites

In 44:1 several Egyptian sites are mentioned. For Tahpanhes and Memphis, see at 2:16 (43:7; 46:14). Memphis, about fifteen miles south of Cairo, was an early capital of Egypt and its largest city for much of its history. Migdol was a city in northern Egypt (46:14). Pathros is a name for upper (or southern) Egypt, an area some three hundred miles south of Memphis. Archaeological excavations have uncovered evidence of Jewish settlements in several areas of Egypt.

Verses 2-6 constitute a review of Israel's idolatrous history and God's persistent efforts to turn them back from their infidelities (for similar brief recollections, see 7:24-26; 25:3-7; 32:29-35; 35:14-15). The only "wickedness" cited is idolatry ("other gods that they had not known," that is, gods unknown in their tradition, 7:9, 19:4). This review begins and ends (vv. 2, 6) with a description

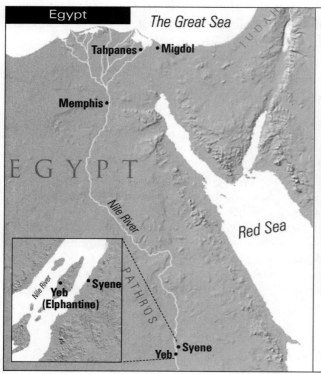

Elephantine Island in the Nile. Pictured above is the outer wall of the ancient nilometer constructed during Roman times on the site of an earlier one. (Credit: Erich Lessing/Art Resource/NY)

of the present situation in Jerusalem and Judah; they have been devastated and are without inhabitant ("as they still are today," v. 6; see vv. 22-23; a recurrent theme, 34:22). Theologically, if not literally, the land is empty, awaiting the restoration of the true people of God.

The people have only themselves to blame; God brought this disaster (*rāʿāh*) upon them because of the wickedness (*rāʿāh*; see **Connections**, ch. 1; **Introduction**) of all involved ("they, you, and your ancestors," v. 3; the people in Egypt are specifically held responsible, but not only them). Because they worshiped other gods, God's anger was provoked and was poured out on them (vv. 3, 6; see 42:18; on anger, see **Connections**, ch. 25). God had persistently sent "all my servants the prophets" (as in 7:25; 26:5; 29:19; 35:15), begging (N.B.!) them not to do the abominable things that God hates (that is, idolatry, see v. 22; 32:35). But they refused to listen and to turn from their evil ways, continuing to worship other deities (vv. 4-5). Because of this idolatry, disaster has taken place (v. 6; this point returns to the theme of v. 2).

Jeremiah then turns to the present situation in Egypt and speaks more specifically to the Judeans who have migrated there. The indictment (vv. 7-10) is followed by the announcement of judgment (vv. 11-14).

The indictment is remarkable in that it consists primarily of questions. [God's Questions] God's indictment takes the form of accusatory laments. First of all, why are they are doing great harm (*rāʿāh*) to themselves and their future by removing every man, woman, and child from Judah (v. 7)? They have emptied the land (theologically, not literally). In doing this, they will leave themselves no remnant (because of the disaster they will experience in making this move). The concern for a "remnant" apparently has to do with providing a nucleus for beginning again, as had been initiated under Gedaliah (40:9-12) and was promised to them earlier (42:10-12). They have cut off their own future by cutting themselves off from the land (see "cut off" in v. 9). Note that they have done great harm (*rāʿāh*) *to themselves*. In other words, the disaster they will experience is self-inflicted. In some sense, this is suicidal behavior. They have only themselves to blame for the disaster that will surely come.

God's Questions

God poses four questions to the audience (vv. 7-9). God's most basic question is: Why?! Though only the first two questions are explicitly so expressed, the last two questions contain an implicit "why"? These questions are not designed to elicit information from the hearers; God knows the situation in all of its horrid detail. Rather, these questions are characteristic of laments and are similar to those that have been addressed earlier by God (see 2:29-32; 8:4-7; 27:13, 17). They might better be considered existential questions, evidencing genuine divine anguish over what has happened. Given the long history of God's attempts to turn the people back to their religious heritage, and given what has happened to Judah and Jerusalem because of their infidelity, God is genuinely baffled at their continuing unfaithful behaviors.

Second, why do they continue to provoke God to anger by worshiping other gods in their Egyptian settlements (v. 8)? Why do they do this so as to cut themselves off (see NIV) from the community of faith and become an object of scorn and ridicule among the nations (see 24:9-10; 42:18; see also 18:16; 19:8; 25:9; 29:18; 34:17)? They no sooner get to a new place than they find new gods to worship or remain attached to old standbys! As in the historical review (vv. 2-6), the focus here and throughout the chapter is on idolatry. The "crimes" of v. 9 also refer to idolatry in view of the parallel reference to idolatrous actions in the "streets of Jerusalem" in vv. 17, 21 (see 7:17). The reference to not walking in "my law and my statutes" in v. 10 (cf. v. 23) may catch up other forms of wickedness, but the fact that idolatry is the only sin named in the entire chapter, and pervasively so, demonstrates the basic issue at stake.

That idolatry is not mentioned in chapters 37–43 as a factor leading to the rejection of these Judeans is striking. It is as if their leaving the land when commanded not to do so is finally deemed an insufficient reason for their rejection and idolatry needs to be added. Yet, the point is more likely that, while leaving the land was the decisive factor (reiterated in vv. 11-14 without reference to idolatry), their infidelity was confirmed by what happened to their worship practices in Egypt. Once again, at the very center of the Yahwistic faith, the people refused to "listen" (v. 16, linked with v. 5), a theme common to chs. 36–43. Not listening to the word of God has become a pattern of life. One point of unfaithfulness has led to another in a downward spiral toward disaster. Finally, their infidelity matches that of their forebears prior to the fall of Jerusalem and they suffer the same fate.

The questions continue in v. 9. How can they have forgotten the long history of wickedness (*rā'āh*; the word appears five times in this verse!) among their forebears, including their kings and their wives (e.g., 1 Kgs 11:1-8)? How can they have forgotten the wickedness of themselves and their wives (see v. 15; notice that the audience is presumed to be male) committed in every place in the land? The admixture of reference in v. 9 to both ancestors and present audience continues in the "they" and "you" of v. 10 ("to this day"). The point is to confront the present audience by showing that their sins are continuous with those of their ancestors that led to the fall of Jerusalem (see [Interpretation across the Generations]). *No one* has shown contrition or the fear of the Lord or walked in the law that God set before them—neither the ancestors, nor "you"!

The announcement of judgment follows in vv. 11-14 ("therefore"). The cascading images of judgment are familiar to the reader (most recently, see 42:15-22; 43:11; 44:8).

The opening statement of divine intention is another instance of correspondence between divine judgment and human wickedness. God is determined (lit., "set my face," see 21:10) to bring disaster (*rā'āh*) upon "you," that is upon "all" Judah (="the remnant of Judah" of v. 12). "Everyone" (v. 12) who has determined (lit., "set their face") to settle in Egypt will perish. God is determined to act because the remnant of Judah is determined to go to Egypt. They shall perish in the land of Egypt and all the devastation that happened in the fall of Jerusalem through sword, famine, and pestilence (note the repetition of these themes in vv. 12-13) will now also happen to them, indeed to all of them. God will "visit" (*pāqad*; NRSV, "punish," v. 13) the sins of the people in Egypt back upon their own head, just as God had "visited" (*pāqad*) Jerusalem.

The strong claim that no one would survive this new devastation, and none would return to the land of Judah, is immediately qualified, but not in a substantive way. There will be survivors who long to go back to the land even if they cannot (raise hopes for themselves that can never be realized); even more, there will be some fugitives who do return (v. 14; so also v. 28). But they will return only as isolated individuals, not as a community, not even as a "remnant" (v. 7; see 42:17). Even with these survivors, the coming disaster will effectively constitute an "end" to this community (vv. 11, 27).

The People Are Defiant, 44:15-18

These verses describe the reaction of the remnant of Judah to Jeremiah's word from God that indicts them and announces judgment upon them. Though "all the Judeans" in various communities in Egypt are said to be gathered in "a great assembly" (v. 1), this is likely a hyperbolic statement in the interests of catching up the entire Judean community in Egypt. Distinctions are made among the respondents—the men who were aware that their wives were making offerings to other gods, all the women who were present to hear Jeremiah speak, and all the Judeans living in Pathros (Upper Egypt).

It is uncertain just how to assign these groups to the speakers of vv. 16-19. It is usually suggested that vv. 16-18 are spoken by everyone mentioned in v. 15 and that v. 19 is added by the women

Worship of the Queen of Heaven

The queen of heaven is to be identified with the Assyro-Babylonian astral deity Ishtar, a goddess of both war and fertility associated with the planet Venus. A form of this deity was worshiped in Canaan under the name of Astarte. She is also mentioned in the indictment against Israelites in the land of Judah (see 7:18), and these Judahites explicitly link what they are doing to the practices of their ancestors (v. 17). Hence, they must have brought these practices with them when they migrated to Egypt.

The goddess Ishtar/Astarte was associated primarily with life and fertility and was thought to assure continuing life for the community through the birth of children and the provision of health and welfare. That this goddess was given a more general designation, "queen of heaven," rather than Ishtar/Astarte, may have been related to various manifestations that this form of worship took in many areas of the ancient world. As such, Jeremiah 44 could serve as a warning for all dispersed Jewish communities who, faced with death and dissolution, might be tempted to assure their future through the adoption of forms of worship linked to this goddess of life and fertility. Syncretism was not an option for any Jewish community if it would be faithful to its heritage.

Dante Gabriel Rossetti. *Astarte Syriaca.* 1877. Oil on canvas. 42"x72". Manchester City Art Gallery. (Credit: Manchester City Art Gallery/Artchive)

(see "our husbands"). This understanding has often led to the addition of "and the women said" at the beginning of v. 19 (e.g., NRSV; NIV; NEB, following the Syriac version, see NRSV footnote). Many other scholars think that the women are the only speakers in vv. 16-19, discounting the general introduction of v. 15.

The basic response (of everyone named in v. 15) is that they are not going to listen to the word that Jeremiah speaks (v. 16). Though Jeremiah speaks in the name of the Lord, and this they do not seem to deny (cf. the "lie" of 43:2), they will not listen to him. He may well be a genuine prophet of God, but they will stubbornly continue with their present practices of worship—making offerings and libations to the queen of heaven (see 7:17-18; 7:2; 44:2)—and they give several reasons for doing so (see Jeremiah's counter-arguments in vv. 20-25). [Worship of the Queen of Heaven] This combination of their recognition that Jeremiah speaks the word of the Lord and their continuing persistence in their idolatrous practice suggests that theirs is a syncretistic worship in which Yahweh continues to play a role (such syncretism is also evident in v. 26). They make their determination in the face of their recognition that Jeremiah may indeed be speaking a word of the Lord. This element in their response recalls the emphasis on Israel's stubbornness in other texts (see **Connections**, ch. 5). Continuing to worship in this way is what they have vowed to do. [The Argument from Experience]

The voices of the women in the group have apparently been heard along with the men in vv. 16-18 (see at v. 15), but now the female voices are heard specifically in v. 19 (see "our husbands"). The specific role of the women is lifted up here in a way that is not the case in 7:17-18 (though that text is inclusive). In effect, they second the voices of vv. 16-18 in almost the same language, but with an additional concern to counter the focus that Jeremiah placed on them (see v. 9; cf. vv. 24-25) for this worship of a goddess. They will go on worshiping the queen of heaven and baking cakes for her (stamped with her image), and besides, they would not be doing these things if their

---

Astarte Syriaca (1877)

Mystery: lo! betwixt the sun and moon
Astarte of the Syrians: Venus Queen
Ere Aphrodite was. In silver sheen
Her twofold girdle clasps the infinite boon
Of bliss whereof the heaven and earth commune:
And from her neck's inclining flower-stem lean
Love-freighted lips and absolute eyes that wean
The pulse of hearts to the sphere's dominant tune.

Torch-bearing, her sweet ministers compel
All thrones of light beyond the sky and sea
The witnesses of Beauty's face to be:
That face, of Love's all-peenetrative spell
Amulet, talisman, and oracle, —
Betwixt the sun and moon a mystery.

Collected Writings of Dante Gabriel Rossetti (Chicago: New Amsterdam Books, 2000), 393.

The Argument from Experience

The reason the people give for refusing to worship the queen of heaven is clear: it is precisely these rituals that make the most sense in view of their experience. These worship practices are what they and their ancestors—including their kings and officials—practiced back in the land of Judah (see 7:17-18), and when they did that they had plenty of food, good fortune, and no experience of evil (*rāʿāh*). It was when they *stopped* worshiping the queen of heaven that their troubles with sword and famine started! This is probably an allusion to the reform of Josiah (see 2 Kngs 22–23), when such idolatrous worship, instituted under King Manasseh, was quashed only to be followed by all the "evil" that led to the fall of Jerusalem. This argument is faulty because it is a *post hoc ergo propter hoc* ("after this, therefore because of this") argument. Just because they experienced the disaster after they ceased worshiping the queen of heaven it does not follow that that was the only or primary causal factor that led to their experience.

The worship of Yahweh as such is not seen to be the problem, but the exclusive worship of Yahweh, the exclusion of that dimension of a syncretistic worship that focused on the queen of heaven (see [The Queen of Heaven]). It is not made clear at what time they picked up the worship of the queen of heaven after the failure of the reform of Josiah. Verse 18 suggests that it was only when they arrived in Egypt that they began to do so, but 7:17-18 indicates that the practice continued both before and after Josiah's reform. But, then, according to their argument, would not the reintroduction of the queen of heaven cult prior to the fall of Jerusalem somehow have prevented the disaster? Yet, their point still stands, even if it is a faulty argument: the fall occurred only after the institution of exclusivist Yahwism (see William McKane, *A Critical and Exegetical Commentary on Jeremiah* [2 vols.; ICC; Edinburgh: T. & T. Clark, 1986], 1089).

husbands were not also very much involved! This inclusion of both male and female is probably intended to reinforce the idea that the entire community had become involved in such idolatrous activity; there were no exceptions, such as might be claimed in a patriarchal culture.

Jeremiah's Final Sermon, 44:20-30

Jeremiah directs his response to "all" the people (note the repetition), including men and women. Unlike the oracles in vv. 2-14, these words are initially not introduced by the messenger formula ("Thus says the LORD"); that introduction comes only with v. 25. First of all, Jeremiah responds to the argument that these offerings were characteristic of their worship in Judah and Jerusalem, as well as the worship of everyone else (vv. 20-21; cf. v. 17). Do not they recall that this is precisely what God remembered? In fact, God took in so much of what they did that he could no longer bear the sight of all their evil (*rōaʿ*) doings and all the horrible things that they had committed. Hence, their good land became wasteland, an accursed thing, without inhabitant "as it is to this day" (v. 22; see vv. 6, 23). Jeremiah then repeats the point, linking it to the law (v. 23). It is precisely in presenting these kinds of offerings that they sinned against the Lord and closed their ears to God's voice, not obeying his laws and statutes. That is why this disaster (*rāʿāh*; the fall of Jerusalem) has befallen them (see 32:23 for "befallen").

Jeremiah's response does not ignore the people's arguments, but states that their *interpretation* of their history is mistaken (there is, of course, no uninterpreted history, though the two versions presented here would not be the only interpretive options). Both interpretations are dependent on a belief that the worship of God (or the queen of heaven) is involved in what happened. For Jeremiah, the worship of the queen of heaven is identified as idolatry and was in fact the problem, not that they had stopped such practices for a time. There is, of course, no way to demonstrate conclusively the rightness or wrongness of either case. Though the *post hoc ergo propter hoc* argument is a logical fallacy, that is not the tack Jeremiah takes in his response (see [The Argument from Experience]). Only if readers hold to Jeremiah's beliefs about God's intention in this situation will they be convinced of his argument.

Second, he responds to their argument that they will be faithful to the vows they have made (v. 25; cf. v. 17). A new introduction is used by the narrator (v. 24) that directs the balance of the sermon to "all the people" and specifically singles out "all the women"

(women are also specifically quoted in v. 25; NRSV, "saying," is feminine; cf. v. 9). Then Jeremiah twice charges (vv. 24, 26) "all the Judeans" to hear the word of the Lord. Jeremiah proceeds by quoting the vow that the people ("you and your wives") have made to present offerings to the queen of heaven. Though the address includes both male and female, the quotation of v. 25 is introduced by a feminine verb, apparently to focus on the women without omitting the men's involvement (see above on vv. 16-19). The quotation suggests that they cannot (!) back away from what they are doing (on stubbornness, see **Connections**, ch. 5). If so, their response is a remarkable recognition that they are enslaved in their own behaviors.

Responding to their claim that they will be faithful to their vow, Jeremiah's counter-argument is deeply ironic, no doubt in view of the vows they made to Jeremiah in 42:4-6 that they would obey whatever word of God Jeremiah spoke. In effect Jeremiah says: you claim that you should keep your vows to present offerings to the queen of heaven; well, you are inconsistent in your concern to keep your vows, so go ahead and keep these (this argument is comparable to that given in 7:21; cf. Rom 1:24-25)! That you have broken one vow and insisted on keeping another will have the same effect.

Verses 26-30 announce the judgment ("therefore") to "all the Judeans." The last words of Jeremiah from an historical perspective are words of judgment. God himself takes an oath in God's own name to follow through on the words that follow. The name of Yahweh shall no longer be pronounced in oath-taking (see 4:2) by the Judeans who remain in the land of Egypt. Because they will not be alive to speak it! This text assumes that the name Yahweh was used by these Judeans, presumably in syncretistic and hence idolatrous practices (similarly, v. 16; 5:2). They will use God in this way no more.

The text at this point reaches back and picks up a key theme from Jeremiah's call/vision, that God is "watching over his word" to perform it (1:12). But, whereas in 31:28 God was "watching over" his word to build and plant the exiles restored to their land (cf. 42:10-12 for comparable language for this very group), in 44:27 God is "watching over" the word to bring harm (*rāʿāh*) rather than good (as in 21:9; 39:16). This language was used in 29:11 in just the reverse order for those in exile in Babylon; for them God had plans for good and not for harm. The effect on the "remnant of Judah" in the land of Egypt would be that they would "*all*" perish by famine and sword. This is somewhat qualified in v. 28 (as in

v. 14); a "few in number" will escape to return to the land of Judah. But, generally, this "remnant" will experience a reversal of God's earlier activity on behalf of Israel in Egypt (see Deut 26:5-8) and a fulfillment of the curse of Deuteronomy 28:68. In the context of chapters 30–33, though, this curse is not a general statement about Israel in its entirety.

The theme of God "watching over his word" is strongly emphasized in vv. 28-29. The remnant of Judah in the land of Egypt shall come to know that God's word would stand rather than theirs (presumably as they were undergoing the experience or in surviving it). Notably, the truth of the words spoken by the people or Jeremiah ("mine or theirs") is not demonstrable by argument. Whether the people have spoken the truth (vv. 17-18) or Jeremiah has done so will have to await events (see the comparable understanding in the conflict between the words of Jeremiah and Hananiah in 28:8-9). This language is commonly cited as an indication that these narratives are finally centered in the word of God and its fulfillment (see **Introduction**).

The sign by which this remnant will know that God would "visit" their sins upon them in this place and that God's word would surely be effected "against you for evil (*rā'āh*)" is the announcement given in v. 30. Pharaoh Hophra, king of Egypt from 589 to 570 BC (see 37:5), will die by the hand of his enemies just as surely as King Zedekiah was given into the hands of the king of Babylon, Nebuchadrezzar. This may have been fulfilled when Hophra was assassinated by Amasis (who became pharaoh in 570 BC). Shortly thereafter Babylon invaded Egypt (see 43:10-13; 46:13-26; Ezek 29:17-20; 30:20-26), though without conclusive results.

CONNECTIONS

Did the "Remnant of Judah" Ever Have a Future?

Walter Brueggemann and others speak of a "sociopolitical function" of chapter 44 (and the larger context),[4] similar to the argument in the book of Ezekiel. It reflects a dispute between Babylonian exiles and those dispersed peoples in Egypt regarding who is the "true carrier of the Jewish tradition" and hence the inheritor of the divine promises (see ch. 30–33). The text "is a witness and party to a conflict about legitimacy." The text (and God's word through Jeremiah) speaks on behalf of the Babylonian exiles as the divinely designated carrier of the future of the people of God. "To say that the process is political does not in principle deny that the final shape is theologically faithful. Theological faithfulness and political interest are not by definition mutually exclusive."[5]

Knowledge of God's will is claimed in stating that the future of Israel is to be identified with the exiles in Babylon. The emphatic use of the word "all" in vv. 1-7 is intended to comprehend all those who are not in Babylonian exile (see [The Emphasis on "All"]). They were "insolent men" and "did not obey the voice of the LORD" spoken by Jeremiah and, hence, they are excluded from the ongoing story of the people of God.

Yet, it needs to be recognized that such a sociopolitical function is nowhere directly stated in the text; it has to be inferred.[6] If the Babylonian exiles (or their sympathizers) were concerned to make this point, then why have they done so in such an indirect way? At the least, great care must be used in advancing this intention behind the text and it certainly should not be considered the primary intention at work. Apart from socio-political realities, R. E. Clements speaks of the "despair" of these persons in flight to Egypt. This despair led them into ever deeper apostasy.[7] Such a perspective gives greater integrity to actual developments within that Egyptian community. The text is more than propaganda. [Discontinuity in Divine Anger]

Those genuine possibilities for the future of the remnant of Judah had now been rejected and the earlier disastrous effects on Jerusalem once again come into view for them. But, it is important to say that this "remnant of Judah" *was not excluded in principle* (as a straightforward propagandistic perspective would imply)! The earlier positive portrayals of this group make the point that, for God, they could have been included in the ongoing community of faith in time, joining the exiles in Babylon in some future shape of Israel. They chose a different path and shaped for themselves a different future, but that was their doing, not God's. [Acting in the Middle]

Discontinuity in Divine Anger

This point regarding ch. 44 may also be considered from another perspective. The chapter is characterized by numerous allusions to other texts in Jeremiah, particularly those having to do with the fall of Jerusalem. The effect of these intertextual references is to show that Israel's prior experience is being replicated among these Judeans in both indictment and judgment (made explicit in vv. 13, 30; see [Interpretation Across the Generations]). At the same time, the move from that period of time to this Egyptian situation is not viewed as being without interruption. God's anger has not been continuous from then to now (42:10). Some new possibilities for this community were indeed put in place, as is evident in the program of Gedaliah (40:9-12) and just before the departure for Egypt (see 42:10-12).

Acting in the Middle

Walter Brueggemann helpfully states, "The recurring problem of biblical faith, upon which the prophets always insist, is that the community of faith must act in the middle of things. This community does not have the luxury of waiting until the end to see how things turn out."

Walter Brueggeman, *A Commentary on Jeremiah: Exile and Homecoming* (Grand Rapids: Eerdmans, 1998), 410-13.

NOTES

[1] See NEB; William McKane, *A Critical and Exegetical Commentary on Jeremiah* (2 vols.; ICC; Edinburgh: T. & T. Clark, 1986), 1055.

[2] Ibid., 1056-57.

[3] See NIV; ibid., 1059-60.

[4] Walter Brueggemann, *A Commentary on Jeremiah: Exile and Homecoming* (Grand Rapids: Eerdmans, 1998), 395-97.

[5] Ibid., 395, fn. 75.

[6] McKane, *Jeremiah*, 1091 and often.

[7] Ronald E. Clements, *Jeremiah* (IBC; Atlanta: John Knox, 1988), 236.

JEREMIAH
COMFORTS BARUCH

45:1-5

This oracle of salvation to Baruch, Jeremiah's scribe, is set in the fourth year of King Jehoiakim (605 BC). This year is identified as the same year in which Jeremiah dictated to his secretary the words of judgment for the first scroll (36:1-4); this chronology also makes connections with chapter 26, also set in the reign of Jehoiakim. Verse 4 is placed chronologically before the fall of Jerusalem and hence before the events of the immediately preceding chapters.

Chapters 36 and 45 are often thought to bracket the memoirs of Baruch in chapters 37–44 (see there). The placement of this chapter at this point may be explained in part by the fact that he had accompanied Jeremiah to Egypt. There he had experienced the sufferings of that exile (43:3-6) and the devastation of that community along with the others (see 42:22). Hence, his experience of pain at the point of the writing of the scroll (ch. 36) has been continued through the rest of his life. Coming after the promised devastation of the Jewish community in Egypt (ch. 44), to which he belonged, God's promise to Baruch at an earlier time is recalled; he will receive his life "as a prize of war," but no more than that. Suffering encloses his life as do chapters 36 and 45 and he may well stand as a symbol of those faithful ones who lived through such a traumatic time in the life of Israel and have been vindicated by a word from God. [Bonhoeffer's Use of Jeremiah 45]

The placement of chapter 45 at this point may be testimony that God's promise, articulated earlier, has in fact been kept, even into the disastrous relationships with the Jews in Egypt (hence the link to ch. 44). This chapter looks forward to chapters 46–51 in its references to "the whole earth" (NRSV, "the whole land") and God's bringing "disaster upon all flesh" (this, in turn, links back to Jeremiah as a "prophet to the nations" in 1:5 and one appointed over nations and kingdoms in 1:10).

Bonhoeffer's Use of Jeremiah 45

In his *Letters and Papers from Prison*, Dietrich Bonhoeffer writes: "I can never get away from Jeremiah 45." In his personal Bible Bonhoeffer had underlined 45:5 several times and has this to say on April 30, 1944: "I think God is about to accomplish something that, even if we take part in it either outwardly or inwardly, we can only receive with the greatest wonder and awe. Somehow it will be clear—for those who have eyes to see—that Ps 58.11b and Ps 9.19f. are true; and we shall have to repeat Jer 45.5 to ourselves every day.

"We realize more clearly than formerly that the world lies under the wrath and grace of God. We read in Jer. 45: 'Thus says the Lord: Behold, what I have built I am breaking down, and what I have planted I am plucking up . . . And do you seek great things for yourself? Seek them not; for, behold, I am bringing evil upon all flesh; . . . but I will give your life as a prize of war in all places to which you may go.' If we can save our souls unscathed out of the wreckage of our material possession, let us be satisfied with that. If the Creator destroys his own handiwork, what right have we to lament the destruction of ours? It will be the task of our generation, not to 'seek great things,' but to save and preserve our souls out of the chaos, and to realize it is the only thing we can carry as a 'prize' from the burning building. 'Keep your heart with all vigilance; for from it flows the spring of life' (Prov 4:23). We shall have to keep our lives rather than shape them, to hope rather than plan, to hold out rather than march forward, but we do want to preserve for you, the rising generation, what will make it possible for you to plan, build up and shape a new and better life."

Dietrich Bonhoeffer, *Letters and Papters from Prison* (London: SCM, 1971), 219, 279, 297.

COMMENTARY

The opening verse of chapter 45 refers to "these words" that Baruch wrote in a scroll. Given the date of 605 BC, this phrase is usually thought to have reference to the scroll that centers the attention of chapter 36. Yet, in the present context, the expression "these words" is somewhat awkward; it could have reference to unspecified words or to Jeremiah's words more generally. The identification of Baruch as the son of Neriah also links this text with 51:59 and the story of another son of Neriah (Seraiah); he is also given a word from the prophet Jeremiah. Both brothers receive charges relative to words that Jeremiah has written. The more personal word given to Baruch becomes a more comprehensive word about the community in 51:59-64.

This text includes the only direct speech by Baruch in the book; he voices a lament over sufferings he has had to endure. Moreover, from his perspective, God has intensified that pain, probably through association with the prophetic announcement of the fall of Jerusalem (v. 3). The "sorrow" voiced by Baruch has also been expressed by Jeremiah (8:18; 20:18) and probably by God as well (8:18; see 4:19). God will deliver Israel from its sorrow in the future (31:13) as well as its "pain" (30:15).

Though the Hebrew word for "weary" is different from that used elsewhere for both Jeremiah (6:11; 20:9) and God (15:6), having this experience in common may be an important dimension of Baruch's troubles. These verbal and thematic linkages to Jeremiah (see also 15:15-18) and Baruch's identification with the prophet's mission suggest that his difficulties are prompted by Jeremiah's experience. Though the antagonism toward Baruch evident in 43:3-6 is set years later, it may reflect earlier struggles. Baruch (like Jeremiah) is clearly identified with the pro-Babylonian perspective and that generated much opposition during the Babylonian threat to Jerusalem and Judah. Baruch, Jeremiah, and God share a commonality of experience and its personal effects.

Specific links with the call of Jeremiah in v. 4 also bring prophet and secretary together within the purposes of God (see 1:10; see also 18:7-9; 24:6; 31:28; 42:10). As with Jeremiah, God catches Baruch up into a devastating future; God is going to pluck up and break down "the whole earth" (this translation is preferred to the NRSV, "the whole land," in view of the phrase "all flesh" in v. 5). The entire region of the Near East seems to be in view, given Babylonian hegemony.

It is not entirely clear what "great things" Baruch has in mind for himself with respect to the future. A common suggestion is that God reprimands Baruch, perhaps even rebukes him (cf. 12:5; 15:19; cf. Ps 131:1), for improper or self-serving ambitions or for seeking special treatment. It seems more likely, however, that the "great things" are parallel to the divine intentions (on the use of "great things" for God's mighty deeds, see Deut 10:21; Ps 71:19). That is, in and through the work of Jeremiah and himself, Baruch had hoped that Israel, which had been built up and planted, could be saved from destruction. He should not seek such a goal, for that future for Israel is no longer possible; God is going to bring disaster (*rā'āh*) on Israel, indeed on all flesh (a reference to all nations, as in 25:31; see 32:27). This is certainly a reference forward to the oracles against the nations in chapters 46–51. This breaking down and plucking up is a pain-filled future in which Baruch will participate with both Jeremiah and God. [The Writings of Baruch] [Gerhard von Rad on Jeremiah 45]

The most that Baruch can expect in view of this coming devastation of land and people is that his life will be spared, wherever he goes (see 43:6). This is a promise also given to the Ethiopian Ebed-melech for saving Jeremiah's life (39:18; see also 21:9; 38:2). Both

🔍 **The Writings of Baruch**

The Letter of Jeremiah (=Baruch ch. 6)
4th–3rd c. BC

Baruch (Apocrypha)
2d–1st C. BC

2 (Syriac Apocalypse of) Baruch
2d C. AD

3 (Greek Apocalypse of) Baruch
1st–3rd C. AD

4 Baruch
1st C. AD

Giotto di Bondone (1266–1336). *The Prophet Baruch.* c.1300. Scrovegni Chapel. Padua, Italy. (Credit: Scala/Art Resource, NY).

Gerhard von Rad on Jeremiah 45

📖 "An undertone of sadness accompanies Jahweh's words: they hint almost at feelings of pain at this work of pulling down what his own hands have built up . . . . The prophet and those about him are drawn in a quite exceptional way into this demolition. . . . They bring the divine demolition to pass; here a human being has in a unique fashion borne a part in the divine suffering."

Gerhard von Rad, *Old Testament Theology* (2 vols; New York: Harper & Row, 1962), 208.

stories give evidence of a concern for the life of specific individuals within the fortunes of the larger group. That is, no other booty or spoil ("prize") will be available after this disaster other than Baruch's own life. This is certainly not the rest for which he longed, but it is life rather than death (see **Connections: Life for the Faithful and Loss for God**).

CONNECTIONS

Life for the Faithful and Loss for God

That the promise in v. 5 links two faithful individuals is important in the context of communal disaster. Through this catastrophe individuals will survive with whom God can begin again. The final phrase, "in every place to which you may go" (v. 5) may be taken to heart by other people of faith who are suffering in the wake of the fall of Jerusalem. They may be scattered throughout that unwelcoming world, without the anchors of land and temple. They may well bemoan their fate, and for good reason given their faithfulness. Yet, they remain alive to begin a new journey embraced by the promise of God. For the God who has had to break down and pluck up has also promised to build and to plant.

This text is also a pointed witness to the painful future that God is facing. What pain it must mean for God to tear down that which God has spent so much time and effort to built up, to pluck up what God has planted and cultivated through the years. In some sense, this is a testimony to divine loss; God's best intentions for Israel have not been realized. In effect, if Baruch thinks he has troubles, think of what God must be going through! [H. Wheeler Robinson on Jeremiah 45]

H. Wheeler Robinson on Jeremiah 45

📖 In Jer 45 "we see comfort brought to the sorrow of man [sic!] by the realization of the sorrow of God. Baruch is overwhelmed by the sense of the failure of the prophet's work and of his own, and the prophet recalls him to the thought of the failure of God. . . . There is hardly a passage in the Old Testament which gives us a more impressive glimpse of the eternal cross in the heart of God."

H. W. Robinson, *The Cross in the Old Testament* (London: SCM Press, 1955), 185.

ORACLES AGAINST EGYPT

46:1-28

The Oracles against the Nations, 46:1–51:64

These chapters are traditionally called the Oracles Against the Nations (OAN), a type of oracle characteristic of several prophetic books (Isa 13–23; Ezek 25–32; Amos 1–2; Nahum; Obadiah). This designation is somewhat of a misnomer, for these oracles are not simply "against" the nations, even if this is predominantly the case. For example, several texts speak of God as one who "restores the fortunes" of some of these nations (e.g., 46:26; 48:47; 49:6; 49:39), who is engaged passionately in their life (e.g., 48:31-32, 36), and uses them as agents for God's purposes (e.g., 46:26). [Salvation for the Nations] This major focus on God's word regarding the future of these nations, whether in judgment or salvation, links up with the call of Jeremiah to be a "prophet to the nations" (1:5, 10). Jeremiah, of

---

Salvation for the Nations

Jeremiah's call specifies that he is appointed over "nations and kingdoms" not simply for the purpose of judgment, but also "to build and to plant" (1:10). In several subsequent texts, God is portrayed as being at work among the nations not simply for purposes of judgment, but also for restoration and salvation (e.g., 3:17; 12:14-16; 16:19-21; cf. 18:7-10, "a nation or a kingdom").

This broad divine purpose means that the issue addressed by these oracles is not simply to claim that God rules over the nations (see the language for God as King in 46:18; 51:57), but that God is about the restoration of the entire creation. Jeremiah's God is no local deity, concerned simply about the people of Israel. God is the Creator God, the "God of all flesh" (32:27; see 25:31; 45:5), who works out the divine purposes for the entire creation in and through the movements of all nations and peoples. As helpful as the metaphor of God as King is, it is simply insufficient to encompass these broad-based purposes. Notably, these texts say not a word about these nations honoring the sovereignty of God, as if they would come to "know" that Israel's God is King in and through the experience of disaster (an apparent exception is 16:21; contrary to Walter Brueggemann, *A Commentary on Jeremiah: Exile and Homecoming* [Grand Rapids: Eerdmans, 1998], 419-20). God will "restore the fortunes" of four of these nations quite apart from their acknowledgment of God as King. While several texts speak of the implications of the destruction of these nations for the salvation of Israel (e.g., 46:27-28; 50:4-5; though only chs. 50–51 indict a nation for mistreatment of Israel), God's salvific purposes for the future include even these nations.

Given the repeated designation of Jeremiah as a "prophet to the nations" (1:5, 10), it is important not to think of these oracles as pertinent only insofar as they are related to Israel and Israelite policies of one kind or another. God is interested in these nations for who they are in themselves, not simply in their relationship to Israel. At the same time, *the particularity of God's work in and through Israel remains intact amid the universality of God's work among the nations.*

Egypt and Mesopotamia

course, has been concerned about nations other than Israel in various parts of the book (e.g., 3:17, 12:14-16; 25:15-38) and God even identifies Nebuchadrezzar as "my servant" (25:9; 27:6; 43:10).

It is this comprehensive theme regarding the nations that links the OAN with the immediately preceding text regarding Baruch. God announces a disaster (*rā'āh*) against "all flesh" and a divine breaking up and plucking up of "the whole earth/land" (45:4-5). In the pattern established throughout the book of Jeremiah, human evil (*rā'āh*) issues in divinely mediated disaster (*rā'āh*; see **Introduction**; **Connections**, ch. 1). Remarkably, unlike the focus on idolatry and infidelity as the key factors leading to judgment on Israel, idolatry is not a focus in these oracles. There are some references to other gods, but idolatry does not become a reason for the judgment (e.g., 46:15, 25). Hence, two reasons for the experience of *rā'āh* come into play: nations so experience disaster because of their own evil (46:8, 17), or the disaster spills over into their lives, not because of their own evil, but because of the wide-ranging effects of the judgment being visited on others (47). Arrogance is the form of human sinfulness most commonly indicted in these oracles (48:26, 29-30, 35, 42; 50:24-27, 31-32; 51:6, 11, 25-26, 56).

Some distinctions within the oracles are important. It is commonly accepted that chapters 46–49 are to be distinguished from chapters 50–51. The judgment experienced by the nations in chapters 46–49 is mediated in and through the Babylonians. The destroyer of these other nations is Babylon. In chapters 50–51 the Babylonians themselves are judged by other nations (Medes and Persians, see 50:9; 51:11). Another difference to be observed is the sheer length of the oracles against Babylon (chs. 50–51) compared to the others. This difference is probably due to the place that Babylon has with respect to the restoration of Israel; Babylon's defeat will be crucial to the return of the exiles. Another factor regarding Babylon relates to the fact that it exceeded its mandate as mediator of divine judgment against Israel (and others?). The prose segment at the end of the OAN (51:59-64) also lifts up Babylon in a special way.[1] There are other differences among the oracles. The oracle against Philistia is not marked by mocking words, or by a statement of their wickedness, but by the sufferings they experience. The oracle against Moab is remarkable for the suffering language used by God for what the Moabites are having to endure. The oracle against Elam, unlike the others, contains no reference to internal realities in that country; the only subject of the verbs is God and what God is going to do.

At the same time, in the midst of these oracles, special attention is given to Israel's place among the nations (46:27-28; 50:4-7, 17-20, 28, 33-34). In these OAN focused attention is given to all the nations with whom Israel has been related in one way of another— Egypt (46:2-26); Philistia (47:1-7); Moab (48:1-47); Ammon (49:1-6); Edom (49:7-22); Syria (49:23-27); Arabia (49:28-33); Elam (49:34-39); Babylon (50–51). The common reference to Jerusalem in the oracles against Babylon (rare in chs. 46–49) is also important. The placement of the oracles against Babylon at the climactic point in the list probably attests not simply to this being the latest of the oracles delivered, but also because the judgment on Babylon opens up the future for Israel. That may be one factor that influences the way in which the book ends, not with a word about the nations, but with a word about Israel among the nations, however tenuously stated (52:1-34).

The location of these oracles at this particular place in the book also suggests a kind of independence. In the Septuagint, this collection of oracles is placed after 25:13a; this is commonly considered to have been their original placement in the book, not least in view of the internal placement of these types of oracles in Isaiah (13–23) and Ezekiel (26–32). Note also the general oracle against the nations in 25:15-38, in the midst of which the nations are listed in 25:19-26. The LXX placement gives a somewhat different rhythm to the book, moving from oracles of judgment against Israel, to those against the nations, to oracles that focus more on hope and promise. Their placement at the end of the book in the Hebrew Bible, especially when integrated with several promises of restoration for Israel and for the nations (see above), gives them a more complex eschatological purpose with universal themes. They demonstrate finally that God's purposes at work in and through complex relationships among these nations are universal in scope. God's work has the world in view. The Hebrew Bible placement of the OAN means that the material regarding the nations in chapter 25 is anticipatory. The rationale for the order in which the oracles appear is uncertain, not least because the order in the LXX is different (see below). Egypt may be included first because it is a major power in that world (and hence brackets the concluding oracles against Babylon), but its placement is also informed by the focus on Egypt in chapters 42–44 (also different from the LXX).

Insofar as the oracles are dated, they are in chronological order (in the LXX, the order is different). This chronology places the delivery of these oracles in the period from the fourth year of King Jehoiakim (605 BC; 46:2, continuing the chronology of 45:1; cf. 46:13; 47:1) to the beginning of the reign of Zedekiah (597 BC; 49:34) to the fourth year of Zedekiah (593 BC; 51:59). The fourth year of Jehoiakim is the same dating as both 25:1 (the context in which the OAN appear in the LXX) and 45:1, the immediately preceding text. This chronology places the dated oracles in the years prior to the fall of Jerusalem (46:13 may reflect events anywhere from 604 to 568–567 BC). This chronology may fit well for the OAN in chapters 46–49, but creates difficulties for the oracles against Babylon in chapters 50–51. That a pre-fall setting (at least according to 51:59) includes the oracles *against* Babylon stands at odds with the "pro-Babylonian" perspective of chapters 27–29 (and 39–40). How could Jeremiah be pro-Babylonian in some texts and anti-Babylonian in chapters 50–51 (see Introduction)?

Moreover, the nations are geographically oriented. The oracles begin with the westernmost nation (Egypt), move to those in the near vicinity of Israel (Philistia, Moab, Ammon, Edom), and finally to those toward the east (Damascus, Arabia, Elam, Babylon). Babylon stands in the climactic position because its fate is most crucial in thinking about the future of Israel. The beginning oracle, against Egypt, is certainly informed by the Egyptian context of chapters 43–44. At the same time, there is a certain generalization that has taken place in these oracles (especially that of Babylon in chs. 50–51) wherein the enemy of God's people can be applied to various historical situations.

These six chapters have their own superscription, identifying them as the word of the Lord concerning the nations (46:1; see also the reference to "book" in 25:13). This heading probably indicates that these oracles had their own history of transmission before being drawn into the book of Jeremiah. Various suggestions regarding their pre-prophetic setting in life (whether military, royal, or worship) have not garnered much support, though it is commonly recognized that the holy war tradition has informed the language and themes of these texts. Only some of the oracles are thought to have originated with the prophet (e.g., 46:3-12), but uncertainty abounds regarding questions of origin and authorship. Certainly the final editors link these oracles with the prophet Jeremiah (46:1, 13; 47:1; 49:34; 50:1; 51:59-64).

God's role in the destruction of these nations is clearly stated in every oracle (see 46:10, 15, 18, 25-28; 47:4, 6-7; 48:10, 12, 26, 33, 35, 38, 44, 47; 49:2, 5, 8, 10, 15-16, 19-20, 27, 32, 35-38). These nations are considered to be the enemies of God and God is certainly considered an agent, though not the only "real" agent.[2] The destroying armies of Babylon (in chs. 46–49, e.g., 49:30) and of the Medes and Persians (in chs. 50–51, e.g., 51:11) are the agents in and through which God works (see 48:10) and they are just as "real" as God even if they are not often mentioned in a specific way (see **Introduction**) (see **Connections: God among the Nations**).

Again and again the parallels between Israel and the nations are drawn out; the judgments on these nations are not exceptional, as if God played favorites and never visited the chosen people with judgment. On the other hand, it is important for Israel, not least an Israel that has experienced great devastation and exile, to know that it has not been divinely singled out and held to a higher standard of behavior than other

Divine Consistency and Accountability

That the predominant theme of the OAN as well as the oracles against Israel is one of judgment bespeaks another word regarding Israel: God is consistent in the way in which God acts in the world. God's word of judgment against Israel is not rooted in caprice, but is part and parcel of God's ways with the nations more generally. Hence, Israel would not be able to claim that God was being unfair, as if they had been singled out for judgment. All nations are accountable to God and God works consistently among them in terms of sin and its consequences (e.g., Egypt for its pride and militarism, 46:8).

One after another, these nations are brought before the bar of justice, accountable to God for who they are and what they have done. And there is not one missing! No matter the justifications or defenses or excuses they might bring to the case, they are called to account. No matter how great their empires, how sophisticated their policies, how brilliant their officials, God will hold all of them accountable. A related purpose of these oracles (at least those in chs. 46–49), depending upon the historical context, may have been to alert Israel that appealing to such nations for help would be a vain exercise. Yet, the texts are remarkably silent about such a purpose. Babylon would sweep across that world and sweep away all nations that stood in its way.

nations. All the nations, chosen or non-chosen, are subject to the judgment of God. [Divine Consistency and Accountability]

COMMENTARY

Two oracles are addressed against Egypt and are related to two different historical situations. Verses 2-12 are set in the fourth year of Jehoiakim (see also 25:1; 36:1; 45:1) and, according to v. 2, pertain to the defeat of Egyptian forces under Pharaoh Neco II at Carchemish by Babylonian armies under King Nebuchadrezzar (605 BC). The battle at Carchemish (a trade center in the upper reaches of the Euphrates valley, vv. 6, 10) was decisive in enabling Babylon to gain control of Syria and Judah. Verses 13-26 probably pertain to a later time (suggestions include 604, 601, 588, and 568 BC) and concern a threat to invade or an actual invasion of Egypt by Babylon under Nebuchadrezzar (see 43:8-13; 44:30). The editors of the chapter probably consider both oracles to have essentially the same historical setting. It is not clear whether the prophet is predicting these encounters between Babylon and Egypt, commenting on current military advances, or reflecting upon recent events. The oracles may well reflect some combination thereof.

These oracles, particularly the first, are remarkable for the range and energy of the similes, metaphors, and word plays used. The poet draws on available images for judgment that are used in other oracles against Egypt (e.g., Isa 19; Ezek 29–32) and judgment language more generally. Readers will be familiar with certain images from other oracles in Jeremiah directed against Israel (e.g., "terror is all around," v. 5, cf. 6:25; 20:3, 10; a time of vengeance, v. 10, cf. 5:9, 29; 9:9; the balm in Gilead, v. 11, cf. 8:22; "shame," v. 12, cf. 2:26, 36; a "waste, a ruin, without inhabitant, v. 19, cf. 9:11). These parallels show that God's entering into judgment with Israel is neither unusual nor unfair. God will hold all peoples accountable and all of them alike will suffer the consequences of their words and deeds. [A Complex Collage]

Notably, the word of judgment is directed against Egypt's leaders (and their gods), not the Egyptians more generally (see vv. 15, 17, 25). There is no demonizing of Egypt in these oracles, as might be

A Complex Collage

AΩ Various efforts have been made to outline these oracles against Egypt in a logical way, but the oracles themselves resist such attempts; this has been made evident not least by the differences among such outlines. It seems best to consider this poetry as more circular in the way it makes its point; the images tumble over one another and give an overall impression rather than moving carefully from one point to the next. The oracles collapse the preparations for battle, the battle itself, as well as the defeat and its shame, into a complex collage. All of the elements associated with the destruction of Egypt are interwoven in such a way that neither logical nor chronological clarity is made available. But the reader knows clearly that a disaster for Egypt has taken place.

expected from those who held an "anti-Egypt" stance in the years before the fall of Jerusalem. At the same time, Egypt is shown to be as helpless as was Judah before the Babylonian armies, confirming the perspectives of those who were opposed to a pro-Egyptian policy. Yet, that point is not made directly and such a confirmation is not used to condemn Egypt in any final way. This open-ended perspective opens the way to the positive statement of v. 26b regarding the future of Egypt.

The placement of the oracle against Egypt may be related to the focus on Egypt in chapters 42–44 and, more generally, to the fact that Egypt is the predominant nation in that world besides Babylon. The opening verse (46:1) introduces all of the oracles and designates all that follows as "the word of the LORD." See above for discussion of the connection that is made between God's word and the history of the nations.

First Oracle against Egypt, 46:2-12

The notes in v. 2 and v. 13 set these oracles in a particular historical situation. Carchemish is located on the border of Syria and Turkey in the upper reaches of the Euphrates river (see vv. 6, 10). From all external appearances these reported events could be explained simply in political and military terms. But the testimony of these oracles is that God is also very much involved; God is working God's purposes in and through these seemingly "secular" events.

The poem begins in the middle of things and it is not immediately clear to the reader what is going on or who is being addressed and described. What follows is certainly not an "eyewitness account," that is, observations made on the actual progress of a military event. The poetry is an imaginative effort to portray what this event *means* for the Egyptians in particular. It is an interpretive exercise. The phrase "in the north by the river Euphrates" (vv. 6, 10) functions as a virtual refrain, closely followed by the image of stumbling and falling warriors (vv. 6, 12). The oracle is almost hymnic in its character.

The oracle begins with the call to Egyptian (rather than Babylonian, in view of vv. 9, 14) military leaders to prepare for war (vv. 3-4), a call that is picked up again in vv. 9, 14 (see also 49:14; 50:14-15, 21, 26-27; 51:11, 27-28). A comparable call had gone out to Israel (4:5-6; 6:1) in the face of an attack from the same Babylonian enemy (Babylon is not specifically mentioned in those contexts either). Though interpreters disagree, it seems best to consider the Egyptians the addressee throughout (as is certainly the case in vv. 14-24).

The "says the Lord" in v. 5 (and v. 1) indicates that God himself is commenting on this military situation! The armies are to deck themselves with the traditional armor (buckler, shield, helmet, breastplates), harness and mount their horses, and draw (or polish) their spears. In view of this finely equipped army, God ironically asks: Why then are they filled with terror? Why are they falling back? Their warriors are beaten and in full retreat. They do not even pause to look back! For them, as for Israel, there is terror all around (6:25; 20:3, 10; cf. 49:29)! The swiftest of the soldiers are not able to escape. There at Carchemish on the Euphrates, every warrior has stumbled and fallen (v. 6).

Once again, God speaks ironically (vv. 7-9). Who are these armies anyway? They make grandiose claims in their arrogance, thinking that they can rise up like their own river Nile during a time of flooding (v. 8 answers v. 7). They speak as if they had the power of the Nile to cover the earth and destroy every city and people in their path (here the imagery of the waters of chaos are drawn upon; cf. Ezek 29:3-10; 32:2). Egypt is making arrogant claims regarding its power to control other nations (this is the key factor that leads to judgment on Egypt). Ironically, the call to battle is heard again, urging the horses to advance, the chariots to dash madly, and the warriors to push forward (v. 9, cf. vv. 3-4). The allies of Egypt (Ethiopia, Put [a region in Libya], and the Ludim [a people from North Africa]) are called upon to bear their shields and draw their bows.

Verse 10 marks a shift in the rhetoric; that shift may best be heard by introducing the verse with a "But" (so NAB, NIV). Babylon is the nation that lies behind the destruction of Egypt (v. 2); at the same time, the poet here links that event to divine activity. [A Day of Retribution] To depict this defeat of the Egyptians, some startling images are used. The sword is personified and portrayed as having killed so many Egyptian warriors that it is satisfied and having drunk so much of their blood that it is full (see vv. 14, 16; 47:6; 48:2; 49:37; 50:35-37; Deut 32:40-42). Even more, this

A Day of Retribution

God's purposes are at work in and through the military disasters experienced by Egypt. These events are referred to in v. 10 as "the day of the Lord God of hosts, a day of retribution" (see "the day of their calamity," v. 21; against Philistia, 47:4). The "day of the LORD" is used in the prophetic literature for a decisive event in the history of Israel or any other nation (see Isa 2:12-17; 13:9; Amos 5:18-20). The effects are either positive or (usually) negative (for the use of "day" in both senses, see Jer 30:7-8). This language is somewhat rare in Jeremiah (see 12:3; 18:17). For the Egyptians, this day of the Lord is a day of vengeance (as it was for Israel, see 5:9, 29; 9:9). That is, it is a day when they reap the consequences of their own deeds and God is shown to be victorious over these ancient enemies so opposed to the divine purposes. The day of the Lord is thus not finally an event in which God alone is active; the people's wickedness has come full term and carries its own effects and God uses historical agents to accomplish the divine purposes.

God's Virgin Daughter Egypt

The oracles against Egypt are remarkable in their repeated reference to the Egyptians as God's "daughter" (46:11, 19, 24); Moab, Ammon, and Babylon are also referred to as God's daughter (48:18; 49:4; 50:42); this language is also used for Sidon and Babylon in Isa 23:12; 47:1. One would, of course, expect that Israel would be referred to in such terms (see Jer 6:23; 18:13; 31:4, 21), but it is theologically significant that Israel is not the only people who are considered to be the children of God. These references are testimony to God as Creator of all people; as such, God as parent is concerned about the welfare of all of God's children, not just God's elect. And that divine concern will be manifested in terms of both judgment and salvation (in the broadest sense of the term). For the latter divine action on behalf of the Egyptians, see Isa 19:24-25 (cf. Jer 46:26), where God refers to Egypt as "my people" (cf. Amos 9:7). All peoples are God's children and God's choice of Israel is ultimately for the sake of all these children.

---

slaughter of Egyptians is portrayed as a sacrifice that God himself offers by the river Euphrates (cf. Ezek 39:17-20)!

Finally, the Egyptians are addressed as God's virgin daughter (v. 11)! [God's Virgin Daughter Egypt] Egypt is called to seek balm in Gilead (applied to Israel in 8:22), but with the sense that no healing salve will be found there; though they have taken many different medicines they have not been healed (historically, Egypt's designs on this territory failed). They themselves will not be the source of their own healing, though they make many efforts to find something to soothe their wounds. Their defeat and the resultant cries and shame will be heard round the world (as also with Israel, 2:36; 13:26; 23:40). The oracle concludes by recalling the last line of v. 6; all of their vaunted warriors, panic-stricken, have stumbled over one another and fallen.

A Second Oracle against Egypt, 46:13-24

As noted, this oracle is set at a time of Babylonian advance against Egypt itself, or at least the threat thereof (dates in 604, 601, 587, and 568 BC have been suggested). As in the first oracle, elements of preparation for war, aspects of the battle itself, and the defeat and resultant shame are combined. This oracle, as with vv. 3-12, is identified as the word of the Lord (v. 13; see "says the LORD" in v. 23).

The initial focus is entirely upon Egypt and its allies (vv. 14-17). God's ironic call to Egypt to prepare for war rings out (v. 14; see vv. 3-4, 9). The sentinels are to call to key Egyptian cities (see 2:16; note 44:1): get ready to defend the country for the sword (=Babylon) has already devoured its neighbors. But then (v. 15), ironically and sarcastically, the prophet asks why Apis (the god of fertility in Memphis, imaged as a black bull) has failed to stand in

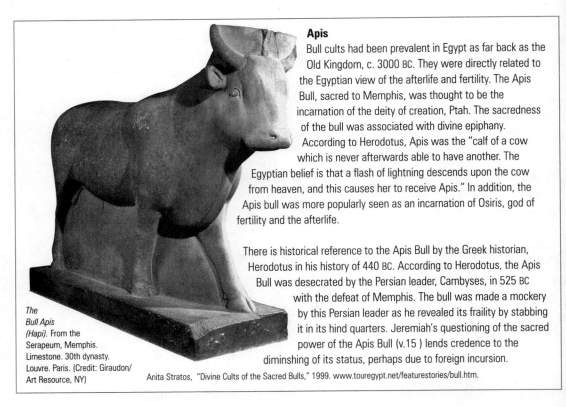

Apis

Bull cults had been prevalent in Egypt as far back as the Old Kingdom, c. 3000 BC. They were directly related to the Egyptian view of the afterlife and fertility. The Apis Bull, sacred to Memphis, was thought to be the incarnation of the deity of creation, Ptah. The sacredness of the bull was associated with divine epiphany. According to Herodotus, Apis was the "calf of a cow which is never afterwards able to have another. The Egyptian belief is that a flash of lightning descends upon the cow from heaven, and this causes her to receive Apis." In addition, the Apis bull was more popularly seen as an incarnation of Osiris, god of fertility and the afterlife.

There is historical reference to the Apis Bull by the Greek historian, Herodotus in his history of 440 BC. According to Herodotus, the Apis Bull was desecrated by the Persian leader, Cambyses, in 525 BC with the defeat of Memphis. The bull was made a mockery by this Persian leader as he revealed its fraility by stabbing it in its hind quarters. Jeremiah's questioning of the sacred power of the Apis Bull (v.15) lends credence to the diminishing of its status, perhaps due to foreign incursion.

The Bull Apis (Hapi). From the Serapeum, Memphis. Limestone. 30th dynasty. Louvre. Paris. (Credit: Giraudon/ Art Resource, NY)

Anita Stratos, "Divine Cults of the Sacred Bulls," 1999. www.touregypt.net/featurestories/bull.htm.

its place and has fled (see v. 25 on judgment against the Egyptians gods; Isa 19:1). The warriors are called to stand, but their god fails to do so! The reason is that Yahweh has already thrown him out! The beginning of v. 16 is textually uncertain, but probably refers to warriors stumbling and falling (as in vv. 6, 10). Those who speak are probably troops beyond the borders of Egypt who urge one another to go back to their homeland in view of the armies that have swallowed up Egypt's neighbors (see v. 14). As their gods flee, so they flee. Not a courageous response to the call to battle!

Verse 17 is a taunt of the Egyptian pharaoh, calling him a braggart or a loudmouth who missed his chance (some see a wordplay on the name of pharaoh Hophra in this taunt). In contrast to the ineffectiveness of the king of Egypt, in v. 18 the King whose name is the Lord of hosts (or armies) swears—a divine oath!—that "one is coming" (that is, Nebuchadrezzar) whose strength is like two mountains in the northern part of Israel (Tabor and Carmel). In the face of this enemy on the horizon the prophet's call goes out to the besieged Egyptians once again (v. 19). God addresses them as "sheltered" (perhaps "inhabited," a play on the last word of the verse) "daughter Egypt" (see v.11; [God's Virgin Daughter Egypt]): pack your bags, you are bound for exile (similarly, Israel in 10:17)! The call to prepare for battle has been followed by a description of

Images for Egypt and Babylon

Jeremiah's use of an amazing variety of images calls for imagination in thinking through the significance of these events for the Egyptians. Egypt is a beautiful heifer, yet helpless, unable to defend itself in the face of a horsefly or gadfly (=Babylon) from the North (vv. 20, 24; as with Israel, 4:6) that lights upon her and stings her. Egypt's mercenaries, hired for just such a military moment, are likened to fatted calves, ready for the slaughter (the bovine images may be related to the images for Egyptian gods). These "helpers" have turned tail and fled, unable to stand against the enemy when disaster comes, the time of their "visitation" (v. 21; this language is also used with Israel's leaders, 8:12; 23:12). The Egyptians are likened to snakes and the sounds they make when they are retreating; they slither away in the face of a swarm of enemies on the march. The Babylonians are like woodchoppers with axes who shall cut down the seemingly impenetrable Egyptian forest because they are more numerous than locusts (vv. 22-23). Such an imaginative use of language is a challenge to all those who would use the biblical text for preaching and teaching.

---

retreating and stumbling warriors and now by the call to prepare for exile. As was the case with Jerusalem (e.g., 9:11; 44:22), so shall Memphis become a waste, without inhabitant (v. 19). The Babylonians have the same effect on Egypt as they had on Judah and Jerusalem.

A series of remarkable images for Egypt and Babylon are now used in ironic and sarcastic ways—heifer, fatted calves, gadfly, snake, woodchoppers, locusts (vv. 20-24). [Images for Egypt and Babylon] Daughter Egypt (see vv. 11, 19; [God's Virgin Daughter Egypt]) will be handed over to the enemy from the North and be violated and put to shame (see v. 12; see images of sexual violation also for Israel at 13:22, 26). Israel also faced this enemy from the North (e.g., 4:6) and the end result for both lands was devastation.

A Prose Commentary, 46:25-26

The following prose verses (vv. 25-26) are probably a later commentary on the basic oracle against Egypt (cf. v. 24b with v. 26a), specifically identifying the enemy from the North and providing an inclusio with the description in v. 13. God, the Lord of hosts (armies) will be "visiting" iniquities (NRSV, "punishment) "upon" (a preposition, *'el* or *'al,* occurs seven times!) everyone and everything imaginable: upon Amon, the sun god, whose temple was in Thebes (the capital city of Egypt during much of its history, located in upper Egypt), upon Pharaoh, upon Egypt, upon its gods, upon its kings, upon Pharaoh (again!), and upon "those who trust in him." This veritable litany speaks of the wide-ranging effects of Egypt's sins upon its life.

In effect, God will give Egypt "into the hand of" (repeated three times) those who seek its life, into the hand of King Nebuchadrezzar, and into the hand of his officers, all of Egypt's godly and royal authorities and all those who trust in them (see 44:30). As is typical for Jeremiah (see **Connections**, ch. 25; **Introduction**) the agency of both God and the Babylonians is highlighted. The word of judgment brought against the gods of Egypt (see v. 15) is certainly intended to show the incomparability of Israel's God and the futility of idol worship, but, strikingly, a special point is not made of the latter. The phrase "those who trust in him" is probably not an oblique reference to those in Israel who sought Egypt as an ally against Babylon; if these oracles were intended to function as a deterrent to such a foreign policy, certainly the point would have been made more directly. [Judgment Not Final for Egypt]

Salvation for Israel, 46:27-28

These verses are virtually identical to 30:10-11, and are similar to several texts in Isaiah (see 41:8-14; 43:1-5), where Israel is also called the servant of the Lord (see Isa 44:1-2). This text has probably been drawn into this context because of the reference to "all the nations" (v. 28; LXX has this text only here). God's judgment on Egypt (and other nations) is not undertaken for the sake of Israel. That judgment is due to Egypt's own particular relationship with God that has been marked by arrogance and its designs on empire building (vv. 8, 17). At the same time, such divine judgments do have a fallout effect on Israel and God's purposes for them. Israel's restoration to the land would be made possible because of such judgments on Egypt and others. It will become

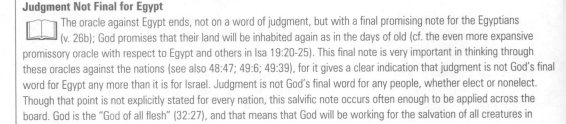

Judgment Not Final for Egypt

The oracle against Egypt ends, not on a word of judgment, but with a final promising note for the Egyptians (v. 26b); God promises that their land will be inhabited again as in the days of old (cf. the even more expansive promissory oracle with respect to Egypt and others in Isa 19:20-25). This final note is very important in thinking through these oracles against the nations (see also 48:47; 49:6; 49:39), for it gives a clear indication that judgment is not God's final word for Egypt any more than it is for Israel. Judgment is not God's final word for any people, whether elect or nonelect. Though that point is not explicitly stated for every nation, this salvific note occurs often enough to be applied across the board. God is the "God of all flesh" (32:27), and that means that God will be working for the salvation of all creatures in every time and place.

That God will make an "end" of all those nations to which Israel has been banished (v. 28) sounds apocalyptic in its tone, but is actually limited in its scope. On the one hand, it pertains only to those nations to which Israel has been exiled. On the other hand, the "end" language must be interpreted in terms of the context in which it is now placed, namely, God's promise to Egypt in v. 26. In view of this future for Egypt, the language of "end" must mean an end to Egyptian rule over Israel or their power more generally, not their annihilation.

clear from texts such as 50:4-5, 17-20 that Babylon's judgment is the most crucial for Israel's return from exile. At the same time, for a restored Israel to live in peace and security (chs. 30–31), the status of other nations in its region (such as Egypt) is an important consideration (see [Judgment not Final for Egypt]).

The repetition of the call to "have no fear" (added from 30:11), the promise that "no one shall make him afraid," and the concern for a rest that is undisturbed, suggests an audience for whom fearfulness and dispiritedness is characteristic. Wherever they have been thrown, God is with them, and is at work among the nations to enable their restoration to rest in the land. As has been promised at various points in the text, no matter how severe the judgment, God will not "make an end of you" (v. 28; see 4:27; 5:10, 18). Even in the promised future, sin will not go unpunished, but God will chastise, not annihilate. Israel can be assured of a future in the purposes of God.

This promise is cross-generational in its range and applicability; it includes not simply those for whom this oracle is written, but also their descendants ("offspring"). While Israel's scattering among these nations is a deserved consequence of their sin, God's purposes are not to kill off this people. God's purposes are to save this people from wherever they may be captive and to bring them home again. Notably, God's purposes are not focused in a (re)establishment of *God's* sovereignty, but of Israel's new life.

CONNECTIONS

God among the Nations

It is not uncommon that communities of faith reduce God to the God of their particular domain. For example, it may be claimed that God's only or primary business is to look after Christian people. God's presence and activity elsewhere in the world, while probably professed in a general way (God is omnipresent), is seldom fully acknowledged or woven into reflections regarding God and the larger world of peoples and nations. But these OAN, so common in the prophetic texts (see also Amos 9:7), testify to the fact that God is not simply present to all peoples, but God is actively at work among them in the pursuance of God's purposes for the entire world. Some such claim is probably the most fundamental theological grounding for these oracles. To put it succinctly: God is present on every occasion and active in every event. All people everywhere have experienced God's presence and activity in their lives. These people may not realize it, of course, but God's activity has indeed been effective.

To make such a claim carries several implications. It means that the people of God must be alert to ways in which God is active among the nations in every time and place. One of our responsibilities, as it was for Jeremiah and other prophetic figures, is to seek to discern how God is at work. There will no doubt be differences among the people of God with respect to issues of discernment, not least because God's activity cannot be factored out in any precise way. At the same time, that ambiguity does not excuse us from the task of discernment.

It would probably be commonly held that God's purposes for the world were well served in the decisions of the Allied armies to stop Hitler; God was active within the hearts and minds of key leaders in leading them to intervene. In a way not unlike Nebuchadrezzar was understood to be God's "servant" for purposes of judgment (e.g., 25:9), so it could be discerned that the Allied armies served a comparable role in World War II. At the same time, even if one would agree with the decision to intervene, it would also be important to ask whether the Allies overextended their mandate in a manner not unlike Babylon by, say, the saturation bombing of certain German cities (e.g., Dresden). In other cases, decisions to intervene in the activities of other nations may be more disputed (e.g., in Yugoslavia or Somalia). In such cases, where ambiguity reigns, leaders will often need to act without the kind of clarity that would be desirable. [Implications for Mission]

Implications for Mission

Another implication of the theological claim that God is active among all the nations of the world relates to the matter of mission. This prophetic perspective would claim that all people have had an experience of God before "we showed up with the Bible in our hand." We do not bring God to the world! God is there before we travel to any particular place, indeed before we even thought about reaching out to others. Again, one of our basic tasks is that of discernment. If we listen carefully to these people we may discern specific ways in which God has been active in their lives. Perhaps it has been an experience of unconditional love, or incredible mercy, or a miraculous deliverance at the individual or communal level. Our responsibility, then, is to name that experience in terms of the God to whom we witness.

NOTES

[1] See Walter Brueggemann, *A Commentary on Jeremiah: Exile and Homecoming* (Grand Rapids: Eerdmans, 1998), 423-24, on the two brothers and the two scrolls.

[2] The use of the word "real" only for Yahweh in Robert Carroll, *Jeremiah* (Philadelphia: Westminster, 1986), 763-64, is unfortunate.

ORACLE AGAINST
THE PHILISTINES

47:1-7

COMMENTARY

The superscription (v. 1) speaks of an attack on the Philistine city of Gaza (on the southern Mediterranean coast) by an unnamed pharaoh (cf. 25:20 and the oracles regarding Philistia in Isa 14:29-32; Ezek 25:15-17; Amos 1:6-8; Zeph 2:4-7; Zech 9:5-7). This attack (reference to which is absent from the LXX) has commonly been associated with the campaigns of Pharaoh Neco II in Israel in 609 BC. On the other hand, the reference to "waters rising out of the north" (v. 2) suggests a Babylonian invasion of Philistia by Nebuchadrezzar in 604 BC (after Carchemish, 46:2). Perhaps an Egyptian attack from the north can be understood in terms of rampaging Egyptian armies returning from their campaigns in the north (e.g., after defeating Josiah at Megiddo in 609 BC or after having been defeated at Carchemish). A Babylonian invasion is also supported by the reference (vv. 5, 7) to the destruction of the Philistine city of Askelon (north of Gaza), destroyed by Nebuchadrezzar in 604 BC. Perhaps Babylonian military activity is in view in that the oracle describes the situation "before" the Egyptian attack, though the "before" may simply signal the predictive character of the oracle. It may be that various incursions into Philistine territory over the years by both Egyptians and Babylonians have contributed to this oracle. [Past, Present, and Future Elided]

A particularly striking aspect of this oracle is the lack of any mention of Philistine wickedness that would occasion the disaster (contrast Amos 1:6-8).

Rather, the oracle simply describes the devastating effects of foreign invasion on these cities. At the same time, these effects are specified

Past, Present, and Future Elided

As with the oracles against Egypt, this oracle is no simple prediction; the destruction of Philistia is portrayed as imminent, in progress, and having been completed. Perhaps this is a way that the speaker projects himself into future events, as if he were living in the midst of what has not yet occurred or has just begun to occur. The effect of this elision of past, present, and future is that readers are brought right into the middle of the maelstrom, as if to relive these disastrous times for the region.

as due to the command of God (v. 7). This command should, however, not be isolated from the larger political situation of that world, particularly the divine judgment on Israel that is mediated in and through military power. Smaller nations such as Philistia, whether they are particularly wicked or not, have gotten caught up in this maelstrom and its disastrous effects. [The Philistines]

Once again, God is the speaker (vv. 1-2). Invading armies are imaged as waters rising out of the north, flowing south toward Philistia, and overflowing the land, devastating cities and inhabitants (v. 2; for this image, see 46:7-8; Isa 8:7-8). The people cry out, mourning over the imminent destruction of their land. Verse 3 picks up more literal images of approaching armies, with a focus on the noise they create— the pounding of the hooves of their steeds and the clatter of the chariots with their rumbling wheels. Fear has so immobilized the populace and engendered such a sense of helplessness that even fathers and mothers do not turn back and rescue their children before they flee.

To this point the oracle has not identified the object of the judgment. That comes in v. 4. The "day" of the Lord is coming, indeed is in progress, for Philistia (v. 4) as it was for Egypt (46:10; see [The Day of Retribution]). Not only will "all the Philistines" be "destroyed"—notice the repetition, with the second phrase introducing God as the subject—but all of their allies will be cut off. Even the helpers are helpless.

Tyre and Sidon were Phoenician cities that allied themselves against Nebuchadrezzar (see 25:22; 27:1-4; cf. Ezek 29:17-21; Amos 1:9-10) and would have been swept up in a Babylonian invasion of this part of the world. It may be speculated that the Philistines were a part of this alliance, and hence opposed to the pro-Babylonian policy of Jeremiah. The Philistines are associated with Caphtor (=Crete) because that is their traditional place of origin (see Amos 9:7 for a remarkable confessional statement about God's involvement in their migration).

The devastation of the Philistines is imaged as being shaved bald (cf. Isa 7:20) and reduced to silence; they are left with only a

The Philistines

The country from which the Philistines migrated into Canaan is still unknown, though the area around the Aegean Sea is a likely point of origin. Known as the "Sea Peoples," conquering Crete (=Caphtor, v. 4) on their way across the Mediterranean Sea, they originally planned to settle in Egypt; defeated by the Egyptians in about 1190 BC, they settled in the coastal cities of Canaan (Gaza, Ashkelon, Ashdod; Ekron, Gath, known as the Philistine pentapolis). They disappeared from history by about the time Israel returned to Canaan during the Persian hegemony. The name Palestine is their primary legacy.

The Philistines are commonly presented as the enemy of Israel in the Old Testament (e.g., Judg 13–16; 1 Sam 4–7), but this text nowhere specifies that Philistia is being destroyed because of this long-standing enmity. In fact, there is a sense in which the wickedness of *Israel* is the reason for the sufferings inflicted on Philistia. Hence, the primary force of this text is to describe the disastrous personal and communal effects suffered by the Philistines in the wake of the judgments against Israel.

Generally, individuals and communities suffer not only because of what they may have done, but also because of what others have done to them (witness what Israel underwent at the hands of the Egyptians in the book of Exodus). Because of Israel's wickedness and the divine judgment it spawns, the map of their entire world gets rearranged—Philistia included.

Philistine plain. (Credit: Mitchell G. Reddish)

"remnant" of their former strength or territory (v. 5). The reference
to gashing themselves is associated with rites of mourning over
their dead (see 16:6); their "baldness" may also be a reference to
such practices or it may refer to the shearing effect of the foreign
invasions. Especially to be noted is the divine lament "how long" in
v. 5b (see v. 6), that is, how long will their times of mourning continue (see below; for other divine laments, see 48:31-32, 36)? [A
Divine Lament for Exilic Readers]

The oracle ends with an image of the sword personified (as in
46:10; 50:35-38), though here it is specifically identified as the
"sword of the LORD" (v. 6), as was also the case for Israel (12:12).
The sword is portrayed as in the process of doing its work, and is
directly addressed in a striking way. Who is the speaker, telling the
sword to cease and desist, to put itself back in its scabbard
(reversing the battle orders)? Who is lamenting with the cry: "how
long" (as in v. 5b)? It has been suggested that the Philistines are
being quoted here, but that is unlikely, given the Yahweh reference
(and other speakers are identified in texts such as 46:16). Other
scholars have suggested that these words are a reflection by the
prophet himself, not least because of the third person reference to
God. Yet, divine oracles often refer to God in the third person. At
the same time, the prophet's own perspective is certainly not
removed from these oracles, so there is some truth is hearing the

---

A Divine Lament for Exilic Readers

The readers of this oracle are not Philistines; they are Babylonian exiles. For one thing, this oracle shows the extent to which that entire world was caught up in the effects of the wickedness (and others). This was an experience of divine judgment mediated through an incredibly violent and merciless foe. Readers are invited to look at all the suffering that was unleashed on Israel's larger world, a world about which God cares (see Amos 9:7) and which God has drawn into the larger divine purposes.

At the same time, this poem is bold to say that things have gotten out of control even for God, a situation about which God laments (see 42:10, for a comparable word with respect to Israel). As such, the point for readers is certainly not centered on "Yahweh's unqualified governance"! A quite different God emerges here, a God filled with pathos. The situation is not such that God can find no way into the future, but that future will not be realized by the flick of the wrist. The divine lament in this text will be more than matched by the portrayal in 48:31-32, 36.

Walter Brueggemann; *A Commentary on Jeremiah: Exile and Homecoming* (Grand Rapids: Eerdmans, 1998), 441.

---

prophet speak at this point (see **Connections: The Sword of the Lord**).

As for the Philistines, these events do prove to be the end of their place in history, at least from all we know from available sources. That may be the reason that there is no qualification that allows for their future, as with Egypt and Moab (46:26; 48:47).

CONNECTIONS

The Sword of the Lord

Because this entire oracle is identified as the word of the Lord (v. 1), it is best to understand the lamenting and questioning of vv. 5-7 as God's own speech, a divine soliloquy or internal divine reflection (see 3:19-20). God's own response to this internal lament comes in v. 7a (see also v. 4 for the use of the third person "LORD"). Yet, even more, given the relationship between divine speech and prophetic speech elsewhere in the book (e.g., 4:19; 8:18), readers may hear the voices of both God and prophet here.

The net effect of understanding these verses as divine/prophetic speech keeps the action of the sword one remove from God himself. The judgment of God is mediated in and through human wielders of the sword. This is the judgment of God (=the sword of the Lord), but the sword is not literally in God's hands, any more than the stallions or chariots or the foe from the North are. Nor is the sword fully in God's control, for God is using human agents to achieve the divine purposes. This explains how it is that judgment eventually comes against Babylonia: it exceeded its divine mandate,

25:12-14; 50–51; these verses suggest that judgment for Babylon comes not only because of Israel, but also because of Philistia and perhaps others who experienced such Babylonian violence. So God himself laments regarding "how long" this will go on for the Philistines, and asks whether they have not experienced enough judgment (see 42:10 for Israel; Zech 1:15). And, remarkably, God seems not fully to know the answer to God's own questioning laments (on absolute divine foreknowledge, see **Connections**, ch. 26).

Finally, v. 7 constitutes a divine recognition (if not resignation) that God has been engaged in the unleashing of the sword in judgment, and that being the case, the armies will proceed to do their work against the Philistines. A kind of divine irony is present here; God has unleashed the judgment, has given over the agency to the invading armies, and they will now see it through to the end. God, involved but not micromanaging, will lament and question the level of the violence that is occurring but will also see it through to the end, indeed, given the choice of agents, *must* see it through to the end.

ORACLES AGAINST MOAB

48:1-47

This chapter consists of several loosely arranged oracles of judgment against Moab, Judah's neighbor to the east of the Dead Sea and with whom Judah shared a kinship relation (Gen 19:37-38). None of the oracles are introduced by a superscription setting them within a particular historical situation, but most are probably related to the advances of the Babylonian armies under Nebuchadrezzar in the period from 604 to 587 BC. The Moabites suffered at Babylonian hands not least because they joined Israel in rebellion against the Babylonians (27:1-11; 595 BC; Josephus mentions that Moab was conquered in 582 BC). At the same time, Israel was periodically at war with the Moabites over the centuries (see 2 Kgs 1:1; 3:3-27; 13:20; 24:2).

For other oracles against Moab, see Isaiah 15–16, Ezekial 25:8-11, Amos 2:1-3, and Zephaniah 2:8-11. Jeremiah 48 is remarkable for its length in comparison to these other oracles; only Babylon receives more attention in Jeremiah (chs. 50–51). The historical relationships between Israel and Moab explain the existence of such oracles, but the reason for the comparative length of Jeremiah 48 is unknown. The oracle does make clear that the interest in Moab goes beyond its specific relation with Israel, which in fact is hardly mentioned. The impact of the Babylonian invasions upon the Moabites themselves stands out in all the language for weeping and wailing.

The reasons behind the judgment on Moab are made clear at various points in the chapter, including trusting in their own strength and wealth (v. 7), self-satisfaction with its treasures (v. 11), and especially pride and arrogance (vv. 14, 26, 29-30, 42). Mistreatment of Israel is given particular attention in v. 27, but this reality is certainly not lifted up for special attention among Moab's sins. It should also be noted that, while Moab's sins are rehearsed, the text spends even more time portraying the great suffering of the Moabites at the hand of Babylonian invaders (e.g., vv. 45-46). Moab and Israel, for all their antipathy to each other, have this great calamity and its disastrous aftermath in common.

These oracles exhibit a remarkable interest in naming specific Moabite cities and towns—more than twenty are mentioned. [Cities

Cities and Towns in Moab

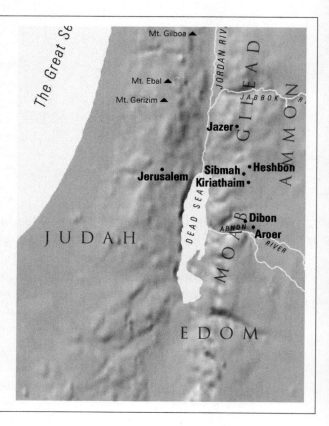

Over twenty Moabite sites are mentioned in these oracles; not many of them can be positively identified, but there is a general movement in the oracles from north to south. Heshbon (vv. 2, 34, 45; modern Hesban) was a key city in northern Moab, some twenty miles east of Jericho. Nebo (vv. 1, 22) was a city (also a mountain) about five miles south of Heshbon. Dibon (vv. 18, 22; modern Dhiban) was an important city in central Moab, some thirteen miles east of the Dead Sea; it was located on the King's Highway, a major caravan route along the Transjordanian Plateau from Damascus to the Gulf of Aqaba. Aroer (v. 19) was a fortress a few miles southeast of Dibon on the Arnon river (v. 20; modern Wadi el-Mujib), which flowed into the Dead Sea from the east. Kir-heres (v. 31; modern Kerak) was a capital city in southern Moab, also situated along the King's Highway. Other lesser towns include: Kiriathaim (vv. 2, 23); Horonaim (vv. 3-4); Luhith (v. 5); Jazer (v. 32); Sibmah (v. 32); eleven towns are mentioned in vv. 21-24 and seven in v. 34.

and Towns in Moab] The first towns named are in northern Moab (vv. 1-2) and, generally speaking, the cities named follow the movement of armies to the South. It is almost as if the prophet wanted readers to hear the fate of every last Moabite town. At the same time, the oracles exhibit an almost complete lack of specificity regarding Moabite history. In their most basic form, these oracles are, of course, not spoken to Moabites but are shaped for exilic readers. For unknown reasons this kind of geographical detail conveyed a word of importance to these readers. Perhaps this specificity was a way of saying that the completeness of the destruction of Moab was comparable to that suffered by Israel. [A Rhetorical Collage]

The chapter's five major segments, somewhat artificially divided, may be characterized as follows: The tumultuous and despairing response of the Moabites to the death-filled invasion of the Babylonians (vv. 1-10) and its imminent destruction (vv. 11-17); a taunt of devastated Moab (vv. 18-28); a lament over destroyed Moab (vv. 29-39); judgment and woe oracles against Moab (vv. 40-46), concluding with a promise of restoration (v. 47).

As with the oracles against Egypt and Philistia, the oracles against Moab reflect various moments of crisis, with invasions anticipated, in progress, and already having worked their devastation on the land (though very little in the way of specific military actions can be discerned). Once again, readers are invited to live themselves into Moab's disastrous situation (all of which would have been past to them). The predominant tone throughout is one of lament and mourning by Moabites, other peoples, and God. Prose insertions at vv. 10, 12-13, 21-27, and 34-39 provide some elaboration on the poetic oracles.

COMMENTARY

The Destruction of Moab, 48:1-10

The opening cry "Alas" sets a tone of mourning and wailing in the midst of death and destruction; it is a consistent rhythm throughout the chapter (see vv. 3-6, 17, 20, 31-39, 46). The cities named in vv. 1-2 are in northern Moab (Madmen is otherwise unknown; see NRSV footnote on a possible wordplay); they would be the first to experience the devastation of the Babylonian armies sweeping in from the north.

A repeated reference to shame stands at the head of these oracles and resounds in what follows (v. 1; see vv. 13, 20, 26, 39; cf. 46:12); this experience is specifically compared to the shame of Israel in 48:13, 27 (cf. 2:26, 36). In the eyes of all of its neighbors, as with Israel, "the renown of Moab is no more" (v. 2). Starting at the northern city Heshbon, the Babylonians are quoted as scheming to end Moab's status as a nation. Their wielding of the sword will reduce the Moabites to silence, deathly silence.

Moving farther down the country, mournful, distressful cries go up from other cities (vv. 3-6; in v. 4 NRSV, "little ones" may be a reference to the city of Zoar, so NAB; see Gen. 19:20-23):

A Rhetorical Collage

The poetry in these oracles is a kind of rhetorical collage, designed to look at Moab's disastrous situation from every angle, as if turning an object in the light and seeing how the light plays off different surfaces. The "argument" of the poem is more circular than linear; it follows no clearly coherent outline. Certain sounds are interwoven throughout, and they are primarily the sounds of wailing and crying on the part of the Moabites, its neighbors, and God. This theme of weeping is interwoven with the staccato beat of devastation, desolation, and death and their effect on the Moabites and their status in the world. These materials tend to evoke different emotions in the reader: a recognition of what pride, arrogance, and self-satisfaction can lead to as well as a sympathy for those who are suffering in the wake of marauding armies. Notably, even God calls for the Moabites to flee from the cities and save themselves (vv. 6, 20)!

"Moab is destroyed!" "Death and Destruction!" All the dwellers of the cities are urged to flee into the wilderness to save themselves, even if it means joining the wild asses (v. 6; see NRSV footnote, the Hebrew refers to still another city, Aroer, as in v. 19).

The mountains of Moab. (Credit: Mitchell G. Reddish)

Because they have trusted in their own strength and their own treasures, they will be captured, and even their chief deity Chemosh and all of his ministers will accompany them into exile (v. 7; see v. 13; according to 1 Kgs 11:7, Solomon introduced Chemosh into Israel's worship; cf. 2 Kgs 23:13). The "destroyer" (=Babylon, an inference drawn from the larger context, also vv. 15, 18) will sweep through every town, and death will visit every plain and valley; "no one will escape" (v. 8). For all the power of the Babylonians at work in this situation, and that military-political reality is not to be discounted, this disaster has happened because "the LORD has spoken." And, then, without skipping a beat, the language of death and destruction resumes (v. 9; similarly Israel, e.g., 26:9; 33:10; 34:22). The call even goes out for the destroyer (see v. 8) to set aside salt for Moab, that is, to make it into a saline wasteland so that its destruction is irreversible (see Zeph 2:9; Judg 9:45).

Verse 10 turns from the Moabites to their enemy. It has a force similar to the personification of the sword at 46:10 and 47:6-7, only the call here is directed to those who wield the sword, namely, the Babylonian armies. The "sword of the LORD" here becomes the "work of the LORD" (see 50:25). And those who are doing the Lord's work are the Babylonians. If they become lax in their carrying out of this work of judgment, if their sword does not draw blood, then they themselves will fall under the curse, which in this context means that they will have the sword wielded against them. This call to the Babylonians is certainly ironic in view of both the vaunted Babylonian violence in their various conquests and the later divine denunciation of Babylon for exceeding its divine mandate (chs. 50–51).

Moab's Complacency, 48:11-17

Verses 11-12 use the imagery of the wine for which Moab was famous (see vv. 32-33; cf. Isa 16:8-10) to portray its settledness in its present ways. Though the wine imagery is not entirely clear,[1] it seems to be a negative image for a complacent Moab (note the "ease" of Israel in Amos 6:1). This interpretation is preferred to a (positive) reference to an extended time of peace (note the following "therefore"). For a wine to mature properly, it should not be allowed to settle on its dregs (lees) in the vessel for too long a time (see Zeph 1:12). After a period of time (forty days or so) on the dregs, wine is to be poured into other vessels and separated from the dregs. Because the wine (which is Moab) has not been properly handled, the flavor and aroma of the wine will stay the same and will not achieve the high quality of which it is capable (NRSV "unspoiled" assumes a more positive sense for the imagery; NIV translates "unchanged"). So Moab has rested back on its laurels, proud of not having been forced into exile (as Israel had been; perhaps a reference to the exile of 597 BC), and has grown complacent with respect to its future.

Given this situation, God announces a judgment on Moab (v. 12; "therefore") and will send decanters (=the Babylonians) to pour out the Moabites. But they shall not be poured into other vessels for proper maturity; rather, those jars will be broken in pieces and the wine will flow out over the ground and be good for nothing. When that happens the Moabites will realize that the strongholds and treasures in which they trusted and their god Chemosh (see v. 7) are of no help to them. They will be disgraced as surely as Israel was when they trusted in the calves that they constructed at Bethel under Jeroboam (v. 13; see 1 Kgs 12:25-33; Amos 7:10-17).

The Moabites are taunted for their claims that they are fearless heroes, valiant in battle (v. 14). Moab's destroyer (see vv. 8, 18) has appeared on the scene and all of its gallant warriors, its finest young men, have been slaughtered. This announcement is made by the King, Yahweh of hosts (armies; see 46:18), in whose name these armies are sent; Moab's calamity or disaster (*rāʿāh*) is poised at its doorstep and its doom will surely and swiftly come (vv. 15-16). The call goes out to Moab's neighbors both to mourn for this fallen people and to mock them (v. 17). They have made such great claims for their glory and strength, and now that has all been broken like a pot. The call for others to mourn for Moab picks up on a prominent theme in the chapter; their mourning will match that of both Moab and God.

Moabite Cities Destroyed, 48:18-28

The mocking or taunting of Moab continues in these verses (on "daughter," see [God's Virgin Daughter Egypt]). With heavy irony, Moab (=Dibon, see [Cities and Towns in Moab]) is invited to come down from its glorious throne and take its seat on the lifeless ground (or possibly, on dung). Look at what has happened! Your destroyer (see vv. 8, 15) has devastated all of your strongholds, your seemingly impregnable fortresses (v. 18). You thought you were so strong!

Again, Moab (=Aroer, see [Cities and Towns in Moab]) is invited to stand by the roads and observe its own compatriots fleeing from the destroyer. Moab is to inquire of these refugees what has happened—the latest news from the front (v. 19). The answer comes back (v. 20): Moab has been disgraced and destroyed, and so the observers are to wail and cry and to get the news out: Moab is ruined.

Verses 21-24 proceed to specify the wide-ranging effects of the destroyer's work; the judgment of God has fallen on virtually every city and town in Moab, far and near. In summary (v. 25), Moab's horn (=posterity, Ps 132:17, is preferable to strength, Ps 18:2) is cut off, his arm (=might) is broken. Verses 26-27 seem to be addressed to Jeremiah and use images from an earlier word of God to the prophet regarding the nations (see discussion at 25:15-16, 27). The word of judgment brought against Moab is likened to their drinking wine, becoming drunk, and vomiting; thereby they are shamed and, as with the inebriated in most cultures, become a laughingstock to all that may pass by (see v. 39). As they had treated Israel (v. 27) so would they themselves be treated. [Reasons for Moab's Judgment]

Reasons for Moab's Judgment

Two related reasons are given for God's judgment of Moab. One, Moab has magnified itself against the God of Israel (also v. 42). This language is either another way of stating its self-promoting pride, which claims a godlikeness that challenges Yahweh whether they realize it or not or, less likely, a reference to its participation in anti-Babylonian counsels in opposition to the will of the Lord (27:3). Two, Moab has made God's people a laughingstock (see Zeph 2:8-10 for some detail) and an object of ridicule (=wagging the head). This Moab had done, even though Israel had not been caught committing a crime (presumably against Moab, for more generally Israel had certainly done so!). This is the only explicit reference in the poem to the mistreatment of Israel by Moab.

Once again (v. 28; see vv. 18, 19), a taunting call is addressed to Moab. They are invited to leave the cities and dwell among the rocks of the wilderness (see v. 6; cf. Israel, 4:29) and live like doves precariously nesting at the edge of a chasm. The reference to doves may be meant to call to mind their moaning (see Ezek 7:16; Nah 2:7; Isa 38:14; 59:11), forever lamenting over what has happened to their great nation.

Divine Lament over Moab, 48:29-39

These verses are set off from what precedes by the use of the first person with God as subject (see the close parallels of vv. 30-33, 36 with Isa 16:6-11). God hears and knows (vv. 29-30); God laments (vv. 31-32, 36), and God judges (vv. 33, 35, 38). The word "therefore," which commonly introduces an announcement of judgment here twice introduces the divine lament (vv. 31, 36). Because of what happens to Moab, God too engages in wailing and weeping (see **Connections: The Divine Lament over Moab**).

Verse 29 is in the first person plural (LXX has first person singular) and may refer to the divine council (see 23:18-22). The pride of Moab in its status and perseverance as a nation has come to the attention of the divine world. Indeed, the fourfold repetition of the root and two synonyms for pride (loftiness, haughtiness) suggests that little else is visible about Moab, even in heavenly places (v. 29). As a result, God truly knows his insolence; he is a liar in both word (boasting) and deed (v. 30).

Five different verbs for weeping and wailing are used in vv. 31-32, 36 (see also Isa 15:5; 16:9, 11; the oracle in Isaiah has even more the character of a lament)! As great as Moab's pride is, the intensity of their fall has been comparably great; yet, equally as intense is God's lament over what has happened to this people. God wails, cries out, mourns for Moab and for individual cities, such as the capital city Kir-heres (see [Cities and Towns in Moab]). A comparison is used in v. 32; God will weep more for the city of Sibmah (whose branches extended to the sea, that is, it was famous for its vineyards and gardens) than for the city of Jazer. The greater intensity of mourning is probably because Sibmah's devastation will be even greater and will include all of its wondrous vegetation (commonly destroyed along with towns and people in that military world; for the negative effect on the land of Israel, see 12:4, 7-13).

The reason for this divine lament is stated succinctly: upon all of Moab, human and nonhuman alike, "the destroyer" has fallen (v. 32; a recurrent theme, vv. 8, 15, 18). The reader will recall God's weeping and wailing for the vegetation, animals, and birds of Israel in 9:10-11. God's lament and God's judgment are comparably linked there as they are in these verses; the claim on the part of some scholars that judgment and lament are incongruous is strange, especially in view of such earlier combinations in Jeremiah and their common juxtaposition in the human analogue, see **Connections**).[2] For God, the internal side of judgment is grief.

The lament then turns from God back to the people once again (vv. 33-39), but the divine lament will reappear in v. 36. The laments of the people and the laments of God remain linked (as with Israel, e.g., ch. 14). The gladness and joy of the Moabites have been taken away (v. 33); their riches have perished (v. 36). The shouts of joy at the treading of the grapes after the harvest have been turned into the shouts of pain and sorrow. That loss of joy is coupled once again with the ruination of the fruitfulness of the land; the vineyards have failed because of God's judgment (v. 33). And now also the water supplies have been turned into dry land (v. 34). As we have seen before in Jeremiah (e.g., 12:4) moral order affects the natural order, and often adversely so. The cries of the Moabites are heard everywhere; the list of cities (v. 34) is a short-hand way of indicating that their cries are heard across the entire land (see vv. 21-24) and in every town square and household (v. 38).

Strong words of divine judgment for Moab (vv. 35, 38b) bracket another divine lament (v. 36) and laments from the Moabites (vv. 37-38a). Their shaving, gashing, and wearing of sackcloth (v. 37) are all signs of mourning and lamentation (cf. the comparable language for Israel in 4:8; 16:6; 41:5; Philistia in 47:5). As with other OAN, the judgment and its effects seem to be past, present, and future in these verses (cf. v. 35 with v. 38b-39), yet not final (v. 47).

Only rarely has the reason for God's judgment been stated in specifically religious terms in the chapter (see vv. 7, 13). Even in

v. 35 the issue of worshiping other gods is somewhat subdued, though the devastating effects are sure: God will bring an end to those in Moab who offer such sacrifices (NRSV translates the same verb as "stopped" in v. 33). But God's word of judgment is immediately accompanied by a look at Yahweh's heart (v. 36; see 32:41). "*Therefore*" God mourns! The moaning of God's heart (one is reminded of the dove in v. 28; see Ezek 7:16) is twice referenced, as if to pick up the actual sound of a moaning flute. The godward side of wrath and judgment is grief; for God, an internal grieving always accompanies wrath and judgment (as is commonly the case in the breakdown of interhuman relationships).

Moab has become a vessel that no one wants (v. 38; as in 22:28 for King Jehoiachin). Moab has been broken like a pot (as was Israel, 19:11). This portrayal voices divine exclamations about Moab's miserable situation as it hides its face in shame (turning its back) and is ridiculed by all of its neighbors (v. 39, as in vv. 1, 13, 17, 26-27).

Moab Destroyed and Restored, 48:40-47

These verses return initially to the destroyer that Moab faces. They reiterate some of the basic themes of the chapter regarding Moab's destruction at the hands of the Babylonians. The onslaught is depicted as in progress. The enemy is imaged as an eagle, a bird of prey, which swoops down with wings spread over a helpless Moab (v. 40, as in 49:22). Town after town, fortress after fortress is seized and devoured. The proud hearts (cf. v. 29) of Moab's warriors—mirrored in the heart of God (v. 36)—suffer anguish and pain like the heart of a woman in labor (v. 41; as with Israel, 6:24; 30:6; cf. Isa 42:14). Moab is being destroyed as a people because of its vaunted pride against the Lord (v. 42, see at v. 26).

Terror, pit, and trap (a play on words in Hebrew) are images used for Moab's desperate situation (v. 43; see the virtually identical language in Isa 24:17-18; cf. Amos 5:18-19). They—and "everyone" is repeated for emphasis—flee from the terror of the marauding armies only to fall into a pit; they climb out of the pit only to be caught in a trap. In other words, their fate is inescapable (v. 44). God is bringing this judgment; the Moabites are faced with the year of their "visitation" from which there is no escape (just as was Israel, 11:23; 23:12). They will flee, but soon fall exhausted, hardly beyond the shadow of the city from which they flee (v. 45).

The northern Moabite city of Heshbon was the first to feel the heat of the army from the north, and from there it flames out and destroys all of Moab (v. 45). The references to "the house of Sihon" and the fire imagery are to be linked to the story of the Amorite king Sihon, whose capital city was Heshbon, and who refused passageway for the journeying Israelites (see Num 21:21-30, especially v. 28; see also Deut 2:24-37; Judg 11:18-22). The references to forehead (cf. Num 24:17) and scalp may be an allusion to the leaders or the king of the unruly people of Moab.

The announcements of judgment against Moab conclude with a woe oracle, as they began (see v. 1; 45:3) and a promise of salvation (vv. 46-47). The woe oracle summarizes the effects of the judgment upon the Moabites; the people of the god Chemosh (see vv. 7, 13) have been ruined because their sons and daughters have been taken captive and shipped off into exile. Their god has been of no help whatsoever.

Yet, in the very next breath God announces a promising future for the Moabites. Using language earlier used for Israel (see 29:14 and often) God will restore the fortunes of Moab (cf. the future of Egypt, Ammon, and Elam, 46:26; 49:6, 39); Isaiah 16:4-5 speaks also of a positive future for Moab. There is no evidence that such a future has ever taken place; Moab's integrity as a nation disappeared soon after Israel returned from exile. This is another, not infrequent instance of a prophecy that has not been fulfilled (see the options spelled out in 18:7-10). The final sentence of v. 37 is an editorial summary.

CONNECTIONS

The Divine Lament over Moab

The interpretation of the lament language in vv. 30-33 (36) is disputed. God seems to utter a sustained lament for the Moabites because of their precipitous fall from the heights of their pride. Though at times denied (probably for theological reasons), God is the subject of the verbs in vv. 30-33 ("says the LORD" in v. 30; only God would be the subject of "stopped" in v. 33; cf. also v. 36).

This lament has been interpreted as ironic or as a way of mocking the fall of this prideful people (see the taunts in earlier verses). Yet, it seems more likely that this is genuine divine lament over the devastation of the Moabites, as was the case with Israel (e.g., 8:18–9:1; and Philistia, 47:5-6); they have fallen so far and their devastation is so great. This divine response would be consonant with God's call to the Moabites to flee from the coming devastation (vv. 6, 20). In addition, it should be noted that elements of lament are common in other oracles against the nations (see especially Isa 13–23; cf. also Ezekiel 25–32).

The sheer range of lament language used by God is remarkable— five different verbs (vv. 31-32, 36; used also in Isa 15:5; 16:9, 11; and in a somewhat different way in Ezekiel, see 2:10, "words of lamentation and mourning and woe"; 27:2; 28:12; 32:2, 16; cf. 30:2; 32:18). This is an intense experience for God (cf. 47:5-7). This language is picked up from the lamentful response of the Moabites themselves over the actual and anticipated devastation of their cities and land (see vv. 4-5, 20, 34, 39); the laments of the Israelites are comparable (14:1-10, 19-22).

The net effect is that God enters into a lament that is as deep and broad as the laments of the people. This interpretation of God's lament places the divine wailing over Moab in parallel with the divine lament over Israel (e.g., 8:18–9:1, 10, 17-19; 13:17; 14:17). As with Israel, so with Moab, God has entered into judgment; but once the judgment has fallen (or is anticipated) God mourns with those who mourn.[3] [God's "Suffering With"]

God's "Suffering With"

In my analysis of divine suffering texts in the Old Testament, I speak of God as suffering because of the people, with the people, and for the people (see T. Fretheim, *The Suffering of God*, 107-48). These laments over Moab seem to fall into the category of "suffering with" the people—either after the destruction or in anticipation of it; the metaphor of God as mourner seems to fit them best. God enters into mourning, not only on behalf of Israel (see Jer 9:17-19), but also on behalf of nonchosen folk who have suffered in comparable ways. Israel has no monopoly on divine empathy; God enters into the suffering of all peoples, whether or not that suffering has been deserved (as certainly was the case with both Israel and Moab).

NOTES

[1] See William McKane, *A Critical and Exegetical Commentary on Jeremiah* (2 vols.; ICC; Edinburgh: T. & T. Clark, 1986), 1166-67.

[2] Contrary to McKane, 1186, 1190.

[3] See Terence Fretheim, *The Suffering of God: An Old Testament Perspective* (Philadelphia: Fortress, 1984), 132-33.

FIVE ORACLES AGAINST
THE NATIONS

49:1-39

This chapter consists of oracles against five nations/peoples: Ammon (vv. 1-6); Edom (vv. 7-22); Damascus/Syria (vv. 23-27); Kedar and Hazor—Arabian tribes (vv. 28-33); and Elam (vv. 34-39). Only the last is given a specific date relative to Israel's history (v. 34; early in Zedekiah's reign, 597–587 BC), though all of these peoples had relations with Israel over the course of their history, often negative (see below). Only the Arabian tribes are related specifically to the campaigns of Nebuchadrezzar (vv. 28, 30), but all of these announcements of judgment are likely to be linked to the movement of Babylonian armies in the years following 605 BC. As with the prior oracles against the nations, the portrayal of judgment is viewed as imminent, in progress, or already having occurred.

COMMENTARY

Oracle against Ammon, 49:1-6

This oracle against Ammon has its counterparts in Amos 1:13-15, Zephaniah 2:8-11, and Ezekiel 25:1-7. [Ammon] As with Moab, Ammon had a kinship relationship with Israel (Gen 19:38). This oracle anticipates that Ammon will be devastated by foreign armies for its territorial expansionism and national pride. In addition, readers will remember the involvement of the king of Ammon in the

---

Ammon

Ammon was a country that lay east of the Jordan river and north of Moab; its territorial boundaries were not well fixed and it was often in conflict with Israel. Its capital city was Rabbah (vv. 2-3; modern Amman, Jordan), located in the valley of the River Jabbok. In the events leading up to the fall of Jerusalem to Babylon in 597 BC, Ammon, having earlier been subjugated by Babylon, joined with Babylon's armies in quelling the revolt under King Jehoiakim (see 2 Kgs 24:2). During the reign of King Zedekiah (probably 594–593 BC), the Ammonites participated with Judah in a rebellion against Babylon (27:3). Ammon continued its rebellion subsequent to the fall of Jerusalem in 587 BC, even supporting Judah's superpatriot Ishmael against the Babylonian appointed governor Gedaliah (see 40:14-41:10). Shortly thereafter Nebuchadrezzar's armies devastated the country (about 582 BC).

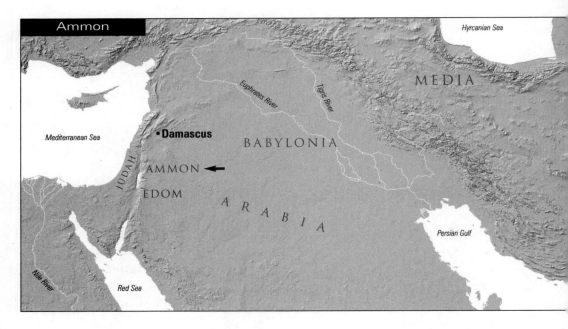

murder of the pious Gedaliah (40:14). Though the specification of time is stated as future (v. 2; "the time is surely coming"), the onslaught is depicted as already in progress (see v. 3).

The opening verse reflects a territorial dispute between the Ammonites and the Israelite tribe of Gad (cf. their conflict over territorial rights in the Transjordan in Judges 11; vv. 23-24 may be reflected in the questions of Jer 49:1). Should the Ammonites and their god Milcom (or Molech) have dispossessed Gad and settled in their towns? The assumption behind the questions in 49:1 is that, as in Jephthah's time, the Ammonites have not honored the territory earlier given to the Israelite tribe Gad (specified in Josh 13:2-28); this may reflect Ammonite expansion into the territory of Gad sometime after the collapse of the northern kingdom.

The point of the opening rhetorical questions is that Israel still has people (the heirs of Gad) living in this territory. Consequently, Gad's right of possession of this land should be honored by the Ammonites. Notably, this text reflects a concern for the future (!) of the people of Israel and their territorial integrity. Because of this Ammonite territorial violation a judgment is announced (v. 2, "therefore"). [The God of the Ammonites]

The announcement of judgment is sounded with a battle alarm against the capital city Rabbah (v. 2). The only explicit action of God initially is to sound the alarm. The capital city will become a desolate mound and the other towns in Ammon will be burned down (see Amos 1:14). Then, after that has occurred (presumably at the hands of Babylon), Israel will dispossess Ammon, just as

The God of the Ammonites

Interestingly, in both this text (Jer 49:1) and Judges 11:23-24 the Ammonite deity (Milcom) is represented as the one involved in the Ammonite actions of possession and dispossession of land. Moreover, v. 3 represents Milcom as going into exile with his attendants. Is the seeming reality given to Milcom simply a rhetorical strategy in order to lift up the superiority of Israel's God (see v. 3)? Or, is it understood that Milcom in fact is a power behind the dispossession of the heirs of Gad? At the least, there is here an honoring of an apparent Ammonite claim that their god is responsible for key events in their history, both victory and defeat.

The god Milcom (or Molech; also identical with the Moabite god Chemosh, see Judg 11:24) is linked to various ancient Near Eastern peoples, including the Canaanites and the Israelites (Baal and Molech seem to be identified, cf. Jer 19:5 with 32:35). Evidence for the name of the god can be traced back to the third millennium BC. King Solomon built a shrine to Milcom and other gods (1 Kgs 11:5-7, 33), introducing this worship into Israelite life. Child sacrifice is associated with this god (see at Jer 7:31; 19:5; 32:35); these practices are explicitly forbidden in Lev 18:21 (see 20:2-5) and Deut 18:10 (see 2 Chr 28:3; 33:6). Both Ahaz and Manasseh are said to have introduced child sacrifice (2 Kgs 16:3; 21:6); Josiah abolished the practice (2 Kgs 23:10) and the shrines associated with the gods Chemosh and Milcom were destroyed (2 Kgs 23:13).

Ammon has dispossessed Israel. Ammon's devastation is expressed in terms of the old adage "what goes around comes around" (v. 2).

God calls upon the inhabitants of several cities in Ammon to lament (Heshbon, see 48:2, is apparently under Ammonite control at some point; Ai is not the city in Israel and is otherwise unknown, but may be a generic reference meaning "ruin"). They are to take up mourning rites with their wailings, sackcloth, and gashing or slashing (the last is an uncertain translation; see 48:37; 16:6; for an alternative, see NIV), for death and exile are coming to Ammon. Even the national deity Milcom with all of his priests will go into exile (v. 3, as with Chemosh, 48:7).

God tauntingly questions Ammon's boasting in its own strength (see 48:29) for, when confronted with this enemy, it has no staying power (v. 4). Remarkably, God calls the Ammonites a faithless (rebellious) *daughter*, as with Egypt (46:11), Babylon (50:42), and especially Israel (e.g., 31:22; see [God's Virgin Daughter Egypt]). This may reflect a fundamental conviction that God's children are to be found in all nations; such familial language by God himself is not reserved for the chosen people. Ammon's boasting was apparently related to its wealth; this contributed to a false trust in itself and a complacent sense that all would go well when faced with any enemy (as with Israel and its prophets, see 23:16-17).

But that trust is misplaced, for God has entered into judgment against Ammon in and through its neighbors round about, especially Babylon presumably (v. 5); notably, these "neighbors" are God's agents in bringing terror. Like Israel (see 29:18), the Ammonites will be scattered headlong, as individuals rather than as a community, among the nations and no one will be available to gather the fugitives and bring them home. But also like Israel

(29:14), God will in time restore the fortunes of the Ammonites (v. 6). Once again (see 46:26; 48:47; 49:39) God is portrayed as having an ongoing relationship with these nations. Even as God brings judgment upon them, so also will God stay with them through the trauma and promises to deliver them in the future. Remarkably, Israel is not the only recipient of God's promises.

Oracle against Edom, 49:7-22

The Edomites were the object of prophetic announcements of judgment more than any other people (see Ps 137; Isa 34:1-17; 63:1-6; Lam 4:21-22; Ezek 25:12-14; 35:1-15; Amos 1:11-12; Obad; Mal 1:2-5). [Edom] These oracles are testimony to considerable levels of antagonism between Israel and Edom over the years, though the text in Jeremiah is surprisingly softer in its tone. This oracle is closely related to several verses in Obadiah (cf. vv. 9-10a with Obadiah 5–6; vv. 14-16 with Obadiah 1–4); which borrows from which is uncertain. Though both texts may be dependent on a third source, the difference in antagonism toward Edom suggests some independence (though the violence in both texts is sharply portrayed). At the same time, the virtual absence of lament themes is striking; this tone is different from the weeping and wailing so evident in other oracles, particularly against Moab. In addition, vv. 18-21 are virtually identical to several verses in the oracle against Babylon (50:40, 44-46), and the image of the eagle in v. 22 parallels that used in the oracle against Moab (48:40-41). The prose elements (vv. 12-13, 17-22) are commonly considered later commentary on the poetic oracles.

As in the other OAN, the images and language used are often general enough to fit a multitude of situations (and hence the linkages to other OAN or to oracles against Israel). No specific historical situations are noted, and the naming of Edomite cities alone enables the determination of the setting. Also as with other OAN, a coherent outline of the material is difficult to perceive (a division between vv. 7-11 and 12-22 is common); it is probably best to understand the text in terms of a collage of images that portray the destruction of Edom. The devastation is portrayed for readers in

Edom

Edom was a country situated to the south and east of Israel and south of Moab and the Dead Sea. Teman (vv. 7, 20) and the capital city Bozrah (vv. 13, 22) were important Edomite centers, used here as metonyms for the entire country (see Ezek 25:13). Sodom and Gomorrah (v. 18) may well have been cities within what later became Edom. The Edomites were, of course, close relatives of Israel, tracing their origins back to Esau (see vv. 8, 10, where Esau=Edom), the twin brother of Jacob (see Gen 25:19-28); their rivalry persisted through the centuries. Edom was subjugated by Babylon shortly after 605 BC and during the time of King Zedekiah joined with Israel in a rebellion against Nebuchadrezzar (27:3). But Edom joined with Babylon in the destruction of Judah and Jerusalem in 587 BC, reveled over their destruction (see Ps 137:7; Lam 4:21-22; Obad), and subsequently extended their territory west and made Hebron their capital. In New Testament times Edom is known as Idumea (Mark 3:8; King Herod was an Idumean).

The mountains of Edom. (Credit: Mitchell G. Reddish)

such a way as to invite them into the midst of the Edomite situation; as such, the destruction is viewed from various perspectives—yet to be initiated, in progress, and having been completed.

God opens the oracle against Edom with rhetorical questions, as with Ammon (v. 1). The questions focus on the wisdom for which Edom was famed (see 1 Kgs 5:11; Obad 8; possibly the book of Job). Has wisdom and understanding perished from Edom (on Teman, see [Edom])? Yes, indeed! Whatever wisdom Edom may have had, it has not been evident in the way they have comported themselves among the nations. The inhabitants of Dedan (a nearby region in north Arabia known for its commercial activity) should keep their caravans away from Edom. They should stay out of the way lest they be adversely affected by the disaster God will "visit" (NRSV, "punish") upon Esau/Edom (v. 8; for Esau, see [Edom]). Using wisdom-like questions, God contrasts this judgment with the work of grape-gatherers and thieves. The latter, having finished their activity, would always leave something behind (v. 9; see Obad 5). Not so with God!

Staying with the image of grape-gathering, God will strip the vines of Esau/Edom bare (v. 10; as with Israel, 6:9). Staying with the image of the thief, there is no hiding place for Edom that God will not be able to discover (see Amos 9:3). The Edomites, including children, relatives, and neighbors (possibly allies), are destroyed; they are no more (v. 10; cf. Israel in 31:15). [A Divine Concern for Edom?]

A Divine Concern for Edom?

Verse 11 is commonly thought to be a quotation of Edom's well-meaning neighbors. Possibly so, but the use of the first person singular, with God as subject, occurs in verses both preceding and following v. 11. Most likely, the first person in v. 11 continues to refer to God, who signals a deep concern for those who are often most deeply affected by such disasters (on God's special concern for orphans and widows, see Deut 10:18). The call to flee (v. 8; cf. 48:6, 28, 30-33, 36) may also reflect this divine concern. This text seems to imply a qualification of the finality of the judgment stated in v. 10; as such, it suggests that there is a future for Edom not unlike that specified for Ammon and Elam (vv. 6, 39).

Verse 12 utilizes the image of judgment as the drinking from a cup; this image is drawn from 25:12-29 (cf. 48:26), where God commands Jeremiah to make all the nations drink. This list of nations given in 25:19-26 includes Edom (see also Lam 4:21; Isa 34:5-6). The possibility of one or more nations avoiding the judgment was raised in 25:28-29 and is here applied to Edom (see **Connections: Judgment on the Undeserving**). God has sworn by himself (v. 13; note the divine oath-taking, as with the judgments on Israel, Egypt, and Babylon in 22:5; 46:18; 51:14) that Bozrah/Edom (see [Edom]) will become an object of ridicule, as with Moab (48:26, 39), Israel (18:16; 19:8), and all nations (25:9). Moreover, their towns will be wastelands forever (as with Israel, 7:34). Verse 17 repeats these themes, bracketing the judgments of vv. 14-16.

Verses 14-16 have many parallels with Obadiah 1–4. The identity of the "I" in v. 14 is uncertain (Obadiah 1 has "we"), but it appears to be Jeremiah's report of a word received from God. The "I" seems to be distinguished from an anonymous messenger (member of the divine council?) who brings the word of the Lord, but the envoy is probably Jeremiah's self-identification (see 1:5, 10 on Jeremiah as a prophet to the nations). The word to be brought to the nations is to prepare for battle as a united front against Edom. God is bringing judgment through them upon Edom, and the effect will be that Edom will become the least among nations and despised by the human race.

The pride of Edom, its presumptuousness of heart, grown in part out of its ability to strike terror in the hearts of other peoples (including Israel), is specified as a key factor for the judgment (v. 16; as with Moab, 48:29, and Ammon, 49:4, and most of the nations). But this is sheer self-deception. Though Edom lives among eagles in a mountainous region (see the fuller detail in Obadiah 3-4), and its pride matches its living spaces, it will be brought down to earth by the judgment of God. In fact, Edom will become like Sodom and Gomorrah (see [Edom]; a comparable word is spoken about Moab and Ammon in Zeph 2:9); it will become a wilderness region wherein no one lives or even wants to live (v. 18; so also Babylon, 50:40; cf. also the language used for Israel in Deut 29:22-23).

Two images from the animal world are used for God's judgmental action against Edom. God is compared to a lion (v. 19), language also used in the oracle against Babylon in 50:44 (cf. the image of lions against Israel, 4:7; 5:6; 50:17). As a lion emerges from its thickets to devour other animals who live in the pasturelands, so God will chase the Edomites and single out the choicest of its rams for slaughter (v. 19; see NRSV footnote). This image continues in the last half of v. 20; like the lions, God in judgment will drag the lambs (=Edomites) away to be devoured and provoke fear among the entire flock. Another image is utilized in v. 22 (also in 48:40-41); God's judgment is compared to the eagle, a bird of prey, who swoops down, spreads its wings over its prey and carries it away. As will be the case with Babylon (see 50:44-46) this judgment is announced as the plan and purpose of God for Teman/Edom (v. 20a; see 32:19 for a more general claim for Israel's God) (see **Connections: God's Plan and Nebuchadrezzar's Plan**).

In the midst of these judgmental images, claims are made regarding the incomparability of Israel's God. Israel's God is a God with whom none can be compared and one whom no one can call to account (v. 19b), themes reminiscent of Second Isaiah (40:18, 25; 45:9-11). No shepherd (that is, earthly leader), let alone any Edomite leader, can remain standing before God in judgment. Indeed, the sound of Edom's fall will resound so loudly that all the nations of the earth will tremble at what God has done (v. 21; see 8:16). In the face of the judgmental activity of Israel's God, the Edomites' reaction becomes a mournful refrain in vv. 20-22. They can only be appalled at their fate; they will cry out so loudly it can be heard all the way to the Red Sea and their pain will be like a woman in travail (see 48:41).

Oracle against Damascus, 49:23-27

Damascus was the capital city of Syria (Aram) and represents that nation. Syria was often at war with Israel (see, e.g., Isa 7:1-8:4), but this conflicted relationship essentially ceased after the destruction of the North in 722 BC. Though Damascus/Aram is not listed among the doomed nations in 25:18-26, this oracle does have parallels in eighth-century prophetic traditions (Isa 17:1-6; Amos 1:3-5). Apparently, the Aramaean armies joined Babylon in the assault on Jerusalem and Judah in 597 BC (see 35:11; 2 Kgs 24:2); that may be the reason for its inclusion here, but we are not informed of any sociohistorical realities in the oracle itself. Once again, the judgment seems to be both imminent, in progress, and completed.

Hamath and Arpad were Syrian cities/states (north of Damascus) that, along with Damascus, were subjugated by the Assyrians in the eighth century (see Isa 10:9-11). This oracle is either set in that time or they are threatened anew in this period and an older poem is used to portray it (by the Babylonians in view of the larger context). These verses describe their response to that threat, though no reason is given, religious or otherwise, for their coming under judgment. Confused and troubled like an agitated sea, Hamath and Arpad lose heart at the bad news; Damascus responds in fear and panic, in anguish and pain as a woman in labor (vv. 23-24; so also Israel, Moab, Edom, and Babylon, 6:24; 48:41; 49:22; 50:43).

Damascus is a famous city, delightful even to God! (see NRSV footnote), but it is forsaken (v. 25; Damascus has in fact been continuously inhabited since ancient times). All of its warriors will fall in its city streets (as with Israel, 9:21). The oracle concludes with a virtual quote from Amos 1:4. God will kindle a fire in Damascus (as in Israel, 11:16; 17:27; 21:14, and Babylon, 50:32) and that fire will consume the palaces/fortresses of King Ben-hadad. This name of at least two Aramaean kings from the ninth–eighth centuries BC, by which the Syrian royal house was more generally known (1 Kgs 15:18-20; 2 Kgs 13:3, 24), represents Syria more generally.

Oracle against Arabian Tribes, 49:28-33

Little is known of these Arabian tribal groups from the south and east of Canaan, perhaps collectively called here "the people of the east." Kedar is a seminomadic people known for commerce (see v. 29; 2:10-11; Ezek 27:21; cf. Gen 25:13 for links to Abraham through Ishmael); Hazor is an otherwise unknown people or desert settlement. An oracle against Kedar is also given in Isa 21:16-17 and various Arabian tribes are mentioned in Jer 25:23-24. Reason for the divine judgment is only alluded to (v. 31; being at "ease," cf. 48:11) and there is only passing reference to lament (v. 29c); no antipathy is expressed toward these peoples in this oracle or elsewhere in the Old Testament.

Alone among the oracles in this chapter, Nebuchadrezzar is explicitly mentioned as the executor of divine judgment. No specific evidence is available as to whether this was in fact the case, though he is known from Babylonian texts to have subjugated Arabian tribes. As in other OAN, the destruction is viewed as both imminent and in progress, though v. 28 may indicate that it was accomplished at the time of writing (cf. NIV). There is an admixture of divine directives given to Babylon's armies (vv. 28b-29b, 31; cf. 46:3-4; 50:14-16, 26-27) and to the inhabitants (v. 30; cf. 48:6, 28; 49:8; 51:6).

God calls upon Nebuchadrezzar and his armies to rise up against Kedar and destroy them as a people (v. 28b). This call is repeated in v. 31. More specifically, they are to plunder their tents (with their curtains, as with Israel, 4:20), goods, and animals (both sheep and camels). In response, these people will cry out regarding the terror that surrounds them (as with Egypt, 46:5), reflecting the kind of response Israel had to Jeremiah's word, both actual and derisive (see 6:25; 20:10).

At this point, God warns the Arabian peoples to flee (v. 30; see also 48:6, 28; 49:8; 50:8; 51:6; cf. the word to Israel in 4:6; 6:1). The regular, if not constant witness in these texts is that God does not desire the total destruction of any people, but provides an opportunity for escape and hence makes eventual restoration possible (e.g., 48:6 with 48:47). The people are to flee because Nebuchadrezzar "has made a plan . . . and formed a purpose" against them, and Nebuchadrezzar is the instrument of the divine plans and purpose (see at v. 20 for the same language used for both God and Nebuchadrezzar; see **Connections**).

Once again (v. 31), God's call goes out to the Babylonians to advance against these people, described here as being complacent and (they think) secure (on a false trust, see v. 4; 48:7; on Israel's complacency, see 22:21). These people live in tents or makeshift dwellings, not in cities (with gates and bars), and they are more independent, not having gathered themselves into sizable communities. Hence, their claim to be secure proves to be deeply ironic.

Verses 32-33 announce the effects of the onslaught. Their animals will become booty for the Babylonians (see v. 29); they will be scattered to every wind (as was Israel, 31:10), and suffer calamity from every side (as did Israel, 18:17; on the shaven temples of these people, see 9:26, 25:23). Hazor will become an eternal wilderness,

Elam

Elam was a country to the east of Babylon at the head of the Persian gulf (present-day Iran); its capital was Susa (see Neh 1:1; Dan 8:2; Esther). Elam may be a general designation for Persia. Elam, subjugated by Assyria, assisted in its war against Israel (Isa 11:11; 21:2; 22:6); it later came under Babylonian and Persian rule. Some evidence exists that Nebuchadrezzar subjugated Elam (see 25:25-26), and that may provide a setting for this text, linking up with Jeremiah's word that "all nations" shall come under the rule of Nebuchadrezzar (25:9; 27:6-7). The oracle also serves to show that even nations to the east of Babylon came under its rule, which was supreme across the entire territory, East and West, North and South. Kings such as Zedekiah (v. 34) could not hope for rebellion against Babylon from any quarter. Elam did eventually contribute to the defeat of Babylon in 540–539 BC. We have no knowledge of a conflict between Israel and Elam.

where no one lives but the jackals (as with Jerusalem, 9:11; 10:22; and Babylon, 51:37).

Oracle against Elam, 49:34-39

This oracle (considered prose in NRSV, poetry in NAB) is surprisingly dated at the beginning of the reign of King Zedekiah (597 BC; the oracle stands first among the OAN in the LXX). On Elam in other oracles, see Ezek 32:24-25. [Elam] This oracle differs in several respects from most of the other OAN, with no directives to the enemy or to the Elamites, no specific names or descriptions of life in Elam, no lamenting, and no actions taken by any human group or character. This reticence may reflect a lack of particular knowledge of Elam on the part of the narrator. This reality may also account for God being the only subject of all the verbs in this segment (eight of them!), though the general statement regarding divine judgment in 25:15-38 is similar.

On the latter point, it is exceedingly important not to think that God is thereby thought to act alone.[1] After all, Elam does have "their enemies" and "those who seek their life" (v. 37). Elsewhere in Jeremiah, God uses the wind as an image of judgment for Israel (4:11-12; 13:24; 18:17; 22:22; cf. v. 32; 10:13=51:16). God elsewhere is said to act in and through the Babylonians to scatter, send into exile (into every nation!), send the sword, terrify/break, bring disaster, consume, and destroy. It is no different here, perhaps for the reason suggested above. ["I Will Set My Throne"]

The divine actions against Elam are comprehensive in scope. Virtually every type of judgment announced against Israel to this point

"I Will Set My Throne"

AΩ The unusual formulation in v. 38, "I will set my throne," is to be explained by the same formulation in 43:10 regarding Egypt, only with Nebuchadrezzar as the subject (see at 43:10). Given the complex understanding of agency in Jeremiah (see **Introduction**), for God to set "my throne" in Elam is another way of speaking of the conqueror of Elam (probably Nebuchadrezzar) setting his throne in Elam. And so this kind of statement could have been made regarding any of the nations that were recipients of divine judgment.

in Jeremiah (noted above) is here gathered and used to speak of the judgment against Elam. To these are added God's breaking of the bow (for which Elam was known, Isa 22:6), an image for shattering military might (as in Hos 1:5; cf. 48:25). Moreover, God will bring the four winds, a vivid way of speaking of a judgment that is far-reaching (see v. 32; 25:32-33; Ezek 37:9; Dan 8:8; Zech 2:6; 6:5). At the same time, it is curious that the comprehensiveness of the judgment is matched by the absolute silence regarding any reason for God's "fierce anger" (v. 37; see 4:8, 26). Reasons are often, but not always (cf. vv. 23-27), given in the other OAN. Also, readers should recall that the general statement of God's judgment against the nations in 25:15-38 is comparable in its reticence regarding the reasons.

Finally (v. 39), God promises to restore the fortunes of Elam "in the latter days," in terms already used for Israel (e.g., 29:14), Moab (48:47), and Ammon (49:6; cf. Egypt in 46:26). Elam did live to see a new day beyond Babylon. Even those nations far removed from Israel, beyond the reach of the chosen people, here become the recipients of the promises of God. Jeremiah is indeed a prophet to the nations (1:5, 10) and God is truly the Creator of all (e.g., 32:27).

CONNECTIONS

Judgment on the Undeserving

Verse 12 recognizes that, in the divine judgment exacted by the Babylonian armies, some people will be undeserving of the suffering they undergo. Edom will not be spared the judgment, not least because other (unnamed) people less deserving have gone through this experience of disaster. It seems clear from Jeremiah's preaching that the people undeserving of judgment is not a reference to Israel generally, but it could refer to righteous/innocent individuals or groups within Israel (and/or within other nations). Interestingly, God is engaged here in comparing sins; Edom's sins are much more deserving of judgment than are others. If the latter are to be caught up in judgment, then certainly Edom should not escape.

The reference to Sodom and Gomorrah in v. 18 (see Gen 18:16–19:38) suggests a linkage to the issue Abraham raises regarding God's judgment undeservedly catching up the righteous/innocent within those cities. It would not be just/right for

Nebuchadrezzer

Reacting against the neo-classicism of his times, William Blake emphasized imagination and emotion in his art. He was a harbinger of romanticism with his emphasis upon visceral emotionalism. His characterization of Nebuchadrezzar's realized dream as interpreted by Daniel (Dan 4:24-25; 31-37) is ghastly in its graphic portrayal of the animal aspects of human nature. Though scholars are not sure this is the same Nebuchadrezzar as referred to in Jeremiah, the point is similar. The king's sovereignty over many territories was ultimately an expression of God's sovereignty over all mortals—anything else is hubris. In this image, it is an understatement to say that Nebuchadrezzar is getting in touch with his creatureliness.

William Blake (1757–1827). *Nebuchadnezzar.* c.1805. Tate Gallery. London. (Credit: Tate Gallery/Art Resource, NY)

God to ignore such a distinction (Gen 18:25). The issue finally for Sodom and Gomorrah is that of *communal* responsibility, namely, that sin and its adverse effects have become so pervasive that the entire community is caught up in it and the righteous/innocent in the city constitute an insufficient critical mass to turn the judgmental situation around.

Implicit in both Genesis and Jeremiah 49:12 is the recognition that, when it comes to communal judgmental disaster, God's judgment does not cut clean. When God has available such realities as natural disasters or armies as means in and through which to exact judgment on a people or nation, that activity will not entail surgical precision. In God's concern for the moral order at a communal level, the righteous will often suffer with the wicked, including children (whether in the fall of Jerusalem or Berlin). The interconnectedness of life means that evil actions will have dire consequences even for those who are not guilty.

It should also be noted that God's judgment, in being less than surgically precise, will also at times allow peoples as deserving as Edom to escape the judgment. The moral order is a loose causal weave; Jeremiah knows well that the deserving may sometimes escape (12:1). Edom does not escape in this situation, but we can be assured that in another time and place such perpetrators of evil may well get off scot-free.

God's Plan and Nebuchadrezzar's Plan

The occurrence of the name "Nebuchadrezzar" in 49:30 is unusual (it is the first occurrence of the name outside of prose introductions, e.g., 49:28) and invites theological reflection. Notably, the language regarding Nebuchadrezzar's "plan" and "purpose" is also used for God (v. 20; cf. 26:3; 36:3). This conformation of language with respect to God and Babylon/Nebuchadrezzar is common in Jeremiah (e.g., 13:14 with 21:7; see chart in **Introduction**). This use of language assumes a certain understanding of agency, namely, God's plans and purposes are embodied in those of Nebuchadrezzar, God's own servant (e.g., 25:9), but without denying the real power of either agent.

From this understanding of agency, it is clear that God is not the sole agent with respect to the downfall and devastation of Israel or any other nation; God acts in and through the agency of Babylon (or other nations). At the same time, the latter will certainly act as kings and armies in that world are wont to act. That is predictable and God knows this from experience with conquerors such as these. This portrayal of God as one whose plans also include Babylon's plans is a kind of extreme realism regarding what is about to happen to the people. And when the people do experience the pillaging, burning, and raping of the Babylonian (and other) armies, readers can be sure that they were real agents. Jeremiah also makes this witness when it describes the actual destruction of Jerusalem (chs. 39; 52) in terms that hardly mention God.

These striking parallels suggest that *the portrayal of God's violent action in Jeremiah is conformed to the means that God uses.* God is portrayed in terms of the means available. God thereby accepts any fallout that may accrue to the divine reputation ("guilt by association").

This perspective is testimony to a fundamentally *relational* understanding of the way in which God acts in the world. There is an ordered freedom in the creation, a degree of openness and unpredictability, wherein God leaves room for genuine human decisions as they exercise their God-given power. Even more, God gives them powers and responsibilities in such a way that *commits* God to a certain kind of relationship with them. This entails a divine constraint and restraint in the exercise of power in relation to these agents (Babylon overdid it!). These texts in Jeremiah are testimony to a divine sovereignty that gives power over to the created for the sake of a relationship of integrity.

NOTE

[1] Contrary to Walter Brueggemann, *A Commentary on Jeremiah: Exile and Homecoming* (Grand Rapids: Eerdmans, 1998), 460, "without any historical agent."

ORACLES AGAINST BABYLON

50:1–51:64

Introduction to the Oracles

These chapters consist of a collection of oracles in poetry, with some prose expansions, that announce judgment against Babylon and salvation for exiled Israelites. These two announcements are linked; the judgment on Babylon enables the restoration of the exiles. Hence, the superscription (50:1) focuses on God's word concerning Babylon. The narrative postscript to these oracles (51:59-64) links these words specifically to the ministry of Jeremiah in the time of King Zedekiah (593 BC). These oracles against Babylon have their parallels in other prophetic books, especially in Isaiah 13–14 and 40–55 (notably, Ezekiel has no oracles directed against Babylon). [A Universal Dimension]

Because of Jeremiah's pro-Babylonian perspective in his encounters with Zedekiah (e.g., 38:17), his assessment of Nebuchadrezzar as God's servant (25:9; 27:6; 43:10), and his links with the exiles in chapters 27–29, it is not clear when this material originated and how much of it can be ascribed to the prophet. Whether and when Jeremiah shifted his perspective cannot be determined, but it may have been after the events of 597 BC. At the same time, references to the destruction of the temple (50:28; 51:11) indicate that the fall and destruction of 587 BC had taken place; it is possible that such texts represent a later editing of earlier oracles (see **Connections: Jeremiah for and against Babylon**).

The oracles against Babylon pick up on a theme struck in 25:12-14, wherein the eventual judgment on Babylon "for their iniquity" is

A Universal Dimension

The nature of the relationship of the oracles against Babylon in chs. 50–51 to the previous OAN in chs. 46–49 is important to consider. The defeat of Babylon means freedom not only for Israel but also for these other nations; this can be seen in the restoration God usually promises them (e.g., 49:39), but not for Babylon, and the common language of God directing these nations to "flee." In one comprehensive statement (50:34; cf. 3:17; 16:19-21; 33:9), God is concerned finally to "give rest to the *earth*."

God's concern, while focused in the future of the exiles, has a more worldwide dimension than is commonly recognized. It is not enough for the prophet to say that the exiles will be delivered from Babylon, he must also go on to say that Babylon will be destroyed. For at least two reasons. One, such a defeat must occur if the future for the exiles is to have any level of peace and security. Two, there is a global moral order with which God is concerned, namely, that sin and evil will not go unchecked in the life of the world and that God's good created order will be put right.

Judgment on Babylon's Way of Waging War

As a way of intensifying God's judgment on Babylon, many verses in chs. 50–51 use language and themes that were earlier applied to Israel (e.g., 50:41-43 is a slightly changed version of 6:22-24) and to other nations (e.g., 50:44-46 applies an earlier oracle against Edom [49:19-21] to Babylon). It is almost as if the worst judgments announced against all other nations have been applied to Babylon. The net effect of this collage of repeated oracles is a judgment of great intensity for Babylon. The worst perpetrator of cruelty in that world will reap the consequences of its own behaviors in spades, not because it waged war, but because of its excessive violence in the mediation of judgment on Israel (and other nations). As such, chs. 50–51 cannot be read as an antiwar piece, but as a critique *of the way in which* Babylon waged war. War will in fact be the means by which God will mediate judgment against Babylon.

---

stated. The nature of its iniquity is specified as excessive pride, oppression of Israel, and devastation of its temple and land (50:16-18, 24, 29-33; 51:24, 34-36, 49). Idolatry is mentioned only in passing (50:38; 51:17-18, a quotation from 10:12-16), as is "sinning" against the Lord (50:14). God's judgment on Babylon is to "do to her as she has done" (50:15; see 51:6, 11, 49, 56). The foe from the North (4:6) that devastated Israel will itself be devastated by a foe from the North (50:3, 9, 41; 51:48) identified as the Medes (51:11, 27-28). [Judgment on Babylon's Way of Waging War]

Generally, many of the words and phrases used for God's judgment against Israel in and through Babylon are now applied to the judgment of Babylon by another instrument of God's judgment (Cyrus of Persia, see 51:20-23 for divine words probably addressed to him or to another such leader). Isaiah 47:1-15 spells out more fully what Babylon's iniquity has been (see also Isa 13:1–14:23; 21:1-10, oracles against Babylon from an earlier age, but made newly applicable during exilic times). Babylon overextended its mandate as God's instrument of judgment and in its self-conceit showed no mercy on those whom it conquered. And so Babylon itself must be judged. [A Failure of Prophecy?]

Remarkable is the extent to which various characters in this drama are directly addressed by God: anonymous messengers (50:2; 51:27-28); the exiles (50:8, 28; 51:6, 8, 24, 36-37, 45-46, 50-51, 54); Babylon (50:11-12a, 24, 31, 41-42; 51:13-14, 25-26); the enemy from the north (50:14-16, 21, 26-27, 29; 51:3, 11-12, 20-23). These direct addresses give a dramatic character to the chapters, as though the various participants were all caught up in a drama and in such a way that their participation truly counted. Readers are brought into the very maelstrom of these events, as though they were watching them occur.

Regarding the structure of these chapters, no scholarly consensus has emerged; indeed, the variety of proposals demonstrates the lack

A Failure of Prophecy?

Upon reading Jer 50–51 (and Isa 13:1–14:23; 21:1-10), the reader gets the distinct impression that Babylon will be devastated in ways similar to the destruction of Jerusalem. But we know from extrabiblical sources that Babylon, decidedly weakened under the reign of Nabonidus (555–539 BC), fell without a battle to the Persians under Cyrus in 539 BC. King Cyrus had earlier subjugated the Medes (549 BC), who were integrated into the Persian empire. The Medes were apparently an especially prominent people within the Persian empire (perhaps because the mother of Cyrus was a Median), and they are mentioned together in several texts (e.g., Esth 1:19; Dan 5:28; 8:20). Yet, Jer 51:11, 28; Isa 13:17 refer only to the Medes as those stirred up by God for the conquest of Babylon (the Persians are not mentioned).

Given these differences between the biblical texts and the historical record, it may be asked whether Jer 50–51 constitute a failure of prophecy. At the least, these texts do not speak with historical precision. It may be that these texts were formulated at a time prior to the rise of the Persians and it was thought that the Medians constituted the decisive threat to Babylon (see [The Enemy of Babylon]). As with prophecy generally, changing circumstances may call for adjustments in prophetic words about the future (see at Jer 18:7-10; examples include 1 Kgs 21:27-29; 2 Kgs 20:1-7).

In addition, the nature of the language needs to be considered. As will be noted throughout the commentary on these two chapters, much of the destructive language is drawn from earlier oracles against Israel. Hence, the language may be considered literary convention, probably informed by an understanding that Babylon will be repaid in kind for its arrogance and excessive violence against Israel (e.g., 51:24). The prominent use of metaphoric language is also to be noted; it opens up the text to several possible levels of interpretation that are less than precise. Readers may compare the powerful use of metaphoric language in Isa 40–55 for the return of the Jews to their homeland and those texts that speak of the actual return in more mundane terms as the effects of Persian royal policies (see Ezra 1–2). As with Isa 40–55, so also Jer 50–51 do not need to be literally descriptive in order to speak the truth about God's actions and be religiously and theologically significant. The basic oracles of judgment are right on target: Babylon fell and disappeared into the mists of history. And the rhetoric used is designed to make it clear to readers that that fall is inevitable. These oracles also reveal that the fall of Babylon was not due to some historical accident; God was using Babylon's enemies as agents for judgment against them. Beyond these basic claims, the reader is not asked to correlate the heightened rhetoric and metaphoric language with historical detail (see [Jeremiah and the Book of Revelation]).

---

of any clear outline. The following identification of units are tentative and provide a convenient way of considering the text (vv. 1-10, 11-24; 25-38, 39-46; see also at ch. 51). Note that a word with respect to the exiles centers each of the first three units (50:4-8, 17-20, v. 28 with vv. 33-34). [The Structure of Jeremiah 50–51]

The repetition in the chapters is rhythmically designed, returning again and again to the fall of Babylon and its effects, negative for Babylon and positive for the exiles. Chapter 50 is punctuated with more specific proclamations of Israel's salvation (vv. 4-8, 16-20, 28, 33-34) amid announcements of Babylon's destruction (which are also salvific for Israel in their own way). Chapter 51 is a more sustained announcement of judgment, but specific encouraging words for Israel have been inserted at key points (see [Judgment on Babylon's Way of Waging War]). As with the prior oracles, the judgment on Babylon is depicted at various stages; the judgment is imminent, in progress, or already having happened. In any case, it is considered inevitable.

The Structure of Jeremiah 50–51

📖 The structure of these chapters may be outlined as follows, with specific words regarding the exiles interwoven throughout the words of judgment. These words that lift up Israel in specific ways consist of lament, words of comfort, and instruction, with a sense of urgency throughout. While this structure is not executed with the kind of precision we might like, it is consistent enough to be revealing of the close link between Babylon's destruction and Israel's restoration.

Jeremiah 50:1-10 — Exiles: 50:4-8
Jeremiah 50:11-24 — Exiles: 50:16b-20
Jeremiah 50:25-38 — Exiles: 50:28, 33-34
Jeremiah 50:39-46 — Exiles: 50:44-46?
Jeremiah 51:1-14 — Exiles: 51:5-6, 9-10
Jeremiah 51:15-19 — Exiles: 51:19
Jeremiah 51:20-26 — Exiles: 51:24?
Jeremiah 51:27-44 — Exiles: 51:34-36
Jeremiah 51:45-49 — Exiles: 51:45-46, 49
Jeremiah 51:50-58 — Exiles: 51:50-51
Jeremiah 51:59-64

For detail, cf. A. O. Bellis, *The Structure and Composition of Jeremiah* 50:2–51:58 (Lewiston NY: Mellen Biblical Press, 1985).

There are several other features of these chapters that stand in some tension with earlier portions of the book. The sharp emphasis on Israel's infidelity is only an echo in these chapters (50:6). The sins of Judah are recognized (50:20, 51:5; indirectly in 50:7), but the depth and breadth of their sinfulness is skimmed over. Even the infidelity of Israel's leaders is passed by with minimal comment (50:6). This material seems to be drawn from a different tradition, but the present form of the text must be taken into account. The basic point would be that the past is truly past for God, that 31:34 has taken over and God will "remember their sin no more" (see 29:10-14). Also minimized is the theme of judgment, especially the role that God played in the fall and destruction of Judah and Jerusalem; only 51:7 could be cited and there it is a general reference to "nations." At the same time, this perspective is also characteristic of the reports of the fall of Jerusalem in chapters 39 and 52; the Babylonian armies are the only agents at work. Again, the point would be that the past is truly past for God; the oracles against Babylon begin to move the people of God into a genuinely new future.

Readers might think that some effort would be made to express gratitude to Babylon for the fact that it served as an agent of divine judgment. Texts such as 29:5-7 could be read from such a perspective, but no texts in chapters 50–51 express such sentiments. There is only joy that Babylon has been defeated (e.g., 51:10).

COMMENTARY

Babylon Is Doomed and Israel Can Go Home, 50:1-10

After the superscription (v. 1), this section is bracketed by the announcement of Babylon's doom at the hands of an enemy from the north (vv. 2-3 , 9-10). Between those announcements is a proclamation of the release of the exiles, the lost sheep of the house of Israel (vv. 4-7), with an urgent call for them to leave Babylon and return home (v. 8).

Marduk

By the time of Nebuchadrezzar's rule, Marduk had become the supreme god of the Mesopotamian pantheon. In Babylonian myth, Marduk was credited with killing Tiamat, a monster who threatened the other gods. From this encounter, Marduk created order out of chaos which included the creation of humankind. It was such symbolic and political power that stood in the face of the oracles that proclaimed the doom of Babylon.

This glazed brick, relief image of the dragon of Marduk is impressive in its combination of profiled formality and linear fluidity. For the most part, the Babylonian figure style was not as heavy and muscular as the Assyrian style, yet the placement of these reliefs served a similar purpose of glorifying the deities and king. The dragon was one of two animal images that decorated the Ishtar Gate which stood at the end of a walled processional way and opened to the temples beyond. The other image was of the bull of Adad and both were alternately interspersed on the glazed brick gate, referring to the gods that were worshiped in the temples.

Dragon of Marduk. Glazed brick relief from the gates of Ishtar at Babylon. c.604–562 BC. Staatliche Museen. Berlin. (Credit: Werner Forman/Art Resource, NY)

The oracles begin with a proclamation that Babylon is doomed; though it has not yet fallen, its end is so sure it can be announced as reality (vv. 2-3). The word about this great empire's fall is to be broadcast across the world; banners are to be prepared to announce this event to every nation. In this context, these "nations" would include all those mentioned in chapters 46–49 and could link up with the promises to restore their fortunes (46:26; 48:47; 49:6, 39). Let no one hold back the news: Babylon has fallen to its enemies (the Medes and the Persians are presumably in mind, see 51:11). Its vaunted god Marduk (Bel is one of Marduk's names, see

51:44; Merodach is Israel's name for Marduk) and all of Babylon's idols have been put to shame. In a remarkably ungodlike way they are all panic-stricken, simply reflecting the panic of their makers. The reason is immediately made clear: a nation has come from the north against Babylon (vv. 9, 41; 51:48; as with the judgment on Israel, 4:6). The effect will be the same as it was for Israel and the other nations (e.g., 33:10; 48:9): the land will become desolate and emptied of its inhabitants as both people and domestic (see v. 39) animals flee (see 51:29, 37).

The most important effect of Babylon's defeat and destruction "in those days and in that time" is what happens to the exiles. The people of Judah and Jerusalem will come out of Babylon, weeping (with joy, see at 31:9, and perhaps penitence) as they seek their God in Zion (see 3:18; 29:13; Ps 126:6). Asking for the way back home, they turn their faces toward Jerusalem. And they will come to Zion and there unite themselves with the Lord in an everlasting covenant (32:40; similarly, 31:31-34), which neither God nor people will ever forget. Notably, the exiles' return to Zion is at the same time a return to their God. It is not that God is geographically located there, but that the return to the land is a symbolization of the divinely reestablished (32:40) covenantal relationship between God and people, a covenant that cannot be broken.

Babylon Not Guilty?

Israel's enemies are quoted in 52:7; probably Babylon is most in mind. These nations felt no guilt in doing what they did to Israel, for they realized that these sheep had sinned against the Lord, their true pasture, and had forsaken the Lord, their ancestral hope (v. 7). It is remarkable that Babylon is represented as having such theological insight into its work as mediator of divine judgment: Israel had sinned against the Lord, the only true resource and firm hope that they had. There is certainly a sense in which these nations are not guilty for what they have done to Israel, for they were the instruments of Israel's God. Yet, other texts will claim that the point made here does not tell the full story, for Babylon exceeded its divine mandate (see 25:12-14; 50:29, 33; 51:24).

God identifies the exiles as "my people" and as "lost sheep" (v. 6). They have been led astray by their shepherds and have lost their way, straggling on the mountains (see 23:1-2, 13; see Isa 53:6; 1 Pet 2:25). They have wandered from hill to mountain worshiping at the shrines of other gods (see 2:20), forgetting the sheepfold to which they truly belonged. As a result of their infidelity, their enemies devoured them (see 5:17), and claim no guilt for doing so (v. 7). [Babylon Not Guilty?]

Given what is about to happen to Babylon, the exiles are told to flee the city and leave the land so as not to be engulfed in that judgment (so also 51:6, 45; Isa 48:20; note the common command to flee in the OAN, e.g., 48:6, 28). The rams (=leaders) of the flock are to lead the way (in contrast to the leaders of v. 6). The narrative returns to the opening verses, giving the reason for Israel's urgent departure from the city (vv. 9-10): God is bringing judgment on Babylon by the instrumentation of the enemy from the north.

These enemies are skilled warriors who will not fail in their objective (="will not return empty-handed"). They will array themselves against Babylon and plunder the city until their appetite for plunder has been satisfied.

The Destruction of Babylon and Restoration of Israel, 50:11-24

This unit is bracketed by God's addresses to Babylon (vv. 11-12a, 24), which are accompanied by descriptions of the dire effects on the city (vv. 12b-13, 22-23). God's address to Babylon's attackers provide an internal bracket (vv. 14-16, 21). The heart of the unit is the announcement of effect of Babylon's destruction on Israel: the restoration of the exiles (vv. 17-20).

God addresses the Babylonian armies as those who have plundered the people/land of Israel (=my heritage, see 12:7). This is their status with God: plunderers! Though they rejoice now, though they frisk like calves and neigh like stallions in prideful exuberance at their successes, their "mother" (a figure of speech for Babylon; see Hos 2:4-5) will soon fall in shame and be utterly disgraced (as was Israel, 15:9, and other nations, 48:39). Its fall will be the "mother" of all disgraces.

Then, turning from direct address to Babylon, God describes its fate for anyone who would listen, especially the exiles (vv. 12b-13). Instead of being the first of the nations, it will be the last; instead of a fruitful land, it will be a desert; instead of a populous city, it will be uninhabited (see 25:12; Isa 13:20-22). As with Israel (e.g.,

18:16; 29:18), other peoples will be appalled at the destruction. Babylon will become an object of horror; people will catch their breath at such horrendous devastation (see v. 23; 51:41-43). This destruction will occur "because of the wrath of the LORD"; these events are not some arbitrary divine move, however. The following verses will be punctuated with the reasons behind the divine wrath (vv. 14-17, 24, 29, 33).

In vv. 14-16 God addresses Babylon's enemy from the North (probably to be identified with Persia under King Cyrus) and does so often in these two chapters (see above). It is almost as though God himself assumes control of the Persian armies and barks out orders to them. The rhythmic orders in vv. 14-16 are accompanied by reasons for so acting (vv. 14b, 15b, 16b; more closely specified in vv. 17, 24, 29, 33), making it clear that the orders are not grounded in a divine caprice.

• The warriors are to take up their positions around Babylon and spare no arrows in their siege of the city (see 51:11). The reason: Babylon has sinned against the Lord.

• The warriors are to raise a victory shout against the city: Babylon has surrendered and its fortifications have been breached (see 51:44, 58; see above on the limited destruction)! The reason: Babylon reaps what it has sown ("do to her as she has done"; see Ps 137:8; see **Introduction**). [Retribution on Babylon?]

• The warriors are to cut the city off from those who sow and harvest the crops (the siege of a city often involved the strategy of

---

Retribution on Babylon?

The "vengeance of the LORD" (v. 15) is defined precisely in "what goes around comes around" terms, as was the case with Israel (5:9, 29; 11:20; 15:15). Babylon reaps the consequences of its own sins, though this understanding is not "naturally" conceived; it is made sharply clear these links between sin and consequence are not fully considered until Israel's God has been factored into the mix. At the same time, that divine involvement is not all-determinative (witness the Babylonian excess, Zech 1:15). This theme becomes almost a refrain in these two chapters (50:29; 51:6, 11, 24, 49). Because these texts have to do with the moral order, however, the language of retribution is not strictly appropriate for describing them. God's involvement does not include placing a penalty on Babylon, that is, introducing something new into the situation; God's engagement is basically understood in terms of "seeing to" the moral order.

It might also be noted in this connection that Babylon's conquerors will not necessarily make the same mistake of excess. At the same time, they may do so, and will in turn reap what they sow. In the history of conflicts among nations, it has been common for them to retaliate excessively (a more contemporary example might be the saturation bombing of certain German cities, e.g., Dresden, by the Allies during World War II).

starvation). The reason: Babylon's destroying sword and oppression of its captives. But v. 16 does not rest with the reason, it moves quickly to attend to the exiles (and other captives) in the city, which in turn sets up vv. 17-20 (v. 17 hooks back to pick up the reasons for Babylon's judgment). They shall flee the oppression of the city and return to their own people (see 46:16; Isa 13:14).

Verses 17-20, the center of this textual unit, link God's destruction of Babylon with its salvific effect for Israel, namely, their restoration to the land. Verse 17 returns to the image of Israel as a lost and hunted sheep (vv. 6-7), driven away from its land by the Babylonian armies (=lions, see 4:7; Isa 5:29). Both Assyria (in the eighth century) and now ("at the end") Babylonia have oppressed Israel, gnawing at their bones like lions (see 5:17). This brief reprise of Israel's centuries of suffering at the hands of oppressive foreign armies issues in a divine "therefore" (v. 18). Whereas the word "therefore" commonly introduces an announcement of judgment (e.g., 5:7, 14), here it introduces an announcement of salvation (cf. 30:16). The God of Israel is going to bring disaster on Babylon (as had been done to Assyria, decisively defeated by the Babylonians at Nineveh in 612 BC; see Isa 10:12) and that judgment has salvific effects for Israel.

Staying with the sheep/shepherd image, God speaks of restoring Israel to its own pasture (v. 19); they will feed on the lush grasses of various pasturelands in Israel and they will never be hungry again (see 23:3; 30-31; Ezek 34:13-14). [The Pasturelands of 50:19] In those days and at that time (see v. 4), when Israel has been restored to its land, God will forgive the sins of the remnant of returned exiles (see 31:34; Isa 43:25; Mic 7:19). Indeed, God's forgiveness of this people will be so thoroughgoing that,

The Pasturelands of 50:19

These four regions of the country are named because of their fertile lands (see Mic 7:14), from Carmel on the Mediterranean coast, to the hills of Ephraim (the former northern kingdom, see 4:15) to Bashan (see 22:20) and Gilead (see 8:22) in the northern regions of the Transjordan.

should anyone look for guilt/sin in them, none will be found. Verse 20 should be related to earlier texts that work with this theme (24:7; 30:15-17; 31:34; 32:40). The point is not that the restored Israelites will no longer be sinners! It is that their guilt and their sin has been forgiven and no longer stands between them and their God. The double reference to "sin" is probably intended to cover guilt for any past sins as well as present sinfulness (hence "guilt" [NAB] is a better translation than "iniquity" [NRSV]). Notably, both Israel and Judah are mentioned, corresponding to Assyria and Babylon as their respective conquerors.

Verse 21 picks up God's address to Babylon's enemies once again (see vv. 14-16, where the imperative is plural), as God the commander-in-chief (v. 21c) of their armies tells them, in effect, to finish the job they have begun. They are to attack and utterly destroy "Merathaim" and "Pekod"; metonymic for Babylon, these names refer to little known regions or tribal groups in or near Babylon (see Ezek 23:23). They are probably used because the words can carry ironic freight: they mean "double rebellion" and "visitation" in Hebrew. Verses 22-23 describe the response of these armies to God's command. The noise of the tramping warriors moves toward Babylon, leaving destruction in their wake (v. 22). Verse 23 is a mocking lament for the fate to which Babylon has fallen. Babylon was the hammer of the entire earth (Persia is similarly named in 51:20), but now that hammer itself has been shattered into many pieces. Babylon has become an object of horror among the nations (see v. 13; 51:41-43). How far Babylon has fallen!

This unit concludes with an ironic address to Babylon (v. 24). Babylon had set out traps for others, but was itself entrapped in them and captured (the NIV translation, "I set a trap for you," is less accurate in this context). And Babylon did not even realize what it had done before it was discovered and seized. A reason for the judgment is given again: Babylon had arrogantly set itself up over against the Lord, apparently a reference to Babylon's violation of God's charge regarding the nature of the judgment to be exacted (see v. 29; cf. 48:26, 42). Babylon insisted on its own way in these matters.

Babylon's Enemy and Israel's Redeemer, 50:25-38

This unit is bracketed by a focus on Babylon's enemies, raised up by God and commanded to destroy everything in their path (vv. 25-27, 29, 35-38). The positive effects of their destruction on the exiles is described in an internal bracket (vv. 28, 33-34). The judgment on Babylon is portrayed in vv. 30-32, including a divine address to Babylon (v. 31); this depiction of disaster is introduced by a renewed call from God to Babylon's enemies (v. 29).

Verse 25 consists of a vivid portrayal of the preparations for battle on the part of God the commander-in-chief: God opens his armory and brings out all "the weapons of his wrath" (see Isa 13:5) to supply the warriors for their attack against the Chaldeans (see 51:11). God "has a task to do," that is, judgment of Babylon, and chooses the most available means to do it: fully supplied warriors of

Babylon's enemy from the north. Having opened the armory, God commands the properly outfitted warriors to attack from every side, open Babylon's granaries, destroy its remaining food supplies (having cut them off from the source of the food, v. 16), and slaughter its animals (vv. 26-27). The destruction of food supplies is linked with images of the destruction of the people; they are to be piled into heaps like grain and destroyed; they are to be slaughtered like the bulls. Babylon's time has come; this is "the time of their visitation" (see 51:18; as with other nations, 46:21; 48:44). As it was for Israel (8:12; 10:15) so it will be for Babylon.

Verse 28 is an interlude between divine directives (vv. 26-27, 29); it could be a word to readers about the positive future these actions provide for the exiles. In effect, pay attention to what is happening! Babylon's captives are being freed to leave exile (see vv. 8, 16; 51:6, 45) and they are on their way to Zion to declare what God has done to Babylon (see 51:10). Babylon will reap what it sowed. What Babylon did to Israel is now being done to Babylon (on "vengeance," see v. 15; see 51:56; [Babylon not Guilty?]). But while there will be no escape for Babylon (v. 29), the exiles will be enabled to escape.

Verse 29 returns to the divine directives to Babylon's enemies of vv. 26-27, and essentially reiterates the directive of v. 14: archers are to be summoned and they are to surround the city so that no one escapes. Verse 29b echoes the point regarding divine vengeance in v. 28b, and restates the meaning of vengeance in the terms of v. 15: these warriors are to do to Babylon what Babylon has done to others. The basic reason for judgment on Babylon is also restated (see v. 24): arrogant defiance of the Holy One of Israel, a theme repeated in vv. 31-32 (see 48:16; 49:16).

Then the announcement of judgment follows (vv. 30-32). Verse 30 repeats 49:26, only this time Babylon will experience the decimation of its youth, both more generally and in the destruction of its armies. God once again addresses Babylon in terms of her most basic identity: "the arrogant one"; in other words, Babylon is arrogance personified. The issue for God is "the unbridled expression of Babylon's overweening imperialist ambitions,"[1] concerned only to establish its own place in that world and willing to do anything to accomplish that end. God repeats (from v. 27b) the announcement regarding this being the day of the Lord for Babylon, the time for the divine visitation against it. The result is inevitable: The strong and steady Babylon will, ironically, stumble and fall (as with Egypt in 46:6, 12, 16), and Babylon will have no helper available to lift it up so as to walk again. God will kindle a fire against Babylon and it will consume everything; as it was with Israel (21:14) and other nations (49:27), so it will be for Babylon.

Verses 33-34 are a description of Israel's captive situation and an announcement that God will be their redeemer. Babylon has refused to let its captives go free (at the end of the seventy years?). Once again, as long ago in Egypt when the pharaoh refused to let the people go, God is the redeemer of the oppressed (see **Connections: God as Redeemer of the Oppressed in Every Age**). In a play on Hebrew words, Israel's captors hold Israel fast (with strength), but Israel's Redeemer God is strong and will deliver them (see 31:11 for a comparable formulation; rare in Jeremiah, common in Isaiah 40–55, e.g., Isa 51:10-11); Israel's God is the Lord of hosts (=armies). Yahweh will surely take up their cause (as would a redeemer [*gōʾēl*]in a legal situation). God will give them rest again in the land (as God did long ago when they wandered in the wilderness, see 31:2). Indeed, God will give rest to all the nations of the earth so devastated by the Babylonian armies (see 25:26-33; 16:19; 33:9), perhaps even to the earth itself (see 4:23, 28). But such rest will come to all only when Babylon has been thrown into a state of unrest and all those held fast in its oppressive fist are freed (see [A Universal Dimension]).

Verses 35-38 return to God's address of Babylon's enemies (see 51:20-23), here personified as a sword, a sword of the Lord (cf. 46:10; 47:6), from God's armory (v. 25). These enemies are directed to take up the sword against Babylon, including everyone and everything in the city. The rhythmic recurrence of the word "sword" cuts a deep swath across Babylon and mows down everything important for waging war (see 4:23-26 for another rhythmic text). [A Sword Litany, (50:35-38)]

The Devastation of Babylon according to Divine Purpose, 50:39-46

This unit is a collage of virtual quotations from preceding verses (and Isa 13) that were applied to Edom (49:18-21) and Israel (6:22-24) especially. See the parallel passages for fuller comment. In linking verses from different contexts, this unit intensifies the judgment experience for Babylon. The unit moves from a portrayal of a devastated Babylon (vv. 39-40) to another look at the coming of the enemy from the north (vv. 41-42) to a description of the king of Babylon upon hearing this news (v. 43). Verses 44-45 cast this entire judgment on Babylon in terms of the divine "I" (as in vv. 9, 18, 31-32) and a specific divine purpose. Verse 46 concludes the

A Sword Litany (50:35-38)

The rhythm of the sword against Babylon begins with references to the people and their leaders—officials and wise men (v. 35); it ends (v. 38b) with a stated reason for the judgment: "for" it is a land filled with images (see v. 2; as was Israel, 8:19) and its inhabitants "go mad" over them. For the lines in between, the sword is to do its work for a specific purpose; each swath renders the war-making capabilities of Babylon incompetent, fearful, and without resources.

- The sword is to strike their diviners so that they can be shown to be fools for the kinds of predictions they have been making (for the idea, see 27:9; 29:8; Isa 44:25).

- The sword is to strike their warriors, so that they may tremble with fear (NAB).

- The sword is to strike horses and chariots and mercenaries so that they become women, that is, melt away before the enemy (see 51:30; 30:6).

- The sword is to "strike" their treasures, so that their resources for carrying on war may be plundered. This use of "sword" is metaphoric.

- The sword is to "strike" their water supplies, so that this indispensable resource for armies is dried up. In this case (v. 38a), "sword" may switch to "drought," though the more difficult reading would be "sword," given the reference to water (NRSV footnote notes that "another reading" [Syriac] is "sword"). As in the last instance, this use of "sword" would be metaphoric.

---

chapter by noting that all the nations will hear and tremble over what has happened to Babylon.

Verses 39-40 are drawn from other contexts (see 49:18, 33; Isa 13:19-22). The basic theme of Babylon becoming a wasteland without inhabitant and the home of wild animals (contrast domestic animals in v. 3; see also 51:29, 37, 43) has been used to portray Edom (49:18), Hazor (49:33), and in many different contexts, Israel (e.g., 9:11). The comparison with Sodom and Gomorrah has been drawn for Edom (49:18) and Israel (23:14). Verses 41-43 are almost identical to 6:22-24, only there applied to Israel. The addressee "against you, O daughter Zion" (6:23) here becomes "against you, O daughter Babylon" (v. 42; see [God's Virgin Daughter Egypt]). Whereas in 6:24 it was the people of Israel who heard the news about a foe from the north and their hands fell helpless so that pain and anguish took hold of them as a woman in labor, here the king of Babylon has that experience (v. 43). Verses 44-46 are virtually identical to a segment from the oracle against Edom (49:19-21), only the news about Babylon will travel farther than the Red Sea; *all* the nations shall hear and tremble. The judgment against Babylon is in accord with the plans and purposes of God (also in 51:12; cf. 49:20, 30).

Judgment against Babylon, 51:1-14

No scholarly consensus exists regarding the structure of this chapter (see introduction to chs. 50–51; [Judgment on Babylon's Way of Waging War]). Tentatively, the following units may be discerned (vv. 1-14, 15-19, 20-26, 27-44, 45-49, 50-58, 59-64). Each of the units has some reference to the exiles and their situation, so that the judgment announced on Babylon is at the same time understood to be deliverance for the exiles. Though the units do not move in a strictly logical or coherent way through the chapter, the renewed rhythms of attack on Babylon, destruction of Babylon, and deliverance of the exiles provide a kind of liturgy that would appeal again and again to the deepest yearnings for freedom and homecoming. The last two sections (vv. 45-49, 50-58), which are similarly structured, call for the exiles to return home in view of the certain fall of Babylon. [The Enemy of Babylon]

This unit (vv. 1-14) begins and ends with an announcement of judgment on Babylon (vv. 1-2, 13-14); the latter is directly addressed to them. A general statement about the depths to which Babylon has fallen punctuates the middle of the unit (vv. 7-8a). Surrounding this general statement about Babylon are specific directives to the exiles (vv. 6, 8b), which in turn are bracketed by theological claims regarding Israel—by God (v. 5) and then, in response to God's directive in v. 8b, by the exiles (vv. 9-10). Directives to Babylon's enemy, here for the first time identified as the Medes (v. 11), provide an internal bracket (vv. 3-4, 11-12; v. 4 describes the effect of v. 3) with theological interpretations inserted at vv. 11b, 12b. The central effect of the destruction of Babylon is God's salvific activity on behalf of the exiles. We have seen this way of centering textual units on God's salvific activity in chapter 50 as well.

The opening verses of this unit draw on two images to describe the judgment on Babylon (they are used together in 4:11 for judgment against Israel; see Isa 41:16). In the first, Babylon's enemy is likened to a destructive wind that, it is implied, will make the city look like a tornado has passed through (v. 1; as with Israel, 13:24; 18:17). [Lēb-qāmai (51:1)] The second is an image drawn from agricultural life, wherein Babylon is

The Enemy of Babylon

AΩ The identification of the enemy of Babylon is something of a mystery throughout ch. 50; in 51:11, 28, however, that identification is made in terms of the Medes, but only in passing (see [The Translation of 51:3a]). Is the author being deliberately vague about the identity for some reason, such as leaving the future open to various possibilities regarding the destroyer of Babylon? This vagueness is also characteristic of Israel's "foe from the North"; this nation is also left unidentified throughout chs. 1–19; the first explicit reference to Babylon comes in 20:4.

Lēb-qāmai (51:1)

AΩ In Hebrew the words *lēb-qāmai* mean "the heart of those who rise up against me," picking up themes of arrogance and rebellion from 50:24, 29-32. The NRSV transliterates the Hebrew and capitalizes it because, as noted in its footnote, this word is a cryptogram for *Kaśdîm*, Chaldea (Babylonia). The cryptogram (or *athbash*), also used in 25:26 (Sheshack for Babylon), hides the true meaning by substituting Hebrew letters in reverse alphabetical order.

likened to a field of standing grain and its enemies are winnowers that will come at the field from every side, cut down the grain, and clear the field (v. 2; as with Israel, 15:7). God is here imaged as the one who stirs up the enemy and then sends it to war against Babylon. The enemy then becomes the subject of the verbs; it comes against the land and clears it. This will be a day of "trouble" or disaster (*rā'āh*) for Babylon, a phrase that stands in the day of the Lord tradition (see Amos 5:18-20). God's directive to Babylon's enemy (v. 3) is, in effect: do not hold back; put on the heavy armor, and utterly destroy its young warriors, indeed, the entire army (see 50:21, 26). [The Translation of 51:3a] Verse 4 indicates the effect on Babylon if that directive is followed (see 50:30).

In vv. 5-10 the exiles are the center of attention, with words to them and from them. Their current situation is explained with specific reference to Babylon. The punctuating note about Babylon's rise and fall (vv. 7-8a) simultaneously explains both Israel's captivity and its new freedom. Babylon was chosen by God to be the instrument of divine judgment; the image of a drinking cup for the pouring out of the divine wrath upon the nations with their resultant drunkenness is that used in 25:15-29 (see Rev 18:3). But now, suddenly, Babylon has fallen! Verses 7-8a are best understood as reassuring words to the exiles, continuing the basic theme of vv. 5-6.

In v. 5 God addresses Israel's situation; they are exiles in the midst of a guilty land (=Babylon, cf. v. 6; 50:7; or is it the land of Israel? Most scholars think it is Babylon) about to experience the judgment of a holy God (God is called holy only twice in Jeremiah, 50:29). The implied question that God addresses, perhaps uttered by the exiles themselves (see first person plural in vv. 9-10), is whether God has forsaken (literally, widowed) them in Babylon and hence they would experience this announced judgment as much as the Babylonians. God reassures the exiles: God has not forsaken Israel and Judah (notice again, both North and South). But they must flee the city in order to escape the coming disaster (v. 6; see vv. 45-46; 50:8, 28; see also 48:6; 49:30, where God is comparably concerned about the welfare of non-Israelites). God urges each individual to leave the city in order to save his/her life, so as not to perish in the judgment now to be visited on a guilty Babylon. God speaks of this time as a time of vengeance (see 50:15, 29; see [Judgment on Babylon's Way of Waging War]) on Babylon for the sins

The Translation of 51:3a

AΩ Verse 3a is textually problematic; in seeking to make sense of it, some translations (e.g., NRSV) insert a "not" before the two verbs ("bend"; "array himself"); some do not (e.g., NAB). With a "not" in the text, the reference is to Babylon (and hence would best be considered a mocking directive); without the "not," the phrases are directives to Babylon's enemy, which then continue in v. 3b. We take the latter position because in no other place in the OAN are those who are objects of judgment asked to lay down their weapons (mockingly or not).

Babylon's Judgment Has Reached Heaven

The exiles recognize that Babylon's judgment has touched heaven (that is, God) and risen to the clouds so that there is no turning back on its disastrous future (v. 9b). This metaphor could be understood concretely in terms of a high pile (so, apparently, Rev 18:5), but other texts regarding matters that come up to God and get the divine attention (e.g., Gen 18:21) may be closer to hand. When the image of judgment (=the effects of Babylon's sins) is drawn in terms of reaching up to heaven, that means that *judgment is at work in Babylon before God picks up on it*. The idea may be similar to that of Ezek 7:27, wherein God judges Israel according to its own judgments. That is, God does not introduce anything new into the situation, but facilitates what is already at work in the effects of the sin. Another way of putting the matter: Babylon's sins have built up consequences to such a point that there can be no other way into the future for Babylon, even for God (as in 27:7; Gen 15:16).

---

it has committed (see 50:14, 24, 29-32). At one time Babylon was God's chosen "servant" for judgment (see 25:9; 27:6; 43:10; **Introduction**), and Israel was the recipient of that judgment, but that time has passed for both Babylon and Israel (vv. 7-8a).

In a remarkable directive to the exiles (v. 8b) God calls upon them to wail for Babylon, to bring balm for its wounds; perhaps it may be healed (for comparable language for a doomed Israel, see 8:22; for Egypt, 46:11). In view of the larger context (see v. 13), this could be interpreted as a mocking taunt, yet Israel's response (v. 9a) suggests a different interpretive direction. They made efforts to bring healing to Babylon, but were not successful. That this was a genuine effort on the part of the exiles is suggested by 29:7; the means they used were prayer and seeking the welfare of the city of Babylon in various, unspecified ways. The wailing is thus probably a genuine lament for the city or a dirge in anticipation of its demise (see 25:34; 47:2; 48:20, 31, 39; 49:3). Having responded to God's directive, the people take up God's call of v. 6 and urge one another to leave Babylon and return to their own land (v. 9a); this is certainly a reference to Israel, but other countries seem to be in mind as well (see 50:16, 28, 34; Isa 13:14). [Babylon's Judgment Has Reached Heaven]

The people then make a clear confession of faith (v. 10); in the judgment on Babylon the Lord has been at work and accomplished "our" salvation or deliverance from exile (*ṣĕdeqāh*; see Isa 46:12-13; 51:5, 8; cf. God as Redeemer in 50:34). They encourage one another to take the steps necessary to declare this work of "the LORD our God" to the people back home in Jerusalem. In effect, this is another encouragement to leave the country, but with the very specific goal of witnessing to other Israelites regarding the work of the Lord in so bringing judgment on Babylon that they are freed from captivity (as in 50:28).

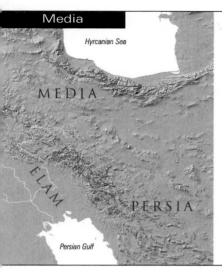

Media

Media was a country north and east of Babylon (in the northwest area of modern Iran), with its capital at Ecbatana (Ezra 6:2; modern Hamadan), located between Tehran and Baghdad. It was a nation that rose to prominence in the 7th century BC, and its cities received exiles from the northern kingdom (2 Kgs 17:6; 18:11). The Medes also participated with Babylon in the defeat of Assyrian Empire. It came under Persian jurisdiction in 549 BC and participated with Persia under Cyrus in the defeat, but not the destruction, of the Babylonian Empire (Jer 51:11, 28; see also 25:25; [A Failure of Prophecy?]). The resultant Persian empire was popularly known as "the Medes and the Persians"; this phrase has been used through the centuries because of the legendary reputation that its laws were considered unalterable (see Esth 1:19; Dan 5:28; 8:20).

In v. 11, God once again directs Babylon's enemies (see v. 3), here identified for the first time as the Medes (see Isa 13:17), to prepare their weapons for battle (comparably, 50:21 follows 50:20). [Media] This directive is given a theological interpretation in the prose segment (v. 11bc): God has stirred up or inspired the Medes to move against Babylon because it is the purpose of the Lord (see v. 12b; 50:45; 49:20; 51:29) to destroy it. This is expressed as divine vengeance for the destruction of the temple by the Babylonians (on vengeance, see at 50:15, 28-29; 51:6, 24, 36). Once again, what goes around comes around; God sees to the moral order in that people reap what they sow.

The divine directive to the Medes continues in v. 12 (see also 50:14-15, 21, 29); they are to prepare for battle with great care, including both watching and waiting in ambush (on "standard," see 4:6), lest the job be bungled. The distinction between God's plan and God's execution of the plan (v. 12b) implies that the human response could affect God's movement from plan to execution. God announces that God has not only spoken (revealing the plan) regarding Babylon, but has followed through on the plan; judgment for Babylon is now a sure thing (see **Connections: God's Planning, the Plan's Execution, and Issues of Divine Temporality**).

In vv. 13-14 God addresses the Babylonians (personified as a woman). They are rich and strong ("mighty waters" is a reference to the Euphrates and Tigris rivers, Isa 8:7, symbolic of their strength), but, ironically, the end of their story has been announced. Their life, seen in terms of the metaphor of a measure of thread, has been cut off (see Isa 38:12). The reason: God has sworn by himself (see

22:5; 49:13), and hence is committed to act by that which has been sworn. That commitment is as sure as God's own life is. Babylon's enemies will fill the city with so many troops it will be like a locust infestation and they will raise a victory shout over the city.

God the Creator Once Again, 51:15-19

These verses describing God as the wise and incomparable Creator are identical to 10:12-16 (see 5:22); the absence of reference to Babylon enables this segment to become applicable in various settings. In 10:12-16 these verses function to make a sharp contrast between Israel's God and the worthless idols of the nations, not least those of Israel. In this context the issue of idolatry is secondary; the idols of Babylon are barely in view (see 50:2, 38; 51:44), and are never explicitly caricatured or condemned. The text's function here may be to make four points.

One, the verses lift up the incomparability of Yahweh, but this portrayal of Israel's God is set over against the mighty empire of Babylon itself rather than its idols (see vv. 7, 13). Babylon itself may be said to have become an idol, at least in its own eyes. God is the Creator of the universe and, indeed, of Babylon.

Second, and related to the first point, God as the Creator of Babylon has the status to stand over Babylon as its judge. Babylon does not have the standing to be its own final evaluator. Because God is Creator of all, and not a local deity, all nations are subject to the rule of Israel's God, including the greatest empire of that world.

Third, the text in this context makes claims for the place of Israel in this Creator's designs for the world. God's very name is "the Portion of Jacob" (see at 10:16) and Israel has been chosen to be God's very own people. The particularity of God's choice of Israel, and God's own self-identification in terms of this people, continues to be confessed amid the universal claims the text makes regarding the work of God in creation and among the nations.

Fourth, the reference to the Lord of hosts in this context may suggest that Israel's God is the commander of armies, including those of the Medes and Persians who now serve as divine instruments for the judgment of Babylon.

God Addresses All the Principals, 51:20-26

This unit consists of three segments, divine addresses to Babylon's enemy (vv. 20-23), to the exiles (v. 24), and to Babylon (vv. 25-26).

The address to the exiles stands at the climactic point, surrounded by material that speaks confidently of the instrument God has chosen for the conquest of Babylon and of Babylon's fate.

Verses 20-23 are addressed to an unnamed individual (the "you" is masculine singular), whose identity is uncertain. Persia (or its king, Cyrus) and Babylon itself have been proposed. The former is most plausible, for Babylon is addressed in the feminine singular in vv. 13-14 as a nation whose end has come and is not described as God's agent in such a sustained way elsewhere in chapters 50–51. The repetitive, rhythmic style is similar to 50:35-38, where Babylon's enemy is addressed. It seems likely that Babylon's enemy is once again here addressed, this time in the person of its leader, probably originally a Median leader, but in time identified with King Cyrus, the conqueror of the Medes (see Isa 41:2-4, 25; 45:1-6). God calls him a war club (a weapon of uncertain identification; the "hammer" in 50:23 is a different word). He is *God's* weapon for war; he is God's agent, raised up for the purpose of destroying Babylon. The rhythm of the following verses includes two agents, Cyrus ("with you") and God ("I"), both of whom are important in the carrying out of God's purposes in this situation. God has chosen to be dependent upon this king, a remarkable and risky, but typical move for the God of Israel.

The verb "to smash, shatter" is used nine times and is applied comprehensively to include (after the initial general reference to nations) Babylonian people in various stations and stages of life as well as their domestic animals (see Isa 13:16-18). Specifically named are: warriors, men and women, old and young males, young men and women (adolescents or children), shepherds and their flocks, farmers and their oxen, governors and other officials of government. This rhythmic cadence vividly portrays the incessant pounding that the enemy directs against Babylon (and its allies), the comprehensiveness of the onslaught, and its deadly effects on their people and animals.

God addresses the exiles in v. 24 ("your"), focusing on a theme that has been a refrain in the oracles against Babylon, namely, vengeance (see 50:15, 29; 51:6, 11; see 25:12-14; 51:49). Because of the wrong that Babylon (and *all* Babylonians) has done in Zion (both city and temple may be in view here, see v. 11), Babylon will have that very wrong visited upon itself. Notably, v. 26 speaks of this wrong as the destruction of "the whole earth"! And this will occur before the very eyes of the exiles; they themselves will see this happen. This point emphasizes the contemporaneity of the fall of Babylon for the readers; the very exiles who read/hear these words

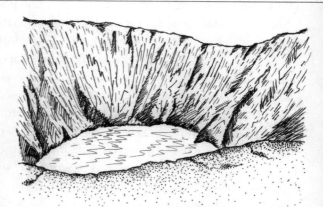

Babylon as Volcano

The use of the mountain image in vv. 25-26 is linked to Babylon's arrogance (50:29-32). But how can the mountain be rolled down the mountain? And what does it mean for the mountain to burn? The usual solution (other than textual emendation) is to think of Babylon as a volcano, out of which spew rocks and coals that roll down the mountainside. A burned-out crater is all that remains. This seems to be correct. While objection has been raised that no volcanoes exist in Mesopotamia, it only takes knowledge of a volcano to make the metaphor work. Verse 26 extends that image even further. No one will take any of these spewed-out stones and use them again to build a cornerstone or a foundation for the city or any building therein (unlike Zion, Isa 28:16). No monument to Babylon's fame will be constructed from what remains.

Illustration of the dormant volcano Irazu in Costa Rica.

are reassured that they will experience the deliverance from captivity that Babylon's destruction will entail.

In vv. 25-26 God once again addresses Babylon. The basic point of the verses is clear: God will destroy Babylon and make it a wasteland as it had destroyed others. The difficulty lies in the function of the metaphor: Babylon is a destroying mountain (or named: The Destroying Mountain) that is itself destroyed. [Babylon as Volcano] The end result (v. 26): this destroyer of so many lands will be a perpetual wasteland, with not even its rocks being good for anything (see 25:12).

Babylon's Pending Judgment, 51:27-44

This segment begins with another (the last!) call to the Medes (see v. 11) to prepare for battle against Babylon (vv. 27-28). It continues with a portrayal of a city sharply weakened and demoralized in the face of this assault (vv. 29-32). Verses 33-40 describe an interaction between God and the exiles regarding Babylon. God announces Babylon's end (v. 33), but the exiles respond uncertainly, with lament and curse, in the face of their horrendous experience with the oppressive might of Babylon (vv. 34-35). God responds in the first person to the voiced concerns of the exiles (vv. 36-40).

The call to Babylon's enemies (vv. 27-28) is somewhat more comprehensive here than in previous directives (cf. v. 12). Here the call goes out to many nations that are part of the Median empire to prepare for battle against Babylon. Three relatively unknown peoples from northern regions of the Median empire are named: Ararat, Minni, Ashkenaz. [Ararat, Minni, Ashkenaz] Troops from these peoples (and other nations in the empire) are to be called up (in numbers likened to locusts, as in v. 14) and prepared for the assault on Babylon.

Babylon is demoralized by this news of an impending attack (vv. 29-32). The land of Babylon is personified as writhing and trembling (as with Israel, 8:16, and the nations, 49:21) under the impact of the news that God's purpose in and through the Medes is directed toward making it desolate and uninhabitable (v. 29; see v. 11; 50:45). The weakening of the city is portrayed first and last (vv. 30, 32) from the perspective of its warriors (see 48:41): they are resigned to defeat and are holed up in their "foxholes"; they have "become women" (see 50:37), that is, they have been sharply weakened; they are in panic. Then the portrayal focuses on the city itself; its houses are on fire and the bars that secure the gates of the city have been broken (v. 30c). Messengers are depicted as scurrying about, trying to get a communication to the king that the city has fallen (v. 31; see 50:43 for his reception of the news). Reed-filled marshes that surround Babylon have been burned and fords for crossing the waterways have been captured by the enemy (v. 32). One can understand why panic rules the day in Babylon.

The demoralization of Babylon can be explained by the news of the attacking armies (vv. 27-28), but v. 33 gives a theological interpretation of this panic ("for"). God has spoken against Babylon and in a short while it will be destroyed. The image used for Babylon is that of a threshing floor especially prepared for the time when it is used to tread the grain of the harvest, which in turn is an image for judgment. This image seems to focus on the timing of the harvest (rather than the actual treading); the harvest will soon come to pass for Babylon (see the language of 27:7; Gen 15:16).

Though God has spoken of the imminent fall of Babylon (v. 33), the exiles respond with uncertainty in the face of their recent experience with its armies (vv. 34-35). The exiles pile up verbs to make their point; the primary image they use is that of being devoured by a monster, mixed with other metaphors of exile. Nebuchadrezzar has devoured them (see 5:17), routed them,

Ararat, Minni, and Ashkenaz

 These are names of peoples who lived in regions to the north and west of Babylon. Ararat (Urartu) is the name of a people that inhabited the territory in modern southeastern Turkey and the northern regions of Iraq and Iran, approximating the range of the Kurdish people. Minni (Mannaya), also known as the Maneans, would be a neighboring people to the Ararat, living in the northwest regions of modern Iran. The identification of Ashkenaz is less certain (see Gen 10:2-3, the genealogy of Japheth); this name probably refers to an Indo-European people from the region of modern Armenia and northeastern Turkey (identified by Herodotus as the Scythians).

emptied the land (=vessel, note that Jerusalem is speaking, v. 35). He has swallowed them like a monster (see Ps 74:13, a reference to chaos in a community lament from the exile), filled his belly with all that they hold dear, and spewed out all that he could not digest. The exiles (=former inhabitants of Zion) cry out to God to avenge their blood (see v. 24; on this use of blood, see Lev 20:9-16); Babylon must be held accountable for the blood it has shed.

God responds to their cries in the first person with an announcement of judgment (vv. 36-44, "therefore"). God will take up the cause of the exiles (as in 50:34) and avenge what Babylon did to them (vv. 6, 11, 24). God will dry up her sea and her fountains; this refers not only to its water supplies and protective lakes (see v. 32), but to its status as an "evil empire" (see v. 34; 47:2). Babylon is viewed as a national embodiment of evil and God is the one who defeats this monster; the specific reference to the Babylonian deity Bel (v. 44; see 50:2) may be ironic, for Bel was worshiped as the conqueror of chaos. Verse 42 will extend this irony in its claim that Babylon itself is swallowed up by the sea. This linkage may help explain the recurrent references to God the Creator in Jeremiah (vv. 15-19; see, e.g., 5:22). Babylon will experience the horror (see 50:13) of what it had done to Israel (see 9:11; 10:22; 18:16; 25:9, 18) and other nations (49:17, 33).

In vv. 38-40 the tables are turned as Babylon, the devourer, becomes the devoured. Babylon is likened to roaring lions (as in 2:15) that gather ferociously at a banquet table. But the Lord has set this table and mixes the drinks; the lions will become inflamed and drink the cup of the Lord's wrath (see 25:15-17, which finally includes Babylon [=Sheshach, 25:26; see 51:41] among the nations, 48:26). Falling into a drunken stupor from which they will never awake, the lions become sacrificial animals (lambs, rams, and goats) and they will be devoured as were the sheep of Israel (50:17).

In a mocking lament, vv. 41-43 portray Babylon (=Sheschah) as a nation already fallen (see 50:23). The nation that had once been the most renowned in the earth for its conquests has itself been seized and made captive. Its renown among the nations has been turned on its head and it is now a horror among those very nations (see v. 37). The embodiment of warring chaos has itself been overwhelmed (see above) and the result is an uninhabited desert land (as in v. 36; 50:12-13). Verse 44 speaks of reversal once again, as the city and its god that swallowed Israel up (v. 34: on Bel, see 50:2) will be forced to disgorge the exiles. The nations will no longer stream to the city as captives, but stream back to their homes through the fallen walls of Babylon. The river of people will now flow in the other direction. As for the exiles, they will stream back to their home in Zion (see Isa 2:2).

Assurance for the Exiles, 51:45-49

The last two units of these oracles are similarly structured, each beginning with God's call to the exiles to return home (vv. 45, 50). They can do so with assurance because the days are surely coming (vv. 47, 52) when Babylon will fall.

This unit begins with God's call to the exiles ("my people"!) to come out of Babylon (see vv. 6, 50; 50:8; Isa 51:17; 52:1-2, 11). By fleeing from the city they will save themselves from the wrath of the Lord, now directed against Babylon and not Israel (see 12:13). The exiles are not to be fainthearted or be dissuaded by all the rumors about violence that thrive among them (their actual response is given in v. 51), probably due to the instability of the Babylonian empire in its last years (v. 46). The days are surely coming (see v. 52) when the judgment announced against Babylon and its images (see v. 52; see Bel, v. 44) will come to pass. All Babylon will be put to shame (see 50:12) and the city will be filled with the slain (see v. 4). When Babylon's fall occurs, at the hands of the destroyer from the north (see vv. 41, 53; 50:3, 9), a victory shout will be heard round the world, indeed even from the hosts of heaven (v. 48; see Isa 44:23; 52:9; 55:12; Ps 96:11-13; Rev 18:20; **Connections**). The fall of Babylon is a global event, with earth-shaking significance. The unit concludes (v. 49) with the now familiar reason why Babylon must fall; it must fall because of the slain of Israel (see 9:1) and the slain of all the other nations that Babylon has conquered (see v. 24; 25:12-14).

Babylon's Final End, 51:50-58

As noted above, this unit is structured very much like that in vv. 45-49. It begins with an address to the exiles, those who survived Babylon's sword. They are to leave the city without hesitation (v. 50). Though they are "in a distant land," that context is not to be decisive for their identity. Rather, they are to fill their minds with thoughts of the Lord and thoughts of home (Jerusalem). Such thoughts will draw the exiles away from the past with its guilt and shame and toward the future with its new possibilities (see 29:11). The exiles respond to this call from the Lord (v. 51; a response is implied in the parallel in v. 46). Their lamenting response suggests that they hesitate to flee and even wonder about their ability to do so because of all the shaming and taunting that they have suffered at Babylon's hands. Moreover, given the fact that the Lord's temple has been violated by the Babylonians (see Ps 74:4-11), does not this imply that their enemies are superior in strength even to Yahweh?

In an initial response to the laments (vv. 52-53) God once again announces that the time is surely coming when ("therefore") judgment will be visited upon Babylon and its idols (as in v. 47; as with Israel, 8:19). Babylonians throughout the land will be groaning because they have been fatally wounded (see v. 47). Though they should scale the heights of heaven with massive towers and strengthen their fortifications, they will not be able to escape the destroyers that God is sending from the North (see v. 48). In light of Isa 14:12-14, these references to heights and heaven may involve more than reinforced buildings; they may entail claims to a certain divine status, or access to deities, that would rival Israel's God (see 50:24, 38). It may be that the story of the tower of Babel is in mind (see Gen 11:1-9).

God continues the response to the exiles by calling them to listen carefully to the noises around them (vv. 54-55; see 50:22, 28). The noises come from two sources, both of which should give reassurance to the exiles. On the one hand, a great cry and a loud clamor is heard from the Babylonians because ("for") God is laying waste their land in and through the "destroyer" (v. 56; see vv. 48, 53; 48:8, 15, 18). On the other hand, the noise is coming from the destroyers, who are likened to waves crashing across the land (see v. 42; see 6:23 for the experience of Israel); their clamor stills Babylon's clamor. As a result, the warriors' bows (=military might, 49:35) are broken and they are taken captive. Once again, God's judgment is seen as a matter of recompense (v. 56; see vv. 6, 11, 24, 35-36, 49). Verse 57 returns to the themes of v. 39; all the intellectual (sages), political (officials, governors, and deputies), and military leaders of Babylon will drink the cup of divine wrath and sleep forever. This is accomplished by Yahweh, the King, the Lord of hosts (as in 46:18; 48:15); it is the kingly rule of Israel's God that will finally prevail over the rule of all earthly kings, including the king of Babylon.

Verse 58 concludes the oracles against Babylon with a sharp and specific statement of what will happen to Babylon and to warring nations more generally. The massive wall of Babylon will be leveled to the ground; its seemingly impenetrable, high gates (as high as thirty meters) will be burned to the ground. Verse 58b may quote Hab 2:13, confirming that the word about the fate of Babylon was on target. These lines have a proverbial character; with Babylon, as with all other nations, all of their wars and rumors of wars are but "sound and fury" in view of the kingly rule of Israel's God. The end that will come for all warring and wearying peoples is, to put it simply: *fire*.

A Symbolic Act against Babylon, 51:59-64

This narrative concludes the oracles against Babylon and specifically ties them back into the earlier narratives in Jeremiah. These verses tell how the oracles against Babylon were written in a book and carried to Babylon. The specific text to which this unit is often linked is 29:3 and the embassy to Babylon that includes Jeremiah's letter to the exiles (the text makes no specific connection, however). King Zedekiah may have gone to Babylon during the fourth year of his reign (593/594 BC) to explain his participation in the conspiracy against Babylon (see 27:3) or to pay tribute in view of it. It is commonly thought that this linkage to the earlier narrative was made in order to assure that the oracles against Babylon were remembered as the words of the prophet Jeremiah. (See the NRSV note in v. 64 that the words of Jeremiah in the Hebrew text are concluded with the phrase, "and they shall weary themselves," as they do in v. 58; this suggests that vv. 59-64 have been spliced into an earlier conclusion of the chapter).

Seraiah, brother of Baruch (see the reference to their father in 32:12) and royal official (a quartermaster, who sees to the details of the journey), was to accompany King Zedekiah on his trip to Babylon. Jeremiah "commanded" Seraiah, obviously a trusted individual, to bring along a scroll on which the prophet had written oracles regarding disasters that would come on Babylon (only in this text does Jeremiah "command" rather than God). As such, these oracles are now the written word of God and have a standing that is comparable to the scroll that was (re)written at Jeremiah's direction in chapter 36.

Jeremiah instructs Seraiah to read aloud all of his recorded words, perhaps to (a representative group of) the exiles, perhaps to no audience at all. The text is not clear on this point; symbolic actions may be private or public (see 13:1-11, also linked to the river Euphrates, only there pertaining to *Israel's* future). Upon reading these words, Seraiah is to pray to the Lord to fulfill the words in terms often used in the oracles themselves, namely, that Babylon will become an uninhabited ruin (see 50:3, 39-40; 51:26, 37). Such a prayer brings together the will of the pray-er (indirectly, Jeremiah) and the will of God; together they are conformed to this future for Babylon. Such a concurrence of the will of God and the will of the prophet shapes the future (in this case, Babylon's) in a more decisive and certain way. Such a concurrence creates an energy that is more focused on its "target" (not unlike Jeremiah having been filled with the wrath of God (6:11; 15:17).

When Seraiah has finished reading the scroll, he is to tie a stone to it and throw it into the Euphrates river that runs through Babylon. In the process of doing this symbolic act, as a representative of the prophet, he is to speak certain words (again, to no known audience). The divine first person ("I" am bringing) indicates that this is a word of God. Babylon shall sink (just as this scroll and rock sink into the river), never to rise again because of the disaster (*rāʿāh*) God is bringing (see Rev 18:21). The reason for this certainty is that God stands behind this word of judgment.

The juxtaposition of these written words against Babylon stands in somewhat startling relationship to the next chapter, which reports Babylon's devastation of Israel.

CONNECTIONS

Jeremiah for and against Babylon

Key to understanding the chronological issues in Jeremiah's words against Babylon are several texts in chapters 25–29, especially those which specify that Israel will serve Babylon for seventy years (25:11-14; 29:10). The sharp conflict between Jeremiah and Hananiah (28:3-4; and other prophets, 27:9-22; 29:21-23) was centered on the issue of the length of time for Israel's subjection to Babylon in the years following 597 BC. The prophets who announced a speedy end of the subjection and return from exile were denounced as false. Hananiah and the other (false) prophets were correct, however, in announcing that God would "break the yoke of the king of Babylon" (28:4). With respect to basic content, that message would be essentially congruent with Jeremiah's message of judgment in chapters 50–51 (Jeremiah expresses a level of agreement with Hananiah in 28:6). Jeremiah recognizes that Babylon's time will come (25:12-14; 27:7; 29:10-14; implicitly 3:14; 24:6; 32:37-44), but that time had not yet arrived. The falseness of the prophets had to do at least in part with issues of timing, that is, the seventy years.

At the same time, it should be recognized that the prophecies of chapters 50–51 are not specifically linked to the seventy years (the

Jeremiah and the Book of Revelation

Interestingly, the book of Revelation has many quotations or allusions to the book of Jeremiah, including about a dozen texts from chs. 50–51. Revelation 18:2-19 (see 14:8) picks up on the theme of wailing over Babylon (=Rome) in a taunting dirge for the fallen city. Just as with Israel, Christians are summoned to flee the city (Rev 18:4). The image of drinking/pouring out the wine of God's wrath, used in 51:7 (see also 25:15-29) is utilized in Rev 18:3. In Rev 18:5, the sins of Babylon are piled so high that they have reached heaven and God remembers their iniquities; in Jer 51:9, it is their judgment (=the effects of their sins) that has reached the heavens. The image of Babylon as a volcano (51:25-26) is also picked up in Rev 18:8-9. The image of the harvest in 51:22 is referred to in Rev 14:14-15. The announcement of judgment on Babylon that its sea would become dry (51:36) may be echoed in the promise of Rev 21:1 that the sea would be no more. The rejoicing of heaven and earth at the defeat of Babylon (51:48) is appropriated by Rev 18:20. The symbolic act of Seraiah in throwing Jeremiah's scroll into the Euphrates (51:59-64) is adapted in Rev 18:21.

The upshot of the parallels drawn between Babylon in Jeremiah and Rome in Revelation is that no country or nation has an eternal standing in God's eyes. Self-importance, arrogance, and overweening pride tend to become characteristic of a people's life over time, and such perspectives sow the seeds for their own destruction. Jeremiah's images live again in Revelation and they may become a lively resource in other times and places. This fluidity in application—first Babylon, then Rome—indicates that no single nation of the world is finally in view in either Jeremiah or Revelation. These texts may be applied to any nation that assumes unto itself a godlike standing in the world, including the United States of America (see also [**A Failure of Prophecy?**]).

LXX insertion of the oracles against the nations right after 25:11-12 would make that linkage much clearer). And so these chapters do stand in no little tension with chapters 25–29. At the same time, it is unlikely that chapters 50–51 were public oracles at the time that Nebuchadrezzar treated Jeremiah so well in the aftermath of the fall of Jerusalem (39:12-14). That they were written private oracles, as 51:59-64 might suggest, softens the tension somewhat, but does not remove all the difficulties.

One might suggest that this tension would have mirrored the experience of exilic readers, who were living between the now and the not yet. Living with unfulfilled promises, not least promises relating to life beyond abuse at the hands of enemies in a hostile world, has been the story of the people of God in every age. Note that Babylon becomes a symbol for such hostile powers in Revelation 14–18, where there are at least twelve quotations or allusions to Jeremiah 50–51. [Jeremiah and the Book of Revelation]

Short of the time of deliverance, Jeremiah's word for the exiles is to settle down in Babylon (29:5-7); his word for those in Judah is to submit to Babylon's yoke and not to rebel (e.g., 38:17-18 and Jeremiah's ongoing counsel to Zedekiah). The importance of continued submission to Babylon is also evident in the years following the events of 587 BC (e.g., 40:9; 42:10-12). Jeremiah does express an understanding of Babylon's eventual downfall in chapters 25–29, but it is certainly not as well developed as it is in chapters 50–51. Whatever anticipatory understandings Jeremiah may have had (see 51:59-64), they have certainly been more fully expanded in chapters 50–51—especially after the fall of 587 BC.

The importance of both chapters 25–29 and chapters 50–51 for exilic readers is considerable. For the time being they are to settle into their place of exile, but at the same time they are being assured that their time in exile in submission to Babylon has temporal limits.

God as Redeemer of the Oppressed in Every Age

The language used for Babylon's oppression of Israel and Judah (vv. 33-34; both kingdoms, as in v. 19) is that used earlier in Jeremiah for *Israel's* oppression of the poor and disadvantaged (6:6; 7:6; 21:12; 22:17). God enters into judgment against any and all nations—chosen or nonchosen—who are guilty of oppression (a divine commitment according to Exod 22:21-27). Israel now finds itself in a situation comparable to that in Egypt (e.g., Exod 1:12). Once again they need to be delivered from an oppressive situation. As with the pharaoh and his officials (Exod 4:23; 7:14, 27; 9:2), once again they are held fast; the Babylonians refuse "to let them go." The reader can see in such formulations how it is that the confession regarding the exodus from Egypt needs to be recast in terms of deliverance from Babylonian captivity (as in 16:14-15=23:7-8).

At the same time, it is important to make a distinction between exodus and exile regarding the nature of Israel's deliverance. Israel's oppression at the hands of the Egyptians had no relationship to its own sin or guilt; Israel was suffering the effects of the sins of other people, namely, the Egyptians. Israel's oppression at the hands of the Babylonians was a more complex reality. It was Israel's own sin that brought them into this situation of oppression; in other words, they were suffering the effects of *their own* sins, most fundamentally. But Babylon had intensified this oppression beyond the judgment that was called for, and God had forgiven Israel its sin (v. 20). Hence, Babylon had become like Egypt and it was to be treated like Egypt had been in order to bring freedom to the exiles.

As often in these oracles, Babylon will experience what Israel (and other nations) have experienced. Neither Israel nor any other nation has been arbitrarily singled out by God for judgment; their sins found them out. All nations, no matter how "religious" or powerful, will experience the dire consequences of their own sins. In judgment, God shows no partiality. And Babylon's sins (both religious and political sins are cited) will reap consequences of a special intensity. Such judgments are necessary in order to restore moral balance to the world.

God's Planning, the Plan's Execution, and Issues of Divine Temporality

God makes an announcement regarding the judgment on Babylon, revealing the divine plans (50:45; 51:12; cf. God's plans in 4:28; 18:11; 26:3; 29:11; 49:20, 30). God's speaking is always a revealing of the divine will (plans). But 51:12 (and similar texts, see Lam 2:17; Isa 48:3) makes it clear that God's speaking does not inevitably entail the fulfillment of what has been spoken. God both plans and executes the divine plans. In other words, there is a temporal distinction between the divine plan and its execution.

This temporal spacing is theologically significant. In the time between the speaking and the execution there could be developments in the pertinent human community, including changes in the relationship between God and people, that could call for a change of the divine plans. God could for example reverse the divine word (see 26:2-3) or, as here, decide to persist (as also with Israel, 4:28). The common language of planning assumes that temporal sequence is important for God, that past, present, and future or "before and after" are important to the divine reflection with respect to any divine planning and subsequent action. [Divine Temporality]

This understanding might be related to a recurrent theme throughout the OAN, namely the call to the enemy to prepare well for battle (e.g., 51:11-12). Such a call is not empty rhetoric; it assumes that the enemy could bungle the job. What God plans and purposes is important and indispensable to accomplish the divine objectives, but what people do with their abilities is understood by God also to be indispensable. God works through means, and the means can make a difference in the outcome, in view of which God may well have to change the divine plans.

> **Divine Temporality**
>
> The God of the Old Testament is "not thought of in terms of timelessness. At least since the creation, the divine life is temporally ordered. God has chosen to enter into the time of the world. God is not above the flow of time and history, as if looking down from some supratemporal mountaintop on all the streams of people through the valleys of the ages. God is 'inside time,' not outside of it. Yet there never was nor will there ever be a time when God is not the living God. There is no moving from birth or toward death for God . . . . The OT witnesses to a God who truly shares in human history as past, present, and future, and in such a way that we must speak of the history of God."
>
> Terence Fretheim, *The Suffering of God: An Old Testament Perspective* (Philadelphia: Fortress, 1984), 43-44.

NOTE

[1] So William McKane, *A Critical and Exegetical Commentary on Jeremiah* (2 vols.; ICC; Edinburgh: T. & T. Clark, 1986), 1282.

THE FALL OF JERUSALEM
AND ITS AFTERMATH

52:1-34

This historical appendix, a shortened form of which is located in 39:1-10, does not mention Jeremiah. It has been taken from 2 Kings 24:18–25:30 with minor changes (a condensed form is also found in 2 Chr 36:11-21; comparably, Isa 36–39 borrows from 2 Kgs 18:13–20:19). This linkage to Kings may indicate that the same school of editors (Deuteronomistic) was involved in the editing of both books. The changes from Kings include several expansions (vv. 10-11 and vv. 21-23 expand 2 Kgs 25:7, 17), one omission (2 Kgs 25:22-26), and one addition (vv. 28-30). The addition, with its enumeration of the number of exiles, is probably intended to provide a sign of hope for the future (vv. 28-30). The omission from 2 Kings 25:22-26 is probably due both to the fact that this information about Gedaliah had already been covered in chapters 40–41 and that this element in the story contained no seeds of hope for the future of the exiles. [The Purpose of Chapter 52]

COMMENTARY

This chapter consists of segments that set the stage (vv. 1-3) and then proceed to portray the Babylonian siege of Jerusalem with King

---

he Purpose of Chapter 52

The primary purpose of this chapter is to provide additional information regarding the decisive events garding which Jeremiah's ministry was so concerned: the bellion of Zedekiah, the fall of Jerusalem, and the exile of populace to Babylon. Even more, these events vindicate remiah and demonstrate the truth of his words (though he not mentioned, as he is in 2 Chr 36:21). And Jeremiah nself speaks not a word in his own defense! The reporting the events just stands there for all to read, with no eological claims made explicit (but much implied, given the eceding chapters).

Even more, because this chapter follows the oracles ainst Babylon (chs. 50–51) with their many hopeful notes

about the future, this judgment on Judah/Jerusalem is given a provisional character. It is as though exilic readers are asked to read about that tragedy again in view of chs. 50–51; the events associated with the fall of Jerusalem certainly had a devastating impact on Israel's life, but they were not God's final word to them. Moreover, the release of King Jehoiachin in vv. 31-34 would concretize for the exiles the positive elements in the oracles of chs. 50–51 (see **Connections**).

Literally, this ending of Jeremiah returns the reader to the beginning of the book. The opening verses had announced the "captivity of Jerusalem" in the reign of Zedekiah (1:3) and included Jeremiah's visionary experience of a foe from the north establishing its throne in Jerusalem (1:14-15).

Agency in Jeremiah 52

Notably, vv. 2-3 contain the only references to God in this chapter; here, the divine agency in this event is explicitly stated in straightforward language: "He expelled them from his presence." At the same time, the actual destruction of city and temple as well as the execution and exiling of the Israelites are all ascribed to Babylonian agency without reference to God. Both theological and military-political factors flow together to bring about this disastrous result. Both divine and human agents are at work; God works in and through the Babylonians to effect the divine purpose in this situation. And, as has been noted at several points (see 25:12-14; 50–51), the Babylonians proved to be overzealous in their destructive activity. This repeated detail shows that these human agents were not somehow micromanaged by God and that they themselves will be judged for their excessive violence.

Zedekiah taken as prisoner (vv. 3b-11), the destruction of homes and the temple, with its furnishings destroyed or taken (vv. 12-23), the execution of various leaders (vv. 24-27), an accounting of the three deportations, with which readers would be able to identify themselves (vv. 28-30), and a conclusion centering on the fate of King Jehoiachin (vv. 31-34).

Setting the Stage, 52:1-3

This announcement of the "evil" of King Zedekiah (597–587 BC), drawn from 2 Kings 24:18-20, also characterizes the populace. This reality arouses the divine anger (see 32:31) that leads to the destruction and exile of Judah and Jerusalem (vv. 1-3a; on Zedekiah's mother and her father Jeremiah of Libnah, see 2 Kgs 23:31; 24:18). Zedekiah finds himself caught between Babylon and a resurgent Egypt; he opts to side with the latter in rebellion against Babylon (v. 3b) and suffers the disastrous consequences. [Agency in Jeremiah 52]

The Siege of Jerusalem, 52:4-11

In response, Babylon attacks Jerusalem, in the ninth year of Zedekiah (see 2 Kgs 25:1-7). The siege of the city, together with accompanying famine (see 37:21), lasts for eighteen months, from January 588 to July 587 BC (vv. 3b-6). When the end becomes obvious, Zedekiah and "all the soldiers" flee the city at night through a breach in the wall and make their way toward the Arabah (the region south of the Dead Sea). The Babylonian armies pursue them and overtake them in the plains of Jericho, the place where Israel had entered the land some 600 years or so earlier. Zedekiah's soldiers scatter, deserting him (vv. 7-8).

Zedekiah, his family, and "all the officers of Judah" are captured and brought before Nebuchadrezzar at Riblah. Sentence is passed upon Zedekiah and his sons and officers are killed in his presence; he is blinded and imprisoned in Babylon for the rest of his life (vv. 9-11; see 39:4-7). His physical blindness may be intended to correspond to his lack of religious insight.

The Destruction and Sacking of the Temple, 52:12-23

In 587 BC (a month after the fall of the city, for unknown reasons) the Babylonian armies, under the command of Nebuzaradan, destroy the temple and the palace, burn down all the houses of Jerusalem, and raze the city walls (vv. 12-14). That this occurred in the nineteenth year of Nebuchadrezzar (v. 12; so also 2 Kgs 25:8; note the switch from Zedekiah's reign in v. 4 to Nebuchadrezzar's here), while v. 28 speaks of his exiling people in the eighteenth year, has received no satisfactory explanation.

Special mention is made of the "great houses" of the city, presumably the homes of the officials and affluent citizens. Nebuzaradan oversees the capture and exile of a second group of Israelites, including some poor people, deserters that had defected to Nebuchadrezzar, the "rest of the artisans," and "the rest of the people who were left in the city." Notably, not only the leading citizens are sent into exile. He leaves only some poor farmers behind to take care of the land and bring in the crops (vv. 15-16; see 39:9-10 and the post-fall activity in 40:11-12). This is an ambiguous reference inasmuch as so few people were actually exiled (at least according to vv. 28-30).

In addition, the armies break up several key temple furnishings (the bronze pillars, sea, and stands) and carry away the bronze and other temple vessels to Babylon as spoil (vv. 17-19; see 1 Kgs 7:13-51 for details; 27:16–28:3 indicates that many of the vessels had been taken in 597 BC). [The Temple Vessels: Continuity and Discontinuity]

Executions and Exile, 52:24-30

Finally, mention is made of the execution—apparently by Nebuchadrezzar personally or at his specific direction (v. 27)—of some seventy-four other priestly, royal, and military officials, and leaders of "the people of the land" who were found in the city. These were apparently persons closely associated with the palace and temple and their leadership. They included the chief priest Seraiah (see 36:26, not the Seraiah of 40:8 or 51:59) and the

The Temple Vessels: Continuity and Discontinuity

The temple vessels are all listed, one by one, as the narrator slowly moves over the dismantling of each and every element of the temple, this most cherished institution in the life of Israel. A poignant way to depict the end of the center of Israel's religious life! The narrator pauses in vv. 20-23 to describe the size, weight, and decorative features of the bronze furnishings that had been broken up. The specific mention of King Solomon (v. 20) makes the point that that glorious chapter in Israel's history has come to an end.

Yet, the fact that many of these items were carried away gave some hope that they might someday be returned. The importance of this hope had already been addressed in the wake of the events of 597 BC (see 27:16-28:3; 2 Kgs 24:13), although this hope was denounced by Jeremiah as premature. He had announced that the temple vessels would again be carried away, but also that God would see to their restoration (27:19-22). The fulfillment of this hope can be observed in Ezra 1:5-11. The emphasis placed on these temple vessels was a concrete way of indicating that God still had a future for Israel, indeed a future for the temple in the life of those who would return.

"second priest" Zephaniah (see 21:1; 29:24-32). It is not known just why these persons were executed and other leaders were exiled. In any case, the leadership of Israel has been decimated and Babylonian rule is in place.

The summary statement in v. 27 makes the essential point: "So Judah went into exile out of its land." Jeremiah has been vindicated and the word of God that he spoke is shown to have been authentic.

Verses 28-30 (not present in 2 Kgs 25) list the numbers of people (=Judeans) exiled, probably in the three deportations of 597, 587, and 582 BC (3,023, 832, and 745 respectively, for a total of 4,600 persons). The first report corresponds to that found in the Babylonian Chronicle. [The Babylonian Chronicle] The discrepancy between the 3,023 persons exiled in 597 BC and the ten and eight thousand of 2 Kgs 24:14, 16 has not been satisfactorily explained (perhaps 3,023 are the adult males). Some have thought this listing to be supplementary rather than a full accounting.[1] The deportation of 582 BC may be linked to the assassination of Gedaliah (see 41:2) but was probably a later event.

The relatively small number of deportees is somewhat surprising (even if they were only adult males). Those exiled certainly included leading citizens of Israel; they may have been viewed as hostages by the Babylonians, providing some leverage for better control of the land. These exiles are the ones in and through whom Israel's hopes for the future are channeled, as stipulated by God's promises (see 24:4-7).

Hope for the Future?, 52:31-34

The final verses of Jeremiah can be dated some twenty-six years after the destruction of Jerusalem (560/561 BC). The interest focuses on the fate of King Jehoiachin, who reigned in Jerusalem only briefly (598–597 BC) and had been carried off to Babylon with his family (2 Kgs 24:15). He is named Coniah elsewhere in Jeremiah and receives an uncompromising judgment from the prophet (22:24, 28; 37:1), though it may be important that he is not represented as rejecting the word of Jeremiah in the way that Jehoiakim and Zedekiah did. Hope is lifted up where even the prophet did not dare to look, such is the surprising way in which his God works. Out of the midst of death, life.

When Jehoiachin was about fifty-three years old (2 Kgs 24:8), he found favor in the eyes of the Babylonian king Evil-Merodach (=Amel-Marduk; 562–560 BC), that is, he was pardoned, perhaps as part of a general amnesty. He was released from prison and given a standing higher than that of captive kings from other countries. He was treated in a kindly manner and given new robes and special provision at the king's table, symbols of honor and power (see 1 Kgs 4:27; his provisions were noted in Babylonian texts). From the perspective of this text, the future remains uncertain.

The Babylonian Chronicle

The Chronicle of the Babylonian king Nebuchadrezzar is only partially preserved. It mentions the removal of king Jehoiachin of Judah and the appointment of his uncle, Zedekiah (597 BC) and the Babylonian destruction of Jerusalem in 587 BC.

Babylonian Chronicle. 598 BC. British Museum. London. (Credit: The British Museum)

Some twenty years remain until King Cyrus of Persia allows the exiles to return home (538 BC; see Ezra 1:1-4) (see **Connections: The Final Verses of Jeremiah**).

CONNECTIONS

The Final Verses of Jeremiah

The interpretation of the final verses in Jeremiah (and in 2 Kings) is much disputed. Do they strike a hopeful note or not? The preponderance of the evidence suggests to this reader that the release from prison of King Jehoiachin, a member of the Davidic line, is meant to end the book on an encouraging note. That Jehoiachin is called "King" is not unimportant, though he sits on no throne and rules over no people, and he dies in exile. His release follows the many hopeful words to the exiles about a life beyond captivity and a return to their homeland in chapters 50–51. If the exiles knew of King Jehoiachin's fate, and there is no reason to think that this would not have been generally known, such a gesture toward him would be a specific, concrete sign of the hopeful oracles in chapters 50–51. These oracles, both in their word about the fall of Babylon and a return from exile, could be seen as taking shape in such an event. [Hope in Judgment]

Hope in Judgment

Also important in thinking through the function of vv. 31-34 is the word about God's connections with the judgment of Israel (v. 3). Israel's judgment was not due to the weakness of their God and the strength of Babylon's gods; the exiles had experienced judgment at the hands of their own God using Babylon as agent. The destruction of Jerusalem/Judah was not an indication that history had somehow gotten beyond their God. Israel's God was the God of the nations. Moreover, that God's wrath had been provoked by Israel's own wickedness indicated that divine wrath is contingent and not an essential characteristic of God. If there were no sin, there would be no wrath. When the claim in v. 3 about divine wrath is read through the lens provided by the hopeful oracles of chs. 50–51, this wrathful response from God is seen not to be God's final word to the exiles. The future belonged to God and not to the Babylonians.

Terence Fretheim *First and Second Kings* (Louisville: West Minster/John Knox, 1999), 224-25.

Finally, it should be noted that, for all of Jeremiah's sharp judgments on Israel's kings, he does not finally claim that the Davidic dynasty will come to an end. Indeed, specific divine promises regarding a future for Israel and the exiles are associated with God's commitment to the Davidic dynasty (23:5-6; 30:8-9; 33:14-26). In that day, God will give them "shepherds after my own heart" (3:15). Such words may be small comfort for the exiles, for it is never easy to live by words alone. But this ending of the book of Jeremiah may begin to put some flesh on those words. The Davidic dynasty is still alive in exile. Yet, even with such a sign of a hopeful future, the exiles know that that future remains in the hands of the God who spoke the promises in the first place. We know from the larger canonical picture that these promises still hold for Israel and those who have been grafted into that tree (see Ezek 37:1-14; Matt 1:10-11).

NOTE

[1] See William McKane, *A Critical and Exegetical Commentary on Jeremiah* (2 vols.; ICC; Edinburgh: T. & T. Clark, 1986), 1381-85.

BIBLIOGRAPHY

Peter Ackroyd. *Exile and Restoration. A Study of Hebrew Thought of the Sixth Century B.C.* London: SCM Press, 1968.

Samuel Balentine, *Prayer in the Hebrew Bible: The Drama of the Divine-Human Dialogue.* Overtures to Biblical Theology. Minneapolis: Fortress, 1993.

Alice Ogden Bellis. *The Structure and Composition of Jeremiah 50.2–51.58.* Lewiston, NY: Edwin Mellen Press, 1995.

Daniel Berrigan. *Jeremiah: The World, The Wound of God.* Minneapolis: Fortress, 1999.

Mark E. Biddle. *Polyphony and Symphony in Prophetic Literature: Rereading Jeremiah 7–20.* Macon GA: Mercer University Press, 1996.

Joseph Blenkinsopp. *A History of Prophecy in Israel.* Rev. ed. Louisville: Westminster John Knox Press, 1996.

Barbara A. Bozak. *Life 'Anew': A Literary-Theological Study of Jer. 30–31.* Rome: Ponfificio Istituto Biblico, 1991.

John Bracke, *Jeremiah 1–29.* Westminster Bible Companion. Louisville: Westminster/John Knox, 2000.

John Bracke. *Jeremiah 30–52 and Lamentations.* Westminster Bible Companion. Louisville: Westminster/John Knox, 2000.

John Bright. *Jeremiah.* 2nd ed. Anchor Bible. Garden City NY: Doubleday, 1978.

Walter Brueggemann, *A Commentary on Jeremiah: Exile and Homecoming.* Grand Rapids MI: Eerdmans, 1998.

Robert Carroll, *From Chaos to Covenant: Prophecy in the Book of Jeremiah.* New York: Crossroad, 1983.

Robert Carroll, *Jeremiah.* Old Testament Library. Philadephia: Westminster Press, 1986.

Brevard S. Childs. *Introduction to the Old Testament as Scripture.* Philadelphia: Fortress, 1979.

Ronald E. Clements. *Jeremiah.* Interpretation. Atlanta: John Knox Press, 1988.

Peter C. Craigie, Page Kelley, and Joel F. Drinkard Jr. *Jeremiah 1–25.* WBC 26; Dallas: Word Books, 1991.

James L. Crenshaw. *Prophetic Conflict: Its Effect upon Israelite Religion.* BZAW 124. Berlin: de Gruyter, 1971.

A. R. Diamond. *The Confessions of Jeremiah in Context: Scenes of a Prophetic Drama.* JSOT Supplement. Sheffield: Sheffield Academic Press, 1987.

A. R. Pete Diamond, Kathleen M. O'Connor, and Louis Stulman, editors. *Troubling Jeremiah.* JSOT Supplement Series. Sheffield: Sheffield Academic Press, 1999.

Terence E. Fretheim. *The Suffering of God: An Old Testament Perspective.* Overtures to Biblical Theology. Philadelphia: Fortress, 1984.

Norman C. Habel. *Jeremiah, Lamentations.* Concordia Commentary. St. Louis: Concordia Publishing House, 1968.

Abraham J. Heschel. *The Prophets.* New York: Harper & Row, 1962.

William L. Holladay, *The Architecture of Jeremiah 1-20.* Lewisburg PA: Bucknell University Press, 1976.

William L. Holladay. *Jeremiah 1.* Hermeneia. Philadelphia: Fortress, 1986.

William L. Holladay. *Jeremiah 2.* Hermeneia. Philadelphia: Fortress, 1989.

J. Gerald Janzen. *Studies in the Text of Jeremiah.* Harvard Semitic Monographs. Cambridge MA: Harvard University Press, 1973.

Douglas R. Jones. *Jeremiah.* New Century Bible. Grand Rapids, MI: Eerdmans, 1992.

G. Keown, P. Scalise, and T. Smothers. *Jeremiah 26–52.* Dallas: Word Books, 1993.

Ralph W. Klein. *Israel in Exile: A Theological Interpretation.* Overtures to Biblical Theology. Philadelphia: Fortress, 1979.

J. R. Lundbom. *Jeremiah: A Study in Ancient Hebrew Rhetoric.* Missoula MT: Scholars Press, 1975.

James L. Mays and Paul J. Achtemeier, editors. *Interpreting the Prophets.* Philadelphia: Fortress, 1987.

J. G. McConville. *Judgment and Promise: An Interpretation of the Book of Jeremiah.* Winona Lake IN: Eisenbrauns, 1993.

William McKane. *A Critical and Exegetical Commentary on Jeremiah.* 2 vols. International Critical Commentary. Edinburgh: T. & T. Clark, 1986.

Patrick D. Miller, Jr. *Sin and Judgment in the Prophets.* SBL Monograph. Chico CA: Scholars Press, 1982.

Ernest W. Nicholson, *Preaching to the Exiles: A Study of the Prose Tradition in the Book of Jeremiah.* Oxford: Blackwell, 1970.

Kathleen M. O'Connor. *The Confessions of Jeremiah: Their Interpretation and Role in Chapters 1–25.* SBL Dissertation Series. Atlanta: Scholars Press, 1988.

Thomas W. Overholt. *The Threat of Falsehood: A Study in the Theology of the Book of Jeremiah.* Studies in Biblical Theology. Naperville IL: Allenson, 1970.

Geoffrey Parke-Taylor. *The Formation of the Book of Jeremiah: Doublets and Recurring Phrases.* SBL Monograph. Atlanta: SBL, 2000.

Leo G. Perdue. *The Collapse of History. Reconstructing Old Testament Theology.* Overtures to Biblical Theology. Minneapolis: Fortress, 1994.

Leo G. Perdue and Brian W. Kovacs, editors. *A Prophet to the Nations: Essays in Jeremiah Studies.* Winona Lake IN: Eisenbrauns, 1984.

Timothy Polk. *The Prophetic Persona: Jeremiah and the Language of the Self.* JSOT Supplement. Sheffield: University of Sheffield Press, 1984.

Thomas M. Raitt, *A Theology of Exile: Judgment/Deliverance in Jeremiah and Ezekiel.* Philadelphia: Fortress, 1977.

Rolf Rendtorff. *Canon and Theology: Overtures to an Old Testament Theology.* Overtures to Biblical Theology. Minneapolis: Fortress, 1993.

Christopher R. Seitz. *Theology in Conflict: Reactions to the Exile in the Book of Jeremiah.* BZAW 176. Berlin: de Gruyter, 1989.

John Skinner. *Prophecy and Religion: Studies in the Life of Jeremiah.* Reprint (1922). New York: Cambridge University Press, 1955.

Mark S. Smith. *The Laments of Jeremiah and their Contexts: A Literary and Redactional Study of Jeremiah 11–20.* SBL Monograph Series. Atlanta: Scholars Press, 1990.

Louis Stulman. *Order Amid Chaos: Jeremiah as Symbolic Tapestry.* Sheffield: Sheffield Academic Press, 1998.

John A. Thompson. *The Book of Jeremiah.* New International Commentary. Grand Rapids, MI: Eerdmans, 1980.

Phyllis Trible. *God and the Rhetoric of Sexuality.* Overtures to Biblical Theology. Philadelphia: Fortress, 1978.

Jeremiah Unterman. *From Repentance to Redemption. Jeremiah's Thought in Transition.* JSOT Supplement. Sheffield: Sheffield Academic Press, 1987,

Gerhard von Rad. *Old Testament Theology.* 2 vols. New York: Harper & Row, 1962, 1965.

Renita J. Weems. *Battered Love: Marriage, Sex, and Violence in the Hebrew Prophets.* Overtures to Biblical Theology. Minneapolis: Fortress, 1995.

Claus Westermann. *Basic Forms of Prophetic Speech.* London; Lutterworth Press, 1967.

Robert R. Wilson. *Prophecy and Society in Ancient Israel.* Philadelphia: Fortress, 1980.

INDEX OF MODERN AUTHORS

JEREMIAH
INDEX OF SIDEBARS

Illustration Sidebars

INDEX OF SCRIPTURES

INDEX OF TOPICS